Neil Miller

OUT OF THE PAST

Gay and Lesbian History from 1869 to the Present

Neil Miller is the former editor of *Boston's Gay Community News* and was a staff writer at the *Boston Phoenix*. His book *In Search of Gay America* won the 1990 American Library Association Prize for lesbian and gay nonfiction, as well as a Lambda Literary Award. He is also the author of the book *Out in the World: Gay and Lesbian Life from Buenos Aires to Bangkok*.

Also by Neil Miller

In Search of Gay America

Out in the World:
Gay and Lesbian Life from Buenos Aires to Bangkok

Out of the Past

*Gay and Lesbian History
from 1869 to the
Present*

by Neil Miller

VINTAGE BOOKS
A Division of Random House, Inc.
New York

First Vintage Books Edition, February 1995

Library of Congress Cataloging-in-Publication Data
Miller, Neil, 1945–
Out of the past : gay and lesbian history from 1869 to the present
/ Neil Miller.—1st ed.
p.   cm.
"A Vintage original."
Includes bibliographical references and index.
ISBN 0-679-74988-8
1. Homosexuality—History.   I. Title.
HQ76.25.M56   1994
306.76'6'09—dc20   94-10739
CIP

Book design by Rebecca Aidlin

Manufactured in the United States of America
10 9 8 7 6 5 4 3 2 1

For Jane and Rob

ACKNOWLEDGMENTS

IN RESEARCHING AND WRITING *Out of the Past,* I was fortunate to have the assistance of a number of people who contributed to making a large and often overwhelming task a reality. I am particularly grateful to Scott Stocker and Mark McGrath, my research assistants at various stages of this project. They performed stellar work—tracking down sources, reading chapters, contributing ideas, and helping to clarify my thinking. Justin Richardson and Steve McCauley also read portions of the manuscript and offered useful suggestions. Jim Marko helped me find various sources and was always encouraging. As usual, I benefited from the stimulation of Michael Bronski's conversation (and the breadth of his knowledge). Scott Elledge and Bill Goldstein—independently—provided the title for the book. I'd also like to thank: Michael Blim, Christopher Bram, Chris Bull, Richard Burns, Phil Canistrarro, George Chauncey, Patrick Cosson, Arlene Donovan, Ann Godoff, Peter Hansen, Michael Harney, Tom Lee, Gary Leupp, Joe Martin, Jay McIntyre, Morgan Mead, Selma and Leon Miller, Sharon O'Brien, Ken Rabb, Sara Rimer, Marsinay Smith, John Stachniewicz, and Jonathan Strong.

Above all, I'm grateful to Robin Desser and Marty Asher, who formulated the idea for this book, shepherded it along a difficult road, and were unceasingly supportive, helpful, and encouraging.

Contents

INTRODUCTION xvii

SECTION I: THE "INVENTION" OF HOMOSEXUALITY 1

CHAPTER 1   THE AGE OF WHITMAN 3

CHAPTER 2   PIONEERS OF SEXOLOGY 13

Two Case Studies from Havelock Ellis's
Sexual Inversion 25

CHAPTER 3   WE'WHA GOES TO WASHINGTON: THE
BERDACHE 29

On the Frontier 40

CHAPTER 4   OSCAR WILDE 44

An Excerpt from Wilde's *De Profundis* 51

Wilde and Bosie in Algiers—An Excerpt
from Gide's *If It Die* 52

CHAPTER 5   ROMANTIC FRIENDSHIPS BETWEEN
WOMEN 55

Willa Cather 64

The Reporter and the First Lady 67

A "Passing Woman": The Strange Case of
Murray Hall 71

CHAPTER 6   SAPPHO COMES TO PARIS 75

An Excerpt from Colette's *The Pure and
the Impure* 82

An Excerpt from Proust's *Sodom and
Gomorrah* 84

An Excerpt from Baudelaire's "Lesbos" 86

André Gide 87

CHAPTER 7   ENGLAND DURING THE GREAT WAR 92

The Sexual Labyrinth of T. E. Lawrence 101

An Excerpt from E. M. Forster's
Maurice 105

J. R. Ackerley and the Quest for the Ideal
Friend 107

Noel Coward 109

CHAPTER 8   GERMANY'S GOLDEN AGE 112
             Strindberg Goes to a Gay Ball in Berlin,
             Circa 1890—An Excerpt from *The
             Cloister* 127
             Christopher Isherwood in Berlin—
             An Excerpt from *Christopher and His
             Kind* 129
             Two Films: *Different from the Others* and
             Mädchen in Uniform 131

SECTION II: FOUR BOHEMIAS 135

CHAPTER 9   GREENWICH VILLAGE 137
             Degenerates of Greenwich Village—from
             the December 1936 Issue of *Current
             Psychology and Psychoanalysis* 146
CHAPTER 10   RENAISSANCE IN HARLEM 148
             A Drag Ball in Harlem 157
CHAPTER 11   PARIS IN THE TWENTIES 159
             Marguerite Yourcenar 167
CHAPTER 12   BLOOMSBURY 170
             Vita and Harold 179
             An Excerpt from Virginia Woolf's
             Orlando 180
CHAPTER 13   *THE WELL OF LONELINESS* 183
             An Excerpt from Radclyffe Hall's *The Well
             of Loneliness* 191
             Quentin Crisp's 1920s 193

SECTION III: THE TRIUMPH OF IDEOLOGY 197

CHAPTER 14   CZARS AND COMMISSARS: HOMOSEXUALITY
             IN RUSSIA 199
             Diaghilev, Nijinsky, and the Ballets
             Russes 208
             Love Between Women in the Gulag—
             An Excerpt from Vasily Grossman's
             Forever Flowing 213
CHAPTER 15   THE NAZI PERSECUTION OF
             HOMOSEXUALS 215
             An Excerpt from Heinz Heger's *The Men
             with the Pink Triangle* 229

CHAPTER 16   THE UNITED STATES IN WORLD WAR II 231
              Homosexuals in Uniform 239
              An Excerpt from Gore Vidal's *The City and
              the Pillar* 241

SECTION IV: BEFORE STONEWALL 245

CHAPTER 17   THE RISE AND FALL OF THE "GAY IS SICK"
              SHRINKS 247
CHAPTER 18   THE AGE OF McCARTHY 258
              Lieutenant Blick of the Vice Squad 273
              Garden of Pansies—The Hand-On-Hip Set
              Wins the Battle of Washington 276
              The Fruit Machine 278
CHAPTER 19   THE STRUGGLE FOR BRITISH LAW REFORM,
              1950–1967 280
              Victim 290
              Alan Turing, Secret Hero 291
              Piccadilly Polari 293
              Canada Reforms Its Laws 295
CHAPTER 20   THE OTHER SIDE OF THE 1950S 297
              Joe Orton in Tangier 307
              Tennessee Williams and Fifties Theater 309
              James Baldwin and *Giovanni's Room* 313
CHAPTER 21   THE OTHER SIDE OF THE FIFTIES,
              PART II: LESBIAN BUTCH/FEMME
              CULTURE 319
              Black Poet in a White Butch/Femme
              World 326
              Lorraine Hansberry 328
CHAPTER 22   THE HOMOPHILES 333
              "The Raid"—An Excerpt from *One*
              Magazine 353
              The Secret Life of J. Edgar Hoover 355
              The Word *Gay* 358
              Bayard Rustin, "Outside Agitator" 360

SECTION V: THE GAY LIBERATION DECADES 363

CHAPTER 23   STONEWALL AND THE BIRTH OF GAY AND
              LESBIAN LIBERATION 365
              "A Gay Manifesto" 384

Lesbianism and the Women's Movement—
An Excerpt from Rita Mae Brown's "The
Shape of Things to Come" 387
Gay Liberation Comes to London 389
Gay Liberation Comes to Paris 392

CHAPTER 24   THE 1970S: THE TIMES OF HARVEY MILK
AND ANITA BRYANT 395
Leonard Matlovich: A Soldier's Story 411
In the Statehouse: Representative Elaine
Noble and Senator Allen Spear 415
The Man Who Saved the President 417
The Rise of the Gay Press 418

CHAPTER 25   SEX AND MUSIC IN THE SEVENTIES 422

CHAPTER 26   LESBIAN NATION AND WOMEN'S MUSIC 431

CHAPTER 27   THE 1980S: THE AGE OF AIDS 439
An Excerpt from Randy Shilts's *And the
Band Played On* 462
The Vatican Cracks Down 464
The Great Lesbian Sex Debates 467
Michel Foucault 470
The Contradictions of the Gay
Conservative: Terry Dolan 473
The Gay Fiction Boom of the 1980s 476

SECTION VI: THE INTERNATIONAL SCENE 481

CHAPTER 28   COMMUNISM AND FASCISM 483

CHAPTER 29   ENGLAND: THE BATTLE OVER
CLAUSE 28 503
Simon Nkoli 512

CHAPTER 30   JAPAN 515
Excerpts from Mishima's *Confessions of a
Mask* and *Forbidden Colors* 522

SECTION VII: THE GAY MOMENT 525

CHAPTER 31   THE CLINTON YEARS 527
Voices from the Military Debate 542
"Whatever Happened to AIDS?" 545
The Many Lives of Martina Navratilova 547
The Year of the Lesbian 551

EPILOGUE 555

NOTES 561

BIBLIOGRAPHICAL SUMMARY 605

BIBLIOGRAPHY 615

INDEX 631

INTRODUCTION

IN THE 1870s, a concept of homosexual identity—or of gay and lesbian community—was barely articulated. It lay dormant, disguised, lost in euphemism—"the love that dare not speak its name." Yet there were some hints of things to come. In 1869, the term "homosexuality" appeared for the first time, in an anonymous pamphlet distributed in Germany advocating repeal of the country's sodomy law. Walt Whitman hiked around the suburbs of Washington, D.C., with his intimate friend, Peter Doyle, writing, vaguely, about "the love of comrades." A few years later, a Scottish woman who called herself Murray Hall came to New York City, where she lived as a man (with another woman as her wife), drinking beer and smoking cigars with fellow Tammany Hall politicians. Students at American women's colleges engaged in violent and passionate "smashes" with their classmates. Two British homosexual pioneers, John Addington Symonds and Edward Carpenter, discovered the delights of carnal love between men—but far from home, in Italy. And Peter Ilych Tchaikovsky, the Russian composer, wrote in his diary about parties where there was much "Z," his private expression for homosexuality.

By the end of the twentieth century, large segments of Western society had been transformed. Hundreds of thousands of self-identified homosexuals marched on Washington, D.C. Lesbian protesters lowered themselves from the public gallery onto the floor of the British House of Lords amid chants of "Lesbians are angry!" There were gay and lesbian pride marches in Paris, Johannesburg, Seattle, and Sacramento. The word *homosexual* had already become passé, retrograde even, to be replaced by *gay* and then by *gay and lesbian* and finally by the once pejorative but increasingly militant *queer*. The most famous female tennis player in the world announced that she was gay, as did two U.S. congressmen, British, Canadian, and German members of Parliament, Britain's leading Shakespearean actor, and Australia's only Nobel Prize–winning author. Books were published and plays and films produced with a gay and/or lesbian audience in mind. Virtually every major American city had its gay neighborhoods, restaurants, bookstores, churches, and synagogues; there was even a gay version of the Olympic Games. Denmark, Norway, and Sweden permitted homosexual couples to have the same legal rights as heterosexual married couples. There was a "gay" disease, too—it had been *thought* to be a gay disease, although now it was increasingly recognized as everyone's problem—called AIDS.

This book traces the making of a gay and lesbian community over the last 125 years in the West. It moves from the period in which gay and lesbian identity was in embryonic form to the "gay moments" of the first years of the Clinton administration. Along the way, the book examines the political events, the social and cultural transformations, the changes in medical, legal, and religious attitudes (and sometimes, the lack of change). Some of these developments have been overt and dramatic—the sensational trials of Oscar Wilde, for example, that in 1895 brought homosexuality into the public eye in England for the first time. Others have been more subtle, more difficult to measure, such as the evolution of gay and lesbian subcultures in large American cities following World War II.

Out of the Past is an introductory survey. It deals primarily with the Western world within a specific time frame—1870 to the present. It makes no pretense to original research: It is the work of a journalist who covered many of the gay and lesbian political events of the 1970s and '80s in the United States, but who is not a professional historian. It depends almost entirely upon the work of scholars who, in the past fifteen years, have opened up a field that, as once was the case with other minorities and women, was neglected, or "hidden from history" (as one anthology of gay and lesbian historical writings is titled). This book would have been impossible without the pioneering work of historians such as Jonathan Ned Katz, Lillian Faderman, John D'Emilio, Martin Duberman, Allan Berube, John Boswell, George Chauncey, Jeffrey Weeks, Carroll Smith-Rosenberg, James Steakley, Richard Plant, and many others; literary critics such as Shari Benstock and Simon Karlinsky; journalists such as Randy Shilts; biographers such as Blanche Wiesen Cook and Sharon O'Brien; sociologists and anthropologists such as Elizabeth Kennedy, Barry D. Adam, Esther Newton, and Walter Williams. In these pages, I have tried to bring together the research of many of these investigators in a lively and accessible narrative that I hope will create a coherent picture of the momentous developments of the past 125 years.

The writing of gay and lesbian history brings up problems, questions, and controversies. As independent historian Will Roscoe notes, "Historians of homosexuality cannot penetrate far into the past (nor anthropologists or sociologists into the 'field') without experiencing the sensation that there is no ground beneath their feet; that instances from different contexts are unconnected; that there may be no logical or legitimate 'unity' to define gay and lesbian studies, as black, Native American, ethnic, and even women's studies have been defined." There is clearly more coherence in the modern period than in homosexual worlds of the more remote past. But there are difficulties that any writer on the subject has to take into account.

For gay and lesbian history incorporates both public events and private lives. It covers subjects like the rise of the homosexual rights movement in Germany in the first decade of the twentieth century; the incarceration of gay men in concentration camps in Hitler's Germany and Castro's Cuba; the death from AIDS of actor Rock Hudson. These are relatively straightforward events, even though chroniclers have often shamefully ignored them. But, like women's history, gay and lesbian history also concerns itself with how men and women conducted their emotional and sexual lives, and what this meant to them and to those around them. And while it is almost always obvious who is black or female or Jewish or Irish-American, it is not always obvious who is gay or lesbian, or even what defines being gay or lesbian.

Much of the difficulty in writing about private lives is due to the fact that, until recently, in the United States and Western Europe, gays and lesbians have been essentially invisible. Those who were open about their sexuality risked the loss of job and family, social ruin, physical harassment, and sometimes arrest. In most cases, religion, medicine, and the law stigmatized homosexuality, causing historical figures and ordinary people alike to hide their sexuality and their relationships; friends, family, lovers, and biographers have helped them do so. Blanche Wiesen Cook, biographer of Eleanor Roosevelt, describes how the First Lady's intimate friend, Lorena Hickok, and other women close to Roosevelt spent hours burning

Roosevelt's letters after her death. The poet Emily Dickinson's niece censored Dickinson's passionate letters to her sister-in-law. But even when diaries and letters survive intact, they have often, until recent years, been dismissed as merely "effusive," as indicative of romantic friendships perhaps, but not of anything more than that. On the other hand, in today's climate, there is the opposite danger that researchers can sometimes interpret letters and diaries in ways that reflect a modern reading but are not at all appropriate for the time when they were written. In our search for the role models long denied us, we run the risk of imposing a gay and lesbian identity upon people who would not perceive themselves that way at all.

Although this is not a book that focuses primarily on famous homosexuals in history, I have traced the lives and relationships of some well-known figures who are presumed to be gay (or bisexual) but whose sexual inclinations cannot conclusively be proven. This group includes Walt Whitman; novelist Willa Cather; black American poet Langston Hughes; and Eleanor Roosevelt. None of them ever stated his or her sexual preference publicly; all lived in an era when a gay or lesbian identity was unarticulated or stigmatized or both. Each case is different: Whitman was most likely gay in the way we would use the term today; Cather had long-term relationships with two women who were unquestionably the emotional, if not the sexual, center of her life; Langston Hughes's closest friends in Harlem in the 1920s were "in the life" and he was reputed to be gay, but there is scant evidence beyond that; Eleanor Roosevelt was a married woman, of course, but her biographer, Blanche Wiesen Cook, argues that her letters to Lorena Hickok are "amorous and specific." Yet to insist on evidence of genital sex or the unearthing of some lost "coming out" manifesto to prove that someone was gay or lesbian in eras of great social and personal reticence sets up a standard of proof that cannot be met. At the very least, the uncertainties surrounding the personal lives of these four people elucidate the lack of sexual clarity of the times in which they lived. Thus, Whitman exemplifies the inchoate sexuality of the period before the sexologists began to classify people as sexual "types"; Cather provides an example of the "Boston marriage" of the late nineteenth and early twentieth centuries; Hughes's reticence reflects the fluidity of sexual identities that was 1920s Harlem. And Eleanor Roosevelt and Lorena Hickok represent, simply, a love story.

One of the problems that I faced in trying to put together this book was the lack of source material about ordinary gays and lesbians (except for medical and legal records) in the late nineteenth and early twentieth centuries. By and large, it has been the wealthy and educated—frequently writers and artists—who have left a "paper trail" of letters and diaries behind; often the only descriptions of gay lives of the past come from them. The experiences of working- and middle-class people, and of people of color, have been difficult to discover and to chronicle, though there are some exceptions to this: the stories of women who "passed" as men in the late nineteenth century and George Chauncey's research into the "fairy" bars of New York's Lower East Side, for example. But the personal documentation of gay history before World War II still largely tells the story of individuals who had the means to free themselves from economic, social, and family constraints. The early chapters of this book, in their focus on cultural figures, reflect this. But the limitations of the material may also represent the truth of the period—that lacking social mobility and the economic means to live on their own, the majority of gays and lesbians remained locked in heterosexual families and heterosexual relationships that prevented them from expressing their homosexual feelings to any great degree. *role models = freedom*

This book takes as its assumption that in the West toward the end of the nineteenth century a modern sense of homosexual identity began to take shape. At that historical moment, it became possible to conceive of oneself as defined by an attraction to people of the same sex—apart from any inversion of gender roles—and, later, to construct a community on that basis. This starting point reflects, to some extent, the division of gay and lesbian historians into two "camps": the "essentialists" and the "social constructivists." Both sides assume that same-sex relations occur across all historical periods and all cultures. But the essentialists believe that a gay and lesbian identity and a homosexual subculture have persisted over time from the ancient Greeks through the Middle Ages forward to our own day. The social constructivists, on the other hand, contend that certain social conditions have to be present before gay men or lesbians can emerge as a social entity; in general, they believe that such conditions only arose toward the end of the nineteenth century in the West. The essentialists would argue that the sexologists of the late nineteenth century "discovered" the homosexual, who had always been there; the constructivists contend that the nineteenth century "created" the homosexual, formulating a person with particular, identifiable characteristics.

There is a rich documentation of the "ancestors" of the modern homosexual—in ancient Greece, Rome, and China; in Western Europe, in the early Middle Ages; in Japan, among medieval samurai warriors and in the teahouses of the Edo period (1603–1868); in England, in the "molly houses" (public houses and taverns frequented by gay men) of the eighteenth century. There were social roles that countenanced same-sex relations in various native cultures in North America, Polynesia, and Siberia: Among many American Indian tribes, for example, there were male (and sometimes female) berdaches, who dressed in the clothes of the opposite sex, often took as spouses members of the same sex, and assumed sacred roles in tribal ceremonies.

By and large, however, I would argue that these identities and subcultures were quite different from our own. In ancient Athens, for example, there appear to have been no particular distinctions between heterosexuality and homosexuality; in most cases, men who were involved with other males were also married to women; same-sex relationships primarily involved older men and younger men and took on a pedagogic character. At the same time, there are few recorded examples of female same-sex relations, beyond the much-celebrated poetess Sappho and the group of women she gathered around her on the island of Lesbos.

In general, it can be assumed that the gay prototypes of antiquity did not view themselves as a minority (and in ancient Athens, they were apparently *not* a minority). They were not stigmatized, not perceived as different or deviant. Above all, they were not defined by their sexual orientation or attractions: The homosexual of the ancient world was Everyman, not a specific "type."

In later historical periods, as Christian prohibitions against sodomy were rigorously enforced—beginning in about 1300, according to historian John Boswell—gay subcultures that may have been more similar to our own were repressed and forced underground. For example, the "molly houses" of eighteenth-century London were the victims of police raids, the most famous being in 1725 when the police arrested forty "notorious sodomites" at Mother Clap's Molly House in Field Lane, Holborn. While the current gay and lesbian world can claim some lineage from these relatively small and hidden subcultures, it is difficult to see today's sense of gay and lesbian identity as a direct outgrowth.

I would argue that the gay identity and culture that began to develop toward the end of the nineteenth century had its own distinct origins and took a particular path that distinguished it from anything before. One crucial factor was the biomedical conceptualization of homosexuality in an age that increasingly classified people by their sexual inclinations—the heterosexual and the homosexual; the fetishist, the sadist, the masochist. This new way of looking at homosexuality tended to stigmatize it, set it apart from the rest of society, and represent it as a medical condition or a symptom of degeneracy. This view, at least early on, insisted that homosexuals possessed characteristics and attributes of the opposite gender.

Another factor was that of economic changes. The emergence of industrial capitalism meant that the old structures of family were breaking down. As historian John D'Emilio writes, "Only when individuals began to make their living through wage labor, instead of as parts of an interdependent family unit, was it possible for homosexual desire to coalesce into a personal identity—an identity based on the ability to remain outside the heterosexual family and to construct a personal life based on attraction to one's own sex." Urbanization pushed people off the farm and into large anonymous cities, where they could find people like themselves. It was now possible to live outside of marriage, outside of the family structure. The homosexual was a distinct being and, in many cases, began to develop a distinct social world as well.

The evolution of liberal and democratic societies in Western Europe and North America was another important factor in the creation of the modern homosexual. In such societies, homosexuals had some legal recourse to acquire, defend, and expand personal rights. In the United States, this was given a particular impetus as "identity politics" came into fashion in the post-1960s period; a gay and lesbian community became viewed as just another minority or constituency group. Once this happened, more and more people felt comfortable in coming out, banding together, and creating their own institutions.

Another way in which the late nineteenth and early twentieth centuries in the West differed from the past was in the improving status of women. In the United States and Western Europe, education and economic possibilities were opening up for women. With economic independence, with less pressure to marry and have children, and with increased social mobility, conditions existed in which women could live without men. If in the past, lack of freedom and social mobility had restricted homosexually inclined women to romantic friendships with friends or family members, the twentieth century marked the first time in Western history that the lesbian was able to emerge as a distinct social identity.

Outside the West, by and large, these trends have not been in evidence until the last decade or so. In most non-Western societies, there has been little social differentiation between heterosexual and homosexual. Lack of economic independence and the existence of powerful family and religious ties made taking on a gay identity difficult, if not impossible. The low status of women in many of these societies has been a social barrier to the growth of lesbian identity. And in countries like China and Japan, where same-sex relations had traditionally been socially accepted, Western missionaries and modernizers brought with them such stigmatizing notions that these traditions went underground. Ideologies such as nationalism and communism, too, tended to repress traditional homosexual patterns. Only in the 1970s and '80s, through economic development, through travel and communication, through the spread of Western notions of gay liberation and feminism, does one observe the cautious beginnings of Western-style gay and lesbian communities in non-Western societies.

During the period I am covering, the development of gay identity and social movements has been almost entirely a phenomenon of the West. The book examines the Native American berdache as an example of a premodern culture in which homosexual relations were enmeshed in the social fabric and which was destroyed by the arrival of the white man and his stigmatizing notions of "homosexuality" and the "homosexual." In the context of the impact of ideologies of communism and fascism, the book also looks at China, Cuba, and Argentina (the latter two societies existing within the Western sphere but having had different political and social experiences from the U.S. and Western Europe). And I examine Japan as an affluent, non-Western society that is beginning to take up Western forms of homosexual identity. Nonetheless, by virtue of its subject matter, this book primarily treats the emergence of gay and lesbian community in Western Europe and North America.

In an effort to make the book readable and accessible, the names of selected historical figures appear in bold type upon first mention. Sidebars provide mini-biographies of notable gays and lesbians and offer brief accounts related to the main narrative; the book also includes excerpts from literary works, magazines, and newspaper articles that illuminate particular periods. Instead of footnotes that interrupt the text, sources are indicated by endnotes at the back of the book. An annotated bibliography describes the sources relied upon for each chapter and offers suggestions for further reading.

I might add a word about terminology here. I have attempted, as much as possible, to use terms for gays and lesbians that reflect each particular era that I am discussing. In writing about much of the early twentieth century, for example, I use the word "homo-sexual." In a social milieu like 1920s Harlem, where there was little sense of discrete homosexual identity, I tried to stay away from any specific label at all, preferring "same sex" relationships or "homo-sexually inclined." By the 1960s, I switched to the word "gay" to describe a more visible, open, affirming community. In covering the past twenty-five years or so, I have tried as much as possible to use the terminology "gay and lesbian," but because of its cumbersome nature, sometimes I have used the word "gay" to mean both men and women.

Somerville, Massachusetts, November 1994

The "Invention" of Homosexuality

Walt Whitman at the docks in Camden, New Jersey, with his nurse, Warren Fritzinger, 1890. (© *The Bettmann Archive*)

CHAPTER I

THE AGE OF WHITMAN

THE CALLING CARD READ, "**Walt Whitman** will be in from 2 till 3½ this afternoon, and will be most happy to see Mr. Wilde and Mr. Stoddart." So on a January day in 1882, the young **Oscar Wilde,** visiting the United States on a lecture tour, and **J. W. Stoddart,** publisher of Gilbert and Sullivan operas, journeyed from Philadelphia to Camden, New Jersey, where Whitman was living at the home of his brother and sister-in-law. At age sixty-two, Whitman was already the "good gray poet," the bearded sage. His *Leaves of Grass,* first published in 1855, had made him the greatest American poet of his time. The *Calamus* poems, celebrating the "love of comrades," had made him the idol of the early British homosexual pioneers. By contrast, the twenty-eight-year-old Irish-born Wilde was still mostly promise and self-promotion. He had yet to write the plays that would make him one of the most admired writers in the English language. But he was already known as a wit and a dandy and as a leader of the Aesthetic Movement—a group of writers and artists who advocated "art for art's sake," as opposed to art whose purpose was moral uplift. The previous year, Gilbert and Sullivan had satirized Wilde in their comic opera *Patience,* a sign of notoriety, at the very least.

"I come as a poet to call on a poet," Wilde announced on his arrival in Camden that afternoon. "I have come to you as one with whom I have been acquainted almost from the cradle." Whitman was flattered. He took out a bottle of his sister-in-law's homemade elderberry wine. "I will call you Oscar," said Whitman. "I like that so much," said Wilde, putting his hand on the great man's knee.

They repaired to Whitman's den—filled with stacks of dusty newspapers—where they talked for two hours. When it was time to go, Whitman insisted that Wilde drink a milk punch. On their way back to Philadelphia, Stoddart, who had been silent for most of their visit, suggested to Wilde that the elderberry wine might have been difficult to get down. "If it had been vinegar I should have drunk it all the same, for I have an admiration for that man which I can hardly express," Wilde replied.

. . .

In both his life and his work, Walt Whitman exemplified premodern attitudes toward homosexuality. If in 1895, four years after Whitman's death, Oscar Wilde would explain to a courtroom in London just exactly what was meant by "the love that dare not speak its name," Whitman was the product of the age in which homosexuality wasn't labeled or understood, the age that "chose the spurious safety of ignorance over the risky benefits of knowledge," in the words of intellectual historian Peter Gay. Whitman himself tried to give the subject a name—"the love of comrades" or "adhesiveness"—but these terms were deliberately vague and ambiguous and imprecise. In his old age, Whitman was to deny that he had any intention of advocating sexual love between men. It was finally left to the sexologists to do the labeling and the cataloging and eventually to pronounce homosexuality as deviant and perverse.

The nineteenth century was a period when romantic friendships between men—and between women—flourished. Sodomy, although against the law, was rarely prosecuted and was viewed as so terrible and so "unnatural" that it was not considered to have any connection with tender, affectionate (and sometimes erotic) relations between men. (In fact, legal opinions in the United States and Germany determined that the laws against sodomy did not apply to oral sex; in England, oral sex only became a crime in 1885.) Students and clerks and professional apprentices were accustomed to sleeping in the same bed, and no one thought it amiss. Bachelor lawyer **Abraham Lincoln** and Illinois storekeeper **Joshua Speed,** close friends and bedmates for three years starting in 1839, are an example of such commonplace sleeping arrangements. (Speed, who had never met Lincoln before, agreed to let Lincoln share his bed as a way of earning a few extra dollars.)

Boundaries between romantic friendship and erotic love were muddy. As E. Anthony Rotundo explains in his book *American Manhood:*

> *A man who kissed or embraced an intimate male friend in bed did not worry about homosexual impulses because he did not assume that he had them. In the Victorian language of touch, a kiss or an embrace was a pure gesture of deep affection at least as much as it was an act of sexual expression. . . .*

As far as sleeping arrangements were concerned, he adds:

Physical contact was an incidental part of sharing a bed, but it happened—and, in the context of a very affectionate relationship, this contact could express warmth or intimacy. It could even express erotic desire. In the absence of a deep cultural anxiety about homosexuality, men did not have to worry about the meaning of those moments of contact.

Rotundo emphasizes that these often intense—and occasionally sexual—relationships between men were restricted to one stage of life, that of youth. They were viewed as a "rehearsal for marriage," at which time such friendships were assumed to come to an end. (This was not the case for women, where lifelong romantic friendships were common—see "Chapter 5: Romantic Friendships Between Women," page 55.) Only toward the end of the century did such relationships begin to be considered deviant. Peter Gay may well be right when he suggests that homosexual lovers were "safer in the earlier days of tight-lipped equivocations than in the later days of clinical inquisitiveness."

Walt Whitman was an impressive man. He stood six feet tall, weighed two hundred pounds, and, in his later years, had white hair and a long, flowing white beard. His friend and literary executor, Maurice Bucke, describes him as "absolutely clean and sweet," with a "simple majesty, such as might be produced by an immense handsome tree, or a large, magnificent, beautiful animal." His biographer Justin Kaplan notes that he liked buckwheat cakes, beef steak, oysters, and strong coffee, and preferred to drink his water directly from the pitcher and his sherry or rum straight out of the bottle. "He had the free and easy manners of someone who worked outdoors," Kaplan writes, "and his closest friends were laborers, drivers, semiliterates, like Peter Doyle, a horse-car conductor and railroad hand, and Harry Stafford, a New Jersey farm boy. He greeted people with 'Howdy' and said goodbye with 'So long,' an idiom he associated with sailors and prostitutes."

Whitman's life (1819–92) spanned virtually the entire nineteenth century. A carpenter's son, he was born on Long Island, went to grammar school in Brooklyn for five years, and then was apprenticed as an office boy. He worked in the printing business, became an itinerant schoolteacher on Long Island, and then a journalist and newspaper editor. In 1855, his *Leaves of Grass*, that song of "himself, his nation, and his century," as Kaplan describes it, was published. Although the first edition achieved only moderate success, it garnered the praise of the influential **Ralph Waldo Emerson,** who pronounced it "the most extraordinary piece of wit & wisdom that America has yet contributed." (The 1860 edition included the homoerotic *Calamus* poems for the first time.)

During the Civil War, Whitman moved to Washington, where he spent time as a "wound dresser" for soldiers in military hospitals in and around the city. After the war, he was employed as a clerk at the Interior Department's Office of Indian Affairs, but he was dismissed when it was revealed that he was the author of an "indecent" book. Later, he worked for seven years in the office of the Solicitor of the Treasury. After the 1868 edition of *Leaves of Grass* appeared (which included his elegy for Abraham Lincoln, "When Lilacs Last in the Dooryard Bloom'd"), Whitman rapidly became a world-famous poet. In 1873, partially paralyzed by a stroke, he moved to Camden, New Jersey, where his brother lived; he remained in Camden until his death in 1892.

Whitman was particularly drawn to young workingmen. "I never knew a case of Walt's being bothered up by a woman," said his intimate friend **Peter Doyle.** "His disposition was different. Woman in that sense never came into his head." These feelings flowered particularly during the Civil War, when he developed deep, emotional attachments to the wounded soldiers he cared for at Armory Square Hospital, in Washington, D.C. There was, for instance, **Lewy Brown,** a twenty-year-old Maryland farm boy, whose left leg was eventually amputated after he was wounded at Rappahannock. "My darling boy," Whitman wrote him when Brown had finally returned home from the hospital, "when you write to me, you must write without ceremony, I like to hear every little thing about yourself & your affairs—you need never care how you write to me, Lewy, if you will only—I never think about literary perfection in letters, either, it is the *man* & the *feeling*." In a letter to another hospital friend, **Tom Sawyer,** Whitman wrote about Brown, "Lew is so good, so affectionate—when I came away, he reached up his face, I put my arm around him, and we gave each other a long kiss, half a minute long."

In fact, it was Sawyer, a soap maker from Cambridge, Massachusetts, who appears to have truly won Whitman's heart. In a letter to Sawyer on April 21, 1863, Whitman writes:

> *Dear comrade, you must not forget me, for I never shall you. My love you have in life or death forever. I don't know how you feel about it, but it is the wish of my heart to have your friendship, and also that if you should come safe out of this war, we should come together again in some place, where we could make our living, and be true comrades and never be separated while life lasts—and take Lew Brown too, and never separate from him. Or if things are not so to be—if you get these lines, my dear, darling comrade, and any thing should go wrong, so that we do not meet again, here on earth, it seems to me, (the way I feel now,) that my soul could never be entirely happy, even in the world to come, without you, dear comrade. What I have written is pretty strong talk, I suppose, but I mean exactly what I say.*

Sawyer's reply to this passionate letter "might just as well have dealt with a proposition involving cast-iron stoves," as Justin Kaplan observes. It went, "I fully reciprocate your friendship as expressed in your letter and it will afford me great pleasure to meet you after the war will have terminated or soon if circumstance will permit."

Soon enough, as Kaplan notes, Whitman was in the throes of yet another tender passion for a wounded Armory Square soldier. "Walt, you will be a second Father to me, won't you?" asked **Elijah Douglass Fox**. "I never before met with a man that I could love as I do you." After Fox had gone home to his wife in Michigan, Whitman answered, "I cannot bear the thought of being separated from you—the blessing of God on you by night & day, my darling boy."

None of these letters imply physical relations, of course (the half-minute kiss, notwithstanding). And it is perhaps possible to view Whitman's language as simply a reflection of the intense, often poetic intimacies between men in wartime. Yet what are we to make of Whitman's notebooks from the fall of 1862 in Brooklyn, and 1863 in Washington, which catalog a list of young men whom he had met, usually on the street, and sometimes "slept with"?:

Dan'l Spencer . . . somewhat feminine . . . told me he had never been in a fight and did not drink at all gone in 2nd NY Lt Artillery deserted, returned to it slept with me Sept. 3d

David Wilson night of Oct. 11, '62 walking up from Middagh—slept with me—works in a blacksmith shop in Navy Yard—lives in Hampden st.—walks together Sunday afternoon & night—is about 19

Horace Ostrander Oct. 22 '62 24 4th Av. from Ostego co. 60 miles west of Albany was in the hospital to see Chas. Green about 28 y'rs age . . . slept with him Dec. 4 '62 . . .

October 9, 1863 Jerry Taylor, (NJ) of 2nd dist reg't slept with me last night weather soft, cool enough, warm enough, heavenly

As historian Jonathan Ned Katz (who reprinted some of these notations in *Gay American History*) observes, even if the expression "slept with" had fairly innocent connotations at the time, "the poet's practice of meeting, taking home, and simply bedding down for the night with male strangers is curious behavior. . . ."

The major relationship of Whitman's life in the years following the Civil War was with Peter Doyle. The Irish-born young workingman—twenty-eight years Whitman's junior—had served in the Confederate Army before he was captured, released, and given a job as a conductor on the Washington and Georgetown street railway. Whitman met him in 1865, and their intimacy continued for almost a decade. In an interview in 1895 after Whitman's death, Doyle described their first meeting:

We felt to each other at once. I was a conductor. The night was very stormy. . . . Walt had his blanket—it was thrown around his shoulders—he seemed like an old sea-captain. He was the only passenger, it was a lonely night, so I thought I would go in and talk with him. Something in me made me do it and something in him drew me that way. He used to say there was something in me had the same effect on him. Anyway, I went into the car. We were familiar at once—I put my hand on his knee—we understood. He did not get out at the end of the trip—in fact went all the way back with me.

For Whitman, his intimacy with Doyle was "the love of comrades" he had been seeking in all those courtships of wounded soldiers. The two took long hikes around Washington, with Whitman whistling, singing, and reciting Shakespeare. They posed for photographs. Whitman sent bouquets of flowers and tender notes. Whitman fretted about a skin disease that Doyle had contracted, fearing it might be syphilis; Doyle threatened to kill himself if it was. The problem turned out to be barber's itch. In that 1895 interview, Doyle recalled, "We were awful close together. In the afternoon I would go up to the Treasury building and wait for him to get through if he was busy. Then we'd stroll out together, often without any plan, going wherever we happened to get. This occurred days in and out, months running."

Over time, it isn't clear whether Doyle returned Whitman's love or if their relationship even had a sexual dimension to it. As Justin Kaplan notes, Whitman commands himself in one notebook entry from 1870, "Depress the adhesive nature. It is in excess—making life a torment . . . diseased feverish disproportionate adhesiveness." "Adhesiveness" was one of Whitman's terms for the love of comrades. In these notes, Whitman tries to cover up Doyle's identity— and his gender. In two entries, Doyle is referred to as "16" and "16.4" (schoolboy numerological code) and in three instances "him" is changed to "her." Whitman wrote,

> Remember where I am most weak, & most lacking. Yet always preserve a kind spirit and demeanor to 16. But pursue her no more.

> July 15- 1870-
> To give up absolutely & for good, from this present hour, this feverish, fluctuating, useless undignified pursuit of 16.4—too long (much too long) persevered in—so humiliating—It must come at last & had better come now—(It cannot possibly be a success).
> Let there from this hour be no faltering, no getting [word erased] at all henceforth, (not once, under any circumstances)— avoid seeing her, or meeting her, or any talk or explanations— or any meeting, whatever, from this hour forth, for life.

Twelve days later, however, when Whitman returned to Brooklyn to visit his mother, he was writing Doyle, "I never dreamed you made so much of having me with you, nor that you could feel so downcast at losing me. I foolishly thought it was all on the other side."

By 1873, their intimacy was waning, however. Whitman had found a new protégé, eighteen-year-old **Harry Stafford,** who worked as an errand boy at a Camden print shop. Whitman referred to him, in various letters, as "my (adopted) son" and "my nephew."

In all these relationships, there is ample evidence of feelings that we would consider homosexual today. Perhaps it was all chaste— the daily walks with Doyle, even the sleeping with strangers encountered on the streets of Brooklyn. In an era where there was no name for such feelings beyond that of friendship (or Whitman's own "love of comrades"), where no labels were assigned for sexual orientations and attractions, it was easy to indulge in "tight-lipped equivocations" and denials—even to oneself.

In the *Calamus* section of *Leaves of Grass,* Whitman writes:

> Resolv'd to sing no songs to-day but those of manly
>   attachment,
> Projecting them along that substantial life,
> Bequeathing hence types of athletic love,
> Afternoon this delicious Ninth-month in my forty-first year,
> I proceed for all who are or have been young men,
> To tell the secret of my nights and days,
> To celebrate the need of comrades.

In *Democratic Vistas,* the poet put similar thoughts into prose:

> Many will say it is a dream, and will not follow my inferences:
> but I confidently expect a time when there will be seen, running
> like a half-hid warp through all the myriad audible and visible
> worldly interests of America, threads of manly friendship, fond
> and loving, pure and sweet, strong and life-long, carried to de-
> grees hitherto unknown. . . .

The imprecise boundaries between romantic friendship and erotic love so prevalent in Victorian America can be seen in Whitman's poetry and prose as well. He seemed to approach and then just stop short of committing himself to an advocacy of same-sex erotic love. Yet there were some, particularly in England, who viewed Whitman's celebrations of "the need of comrades" and of "athletic" and "manly friendship" as constituting a kind of early homosexual manifesto. For many years, Whitman did nothing to disabuse them of such ideas. So **Edward Carpenter,** the English essayist and poet (later dubbed "England's Whitman"), wrote in 1874 to thank Whitman for legitimatizing the "love of men." "You have made men to be not ashamed of the noblest instinct of their nature," he wrote. "Women are beautiful; but, to some, there is that which passes the love of women." Three years later, he was knocking on Whitman's door in Camden. Meanwhile, **Charles Warren Stoddard,** a young American writer, was corresponding with Whitman about his travels in the South Seas. There, "for the first time I act as my nature prompts me," he noted. In one letter, he described a night spent with a young man there, wakening to find him watching him with "earnest, patient looks, his arm over my breast and around me." Stoddard added, "You will easily imagine, my dear sir, how delightful I find this life. I read your Poems with a new spirit, to understand them as few may be able to."

One of the people most responsive to the homoerotic elements in Whitman's writing was **John Addington Symonds** (1840–93), historian of Renaissance Italy and investigator into same-sex love in ancient Greece. "I might have been a mere English gentleman had I not read *Leaves of Grass* in time," he said. "It revolutionalized my previous conceptions, and made another man of me." One of the changes it wrought in his life was that, although married, Symonds began frequenting soldiers' barracks and male brothels. (He also developed a particular fondness for Venetian gondoliers, one of whom he brought to England in 1892.)

Unlike Whitman's other homosexual admirers, however, Symonds was determined to pin Whitman down as to his meanings. "I have pored for continuous hours over the pages of Calamus (as I used to pore over the pages of Plato), longing to hear you speak, *burning* for a revelation of your more developed meaning. . . ." he wrote Whitman in 1872. "Some day, perhaps—in some form, I know not what, but in your own chosen form—you will tell me more about the Love of Friends!"

Symonds continued writing, and Whitman went on being evasive. In an August 1890 letter, Symonds observed to Whitman that some of his friends objected to the *Calamus* poems as "praising and propogating a passionate affection between men" which might "bring people into criminality." Did Whitman contemplate "the possible intrusion of those semi-sexual emotions and actions which no doubt do occur between men?" In response, the seventy-two-year-old Whitman finally answered Symonds, emphatically denying any homosexual content in his work:

> *Ab't the questions on Calamus pieces &c: they quite daze me. L of G. [Leaves of Grass] is only to be rightly construed by and within its own atmosphere and essential character . . . that the calamus part has even allow'd the possibility of such construction as mention'd is terrible—I am fain to hope the pages themselves are not to be even mention'd for such gratuitous and quite at the time entirely undream'd & unreck'd possibility of morbid inferences—wh' are disavow'd by me & seem damnable. Then one great difference between you and me, temperament & theory, is restraint . . .*

In the same letter, Whitman also claimed to have fathered six children, a fact not substantiated by any of his biographers. As for Symonds, he was so stunned by the vehemence of the reply that he dismissed Whitman as having feelings "at least as hostile to sexual inversion as any law-abiding humdrum Anglo-Saxon could desire."

It is doubtful, however, whether Whitman's letter to Symonds can really be construed as the last word on the subject. The letter is contradictory: On the one hand, Whitman tries to give the impression that physical love between men never entered his mind, while, on the other hand, he counsels Symonds in restraint. For his part, Edward Carpenter criticized Symonds for the way he posed the question: "Why, he [Whitman] knew that the moment he said such a thing he would have the whole American Press at his heels, snarling and slandering, and distorting his words in every possible way." Carpenter noted that Whitman, despite a reputation for candidness, was also the most cautious of men. "There is no doubt in my mind," wrote Carpenter, "that Walt Whitman was before all a lover of the Male. His thought turned towards Men first and foremost, and it is no good disguising that fact. A thousand passages in his poems might be quoted in support of that contention."

As for Oscar Wilde, four months after his first visit to Camden, he returned again to call on Whitman. On that occasion, Wilde claims that Whitman talked freely about his attractions to other men. The "kiss of Walt Whitman," Wilde would say later, "is still on my lips."

CHAPTER 2

PIONEERS OF SEXOLOGY

IT WAS THE SEXOLOGISTS, not the poets, who were to define same-sex love, to give it a name. The term *homosexuality (Homosexualität)* was actually used for the first time in 1869 by **Karl Maria Kertbeny,** a German-Hungarian campaigner for the abolition of Prussia's laws that criminalized sexual relations between men. Homosexuality was not the only word that the late nineteenth century found to describe sexual relations between persons of the same sex. The term *inversion* was even more widely used (the "invert," male or female, was the practitioner of inversion). And in 1870, the German physician **Karl Westphal** invented the phrase "contrary sexual feeling" *(Die Conträre Sexualempfindung),* in detailing the history of a young lesbian. These expressions all had a clinical tinge to them. Then there were the more sympathetic, but no less problematic, terms—the "third sex" and the "intermediate sex."

These terms reflect an evolution in nineteenth-century thought from a moral and religious attitude toward same-sex relations to a scientific one. As the century wore on, sodomy, the sin, was transformed into homosexuality, the medical category. The French philosopher and historian **Michel Foucault** points out that, before this time, sodomy had been simply a category of forbidden acts, defined by ancient civil or canonical codes. The person who committed such acts, notes Foucault, was nothing more than the legal subject of them. The acts did not define him as a person or provide him with an identity. But the nineteenth century's mania for classification and compilation changed all this. Once homosexuality became constituted as a medical category, the homosexual himself became, in Foucault's words, "a personage, a past, a case history, and a childhood." Foucault elaborated:

Nothing that went into his [the homosexual's] total composition was unaffected by his sexuality. It was everywhere present in him: at the root of all his actions because it was their insidious and indefinitely active principle; written immodestly on his face and body because it was a secret that always gave itself away . . . The sodomite had been a temporary aberration; the homosexual was now a species.

But how to explain the "species"? The late nineteenth century was fascinated by the question. One of the first to offer an explanation was **Karl Heinrich Ulrichs** (1825–95), a German lawyer and assessor for the German kingdom of Hanover. Ulrichs, who was homosexual himself, wrote under the name of Numa Numantius. In 1864, he published the first of many pamphlets that contended that male and female homosexuals constituted a third, or "intermediate," sex. According to Ulrichs's theory, a male homosexual was essentially a female soul in a male body; a lesbian was a male soul in a female body. Ulrichs developed his theory in the wake of the belief at the time that the human embryo possessed both male and female sex organs, losing one as it developed in the uterus. He theorized that male homosexuality came about when the embryo shed the female sex organ, but the same change did not occur in the part of the brain that regulates the sex drive. (Again, the situation was reversed in the case of female homosexuality.)

Ulrichs assumed that because male homosexuals had a female soul in a male body, they therefore possessed the personality characteristics of women. Likewise, female homosexuals had the personality characteristics of men. According to him, homosexuality was not just an "inversion" in the choice of sexual object but an "inversion" of one's broader gender characteristics as well. This idea did not originate with Ulrichs, to be sure. But his theory of the "third sex" gave these gender stereotypes a quasi-scientific basis, confounding sexual orientation with gender and homosexuals with hermaphrodites. The German gay rights movement—the first in the world—accepted Ulrichs's theory, and the notion of homosexuals as a "third sex" became quite widespread in Germany and throughout Europe in the first decades of the twentieth century.

Ulrichs contended that homosexuality was an inborn and innate trait that could not be eradicated; this was a complete change from the "temporary" nature of the sodomite and his sin. By arguing that homosexuality was inborn, Ulrichs could insist that it was neither criminal nor sinful. He became a crusader for the removal of legal penalties against homosexual acts throughout Germany (Bavaria and his native Hanover were the only German states at the time that didn't have such penalties). Unhappy with terms like *sodomite* and *pederast,* Ulrichs turned to Plato's *Symposium* for new terminology, using the word *urning* for members of the "third sex." In English, the term *Uranian* (Plato's term for "heavenly love") began to be widely used.

If Ulrichs viewed the "third sex" as a harmless product of heredity, other early sexologists saw a genetic component that was not so benign. They insisted that homosexuality was a symptom of "degeneration." Degeneracy theory, which was particularly influential in France, contended that medical, psychiatric, and social problems were transmitted from generation to generation. Progressive degeneracy was offered as an explanation for poverty, insanity, and alcoholism, as well as for political and military failures—the defeat of the French army in the Franco-Prussian war, for example.

Richard von Krafft-Ebing (1840–1902), a professor of psychiatry at the University of Vienna, subscribed to the degeneracy theory. In his 1886 *Psychopathia Sexualis* he compiled some two hundred case histories of sexual behaviors or interests that differed from the norm, labeling individuals as to types—sadism, masochism, assorted fetishisms, and "antipathic sexual instinct," his term for homosexuality. Nonetheless, Krafft-Ebing was circumspect in his writing, using technical language or Latin whenever descriptions threatened to become too racy. Peter Gay, in his book *The Tender Passion,* offers one example in which Krafft-Ebing relates the story of a thirty-year-old homosexual physician:

> *One evening I was seated at the opera next to an elderly gentleman. He courted me. I laughed heartily at the foolish old man and entered into his sport. Exinopinato genitalia mea prehendit, quo facto statim penis meus se erexit . . . He told me that he was in love with me. Since I had heard of hermaphrodites in the hospital, I thought I had to do with one of them here, curiosus factus genitalia eius videre volui. Sicuti penem maximum eius erectus adspexi, perterritus effugi.*

Gay adds dryly, "Whether this sort of prose encouraged the study of Latin is not on record."

Krafft-Ebing's description of homosexuals tended to emphasize gender stereotypes—in virtually every case study, he saw the characteristics of the opposite sex. He explained this, not by the existence of some third sex, but as being in line with the degeneracy theory of the time. "In almost all cases [of homosexuals]," he main-

tained, "where an examination of the physical and mental pecul-
iarities of the ancestors and blood relations has been possible,
neuroses, psychoses, degenerative signs etc. have been found in the
families." In the last edition of his work, in 1900, however, his
views changed considerably. By then he regarded "inversion" to be
a congenital anomaly, but saw no sign of degeneration or morbidity.
Krafft-Ebing lent his support to the campaign to repeal Paragraph
175, the German law that criminalized sexual relations between
adult males.

The British sexologist **Havelock Ellis** (1859–1939) was clearly
indebted to Krafft-Ebing's use of case studies, but his approach was
quite different: He wanted to promote the acceptance of homosexuals. As his biographer Phyllis Grosskurth notes, he was the first
person to write a book in English that treated homosexuality neither
as a disease nor a crime. The book was the extremely comprehensive
Sexual Inversion, the first of the *Studies in the Psychology of Sex.*
It was published in Germany in 1897, but it was banned in England
in the aftermath of the Oscar Wilde trial.

Like Ulrichs, Ellis believed homosexuality to be inherited. But
he rejected the theory of the male "invert" as a woman trapped in
a man's body and vice versa. He also dismissed the idea that homosexuality was a sign of moral degeneracy. To him, homosexuality
was simply an anomaly of nature, something that appeared throughout the animal kingdom and had been present in ancient times. To
debunk the degeneracy theory, he pointed out the number of homosexuals of unusual intellectual ability and moral leadership—**Erasmus, Leonardo da Vinci, Michelangelo, Cellini,** and **Sappho.** He
estimated the number of homosexuals as being somewhere between
1 and 10 percent—and probably slightly over 2 percent—of the
population at large.

Of all the early sexologists, notes Peter Gay, Ellis was the one
who most enjoyed his work. The heterosexual Ellis discovered "tantalizing and troubling materials for his life's work in his own ap-
petites and at his own hearth," says Gay. "The most arousing sight,
to him, was a woman urinating. His wife turned out to be a lesbian."
Havelock Ellis was born of lower-middle-class parents in Croydon,
outside London. After a brief stint as a teacher in Australia, Ellis
returned to England, where he immersed himself in Socialist and
intellectual circles, becoming friends with **Karl Marx**'s daughter,
Eleanor, the early Fabian Socialists, and the South African feminist
and novelist **Olive Schreiner,** whom he loved (unrequitedly) for

Havelock Ellis, just before his seventy-third birthday, 1932. (© *Hulton Deutsch Collection Ltd.*)

much of his life. Ellis was an enthusiast for progress and for social change, and his first book, *The New Spirit,* published in 1890, expressed his belief in a new age that would see the triumph of science, the emancipation of women, and the growth of social democracy. His views on sex were part of his liberal, ameliorative approach to social issues. "Sex lies at the root of life," he wrote, "and we can never learn to reverence life, until we know how to understand sex."

In 1892, Ellis was approached by John Addington Symonds with the idea of coauthoring a book about homosexuality. Symonds had written two privately printed books on the subject, *A Problem in Greek Ethics* and *A Problem in Modern Ethics* (in the second book, published in 1891, he talked about "homosexual instincts," believed to be the first use of the term *homosexual* in English). Symonds thought a book coauthored with Ellis would have substantial weight, given Ellis's reputation—and heterosexuality. Ellis agreed to collaborate. The original plan was that Symonds would write about homosexuality in ancient Greece, while Ellis would discuss its medical and scientific aspects. Symonds died the following year, however, and Ellis went forward without him. When Ellis's *Sexual Inversion* was first published in Germany, in 1897, Symonds's essay on Greece and many of his ideas were incorporated in the book. A year later, a similar version was published in England, with both Symonds and Ellis listed as coauthors, but after pressure from Symonds's literary executor, all references to Symonds and all extracts from his work were expunged from the British edition. When Ellis tried to find a publisher for the new version, he ran into trouble and the book was eventually banned by British authorities.

Sexual Inversion contained thirty-three case studies, although many of the subjects, it turned out, were literary and scientific acquaintances of Ellis. Six were lesbians. It was the first time any of the sexologists attempted to deal with female homosexuality in a serious manner. One of the case studies was that of Ellis's wife, **Edith Lees** (see "Two Case Studies from Havelock Ellis's *Sexual Inversion,* page 25). When Ellis first met her in 1890, Lees (1861–1916) was giving feminist lectures and was secretary of the Fellowship of the New Life, predecessor to the Fabian Society. To Ellis, she exemplified the "New Woman" of the time, full of independence and self-confidence. In fact, she was emotionally fragile and was later to suffer from hysteria and breakdowns. It wasn't until after their marriage in 1891 that Ellis learned of her attraction to other women. Although he was shocked and distressed at first (he was particularly mystified because Edith did not possess the masculine traits he associated with lesbianism), he eventually reconciled himself to her passionate friendships with women. They remained married for twenty-five years, until her death in 1916.

Perhaps the most important aspect of Ellis's research was his discovery that male "inverts" did not necessarily conform to stereotypes; by and large, they appeared and acted like most other men. (He did find greater artistic and dramatic aptitudes among them, however, although he admitted this might be partly due to the circumstances of their lives.) His findings redefined male homosexuality in narrow terms of sexual object choice, taking it out of the broader realm of gender inversion, transvestism, and "character."

But if he removed the male homosexual from gender stereotypes, he kept to a more traditional view of lesbians. As historian George Chauncey points out, Ellis and other sexologists continued to assert that "character inversion" was a feature of female homosexuality. The late-Victorian notion of the natural "passivity" of women was something that was just too ingrained to give up, even for iconoclastic thinkers like Ellis. Ellis's biographer Phyllis Grosskurth notes that in Ellis's work "the female emerges as someone distinctly nervy, boyish in appearance, with a deep voice . . . someone, in fact, rather like Edith." Ellis himself characterizes lesbians this way:

> *The brusque, energetic movements, the attitude of the arms, the direct speech, the inflections of the voice, the masculine straightforwardness and sense of honor . . . will often suggest the underlying psychic abnormality to a keen observer. In the habits not only is there frequently a pronounced taste for smoking cigarettes, often found in quite feminine women, but also a decided taste and tolerance for cigars. There is also a dislike and sometimes incapacity for needlework and other domestic occupations, while there is often some capacity for athletics.*

In addition to his stereotypical views of lesbians, many of Ellis's conclusions appear almost comical today. Among them were:

- Green is the favorite color of inverts (but not of the general population, who, according to Ellis, prefer blue or red).
- A large percentage of male inverts are unable to whistle (a

manly trait, in Ellis's estimation); female inverts, on the other hand, can whistle "admirably."
• Inverts of both sexes are often characterized by youthfulness of appearance and childlike faces.

Ellis often seemed to contradict himself or straddle the fence on controversial issues. For example, he argued that inversion was not a sign of degeneracy, yet at the same time he saw it as dangerous to encourage inverts to have children, fearing it would lead to off-spring of "neurotic and falling stock." He believed strongly in the hereditary nature of inversion but at the same time argued that there was a latent bisexuality in all people. And although inversion was hereditary, in his view, it could lie dormant and be aroused by a specific situation—a school "crush," a seduction, or a disap-pointment in heterosexual love. He believed that women who were not congenitally inverted could be encouraged in that direction by "true" inverts. (This seemed to be his way of explaining away the existence of lesbians who didn't reflect gender stereotypes.) Thus, he feared that the modern feminist movement—which he described as "on the whole, a wholesome and inevitable movement"—might push some women toward inversion. "These unquestionable influ-ences of modern movements cannot directly cause sexual inver-sion," he said, "but they develop the germs of it, and they probably cause a spurious imitation. This spurious imitation is due to the fact that the congenital anomaly occurs with special frequency in women of high intelligence who, voluntarily or involuntarily, influ-ence others."

Ellis strongly opposed English laws that punished private, con-senting acts between men. Although he argued that heterosexual marriage was the preferable state for all individuals, he found more damage was done by trying to cure inverts than by leaving them alone. Society would do better to learn tolerance of their existence, he believed. This opposition to forcing homosexuals to "change" from homosexual to heterosexual put him at odds with many in his own time.

It was another English sexological pioneer, Edward Carpenter (1844–1929), a friend of both Ellises, who would bring homosex-uality from a clinical to a more spiritual plane. Socialist, feminist, and vegetarian, Carpenter was born in an upper-class Brighton family and, after studying at Cambridge, took orders in the church and became a curate. In his late twenties, he lost his faith and decided to change his way of life. What he needed, he felt, was to "work down among the mass-people." In 1883, he bought some land at Millthorpe in Derbyshire, southeast of Manchester. There he embraced a life of outdoor physical labor, sandal-making, and writing, eschewing meat and alcohol.

Carpenter was homosexual—in his later years, openly so—and part of the inspiration for the change in his life was his reading of Whitman's poetry. "It was not till (at the age of twenty five) I read Whitman—and then with a great leap of joy—that I met with the treatment of sex which accorded with my own sentiments." He soon became the leading exponent of all kinds of new ideas—Hindu mysticism, vegetarianism, and sexual reform, among them.

In his writings, Carpenter expounded the notion of the third sex, and campaigned for the acceptance and understanding of Uranism, a term he tried to popularize. The sexes, he contended, represented two poles of the human race, with a middle group—the interme-diate sex—where men and women are "by emotion and tempera-ment very near to each other." The male of this middle group tended to be of "a rather gentle, emotional disposition" with defects in the direction of "subtlety, evasiveness, timidity, vanity"; the female, on the other hand, was "fiery, active, bold, and truthful," with defects running toward "brusqueness and coarseness." Although Carpenter returned homosexuals to the stereotypical categories from which Ellis attempted to free them, he viewed the "Uranian temperament" as a "forward force in human evolution" because it did not fit into conventional male/female dichotomies. In fact, his writings can be seen as an early example of gay pride. Uranians, he contended, were "remarkable and indispensable types" who, because of "the union or balance of feminine and masculine qualities," bridged the gap between men and women, becoming "the interpreters of men and women to each other." They were "dreamers, thinkers, discover-ers." In many cultures, he noted, those endowed with a "Uranian temperament" became inventors, teachers, musicians, medicine men, and priests.

Carpenter met his lover, **George Merrill**, a young man from the slums of nearby Sheffield, in a railway car in 1891. The two re-mained together until Merrill's death in 1927. It was not until several years after they first became involved that they began to live together openly at his Millthorpe home, a rather bold step that aroused a great deal of criticism. "He believes and practices the physical very frankly," wrote Oxford don **Goldsworthy Lowes Dick-**

inson. "How it is that public opinion hasn't managed to get him to prison and murder him is a mystery." Carpenter himself wrote:

> *I received no end of letters, kindly meant, but full of warnings and advice—deprecating the idea of a menage without a woman, as a thing unheard of, and a step entered on, it was supposed, in a rash moment, and without due consideration: hinting at the risk to my health, to my comfort, at bad cooking, untidy rooms, and abundance of cobwebs, not to mention the queer look of the thing, the remarks of neighbors, the certainty that the arrangement could not last long, and so forth.*

Carpenter was a charismatic figure, a bearded sage in the Walt Whitman manner. His Millthorpe house became a center of pilgrimage to many in the labor and progressive movements. It also became a place of refuge for many homosexuals. Edith Lees, Havelock Ellis's wife, spent a good deal of time there, mending socks by the fire or talking about livestock with local farmers in the pub. Carpenter recounts in his autobiography that one farmer asked, referring to Edith, "When is that little lady coming again with that curly hair, like a lad's, and them blue eyes, what talked about pigs and cows? I shall never forget her." Another person who experienced the force of Carpenter's personality was the novelist E. M. Forster, who was inspired to write *Maurice,* his novel about homosexual love, after a visit to Millthorpe. (See "Chapter 12: Bloomsbury," page 170).

Carpenter differed from the other sexologists in his emphasis on the spiritual and emotional aspects of same-sex love, using Whitmanesque language like the "love of comrades" and "adhesiveness." Yet he is important for that reason. As British historian Jeffrey Weeks writes, "Carpenter was almost alone . . . in publicly asserting the possibly higher moral possibilities of homosexuality. Its flavor, of course, came from an emphasis on the spiritual qualities of a Whitmanite comradeship rather than an advocacy of sexual license, but it was a potent brew."

Sexual pioneers like Ulrichs, Ellis, and Carpenter all tried to combine an understanding of homosexuality and its causes with a plea for toleration of homosexuals. They assumed that positing same-sex attraction as an inherited characteristic was helpful in this regard, removing homosexuality from the category of sin or illness. The concept of homosexuals as some "third" or "intermediate" sex was very appealing, and the early gay rights movement in Germany particularly identified with it. Yet at the same time, the idea of the "third sex" tended to encourage stereotypes that marginalized homosexuals. And Ellis, the only sexologist who removed male homosexuals from gender stereotypes, did not do so in the case of lesbians, perpetuating notions of female homosexuals as having a masculine appearance and personality traits.

The overall biomedical conceptualization of homosexuality was also double-edged. Although it created a "species" and an identity and the possibility of the formation of support systems and communities, it also had its negative effects. Not everyone accepted the idea that the new category of homosexual or invert was either hereditary or harmless. Thus efforts to transform "tortured" homosexuals into "well-adjusted" heterosexuals gained currency. Krafft-Ebing, for example, used hypnosis as behavior modification, urging the male patient to think of women in the sexual act. Other methods of behavior change were not so benign, however. Jeffrey Weeks writes that in 1898 an asylum in the American state of Kansas reported that forty-eight men had been castrated; castration was used on sex offenders and homosexuals in Switzerland in the early years of the century and in the 1930s in Denmark. Hormone treatments and aversion therapies were later adopted. Despite the "special pleading" of polemicists like Ulrichs, Ellis, and Carpenter, the creation of homosexuality as a category often meant turning it into a medical condition to be cured.

With the advent of the psychoanalytic theory of **Sigmund Freud** (1856–1939), much of the thinking of the late-nineteenth- and early-twentieth-century sexologists was eclipsed. Freud rejected the congenital theories both of the "degeneracy" theorists and the "third sex" advocates, arguing instead that a combination of nature and nurture was responsible for creating gay men and lesbians. He believed that a homosexual orientation was the result of "arrested development" at an early developmental stage that prevented the young man or woman from moving on to "normal" attraction to members of the opposite sex. Nonetheless, Freud believed that all human beings were essentially bisexual and that sexual feelings for the same gender could be experienced (although often sublimated) in all stages of life. Heterosexuality, however, was the goal, and the homosexual had failed to reach it. As Peter Gay puts it, "For Freud, heterosexual, genital lovemaking was not a matter of course, but an achievement, the culmination of a long, never painless, and never quite complete evolution."

Why did some individuals remain "stalled" at the homosexual phase of their psychosexual development? Freud was never sure. In his writings, he offered a number of possible ideas, ranging from an obsession with one's own genitals (males), to penis envy (females), to a family constellation of seductive mother and weak father (males). After Freud's death, some of his disciples tried to turn the last hypothesis into dogma.

Despite the negative connotations of "arrested development," Freud himself tried to remove the moral and legal opprobrium from homosexuality and homosexuals. He contended that, incomplete as they might be in their sex life, in other parts of their lives, homosexuals functioned quite well; in fact, they were often characterized by "specially high intellectual development and ethical culture." He opposed legal penalties against same-sex relations and rejected proposals that homosexuals be barred from membership in psychoanalytic societies. He was extremely dubious about the argument that homosexuals could be "cured"—turned into heterosexuals—contending that the possibilities of doing so were "not much more promising than to do the reverse." Because homosexual sex was a source of pleasure, homosexuality could not be changed easily, he believed. Change could only occur in rare cases in which homosexual object-choice was weak or where there remained "considerable rudiments and vestiges of a heterosexual choice of object."

In his famous 1935 "Letter to an American mother" (of a gay son), Freud summed up his ideas on the subject:

> Homosexuality is assuredly no advantage but it is nothing to be ashamed of, no vice, no degradation, it cannot be classified as an illness; we consider it to be a variation of the sexual function produced by a certain arrest of sexual development. Many highly respectable individuals of ancient and modern times have been homosexuals, several of the greatest men among them (Plato, Michelangelo, Leonardo da Vinci, etc). It is a great injustice to persecute homosexuality as a crime, and cruelty too. . . .
>
> By asking me if I can help, you mean, I suppose, if I can abolish homosexuality and make normal heterosexuality take its

place. The answer is, in a general way, we cannot promise to achieve it. In a certain number of cases we succeed in developing the blighted germs of heterosexual tendencies which are present in every homosexual, in the majority of cases it is no more possible. . . .

What analysis can do for your son runs in a different line. If he is unhappy, neurotic, torn by conflicts, inhibited in his social life, analysis may bring him harmony, peace of mind, full efficiency whether he remains a homosexual or gets changed. . . .

Few of Freud's followers continued in line with his relatively compassionate approach, however. "Arrested development" eventually became a term of opprobrium of its own that meant that homosexuals were somehow not fully mature adults. If homosexuality wasn't congenital, Freud's followers argued, then perhaps, despite what the master said, homosexuals could till be changed. Treatment whose aim was undoing childhood "damage," overcoming the fixation of arrested development, became the focus. This opened the way for the emergence of all sorts of nonanalytic techniques to try and change homosexuals into heterosexuals—aversion therapy, shock treatment, lobotomies, and the like. The era of stigmatization, of "gay is sick," had arrived.

Two Case Studies from Havelock Ellis's *Sexual Inversion*

These two case studies from Havelock Ellis's Sexual Inversion, *first published in 1897, illustrate the sexologist's methodology and technique in attempting to understand and classify homosexual behavior. The subject of Case History XXXVI—one of the six case histories of lesbians in the book—is widely assumed to be Ellis's wife, Edith Lees.*

HISTORY XXXVI—MISS H, AGED 30. Among her paternal relatives there is a tendency to eccentricity and to nervous disease. Her grandfather drank; her father was eccentric and hypochondriacal, and suffered from obsessions. Her mother and mother's relatives were entirely healthy, and normal in disposition. . . .

When she was about 8 she used to see various nurse-maids uncover their children's sexual parts and show them to each other. She used to think about this when alone, and also about whipping. She never cared to play with dolls, and in her games always took the part of a man. Her first rudimentary sex-feelings appeared at the age of 8 or 9, and were associated with dreams of whipping and being whipped, which were most vivid between the ages of 11 and 14, when they died away on the appearance of affection for girls. She menstruated at 12.

Her earliest affection, at the age of 13, was for a schoolfellow, a graceful, coquettish girl with long golden hair and blue eyes. Her affection displayed itself in performing all sorts of small services for this girl, in constantly thinking about her, and in feeling deliciously grateful for the smallest return. At the age of 14 she had a similar passion for a girl cousin; she used to look forward with ecstasy to her visits and especially to the rare occasions when the cousin slept with her; her excitement was then so great that she could not sleep, but there was no conscious sexual excitement. At the age of 15 or 16, she fell in love with another cousin; her experiences with this girl were full of delicious sensations; if the cousin only touched her neck, a thrill went through her body which she now regards as sexual. . . . On leaving school at the age of 19 she met a girl of about the same age as herself, very womanly, but not much attracted to men. . . . This relation became vaguely physical, Miss H taking the initiative, but her friend desiring such relations and taking extreme pleasure in them; they used to touch and kiss each other tenderly (especially on the *mons veneris*), with equal ardor. They each experienced a strong pleasurable feeling in doing this, and sexual erethism, but no orgasm, and it does not appear that this ever occured. Their general behavior to each other was that of lovers, but they endeavored, as far as possible, to hide this fact from the world. . . .

Her feeling toward men is friendly, but she has never had sexual attraction towards a man. She likes them as good comrades, as men like each other. . . . Her feeling toward marriage has always been one of repugnance. She can, however, imagine a man whom she could love or marry. . . .

She believes that homosexual love is morally right when it is really part of a person's nature, and provided that the nature of homosexual love is always made plain to the object of such affection. . . . The effect of her loving women is distinctly good, she asserts, both spiritually and physically, while repression leads to morbidity and hysteria. She has suffered much from neurasthenia at various periods, but under appropriate treatment it has slowly diminished. The inverted instinct is too deeply rooted to eradicate, but it is well under control.

HISTORY XII—AGED 24. Father and mother both living; the latter is of a better social standing than the father. He is much attached to his mother, and she gives him some sympathy. He has a brother who is normally attracted to women. He himself has never been attracted to women, and takes no interest in them nor in their society.

At the age of 4 he first became conscious of an attraction for older males. From the ages of 11 and 19, at a large grammar-school, he had relationships with about one hundred boys. Needless to add, he considers homosexuality extremely common in schools. It was, however, the Oscar Wilde case which first opened his eyes to the wide prevalence of homosexuality, and he considers that the publicity of that case has done much, if not to increase homosexuality, at all events to make it more conspicuous and outspoken.

He is now attracted to youths about 5 or 6 years younger than himself; they must be good-looking. He has never perverted a boy not already inclined to homosexuality. In his relationship he does not feel exclusively like a male or female: sometimes one, sometimes the other. He is often liked, he says, because of his masculine character.

He is fully developed and healthy, well over middle height, inclined to be plump, with a full face and small mustache. He smokes many cigarettes and cannot get on without them. Though his manners are very slightly if at all feminine, he acknowledges many feminine ways. He is fond of jewelry, until lately always wore a bangle, and likes women's rings; he is very particular about fine ties, and uses very delicate women's handkerchiefs. He has always had a taste for music, and sings. He has a special predilection for green; it is the predominant color in the decoration of his room, and everything green appeals to him. He finds the love of green (and also of violet and purple) is very widespread among his inverted friends.

CHAPTER 3

WE'WHA GOES TO WASHINGTON: THE BERDACHE

*I know not through what superstition some Illinois, as well as some
Nadouessi, while still young, assume the garb of women, and retain
it throughout their lives. . . . They never marry, and glory in demeaning themselves to do everything that the women do. . . . They
are summoned to the Councils, and nothing can be decided without their advice. Finally, through their profession of leading an
Extraordinary life, they pass for Manitous—That is to say, for
Spirits,—or persons of Consequence.*

—from Father Jacques Marquette's account of his voyage
down the Mississippi, 1673–77

IN THE YEAR 1886, the Zuni Indian berdache **We'wha** (1849–
96) came to Washington, D.C. He stayed for six months, as a guest
of his friend, the anthropologist **Matilda Coxe Stevenson**, and cap-
tivated Washington society. He demonstrated Zuni weaving at the
Smithsonian. He appeared at the National Theatre in an amateur
theatrical event, at which he received "deafening" applause from
an audience of senators, congressmen, and other luminaries. He
became friends with the Speaker of the House of Representatives
and his wife and also called on President **Grover Cleveland,** to whom
he presented a gift of his handiwork.

We'wha was known for his pottery and for his weaving; sales
of his work to various collectors made him one of the first Zunis
to earn cash. He was "the most intelligent of the Zuni tribe," with
an "indomitable will and an insatiable thirst for knowledge," according to Stevenson, who spent a number of years in the New
Mexico pueblo where he lived. He was also, she noted, "perhaps
the tallest person in Zuni: certainly the strongest both mentally and
physically."

Despite We'wha's strength and stature, President Cleveland and

Zuni Indian berdache We'wha. (© *National Anthropological Archives, Smithsonian Institution*)

all of Washington society mistakenly believed him to be a woman. We'wha apparently never indicated anything to the contrary. For many years, Stevenson shared this misapprehension—even after she learned the truth, in her writings she always referred to We'wha as "she." The Washington *Evening Star* described We'wha's appearance at the National Theatre as follows:

> *Folks who have formed poetic ideals of Indian maidens, after the pattern of Pocahontas or Minnehaha, might be disappointed in Wa-Wah [sic] on first sight. Her features, and especially her mouth, are rather large; her figure and carriage rather masculine.*

For his part, We'wha was disillusioned with the white women he met in Washington. He had seen them, in the ladies' rooms, removing their false teeth and the "rats" from their hair.

Berdaches represented a special category among many Native American tribes. They were men who wore women's clothing, occupied themselves with "women's work" such as pottery and basket weaving, and took a sacred role in tribal rituals. In some tribes, young boys were initiated into berdache status at a special ceremony. A berdache had sex with other men, often marrying one or, in a polygamous marriage, becoming a secondary wife to a male who was already married to one or more women. Anthropologist Stevenson was particularly reticent in describing the sexuality of the berdache: "There is a side to the lives of these men which must remain untold. They never marry women, and it is understood that they seldom have any relations with them." In some Native American tribes, there was a female equivalent of the male berdache, although it was apparently far less common.

The berdache status could be found in 130 different Native American tribes. In his book, *The Spirit and the Flesh,* ethnohistorian Walter L. Williams noted that the institution of the berdache was well-established throughout the continental United States, with the apparent exception of the Northeast. Some particularly warlike tribes like Comanches and the Apaches looked down on berdaches; others, such as the Navajo, revered them. Equivalents of the berdache can also be found in a variety of non-Western cultures, from the "soft men" of Siberia to the *mahus* of Polynesia. In North America, with the arrival of the white man—particularly the missionaries—berdaches largely went underground. By the twentieth century they had almost vanished altogether.

Berdaches have posed a major problem for Western historians because they don't fit into neat categories of sexuality and gender. They illustrate the problems in trying to impose Western notions of sexuality on non-Western cultures and on premodern sensibilities. Berdaches had sex (apparently almost always passive anal sex) exclusively with other men who were not berdache. They dressed in women's clothing or a mix of men's and women's clothing. They had a recognized social status that incorporated both male and female attributes and led many Indians to describe them as "half men, half women." Yet to label them as homosexual or transvestite or as representing some third sex is to miss the complexity of their role in tribal society.

What is clear is that the berdache functioned outside the heterosexual and homosexual dichotomies that came to dominate thinking about sex in the West by the end of the nineteenth century. Berdaches inhabited a world in which individuals were not classified on the basis of sexual orientation. Will Roscoe, who wrote about We'wha in an article that appeared in the gay and lesbian magazine *OUT/LOOK* emphasizes that occupational pursuits and social behavior, rather than whether one was attracted to members of the same sex, determined who was a berdache. Walter Williams contends similarly that in Native American culture, people are classified primarily by "character," not by sexual orientation. He suggests that the contemporary Western equivalent of the male berdache is "a subgroup" of homosexuals, "known in the vernacular of the gay community as queens." The major difference, he argues, between the berdache and the modern "queen" was the sacred and spiritual role of the berdache.

The sexual partner of the male berdache was always a masculine man. The idea of two berdaches having sex together represented a kind of "incest" that was unthinkable to the Indian mind. Nor are there many recorded instances of two non-berdache men having a sexual relationship. Husbands of berdaches were often the object of joking and teasing, but otherwise were in no way viewed as strange or unusual. They were not labeled in any way; no social category was created for them. Anthropologist Stevenson noted that in the 1880s a berdache who was the richest man in the Zuni pueblo where Stevenson lived "allied himself to a man." Seventeen years later, when Stevenson left the pueblo, the couple "were living together, and they were two of the hardest workers in the pueblo and among the most prosperous."

Recognized marriages between a berdache and another man were apparently commonplace. In 1542, the Spanish explorer **Cabeza de Vaca,** who spent five years among the Timucua Indians of Florida, reported, "During the time I was thus among these people I saw a devilish thing, and it is that I saw one man married to another." A survey of California Indian cultures as late as the 1930s found that all but one of the tribal groups that recognized berdache status also recognized marriage between a berdache and another man. In polygamous marriages, a Native American man might have a berdache wife as well as female wives. The Lakota Sioux chief **Crazy Horse** is said to have had one or two *winktes* (the Sioux term for berdache) in addition to his female wives. In these marriages, the berdache was expected to do women's work and be the receptive partner during sex.

Men took on berdache status in a number of ways. Sometimes they became berdaches as a result of dreams. In some tribes, male children who seemed to prefer female pursuits would be tested to see if they should take on the berdache role. Among the Mohave of the American Southwest, such a boy (usually of age ten) would be surrounded by members of the tribe, and a singer, hidden from sight, would perform particular songs. If the boy began to dance like a woman (meaning with great intensity), he assumed berdache status. He was bathed, given a skirt, and led back to the dance ground, where he would announce his new female name to the crowd. Among the Papago Indians of Arizona, as late as the 1930s, such a test involved building a small brush enclosure in which members of the tribe placed a man's bow and arrows and a woman's basket. A boy who displayed berdache inclinations was brought to the enclosure and told to enter, as the adults watched. Once he was inside, the adults set fire to the enclosure. They watched what the child took with him as he fled: If he took the woman's basket, he would become a berdache. As Williams points out, the berdache role was not forced on a boy. Rather, in assuming such a role, he was viewed as acting out his "basic character."

Male berdaches had a variety of ceremonial and other roles. Among the Navajo they were often responsible for the preparation and cooking of sacred food at tribal gatherings. The Crow berdache chopped down the first tree for the sun dance. Among the Lakota Sioux, the *winkte* would offer the male child a sacred name; this spiritual protection ensured good health and long life. Berdaches were also seen as having powers to cure illnesses. Cheyenne war parties, for example, almost always took a berdache along to care for the wounded. The sacred character of the berdache is exemplified by a myth about a warrior who tried to force a berdache to abandon women's clothing. The berdache resisted, and the warrior shot him with an arrow. Immediately, the berdache disappeared; all that was left was a pile of stones with the arrow in them. Since that time, no Indian would show disrespect to a berdache.

The berdache often functioned as a mediator between the world of women and men. Among the Navajo, berdaches were often asked to resolve conflicts between married couples. In some tribes, they were used as matchmakers. Among the Cheyenne, they would direct the scalp dance, in which they matched up all the unmarried young men with the young women. George Grinnell, who wrote about the Cheyenne, gave the following description of the scalp dance:

> These old time scalp dances were directed by a little group of men called Hee man eh', "halfmen-halfwomen," who usually dressed as old men. . . . They were very popular and especial favorites of the young people, whether married or not, for they were noted matchmakers. They were fine love-talkers. If a man wanted to get a girl to run away with him and could get one of these people to help him, he seldom failed. When a young man wanted to send gifts for a young woman, one of these halfmen-halfwomen was sent to the girl's relative to do the talking in making the marriage. . . .

Sometimes they participated in warfare. A Crow berdache put on men's clothes for a day and attacked a Sioux war party during the Battle of the Rosebud in 1876. For his exploits, the berdache received the name **Osh-Tisch** (Finds Them and Kills Them). More often, when berdaches went to war, they did so in support capacities. Among the Sioux, berdaches would take care of the camp, do the cooking, and cure the sick. Among the Cheyenne, one or two berdaches always went on a raiding party for good luck—in addition to their role in caring for the wounded.

This sacred, often revered status, was in sharp contrast to the deviant label increasingly imposed on homosexuals and transvestites in Western culture. "If a *winkte* is in a family, that family would feel fortunate," one Sioux informant told Walter Williams. And Maltilda Coxe Stevenson relates how the death of We'wha in 1896 caused "universal regret and distress" among the Zuni:

> We'wha's death was regarded as a calamity, and the remains lay
> in state for an hour or more, during which time not only members
> of the clans to which she was allied, but the rain priests and
> theurgists and many others, including children, viewed them.
> When the blanket was finally closed, a fresh outburst of grief
> was heard. . . .

When he died, We'wha was buried in both men's and women's
clothing.

When the Portuguese explorer **Pedro de Magalhães de Gandavo**
traveled through northeastern Brazil in 1576, he found an unusual
group of female warriors among one of the tribes in the region.
"They wear the hair cut in the same way as men, and go to war
with bows and arrows and pursue game, always in company with
men," he wrote. "Each has a woman to serve her, to whom she
says she is married; and they treat each other and speak with each
other as man and wife." The explorer named the river that flowed
through the area the Amazon, after the ancient Greek legend about
female warriors.

Some thirty tribes are said to have had a special status for female
berdaches, but very little is known about them. One tribe that had
this kind of status were the Mohave, who called such women
hwame. As young girls, *hwame* were said to discard their dolls and
to prefer boys' tasks and games. As in the case of boys, there was
a ritual test, and if they passed, the young girls would take a masculine name, wear male clothing, and learn the same skills as boys.
In one documented case, a late-nineteenth-century Mohave *hwame*
named **Sahaykwisa** dressed more like a woman than a man and
engaged in both farming (a woman's occupation) and hunting (a
man's). *Hwame* were expected to marry a woman when they got
older. As with husbands of the male berdache, there was no label
or stigma assigned to the wife of *hwame*. (In Sahaykwisa's case,
her first wife seems to have been teased unmercifully, however.) If
the wife had a child from a previous marriage, the *hwame* would
become the child's parent.

Among the Indians of the Great Plains, there does not appear
to have been an accepted berdache status for women, as there was
for men. Nonetheless, within Plains Indian culture, there was at
least one nineteenth-century woman who took on a traditionally

male role (and female wives). She was known only as the Woman Chief of the Crow Indians of the upper Missouri. As a young girl, she was a member of another tribe, the Gros Ventres, but was taken prisoner by the Crow at age ten and adopted by a Crow warrior. Edwin T. Denig, a white frontiersman who lived with the Crow and knew her for twelve years, describes how as a young girl she desired to acquire "manly accomplishments." Her Crow foster father encouraged her in this, permitting her to guard the horses, presenting her with bow and arrows, and teaching her to ride fearlessly. She later carried a gun, learned to shoot, and was the "equal if not the superior" to any of the men in hunting. "Long before she had ventured on the warpath," Denig wrote, "she could rival any of the young men in all amusements and occupations, was a capital shot with the rifle, and would spend most of her time killing deer and bighorn, which she butchered and carried home on her back when hunting on foot." She never wore men's clothes, however, except for her hunting arms. After the death of her foster father, she assumed responsibility for his lodge and family.

When the Blackfeet made a charge on the Crow lodges, she single-handedly led a counterattack against them, killing one with a gun and shooting arrows into two more. This act made her a hero to the entire Crow Nation. The following year, she led a number of young men on their first war excursion against the Blackfeet, returning with seventy horses and two scalps. Other successful raids followed. As Denig wrote:

> Old men began to believe she bore a charmed life which, with her daring feats, elevated her to a point of honor and respect not often reached by male warriors, certainly never before conferred upon a female of the Crow Nation. The Indians seemed to be proud of her, sung forth her praise in songs composed by them after each of her brave deeds. When council was held and all the chiefs and warriors assembled, she took her place among the former, ranking third person in the band of 160 lodges.

Soon after, she married a woman, and later added three more wives. Before taking a young woman in marriage, she always went through the expected procedure of giving horses to the family of her intended. Denig thought there was a practical reason for her marrying women: Given her rank as a warrior and hunter, she viewed women's work as beneath her. Thus, marriage to a man would be inappropriate to her status. He added, "Strange country this, where males assume the dress and perform the duties of females, while women turn men and mate with own sex!"

For twenty years the Woman Chief seems to have "conducted herself well in all things appertaining to war and a hunter's life," as Denig put it. Then, in the summer of 1854, she was killed while on a peacemaking expedition to the Gros Ventres tribe. "Thus closed the earthly career of this singular woman," wrote Denig. "Neither has there since appeared another of her sex who preferred the warrior's life to that of domestic duties."

With the arrival of the white man, the status of berdaches—sometimes their very lives—was in peril. The Spanish, in particular, extending the brutal excesses of the Inquisition to the New World, were eager to wipe out indigenous traditions; the association of berdaches with the sin of sodomy gave the Spanish a particular reason to eradicate them. In 1519, the conquistador **Hernán Cortés** wrote to the Emperor Charles V that the Indians of Mexico "are all sodomites and have recourse to that abominable sin." In 1530, another conquistador, **Nuno de Guzman,** recalled that the last person captured in battle, and who had "fought most courageously, was a man in the habit of a woman, which confessed that from a child he had gotten his living by that filthiness, which I caused him to be burned." On his expedition across Panama, the explorer **Vasco Núñez de Balboa** saw men dressed as women. Upon learning that they were "sodomites," he ordered forty of them to be eaten by his dogs, "a fine action of an honorable and Catholic Spaniard," as one chronicler described it.

An account by a Spanish missionary, reprinted in Jonathan Ned Katz's *Gay American History,* illustrates later Spanish attitudes. The missionary describes the visit in the 1780s of *Joya* (a native word for berdache) and his husband to another Indian, a convert who was living at a mission near Santa Barbara, California. The suspicious head of the mission went to their quarters, along with a sentry and soldier, and found the couple "in the act of committing the nefarious sin." The couple were punished (although mildly), and, in his defense, the man informed the priest that the berdache was his wife. After this, the couple vanished from sight. The missionary noted that "many *Joyas* can be seen in the area . . . almost every village has two or three." He continued, "But we place our trust in God and expect that these accursed people will disappear with the growth of the missions. The abominable vice will be eliminated to the extent that the Catholic faith and all the other virtues are firmly implanted there. . . ."

The Spanish began a major attempt to wipe out the berdache in California. By the 1820s another missionary at San Juan Capistrano was able to report that while berdaches had once been very numerous, "at the present time this horrible custom is entirely unknown among them."

In the Great Plains and the American West, as they tried to assimilate the Indians into white man's culture, the Indian agents of the U.S. government also attempted to eliminate the berdache. At the end of the nineteenth century, one particular Indian agent reportedly incarcerated Crow berdaches (known as *badé*), forced them to cut their hair, and made them wear men's clothing. The agent was told to leave the reservation. Because of his great prestige, Osh-Tisch (1854–1929), the hero of the Battle of the Rosebud, was a particular target of attempts to undermine the Crow berdache. In 1903, a Baptist minister came to his reservation. One Indian informant told Walter Williams that the minister "condemned our traditions, including the badé. He told congregation members to stay away from Osh-Tisch and the other badés. He continued to condemn Osh-Tisch until his death. . . . That may be the reason why no others took up the badé role after Osh-Tisch died."

Indian boarding schools were a focus for the assimilation of Indians into white culture. Williams tells how a young Navajo berdache was taken, along with other children of his tribe, to the Carlisle Indian School in Pennsylvania. Since he was dressed as a girl, he was assumed to be female and placed in a girls' dormitory; the other Navajo students protected him. However, during a lice infestation in which all the girls were scrubbed, it was discovered that this student was actually a male. He was removed from school and never seen again.

In Canada, a similar situation prevailed. A Kwakiutl chief in British Columbia recalled what happened when his berdache lover was forced to abandon his female role in about 1900:

The Indian agent wrote to Victoria [the provincial government] telling the officials what she was doing [dressing as a woman]. She was taken to Victoria, and the policeman took her clothes off and found she was a man, so they gave him a suit of clothes and cut off his hair and sent him back home. When I saw him again, he was a man. He was no more my sweetheart.

In 1883 the United States Department of the Interior set up Courts of Indian Offenses, run by cooperative Indians, in order to deal with minor crimes. The courts were responsible for the majority of cases on reservations at the end of the nineteenth and the beginning of the twentieth centuries. Williams notes that court records are full of cases of adultery, polygamy, licentiousness, and fornication. Yet, as long as the court system was managed by Indians, sodomy cases were notably absent. This indicates that Indians tended to protect berdaches, in particular because of their sacred status.

Nonetheless, the acculturation of the younger generation of Indians into white society eventually had a negative effect on attitudes toward the berdache. A Lakota Sioux medicine man described to Williams how in the early twentieth century, as Indian people came under the influence of missions and boarding schools, they began to forget the traditional ways:

> *They began to look down on the* winkte *and lose respect. The missionaries and the government agents said* winktes *were no good, and tried to get them to change their ways. Some did, and put on men's clothing. But others, rather than change, went out and hanged themselves. I remember the sad stories that were told about this.*

Throughout much of the twentieth century, many Indians viewed traditional culture in negative terms. Homosexuality was viewed as "the white man's disease." Berdaches were perceived as deviant— both in their sexual behavior and in their cross-dressing. They began to die out. This was true even among the Navajo, a tribe in which berdaches had been held in particularly high esteem. In the late 1940s, anthropologists were reporting that the remaining Navajo berdaches were all middle-aged and older: "It may be that the bachelors in their thirties who live in various communities today are [secretly berdaches] . . . who fear the ridicule of white persons and so do not change clothing."

With the resurgence of interest in traditional culture among a new generation of Indians in the 1970s and '80s, attitudes toward berdaches began to change yet again. Gay historians and anthropologists rediscovered the berdache. Many gay Indians—who had become urbanized and taken up more "modern" approaches toward being gay—began to search for their cultural roots. They saw berdaches as role models, even if they weren't gay in the contemporary sense. In any event, the berdache shows how certain premodern societies took people who would probably be considered homosexual today and affirmed them, instead of stigmatizing them, giving them important—even sacred—cultural roles.

On the Frontier

MRS. NASH WAS THE COMPANY LAUNDRESS of General George Armstrong Custer's Seventh U.S. Cavalry. She remained with the regiment from 1868 to 1878, married to one soldier after another. In the summer of 1878, Mrs. Nash died at Fort Meade, in Dakota Territory, while the corporal she had been living with was off fighting Indians. The ladies of the garrison prepared her body for burial, and it was then that they made an astonishing discovery: Mrs. Nash was a man. (She had always been heavily veiled when she appeared in public.) When her corporal-lover returned home, he was ridiculed unceasingly by his fellow soldiers. He shot himself to death.

This odd story—with echoes of M. Butterfly—is one of the few documented incidents of homosexual relationships among white men in the Old West. The American West was a largely male society, with few available women. Neither soldiers nor cowboys were known for their chastity. As the Topeka Daily Commonwealth newspaper wrote in 1871, "They [cowboys] drink, swear, and fight, and life with them is a round of boisterous gayety [sic] and indulgence in sensual pleasure." One turn-of-the-century observer noted that most cowboys "were burned out with bad whiskey and disease." During the winter months, some were "pimps, living off some cheap prostitutes. . . . Most of them had a dose of clap or pox and some had a double dose. All in all, most of the old-time cowhands were a scrubby bunch."

Although homosexual relations are reputed to be commonplace

in other all-male societies—prisoners, pirates, sailors—there is little documented evidence about their existence on the frontier. As Australian gay historian Robert French pointed out, when asked if "mateship" among Australian bushrangers (their version of the cowboy) involved homosexual relationships, "We just don't know. They didn't write letters out there in the bush." That applies to the American cowboy, as well. Given the aura of romantic myth about the frontier—and the assumption that the rough-and-tough masculinity of that world excluded homosexuality—historians have chosen not to investigate the subject too thoroughly.

Yet in some cases cowboys attending dances where few if any women were present would tag a male partner with a scarf tied to his arm. In *Reminiscences of a Ranchman*, Edgar Beecher Bronson describes the antics of a "six-foot two blond giant" named **Jake DePuyster** at a dance in 1882 at The Cowboys' Rest in Ogallala, Nebraska, northern terminus of the great Texas trail. With "not enough gals around," Jake decides to remedy the situation. He leaves the bar and returns ten minutes later, still in his wide chaps, spurred heels, and belt, but otherwise "the most remarkably clad figure that ever entered even a frontier dance hall." For,

> *Cocked jauntily over his right eye he wore a bright red toque with a faded wreath of pale blue flowers, from which a bedraggled green feather drooped wearily over his left ear; about his waist wrinkled a broad pink sash, tied in a great double-knot set squarely in front, while fastened also about his waist, pendent no more than mid-way of his long thighs, hung a garment white of colour, filmy of fabric, bifurcated of form, richly ruffled of extremity. . . .*

The bearded Jake then sidles up to his mate, Buck, and, with a broad grin, shyly murmurs that he would like the privilege of the next quadrille. After initial hesitation, Buck accepts. The author observes:

> *While there were better dancers and prettier, that first quadrille made "Miss DePuyster" the belle of the ball for the rest of the day and night, and not a few serious affrays over disputes for an early chance of a "round" or a "square" with her were narrowly avoided.*

Then there is the case of U.S. marshal, soldier, and scout **James Butler "Wild Bill" Hickok** (1837–76). One chronicler of the West, Stuart Henry, remarks Hickok's "feminine looks and bearing," his "hermaphroditism" and "epicene pattern." Henry continues, "His looks surprise one. That softly rounded contour, that rather angelic countenance, were quite opposite of the thin, rawboned Texan model."

In *The Spirit and the Flesh*, Walter Williams suggests that migration to the frontier might have been a common pattern for men who were attracted to other men. Such men might have been drawn to the frontier because it was a virtually all-male society and because sodomy was associated with the Indians. "This is not to suggest that most men went west with these more or less conscious notions," writes Williams. "But it does suggest that those historians who do not consider this motivation ignore an important facet of frontier life."

What about romance between two men in the vast and lonesome spaces of the Great Plains or the American Southwest? Again, few sources exist. But the following poem, "The Lost Pardner," published in 1915 in a collection of Western poetry by **Badger Clark**, an Arizona rancher, gives some clues:

> *I hate the steady sun that glares and glares!*
> *The bird songs make me sore.*
> *I seem the only thing on earth that cares*
> *'Cause Al ain't here no more!*
>
> *And him so strong, and yet so quick he died*
> *And after year on year*
> *When we had always trailed it side by side,*
> *He went—and left me here!*
>
> *We loved each other in the way men do*
> *And never spoke about it, Al and me.*
> *But we both knowed, and knowin' it so true*
> *Was more than any woman's kiss could be . . .*
>
> *The range is empty and the trails are blind,*
> *And I don't seem but half myself today.*
> *I wait to hear him ridin' up behind*
> *And feel his knee rub mine the good old way.*

Even in this seemingly explicit poem, it isn't clear whether the relationship between the two men was sexual or just one of innocent mateship. But only in a period before a sense of male homosexual identity was firmly established could a poem of such romantic feeling be written about intimacy between ostensibly heterosexual men.

CHAPTER 4

OSCAR WILDE

AMONG THE MOST SENSATIONAL EVENTS of the end of the nineteenth century were the trials, in London, of the flamboyant genius Oscar Wilde (1854–1900). The poet and playwright first made his name by going around London in the evening in knee britches and silk stockings, wearing a green carnation in his buttonhole, and extolling the work of a little-known French poet named **Baudelaire.** He mocked the moral seriousness of his age, glorifying pleasure, even shallowness, arguing that aesthetics were more important than ethics, and promoting art for art's sake. "Books are not good or bad, only well or badly written," went one of his famous aphorisms. He was witty, arrogant, always striking a pose. When he arrived in New York on his 1882 lecture tour, he told customs officials, "I have nothing to declare except my genius."

By the mid-1890s, Wilde was at the height of his fame. His comic plays *Lady Windermere's Fan* and *A Woman of No Importance* had been extolled by critics and audiences alike; *The Importance of Being Earnest,* his most famous work, was soon to come. Young men slavishly imitated everything he did, arriving at the theater on the opening night of *Lady Windermere's Fan,* for example, wearing Wilde's trademark green carnation in their buttonholes. But his novel *The Picture of Dorian Gray,* seeming to revel in decadence and sensation, showed another side of Wilde that was disquieting in an era that prized reticence and respectability above all else. Although married and the father of two children, Wilde was homosexual. And reticence was completely antithetical to his nature.

Homosexuality was certainly not unknown in Britain at the time. The preparatory schools and universities were rife with it. John Addington Symonds wrote that at Harrow, among the most famous of the public schools, in the 1850s, "The talk in dormitories and studies was incredibly obscene. Here and there one could not avoid seeing acts of onanism, mutual masturbation, and the sport of naked boys in bed together." Years later, the poet **Robert Graves** was to observe that for every one "born" homosexual, there were at least ten permanent homosexuals "made" by the public-school

Oscar Wilde (left) and Lord Alfred Douglas (right) in Oxford, about 1893. (© *The Bettmann Archive*)

system. At Oxford and Cambridge, dons were not allowed to marry until 1882, and for many years after, few availed themselves of the opportunity. The cult of romantic friendship flourished, virtually canonized in **Tennyson**'s great poem "In Memoriam." In examining the papers of the Apostles, the most elite and intellectual society at Cambridge, the biographer **Lytton Strachey** became convinced that many of the past Apostles had been secret although chaste homosexuals. But sex between men was not just restricted to the upper classes. The Cleveland Street scandal of 1889–90, involving aristocrats and working-class male prostitutes, showed that sex between men knew no class boundaries.

Wilde apparently had his first homosexual experience, with **Robbie Ross** (later to be his literary executor), at Oxford in 1886. In 1891 he met **Lord Alfred Douglas** (1870–1945), with whom he began a relationship that was to dominate his life and prove his undoing. The two became lovers when Wilde was thirty-six and Douglas, known as "Bosie," was just twenty-one. By the time Bosie first met Wilde, he had read *The Picture of Dorian Gray* nine times over. Wilde's biographer Richard Ellmann describes Bosie this way:

> *The youngest son of the Marquess of Queensberry had a pale alabaster face and blonde hair. . . . His friends—and he never lacked friends—thought him charming. In temperament, he was totally spoiled, reckless, insolent, and, when thwarted, fiercely vindictive. Wilde could only see his beauty. . . .*

Although their sexual relationship soon ended, Wilde and Bosie became inseparable; there was a romantic and passionate quality to their friendship that continued for the next few years. Bosie wrote sonnets and edited an Oxford literary magazine, in whose pages he urged acceptance of homosexual relationships. He introduced Wilde to the aristocracy, as well as to the world of young working-class men—stable boys, clerks, and domestic servants—who were sexually available for a few pounds or a good dinner. Wilde called this "feasting with panthers."

Under the influence of the vain and extravagant Bosie, Wilde became increasingly less discreet. He began residing in various hotels, ostensibly to write, but really because it was a convenient place to bring young men—young working-class men, in particular. Frank Harris, Wilde's friend and biographer, reports encountering Wilde one evening at the Café Royal sitting between two youths, who "looked like grooms." Harris was playing chess at the table just opposite. "To my astonishment," writes Harris, "he was talking as if he had a picked audience, talking, if you please, about the Olympic Games [in ancient Greece], telling how the youths wrestled and were scraped with strigulae and threw the discus and ran races and won the myrtle-wreath. . . ." Suddenly, the younger of the boys asked:

> 'Did you sy they was niked?'
> Of course, Oscar replied, 'nude, clothed only in sunshine and beauty.'
> 'Oh, my,' giggled the lad in his unspeakable Cockney way.

Harris, feeling in an "impossible position," left the cafe. It is not clear what bothered him the most—the homosexual implications of the encounter or the fact that the young men were obviously from the working class.

For his part, the often careless Bosie permitted some love letters from Wilde to fall into the hands of one such young man. This lack of discretion on both their parts was extremely unwise. An 1885 law called the Labouchere Amendment had widened legal prohibitions against male homosexual acts. Up until then, only sodomy had been a punishable offense—by death, until 1861; no other sexual acts between males had been penalized. Now the law extended to "indecency between males" (oral sex) as well, an offense punishable with two years in prison. The new law was widely called the "Blackmailer's Charter." Nonetheless, Wilde remained convinced that the law would not touch him. "The Treasury will always give me twenty-four hours to leave the country," he assured one intimate.

Bosie's father was the combative and sometimes violent **Marquess of Queensberry,** a boxing enthusiast who at the age of twenty-four had invented the rules of the sport that are used to this day. He forbade his son to see Wilde. Bosie refused to obey and replied with insults. Queensberry then began to harass Wilde. He plotted to disrupt the opening-night performance of *The Importance of Being Earnest* but was foiled. On another occasion, he left his card at Wilde's club, with the writing, "To Oscar Wilde, ponce and Somdomite [sic]." If it was a trap, Wilde fell into it. Wilde sued for libel. Friends pleaded with him to drop the case, but Bosie encouraged him, viewing the suit as a weapon to use against his father.

The libel action was a fatal error, as Queensberry's lawyers had obtained the names of ten young men willing to testify that Wilde had solicited them to commit sodomy. Shortly after the trial opened on April 3, 1895, Wilde himself took the stand. His disdainful manner did him little good. When Queensberry's lawyer, **Sir Edward Carson,** read a passage from *The Picture of Dorian Gray* during his cross-examination of Wilde, the following exchange occurred:

> *Carson: The affection and love of the artist of Dorian Gray might lead an ordinary individual to believe that it might have a certain tendency?*
> *Wilde: I have no knowledge of the views of ordinary individuals.*
> *Carson: Have you ever adored a young man madly?*
> *Wilde: No, not madly. I prefer love—that is a higher form.*
> *Carson: Never mind about that. Let us keep down to the level we are at now.*
> *Wilde: I have never given adoration to anybody except myself.*

The judge threw out the case, vindicating Queensberry. Within hours of the decision, Wilde was arrested and charged with sodomy and indecent behavior.

Wilde was taken to prison and denied bail. His name was removed from the bills of two theaters where *An Ideal Husband* and *The Importance of Being Earnest* were being performed. The plays themselves were soon closed, and an American tour of his play *A Woman of No Importance* was canceled. Bosie fled to France, where, under the Code Napoléon, there were no penalties for sodomy. Apparently, many others who shared Wilde and Douglas's sexual proclivities did so as well: One night, some six hundred men made the Channel crossing from Dover to Calais, when typically only sixty would have done so, according to Frank Harris. "Never was Paris so crowded with members of the English governing classes," Harris wrote. "It was even said that a celebrated English actor took a return ticket for four days in Paris, just to be in the fashion. The mummer returned quickly; but the majority of the migrants stayed abroad for some time. The wind of terror which had swept them across the Channel opposed their return, and they scattered over the Continent from Naples to Monte Carlo and from Palermo to Seville under all sorts of pretexts."

Wilde's trial, which opened just three weeks after the libel decision, featured testimony by young male prostitutes that Wilde had indeed solicited sex from them. Looking "careworn and anxious," as *The New York Times* described him, Wilde was significantly less disdainful when he took the stand this time around. He admitted he knew the boys, but denied that he had had sex with them. During the cross-examination, he was asked, "What is the 'Love that dare not speak its name'?" In perhaps the first public defense of homosexuality in England, Wilde replied:

> The 'Love that dare not speak its name' in this century is such a great affection of an elder for a younger man as there was between David and Jonathan, such as Plato made the very basis of his philosophy, and such as you find in the sonnets of Michaelangelo and Shakespeare. It is that deep, spiritual affection that is as pure as it is perfect.... It is beautiful, it is fine, it is the noblest form of affection. There is nothing unnatural about it. It is intellectual, and it repeatedly exists between an elder and a younger man, when the elder man has intellect, and the younger man has all the joy, hope and glamour of life before him. That it should be so the world does not understand. The world mocks at it and sometimes puts one in the pillory for it.

At the conclusion of his speech, the courtroom spectators burst into applause. Perhaps because of Wilde's eloquence, the jury failed to reach a verdict and a new trial was ordered. During the period between the trials, Wilde was released on bail. His friends tried to persuade him to flee to France, even hiring a yacht for his escape. Wilde refused. At the second trial, he was found guilty and sentenced to two years in prison and hard labor. The judge pronounced it "the worst case I have ever tried" and accused Wilde of being "the centre of a circle of extensive corruption of the most hideous kind among young men." To make his downfall complete, Wilde lost all his possessions in bankruptcy proceedings after he was forced to pay the Marquess of Queensberry's court costs for the original libel action.

Wilde spent two utterly miserable years in prison at a time when conditions in English jails were unspeakable. "Three permanent punishments authorized by law," Wilde wrote, were "1. Hunger, 2. Insomnia, and 3. Disease." At first he was denied pen and paper. Eventually, however, he embraced his suffering and completed his great *De Profundis* (see excerpt, page 51), a cry of bitterness and remorse and a work of philosophy. When he was released from prison, he immediately left for France. After brief attempts at reconciliation with Bosie, Wilde died a broken man in Paris in 1900 at the age of forty-six.

Throughout this period Wilde's feelings toward Bosie were complicated. In a letter to him on the last day of his libel trial, Wilde wrote, "My dearest boy, This is to assure you of my immortal, my eternal love for you. . . . If one day, at Corfu or in some enchanted isle, there were a little house where we could live together, oh! life would be sweeter than it has ever been. . . . Our love was always beautiful and noble, and if I have been the butt of a terrible tragedy, it is because the nature of that love has not been understood." Yet in *De Profundis*, written in the form of a letter to Bosie, he blames himself—but Bosie, as well—for destroying his life. "The basis of character is will power," he wrote, "and my will power became absolutely subject to yours." After he left prison, he resisted Bosie's entreaties that they meet, although eventually he relented. They spent two months together in Naples, which ended disastrously. Later Bosie married, converted to Roman Catholicism, and became a staunch, even fanatical, opponent of "the love that dare not speak its name."

The effects of the trials were immense. Wilde became the object of such great revulsion in England that the word *Oscar* became a popular term of contempt. Meanwhile, in America, some nine hundred sermons were said to have been preached against Wilde from 1895 to 1900. By 1899, also in America, an enterprising businessman was selling undergraduates—for twenty dollars—a set of pornographic photographs (with a scarlet cover) entitled "The Sins of Oscar Wilde." A story of the time relates how a young American from Hot Springs, Arkansas, was sitting reading the *New York Herald* at a Paris cafe when a rather tall Englishman asked him for a match. They struck up a conversation and emptied two bottles of wine together. As they were in the middle of the third bottle, a waiter dropped a card at the young American's elbow that read, "That is Oscar Wilde." When the young man wrote his mother in Hot Springs that he had met the famous Oscar Wilde, she ordered him home on the next boat. The tale may be apocryphal, but it captures the atmosphere of the years following the trial.

In an article penned while Wilde was in prison, Bosie wrote, "Wilde is now suffering for being a Uranian, a Greek, a sexual man. . . . I have already said such men are the salt of the earth." Despite the revulsion caused by the trials—and the fear that they inspired within many homosexual men—"the love that dare not speak its name" was given a name, a voice, a face. "I'm an unspeakable of the Oscar Wilde sort," says the title character in E. M. Forster's novel *Maurice,* written almost twenty years later. Havelock Ellis wrote that the celebrity of Wilde and the publicity surrounding the trials "may have brought conviction of their perversion to many inverts who were before only vaguely conscious of their abnormality, and paradoxical though it may seem, have imparted greater courage to others." In that sense, the downfall of Wilde may been as significant as all the case histories and the classifications of the sexologists. Thanks to Oscar Wilde, homosexuality and homosexuals now possessed an identity—one that was witty, frivolous, dandified, with an epigram on its lips and a green carnation in its buttonhole. This image set the tone for male homosexual style in the English-speaking world throughout much of the twentieth century.

An Excerpt from Wilde's *De Profundis*

Wilde's De Profundis *was written while he was in prison, in the form of a letter to Lord Alfred Douglas (Bosie). Part philosophical work, part* cri de coeur, *it remains one of his greatest achievements.*

THE GODS had given me almost everything. I had genius, a distinguished name, high social position, brilliancy, intellectual daring; I made art a philosophy and philosophy an art: I altered the minds of men and the colours of things; there was nothing I said or did that did not make people wonder. . . . Drama, novel, poem in prose, poem in rhyme, subtle or fantastic dialogue, whatever I touched, I made beautiful in a new mode of beauty: to truth itself I gave what is false no less than what is true as its rightful province, and showed that the false and the true are merely forms of intellectual existence. I treated art as the supreme reality and life as a mere mode of fiction. I awoke the imagination of my century so that it created myth and legend around me. I summed up all systems in a phrase and all existence in an epigram. Along with these things I had things that were different. But I let myself be lured into long spells of senseless and sensual ease. I amused myself with being a *flâneur,* a dandy, a man of fashion. I surrounded myself with the smaller natures and the meaner minds. I became the spendthrift of my own genius, and to waste an eternal youth gave me a curious joy. Tired of being on the heights, I deliberately went to the depths in the search for new sensation. What the paradox was to me in the sphere of thought, perversity became to me in the sphere of passion. Desire, at the end, was a malady, or a madness, or both. I grew careless of the lives of others. I took pleasure where it pleased me, and passed on. I forgot that every little action of the common day makes or unmakes character, and that therefore what one has done in the secret chamber one has some day to cry aloud on the house-tops. I ceased to be lord over myself. I was no longer the captain of my soul, and did not know it. I allowed pleasure to dominate me. I ended in horrible disgrace. There is only one thing for me now, absolute humility.

Wilde and Bosie in Algiers—An Excerpt from Gide's *If It Die*

André Gide, the young French writer, first met Oscar Wilde in Paris in 1891. In 1895, shortly before Wilde's libel suit against the Marquess of Queensberry, he encountered Wilde again in Algiers, where Wilde and Bosie had gone in search of boys. (Gide himself had his first homosexual experience in Algeria, under Wilde's tutelage—see "André Gide," page 87). Gide was able to spend time with Wilde in the days just before Wilde's downfall

*and also had an intimate glimpse of the Wilde-Bosie relationship.
The following excerpt comes from Gide's autobiography,* If It
Die, *published in 1924.*

AT THE BACK of all Wilde's obvious faults, it is his greatness I am
chiefly conscious of. No doubt nothing was more exasperating than
the paradoxes he was continually firing off out of an unceasing
desire to appear witty. But some people, when they heard him
exclaim at the sight of a furniture brocade: "I should like to have
a waistcoat of it," or at the sight of a waistcoat material, "I should
like to hang my drawing-room with it," too easily forget how much
truth, wisdom, and in a more subtle fashion, how much personal
revelation, lay behind his mask of conceits. But with me, as I have
said, Wilde had now thrown aside his mask. It was the man himself
I saw at last; for no doubt he had realised there was no further
need for pretence and that the very thing that would have made
others recoil was precisely what attracted me. Douglas had returned
to Algiers with him; but Wilde seemed trying to avoid him.

I remember particularly one late afternoon coming across him
in a bar. When I went in, he was sitting in front of a sherry-cobbler,
with his elbows on a table strewed with papers.

"Excuse me," he said, "these letters have just come. . . .

"Oh! this one is from a young . . . what do you call it . . . acrobat?
yes; acrobat; absolutely delicious." (He put an exaggerated emphasis on the second syllable of the word; I can hear him still.)
Then he laughed, bridled, and seemed highly amused with himself,
"It's the first time he has written to me, so he doesn't like to spell
properly. What a pity you don't know English! You would see. . . ."

He was continuing to laugh and joke, when suddenly Douglas
came into the bar, wrapped in a fur coat, with the collar turned
up, so that nothing was to be seen of him but his nose and the
glance of his eyes. He brushed past me as though he didn't recognise
me, planted himself in front of Wilde and in a hissing, withering,
savage voice, rapped out a few sentences, of which I understood
not a single word, then turning on his heels, went out. Wilde had
let the storm pass over him without a word; but he had turned very
pale and after Bosy [sic] had gone neither of us spoke for some
time. . . .

Indeed Douglas's personality seemed much stronger and much
more marked than Wilde's; yes, Douglas's personality was over-

weening; a sort of fatality swept him along; at times he seemed almost irresponsible; and as he never attempted to resist himself, he would not put up with anyone or anything resisting him either. To tell the truth Bosy interested me extremely; but "terrible" he certainly was, and in my opinion it is he who ought to be held responsible for all that was disastrous in Wilde's career. Wilde beside him seemed gentle, wavering, and weak-willed. Douglas was possessed by the perverse instinct that drives a child to break his finest toy; nothing ever satisfied him; he always wanted to go one better. The following example will show to what lengths his effrontery would go: I was questioning him one day about Wilde's two sons; he laid great stress on the beauty of Cyril (I think), who was quite young at the time, and then whispered with a self-satisfied smile, "He will be for me. . . ."

The next day or the day after, Douglas returned to Blidah, where he was making arrangements to elope with a young *caouadji* [a boy who makes coffee in a cafe] he wanted to take with him to [the oasis of] Biskra. . . . But to run away with an Arab is not such an easy thing as he had thought at first; he had to get the parents' consent, sign papers at the Arab office, at the police-station etc.; there was work enough to keep him at Blidah for several days; during this time Wilde was more at liberty and able to talk to me more intimately than he had hitherto done. . . . I have described his excessive assurance, the hoarseness of his laugh, the fierceness of his joy; I have also said that a growing uneasiness sometimes showed through all this extreme vehemence. Some of his friends have maintained that Wilde at this time had no idea what was awaiting him in London, where he returned a few days after our meeting in Algiers; they speak of Wilde's confidence and declare he kept it unshaken until the fatal upshot of the libel case. I beg leave to set against his, not my own personal impression, but Wilde's actual words, which I transcribed with absolute fidelity. They bear witness to a kind of vague apprehension, a presentiment of some kind of tragic event which he dreaded, but at the same time almost longed for.

"I have been as far as possible along my own road," he repeated. "I can't go any farther. *Something* must happen now."

CHAPTER 5

ROMANTIC FRIENDSHIPS
BETWEEN WOMEN

THE LATE NINETEENTH CENTURY was a period of major change in the lives of women in the United States and Western Europe. Middle-class women were emerging from the world of compulsory domesticity to one in which independence was increasingly possible. Economic and educational opportunities were growing. At the same time, romantic friendships between women continued to flourish, as they had through the centuries. Sexual identities were not fixed, and women still were not perceived as sexual beings, in any event. The tradition of female romantic friendships, combined with women's growing economic independence, created the possibility of two women living together in a primary relationship without men.

As with male romantic friendships, these women apparently didn't perceive such unions as deviant. Their relationships differed from male romantic friendships in that they were often lifelong, not just restricted to some youthful premarital period. Some of these women were married, but, as the century progressed and the economic opportunities for women widened, many remained unmarried. But when sexual innocence was replaced by the case histories of the sexologists and the heightened sexual and psychological awarenesses of the Freudian age, these relationships became suspect. Once the dire words *lesbian* and *female invert* were spoken, once Krafft-Ebing had completed his cataloging of sexual pathologies, everything began to change. In fact, feminist historian Nancy Sahli refers to this social and cultural shift as "the fall."

Much of the documentation of these relationships comes from letters exchanged between women at the time. Like Whitman's correspondence with his young soldier friends, these letters often display an emotional intensity that modern readers are unaccustomed to seeing outside love relationships. **Anna E. Dickinson,** American orator, actress, and political activist, was the recipient of a number of such letters from female admirers in the 1860s and 1870s. (These

Frances Kellor (1873–1952), in the driver's seat, with her lifelong friend, Mary Elisabeth Dreier (1875–1963). Kellor was an expert in arbitration; Dreier was president of the New York Women's Trade Union League. (© *Mary E. Dreier Papers, Schlesinger Library, Radcliffe College*)

letters appear in Nancy Sahli's essay "Smashing: Women's Relationships Before the Fall.") Dickinson, who was unmarried, received the following letter from **Louise Brackett,** wife of a Boston artist:

> *How much I want to see you: as your letter gave me such exquisite pleasures indeed! I will marry you—run off any where with you, for you are such a darling—I can feel your soul—if not your body sweet Anna—do I offend your delicacy?*

Susan B. Anthony, the suffrage leader, was a particular admirer:

> *Now when are you coming to New York—do let it be soon—I have plain quarters—at 44 Bond Street—double bed—and big enough and good enough to take you in— . . . I do so long for the scolding & pinched ears & every thing I know awaits me— what worlds of experience since I last snuggled the wee child in my long arms. . . . Your loving friend Susan.*

Another letter writer was **Laura Curtis Bullard,** a married woman and editor of a suffragette-backed paper called *Revolution:*

> *I am so glad that I have got you for my darling that I can't find words to express my delight in my new love.*

What is one to make of letters like these? Just how "passionless" really were these relationships? And how should we interpret alliances between women of this period, some of which lasted for decades? It is, of course, easy to take passages from these letters and read them as if they were written today, with the assumption that the correspondents were involved in sexual unions. But that is to impose the ideas of the late twentieth century on a far more reticent era. (At that time, for example, the idea of two women sharing a bed—as in the case of two men—was perfectly acceptable and did not imply a sexual relationship.) Historians themselves are unsure about the nature of these relationships; Lillian Faderman and Carroll Smith-Rosenberg, who both have written extensively on the subject, cast doubt on whether such relationships included genital intimacy.

In the end, the answer is probably not that important. Blanche Wiesen Cook, a women's historian (and biographer of **Eleanor Roosevelt**), has written, "Women who love women, who choose women to nurture and support and to create a living environment in which to work creatively and independently, are lesbians." Whether one agrees with Cook's definition or not, there is ample evidence that these relationships were perceived by the women involved as the central emotional bonds of their lives, just as similar relationships would be viewed by lesbian partners today. On the other hand, none of these women identified themselves publicly as lesbians and it is doubtful if they used the term in thinking about themselves.

The evolution of female romantic friendships in nineteenth-century America must be seen in the context of the emergence of the "New Woman." Carroll Smith-Rosenberg describes the phenomenon as "a cohort of middle- and upper-middle-class American women born between the late 1850s and the early 1900s, who were educated, ambitious, and most frequently, single. By the early twentieth century, they had established places for themselves within the new professions and within government and reform agencies. . . . Their emergence within middle-class rhetoric signaled the symbolic death of that earlier female subject, the refined and confined Victorian lady."

There were a number of reasons for the emergence of the New Woman: the growth of the feminist, abolitionist, and temperance movements, which awakened women politically; widening educational opportunities; and an expanding middle class, which held out more possibilities of economic independence to women.

In the United States, with the emergence of the New Woman came an increasing number of new living arrangements, dubbed "Boston marriages." The term described a long-term relationship between two unmarried women. (In notes for his novel about one such relationship, *The Bostonians,* published in 1886, **Henry James** referred to "one of those friendships between women so common in New England.") Lillian Faderman observes that such women were usually feminists, most often financially independent because of inheritance or career, and frequently involved in the "social betterment" movements of the day. It should be stressed that "Boston marriages" were primarily an upper- and middle-class phenomenon; there are few records of these kinds of alliances existing between poorer women.

Some of the most admired and successful women of the period participated or lived in such arrangements. **Jane Addams,** founder of the settlement house movement in the United States, never married and had an intimate relationship first with **Ellen Starr** and then for forty years with **Mary Rozet Smith,** with whom she owned a house in Bar Harbor, Maine; **M. Carey Thomas,** president of Bryn Mawr College, had two close companions: **Mary Gwinn,** a girlhood friend who lived with her in the college deanery, and later **Mary Garrett,** a millionaire philanthropist who lived with her on the Bryn Mawr campus after 1906 and made large gifts to the college; the novelist **Sarah Orne Jewett** (author of *In the Country of the Pointed Fires*) and **Annie Fields** were intimately involved for thirty years after the death of Fields's husband and lived together in Boston for part of each year; novelist **Willa Cather** and her companion, **Edith Lewis,** had a relationship of almost forty years (see "Willa Cather," page 64); and **Mary Wooley,** president of Mount Holyoke College, lived for fifty-five years with her devoted companion, **Jeanette Marks,** a Mount Holyoke professor.

In England, too, there were numerous examples of such unions, as well as networks of women involved in settlement houses, education, and the theatre. **Octavia Hill,** founder of the University

Women's Settlement, never married, and lived for the last thirty-five years of her life with **Harriot Yorke;** the two women are buried together. **Lilian Baylis,** who managed the Old Vic and Sadler's Wells theatres and turned them into centers of national culture, was part of a close group of unmarried women in the first decades of the twentieth century. Edward Carpenter saw a connection between the feminist movement, the New Woman, and the growth of such relationships, commenting, "It is pretty certain that such comrade-alliances—of a quite devoted kind—are becoming increasingly common, and especially perhaps among the more cultured classes of women who are working out the great cause of their own sex's liberation."

The American temperance leader **Frances Willard,** who had a number of romantic attachments with women, noted in her autobiography:

> *The loves of women for each other grow more numerous each day, and I have pondered much why these things were. That so little should be said about them surprises me, for they are everywhere. . . . In these days, when any capable and careful woman can honorably own her own support, there is no village that has not its examples of "two hearts in counsel" both of which are feminine. Oftentimes these joint-proprietors have been unfortunately married, and so have failed to "better their condition" until, thus clasping hands, they have taken each other "for better or worse." These are the tokens of a transition age.*

Willard had her own opinion as to why these all-women alliances were occurring. She blamed drink and tobacco, "the great separatists between women and men."

Historian Faderman takes a different view, however. "More than any phenomenon, education may be said to have been responsible for the spread among middle-class women of what eventually came to be called lesbianism," she writes in her book *Odd Girls and Twilight Lovers.* Mount Holyoke, the first women's college in the United States, was founded in 1837. Throughout the second half of the nineteenth century, the number of women's colleges grew: Vassar opened in 1865, Smith in 1872, Wellesley in 1875, and Bryn Mawr in 1886. Some traditionally male colleges also began to admit women: Oberlin College did so in the 1830s; Cornell and the University of Michigan became coed in the 1870s. Faderman notes that while only 10 percent of American women remained unmarried between 1880 and 1900, about 50 percent of American female college graduates fell into that category. Fifty-seven percent of the Smith class of 1884 never married. Of the women who received Ph.D.s from U.S. universities from 1877 to 1924, three-quarters remained single. One can argue that a man of that period might not be overly eager to marry a highly educated woman, especially one with a Ph.D., but the statistics would indicate that there were a large number of female college graduates who declined to marry of their own volition.

One aspect of the women's college experience that clearly had an impact on the prevalence of these relationships was "smashing," the romantic crushes, presumably nonsexual (but perhaps not?), that flourished in closed same-sex environments. An 1873 letter to the *Yale Courant* described the practice as follows:

> *When a Vassar girl takes a shine to another, she straightway enters upon a regular course of bouquet sendings, interspersed with tinted notes, mysterious packages of "Ridley's Mixed Candies," locks of hair perhaps, and many other tender tokens, until at last the object of her attentions is captured, the two become inseparable, and the aggressor is considered by her circle of acquaintances as—smashed.*

The dismayed letter writer continued:

> *One young lady, the "Irrepressible," rejoices in more than thirty [smashes]. She keeps a list of them, in illuminated text, framed and hung up in her room like a Society poster. How ... such a custom should have come into vogue, passes masculine comprehension. But the solemn fact remains, and Vassar numbers her smashes by the score.*

In the early 1880s, the Association of Collegiate Alumnae (known today as the American Association of University Women) appointed a research committee to study what they saw as the problem of "smashing." A member of the committee, **Alice Stone Blackwell,** commented on committee discussions in an 1882 letter, noting strong arguments that "one thing which damaged the health of the girls seriously was "smashes"—an extraordinary habit which they have of falling violently in love with each other, and suffering all the pangs of unrequited attachment, desperate jealousy &c &c with as much energy as if one of them were a man." She reported a certain Miss Brown on her committee relating how, while at Smith, "a 'veteran smasher' attacked her & captured her, & soon deserted her for someone else; & she used to cry herself to sleep night after night, & wake up with a headache in the morning. And they write each other the wildest love-letters & send presents, confectionary, all sorts of things, like a real courting of the Shakespearean style." Blackwell, who had graduated from coed Boston University, contended that smashes were rare there, perhaps, she speculated, because there were other outlets for sentimental relationships (i.e., men).

When Blackwell's committee published its final report in 1885, it made no mention of "smashing" by name, referring instead to such conditions as "weakness of the nervous system" and "emotional strain." It did point out, nonetheless, that "only a few of the students were so situated as to be able to enter into a society other than the companionship of their fellow-students."

But even the passionate attachments found in women's colleges could not survive the growing sexual sophistication of the early twentieth century. Faderman cites **Wanda Fraiken Neff**'s 1928 novel about Vassar, *We Sing Diana,* which charts an undergraduate's return to Vassar to teach there. In 1913, when the character is first at Vassar, intense crushes between young women were considered "the great human experience." But seven years later, when she returns, the atmosphere has changed dramatically: Everything is attributed to sex, and Freud and Freudian terminology dominate everyone's thinking and speech. "Intimacy between two girls was watched with keen distrustful eyes," Neff writes in the novel. "Among one's classmates, one looked for the bisexual type, the masculine girl searching for a feminine counterpart, and one ridiculed their devotions."

In fact, changes in social attitudes came about even before the period the book chronicles. The year 1892 finds the budding novelist Willa Cather writing to **Louise Pound,** a fellow University of Nebraska student with whom she was quite enamored, "What a shame that feminine friendship should be unnatural." Three years later, the popular writer **Ruth Ashmore,** writing in the *Ladies' Home Journal,* was warning female readers against forming romantic bonds with other women. "I like a girl to have many girl-friends; I do not like her to have a girl sweetheart," she advised. In 1908, Mount Holyoke professor Jeanette Marks, herself a partner in a lifelong Boston marriage, cautioned in an essay against "unwise college friendships," calling them "pleasant or worse" and a sickness requiring a "moral antiseptic."

Historians such as Faderman and Smith-Rosenberg tend to blame the sexologists for creating lesbianism as a deviant category and using it to attack the New Woman and the feminist and reform movements. An example was Havelock Ellis's distinction between women who were "true inverts" and those for whom homosexuality was an acquired characteristic that could be prevented. (In line with his congenital theories, he argued rather lamely that the latter group had a genetic predisposition for the advances of other women.) According to Ellis, all-female environments—a women's college or a settlement house—could provide the place where such a susceptible woman could succumb to the invert's influence. And, as we noted earlier, he feared that feminism could push some women toward inversion.

As the social mood shifted, there was an attempt to censor the letters and works of women involved in romantic friendships. When Annie Fields, longtime companion of novelist Sarah Orne Jewett, wanted to bring out a book of Jewett's letters after the novelist's death in 1911, Jewett's biographer suggested omitting four-fifths of the affectionate references in them to Fields out of concern for "all sorts of people reading them wrong." Similarly, in the 1920s, the poet **Emily Dickinson**'s niece censored the passionate letters Dickinson wrote to Dickinson's sister-in-law, **Sue Gilbert.** Among the casualties were lines such as "If you were here—and Oh that you were, my Susie—we need not talk at all, our eyes would whisper for us, and your hand fast in mine, we would not ask for language." While these kinds of feelings and their expression were perfectly acceptable in the mid-to-late 1800s, by the early twentieth century, they carried connotations of deviance. Such censorship by family members and literary executors makes it even harder to understand the true nature of the relationships in question. Significantly, Henry James's novel about the subject, *The Bostonians,* was omitted from the twenty-six-volume Scribner edition of his works published between 1907 and 1917. The work was not reissued in the United States until 1945.

Some feminist historians contend that the threat to male dominance led American culture to clamp down on women's relationships, the feminist movement, and women's institutions early in the
twentieth century. "As long as women loved each other as they did
for much of the nineteenth century, without threatening the system
itself, their relationships either were simply ignored by men or were
regarded as an acceptable part of the female sphere," writes Nancy
Sahli. "Feminists, college graduates, and other independent women,
however, were a real threat to the established order, and one way
to control these sexless termites, hermaphroditic spinsters, or whatever one might call them, was to condemn their love relationships—
the one aspect of their behavior which, regardless of their other
social, political, or economic activities, posed a basic threat to a
system where the fundamental exercise of power was that of one
sex over another."

Other factors clearly played a role as well. As women began to
be viewed as "sexual" in the age of Freud, as birth control became
more accessible in the 1920s and heterosexual sex didn't have to
end in babies, the pressure grew for women to abandon these romantic friendships and give themselves totally to their husbands.
The new awareness of women's sexuality made it harder for women
to hide their attractions to members of the same sex in some asexual
guise.

Whatever the reasons for the social turnabout, it is evident that
for a brief period at the end of the last century, social innocence—
or denial—about female sexuality, combined with increased economic opportunities and independence, permitted a generation of
middle- and upper-class women to make intimate same-sex relationships the emotional, if not the erotic, center of their lives. They
did so within the bounds of social acceptance but, increasingly,
outside the bounds of heterosexual marriage. And it is also evident
that, in the early decades of the twentieth century, social attitudes
turned abruptly against these women and against such unions, denying their importance and condemning them. Soon the only places
where they could survive were in artistic or bohemian pockets,
where social rules were relaxed and unconventionality was prized.

Willa Cather

IN 1916, when **Isabelle McClung,** writer Willa Cather's intimate friend of many years, announced that she was getting married, Cather fell into a depression that lasted several months. She couldn't write; she took a trip out West for a change of scene; her face was "bleak" and "vacant" when she told another friend of the news. Seven years later, when she spent a summer in France at the home of McClung and her husband, Cather developed neuritis in her arm and shoulder so severe that it was impossible for her to work. Later she destroyed all her correspondence with McClung.

The life of Willa Cather (1873–1947), author of such classic American novels as *My Ántonia* and *Death Comes for the Archbishop,* illustrates changing social attitudes as the era of passionate women's friendships waned. During her first two years at the University of Nebraska, beginning in 1890, Cather was very much the rebel: She dressed in men's clothes, insisted on using the men's cloakroom, and called herself "William Cather." "She was the first girl that I ever saw in suspenders," noted one of her classmates, quoted in Sharon O'Brien's book *Willa Cather: The Emerging Voice.* Another classmate recalled a first impression of Cather:

> While the students were sitting in the classroom waiting for the instructor to arrive, the door opened and a head appeared with short hair and straw hat. A masculine voice inquired if this were the beginning Greek class, and when someone said it was, the body attached to the head and hat opened the door wider and came in. The masculine head and voice were attached to a girl's body and skirts. The entire class laughed, but Willa Cather, apparently unperturbed, took her seat and joined the waiting students.

During her undergraduate years, Cather became infatuated with the brilliant and sportsy Louise Pound, who was three years ahead of her in school. (Pound was the university tennis champion in 1891 and 1892, defeating male opponents to win the prize; years later she became the first female president of the Modern Language Association.) Cather wrote adoring letters to Pound, signing them "William." But Cather was aware of the changing social mores in which women's friendships were increasingly viewed as deviant. This evident in the letter she wrote Pound, complaining how unfair it was that feminine friendship should be considered "unnatural."

Willa Cather. (© *Schlesinger Library, Radcliffe College*)

Perhaps it was Cather's own ambivalence about the subject that led her to be so reticent about her sexuality both in life and art. There is no indication in her letters or papers that she ever had sexual relations with another woman (although the letters to McClung, had they survived, might have given a different impression). She never identified herself as lesbian or wrote about lesbianism; the only time she approached a homosexual theme was in "Paul's Case," the story of a sensitive, misunderstood boy who wears a red carnation in his buttonhole and throws himself under a train. Until O'Brien's book was published in 1987, her biographers insisted that Cather's dilemma was being forced to choose between two exclusive alternatives—personal relationships (heterosexual marriage) and the lonely life of the artist—and that she chose the latter. But in fact, the two central relationships of her life were with women.

After college, Cather moved to Pittsburgh, where she got a job on a newspaper and later became a schoolteacher. It was there that she met Isabelle McClung; in 1901, she moved in with McClung and her family. At first McClung's parents, members of Pittsburgh's wealthy elite, were hesitant about permitting Cather to live in the house. But their daughter's wishes prevailed, and Cather lived there for five years before leaving to take a job with the muckraking *McClure's* magazine in New York City. For several years after she left Pittsburgh, she and McClung would take vacations together, and Cather would come to Pittsburgh for long visits, periods in which she wrote substantial portions of *O Pioneers!* and *The Song of the Lark*.

Once she moved to New York, Cather found another woman with whom to share her life, Edith Lewis. The two set up house in 1908 and lived together until Cather's death in 1947. During the early years of their relationship, Cather's major attachment still lay with McClung. But after McClung married, Lewis began to take a much more important role in Cather's life. If, in Sharon O'Brien's view, McClung was Cather's "grand romance, her muse, her ideal reader," Lewis fulfilled a different role, offering Cather "tranquillity and protection, not passionate intensity." She was Cather's Alice B. Toklas. After Cather died, Lewis spent much of her time protecting Cather's memory and furthering her friend's literary reputation. Until Lewis's own death in 1972, she kept their Park Avenue apartment exactly as it had been when Cather was alive. The two women are buried next to each other in a cemetery in Jaffrey, New

Hampshire. But surrounding the details of their life together, there remains only silence.

The Reporter and the First Lady

DURING THE 1932 PRESIDENTIAL CAMPAIGN when it became obvious that Franklin D. Roosevelt would be elected president of the United States, the political reporter for the Associated Press, **Lorena "Hick" Hickok** (1893–1968), was moved from covering the candidate to covering the candidate's outspoken and activist wife. At first, reporting about Eleanor Roosevelt (1884–1962) turned out to be less momentous than Hick had anticipated. As Blanche Wiesen Cook tells it in her biography *Eleanor Roosevelt,* days would go by with Hick "cooling her heels, waiting for a tidbit outside her office," and wondering whether this new assignment was worth her employer's money. For her part, Mrs. Roosevelt was dismayed by the loss of privacy. After a while, however, Hick's admiration for the First Lady-to-be grew ("THE DAME HAS TREMENDOUS DIGNITY. SHE'S A PERSON," Hick cabled the Associated Press on one particularly slow news day), and Mrs. Roosevelt began to trust Hick. As election day neared, on a night train trip home from a campaign swing, she told Hick the story of her life. As Cook writes, "More than a political interview, that evening on the train was the beginning of the most intimate friendship of their adult years." From that point on, Hick became a part of the Roosevelt family circle, and FDR, busy with his own romantic affairs, didn't seem to mind.

They were an odd couple—Eleanor Roosevelt, with her aristocratic background, her humane and internationalist politics, her children and grandchildren, and Lorena Hickok, the hard-boiled, self-made reporter who was born on a dairy farm in Wisconsin and grew up with an out-of-work and abusive father in a series of dismal Dakota prairie towns. Hick was a crack reporter who received some of the most coveted assignments (the kidnapping of the Lindbergh baby, for example) and earned a higher salary than any other female reporter in America. She stood five feet eight and weighed two

Eleanor Roosevelt (left) and her devoted friend newspaperwoman Lorena "Hick" Hickok (right), photographed in 1934 when the First Lady was on a speaking tour. *(©UPI /Bettmann Newsphotos)*

hundred pounds, smoked cigarettes, cigars, and pipes. She hung out with her male colleagues, playing poker and drinking—mostly bourbon on the rocks. Cook writes of Hick's relationship with "E.R.," as she calls Mrs. Roosevelt:

> Theirs was a powerful attraction, in the beginning based on work and political interests. . . . [E.R.] welcomed Hick's shrewd advice, comforting directness, and sharp political insights. She was charmed by her pungent and often startling sense of humor, her quick and robust capacity for fury. . . . The period of passion soared and mellowed, and did not last very long, though longer than either would have predicted. Still, their happiness seemed worth all the trouble. And their friendship ended only with death.

The timing of their relationship was problematic, however. Shortly after they met, Mrs. Roosevelt was to move into the White House and to become the most public—and most admired—woman in the United States. The two were often separated. Mrs. Roosevelt would write Hick daily letters of ten to twenty pages in length. Hick persuaded her to transform the "diary" portions of these letters—which described the First Lady's hour-by-hour activities—into a syndicated newspaper column that became known as "My Day." (She also convinced Mrs. Roosevelt to hold news conferences restricted to female reporters.) Mrs. Roosevelt kept all of Hickok's letters to her. In one, written in 1933, Hick writes:

> I've been trying today to bring back your face—to remember just how you look. Funny how even the dearest face will fade away in time. Most clearly I remember your eyes, with a kind of teasing smile in them, and the feeling of that soft spot just north-east of the corner of your mouth against my lips.

Hickok ends her letter.:

> Good night, dear one, I want to put my arms around you, and kiss you at the corner of your mouth. And in a little more than a week now—I shall!

For her part, Mrs. Roosevelt wrote Hick on March 7, 1933, Hick's fortieth birthday:

Hick darling, All day I've thought of you & another birthday I will be with you & yet tonite you sounded so far away & formal. Oh! I want to put my arms around you. I ache to hold you close. Your ring is a great comfort. I look at it and think she does love me, or I wouldn't be wearing it.

In 1933, Hick quit her newspaper job to take a New Deal post in Washington in order to be near the First Lady. Within a few years, however, the passion seems to have gone out of their relationship, at least on Mrs. Roosevelt's side. In January 1941, Hick moved into the White House, but things were not as they had been. As historian Doris Kearns Goodwin writes, "Though she [Hick] had come to accept that she could never mean to Eleanor what Eleanor meant to her, the yearning in her soul was still too powerful to allow her to break away. Accepting Eleanor's invitation was in some ways a self-destructive act, but, by living so close, she rationalized, she would at least have the chance to share an occasional breakfast with Eleanor in the morning or talk with her late at night. It was not enough, but it was better than nothing."

Although the post-Freudian 1930s are some distance from the era of nineteenth-century passionate friendships, some of the same uncertainties of interpretation remain in the Hickok-Roosevelt relationship as in women's friendships of previous generations. Hick destroyed many of Mrs. Roosevelt's letters to her and removed personal references in others. Still, Cook considers the thousands of letters that remain to be "amorous and specific." And she also points out that, during the 1920s, Mrs. Roosevelt's closest friends were two lesbian couples, active in women's political and international peace organizations. During the 1920s at Val-Kill, next door to Hyde Park, where she and her friends **Marion Dickerman** and **Nancy Cook** built a cottage, Mrs. Roosevelt had towels and linens embroidered with the initials of all three—EMN. During her years as First Lady, she rented a "hiding house" from another lesbian friend, **Esther Lape,** in Greenwich Village, to which she could slip away from the pressures of public life. Dickerman, Cook, Lape, and Lape's partner, **Elizabeth Read,** functioned as a virtual second "family" for Mrs. Roosevelt, and yet none of her letters to these friends survive. What remained instead was the myth of Eleanor Roosevelt as the Victorian wife who didn't enjoy sex and responded to her husband's infidelities by becoming even more the social activist.

But biographer Cook, for one, is convinced that the relationship between Mrs. Roosevelt and Hick cannot be dismissed as a chaste romantic friendship of the old school:

The fact is that E.R. and Hick were not involved in a schoolgirl "smash." They did not meet in a nineteenth-century storybook, or swoon unrequitedly upon a nineteenth-century campus. They were neither saints nor adolescents. Nor were they virgins or mermaids. They were two adult women, in the prime of their lives, committed to working out a relationship under very difficult circumstances. They had each already lived several other lives. They knew the score. . . . They touched each other deeply, loved profoundly, and moved on. They sought to avoid gossip. And, for the most part, they succeeded. They wrote to each other exactly what they meant to write.

Cook concludes, "Sigmund Freud notwithstanding: A cigar may not always be a cigar, but the 'north-east corner of your mouth against my lips' is always the northeast corner."

A "Passing Woman": The Strange Case of Murray Hall

THE PHENOMENON of women who "passed" as men—particularly in the nineteenth and early twentieth centuries—has fascinated gay and feminist historians. In his book *Gay American History,* Jonathan Ned Katz documented an impressive number of such stories from all social classes, including a Revolutionary War soldier, a hunter, an innkeeper, three Civil War soldiers, three doctors, a boilermaker's apprentice, a sailor, a railroad cook, a society gentleman, and a Tammany Hall politician. Lillian Faderman cites reports by Union Army doctors that approximately four hundred women masquerading as men fought in the Civil War. At least eleven "passing" women were reported to have worked for the New York Central Railroad at the turn of the century.

In many cases, the true identities of these women were only

revealed when they became ill (and were forced to consult a physician) or died. "There must have been thousands of women wandering around America in the latter part of the nineteenth century and the early twentieth century who were passing as men," Faderman suggests. She notes that it was relatively easy to do so because in that era women never wore pants. Anyone who did wear pants was assumed to be male, and no one bothered to investigate further.

Many of these women pretended to be men for economic reasons. While there were new economic opportunities becoming available for middle-class women during this period, most women were still relegated to low-paying jobs in factories and as domestic servants. Furthermore, a woman who masqueraded as a man was able to do things that other women were unable to do: open a bank account, own property, and vote.

As Katz points out, such women represent a kind of "early form of female revolt" in a society in which women could only live in circumscribed ways. **Cora Anderson,** a Native American woman who lived for thirteen years in Milwaukee as Ralph Kerwinieo with her longtime companion, Marie White, explained her masquerade in a 1914 article that appeared in a Chicago tabloid:

> *This world is made by man—for man alone. . . .*
> *Do you blame me for wanting to be a man—free to live life as a man in a man-made world?*
> *Do you blame me for hating to again resume a woman's clothes and just belong?*

The long tenure of many women in men's garb—sometimes marrying or being in couple relationships with other women—brings up many of the same issues as "Boston marriages." Were these women having sex with their female "wives" or partners? Did such women consider themselves as "inverted" or lesbian? How much of their motivation for passing was psychological or sexual, and how much was economic? The reality is that for one member of a female couple to present herself to the world as a man was one of the few ways that two working-class women could live together openly.

One of the most intriguing cases of "passing women" was that of Tammany Hall politician and bail bondsman Murray Hall (a.k.a., Mary Anderson), whose impersonation of a man was discovered only upon her death in 1901. She had lived as a man in New York

City for some twenty-five to thirty years. Hall had been a member of the General Committee of Tammany Hall—the political "machine" that governed New York politics. A friend of State Senator **"Barney" Martin,** she had been one of the most active Tammany members within her district. She had considerable political influence within Tammany Hall, often finding jobs for friends, and apparently never arousing the remotest suspicion as to her real gender. As *The New York Times* wrote in an article headlined MURRAY HALL FOOLED MANY SHREWD MEN, "She played poker at the clubs with city and State officials and politicians who flatter themselves on their cleverness and perspicacity, drank whisky and wine and smoked the regulation 'big black cigar' with the apparent relish and gusto of the real man-about-town."

The political associates whom the *Times* interviewed all expressed astonishment at the discovery of Hall's true identity. State Senator Martin said, "Truly, it's most wonderful. . . . Suspect he was a woman? Never. He dressed like a man and talked like a very sensible one." The only thing that Martin had ever found to be eccentric was Hall's clothing: Hall would wear a coat that was a size or two too large. "Now that they say he's a woman, I can see through that," he said. Joseph Young, one of Martin's aides, was quoted as exclaiming, "A woman? Why, he'd line up to the bar and take his whisky like any veteran, and didn't make faces over it, either. If he was a woman he ought to have been born a man, for he lived and looked like one."

Hall's origins were unclear, although the sexologist Havelock Ellis claimed she was born in Govan, Scotland, and was left an orphan. When her only brother died, she put on his clothes and went to Edinburgh, where she worked as a man. Then, after her secret was discovered during an illness, she emigrated to America. In New York, she opened an employment agency on Sixth Avenue. At that time, she had a woman with her whom she introduced as her wife.

Hall, in fact, was married twice—the first time for three years and the second time for about eight years. (Ellis, quoting Scottish sources, says her second marriage actually lasted twenty years.) She also had an adopted daughter, Minnie, who was twenty-two at the time of Hall's death. According to neighbors, both her marriages broke up because Hall paid too much attention to other women. Newspaper accounts after her death did not include comments from these ex-wives. Her daughter, however, insisted that she had never remotely suspected that her father was a woman. The cause of Hall's death (she was said to be seventy when she died) was listed as breast cancer, but when her physican, Dr. **W. C. Gallagher**—who had been treating her for about a year—was asked if he knew that she was female when she first came to him as a patient, he declined to answer. Indeed, she seems to have postponed seeing a doctor for a long time because of her fear of discovery.

"How a woman could for so many years impersonate a man without detection," *The New York Times* marveled, "deceiving even her physician and some of the cleverest men and women in New York with whom she frequently came in contact, though the secret must have been known to at least two others—the wives—is a mystery quite as inexplicable as the character that accomplished the feat." But as a strategy for women's survival (and perhaps especially lesbian survival), Hall's masquerade may not have been as inexplicable—or unusual—as the newspaper believed.

CHAPTER 6

SAPPHO COMES TO PARIS

> *Then I replied to them, the delightful women,*
> *"How you will remember till you are old, our*
> *Life together there in the splendid time of*
> *   Youth, for we did so*
>
> *Many pure and beautiful things together*
> *Then, and now that you are all departing*
> *Amorous passion gathers up my heart and*
> *   Wrings it with anguish."*
>
> —Sappho

IN 1879, in the oasis of El Faiyum, southwest of Cairo, archae-
ologists came upon a remarkable find: eighth-century manuscripts
that proved to be the poems of Sappho. Twenty years later, also in
Egypt, more fragments of Sappho's work were discovered; these
had been written on papyrus rolls used as lining in mummies and
wadded into the carcasses of crocodiles and other sacred animals.
Born in the seventh century B.C. on the Greek island of Lesbos,
Sappho was regarded as the greatest woman poet of antiquity. She
was also known for love poems to other women and for the female
circle of poets she gathered around her on Lesbos (hence the term
lesbian). By the Middle Ages, though, very little of her poetry remained extant—all but a few fragments are said to have been destroyed by **Pope Gregory VII** in 1073—and she was mostly known
through quotations of her work by other poets. Her life—and death,
supposedly by leaping into the Aegean after a failed love affair—
remained shrouded in mystery.

At the time of her rediscovery, a fascination with Sappho and
Sapphic sexuality emerged in France. Earlier in the century, writers
such as **Gautier,** Baudelaire, and **Verlaine** had laid the groundwork
in novels and poetry. In 1894, **Pierre Louÿs** published *Songs of*

Bilitis, a book that included passionate love poems between two women, supposedly written by a contemporary of Sappho. The book, which was wildly popular, was in fact an elaborate literary hoax—with invented bibliography and textual notes. (Composer **Claude Debussy** wrote a number of songs based on the work, and the Daughters of Bilitis, the lesbian organization founded in the United States in the 1950s, took its name from it.) The authors of these works—all men—tended to link lesbianism with decadence. Soon, women who shared Sappho's sexuality discovered her as well, and like the model for contemporary male homosexuality that British gay pioneers such as John Addington Symonds sought in classical Greece, Sappho became a focus for a new, affirming sense of lesbian identity.

Paris at the end of the nineteenth century was an appropriate place for the Sapphic revival. It was the period of the "Belle Époque," with its relaxed moral climate and its androgynous aesthetic. In the salons of the period, "women of the *demi-monde* mixed with aged duchesses," and "homosexual men appeared in rouge and wigs and homosexual women wore tuxedos with monocles tucked in the pockets," writes Shari Benstock in her book, *Women of the Left Bank.* In France, the penal code of 1791, following the revolution, and the Code Napoléon, two decades later, had decriminalized homosexuality. (In 1863, the age of consent was established at thirteen.) If the law and social attitudes in France were far more liberal than in England, male homosexual relationships were still viewed with disdain, if not moral censure. But lesbianism was viewed quite differently, at least among the upper classes. As George Painter, the biographer of **Marcel Proust,** noted, lesbians were spared "the unjust stigma which condemned the natives of Sodom [homosexual men] to a furtive or defiant criminality . . . they seemed to the world, as indeed they were, an innocent, proud, eccentric, indispensable leavening in a monotonous society." Indeed, in certain circles, lesbian relationships were almost fashionable. As one salon hostess of the time put it, "All the noteworthy women are doing it."

Female-to-male cross-dressing was very much in vogue, even though it was illegal, due to a hundred-year-old ordinance that was stringently enforced by the Paris prefect of police, **M. Lépine.** Rich women could hide their male attire under their cloaks as they stepped out of coaches. But lesbianism was primarily something that fin de siècle Paris society toyed with. Women were still expected to marry. Lesbianism might be intriguing to the habitués of salon society, but it did not represent a personal or social alternative to heterosexual relationships. It didn't yet constitute a recognized identity.

The limits to the acceptance of lesbianism among the upper classes can be seen in a 1907 scandal in which the novelist **Colette** (1873–1954) featured prominently. Colette was separated from her first husband, the music critic **Henri Gauthier-Villars,** better known by his professional pseudonym, **"Willy."** At the time, she was living with the **Marquise de Belbeuf** (**"Missy"**), a woman quite a bit older than she. The Marquise, who had obtained a separation from her husband, the **Duc de Belbeuf,** four years earlier, was a member of the Napoleonic aristocracy; her father was the bastard half-brother of Napoleon III, whom he had served as foreign minister. She was famous for her cross-dressing, particularly as an automobile mechanic. One biographer of Colette describes the Marquise as wearing "an assortment of shirts and woolen waistcoats that made her look a bit like a teddy bear." (Because she had very small feet, she used to wear several pairs of socks to fill up her men's shoes.) In later life, the Marquise lived in the Passy quarter of Paris, always as a man. It is said that Willy, Colette's husband, amused himself by traveling in "ladies' only" compartments on trains; when a passenger objected he would explain, "I am the Marquise of Belbeuf."

It was Willy, known for his self-promotion (and for claiming his wife's novels as his own), who is said to have convinced the Marquise and Colette to appear onstage at the Moulin Rouge in a pantomime called *Rêve d'Égypte* (An Egyptian Dream). In the pantomime, set in the time of the Pharaohs, a mummy (played by Colette) emerges from her sarcophagus and, virtually naked, mimes the tale of her former loves. She charms an elderly scholar (the Marquise, dressed in a blue velvet suit) and the two kiss passionately. On opening night, the Moulin Rouge was filled with some of the most elegant people in Paris, but it also included thugs, hired by the family of the Marquise's former husband. The family was apparently so dismayed by the possibility of scandal that it was determined to create an even greater scandal. When the moment arrived that the two women kissed, the outraged audience threw orange peels, cigarettes, matchboxes, and vegetables onto the stage. Willy then stood up in his box and began to applaud. The audience booed and cried, "Cuckold," and Willy fled.

The following day, the prefect of police banned further performances. Willy was fired from his job as music critic at *L'Echo de Paris,* and two weeks later, he applied for a legal separation from Colette. Social pressure forced Colette to stop living openly with the Marquise de Belbeuf (although they continued to be involved for four more years). Parisian law and society had exacted its revenge on those who would transgress its norms.

Colette's life with the Marquise de Belbeuf gave her a window on the world of aristocratic Parisian lesbians. It is through her elaborately wrought prose that we get the best view of Paris lesbian life of the time, at least among the upper classes. In her fictionalized memoir, *The Pure and the Impure,* Colette describes the members of the Marquise's lesbian circle—ranging from lady cousins of the Czars to illegimate daughters of grand-dukes to horsewomen of the Austrian aristocracy—and the young women who were their protégées:

> *Some of these ladies fondly kept in their protective and jealous shadow women younger than they, clever young actresses, the next to the last authentic demimondaine of the epoch, a music hall star. . . . You heard them in whispered conversation, but to the great disappointment of the curious ear, the dialogue was banal. "How did your lesson go? Do you have it now, your Chopin waltz?" "Take your furs off here, you will get hot and won't be in voice this evening."*

Some of these women "wore a monocle, a white carnation in the buttonhole, took the name of God in vain and discussed horses competently," Colette noted. In fact, they seemed almost as fond of horses as they were of their young protégées. "The exciting scent of horses, that so masculine odor, never quite left these women, but lingered on after the ride . . ." she wrote. "With their strong slender hands they were able to break in and subjugate a horse, and when age and hard times deprived them of the whip and the hunting crop, they lost their final scepter."

During these years, Colette became friendly with her neighbor **Renée Vivien** (1877–1909), the alcoholic decadent poet who for many epitomized the atmosphere of lesbian Paris in the years before World War I. Vivien, an Englishwoman whose real name was Pauline Tarn, lived in a vast and dark flat filled with gigantic Buddhas. Colette describes Vivien wandering through the apartment, "veiled in black or purple, almost invisible in the scented darkness of the immense rooms barricaded with leaded windows, the air heavy with curtains and incense." At one point in their friendship, Vivien was supposed to appear in a *tableau vivant* at a costume ball and discovered that, to her horror, she had gained ten pounds. Determined to lose the extra pounds in the ten days remaining before the ball, Vivien sought seclusion in the Pavillion Henri IV in Saint-Germain. There, she would drink only a glass of tea in the morning and then walk in the forest until she was exhausted. Later, she would drink more tea, with alcohol, and go to bed. This starvation regime continued for ten days. On the night of the ball, she arrived at the Theatre des Arts "powdered and rouged, hollow-eyed, her hair loose on one shoulder. . . ." She played her part in the *tableau vivant*, but afterward, she fainted backstage. She recovered but was dead before she was thirty, of drugs, drink, and starvation, as if she had been determined to live out the image of the lesbian of a poem by Baudelaire or Verlaine—tragic and doomed.

But Vivien did more than spend her life in some overscented stupor. Along with her lover at the time, the American writer **Natalie Barney** (1876–1972), she was determined to remove male interpretations from Sappho's life and reclaim the Greek poet as someone whose writings celebrated women's love and friendship. Vivien wrote four poetic plays about Sappho (Barney wrote one as well), recreating Sappho as indisputably lesbian. Both Vivien and Barney learned ancient Greek, and Vivien eventually translated the work of a number of minor Greek poets. In 1904, both journeyed to the island of Lesbos itself, a kind of pilgrimage to sacred soil, but were quickly disillusioned. When they arrived on the island, they were greeted by noisy, blaring music. Lesbos was dirty; the inhabitants were already corrupted by the modern age. Despite her expertise in the classics, Vivien could not understand modern Greek. Barney wrote her mother, complaining that the ancient Greeks "must have been in reality horrid, dirty people—the sight of so many tarnished feet quite ruins our illusions about the Greeks." The two women nonetheless bought two houses on the island and decided to establish a Sapphic school of poetry, but Vivien soon retreated to Constantinople, at the call of another lover, the **Baroness de Zuylan.** For her part, Barney decided it was more realistic to revive Lesbos in Paris, instead.

Natalie Clifford Barney, "the wild girl from Cincinnati," as she was called, was the daughter of an American railway car magnate who had left her a fortune of $2.5 million when he died in 1902. Barney had been brought up in Europe, made a quick foray back to America for a semester at Bryn Mawr, and was engaged briefly to Lord Alfred Douglas ("Bosie")—largely to antagonize her father. Eventually she settled in Paris, "the only city where you can live and express yourself as you please," as she put it. Her expatriate status and inherited wealth combined to assure her of an unusual degree of personal and financial independence for a woman of the period. She wrote poetry in French, in a romantic style that was anachronistic even at the time. Her work was printed in limited editions through small Paris publishing houses. When her first book of poetry was published in 1901 (with a cover featuring Barney dressed as a Renaissance page), her father bought up all the copies and the typesetting plates.

Authors ranging from **Ronald Firbank** to **Radclyffe Hall** to **Djuna Barnes** all used Barney as a model for characters in their novels. She had a reputation as a female Don Juan and had affairs with **Liane de Pougy,** the most famous courtesan of the era, and later with Oscar Wilde's niece **Dolly.** In her novel *The Well of Loneliness,* Radclyffe Hall described Valerie Seymour, the character based on Barney, as "a creature born out of her epoch, a pagan chained to an age that was Christian." In the Barney character's luminous eyes could be discerned "the pale yet ardent light of the fanatic."

Colette's references to horse-obsessed women could have applied to Barney. She became known for riding every morning in the Bois de Boulogne in a bowler hat, bow tie, and waistcoat. She kept a glass coach and horses and didn't buy a car until after World War II.

Barney never quite recreated a Sapphic circle in Paris. Nonetheless, in the garden of her Neuilly home, Sapphic plays were performed, with guests and performers ranging from Colette to **Mata Hari.** It was a Lesbos of the imagination. In an era when many lesbians were attracted by mannish attire and cross-dressing, Barney preferred a pre-Raphaelite, more delicate look. Benstock describes "her wild, overgrown garden" where "slim-hipped, long-legged, small-breasted women danced for each other . . . [Barney] celebrated this female figure, separating it from the morbidity and misogyny that underwrote the male conception of it. . . . [She] feminized this body, draped it in Grecian robes or photographed its lithe contours by moonlight."

As the years passed and the Belle Époque faded into World War I, Barney's life began to change as well. In 1915, she met the painter **Romaine Brooks,** who became her lover, and despite Barney's infidelities, the two remained together until both were well into their nineties. By the end of the war, in 1918, as Benstock points out, Barney was forty-two and "no longer resembled the wood nymphs, shepherdesses, or court pages that constituted the poses of her youth."

But as the postwar era dawned, Barney found another role—presiding over one of the most famous salons in Paris. Pagan nudity by moonlight gave way to Friday-afternoon teas held in her backyard Temple of Friendship—a structure with a domed glass ceiling, an alcove hung with tapestries where recitations took place, and four harps. There, Paris's leading literary lights assembled, ate cucumber sandwiches and strawberry and raspberry tarts, and read from their works. As **Sylvia Beach,** the American expatriate of the 1920s, wrote, at such teas one met, among others, lesbians:

> *Paris ones and those only passing through town . . . ladies with high collars and monocles, though Miss Barney herself was so feminine. Unfortunately, I missed the chance to make the acquaintance at her salon of the authoress of* The Well of Loneliness *in which she concluded that if inverted couples could be united at the altar, all their problems would be solved.*

The idea of "inverted couples" being "united at the altar" was a long way from the view of female same-sex relations as fashionable diversions so commonplace in the early days of the Belle Époque. A very different view of lesbian relations was emerging—often promoted by British and American expatriates, who had money and independence and a determination to follow their own natures, not social convention. And so the Sapphic world of prewar Paris moved into the decade of the 1920s.

An Excerpt from Colette's
The Pure and the Impure

Colette's fictionalized memoir, The Pure and the Impure *(originally titled* Les Plaisirs*), details the novelist's brief sojourn in Paris's lesbian world, during the period of her affair with the Marquise de Belbeuf. The book includes portraits of the decadent poet Renée Vivien, and of the famous Ladies of Llangollen, two well-born English ladies who in 1778 ran away to live together in a small town in Wales. Colette's portrayal of lesbian Paris is quite different from that of French male writers, who linked lesbianism and decadence. As her biographer Michèle Sarde notes, "Colette's Lesbos is a more comforting womb or a mild eighteenth-century convent than it is a debauched Gomorrah. It is placid, even cozy. . . ." What follows is Colette's description of a Paris lesbian bar during the first decade of the twentieth century:*

THERE WAS ALSO a cellar in Montmartre that welcomed these uneasy women, haunted by their own solitude, who felt safe within the low-ceilinged room beneath the eye of a frank proprietress who shared their predilections, while an unctuous and authentic cheese fondue sputtered and the loud contralto of an artiste, one of their familiars, sang to them the romantic ballads of Augusta Holmes. . . . The same need for a refuge, warmth, and darkness, the same fear of intruders and sightseers assembled here these women whose faces, if not their names, soon became familiar to me. Literature and the makers of literature were absent from these gatherings and I delighted in that absence, along with the empty gaiety of the chatter and the diverting and challenging exchange of glances, the cryptic reference to certain treasons, comprehended at once, and the sudden outbursts of ferocity. I reveled in the admirable quickness of their half-spoken language, the exchange of threats, of promises, as if, once the slow-thinking male had been banished, every message

Colette, in her early days. (© *The Bettmann Archive*)

from woman to woman became clear and overwhelming, restricted to a small but infallible number of signs. . . .

All amours tend to create a dead-end atmosphere. "There! It's finished, we've arrived, and beyond us two there is nothing now, not even an opening for escape," murmurs one woman to her protégée, using the language of a lover. And as a proof, she indicates the low ceiling, the dim light, the women who are their counterparts, making her listen to the masculine rumble of the outside world and hear how it is reduced to the booming of a distant danger.

An Excerpt from Proust's
Sodom and Gomorrah

Marcel Proust (1871–1922) was, by common consent, one of the greatest writers of the twentieth century. He began writing his six-volume masterpiece, Remembrance of Things Past *in 1908. The first volume,* Swann's Way, *was published in 1913. Proust was homosexual, and the fourth volume,* **Cities of the Plain** *(in its most recent English translation called* **Sodom and Gomorrah***), offered the richest array of gay and lesbian characters in literature up to that point. It was published in 1921. The book is certainly not a work of "special pleading"; Proust's gay and bisexual characters present a depressing spectacle, and his view of homosexual love and the possibilities for gay community is rather hopeless. As historian Peter Gay notes, "Proust consciously treated homosexual urges as a curse, invincible, and ineradicable, imposed by a blighted heredity and a poisonous environment." Still, as Gay notes, this portrayal was not altogether unhelpful to the homosexuals of his time—after all, "a fate is not a vice." What follows is the great novelist's exposition of homosexuality from* Sodom and Gomorrah:

I NOW UNDERSTOOD, moreover, why earlier, when I had seen him coming away from Mme. de Villeparisis's, I had managed to arrive at the conclusion that M. de Charlus looked like a woman: he was one! He belonged to that race of beings, less paradoxical than they appear, whose ideal is manly precisely because their temperament is feminine, and who in ordinary life resemble other men in appearance only. . . .

A race upon which a curse is laid and which must live in falsehood and perjury because it knows that its desire, that which constitutes life's dearest pleasure, is held to be punishable, shameful, an inadmissable thing; . . . sons without a mother, to whom they are obliged to lie even in the hour when they close her dying eyes; friends without friendships . . . lovers who are almost precluded from the possibility of that love the hope of which gives them the strength to endure so many risks and so much loneliness, since they are enamoured of precisely the type of man who has nothing feminine about him, who is not an invert and consequently cannot love them in return. . . .

Their honour precarious, their liberty provisional, lasting only until the discovery of their crime; their position unstable, like that of the poet one day fêted in every drawing room and applauded in every theatre in London, and the next driven from every lodging, unable to find a pillow upon which to lay his head . . .

What they have been calling their love . . . springs not from an ideal of beauty which they have chosen but from an incurable disease; like the Jews . . . shunning one another, seeking out those who are most directly their opposite, who do not want their company . . . brought into company of their own kind by the ostracism to which they are subjected, the opprobrium into which they have fallen, having finally been invested, by a persecution similar to that of Israel, with the physical and moral characteristics of a race, sometimes beautiful, often hideous, finding . . . a relief in frequenting the society of their kind, and even some support in their existence . . . and seeking out (as a doctor seeks out cases of appendicitis) cases of inversion in history, taking pleasure in recalling that Socrates was one of themselves, as Jews claim that Jesus was one of them, without reflecting that there were no abnormal people when homosexuality was the norm . . . forming a freemasonry far more extensive, more effective and less suspected than that of the Lodges, for it rests upon an identity of tastes, needs, habits, dangers, apprenticeship, knowledge, traffic, vocabulary, and one in which even members who do not wish to know one another recognise one another immediately by natural or conventional, involuntary or deliberate signs. . . .

These descendents of the Sodomites . . . have established themselves throughout the entire world; they have had access to every profession and are so readily admitted into the most exclusive clubs that, whenever a Sodomite fails to secure election, the black balls are for the most part cast by other Sodomites, who make a point of condemning sodomy, having inherited the mendacity that enabled their ancestors to escape from the accursed city. It is possible that they may return there one day. Certainly, they form in every land an oriental colony, cultured, musical, malicious, which has charming qualities and intolerable defects. . . .

I have thought it as well to utter here a provisional warning against the lamentable error of proposing (just as people have encouraged a Zionist movement) to create a Sodomist movement and to rebuild Sodom. For, no sooner had they arrived there than the Sodomites would leave the town so as not to have the appearance of belonging to it, would take wives, keep mistresses in other cities where they would find, incidentally, every diversion that appealed to them. They would repair to Sodom only on days of supreme necessity, when their own town was empty, at those seasons when hunger drives the wolf from the woods. In other words, everything would go on very much as it does today in London, Berlin, Rome, Petrograd or Paris.

An Excerpt from Baudelaire's "Lesbos"

If writing about homosexual love was essentially taboo in England and the United States during much of the nineteenth century, that wasn't true in France. There, lesbianism was a topic of increasing fascination. But, as already noted, the French writers who wrote about lesbianism, all of them male, tended to view it as the "other"—exotic, hypersensual, occuring in distant times and places, transgressing moral laws. The decadent poet Charles Baudelaire (1821–67) titled one poem about the lesbian lovers Delphine and Hippolyta "Femmes Damnées" ("Damned Women"). In another poem, "Lesbos," from Les Fleurs du Mal *(The Flowers of Evil), first published in 1857, Baudelaire makes reference to "virile Sappho, the lover and poet." What follows are some stanzas from that poem:*

> *Mother of Latin games and Greek delights.*
> *Lesbos! where the kisses, languid or rapt,*
> *cool as melons, burning as the sun,*
> *adorn the dark and gild the shining days*
> *given to Latin games and Greek delights . . .*
>
> *Lesbos, where on suffocating nights*
> *before their mirrors, girls with hollow eyes*
> *caress their ripened limbs in sterile joy*
> *and taste the fruit of their nubility*
> *on Lesbos during suffocating nights!*
>
> *What if old Plato's scowling eyes condemn?*
> *Kisses absolve you by their sweet excess*
> *whose subtleties are inexhaustible!*
> *Queen of the tender Archipelago,*
> *pursue what Plato's scowling eyes condemn . . .*
>
> *What use to us are laws of right and wrong?*
> *High-hearted virgins, honor of the Isles,*
> *your altars are august as any: love*
> *will laugh at Heaven as it laughs at Hell!*
> *What use to us are laws of right and wrong?*

André Gide

IT WAS OSCAR WILDE who first introduced the French writer André Gide to homosexuality. This happened in 1895, in Algiers, just weeks before Wilde, falling into the Marquess of Queensberry's trap, brought the disastrous libel action against him. Gide, who was then twenty-six, had been dazzled and unsettled by Wilde when he met him in Paris a few years before. (A mutual friend thought he was in love with Wilde.) In his January 1, 1892, diary entry, Gide wrote, "Wilde, I believe, did me nothing but harm. In his company I had lost the habit of thinking. I had more varied emotions, but had forgotten how to bring order to them." Four years later, when Gide first saw the names of Wilde and Lord Alfred Douglas on the registry of his hotel outside Algiers, he tried to erase his own name and flee. But later he returned.

Douglas left Algiers a few days later, and Wilde took Gide to an Arab cafe to hear music. Gide recounted in his autobiography, *If It Die (Si le grain ne meurt)*, that as he and Wilde awaited their tea, there appeared in the half-opened doorway of the cafe "a marvellous youth" who took a reed flute out of his waistcoat and began to play. The song of the flute "flowed on through an extraordinary stillness, like a limpid steady stream of water, and you forgot the time and the place, and who you were and all the troubles of this world." Wilde took Gide outside, placed his hand on Gide's shoulder, and asked in a whisper: "*Dear,* would you like the little musician?" Gide recalled:

> *Oh! how dark the alley was! I thought my heart would fail me; and what a dreadful effort of courage it needed to answer: "Yes," and with what a choking voice!*

The two went to yet another cafe, where Wilde burst into laughter at Gide's tortured assent to his proposal—"a resounding laugh, more of a triumph of pleasure, an interminable, uncontrollable, insolent laugh." Wilde's amusement was that of "a child and a devil," thought Gide. What Wilde didn't know was that Gide had had a previous encounter with an Arab boy in Tunisia that had almost—although not quite—led to orgasm. In any event, later that evening Wilde brought Gide to a certain house and the musician (who was fourteen years old) was produced. "Every time since then that I have sought after pleasure, it is the memory of that night I have pursued," Gide wrote, adding:

> *It was now that I found my normal. There was nothing constrained here, nothing precipitate, nothing doubtful; there is no*

taste of ashes in the memory I keep. My joy was unbounded, and I cannot imagine it greater, even if love had been added. . . .

André Gide (1869–1951) was a figure of great stature and influence. By the time of his death at age eighty-one, he was one of the major French literary figures of the century. (He was awarded the Nobel Prize for literature in 1947.) He was famous for reverses of intellectual and political direction: After a trip to Africa he was so disgusted with colonialism that he became a Communist; then, after a trip to the Soviet Union, he rejected communism. A committed antifascist, he opposed the Nazis when other French intellectuals collaborated. Yet he remained a somewhat puzzling and distant figure, even to his admirers. Writer **Edmund White** noted that "many people found that Gide resembled a Protestant minister with his long oval face, severe manner, and the extravagant austerity of his clothes and surroundings." E. M. Forster described him as "slippery as a trout" and recalled an evening in Paris in 1935 when Gide invited Forster and a friend to dinner and then, as the coffee arrived, mysteriously vanished. Still, Forster wrote, upon Gide's death, "He has taught thousands of people to mistrust façades, to call the bluff, to be brave without bounce and inconsistent without frivolity. He is the humanist of our age. . . ."

Gide grew up in Paris in a Protestant gentry family, raised by three aging women—his mother, his aunt, and a spinster kept by charity—all dressed in black. His upbringing was austere and joyless, and taught him that "it was my duty to deny my desire *everything*," as he wrote in *If It Die*. The values of his childhood were very much at variance with his homosexual attractions and caused him great conflict. The tension between Puritan morality and a desire to follow his own nature characterizes much of Gide's work.

Eighteen ninety-five was not merely the year of his first homosexual experience. It was also the year of the death of his mother. Perhaps it was the confluence of those events that led Gide to marry his pious and melancholy cousin **Madeleine** (Emmanuele) in that same year. He wrote:

> There was nothing now I could attach myself to but my love for my cousin; my determination to marry her was the only light left me by which to guide my life. . . .
>
> [I]n loving Emmanuele, was it not virtue itself I loved? It was the marriage of Heaven with my insatiable Hell; but at the actual

*moment, my Hell was in abeyance; the tears of my mourning
had extinguished all its fires; I was dazzled as by the blaze of
azure and the things I refused to see had ceased to exist for
me. . . . Shortly after this, we became engaged.*

Gide seems to have worshipped Madeleine as a spiritual ideal
rather than loved her as a woman. Their marriage was never con-
summated, although they remained married until Madeleine's
death, in 1938. During the intervening years, Gide had a love affair
with **Elisabeth van Rysselberghe,** the daughter of an old friend, who
bore him a daughter. He also had a lasting relationship—one that
was both physical and spiritual—with **Marc Allégret,** son of his
former tutor, beginning in 1917 when Allégret was fifteen. Angered
by a trip that Gide and Allégret took to England in the summer
and fall of 1918, Mme. Gide burned all the letters that Gide had
written her before and after their marriage. "I read every one before
destroying them," she said. "They were my dearest possession on
earth."

Gide was a defender of homosexuality and one of the few literary
figures of his time to write about his own homosexual experiences.
His 1902 novel, *The Immoralist*—which bears a number of similarities to the author's own life—tells the story of a young man
who goes to Algeria to recover from tuberculosis and in his con-
valescence comes to rebel against bourgeois morality, a rebellion
linked at least in part to a desire for Arab boys. Significantly, the
protagonist's regeneration comes at the price of the illness of his
wife. If *The Immoralist* alluded to his homosexual attractions, Gide
discussed the subject frankly in *If It Die,* published privately in
1920 and by a major French publishing house in 1924.

His most famous work on the subject of homosexuality was
Corydon, a series of four Socratic dialogues between Corydon, a
homosexual physician, and the narrator, a critic of homosexuality.
The first two dialogues of *Corydon* were printed in 1911 in an
unsigned private edition of twelve copies and shut away in a drawer;
another private edition of twenty-one copies was published in 1920.
A commercial edition—under Gide's name—was finally brought
out in France in 1924. Gide referred to it as "the most important
of my books" and wrote in his journals that no other undertaking
of his middle years thrilled and elated him as did the writing of
Corydon.

The book adopts a quasiscientific approach, taking great pains to portray male homosexuality as normal and natural (lesbianism is barely alluded to). Corydon, Gide's spokesman, attempts to distinguish between the "invert" (the effeminate homosexual) and the "normal homosexual" (the lover of youth, in the Greek manner). Corydon tells the narrator:

> You understand that in homosexuality, just as in heterosexuality, there are all shades and degrees, from Platonic love to lust, from self-denial to sadism, from radiant health to sullen sickliness, from simple expansiveness to all the refinements of vice. Inversion is only one expression. Besides, between exclusive homosexuality and exclusive heterosexuality there is every intermediate shading. But most people simply draw the lines between normal love and a love alleged to be contra naturam— and for convenience's sake, all the happiness, all the noble or tragic passions, all the beauty of action and thought are put on one side, and to the other are relegated all the filthy dregs of love. . . .

Despite Gide's own enthusiasm for the book, many who might have been thought to be sympathetic were critical of *Corydon*. Edmund White dismisses it as "a faintly ridiculous defence of homosexuality, which argues that homosexuality is completely natural since it can be observed in several other species." The American novelist and critic **James Baldwin** wrote of Gide, "He ought to have leaned less heavily on the examples of dead, great men, of vanished cultures, and he ought certainly to have known that the examples provided by natural history do not go far toward illuminating the physical, psychological, and moral complexities faced by men. If he were going to talk about homosexuality at all, he ought, in a word, to have sounded a little less *disturbed*."

Nonetheless, *Corydon* was one of the earliest efforts to mount an intellectual defense of homosexuality, and the fact that it was written by one of France's most respected cultural luminaries was quite significant at the time. As for Gide himself, E. M. Forster noted that he did not have a great mind but a "free mind," and "free minds are as rare as great, and even more valuable at the present moment."

CHAPTER 7

ENGLAND DURING
THE GREAT WAR

T HE ADVENT of World War I brought into sharp relief the contradictions of English attitudes toward homosexuality. On the homefront, the War began with veiled and not-so-veiled antigay rhetoric and ended with a sensational libel trial that equated homosexuality with treason. Meanwhile, in the trenches of France, male romantic friendships flourished. Never has any war, before or since, chronicled such a degree of tender passion between men.

As the historian Samuel Hynes notes, many saw the outbreak of war as an opportunity to restore a manly, martial Britain, to free it from soft, decadent, i.e., homosexual influences. At least one thinker, **Selwyn Image,** a professor of fine art at Oxford, accused the art-for-art's sake movement—closely associated with Oscar Wilde—as somehow helping to bring on the War; he called for a "cleansing purge." Yet only war, he argued, could give art and conduct "the salutary shock." Some even portrayed "the love that dare not speak its name" to be as great a menace as the Kaiser. Wilde's erstwhile lover Lord Alfred Douglas, now married, a convert to Roman Catholicism, and reborn as the great scourge of homosexuality, warned, "It is just as important to civilization that Literary England should be cleansed of sex-mongers and peddlers of the perverse, as that Flanders should be cleared of Germans."

Despite the homefront rhetoric, the atmosphere of homoeroticism that suffused the experience of British soldiers on the battlefield is apparent in the poems, diaries, and letters of the period. The two greatest of the war poets—**Siegfried Sassoon** (1886–1967) and **Wilfred Owen** (1893–1918)—were both homosexual. But the glorification of romantic male friendship extended beyond homosexual poet-soldiers. As Paul Fussell writes in his book *The Great War and Modern Memory,* "No one turning from the poetry of the Second War back to that of the First can fail to notice there the unique physical tenderness, the readiness to admire openly the bodily beauty of young men, the unapologetic recognition that men may be in love with each other."

One explanation may lie in the unprecedented mass slaughter of a stalemated war; this shared experience bound men together in a way that brought out deep—sometimes forbidden—feelings, similar to those Whitman experienced in the hospitals of Civil War Washington, D.C. The Victorian tradition of romantic same-sex friendships—nurtured in the public schools and at Oxford and Cambridge—was another factor. What inspired such passions, Fussel writes, "was—as always—faunlike good looks, innocence, vulnerability, and 'charm.' The object was mutual affection, protection and admiration. In war as at school, such passions were antidotes against loneliness and terror." Fussell continues:

> Do the British have a special talent for such passions? An inquirer turning over the names of the late nineteenth and early twentieth century literary worthies might be led to think so as he encounters Wilde, Samuel Butler, Edward Fitzgerald, Houseman, Hopkins, Symonds, Strachey, Edward Marsh, William Johnson Cory (author of the "Eton Boating Song"), Hugh Walpole, John Maynard Keynes, E. M. Forster and J. R. Ackerley. Even such professionally manly figures as Cecil Rhodes and Sir Richard Burton proved homoerotically excitable.... Of the sainted Lord Kitchener Queen Victoria once said, "They say he dislikes women, but I can only say he was very nice to me."

In the trenches, however, there was little recognition that passionate feelings toward another soldier labeled or stigmatized one in any way. The concept of the homosexual as "species" or personality type was still not widespread, despite the best efforts of the sexologists. If the flamboyant Oscar Wilde was the public face of homosexuality, few soldiers—whatever their sexual inclinations—identified with it. "We did not call it love; we did not acknowledge its existence; it was sacramental and therefore secret," wrote the poet **Herbert Read**. The gay novelist and memoirist **J. R. Ackerley** recalled that he never met "a recognisable or self-confessed adult homosexual" until after the War. To him, relationships between soldiers were simply an extension of those of public school—that is, unspoken and almost entirely chaste. Ackerley, who served as an officer in France (and was later a prisoner of war), admits,

"My personal runners and servants were usually chosen for their looks; indeed this tendency in war to have the prettiest soldiers about one was observable in many other officers; whether they took more advantage than I dared of this close, homogeneous, almost paternal relationship I do not know." Ackerley's biographer, Peter Parker, suggests that the well-known predilection of British upper-class homosexuals for working-class men may have been influenced by the war experience, in which public-school officers, like Ackerley, learned to love, and sometimes to romanticize, the men who served under them.

By all accounts, in fact, there was little or no sex in the trenches. The lack of privacy and the dreadful physical conditions seem to have made it virtually impossible. The military code punished sodomy with ten years to life in prison and gross indecency (oral sex) with two years. Yet with three million British men under arms, only 22 officers and 270 ordinary soldiers were court-martialed for gross indecency during the course of the War and in the year following.

What the War did, however, was to legitimatize the celebration of male youth and beauty. Homosexually inclined writers could yearn for their fallen comrades in their poetry as they would a lover and be considered patriotic rather than immoral. The American poet **Edna St. Vincent Millay** was quick to realize the erotic impulse behind much of the writing of the time when she attended a poetry reading by Siegfried Sassoon in New York after the War. "I wonder whether he would have cared so much if it were a thousand virgins who had been slaughtered," she mused, rather cruelly.

Sassoon, who was almost twenty-eight when he enlisted in 1914, had spent the prewar years fox-hunting, playing cricket, and writing minor verse. He was wounded in France and was the recipient of the Military Cross. As casualties mounted at an appalling rate and the War seemed increasingly pointless, he became a fierce opponent of it. A protest letter that he sent to newspaper editors and members of Parliament landed him in a hospital for shell-shocked soldiers. He wrote his poetry in a realistic, unsentimental style. But at the root of the antiwar passion and the fury of his best poems were more personal feelings. As he wrote in his April 6, 1916, diary entry:

Tommy dead; and Bobbie Hanmer at Salonika; I can't keep them clear in memory; they fade, with their bright hair and happy eyes. I cannot recall the tones of their voices. And yet, when they were with me, I always tried to learn them by heart, like music, and said to myself, "Only a little while; get all you can from them; make them happy if you can. . . ."

In another diary entry, June 5, 1918, he describes encountering a soldier who was doing fieldwork as punishment for getting drunk in Marseilles:

Then I saw him, digging away at road-mending, and he'd got a rotten pair of boots, which were an excuse for conversation, and I've loved him ever since (it is just as well he's not in my present Company). And when he got into trouble I longed to be kind to him. And I talked to him about "making a fresh start, and not doing anything silly again," while he stood in front of me with his white face, and eyes full of tears. I suppose I'd have done the same for any man in the Company who had a good character. But there was a great deal of sex floating about in this particular effort. No doubt he dreams about "saving my life." I wish I could save his.

In his reference to "sex floating about," Sassoon was more honest with himself than most. But the fact that erotic feeling remained just below the surface, that it was all rather vague and ethereal and idealized, protected many of these soliders from having to come to grips with the implications of such relationships. When they did, as Martin Taylor points out in his book, *Lads: Love Poetry of the Trenches,* such a realization often precipitated a personal crisis. For example, the poet Robert Graves had had an intimate but chaste friendship with a young man he called "Peter" [**G. H. Johnstone**], whom he had been close to at school. His correspondence with Johnstone (who remained at home) had been his "greatest stand-by" early in the War, "something solid and clean to set off against the impermanence of trench life and the uncleanness of sex-life in billets," as he described it. But when Graves read in a newspaper that Johnstone had been found guilty of making a sexual proposal to a corporal in a Canadian regiment, he was devastated. "This news," he wrote twelve years later, "was nearly the end of me. I decided that [Johnstone] had been driven out of his mind by the war. There was madness in the family, I knew; he had once showed me a letter from his grandfather scrawled in circles all over the page. It would be easy to think of him as dead." Shortly thereafter, in a kind of panic, Graves married. After such a narrow escape from his "pseudo-homosexual" period, as he referred to it, he never communicated with Johnstone again.

Because there was little or no acknowledgment of the homoerotic impulse behind so many of the relationships at the front—even on the part of homosexually inclined soldiers—the War did little to advance any kind of gay self-definition and solidarity.

For some soldiers, though, the intense feelings of wartime comradeship would forever seem grander, nobler than the pleasures of peacetime sexual love. In the midst of an affair with a young man named **Gabriel Atkin** in 1920, after the War, Sassoon describes how one evening upon returning home from a concert, he pulled out his old War notebooks. He read his account of midnight wire-cutting just before the attack on the Somme and the face of a man named Gibson in the first gray light of dawn:

> *Gibson is a ghost, but he is more real to-night than the pianist who played Scriabin with such delicate adroitness. I wish I could "find the moral equivalent for war." To-night I feel as I were only half-alive. Part of me died with all the Gibsons I used to know. Their memory makes Gabriel [his peacetime lover] taste like a cheap liqueur.*

Although he carried on an affair with the dandyish **Stephen Tennant** throughout much of the 1920s, Sassoon never quite found his place as a gay man in the postwar world. He married in 1933, much to the puzzlement and disapproval of his homosexual friends (the marriage was a failure), and later converted to Roman Catholicism.

In his June 2, 1918, diary entry, while in France, Sassoon wrote, "The papers are full of this foul 'Billing Case.' Makes one glad to be away from 'normal conditions.' And the Germans are on the Marne and claim 4500 more prisoners. The world is stark staring mad. . . ."

National disapproval of homosexuality was transformed into near-hysteria toward the end of the War, when **Noel Pemberton Billing,** an independent member of Parliament, made the stunning claim that the German Secret Service possessed a "Black Book" containing the names of 47,000 prominent English citizens who were engaged in "the propagation of evils which all decent men thought had perished in Sodom and Lesbos." This list was supposedly kept for the purpose of blackmailing English men and women in high places into helping the German war effort. Billing made this charge in an article in the January 26, 1918, issue of his magazine, *The Vigilante,* in an article called "The First 47,000."

Billing himself cut a rather dashing figure. Thirty-eight years old, tall and good looking, he wore a monocle and a long pointed collar without a necktie and drove a yellow Rolls-Royce. He had been a sailor, a mounted police trooper, a pilot, and an inventor. As a young man he had designed his own airplane and flown it; he was elected to Parliament for the first time in 1916 on a platform emphasizing greater use of airpower in the war. His magazine, *The Vigilante,* was known for attacking Jews, German music, pacifism, Fabian Socialism, and financiers. He described the Black Book in his journal as "a most Catholic miscellany. The names of Privy councillors, youths of the chorus, wives of Cabinet ministers, dancing girls, even Cabinet ministers themselves, diplomats, poets, bankers, editors, newspaper proprietors and members of his Majesty's household follow each other with no order of precedence." In February 1918, Billing made the same claim in a speech before the House of Commons.

It so happened that early that same year, a producer named **J. T. Grein** had been planning a production of Oscar Wilde's play *Salomé,* with dancer **Maud Allen** in the title role. The performance was to be private, and tickets were sold by subscription. The February 1918 issue of Billing's *The Vigilante* reported it this way:

THE CULT OF THE CLITORIS
To be a member of Maud Allan's [sic] private performance in Oscar Wilde's Salomé one has to apply to a Miss Valetta of 9, Duke Street, Adelphi, W.C. If Scotland Yard were to seize a list of these members, I have no doubt they would secure the names of several thousand of the first 47,000.

Maud Allen was not amused. The implication was that she herself was one of "the first 47,000." She sued Billing for criminal libel.

The trial, which took place before **Justice Darling** and a jury, was held at the Old Bailey and began on May 29, 1918. Billing conducted his own defense. It lasted for six days and quickly became the talk of London. As Samuel Hynes notes in his book *A War*

Imagined, "It was at no point a trial of the accused on the charge of libel; it was, rather, yet another trial of Oscar Wilde, and of 47,000 putative English perverts." The term "the first 47,000" became a byword.

Justice Darling lost control of his courtroom early on, and the trial turned out to be one of the most raucous in the Old Bailey's history. The first witness for Billing and the defense was a woman named **Eileen Villiers Stuart.** She testified that she had seen the Black Book and that among the names were not just the prime minister and his wife, but also the presiding judge himself. This announcement was followed by cheers, laughter, and general uproar in the courtroom. Later that year, Stuart was convicted of bigamy and went to prison for nine months. (It was also revealed that she was Billing's mistress.)

Next came Captain **Harold Spencer,** Billing's assistant editor and the author of the allegedly defamatory article. Spencer, an American, had previously worked for the British Secret Intelligence Service but had been discharged, apparently on mental grounds. He claimed that he had discovered the Black Book while serving as an aide to Prince **William of Wied,** a German who had occupied the throne of Albania briefly in 1914. Spencer had seen the book in the King's private rooms at his palace in the Adriatic port city of Durazzo (now Durrës). The witness confirmed some of the names in the book, including that of the prime minister.

And so it went. One of the more bizarre witnesses was Lord Alfred Douglas himself. He was called not because of any personal knowledge of the Black Book, but because of the relationship of the trial to Wilde's *Salomé.* (Bosie had translated the play from the original French to English.) On the stand, Bosie dismissed Wilde as "a good second-rate literrateur, tremendously over-rated." Pemberton Billing then asked him if he regretted having known Wilde. Bosie replied, "I do. He had a diabolical influence on everyone. I think he was the greatest force for evil in Europe for the last 350 years."

The trial continued in an atmosphere that one observer described as alternating "between intermittent uproar and opera bouffe." In questioning Maud Allen, Billing noted that her brother had been executed in San Francisco for murdering two young girls. He justified his questions on the ground that depraved practices might be prevalent in her family. Various individuals were ordered removed from the courtroom for disruption, including Bosie. Amid cheering, hissing, and other interruptions, Justice Darling digressed from his summing-up of the case to launch an attack on Oscar Wilde:

> Oscar Wilde wrote filthy works, as you know: he was guilty of filthy practices; he was convicted in this Court and suffered imprisonment, and social extinction, and death in due course. . . . Well, gentlemen, it is possible to regard him as a great artiste, but he certainly was a great beast; there is no doubt about that.

When the jury announced its verdict—not guilty—the courtroom burst out into wild applause. It was a victory for Pemberton Billing and the Black Book. Maud Allen and J. T. Grein, *Salomé*'s producer, were ordered to pay Billing's court costs.

The British public viewed Billing as more than just a crank. In fact, he had widespread approval at a time when an increasingly disillusioned public believed that it had been deceived by government figures who prosecuted the war. The respected novelist **Arnold Bennett** wrote, "There can be no doubt that Mr. Pemberton Billing had a very great deal of support from plain people throughout the country. These people said: 'He is not attacking; he is defending himself. And what has he to gain from his attempt to expose an alleged huge conspiracy of vice and pro-Germanism? Nothing. Hence he must be a patriot.'" Robbie Ross, Oscar Wilde's literary executor, saw the trial similarly. "For a few days London forgot all about the War in its excitement about the case," he wrote to a friend in India. "The populace were entirely on the side of Billing and, as he succeeded in the trial, are quite convinced that all he says must be true. Kicking the corpse of Wilde has also been a pleasure to the English people even if they disapprove of Billing's methods."

The Billing case furthered the impression that homosexuality, decadence, and disloyalty were all related (with Oscar Wilde seemingly orchestrating everything from beyond the grave, as Samuel Hynes points out). In fact, the equation between homosexuality and disloyalty was to be a running theme throughout Western European and American history in the twentieth century. The Redl affair, in prewar Vienna, in which an intelligence officer sold secrets to the Russians in order to obtain money to buy a car for his male lover, gained widespread attention. German nationalists linked Jews and homosexuals to the "stab in the back" that supposedly caused them to lose World War I. The issue would resurface in England in the spy case of **Guy Burgess** and **Donald Maclean** in the 1950s. In the United States, Senator **Joseph McCarthy** would accuse "perverts" of disloyalty in the 1950s, and homosexuals would be purged from the American State Department as "security risks." Gays and lesbians would continue to be barred from the U.S. military—and the military of other countries as well. Weak and despised groups were somehow to blame for the errors of generals and politicians. The Billing case, despite its absurdities and comic elements, furthered the stereotype of the homosexual as untrustworthy, if not a national menace.

By the 1920s, decadence and art-for-art's-sake aestheticism were once again in vogue in university and sophisticated upper-class circles. Oscar Wilde was increasingly viewed as a martyr and symbol of intolerance; aesthetes like **Harold Acton** and **Brian Howard** became important figures at Oxford, where homosexuality was widespread during these years: "The romantic mood of the place—by almost universal testimony—was oriented toward young men," writes Martin Green in his book *Children of the Sun*. Oxford male student life was divided into two factions—the "hearties" and the "aesthetes." The "hearties went in for beer, sports, and picking up girls on Saturday nights; and the aesthetes, in general, went in for poetry, homosexuality, and a modified Baudelairian dandyism," according to Green. Meanwhile, Proust's novels, the first major works of art to address the subject of homosexuality, were widely read, and **Noel Coward's** plays were all the rage in London. The homosexual content of some of these works remained encoded, but a sensibility that we would recognize as "gay" began to make its mark on English cultural life.

Chroniclers of the period, perhaps giving too much weight to these cultural changes, take a relatively positive view of 1920s attitudes toward homosexuality. "The homosexuals of the twenties came out of the closet and into the drawing room," writes Noel Annan in *Our Age*, his portrait of British intellectual life between the wars. "They did not—or very few of them did—'come out,' i.e. write manifestoes and boast of what then was criminal conduct. But many did not try to hide the difference between them and the other guests—in their manners, their tone of voice or their clothes." In *The Long Weekend*, a social history of Great Britain in the 1920s and '30s, authors Robert Graves and Alan Hodge viewed the period this way:

> So long as one acted consistently in accordance with one's personal hypothesis, and was not ashamed of what one did, all was well. . . . When anti-French feeling in 1922 caused a revulsion in favour of the poor downtrodden Germans, the more openly practised homosexuality of Berlin seemed brave and honest: in certain Berlin dancing-halls, it was pointed out, women danced only with women and men with men. Germany land of the free! The Lesbians took heart and followed suit, first in Chelsea and St. John's Wood and then in the less exotic suburbs of London.

But antigay feelings lay just below the witty surface of upper-class "tolerance." If attitudes were beginning to ease, even just a bit, this change did not last long. By the end of the twenties came the prosecution, on charges of obscenity, of Radclyffe Hall's novel *The Well of Loneliness,* and long-standing fears and prejudices began to surface once again. It was as if each generation insisted on playing out its own version of the Oscar Wilde trial.

The Sexual Labyrinth of T. E. Lawrence

WHILE ALLIED TROOPS LAY MIRED in the endless stalemate of the Western Front, a thousand miles to the East on the Arabian peninsula, a Bedouin army, led by a British scholar-soldier dressed in the flowing robes of an Arab prince, was putting the Ottoman Turks to flight. Blowing up trains and dynamiting bridges, swooping down upon Turkish patrols and then disappearing into the desert, the ragtag Arab army fought the first successful guerrilla insurgency of the century. It was perhaps the most romantic episode of a war that produced great slaughter and few heroes. The leader of the insurgency, **T. E. Lawrence** (1888–1935), was a five-foot-three Irishman who was twenty-six years old when the War broke out. Before he vanished into the desert, he was working as a report-writer and cartographer for British military intelligence in Cairo.

T. E. Lawrence, photographed in 1927 in the Arab garb he was
famous for wearing during the War. *(© UPI/Bettmann)*

By the end of the War, he was a legend in his own time, "Lawrence of Arabia." In yet another transformation, he became Airman Shaw of the Royal Air Force, seeking obscurity by working as an ordinary mechanic and sleeping in a bunkhouse along with nineteen other men. He was also a literary figure, on intimate terms with people like E. M. Forster and Siegfried Sassoon. He died in 1935 in a motorcycle accident.

In his book *Seven Pillars of Wisdom* (privately circulated during his life and published only after his death), Lawrence wrote approvingly of wartime homosexuality. With few women to be encountered in their wanderings through the Arabian desert, Lawrence noted:

> . . . *our youths began indifferently to slake one another's few needs in their own clean bodies—a cold convenience that . . . seemed sexless and even pure. Later, some began to justify this sterile process, and swore that friends quivering together in the yielding sand with intimate hot limbs in supreme embrace, found there hidden in the darkness a sensual co-efficient of the mental passion which was welding our souls and spirits in one flaming effort. Several, thirsting to punish appetites they could not wholly prevent, took a savage pride in degrading the body, and offered themselves fiercely in any habit which promised physical pain or filth.*

Perhaps Lawrence fit the last category. In November 1917, while on a reconnaissance mission to Turkish-occupied Dera, south of Damascus, he was beaten and raped by the governor and his underlings. For Lawrence, the experience had a pleasurable aspect to it, despite—or because of—the pain. "I remembered the corporal kicking with his nailed boot to get me up," he writes in *Seven Pillars*. "I remembered smiling idly at him, for a delicious warmth, probably sexual, was swelling through me. . . ." Lawrence became fixated on the experience and determined to repeat it as often as possible. From 1923 to 1934, in England, he employed young men on a regular basis to beat him with a whip until he reached orgasm.

What appears to be Lawrence's homosexual masochism has fascinated generations of biographers and psycho-historians. Was he a victim of a trauma that he attempted to exorcise by a repetition of the experience? Or was he trying to exorcise something else—perhaps some loathing of his own sexual desires, perhaps deeper conflicts and feelings—through pain and punishment? Were his truest sexual inclinations awakened in the desert, inclinations so opposed to social norms that he could never have experienced them in England? And did the rape at Dera ever happen at all? A recent biographer of Lawrence, Lawrence James, makes the case that Lawrence could never have been at Dera when he said he was. He argues that the incident was either a transposition of something that happened elsewhere or perhaps a mere erotic fantasy concocted to "justify" Lawrence's sexual inclinations. Such a fabrication might have had a political purpose as well: to deflect attention from atrocities by Lawrence's Arab troops by focusing attention on the supposed brutality of the Turks.

Certainly, Lawrence never identified himself as homosexual (although neither did he show any interest in women at any time during his life). After reading a homosexual story by E. M. Forster, he wrote Forster:

> The Turks, as you probably know (or have guessed, through the reticences of the Seven Pillars) did it to me, by force: and since then I have gone about whimpering to myself unclean, unclean. Now I don't know. Perhaps, there is another side, your side, to the story. I couldn't ever do it, I believe: the impulse strong enough to make me touch another creature has not yet been born in me . . .

Lawrence remains a puzzle. Whatever the exact nature of his sexuality, he was able to discover truths about his psychological and sexual makeup in wartime, when sexual restraints were loosened, and in an alien culture where the social expectations and restrictions of home were absent and sexual relations between men less stigmatized. In this, he was like many other Western homosexual men: Gide, who discovered his attraction to young men in the oases of Algeria; Forster, who had his first gay relationship in Cairo, also during the War, with a tram conductor; and countless numbers of literary travelers and explorers (gay and bisexual) of the past two centuries, from **Lord Byron** to **Bruce Chatwin**. In Lawrence's case, his sexual "outsiderness" helped to transform him into a romantic hero. Perhaps what appear to be the complexities of his personality are more than anything a reflection of British (and Northern European) sexual repression.

An Excerpt from E. M. Forster's *Maurice*

E. M. Forster's novel Maurice *was written in 1913, just before the outbreak of World War I. The novel, the only one in which the author of* Howard's End *and* A Passage to India *deals overtly with homosexuality, tells the story of a young suburban stockbroker and his struggle for sexual acceptance and self-acceptance. The novel takes him through two relationships—one with the cerebral, inhibited Clive; the other with the idealized, working-class Alec. Forster himself wrote, "In Maurice I tried to create a character who was completely unlike myself or what I supposed myself to be: someone handsome, healthy, bodily attractive, mentally torpid, not a bad business man and rather a snob. Into this mixture I dropped an ingredient that puzzles him, wakes him up, torments him and finally saves him." At first, there was no question in Forster's mind of publishing* Maurice. *That could not happen "until my death and England's," as he put it. He showed the book to selected friends and revised parts of it on three different occasions, the last revision taking place between 1959 and 1960. It was finally published in 1972, the year Forster died. The section excerpted here, in which Maurice consults a doctor about his sexual conflicts, exemplifies Edwardian attitudes toward male homosexuality:*

AS THE SPRING WORE AWAY, he [Maurice] decided to consult a doctor. . . . He loathed the idea of a doctor, but he had failed to kill lust single-handed. As crude as in his boyhood, it was many times as strong, and raged in his empty soul. He might "keep away from young men," as he had naively resolved, but he could not keep away from their images, and hourly committed sin in his heart. Any punishment was preferable, for he assumed a doctor would punish him. He could undergo any course of treatment on the chance of being cured, and even if he wasn't he would be occupied and have fewer minutes for brooding.

Whom should he consult? Young Jowitt was the only doctor he knew well, and the day after that railway journey he managed to remark to him in casual tones, "I say, in your rounds here, do you come across unspeakables of the Oscar Wilde sort?" But Jowitt replied, "No, that's in the asylum work, thank God" . . .

In the end he braved a visit to Dr. Barry. He knew he should have a bad time, but the old man, though a bully and a tease, was absolutely trustworthy. . . .

"I'm afraid I want to speak to you, sir," he said with an emotion so intense that he felt he should never accomplish the real words at all.

"Well, speak away."

"I mean professionally."

"Lord, man, I've retired from practice for the last six years. You go to Jericho or Jowitt. Sit down, Maurice. Glad to see you, shouldn't have guessed you were dying. Polly! Whisky for this fading flower" . . .

The ugliness of the interview overcame him. . . . Unable to say the right words, he muttered, "It's about women—"

[The doctor orders Maurice to strip and examines him for venereal disease and impotence.]

"You're all right," repeated the other [Dr. Barry]. "You can marry tomorrow if you like, and if you take an old man's advice you will. Cover up now, it's so draughty. What put all this into your head?"

"So you've never guessed," he said, with a touch of scorn in his terror. "I'm an unspeakable of the Oscar Wilde sort." His eyes closed, and driving clenched fists against them he sat motionless, having appealed to Caesar.

At last judgement came. He could scarcely believe his ears. It was "Rubbish, rubbish!" He had expected many things, but not this; for if his words were rubbish his life was a dream.

"Dr. Barry, I can't have explained—"

"Now, listen to me, Maurice, never let that evil hallucination, that temptation from the devil, occur to you again."

The voice impressed him, and was not Science speaking?

"Who put that lie into your head? You whom I see and know to be a decent fellow! We'll never mention it again. No—I'll not discuss. I'll not discuss. The worst thing I could do for you is to discuss it."

"I want advice," said Maurice, struggling against the overwhelming manner. "It's not rubbish to me, but my life."

"Rubbish," came the voice authoritatively.

"I've been like this ever since I can remember without knowing why. What is it? Am I diseased? If I am, I want to be cured, I can't put up with loneliness any more, the last six months specially. Anything you tell me, I'll do. That's all. You must help me."

He fell back into his original position, gazing body and soul into the fire.

"Come! Dress yourself."

"I'm sorry," he murmured, and obeyed. Then Dr. Barry unlocked the door and called, "Polly! Whisky!" The consultation was over.

J. R. Ackerley and the Quest for the Ideal Friend

The British novelist, playwright, memoirist, and editor J. R. Ackerley (1896–1967) first became aware of his homosexuality while he was interned in Switzerland after being taken prisoner during World War I. A fellow internee named Arthur Lunn asked him, somewhat mischievously, if he was "homo" or "hetero." Ackerley had never heard of these terms before. Once Lunn explained them, Ackerley realized there was only one answer. Lunn (who was "hetero" himself) recommended books for him to read— Plutarch and Edward Carpenter, among others. Soon enough, Ackerley was "on the sexual map" and proud of his place on it. He became convinced that true love took place only between men. In time he became "something of a publicist for the rights of that love that dare not speak its name"—in a critically acclaimed play called Prisoners of War, *first staged in 1925, and, most notably, in his memoir,* My Father and Myself, *published shortly after his death in 1967. In* My Father and Myself, *he contrasted his own secret life as a homosexual with that of his father, a fruit magnate whom Ackerley later discovered had had another wife and children and maintained a second household throughout the entire period he was married to Ackerley's mother.*

The younger Ackerley led a varied life, public and private—as secretary to the maharaja of the Indian state of Chhatarpur (the maharaja shared his sexual inclinations and Ackerley made him the central figure of his zany travel book, Hindoo Holiday)*, as literary editor (from 1935–59), of* The Listener, *one of England's most influential magazines, and as best friend and confidant of E. M. Forster. Like Forster and like so many of his generation of British upper-class homosexuals, the strikingly handsome Ackerley was exclusively attracted to working-class men. He was perpetually searching for the "Ideal Friend," and although by his own count, two or three hundred young men were to share his bed over the years, he insisted that he considered himself of a monogamous cast of mind. Some of these young men married and had children, and Ackerley remained loyal to them long after any sexual relationship had faded. In the 1940s, one of these friends was sentenced to prison, and Ackerley became the guardian of his dog, an Alsatian named Queenie. Queenie became the emotional center of Ackerley's later years and the subject of his book* My Dog Tulip. *When the dog died in 1961, Ackerley proclaimed it the saddest day of his life. His biographer Peter Parker noted that "like many widowers, he went into a slow decline thereafter."*

In the following excerpt from My Father and Myself, *Ackerley offers this description of the Ideal Friend that he searched for over so many years:*

HE SHOULD NOT BE EFFEMINATE, indeed preferably normal; I did not exclude education but did not want it, I could supply all that myself and in the loved one it had always seemed to get in the way; he should admit me but no one else; he should be physically attractive to me and younger than myself—the younger the better, as closer to innocence; finally he should be on the small side, lusty, circumcised, physically healthy and clean: no phimosis, halitosis, bromidrosis. It may be thought that I had set myself a task so difficult of accomplishment as almost to put success purposely beyond my reach; it may be thought too that the reason why this search was taking me out of my own class into the working class . . . was that guilt in sex obliged me to work it off on my social inferiors.

This occurred to me only as a latter-day question and the answer may be true, I cannot tell; if asked then I would probably have said that working-class boys were more unreserved and understanding, and that friendship with them opened up interesting areas of life, hitherto unknown.

Noel Coward

IF ANY ONE INDIVIDUAL incarnated the rebellious sensibility of England in the 1920s, it was the actor, playwright, and songwriter Noel Coward (1899–1973). Coward's image was fixed in the public mind in 1924 at the time of the production of his first successful play, *The Vortex*. A publicity photo showed Coward in bed, "wearing a Chinese dressing gown in a scarlet bedroom decorated with nudes, his expression being one of advanced degeneracy," as Robert Graves and Alan Hodge described it in their social history, *The Long Weekend. The Vortex*, a drama about a drug-taking son (played by Coward) and a mother who is having an affair with a much younger man, was considered shocking (and overly sympathetic toward its "immoral" characters). It was followed by a series of sleek, sophisticated comedies—*Private Lives, Hay Fever, Blithe Spirit, Design for Living*—as well as revues like *This Year of Grace* and operettas like *Bitter Sweet*. Graves and Hodge describe Coward as "the dramatist of disillusion. . . . The main theme of the revues that Coward wrote for C. B. Cochran was that one now knew a little too much for happiness. . . . His songs 'World-Weary' and 'Dance, Dance, Dance, Little Lady' were felt to reflect the mood of his time. . . ."

With his wit, his genius for light comedy, and his dandyish pose, Coward could be seen as a 1920s version of Oscar Wilde. Unlike Wilde, however, Coward was relatively circumspect about his homosexuality. Thus **Rebecca West** could write, "He was a very dignified man. . . . There was impeccable dignity in his sexual life, which was reticent but untainted by pretense." He rarely wrote overtly about homosexuality in his work, preferring to toy with his audiences, while seeming daring at the same time. A relative ex-

Noel Coward. (© *The Bettmann Archive*)

ception was his 1933 play *Design for Living,* about a ménage à trois, in which one of the two men explains to the woman: "I love you. You love me. You love Otto. I love Otto. Otto loves you. Otto loves me." As cultural critic Michael Bronski writes in his book, *Culture Clash: The Making of Gay Sensibility,* "Hiding behind his dandy prose and sophisticated wit, Coward got away with it." Bronski also notes the "in jokes" and coded language in several verses of Coward's 1932 song "Mad About the Boy," a ballad sung by several women about a matinee idol who has "a gay appeal/ That makes me feel/There's maybe something sad about the boy."

Coward was more direct in the song "Green Carnation" from his 1929 operetta *Bitter Sweet,* in which he satirized the decadent, self-consciously shallow gay men who followed in Oscar Wilde's footsteps. In that song, he makes fun of "pretty, witty" boys who have a preference for porphyry bowls and chandeliers and are invited out to dine by wealthy matrons. Of course, they all wear Wilde's trademark green carnation.

As the years passed, Coward became increasingly associated with the values of the British upper classes, and his politics moved rightward. The enfant terrible of 1924 became a defender of British imperialism, saw postwar England as going down the drain, and was convinced there were "bad times just around the corner," as one of his song lyrics went. As Bronski notes, "Coward's career floundered during the last 30 years of his life because although he maintained the pose of the dandy, he repudiated its rebellious history; for him it had become an empty posture."

CHAPTER 8

GERMANY'S GOLDEN AGE

IN GERMANY, as in England, male homosexual acts were against the law. Paragraph 175 of the German legal code, enacted in 1871 after the unification of the German states, stipulated that "a male who indulges in criminally indecent activities with another male or who allows himself to participate in such activities will be punished with jail." There were no such laws regarding sex between women. Under the influence of the French Revolution, the state of Bavaria had abolished laws in 1813 criminalizing homosexual acts between consenting adults. Hannover had done the same in 1840. But with unification, the law of Prussia, outlawing "unnatural sexual acts between men and men, and men and beasts," became the basis for the law of the unified Germany.

In December 1897, Dr. **Magnus Hirschfeld,** a Berlin physician, petitioned the Reichstag, the German parliament, to abolish Paragraph 175. The Reichstag rejected the petition, but not before the leader of the opposition Social Democratic Party, **August Bebel,** gave a ringing speech on its behalf, probably the first defense of homosexual rights ever made before a legislative body. By the following year, Hirschfeld's petition listed more than two thousand names, including intellectual luminaries such as **Thomas** and **Heinrich Mann, Rainer Maria Rilke,** and **Gerhart Hauptmann.**

Hirschfeld (1868–1935) was to spend the rest of his life crusading for the repeal of Paragraph 175, through his voluminous writings, his Scientific Humanitarian Committee, and his Institute for Sexual Research and World League for Sexual Reform. In the process, the earliest and strongest gay movement in Europe emerged. Hirschfeld came from an assimilated Jewish family (his father was a physician) and grew up in the seaside spa of Kolberg. He studied medicine in Berlin and Munich, first setting up practice in the city of Magdeburg, near Berlin. There, one of his patients, an officer, shot himself through the head on the eve of his marriage. The following day, Hirschfeld received a letter from him telling the story of his suicide: The officer described his feeling that his homosexuality was a "curse" and said he had decided to kill himself when the strain of leading a double life became unbearable. He asked Hirschfeld to publish the story. The officer's agony convinced Hirschfeld, who was also homosexual, that something needed to be done. So, in 1896, the year after Oscar Wilde's trial, Hirschfeld published a thirty-four-page pamphlet called "Sappho and Socrates: How Can One Explain the Love of Men and Women for People of Their Own Sex?" He wrote it under the pseudonym of Dr med. Th. Ramien. According to his biographer, Charlotte Wolff, by 1902–03, Hirschfeld had saved twenty German gay men from suicide.

Strongly influenced by the early sexologist Karl Heinrich Ulrichs, Hirschfeld believed that homosexuality had a biological basis and that homosexuals represented a "third," or "intermediate," sex. He believed that it could be determined whether someone was a member of the third sex by measuring their hips: "Urnings" (male homosexuals) had wider hips than heterosexual men, while "urinden" (lesbians) had narrower hips than heterosexual women. As curious

Magnus Hirschfeld (seated, center) surrounded by friends and colleagues. *(© UPI/ Bettmann)*

(and inaccurate) as these ideas appear today, they seem to have had wide currency at the time; three decades later, the Nazis would use measurement of head size and facial features to distinguish Aryans from Jews. In any event, the belief of Hirschfeld and others that homosexuality was inborn and represented a third sex may have helped establish a stronger sense of gay identity in Germany than elsewhere in Europe.

To those who met him, Hirschfeld himself did not give any indication of being a member of some intermediate sex. He looked like a well-to-do Jewish bourgeois, who, as Charlotte Wolff put it, "could easily have been taken for a businessman or a banker."

Following unification in 1871, the new Germany rapidly became the most dynamic country in Europe. The population of the nation's cities doubled. By the 1890s, with massive overcrowding of urban areas and a deterioration in the quality of life, the German middle class was turning to a variety of social movements as antidotes to growing social problems. These ranged from women's and youth movements to Eastern religions and meditation to the nudity and home vegetable garden movements. This atmosphere of openness to new ideas helped create a climate conducive to the establishment of the gay movement. The general migration into cities also facilitated the establishment of urban gay subcultures. The police of Berlin, in particular, had a long-standing tradition of tolerance toward homosexuality. By 1914, the city was said to be home to forty gay and lesbian bars, as well as to one to two thousand male prostitutes.

It was his attempt to discover just how many homosexuals there actually were in Berlin that made Hirschfeld a figure of controversy for the first time. In 1903, he sent questionnaires to three thousand male students of the Charlottenburger Technical High School in Berlin asking them whether they were attracted exclusively to women, to both men and women, or just to other men. Included was a postcard, to be returned anonymously, with a W (indicating attraction for women) printed on the left-hand side, an M (for men) in the middle, and a $W + M$ (indicating bisexuality) on the right. Of those who replied, 1.5 percent stated that they were attracted to members of the same sex, while another 4.5 percent said that they were attracted to both sexes. The following year, similar questionnaires were sent to five thousand metal workers at a factory at which Hirschfeld had given a lecture on homosexuality. There, the numbers were slightly lower than among the students: 1.15 percent replied that they were inclined to the same sex, while another 3.19 percent said they were attracted to members of both sexes. (By contrast, in 1864, Ulrichs had suggested that Uranians might constitute as much as .002 percent of the German population.)

The results of Hirschfeld's survey were quickly overshadowed by criticism. The right-wing press denounced the distribution of this kind of questionnaire among "impressionable" students and accused Hirschfeld of attempting to lure young people into homosexuality. Six students took him to court, charging him with disseminating obscene material. Hirschfeld was found guilty and forced to pay a fine and court costs.

In the course of the trial, Hirschfeld gave an impassioned defense:

At the beginning of this very week, a well-known homosexual student at the School of Technology poisoned himself because of his homosexuality. In my medical practice, I have at present a student in the same school who shot himself in the heart. Just a few weeks ago, in this very room, I attended a case against two blackmailers who had driven a homosexual gentleman— one of the most honorable men whom I knew—to suicide. . . . I could present hundreds of cases like this, and others similar to it. I felt it was necessary to bring about this inquiry in order to free humanity of a blemish that it will some day think back on with the deepest sense of shame.

Despite the court decision, ideas about the third sex were very much in the air in Germany. For example, a cartoon that appeared in a 1905 issue of the Munich cultural weekly *Jugend* shows a bourgeois family in their garden being asked questions by a uniformed census official. The patriarchal-looking father sits in a rocking chair, while the mother stands with two children under her arms; other children look on inquisitively. "How many children?" asks the census taker. "Two daughters, one boy, one Uranian, and three homosexual intermediates," replies the mother. The cartoon was captioned "Census, Modern Style."

But the concept of gay men and women as a third sex was far from universally accepted, even among German homosexuals. Nor was the equation of homosexuality and decadence, so pronounced in England and France, especially after the Wilde Trial, widespread. One group of German homosexual men took a different path entirely, in 1903 forming an organization called the Committee of the

Special. It combined advocacy of relationships between older and younger men, idealization of ancient Greek culture, and male supremacy. The group also advocated bisexuality, following the Greek model; many of its members were married. Unlike with Hirschfeld's group, no lesbians were permitted to join. Instead of constituting a third sex, it contended instead that homosexuality was among the most "manly" of pursuits. The Committee's major theorist, **Benedikt Friedländer** (1866–1908), criticized Ulrich's theory of the third sex for proceeding from the "false premise that love of a male being is an exclusively female characteristic." It was unacceptable, he wrote, "to attribute such an extremely frequent phenomenon as homosexuality and bisexuality to such a rare phenomenon as partial hermaphroditism. . . . Thus we shall not speak of 'Urnings' nor of the 'third sex,' nor yet of 'sexual intermediates' . . ."

Friedländer, a wealthy philosopher and biologist who was himself married, was also critical of the medicalization of same-sex relationships. Because of their professional training, he argued, doctors tended to classify everything under the rubric of sickness or pathology. In Friedländer's view, homosexuality was neither an illness nor an abnormality. "Most cases of same-sex love are not in the least pathological, but are rather completely normal," he maintained. In 1906, his group seceded from Hirschfeld's Scientific Humanitarian Committee. By 1910, perhaps in response to this increasing criticism, Hirschfeld had essentially discarded his notion of the third sex.

Although some lesbians were members of Hirschfeld's Scientific Humanitarian Committee and Berlin featured lesbian balls and lesbian cafes (including one called the Café Dorian Gray, after Wilde's novel), in general lesbians were less visible than gay men. Many were married. The fact that Paragraph 175 did not punish sexual relations between women lessened the urgency of lesbian political involvement. At the same time, the growing women's movement was reluctant to take up the issue of lesbian equality. In a speech given to Hirschfeld's group at its annual conference in Berlin in 1904, **Anna Rueling** was critical of the women's movement, expressing dismay that "the large and influential organizations of the movement have never lifted a finger to improve the civil rights and social standing of their numerous Uranian members. It is amazing that they have done nothing, absolutely nothing, to protect many of their best-known and most deserving leaders from ridicule and scorn by enlightening the general public about the true nature of Uranism." It was not until 1911, when the Reichstag was considering a proposal extending Paragraph 175 to lesbians, that the women's movement began to pay attention.

Meanwhile, Hirschfeld's Scientific Humanitarian Committee continued to seek passage of repeal of Paragraph 175 but without success. Frustration was mounting, and new—and more imaginative—tactics were proposed. In 1905, for example, the group considered a plan in which a thousand homosexuals would turn themselves into the police and insist that charges be placed against them for violating Paragraph 175. In the end, the plan was shelved as unworkable.

Then, eighty years before it was to become chic in the United States, came the first instance of "outing." **Adolf Brand** (1874–1945), the editor of the gay magazine *Der Eigene,* published a pamphlet that claimed that **Kaplan Dasbach,** the leader of the Catholic Center Party, which strongly opposed repeal of Paragraph 175, was attracted to men and had been the blackmail victim of a male prostitute. Brand had assumed that Hirschfeld and his committee would support his action, but they quickly repudiated such a radical approach.

The origin of Brand's tactics was the scandal a few years before involving the richest man in Germany, **Alfred Krupp.** In 1902, the Social Democratic Party newspaper *Vorwärts,* revealed that Krupp had been engaged in sexual activities with young men on the Italian island of Capri, where he maintained a villa. Although the Social Democrats were the one major political party to support repeal of Paragraph 175, they couldn't resist the temptation to attack the leading industrialist in Germany and the country's leading producer of armaments. After the failure of various efforts to cover up the affair—including the commitment of Krupp's wife to a mental hospital in an effort to silence her—Krupp committed suicide. At his funeral, Krupp's friend **Kaiser Wilhelm II** accused the Social Democratic newspaper of "intellectual murder" and announced that he had come "to raise the shield of the German emperor over the house and memory of Krupp."

Rapidly, the use of accusations of homosexuality to destroy political opponents became a characteristic of Imperial German politics. The culmination was the Eulenburg affair, in which members of the entourage of Kaiser Wilhelm II were named in the most widespread and publicized homosexual scandal in European history. In the process, the gay movement in Germany suffered a major setback.

The major figure in the scandal and the man who gave it its name was Prince **Phillip zu Eulenburg.** Eulenburg had become a close friend of the Kaiser beginning in 1886, when the Kaiser was still a prince. They were drawn together because of a mutual interest in music and the arts. Eulenburg was an extremely accomplished man. He wrote children's stories; his plays were professionally produced in Berlin and Munich; and his songs, the "Rosenlieder," went through three hundred printings over a span of twenty-five years, selling five hundred thousand copies. Writer Anne Topham describes him as "a pale, grey-haired, somewhat weary-looking man with a pallid, fleeting smile, something of a visionary . . . who told his tales in a quiet, soft, subtle voice with a grave smile and a certain fascinating charm of manner." The young Kaiser appears to have idolized him. When Eulenburg played the piano, the Kaiser turned the pages. The Kaiser introduced Eulenburg to his former tutor as "my bosom friend, the only one I have" and recalled later, "Whenever he [Eulenburg] came into our Potsdam home, it was like a flood of sunshine on the routine of life."

Two years after they met, the Kaiser's father died and he became Wilhelm II. Initially, after ascending the imperial throne, his relationship with Eulenburg remained as close as ever. These close ties caused Eulenburg to be dubbed the "ambassador of the German government to the Kaiser." On the Kaiser's boat, the *Meteor,* a picture of Eulenburg sat on the desk in the Kaiser's stateroom— the only photo. On the cruises that the Kaiser took every summer, Eulenburg's cabin was next to his.

Eulenburg tried his best to counter the German military's influence over the Kaiser, which was growing in the 1890s. As time passed, however, the Kaiser began to rely less and less on his old friend. Eulenburg served as ambassador to Vienna and then came home to his estate in Liebenberg. Still, the two men remained friends, and by the early 1900s, Eulenburg's political star seemed on the ascendent once again. The scandal that was to lead to Eulenburg's downfall began in 1905 when he lunched with the Kaiser. By coincidence, on that same day, **Friedrich von Holstein** was removed from office as the Kaiser's First Counselor. Holstein blamed Eulenburg, merely on the basis that Eulenburg had been the Kaiser's lunching companion on the day of his dismissal. Holstein was determined to revenge himself on Eulenburg.

Holstein found an ally in **Maximilian Harden,** a prominent journalist who was known for his hostility to the Kaiser and to "official Germany." But Harden was sympathetic to Holstein's policy of humiliating France and attempting to disrupt the French-British alliance; he was convinced that Eulenburg and the "Liebenberg roundtable" were encouraging the Kaiser to take a more conciliatory line toward France. So Harden's weekly newspaper, *Die Zukunft* (The Future), launched a series of attacks on alleged sinister influences around the Kaiser, taking aim at Eulenburg as an "unhealthy, late romantic and clairvoyant" and as "leader of a sinister and effeminate camarilla." Harden linked Eulenburg to General **Kuno Count von Moltke,** military commandant of Berlin: An article in *Die Zukunft* referred to Eulenburg as "the Harpist" and Moltke as "Sweetie," implying a homosexual relationship. In 1907, Harden named three of the Kaiser's military aides-de-camp, all members of the so-called Liebenberg group, as homosexuals. The crown prince was chosen to inform the Kaiser, who refused to read *Die Zukunft* on principle. The Kaiser was mortified at the accusations. He insisted that Molkte and several others resign their commissions and that his dear friend Eulenburg leave the diplomatic service and return the Order of the Black Eagle, the highest decoration awarded by the state of Prussia.

Moltke, the Berlin commandant, brought a civil suit against Harden. Shortly afterward, Adolf Brand, the gay activist who had attempted to "out" the Center Party politician a few years before, added to the litany of accusations. He accused the Chancellor of Germany, **Bernhard Prince von Bülow,** of being romantically involved with his male secretary. Brand again claimed he was doing so for poiltical reasons. Bülow sued him for libel.

The *Moltke v. Harden* trial opened on October 23, 1907, in Berlin Municipal Court. The magistrate was experienced; his sheriffs consisted of a butcher and a milkman. Although not officially involved in the case, Eulenburg was clearly the defense's main target. Moltke's former wife was the star witness. She and her former husband had had conjugal relations only twice in their two years of marriage, she testified; Moltke had sometimes put a pan of water between them in bed to ward off her advances. She also revealed that her husband had once found a handkerchief left behind by

Eulenburg and had pressed it to his lips, murmuring, "Phili, my Phili." According to her testimony, Moltke referred to Eulenburg as "my soulmate, my old boy, and my one and only cuddly bear." Although her husband seemed to spend more time with Eulenburg than with her, she had suspected nothing, she said. At that time she had no idea that there was even such a thing as homosexuality.

The trial caused a sensation. With the number of spectators growing larger by the day, the final witness was none other than homosexual rights campaigner Magnus Hirschfeld, called as an "expert" witness. In his testimony, Hirschfeld asserted that Moltke had his "feminine side." He based this statement on his observations of Moltke's behavior in the courtroom and on the testimony of his ex-wife. Hirschfeld suggested that Moltke's treatment of his wife, his sensitivity toward the arts, and his use of makeup all indicated that his "unconscious orientation" was "homosexual."

On October 29, the court acquitted Harden of libel. As far as the magistrate was concerned, Moltke's homosexuality had been proven. But many felt the courtroom histrionics had turned the trial into a farce. The verdict was overturned and a new trial was ordered.

A few days later, proceedings opened in the libel suit of Chancellor Bülow against the gay activist Adolf Brand. Testifying on his own behalf, Brand insisted that he wasn't trying to insult Bülow at all by calling him homosexual. He had exposed the Chancellor, he testified, to hasten the repeal of Paragraph 175. It was the strategy of the "path over corpses." The court was unimpressed and handed Brand an eighteen-month jail sentence.

Soon afterward, at the retrial of Moltke, medical experts declared his wife a hysterical witness, and Hirschfeld withdrew his "expert" opinion. Moltke was cleared. Harden, his accuser, was found guilty of libel and sentenced to four months in prison. For the moment, the reputation of the aristocracy was preserved.

Once he was released from prison, however, Harden continued his campaign against Eulenburg. Eventually, Eulenburg himself was put on trial for perjury, but as the trial was about to begin, he became ill and was hospitalized. One by one, potential witnesses were brought to his hospital room to make an identification. In the end, the witnesses were reduced to two—both of them boatmen in Munich who claimed to have had sexual relations with him. One had thirty-two convictions on his record and, even while the trial was in progress, tried to blackmail Eulenburg. The other, a former house servant of Eulenburg, testified that in 1883—twenty-five years before—the Prince had made advances to him on a boat and the two had had sex. As the trial continued, Eulenburg, suffering from heart problems and severe rheumatoid arthritis, had to be brought into court on a stretcher. Although his wife had prepared a ringing defense, just before she was to testify, Eulenburg fainted in the courtroom. The case was postponed, and postponements continued year after year because of Eulenburg's health. The case was never concluded.

Eulenburg wasn't the only person whose health was affected by the scandal. After the first Moltke-Harden trial, the Kaiser himself suffered a nervous collapse and took to his bed for two days. In a letter at Christmas 1907, he wrote, "It has been a very difficult year which has caused me an infinite amount of worry. A trusted group of friends was suddenly broken up through . . . insolence, slander, and lying. To have to see the names of one's friends dragged through all the gutters of Europe without being able or entitled to help is terrible." The Kaiser never saw Eulenburg again; in 1927, he wrote Eulenburg's son that he believed the Prince had been "absolutely innocent." Although some have said that the fall of Eulenburg and his circle pushed the Kaiser toward a more militaristic foreign policy and hastened the onset of World War I, most historians do not give this view much credence.

The Eulenburg affair was important in another way, however. It could be viewed as one more indication of the end to the era of passionate friendships, of florid expressions of male affection. Eulenburg himself expressed this in a letter to Moltke on the eve of the latter's first trial: "At the moment when the freshest example of the modern age, a Harden, criticized our nature, stripped our ideal friendship, laid bare the form of our thinking and feeling which we had justifiably regarded all our lives as something obvious and natural, in that moment, the modern age, laughing cold-bloodedly, broke our necks."

As much as the trials brought homosexuality into public view, the short-term effects on German gay life and the fledgling homosexual rights movement were extremely negative. Prosecutions for violations of Paragraph 175 increased from an average of 363 in the years from 1903 to 1907 to an average of 542 in the years from 1909 to 1913, according to historian James Steakley. At the same time, the homosexual rights movement was driven into quiescence, from which it never really emerged until the end of World War I. Hirschfeld's labeling of Moltke as homosexual on such flimsy grounds and Hirschfeld's later recantation had discredited the gay rights campaigner. The testimony was "an amazing tactical blunder," Steakley asserts. After Hirschfeld's courtroom appearance, financial support from upper-class, pro-monarchist homosexuals for Hirschfeld's organization decreased by about two-thirds from 1907 to 1909. Perhaps, Steakley suggests, wealthy contributors feared that Hirschfeld might someday testify against *them*, suggesting they were homosexual by virture of their mannerisms or makeup, as he had done at the Moltke trial.

The scandals hurt the gay movement in the longer term as well. The Eulenburg affair was widely publicized throughout Europe, equating Germany with homosexuality and offering a propaganda bonanza to anti-German elements. This was particularly true in France, where homosexuality began to be popularly known as *"le vice allemand"* and the question "Are you German?" could be found scrawled on the walls of the public urinals of Paris. The fact that Harden, the newspaper editor who initiated the scandals, was Jewish and that Hirschfeld, the "expert" witness, was Jewish *and* homosexual, encouraged the notion that Jews and homosexuals were linked in a plot to slander the Kaiser and the German ruling class. When German nationalists tried to find scapegoats for the country's defeat in World War I, it was convenient to blame Jews and homosexuals for the "stab in the back." (In 1927, Kaiser Wilhelm himself claimed that the scandal had been started by "international Jewry" and marked the "first step" of a conspiracy that led to the defeat of Germany.) Although one wouldn't want to overestimate the legacy of the Eulenburg affair, it unquestionably helped to fuel the fires of anti-Semitic and antigay nationalism.

Part of the immediate backlash to the trials was a legislative effort to extend the penalties of Paragraph 175 to lesbian sexual relations. In an effort to counter this, Hirschfeld's Scientific Humanitarian League allied itself with one of the more conservative factions of the women's movement, the League for the Protection of Maternity and Sexual Reform. In February 1911, a meeting took place in which Hirschfeld and **Helene Stöcker,** head of the league, spoke. The league adopted a resolution that may well be the first by any women's group on the subject of homosexuality. Terming the proposed criminalization of sexual acts between women a "grave error," the statement continued that such a law "would not remove inequality [of the sexes] but double injustice. The door would be thrown open to informers and blackmailers, and unmarried working women who live together would be shamefully harassed without protecting any legal interests." In the end, the attempt to include women under Paragraph 175 failed.

The year 1911 also marked the establishment of the first gay rights organization outside Germany, the Dutch Scientific Humanitarian Committee (Nederlandsch Wetenschappelijk Humanitair Komitee, or NWHK). Although the Netherlands had abolished its sodomy laws a hundred years before, in 1911 a new government coalition of Catholic and Calvinist religious parties raised the age of consent for homosexual activity from sixteen to twenty-one. The Dutch Scientific Humanitarian Committee was formed as a result, under the leadership of the liberal jurist **Jacob Schorer**. Modeled on Hirschfeld's group, the NWHK was relatively low-key and educational in nature and never achieved the visibility of its German counterpart. But its establishment helped create a climate that made Holland the most tolerant country in Europe concerning homosexuality for much of the latter part of the century.

Germany's defeat in World War I and the ensuing abdication of the Kaiser seemed to usher in a hopeful new era for German gays and lesbians. The day before the armistice was announced, Magnus Hirschfeld was one of a number of speakers at a rally of five thousand people gathered around the Bismarck monument in the Reichstagplatz in Berlin. The rally demanded the immediate dissolution of the Reichstag and the election of a national assembly (it had nothing to do with homosexual rights). Suddenly, monarchist soldiers began firing at "red" soldiers guarding the demonstration, and a gun battle ensued.

The outdoor meeting was symbolic of what was to follow. In the liberal atmosphere of the Weimar Republic of the 1920s, Germany witnessed the flowering of homosexual life and culture. Yet at the same time, the country became increasingly polarized between Left and Right, a polarization that was to prove disastrous for the country—and for German gays and lesbians, in particular.

Under the Weimar Republic, Berlin rapidly acquired the reputation as the "gayest" city in Europe. A homosexual group called the German Friendship Association established an activities center in Berlin, sponsored dances, and published a weekly newspaper. Throughout the 1920s there were some thirty different gay publications, part of expanded freedom of the press under Weimar. A homosexual theater group, the Eros Theatre, was founded. The first film on a gay subject—*Different from the Others*—starring **Conrad Veidt,** one of the leading actors of Weimar Germany, was released. Hirschfeld himself appeared in a cameo role (see "Two Films," page 131). There was even talk of starting a gay political party—under the Weimar constitution, any group able to muster sixty thousand votes could legally constitute itself a political party and send a representative to the Reichstag. But this never happened.

The scale of the homosexual subculture dazzled foreign visitors. The Austrian writer **Stefan Zweig** wrote of 1920s Berlin, "Along the entire *Kunfurstendamm* powdered and rouged young men sauntered . . . and in the dim-lit bars one might see government officials and men of finance tenderly courting drunken sailors without any shame." Cooks Tours of Berlin included visits to lesbian bars. In an article in *La Mercure de France,* French diplomat **Ambroise Got** described gay Berlin as "a mad whirl of pleasure, a wild rush to enjoyment." In a visit to the Kleist casino, Got found a middle-class gay clientele and "a tiny orchestra consisting of piano and a violin, playing soothingly sentimental and languorous airs . . . some chat, hand in hand; others touch, caress and look longingly at each other." The diplomat attended an adaptation of Marlowe's *Edward II* at the gay Eros Theatre, as well as a play about a woman who leaves home and child for another woman. **Robert McAlmon,** the heterosexual American chronicler of expatriate Paris, offered a more bizarre vision of Berlin during a short visit in 1923:

> *Hirschfeld was conducting his psychoanalytic school and a number of souls unsure of their sexes or of their inhibitions competed with each other in looking or acting freakishly, several Germans declared themselves authentic hermaphrodites, and one elderly variant loved to arrive at the smart cabarets each time as a different type of woman: elegant, or as a washwoman, or a street vendor, or as a modest mother of a family. He was very comical and his presence always made for hilarity, as did the presence of a chorus boy from New York. The chorus boy was on in years, but he fancied himself Bert Savoy [a famous drag entertainer] and was ribaldly outright and extremely weird.*

For the young novelist **Christopher Isherwood** (1904–86), eager to escape the sexually repressive environment of his native Britain,

"Berlin meant boys." He arrived in Berlin in 1928 and, like the hero of his *Berlin Stories,* earned his living by giving English lessons. Isherwood tended to prefer working-class bars that featured photographs of boxers and racing cyclists above the bar and where "boys stripped off their sweaters or leather jackets and sat around with their shirts unbuttoned to the navel and their sleeves rolled up to the armpits." But he also frequented some of the more bourgeois gay clubs. Such establishments were "governed by the code of heterosexual middle-class propriety," he observed. "If two boys were sitting together and you wanted to dance with one of them, you bowed to both before asking, 'May I?' Then, if the boy said yes, you bowed again to the other boy, as though he were the escort of a girl and had just given you his permission to dance with her."

Berlin did its best to live up to its reputation. At dens of "pseudo-vice" catering to heterosexual tourists, Isherwood found screaming boys in drag and monocled girls in dinner jackets playacting "the high jinks of Sodom and Gomorrah." The idea was to horrify the onlookers and reassure everyone that Berlin was still the most decadent city in Europe. Isherwood was convinced that much of this was commercial hype. Paris had cornered the "straight girl–market," so what was left for Berlin, he suggested, to offer its visitors "but a masquerade of perversions"?

While gay Berliners and foreign sex tourists were busily entertaining themselves, efforts to repeal Paragraph 175 continued. Hirschfeld himself began increasingly to devote himself to the movement for broader sexual reform. On July 1, 1919, he inaugurated the Institute for Sexual Science at a palatial Berlin mansion. It was staffed by four physicians and their assistants and housed clinical and research facilities. It was not exclusively concerned with homosexuality: Among the services the institute offered were marriage and career counseling, VD testing and treatment, family planning and sex education programs, and psychiatric therapy. A legal department advised men who were arrested for violating Paragraph 175 and other laws regarding sexual offenses. The institute also had a library and museum and collections of social and ethnological materials.

But Germany of the 1920s was in the midst of an increasingly darkening period, with rampaging inflation and economic gloom and the rising specter of Nazism. The nationalistic Right emphasized the *Volk,* the purity of race, blood, and soil, and the sanctity of family life. The Weimar Republic was denounced for giving free rein to sexual license of all sorts: **Hitler** condemned the young democracy as a "hothouse for the forced growth of sexual notions and incitement." As both a Jew and a homosexual, Hirschfeld was the ideal target for right-wing groups. He was assaulted by anti-Semites in Munich in 1920; in a similar incident in the same city in 1921, he was left for dead with a fractured skull (some newspapers, in fact, even reported his death). In 1923, a youth opened fire at a lecture Hirschfeld was giving in Vienna, wounding several people in the audience. After the first physical attack on Hirschfeld, a Nazi commentator gloated, "It is not without charm to know that . . . Hirschfeld was so beaten that his eloquent mouth could never again be kissed by one of his disciples."

Increasingly, Hirschfeld was seen as a liability in the law reform movement (now led by his disciple, **Kurt Hiller**). As it was, he began to lose faith that homosexuals could ever represent an effective political force. "Except for a few minor cliques, homosexuals are in reality almost totally lacking in feelings of solidarity," Hirschfeld complained in 1927. "In fact, it would be difficult to find another class of mankind which has proved so incapable of organizing to secure its basic rights." Meanwhile, the gay movement increasingly allied itself with the Communists, further antagonizing the nationalistic right. Hirschfeld visited the Soviet Union in 1926 and was impressed by its enlightened attitudes toward marriage and prostitution and its repeal of legal penalties against homosexual acts. The German Communist Party responded by becoming the strongest supporter in the Reichstag of the repeal of Paragraph 175. But the gay movement's sympathy for the Soviet Union waned as Soviet policies themselves began to shift under Stalin and rumors spread that the authorities there were incarcerating homosexuals in mental hospitals.

Still, in 1929, the long-sought effort to repeal Paragraph 175 seemed within reach. Supported by the Communists and the Social Democrats, a Reichstag committee approved repeal by a narrow 15–13 vote. Passage by the entire parliamentary body appeared likely. But 1929 was the year of the stock market crash and the beginning of the international Depression. Economic problems became such a national preoccupation that repeal never came up for a vote before the full Reichstag.

After the Reichstag committee vote, Hitler's official newspaper wrote:

*We congratulate you, Mr. Hirschfeld, on the victory in commit-
tee. But don't think that we Germans will allow these laws to
stand for a single day after we have come to power. . . . Among
the many evil instincts that characterize the Jewish race, one that
is especially pernicious has to do with sexual relationships. The
Jews are forever trying to propagandize sexual relations between
siblings, men and animals, and men and men. We National Socialists will soon unmask and condemn them by law. These efforts are nothing but vulgar, perverted crimes and we will punish
them by banishment or hanging.*

A new era was about to dawn in Germany.

Strindberg Goes to a Gay Ball in Berlin, Circa 1890—An Excerpt from *The Cloister*

*One of the first writers to treat homosexuality sympathetically
was the Swedish playwright and novelist **August Strindberg**
(1849–1912). In his 1885 short story, "Nature the Criminal,"
published in his collection* Getting Married, *he tells of a homosexual encounter between a chief of a frigate and a young cadet.
Strindberg never uses the word* homosexuality, *but it is clear
what he is writing about: "By this time, human beings should be
enlightened enough not to punish disabilities," one character
says, adding, "Why, in France, a law has already been proposed
in both chambers that would annul the paragraph that deals with
this supposed crime." (In fact, no such law existed in France.) In
his novel* The Cloister, *written in 1891, Strindberg offers a description of a gay ball in Berlin that has all the features of a documentary account. Combining shock and sympathy, it is
probably the first description of a homosexual ball ever published.*

BEFORE GOING to the Café National he had been to a "Viennese Ball" as an onlooker. He, and a consular secretary, and a doctor had been invited there by an Inspector of Police. It was the most horrible thing he had ever seen. In order that a better check might be kept on them the perverts of the capital had been given permission to hold a fancy-dress ball. When it opened everyone behaved ceremoniously, almost as if they were in a madhouse. Men danced with men, mournfully, with deadly seriousness, as if they were doing something they had been ordered to do, without pleasure, without a smile. Between the dances the couples sat gazing into each other's eyes, as if in them they could read their fate. The one playing the lady's role might have the mustache of a cavalryman and pince-nez, he might be ugly, with coarse, masculine features, and not even a trace of femininity to serve as an apology.

The gods had struck them mad, so that they saw what was not there, were drawn towards what they did not wish and might not have. It was punishment for unknown sins and certainly not what you would call vice or sensuality, for they looked like outcasts and were incredibly clever at avoiding seeing the Police Inspector and his guests who had seated themselves at a table in the centre of one end of the room, close to which all the couples had to pass. Pandemonium, the seventh circle of Hell, for the unblessed, the wretched, the mentally sick. And they were treated as criminals. The Inspector called them by their Christian names and summoned some of the most interesting among them to his table, so that the author could study them! Some of them approached with funereal faces, unwilling, colourless, and answered evasively. Others were shy, and made childish little gestures, as if they were playing a game.

Most of them appeared to be in love, but in a purely psychic sense. They were bound together by unfathomable sympathy, and the same couples danced every dance together, did not leave each other for an instant, faithful to the death, and jealous. While the ball was in progress the respected old doctor rose in distress and left the table, but returned in a moment still more upset. He had seen his best friend, a highly-placed Civil Servant, whom it was true he had suspected, but without having any proof.

In the female section, where women danced with women, the most noteworthy person was a stately lady, beautiful, distinguished-looking, well-dressed, but not in fancy dress, who conducted herself with the dignity of a lady-in-waiting. Her truly noble features diffused modesty and pain for something, she knew not what, as her eyes followed a radiant young blonde. The Inspector informed them that the two were bound together by a passionate love for each other, and that, as the elder woman was poor, the younger one supported her by selling herself to men she abhorred. Martyrdom here too, self-sacrifice, faithfulness, all the virtues in the midst of vice!

When they left that hell he took with him an impression of something inexplicable, which neither pathology nor psychiatry could explain. It seemed to him that the most horrible thing of all was that everything was done so seriously, and that it was all so respectable!

Christopher Isherwood in Berlin—An Excerpt from *Christopher and His Kind*

The British novelist Christopher Isherwood first came to Berlin in 1928, in the waning days of the Weimar Republic. He lived there, on and off, for the next few years, teaching English and gathering material for his Berlin Stories. *In his autobiography,* Christopher and His Kind, *he provides a vivid portrait of gay life in Berlin during this period. At one point he lived next door to Magnus Hirschfeld's Institute for Sexual Science, which he described as follows:*

THE BUILDING which was now occupied by the Hirschfeld Institute had belonged, at the turn of the century, to the famous violinist Joseph Joachim; its public rooms still had an atmosphere which Christopher somehow associated with Joachim's hero, Brahms. Their furniture was classic, pillared, garlanded, their marble massive, their curtains solemnly sculpted, their engravings grave. Lunch was a meal of decorum and gracious smiles, presided over by a sweetly dignified lady with silver hair: a living guarantee that sex, in this sanctuary, was being treated with seriousness. How could it not be? Over the entrance to the Institute was an inscription in Latin which meant: Sacred to Love and to Sorrow.

Dr. Hirschfeld seldom ate with them. He was represented by Karl Giese, his secretary and long-time lover. Also present were the doctors of the staff and the patients or guests, whichever you chose to call them, hiding their individual problems behind silence or polite table chatter, according to their temperaments. I remember the shock with which Christopher first realized that one of the apparently female guests was a man. He had pictured transvestites as loud, screaming, willfully unnatural creatures. This one seemed as quietly natural as an animal and his disguise was accepted by everyone else as a matter of course. Christopher had been telling himself that he had rejected respectability and that he now regarded it with amused contempt. But the Hirschfeld kind of respectability disturbed his latent puritanism. During those early days, he found lunch at the Institute a bit uncanny.

Christopher giggled nervously when Karl Giese and Francis [Christopher's friend] took him through the Institute's museum. Here were whips and chains and torture instruments, designed for the practitioners of pleasure-pain; high-heeled, intricately decorated boots for the fetishists; lacy female undies which had been worn by ferociously masculine Prussian officers beneath their uniforms. Here were the lower halves of trouser legs with elastic bands to hold them in position between knee and ankle. In these and nothing else but an overcoat and a pair of shoes, you could walk the streets and seem fully clothed, giving a camera-quick exposure whenever a suitable viewer appeared.

Here were fantasy pictures, drawn and painted by Hirschfeld's patients. Scenes from the court of a priapic king who sprawled on a throne with his own phallus for a scepter and watched the grotesque matings of his courtiers. Strange sad bedroom scenes in which the faces of the copulators expressed only dismay and agony.

And here was a gallery of photographs, ranging in subject matter from the sexual organs of quasi-hermaphrodites to famous homosexual couples—Wilde with Alfred Douglas, Whitman with Peter Doyle, Ludwig of Bavaria with Kainz, Edward Carpenter with George Merrill.

Christopher giggled because he was embarrassed. He was embarrassed because, at last, he was being brought face to face with his tribe. Up to now, he had behaved as though the tribe didn't exist and homosexuality were a private way of life discovered by himself and a few friends. He had always known, of course, that this wasn't true. But now he was forced to admit kinship with these freakish fellow tribesmen and their distasteful customs. And he didn't like it. His first reaction was to blame the Institute. He said to himself: How can they take this stuff so *seriously?*

Then, one afternoon, André Gide paid them a visit. He was taken on a tour of the premises personally conducted by Hirschfeld. Live exhibits were introduced with such comments as: "Intergrade. Third Division." One of these was a young man who opened his shirt with a modest smile to display two perfectly formed female breasts. Gide looked on, making a minimum of polite comment, judiciously fingering his chin. He was in full costume as the Great French Novelist, complete with cape. No doubt he thought Hirschfeld's performance hopelessly crude and un-French. Christopher's Gallophobia flared up. Sneering, culture-conceited frog! Suddenly he loved Hirschfeld—at whom he himself had been sneering, a moment before—the silly solemn old professor with his doggy mustache, thick peering spectacles, and clumsy German-Jewish boots. . . . Nevertheless, they were all three of them on the same side, whether Christopher liked it or not. And later he would learn to honor them both, as heroic leaders of his tribe.

Two Films: *Different from the Others* and *Mädchen in Uniform*

THE LIBERAL ATMOSPHERE of Weimar Germany provided the setting for the earliest films on gay and lesbian themes. In fact, the first feature film on a gay subject was a product of the German homosexual rights movement. Produced with the cooperation (and participation) of Magnus Hirschfeld, the silent film *Different from the Others (Anders als die Andern)* was released commercially in 1919. The film, both a love story and a polemic, starred Conrad Veidt as a gay violinist who is loved by two women but in fact loves a young man. He is blackmailed by yet another man, whom he had met years before at a gay ball, and arrested for violating Paragraph 175. After the blackmailer testifies against him, the violinist is sentenced to prison. He commits suicide. Meanwhile, the young man whom he loves, unable to face life without him, decides to kill himself as well. Dr. Hirschfeld, playing himself, talks the youth out of it. In the process, Hirschfeld gives an impassioned speech against the evils of Paragraph 175, the law that was indirectly responsible for the violinist's suicide. The youth decides to devote his life to the fight to repeal Paragraph 175.

Different from the Others was first shown on May 14, 1919, at a Berlin theater, introduced by Dr. Hirschfeld himself. It was swiftly banned in several German cities. Later that year, the movie was given a special showing at Hirschfeld's Institute for Sexual Science for the benefit of government ministers and high-ranking civil servants. But the attacks by right-wing newspapers and nationalist hoodlums took their toll; in 1920, the Weimar government banned the film outright. In 1927, *Different from the Others* was remade as *Laws of Love (Gesetze der Liebe)* with the Hirschfeld part removed, a sign of Hirschfeld's growing unpopularity.

Christopher Isherwood described seeing both films at Hirschfeld's institute when he lived in Berlin in 1930. He recalled one scene in which the violinist, while in jail, has a vision of a "long procession of kings, poets, scientists, philosophers and other famous victims of homophobia," moving somberly across the screen, heads bowed. Each cringes as he passes under a banner inscribed PARAGRAPH 175. In the final scene, Dr. Hirschfeld appears with the corpse of the violinist lying in the background and delivers a speech appealing for justice for the third sex. Isherwood found that moment "like the appearance of Dickens beside the corpse of Jo, in *Bleak House,* to deliver the splendid diatribe which begins: 'Dead, your Majesty . . .' "

On another occasion Isherwood saw Conrad Veidt, star of both films, at a gay ball in Berlin. Veidt sat apart at his own table, in evening dress, sipping champagne, smoking a cigarette out of a long holder, and watching the dancing through his monocle. Partygoers dropped by his table to pay their respects, but none was bold enough to sit with him. To Isherwood he appeared "a supernatural figure, the guardian god of these festivities, who was graciously manifesting himself to his devotees."

Only one partial print of *Different from the Others,* discovered in the Ukraine in 1979, survives. All other prints were destroyed by the Nazis.

A lesbian character appeared for the first time on screen in G. W. Pabst's 1929 film, *Pandora's Box,* but it was in the film *Mädchen in Uniform* that the lesbian theme took center stage. Released in 1931, *Mädchen* was adapted from a play by German lesbian writer and sculptor **Christa Winsloe** (1888–1944) and was directed by **Leontine Sagan** with an all-female cast. Although historian George Mosse calls it "the most famous plea for lesbian liberation in Germany . . . straightforward and forceful," its subject matter is as much antiauthoritarian as it is pro-gay. Set in a boarding school for daughters of poor officers of the Prussian aristocracy much like one attended by Winsloe herself, *Mädchen* tells the story of the love of a sensitive and high-spirited student, Manuela (played by **Hertha Thiele**), for her teacher, Fräulein von Bernburg (**Dorothea Weick**). In a school run by an authoritarian headmistress, Fräulein von Bernburg is a sympathetic voice, telling the headmistress, "I cannot stand the way you transform the children into frightened creatures." After a school play to celebrate the headmistress's birthday, an intoxicated Manuela blurts out her love for her teacher and then swoons. The headmistress is shocked. She shouts, *"Ein scandale,"* ostracizing Manuela and forbidding anyone to speak to her. In the play, Manuela commits suicide, jumping to her death from the school's second-floor window. The film has a happy ending, however, in which the other students prevent the suicide attempt, and the abashed headmistress seems to lose her authority.

Germans responded to the film as an attack on the rigid Prussian system of discipline, and it was immensely popular, considered the best film of the year in Germany. But when it was screened in the United States, *Mädchen* was rejected by the censors, and was shown only after cuts were made that effectively obscured the lesbian content. Eliminations included a scene in which the headmistress calls Manuela's passion "a sin" and the teacher, Fräulein von Bernburg, replies, "What you call sins, Principal, I call the great spirit of love, which has thousands of forms." American film critic Vito Russo notes that "this deletion, a political act, effectively removed any defense of such emotions and thereby perverted the intent of both Winsloe and Sagan."

Christa Winsloe turned *Mädchen* into a novel, called *The Child*

In the 1931 film *Mädchen in Uniform*, an adoring Manuela, played by Hertha Thiele (right), clasps the hand of her teacher, Fräulein von Bernburg, played by Dorothea Weick (left). (© *Museum of Modern Art/Film Stills Archive*)

Manuela. It was published in 1933, making it apparently one of the last gay-themed novels to be published after Hitler came to power. The former wife of a Hungarian baron, Winsloe left Germany after the Nazi takeover and had a passionate relationship with American journalist **Dorothy Thompson,** who was madly in love with her. Winsloe went to Hollywood to write scripts, including one about a young boy's struggle with his homosexuality. None were ever produced, however, and she returned to Europe in 1935. She and her female lover, **Simone Gentet,** were murdered in 1944 in disturbances that followed the liberation of Paris. A remake of *Mädchen in Uniform* starring **Romy Schneider** was released in 1958.

FOUR BOHEMIAS

CHAPTER 9

GREENWICH VILLAGE

ARTISTIC AND BOHEMIAN ENCLAVES were among the places where a modern sense of gay and lesbian community first began to emerge. Whether they be New York's Greenwich Village or Jazz Age Harlem or Left Bank Paris, bohemias were self-enclosed geographical and spiritual worlds where unconventionality was prized and new ideas venerated; where women experienced an enhanced degree of freedom; where the power of religion and family to enforce cultural, political, and sexual conformity was limited. Often these bohemias became magnets for gays and lesbians from provincial cities and towns. Yet even in such relatively enlightened environments, the norms of the rest of society were not totally absent, and acceptance of homosexual relationships and identity often involved struggle and compromise.

In the 1910s and '20s, Greenwich Village was a pocket of political radicalism and sexual freedom and, above all, of art and artists. With its crooked streets and relative isolation, the Village escaped the growth and development inflicted upon much of the rest of Manhattan in the late nineteenth century. By the early 1900s, it was a declining residential neighborhood where, as literary critic **Malcolm Cowley** put it, "you could rent a furnished hall-bedroom for two or three dollars weekly or the top floor of a rickety house for thirty dollars a month." The cheap living, in addition to the area's old-world charm (it was largely populated by Italian immigrants), made the Village appealing to artists of all stripes. This combination also made it attractive to gays and lesbians, who could blend in among the other nonconformists of the Village. After all, in popular parlance, "artistic" was often a code word for homosexual.

In its heyday, before and just after the outbreak of World War I, the Village was a hotbed of all things new and "un-American": socialism and psychoanalysis, feminism and free love. **Emma Goldman** advocated anarchism, and **Margaret Sanger** birth control; the dancer **Isadora Duncan** was the symbol of paganism; **Eugene O'Neill**'s plays transformed the modern stage; *The Masses*, "the

Socialist magazine of Free Expression," chronicled the intellectual ferment of the period and wound up in court for opposing American participation in World War I; the romantic **John Reed** prepared to go off to Russia to chronicle ten revolutionary days that shook the world. In the Village they even dressed differently: the men in flannel shirts with soft rolled collars, the women in smocks and loose-fitting suits with bright colors. The men wore their hair long; the women smoked cigarettes in public and drank alcohol in cafes. One local figure of the time described the geography of the prewar Village this way: "It is bounded on the North by the Feminist Movement, on the East by Old World Bohemia . . . on the South by the Artistic Temperament and on the West by the IWW [International Workers of the World]."

Puritanism was the great enemy; Malcolm Cowley wrote of the "private war between Greenwich Village and the *Saturday Evening Post.*" Long before the Kinsey Report, Villagers presumed that women had sex lives and the same rights as men to sexual gratification inside or outside marriage. In fact, marriage and monogamy were held in such disrepute and sexual unconventionality so romanticized that there was "a fatal tendency to assume that all mothers who bore children out of wedlock were modern madonnas and that their offspring were of superior stock to those more traditionally conceived," notes Leslie Fishbein in her book *Rebels in Bohemia.*

Homosexuality and homosexual relationships were part of the unconventional Village stew. **Mabel Dodge Luhan**, the Village's chief party-giver in the early 1910s, had had lesbian relationships in her younger days that she wrote about quite frankly in her memoirs. ("It was a more delicious life I felt in me than I had ever felt before," she wrote of her love for **Violet Shillito**. "I thought it was a superior kind of living, too.") **Carl Van Vechten**, who wrote a weekly column for *The New York Times* and later popularized the Harlem Renaissance, introduced Dodge to bohemian circles and helped plan her parties. Although married, Van Vechten had a taste for men. Gay painters **Charles Demuth** and **Marsden Hartley** were very much in evidence, and the dandyish Demuth—whose work was a precursor of the pop art of the 1950s and '60s—painted homosexual tearooms, bathhouses, and, of course, sailors. **Margaret Anderson** and her lover, **Jane Heap**, moved their modernist literary magazine, *The Little Review,* from Chicago to the Village and published **James Joyce**'s *Ulysses* in serial form. The poet Edna

St. Vincent Millay (1892–1950), fresh from her Vassar "smashes," rapidly became the darling of the Village—and later the most popular female poet in the United States.

"It was bohemian chic for a woman to admit to a touch of lesbianism," notes historian Lillian Faderman. Faderman cites a conversation that Edna St. Vincent Millay had at a Village party with a psychoanalyst who was attempting to help her figure out the cause of a headache Millay was complaining of. The psychoanalyst asked, "I wonder if it has ever occurred to you that you might perhaps, although you are hardly conscious of it, have an occasional impulse toward a person of your own sex?" Millay is said to have responded, "Oh, you mean I'm homosexual! Of course I am, and heterosexual too, but what's that got to do with my headache?"

Despite Millay's casual response, Village attitudes were actually more complicated. While an undergraduate at Vassar, from 1913 to 1917, Millay gathered her own Sapphic circle around her, some of them young women who were her "smashes." Her play *The Lamp and the Bell* captures the spirit of those days, celebrating love between women and commenting on one female couple, "I vow I never knew a pair of lovers more constant than those two." Yet when Millay came to Greenwich Village, she was subjected to great pressure from the local bohemian males to abandon her exclusive interest in women. Freudian thinking—with its view of homosexuality as "arrested development"—was in vogue. According to the Freudians, lesbian relationships weren't sufficiently serious: A truly "adult" relationship was a heterosexual one. **Floyd Dell**, one of the Village's most prominent figures and Millay's first suitor there, accused her of being trapped in "the enchanted garden of childhood," where men were barred. She was "terrified at the bogeys which haunt the realm of grown up man-and-woman love," he claimed. Dell urged her to seek psychoanalysis to overcome her lesbianism. Millay declined. Freudian ideas, she replied, were "a Teutonic attempt to lock women up in the home and restrict them to cooking and baby-tending."

Nonetheless, Dell became Millay's first male lover. Although she later married a Dutch-born coffee importer twelve years her senior, her inclinations toward other women did not vanish entirely. Shortly before her marriage, she had a brief affair with the sculptor **Thelma Wood**, who was later to be the lover of the novelist Djuna Barnes. Millay's experience in the Village was typical of the period: As in Belle Époque Paris, lesbian love was acceptable as a "phase" or as a diversion, but it was still considered inferior to heterosexual love and not perceived as a basis for sustaining lifelong relationships.

As Lillian Faderman observes, Village attitudes toward homosexuality in general were more ambivalent than one might expect, given all the local emphasis on "free love." Self-described feminist Floyd Dell believed that homosexuality was a characteristic of patriarchal societies in which women were subordinated to men; in the modern age of free love, he argued, it represented a social anachronism and personal regression. Others were concerned that the popular equation of homosexual and artistic tarnished heterosexual Villagers with the "queer" brush. Malcolm Cowley recalls that while editing a magazine called *Broom* in the 1920s, he started receiving letters at the publication's 45 King Street office addressed to "45 Queer Street." "I came to believe," he wrote, "that a general offensive was about to be made against modern art, an offensive based on the theory that all modern writers, painters, and musicians were homosexual." He started to view "pansipoetical poets" as the enemy, fantasizing about a writer's revolution in which "you would set about hanging policemen from the lamp posts . . . and beside each policeman would be hanged a Methodist preacher, and beside each preacher a pansy poet."

One of the few Villagers to take a strong and public stance in defense of homosexuality was the Russian-born anarchist Emma Goldman. Although Goldman herself was not gay, the subject featured prominently in her national lecture tours, which displeased the "censors" within the ranks of the anarchist movement, who thought that anarchism was misunderstood enough without their taking up the issue of homosexuality. But that only made Goldman "surer of myself, more determined to plead for every victim, be it one of social wrong or of moral prejudice," as she wrote in her autobiography. When she would give a lecture in which she mentioned homosexuality, a number of people would come up to her afterward, relating their personal anguish and isolation. Their stories confirmed to Goldman that she was on the right path. "To me anarchism was not a mere theory for a distant future," she wrote. "It was a living influence to free us from inhibitions, internal no less than external, and from the destructive barriers that separate man from man."

·   ·   ·

During World War I, among the major Village social events were the all-night costume balls held at Webster Hall on East Eleventh Street near Third Avenue. The dances were organized to benefit various Village groups and organizations: There was the Liberal Club's "Arabian Nights" and *The Masses*' "Futurists' Ball; even Emma Goldman hosted one called the "Red Revel," for which she dressed as a nun and demonstrated a dance step she called the "Anarchist's Slide." The balls, which began in 1914, proved to be immensely popular. In reading reports submitted by agents investigating "vice conditions" in the wartime Village, historian George Chauncey found some interesting material regarding the Webster Hall dances. In 1917, a police investigator was writing that the balls were becoming quite popular because "most of those present at the dances being liberals and radicals, one is not surprised when he finds a young lady who will talk freely with him on Birth Control or sex psychology." A year later, the investigator was taking a different slant. An increasingly "prominent feature of these dances is the number of male perverts who attend them," he noted. "These phenomenal men . . . wear expensive gowns[,] employ rouge[,] use wigs[,] and in short make up an appearance which looks for everything like a young lady."

The Webster Hall dances did not mark the first time that men dressed in women's clothing appeared in public in lower Manhattan. As Chauncey documents, certain working-class bars on the Bowery at the turn of the century catered to "fairies"—a term that Chauncey uses to describe effeminate men who characterized themselves not so much by their sexual orientation as by the gender role they assumed. Bars like the Slide on Bleecker Street and Paresis Hall in Cooper Square were quite notorious as "fairy" hangouts. In an 1890 publication called *Vices of a Big City,* the Slide was described as "the lowest and most disgusting place. The place is filled nightly with from one hundred to three hundred people, most of whom are males, but unworthy of the name of men. They are effeminate, degraded, and addicted to vices which are inhuman and unnatural." Clearly, some of this early "fairy" subculture survived into the Webster Hall dances.

By the 1920s, gays were holding their own dances at Webster Hall, although they were advertised circumspectly. (One 1923 Webster Hall ball promoted itself with "Come all ye Revelers!—Dance the night unto dawn—come when you like, with whom you like—

A costume ball at Greenwich Village's popular Webster Hall, site of gay balls in the 1920s. (© *Schlesinger Library, Radcliffe College*)

wear what you like—Unconventional? Oh, to be sure—only do be discreet.") As Chauncey notes, the gay balls of the 1920s were part of the emergence of a more middle-class gay community with its own particular meeting places. There, he notes, "fairies" and more conventionally masculine gay men socialized together. This had not been the case in the past, and signaled the advent of a "modern" gay culture in which homosexuality—not gender role—was the unifying factor.

In part, the emergence of this expanding subculture was related to changes within the Village itself. At the end of the War, the subway lines were extended along Sixth and Seventh Avenues in the Village, ending the area's isolation. The era of the great Village bohemian period drew to a close as commercialization became endemic. The Village's reputation as the headquarters of "free love" spread; a homosexual migration from the hinterlands began. At the same time, the onset of Prohibition made every establishment that served liquor an "outlaw" establishment and paradoxically encouraged the opening of tearooms and speakeasies that catered to gays and lesbians.

The most well-known of the gay Village speakeasies was Paul and Joe's, located on the corner of Sixth Avenue and Ninth Street (and later in nearby Chelsea). The *Greenwich Village Quill* newspaper described the club as a "hangout of dainty elves and stern women." By the mid-twenties, Chauncey notes, a number of gay clubs existed in the area south of Washington Square, along MacDougal Street. One of the most famous, the Black Rabbit, was run by a Polish Jewish émigré named **Eva Kotchover**, known as **Eve Addams**. One newspaper dubbed her "the Queen of the Third Sex," and an ad in a Village guide described the place as "Eve's Hangout. Where ladies prefer each other. Not very healthy for she-adolescents, nor comfortable for he-men." After a 1926 police raid, however, Addams was charged with disorderly conduct and with writing an obscene book called *Lesbian Love*. She was deported the following year and is said to have opened a lesbian club in Montmartre.

Then, there were the gay baths, the most famous being the Everard, north of the Village, on West Twenty-Eighth Street. Originally a church, the Everard was converted into a bathhouse in 1888. According to Chauncey, gay men started patronizing the Everard by World War I. In the 1920s, it was still considered one of the leading Turkish bathhouses in New York, catering to a wealthy and middle-class clientele. Despite police raids in the immediate postwar period, by the 1930s the Everard had established itself as the "classiest, safest, and best known of the baths," according to Chauncey. (It was destroyed by fire in 1977.) There were other gay bathhouses as well. Popular in the 1910s were the Produce Exchange Baths and the Lafayette Baths (said to be a favorite haunt of painter Charles Demuth); both were south of Cooper Square. The Penn Post Baths, located in the basement of a seedy hotel a few blocks from the Everard, was a much-frequented spot for gay sexual encounters in the 1920s.

The image of Greenwich Village as bohemian-cum-homosexual haven is confirmed by a 1932 film, *Call Her Savage,* starring **Clara Bow**. In the film, Bow's suitor, a hired gigolo who is really a wealthy capitalist in disguise, takes her out for an evening to a place "down in the Village where only wild poets and anarchists eat. It's pretty rough." The place turns out to be a smoky nightclub inhabited by bearded artists and revolutionaries as well as pairs of neatly dressed male and female couples, their arms around one another. Two men in white aprons and maids' caps, carrying feather dusters, sing:

> If a sailor in pajamas I should see
> I know he'll scare the life out of me
> But on a great big battleship
> We'd like to be
> Working as chamber maids!

After a few moments of entertainment, a young socialist in the crowd identifies Bow's date as a wealthy industrialist, and Bow and her escort are forced to flee the restaurant in a shower of plates and bottles.

Despite the emergence of a gay subculture and gay institutions in the Village, there were no political organizations nor any attempt to assert gay power on a political stage. Police crackdowns on homosexuals were quite extensive in the 1920s. For example, in 1926, some six hundred men were arrested for cruising New York's parks, subway washrooms, and public squares. The following year, a performance of *The Captive,* a French play written by **Edouard Bourdet** about lesbianism, was raided and the producer and cast arrested. This was part of a campaign against "immoral" plays by New York Mayor **James "Gentleman Jimmy" Walker.** (Among the casualties of Walker's campaign was a planned production of **Mae West's** *The Drag,* a play that purported to show that "certain persons are more to be pitied than censured," as *The New York Times* put it; the cast of *The Drag* included forty gay chorus boys whom West was said to have recruited at a Greenwich Village speakeasy.) Two months after the raid on *The Captive,* the New York state legislature enacted a law outlawing the presentation of any work "depicting or dealing with, the subject of sex degeneracy, or sex perversion." The law remained on the books until 1967.

In his book, *Gay New York,* George Chauncey argues that before the 1930s, an informal "understanding" between gay men and the authorities in New York City, particularly in the Village and Times Square, enabled male homosexuals to socialize in public as long as they did little to draw attention to themselves. "Restaurants, speak-easies, and even bathhouses patronized by gay men were able to flourish so long as they kept out of public view," he writes. Even with the theater crackdown, a brief craze for "pansy" entertainers moved uptown from the Village to Times Square nightclubs in the waning days of Prohibition. (Chauncey reports that one nightspot called the Pansy Club opened at 48th Street and Broadway in 1930, featuring female impersonators, a pansy chorus line, and a largely straight clientele.)

However, the police-homosexual compact—and the growing visibility of homosexual culture—declined by the early 1930s with the enactment of various antigay regulations: the theater censorship law, the Motion Picture Code banning depictions of "sexual perversion" in the movies, and especially the decision by the New York State Liquor Authority (SLA), following the repeal of Prohibition, that prohibited bars and restaurants from serving liquor to gay and lesbian patrons. In New York City, throughout the next two and a half decades, Chauncey notes, the SLA "closed literally hundreds of bars that welcomed, tolerated, or simply failed to notice the patronage of gay men or lesbians. As a result, while the number of gay bars proliferated in the 1930s, '40s, and '50s, most of them lasted only a few months or years, and gay men were forced to move constantly from place to place, dependent on the grapevine to inform them of where the new meeting places were."

If the public homosexual presence began to take on a more clandestine character by the 1930s, nonetheless the beginnings of a community based on shared sexual orientation had been forged in Greenwich Village, one that has continued to the present day. It is no surprise that the Stonewall riots that launched the gay and lesbian liberation movement of the 1970s and '80s took place in the heart of the Village.

Degenerates of Greenwich Village— from the December 1936 Issue of *Current Psychology and Psychoanalysis*

Despite the growing visibility of a gay and lesbian subculture in New York's Greenwich Village (and increasingly, in the Times Square area), by the 1930s the social climate was beginning to change for the worse. This was evident not just in police crackdowns but in popular attitudes, as well. The following excerpt from a 1936 issue of the magazine Current Psychology and Psychoanalysis *offers an example of how the larger culture viewed homosexuality. (A longer version of this article was published in Martin Duberman's book* About Time.)

A NEW YORKER who returned to his native city after an absence of two decades was astounded at the changes that had come over New York and, in particular, Greenwich Village. A few weeks before he returned, police had raided a large, brightly-lighted cafeteria in the heart of the Village. The place had been infamous for the past few years as the meeting place of exhibitionists and degenerates of all types. Sight-seers from all parts of the city made pilgrimages to view these misfits on parade.

. . . Greenwich Village, which was once a happy, carefree abode of struggling young writers and artists, inhabited by many of America's literati, is now a roped-off section of what showmen would call "Freak Exhibits" . . .

Forming an important division within this group are the sexual inverts—members of the third sex. Persons with abnormal sex habits flaunt their traits in the Village. One sees many of them—the boy assuming the usual feminine characteristics and obligations, the girl the Lesbian, who apes her brother.

"Lady Lovers," as they are termed on Broadway, are plentiful. Girls, many in their teens, with their "wives," rove both the dark streets and alleys and the well-lighted avenues arm-in-arm. Often it is difficult to tell whether these creatures are boys or not. Clothed in mannish togs, flat-chested, hair slicked tightly back and closely cropped, seen in a restaurant or bar room, one often ponders minutes before hazarding a guess as to "its" sex. Faces thin, often hard, voices low as a man's, their features have masculine characteristics, although few shave. Make-up is not used in an obvious fashion as it is by most women.

Boys, usually known as "pansies," are seen with make-up; heavy mascara, rouge and lipstick. In high-pitched voices, these exhibitionists smirk indecent suggestions at each other.

The center meeting place has been, for a long time, a cafeteria. It is a large place—one of the largest self-service restaurants in town. Brilliantly lighted, fully exposed to two streets, it operates day and night. Here, sipping coffee and munching sandwiches, is the most curious restaurant gathering to be found in all America. The Park Avenue deb with the Wall Street boy friend nibbles cheap pastry and stares and jibes at the "show" . . .

There is a wide-spread use of strange slang among some of these human misfits. Once I heard one say: "That queen over there is camping for jam." I was puzzled. Investigation showed that neither royalty, the wide open spaces nor the household delicacy were involved. The statement meant that a ringleader (queen) of a group of homosexuals was making a play (exhibiting-camping) for a young boy (jam-virgin). . . .

There are other "nice" places, newly decorated. . . . I think of a place that is well known, near Sheridan Square. . . .

At the tables may be seated a score or so of Lesbians. They talk quietly, in deep, low voices. Their outstanding characteristic is their jealousy. They are vicious with the green-eyed god of envy. If one's "girl-friend" is seen talking with another, if idle rumors tell of "unfaithfulness" there is apt to be as mad a hair-pulling, face-scratching and punching scene as could be found in a month's tour of alley brawls. A real Kilkenny cat fight. Black eyes are often in evidence.

Many of these creatures are actually paid for displaying themselves in night clubs to sensation-hungry guests. They revel in their own perculiarities, and are never so happy as when they have a good audience. They are possessed by one craving: to be noticed. They have never grown up.

CHAPTER 10

RENAISSANCE IN HARLEM

There's two things got me puzzled, there's two things
    I can't understand
That's a mannish-actin' woman, and a skippin', twistin'
    woman-actin' man.

           —Bessie Smith, "Foolish Man Blues"

A LARGE MIGRATION of Southern blacks in the opening decades of the twentieth century transformed Harlem, the neighborhood north of Manhattan's Central Park, into the most populous African-American community in the United States. By the 1920s, Harlem had blossomed as a center of nightlife, for whites as well as blacks. It also emerged as a center of black American music, literature, and art, a cultural movement known as the Harlem Renaissance. Jazz Age Harlem offered a combination of license and sexual ambiguity that provided a comfortable environment for those attracted to members of their own sex. You didn't mention the word *homosexual* in Harlem in those years, even if you were a "mannish-actin' woman" or a "skippin', twistin' woman-actin' man." Yet it was another bohemia where gays and lesbians could flourish.

For the new black migrants, Harlem was a place of promise, where they believed they could free themselves from the racism and poverty of the South. "I was in love with Harlem long before I got there," recalled the poet **Langston Hughes** (1902–67), who was born in Joplin, Missouri. "Had I been a rich young man, I would have bought a house in Harlem and built musical steps up to the front door, and installed chimes that at the press of a button played Ellington tunes." For white visitors, Harlem represented the exotic, where social restrictions and personal inhibitions could be jettisoned. For them, "slumming" or going "uptown" became a fashionable pastime. Whites went to basement speakeasies and to cabarets such as the Cotton Club, where black entertainers performed. "Whites snickered and leered in places that specialized in double entendre songs. They peeked into or participated in sex circuses and marijuana parlors," writes Lillian Faderman. "And they went to Harlem to experience homosexuality as the epitome of the forbidden: they watched transvestite floor shows; they rubbed shoulders with homosexuals; they were gay themselves in mixed bars that catered to black and white, heterosexual and homosexual."

Langston Hughes, during a 1938 visit to France.
(© UPI/ Bettmann Newsphotos)

An aura of sexual ambivalence pervaded Harlem nightlife. Male impersonator **Gladys Bentley** performed at Harry Hansberry's Clam House; drag balls took place at the Rockland Palace and Savoy ballrooms. Some places catered specifically to men interested in other men: There was an "open" speakeasy at 126th Street and Seventh Avenue, for example, that Renaissance figure **Bruce Nugent** described as attracting "rough trade"—"the kind that fought better than truckdrivers and swished better than Mae West," as he put it.

In the "anything goes" atmosphere of Prohibition, various kinds of private parties sprung up, part of an underground system that was ignored by the authorities. There were "rent parties," known for their wild, sexually charged atmosphere and bootleg liquor. Then, there were "buffet flats," apartments converted into sex clubs that featured shows and prostitution. Although they began primarily as a heterosexual institution, buffet flats spread to those interested in their own sex. **Ruby Walker**—niece of blues singer **Bessie Smith**—recalled one buffet flat where there were "nothing but faggots and bulldaggers . . . everybody that's in the life . . . everything goes. . . . They had shows in every room, two women goin' together, a man and a man goin' together . . . and if you interested they do the same thing to you."

Sexual identities were fluid in Harlem. Those who engaged in same-sex relations rarely defined themselves as homosexual. A concept of exclusive gay or lesbian identity was weak and was not socially acceptable. Men and women were expected to marry, even in bohemian circles. Yet performers such as Bessie Smith, **Ma Rainey, Alberta Hunter, Jackie "Moms" Mabley, Josephine Baker,** and **Ethel Waters** all cultivated a bisexual image. For female jazz and blues singers, attraction to other women was chic. As Faderman notes, "Although unalloyed homosexuality may still have connoted in 1920s Harlem the abnormality of a 'man trapped in a woman's body,' bisexuality seems to have suggested that a woman was super-sexy."

The legendary blues singer Ma Rainey got into trouble with the police for her lesbian behavior in 1925, when she was arrested for taking part in an orgy at her home involving the women in her chorus. She was charged with running an indecent party; Bessie Smith came and bailed her out of jail the following morning. Faderman writes that the album for Ma Rainey's song "Prove It to Me Blues," a monologue about a woman who prefers women, made reference to the event by featuring "a plump black woman, looking much like Ma Rainey, in a man's hat, tie, and jacket, talking to two entranced flappers. In the distance, observing them, is a policeman. The copy reads, 'What's all this? Scandal? Maybe so, you wouldn't have thought it of Ma Rainey. But look at that cop watching her? What does it all mean?'" The song goes:

> Went out last night with a crowd of my friends
> They must've been women, 'cause I don't like no men . . .
> They say I do it, ain't nobody caught me,
> They sure got to prove it on me . . .

Ma Rainey originally "discovered" Bessie Smith, "The Empress of the Blues," when Smith was singing at a club in a small Georgia town. Although married to a man, Smith didn't hide her interest in other women; while on the road away from her husband, she had an ongoing affair with a chorus girl named **Lillian Simpson.** In Chris Albertson's biography, *Bessie,* the singer's niece, Ruby Walker, relates an incident in Detroit that followed a quarrel between Smith and her lover. The singer went on a drinking binge, winding up at a buffet flat with an entourage of five women from her chorus, including Walker. Shortly after Smith returned to her motel, her husband made a surprise appearance and discovered her in a "compromising situation" with one of the chorus girls. A noisy scene followed, and Smith and the women fled in Smith's private train-car. Ruby Walker recalled that they had to make such a quick getaway that they left many of their possessions behind at the motel. "That's how I lost the only fur coat I ever had," she said. "Bessie took us out of Detroit almost naked."

In his book *Culture Clash,* Michael Bronski contends that blues and jazz, especially when performed by female vocalists, played an important role in the formation of white gay male sensibility. "Because so much of popular culture is concerned with unrequited love, lost love, or just plain fouled up love," he noted, "jazz singers with a background in blues hit upon a powerful combination. A black woman singing about unhappiness in love with the consciousness that she was [an] outcast because of her race, was sure to attract the attention and empathy of gay men."

One of the best-known performers of the time was Gladys Bentley, a three-hundred-pound singer and piano player who dressed in white tuxedo and top hat during performances at Harry Hansberry's Clam House. Langston Hughes relates that "for two or three amazing years, Miss Bentley sat, and played a big piano all night long, literally all night, without stopping—singing songs like 'The St. James Infirmary,' from ten in the evening until dawn, with scarcely a break between the notes, sliding from one song to another, with a powerful and continuous underbeat of jungle rhythm." Later, Bentley was famous for inventing obscene lyrics to popular songs. She is said to have married another woman in a New Jersey ceremony.

In a 1952 *Ebony* magazine article entitled "I Am a Woman Again: Fabulous entertainer tells how she found happiness in love after medical treatment to correct her strange affliction," Bentley offered a revisionist account of those years. "For many years I lived in a personal hell," she wrote. "Like a great number of lost souls,

I inhabited that half-shadow no-man's land which exists between the boundaries of the two sexes." While she was enjoying critical acclaim and popular success, "still, in my secret heart I was weeping and wounded because I was traveling the wrong road to true happiness." By the 1950s, with the assistance of hormone treatments and a good man, Bentley found herself on the road to heterosexuality: The *Ebony* article pictured her turning down the covers on the marital bed and taste-testing a dinner she had prepared for her husband (identified as a well-known West Coast theatrical columnist).

Later, Bentley divorced her husband and became very involved in the Temple of Love in Christ. In January 1960, shortly before she was to be ordained as a minister, she died at the age of fifty-two.

The Jazz Age was a period of political and intellectual ferment in Harlem. **W. E. B. Du Bois** founded the NAACP; **Marcus Garvey** preached his doctrine of the establishment of an African homeland for the American Negro. The novelist **Zora Neale Hurston** rediscovered black folk traditions; **Paul Robeson** revived the Negro spiritual. The poets Langston Hughes and **Countee Cullen** combined blues and jazz rhythms with modernist poetical modes. All this activity fostered a growing sense of black pride. As Hughes wrote in his essay "The Negro Artist and the Racial Mountain":

> ... *We younger Negro artists who create now intend to express our individual dark-skinned selves without fear or shame. If white people are pleased we are glad. If they are not, it doesn't matter. We know we are beautiful. And ugly too. The tom-tom cries and the tom-tom laughs. If colored people are pleased we are glad. If they are not, it doesn't matter either. We build our temples for tomorrow, strong as we know how, and we stand on top of the mountain, free within ourselves.*

Many of the leading intellectual figures of the Harlem Renaissance were primarily inclined toward members of their own sex. They were "in the life," as they called it in Harlem. This group included **Alain Leroy Locke**, the editor of the *New Negro*, the anthology that first brought black writers to a wider public; Countee Cullen, along with Hughes, considered one of the leading poets of the Renaissance; poet and artist Bruce Nugent; and the journalist, dramatist, and novelist **Wallace Thurman,** whose play *Harlem* was a Broadway sensation. Thurman, Nugent, and Langston Hughes all rented rooms in a 137th Street rooming house they called "Niggerati Manor."

The sexuality of Hughes, the most-admired black American poet of his generation, is less clear, however. Certainly his closest friends, at least in the 1920s, were "in the life." In his later years, Hughes, who seemed always to be in the company of some handsome young man, was widely assumed to be gay, according to his biographer Arnold Rampersad. (Hughes remained a lifelong bachelor.) Rampersad quotes one man who knew Hughes in Harlem in the 1960s as saying, "We just took it for granted, as a fact. He was gay, and there was no two ways about it." Yet Hughes was never explicit about his sexuality and rarely addressed gay themes in his work. His sexual proclivities seem to have remained a mystery even to his closest friends. Bruce Nugent, who was close to Hughes during the twenties, says he always assumed Hughes was asexual. Nugent recalls sitting in a gay bar in Harlem one day when the poet passed by the open front door. Nugent invited him in, but Hughes only laughed. "He was definitely curious about what might have been going on," Nugent says. "But that kind of curiousness is more a sign of a basic lack of real interest than of anything else. In any event, I never saw him inside." For his part, the writer Carl Van Vechten found Hughes one of the few men he'd known "who seemed to thrive without having sex in their lives" and who gave no indication of being either heterosexual or homosexual. Whether friends like Nugent and Van Vechten were simply "covering up" for Hughes is anyone's guess.

If Hughes was in fact gay, his reticence about the subject is not surprising. For just as primarily lesbian blues singers had to appear bisexual, at least in their public image, the black gay literati were equally cautious. The poet Countee Cullen married W. E. B. Du Bois's daughter **Yolande** before 3,000 people in what was the major social event of 1928. The marriage was over before it began, and two months later, Cullen sailed for Europe with **Harold Jackman,** his closest friend. GROOM SAILS WITH BEST MAN, was the wry headline in one black newspaper. The homosexually inclined playwright Wallace Thurman, who had been arrested in a men's lavatory on the day he arrived in New York in 1925, married as well. The marriage lasted only a few weeks.

Like Greenwich Village a decade earlier, Harlem of the period had its salons. Perhaps the most famous was presided over by **A'Lelia Walker**, "a gorgeous dark Amazon, in a silver turban," as Hughes described her. Walker's mother, a washerwoman, had made a fortune from the development of the Madame Walker Hair Straightening Process. Walker was known for her lavish parties at her Hudson River estate and her apartment on 136th Street in Manhattan. Her parties, "crowded as the New York subway at the rush hour," were places where "Negro poets and Negro number bankers mingled with downtown poets and seat-on-the-stock-exchange racketeers," in Hughes's words. Later, she opened a combination tearoom-salon called The Dark Tower, decorated with rosewood furniture, a rosewood piano, rose-colored curtains, and framed verses by Countee Cullen and Langston Hughes on the walls. "Because A'Lelia adored the company of lesbians and gay men, her parties had a distinctly gay flavor," writes Eric Garber in his essay "Spectacle in Color: The Lesbian and Gay Subculture of Jazz Age Harlem." Walker, who is said to have had affairs with women, was instrumental in bringing about the acceptance of gays and lesbians in Harlem social circles.

Another important promoter of the Harlem Renaissance was the white writer and critic Carl Van Vechten. He invited black artists and public figures to his home for parties—a daring thing to do in those days—and his interest in Harlem and black culture led him to write the controversial, best-selling novel *Nigger Heaven*. Van Vechten championed jazz and blues and Negro spirituals, and was responsible for the publication of Langston Hughes's first book of poetry, *The Weary Blues*. Gladys Bentley noted that a visit by Van Vechten to the club where she was performing represented "the beginning of patronage by top-drawer society folk from downtown." Although married twice, Van Vechten is said to have been predominately homosexual and featured gay characters in his novels. He served as a judge at drag balls at the Rockland Palace casino and at the Savoy ballroom. On one occasion, he awarded first prize at a Savoy ball to a boy "stark naked, save for a decorative *cache sex* and silver sandals and . . . [he was] painted a kind of apple green."

Despite the atmosphere of relative tolerance toward those "in the life," the emphasis of the Harlem Renaissance was on blackness, not sexuality. The idea of addressing same-sex love publicly was frowned upon. One man who did so was Bruce Nugent, whose story "Smoke, Lillies, and Jade" in *Fire!!*, a 1926 literary quarterly, is believed to be the first to treat black homosexuality. In the story, a Harlem artist falls in love with a Latin man he called Beauty and discovers, after a night of passion, that:

> He loved them both . . . there . . . he had thought it . . . actually dared to think it . . . one can love two [sexes] at the same time . . . one can. . . . Beauty's hair was so black and soft . . . was that why he loved Beauty . . . one can . . . or because his body was beautiful . . . and white and warm . . . or because his eyes . . . one can love . . . [ellipses in original text]

The attempt to shock was deliberate. "Wally [Thurman] and I thought that the magazine would get bigger sales if it was banned in Boston," said Nugent later. "So we flipped a coin to see who wrote bannable material. The only two things we could think of that was bannable were a story about prostitution or about homosexuality." The anthology did in fact create controversy. "I have just tossed the first issue of *Fire!!* into the fire," announced the reviewer of the *Baltimore Afro-American*. But *Fire!!* lasted only one issue. Despite its deliberately controversial content, white critics ignored it. There was no way of distributing it and, as a result, Nugent took copies around New York on foot, eventually getting it displayed in some Greenwich Village bookshops. But Nugent, who had no money and no job, would eat up the profits before he returned to Harlem.

Nugent wrote "Smoke, Lillies, and Jade" under the pseudonym of Richard Bruce, out of deference to his family. But he claims that being a gay man in Harlem in the twenties resulted in very little social disapproval. Even after the publication of his erotic story, he was ostracized for only "about two days." "I've always been flamboyant," Nugent recalled years later in an interview that appeared in the black gay anthology *In the Life*. At that time, in Harlem, he assumed everyone he met was "in the life." His attitude was, "If you can't take me the way I am, it's your problem. It's certainly not mine." Yet Nugent himself was a product of his time. Author **Samuel Delaney** recalls Nugent saying in later life, "I just don't see why everyone has to be labeled. I just don't think words like homosexual—or gay—*do* anything for anybody." Nugent married in

1952, although during his seventeen years of marriage he continued to sleep with men. Referring to his wife, he said, "There is a great difference between lust and love. I loved her but I did not lust after her."

Though Harlem provided a refuge for those "in the life," it had, nonetheless, no separate community based on shared sexual orientation; what united it was the revival and development of black culture. The emphasis on marriage made it more difficult for a distinctly gay and lesbian subculture to emerge. The fact that, even today, a distinct sense of gay identity has generally been slower to emerge among many black Americans than among whites is reflected in Jazz Age Harlem. Still, Harlem of the 1920s offered those inclined toward their own sex an arena for experimentation; it gave blues and jazz singers and intellectuals a world in which their sexuality—and their art—could express itself and find recognition.

With the advent of the Great Depression, the Harlem Renaissance faded. Whites stopped journeying uptown, Harlem's economy deteriorated, and the creative flowering played itself out. **Adam Clayton Powell, Sr.,** Harlem's most powerful minister, was thundering against the evils of "perversion" from the pulpit of his Abyssinian Baptist Church. Even before the Crash, Langston Hughes expressed disillusion when he returned to Harlem from Lincoln University in Pennsylvania for a two-week vacation in 1929. The Harlem he had known—the world of the "New Negroes," of midnight visits to speakeasies—was barely recognizable. The cabarets had gone mostly white; Carl Van Vechten was off in Europe; Bruce Nugent was "strutting about in a modish English suit"; the fortunes of his friends, authors Alain Locke and Wallace Thurman, were declining. "Awfully bad colored shows are being put on Broadway every week or so," he wrote to his friend **Claude McKay.** "They fail—as they deserve to. Some of the colored Victrola records are unbearably vulgar, too. Not even funny or half-sad any more."

A Drag Ball in Harlem

During the 1920s and '30s, one of Harlem's major social events was the annual Hamilton Lodge Ball, organized by Lodge No. 710 of the Grand United Order of Odd Fellows. According to historian George Chauncey, sometime during the 1920s, the "gay element" apparently became prominent among the organizers. The event soon became widely known as the "Faggots' Ball," attracting large numbers of female impersonators. By 1929, some two thousand dancers and three thousand spectators attended— mostly blacks, but some whites, as well. (The majority of the participants were apparently young workingmen.) The popularity of the balls grew, and, by 1937, attendance reached eight thousand. Singer Ethel Waters is said to have attended the balls at the beginning of her career, even loaning her gowns to prize-winning drag queens, according to Chauncey. Harlem's leading newspaper, the Amsterdam News, *printed pictures of winning contestants. In his autobiography,* The Big Sea, *first published in 1940, Langston Hughes describes one of the balls:*

STRANGEST AND GAUDIEST of all Harlem spectacles in the '20s, and still the strangest and gaudiest, is the annual Hamilton Club Lodge Ball at Rockland Palace Casino. I once attended as a guest of A'Lelia Walker. It is the ball where men dress as women and women dress as men. During the height of the New Negro era and the tourist invasion of Harlem, it was fashionable for the intelligentsia and social leaders of both Harlem and the downtown area to occupy the boxes at this ball and look down from above at the queerly assorted throng on the dancing floor, males in flowing gowns and feathered headdresses and females in tuxedoes and box-black suits.

For the men, there is a fashion parade. Prizes are given to the most gorgeously gowned of the whites and Negroes who, powdered, wigged, and rouged, mingle and compete for awards. From the boxes these men look for all the world like very pretty chorus girls parading across the raised platform in the center of the floor. But up close, most of them look as if they need a shave, and some of their evening gowns, cut too low, show hair on the chest.

The pathetic touch about the show is given by the presence there of many former "queens" of the ball, prize winners of years gone by, for this dance has been going on a long time, and it is very famous among the male masqueraders of the eastern seaboard, who come from Boston and Philadelphia, Pittsburgh and Atlantic City to attend. These former queens of the ball, some of them aged men, still wearing the costumes that won for them a fleeting fame in years gone by, stand on the sidelines now in their same old clothes—wide picture hats with plumes, and out-of-style dresses with sweeping velvet trains. And nobody pays them any mind—for the spotlights are focused on the stage, where today's younger competitors, in their smart creations, bid for applause.

CHAPTER 11

PARIS IN THE TWENTIES

IT WAS Natalie Barney, Sapphist of the Belle Époque, who said that Paris was the one place where you could live and express yourself as you pleased. That was perhaps never more true than in the boom years of the 1920s when Paris was the undisputed cultural capital of the Western world. In some quarters of town, artists appeared to outnumber the "working population," as **George Orwell** noted. By the end of the decade, there were as many as thirty thousand painters in Paris, most of them, in Orwell's view, imposters. "The populace had grown so hardened to artists," he wrote, "that gruff-voiced lesbians in corduroy breaches and young men in Grecian or medieval costume could walk the streets without attracting a glance, and along the Seine banks by Notre Dame it was almost impossible to pick one's way between the sketching stools."

Gertrude Stein (1874–1946) and **Alice B. Toklas** (1877–1967) had learned to pick their way between the sketching stools, of course. In the process, they purchased a virtual museum-full of paintings by artists like Cézanne, Picasso, Braque, and Matisse for a pittance. Stein and Toklas had arrived in Paris, where they met, well before World War I. Natalie Barney had made Paris her home by 1902. The 1920s brought a flood of expatriate lesbians from the United States and England—the novelist Djuna Barnes; the poet and founder of the Imagist school of poetry, **Hilda Doolittle (H.D.)**, and her lover, the publisher **Bryher (Winifred Ellerman)**; bookseller and publisher Sylvia Beach; magazine editor Margaret Anderson; journalist **Janet Flanner**, and others. Still others dropped by for extended visits—Radclyffe Hall, author of *The Well of Loneliness*, and her lover, **Una Troubridge**, for example.

At least some of these expatriates—Stein and Barney, in particular—were wealthy. Even for those who weren't wealthy, the value of the dollar was so high that expatriates, American ones in particular, could live rather comfortably. Many had little contact with French society (in some cases they didn't even speak the language). With the freedom that came with expatriation, with economic independence, and with the tolerant atmosphere offered by a bohe-

Two friends, Paris. (© *Estate Brassaï*)

mian subculture, these women were able to create a more public sense of lesbian relationships than had been seen before.

Still, the lesbian expatriates didn't attempt to create the separate Sapphic culture that Natalie Barney had envisioned in her prewar soirees by moonlight. Although they formed close bonds among themselves, they became part of the primarily (heterosexual) male expatriate community. Above all, what is striking about the lesbians of the Left Bank of Paris in the twenties was the extraordinary role they played in the creation of modernism in art and literature. This was evident in their own works—the experimental prose of Gertrude Stein and Djuna Barnes, for example—but equally important was their role as promoters of other modernists.

Suddenly arriving on the Left Bank from the apocryphal Hot Fudge, Nebraska, or Agamemnon, Iowa, didn't necessarily bring about a transformation of personal attitudes toward sexuality, however. Natalie Barney, who had grown up in Europe, had probably the most positive self-image as a lesbian of any of these women: "I considered myself without shame: albinos aren't reproached for having pink eyes and whitish hair; why should they hold it against me for being a lesbian?" she wrote in her autobiography. "It's a question of Nature. My queerness isn't a vice, isn't deliberate, and harms no one." In her book *Women of the Left Bank,* Shari Benstock divides the lesbians of this period into two groups: the "mannish lesbian," perceived as a doomed misfit, a man trapped in a woman's body; and the free-spirited lesbian, who imitated Sappho. Radclyffe Hall and Barney's lover Romaine Brooks exemplified the first group; Natalie Barney was the prototype of the second.

Gertrude Stein and Alice B. Toklas didn't fit into either of these categories. They didn't dress in suits or wear monocles; in style, they probably most resembled the hippies of the 1960s. And they certainly weren't imitating Sappho; Stein considered herself too great a genius to be imitating anyone. Sylvia Beach, owner of the bookstore Shakespeare and Company, described her first glimpse of Stein and Toklas this way: "Not long after I had opened my bookshop two women came walking down the Rue Dupuytren. One of them [Stein], with a very fine face, was stout, wore a long robe, and, on her head, a most becoming top of a basket. She was accompanied by a slim, dark, whimsical woman [Toklas]; she reminded me of a gypsy."

Stein and Toklas met in 1907, when Toklas was fresh from San Francisco, and they remained together until Stein's death in 1946.

The roles in their relationship were well-defined. Stein was the genius and Toklas was her "editor, amanuensis, secretary, housekeeper, lover, wife, and friend," as their biographer Diana Souhami describes it. When Picasso, Braque, Apollinaire, and other French avant-gardists came to dinner, Stein would sit with the men and Toklas would be sent into exile with their wives and girlfriends in the other room. Souhami describes their stay on the island of Majorca: "Most of the time, though, Gertrude and Alice were totally absorbed in their work and each other, 'she with a sheet of linen and he with a sheet of paper.' The roles polarised into husband and wife. And their use of the words 'husband' and 'wife' and 'he' and 'she' determined their obligation to each other: Gertrude was to dictate and protect, Alice was to serve and to please."

Although Stein and Toklas had many lesbian friends, they made

Gertrude Stein (left) and Alice B. Toklas (right) on board the SS *Champlain*, arriving in New York for Stein's American lecture tour, 1934. (© *The Bettmann Archive*)

no attempt to gather a lesbian community around them. Sex, Stein was quoted as saying early in her life, was "an individual problem that each one had to solve for herself or himself." She was contemptuous of male homosexuals. **Ernest Hemingway** recounts Stein telling him:

> *The act that male homosexuals commit is ugly and repugnant and afterwards they are disgusted with themselves. They drink and take drugs to palliate this, but they are disgusted with the act and they are always changing partners and cannot be really happy. . . . In women it is the opposite. They do nothing that they are disgusted by and nothing that is repulsive and afterwards they are happy and they can lead happy lives together.*

Whatever Stein's stated views, the Stein-Toklas relationship was that of an openly lesbian couple. And, in sexual terms, theirs was clearly no platonic Boston marriage. According to Souhami, Stein described Alice as "her gay, kitten, pussy, baby, queen, cherubim, cake, lobster, wife, Daisy and her little jew." Gertrude herself was "king, husband, hubbie, Mount fattie and fattuski." In the mellifluous style she made famous, Stein wrote of her love for Alice:

> *I marvel at my baby. I marvel at her beauty I marvel at her perfection I marvel at her purity I marvel at her tenderness. I marvel at her charm I marvel at her vanity . . . I marvel at her industry I marvel at her humor I marvel at her intelligence I marvel at her rapidity I marvel at her brilliance I marvel at her sweetness I marvel at her delicacy, I marvel at her generosity, I marvel at her cow.*

In Stein and Toklas's playful, private language, a cow is apparently an orgasm. "Cows are very nice," Stein wrote. "They are between legs."

Another prominent American expatriate lesbian writer in Paris was Djuna Barnes (1892–1982), whose highly praised novel *Nightwood*, published in 1936, offers a rather grim view of lesbian life and relationships. In an introduction to the book, **T. S. Eliot** praised *Nightwood* for "the great achievement of a style, the beauty of phrasing, the brilliance of wit and characterization, and a quality of horror and doom very nearly related to that of Elizabethan tragedy." Barnes's *Ladies Almanack,* a curious and comic book featuring pen-and-ink drawings by the author (and including yet another portrait of Natalie Barney), became an underground lesbian classic. She did not publish it under her own name, however, but as the work of a "Lady of Fashion." Barnes was known for her beauty, her wit, her drinking, and later for her breakdowns and reclusiveness. One fellow writer called her "the most unbourgeois woman" he had ever met and claimed she couldn't boil an egg. Barnes's most famous comment, made shortly after arriving in Europe, was "I came to Europe to get culture. Is this culture I'm getting? Then I might as well go back to Greenwich Village and rot there." Her biographer Andrew Field described her as "one of the great expatriate solitaries" and noted her "incredibly long silences in the cafés."

Next to James Joyce, Barnes was considered by her peers to be the most important writer of the expatriate Paris community. She and her lover, the sculptor Thelma Wood (on whom Barnes based the character of Robin Vote in *Nightwood*), had a stormy relationship. Field writes of the two women: "They walked down 1922 and the boulevard du Montparnasse with their legs coming forward in perfect coordination as though they were one. They were dressed in black and they did not stop until 1931." Barnes was ambivalent about her sexuality. "I'm not a lesbian," she said in later life. "I just loved Thelma." But in a 1936 letter, she wrote, "I am not offended in the least to be thought lesbian—it's simply that I am very reticent about my personal life, a little English perhaps."

According to Andrew Field, there were three gateways through which English- and French-speaking writers in Paris met one another—and two of the gate-keepers were lesbians. One was Natalie Barney's salon, which was quite influential and important throughout the 1920s; the other was Sylvia Beach's bookshop, Shakespeare and Company. Paris salons were not just a center for an exchange of ideas and styles but were also surrogates for family and country. Shakespeare and Company, located on the rue de l'Odéon, between the boulevard du Montparnasse and the Seine, was, in Field's words, the "parliament of the expatriation." It was the first combination English-language bookstore and lending library in Paris, functioning as meeting place, post office, money exchange, and reading room. Homey and picturesque, it was decorated with black and white Serbian rugs on the floor and antique furniture, plus racks full of English and American literary reviews. On the walls were

Blake drawings, Whitman manuscripts, and pictures of Edgar Allan Poe, Whitman, and Oscar Wilde.

Beach, who had grown up in Princeton, New Jersey, and was the daughter and granddaughter of Presbyterian ministers, founded the bookstore in 1921. Her lover, **Adrienne Monnier**, had established the first lending library in France just across the street six years before. Beach was thirty and Monnier twenty-six when they met in 1917. "My loves were Adrienne Monnier and James Joyce and Shakespeare and Company," Beach wrote. But more than selling books or running a bookstore/salon, Beach promoted culture in another way: In 1922, she published James Joyce's *Ulysses,* arguably the greatest novel in English in the twentieth century, at a time when it was banned in England, Ireland, and the United States. Beach raised the funds for publication through subscriptions to her bookshop and helped Joyce smuggle copies into the United States. She continued to publish *Ulysses* through a number of printings until 1932 and supported Joyce personally and financially. Monnier, meanwhile, published the first French translation of *Ulysses* in 1929, and her magazine, *Le Navire d'Argent,* published prominent French writers and introduced English-language writers like T. S. Eliot to the French public. In 1941, during the Occupation, Shakespeare and Company was shut down after Beach refused to sell a Nazi officer her only copy of Joyce's *Finnegan's Wake.*

Beach and Monnier were not the only lesbians who encouraged modernist literature and art in twenties Paris. Gertrude Stein promoted artists and writers from Picasso to Hemingway; she is given credit for sending writer and composer **Paul Bowles** off to Tangier, where he played a role in the establishment of yet another expatriate colony (see "Chapter 20: The Other Side of the 1950s," page 297). Margaret Anderson and her former lover Jane Heap moved *The Little Review,* the most influential literary publication of its time, to Paris after being convicted on obscenity charges for publishing *Ulysses* in serial form in New York. In Paris, Anderson published surrealists and Dadaists. Meanwhile, Bryher (Winifred Ellerman), the lover of the poet H.D., financially supported Djuna Barnes and arranged for the publication of Gertrude Stein's *The Making of Americans.* Although a lesbian, Bryher married Robert McAlmon, an American expatriate who ran the Contact Press; she did this to appease her parents—her father, a shipping magnate, was the richest man in England. With Bryher's money and editorial help, the Contact Press published writers ranging from **Ezra Pound** to **William Carlos Williams**. Meanwhile, Janet Flanner, the influential lesbian journalist, interpreted Paris and promoted an image of Paris as the cultural center of the world for an entire generation of Americans through her "Letter from Paris," which appeared in *The New Yorker* magazine starting in 1925 under the pseudonym of Genêt. (In the 1930s, Flanner used the "Letter from Paris" to document the rise of fascism in Europe and to build sympathy in America for the antifascist cause.)

Although these women attached themselves to an artistic community because it was perceived as relatively liberal, many of them found that Paris's expatriate world, like that of Greenwich Village, was still dominated by men. Except for "geniuses" like Stein and perhaps Djuna Barnes, they tended to use their creativity behind the scenes in a minisociety that, for all its pretenses, still devalued women. Nonetheless, expatriate Paris in the 1920s was an early example of a community where a number of long-standing lesbian couples were visible and played admired social roles. These women were not just flirting with lesbianism before making a "serious" commitment to heterosexual marriage, as had been the experience of women in the Belle Époque and even in Edna St. Vincent Millay's Greenwich Village. In Paris in the twenties, they could live as lesbian couples in a way that wasn't possible even in other bohemias, in part because of the groundwork Natalie Barney and Renée Vivien and Colette had laid a generation before.

But artistic and expatriate bohemias rarely reflect the larger society. Despite France's reputation for tolerance, the country's first gay publication, *Inversions,* was shut down by the police in 1924, after five issues, as an "outrage to good morals." When the publication was revived as *L'Amitié,* the two founders, **Gustave-Léon Beyria** and **Gaston Lestrade**, were hauled into court and charged with publishing "propaganda liable to compromise the future of the race." Beyria received ten months in prison, and Lestrade six months. Ironically, it was during this period that Weimar Germany boasted some thirty gay publications. And when **Jean Cocteau's** book of erotic adventures, *Le Livre Blanc* (*The White Paper*), was published in 1928, the author remained anonymous, despite Cocteau's reputation for flamboyance and despite the book's closing line—"I'm not willing just to be tolerated."

As the Depression deepened in the early 1930s, the Paris expatriate scene was breaking up. Americans like Djuna Barnes packed up and went home; Shakespeare and Company was struggling to survive; storm clouds were gathering over Europe. When the Germans occupied Paris, Sylvia Beach was interned, and Gertrude Stein and Alice B. Toklas took refuge in the countryside. For her part, Natalie Barney, who had turned Fascist in her later years, spent the war in Italy. Over time, the expatriate decades have acquired a sense of romance and mystique. As Djuna Barnes wrote in a letter to Natalie Barney in 1972, "I think of all of us with amazement and antique amused affection—what a far-off unlike our present that world was . . . long hair and all, capes, our polemics for and against freedom and love!"

Marguerite Yourcenar

IN 1929, a twenty-six-year-old Frenchwoman who called herself **Marguerite Yourcenar** published one of the first novels about male homosexuality written by a woman. Entitled *Alexis* (the French title is *Alexis ou le traité de vain combat*), the novel is written in the form of a letter by a young homosexual musician, Alexis, to his wife, Monique, in which he reveals his homosexuality for the first time. Alexis tells his wife that he cannot continue to live with her (and their child) any longer, that he must live out his sexual destiny. Written in the elegant, almost classical style that was to become Yourcenar's hallmark, *Alexis* launched the career of one of France's most admired novelists, "the last echo of a heroic chorus of European writers that included Thomas Mann and André Gide," in the words of Edmund White.

Yourcenar (1903–87) was a lesbian, who lived for forty years almost entirely in the United States with the American academic **Grace Frick**. (In 1950, Yourcenar and Frick bought a cottage on Mount Desert Island in Maine, which became their primary residence.) In both her life and her work, Yourcenar was fascinated with male homosexuality. In the 1930s, before she met Frick, she fell passionately in love with her editor, André Fraigneau, a gay man. "She was the very epitome of a woman who loves women," Fraigneau told Yourcenar's biographer Josyane Savigneau. "Nonetheless, I soon realized that she dreamed of being the mistress of men who love men." The result of her unrequited passion for Fraigneau was her masterful short novel *Coup de Grace* (1939), which tells the story of a man who rejects the affections of the sister of the man he loves. *Memoirs of Hadrian* (1951), considered her greatest work, chronicles the Roman emperor's passion for his Greek male lover. She also wrote essays about the Greek poet **Constantine Cavafy** and Japanese novelist **Yukio Mishima**, both homosexual. After Frick died in 1980, Yourcenar spent her last years in the company of a young American gay man, **Jerry Wilson**, with whom she was apparently in love.

In the early 1950s, Yourcenar and Frick became friends with Natalie Barney, lesbian salon hostess of Belle Époque and 1920s Paris, and she added her voice to the many portraits that Barney inspired. In a 1963 letter to Barney, Yourcenar wrote:

> *I have been particularly grateful to you for having escaped the intellectual viruses of this half-century, for having been neither psychoanalyzed, nor an existentialist, nor busy performing gratuitous acts, but for having remained faithful on the contrary to what your mind, your senses, and indeed your good sense told you. I cannot stop myself from comparing your existence with my own, which will not, in the end, have been a work of art, but rather so much more subjected to happenstance events, rapid or slow, complicated or simple. . . .*

Happenstance or not, Yourcenar achieved one thing that Barney never was able to achieve—a revered position in twentieth-century French literature. In 1981, she became the first woman admitted to the French Academy and was one of the first living French authors to have her complete works published in Pleiade editions, an honor usually reserved for the classics.

The following passage from *Alexis* offers a glimpse of Yourcenar's literary style as well as her view of homosexuality, circa 1929. Here, Alexis describes his growing up in a house full of sisters, a situation he believes contributed to his attractions toward other men. Yourcenar echoes the popular notion that if gay men were not quite men trapped in the body of a woman, they did have more in common with women than with heterosexual men:

... *Naturally, I was much too young for them [his sisters] to confide in me; but I guessed what they were feeling and shared in their sorrows. When the man they were in love with would arrive unexpectedly, my heart raced, posssibly more than theirs. It is dangerous, I am sure, for a sensitive adolescent to learn to view love through the dreams of young girls, even when they seem to be pure and he imagines himself to be pure also.* ...

To be sure, my sisters also had girlfriends who lived with us almost like members of the family and of whom I came to think of myself the younger brother. Nothing would appear to have prevented me from loving one of these girls, and perhaps you yourself find it strange that I did not. Yet the fact is, it was impossible. An intimacy so familial, so peaceful, took away the curiosities and inquietudes of desire, even supposing I had been capable of them. ... *I already had a suspicion (I even exaggerated it to myself) of how brutal the physical acts of love can be. It would have repelled me to join these images of domestic, rational, perfectly austere and pure life with other more passionate ones. One does not lose one's heart to what one respects, nor perhaps even to what one loves; above all, one does not lose one's heart to what resembles oneself—and it was not women I was most different from.*

CHAPTER 12

BLOOMSBURY

ONE SPRING EVENING in 1908, sex—or more accurately, talk about sex—entered the Edwardian drawing room of **Virginia Woolf** (at the time the still-unmarried Virginia Stephen). Her friend Lytton Strachey stood at the threshold and pointed his finger at a stain on the dress of Virginia's sister, **Vanessa**. "Semen?" he inquired. The two sisters burst into laughter. Virginia Woolf wrote:

> With that one word all barriers of reticence and reserve went down. A flood of the sacred fluid seemed to overwhelm us. Sex permeated our conversation. The word bugger was never far from our lips. We discussed copulation with the same excitement and openness that we had discussed the nature of the good. It is strange to think how reticent, how reserved we had been and for how long.

Woolf's nephew and biographer, Quentin Bell, describes Strachey's utterance as an important moment in the mores of Bloomsbury and the British middle class. For almost everything concerning Bloomsbury—the legendary group of British liberal intellectuals during the period before and after World War I—influenced the wider world. Bloomsbury began as a small group of friends, with a core of twenty or so that fluctuated over the years. Starting in 1906, the group met every Thursday evening at the home of Virginia Woolf and her brother Adrian (and on Friday afternoons at the home of their sister, Vanessa) in the Bloomsbury section of London. One of the things that was shocking about those early Bloomsbury salons—even before the arrival of sex-talk—was the idea of unmarried men and women sitting together and talking until late in the night. But in the early days of Bloomsbury, sexual tension was not in the air—at least not between men and women. Wrote Woolf, "It never struck me that the abstractness, the simplicity which had been so great a relief . . . were largely due to the fact that the majority of young men who came there were not attracted by young women." Later, she put it another way: "I knew there were buggers in Plato's Greece. But it never occurred to me that there were buggers even now in the Stephen sitting-room in Gordon Square."

In its first phase, the Bloomsbury group had an adolescent quality about it: "a mixture of homosexuals with young virgins on the neutral ground of 'the Beautiful' and 'the Good'" as Leon Edel relates in his collective biography, *Bloomsbury: A House of Lions*. Soon, Bloomsbury was creating its own institutions—a play-reading club, an art club, and, after the war, the famous Memoir Club. Bloomsbury painter **Roger Fry** founded the Omega Workshops in order to give employment to artists who were having trouble making ends meet; Omega specialized in the decorative arts: furniture design, carpet and china patterns, and murals for private homes. (Fry was also largely responsible for the "Art-quake of 1910," the exhibit that introduced Cézanne, van Gogh, Gauguin, and Picasso to the British public.) Bloomsbury produced some of the century's most important writers and thinkers—Virginia Woolf; **John Maynard Keynes**, the economist whose theories saved capitalism during the Great Depression; and Lytton Strachey, whose book *Eminent Victorians* revolutionalized the art of biography. E. M. Forster, author of *Howard's End* and *A Passage to India* (and the gay novel *Maurice*), was somewhat removed from Bloomsbury but is still considered among the core group of twenty.

In addition to producing art and artists (and economic theory), Bloomsbury began to develop a coherent view of the world—pacifist during World War I, hostile to organized religion and authority, tolerant in matters of sex. It was liberal and humanistic in its outlook, emphasizing honesty in conversation and in personal relationships; it was suspicious of political dogmas, whether of the left or right. Yet at the same time Bloomsbury was rather snobbish— as evidenced by the initial hesitation it displayed in taking up the cause of Radclyffe Hall's lesbian novel, *The Well of Loneliness,* because the book was viewed as not being up to Bloomsbury's artistic standards.

Although Bloomsbury attracted gay men, especially in its earliest years, many prominent Bloomsberries weren't homosexual or inclined in that direction at all: Virginia Woolf's sister Vanessa and her husband **Clive Bell**; Virginia's husband, **Leonard Woolf**; and the painter Roger Fry, to name a few. Sexuality was fluid in Bloomsbury, as in other bohemias. Some of its most prominent homosexually inclined men—Keynes and Strachey, for example—eventually wound up involved with women. The painter **Duncan Grant**, who had been Keynes's lover, fell in love with Vanessa. Sexual and affectional ambivalences could go in the other direction as well: Witness Virgina Woolf's passionate friendship in her later years with the aristocratic **Vita Sackville-West**.

Yet Bloomsbury was a movement in which homosexuals were influential and taken for granted. Lytton Strachey expressed the flavor of Bloomsbury's homosexual side when he went before a tribunal to seek conscientious-objector status during World War I. Leon Edel described Strachey's appearance there:

> *Suffering from hemorrhoids, he brought a rubber cushion which he inflated as if he were blowing a bugle. . . . [A military interrogator] asked Lytton what he would do if a German soldier attempted to rape his sister. Lytton's homoerotic being provided the prompt answer. He would "try and interpose my own body." The Tribunal reserved judgement pending Lytton's physical. He sat, reading a history of England, in a congerie of unclad youths destined for the trenches. The doctors pronounced him unfit for service. He returned to the writing of* Eminent Victorians.

The son of a general, Strachey (1880–1932) was perhaps the most eccentric of the Bloomsberries. Edel writes that had he been a woman, Strachey "would have become a Victorian invalid, with smelling salts, a corner chair, a pile of novels." In 1905, while working on his thesis, Strachey fell passionately in love with his cousin Duncan Grant, five years younger. He confided to his friend John Maynard Keynes, "He [Duncan] is the full moon of heaven. I rave, and you may judge of my condition when I tell you that it's 4 p.m.—the most utterly prosaic hour of the day."

The frankness of Strachey and Keynes's correspondence seems "to uncover a state of affairs within Cambridge [where both were students] which would have provoked curiosity in Gomorrah and caused the inhabitants of Sodom to sit up and take note," according to Strachey's biographer Michael Holroyd. But Holroyd suggests that there was probably more talk between them than anything else. He observes that the word "propose," for example, might mean little more than the "slight ambiguous pressure of one hand upon another"; to "rape" and even to "bugger" usually meant "a peck on the cheek, or a dubious embrace." Holroyd continues, "[I]n a society which regarded homosexuality as more grave than murder, what Lytton and Keynes were looking for almost as urgently as love itself, was a discreet and sympathetic source of disclosure."

But Strachey's faith in Keynes as a confidant proved misplaced when it was revealed that Keynes and Grant had become lovers. Strachey felt betrayed, and the rather low esteem in which Bloomsbury held Keynes throughout the years had its origin in Strachey's jealousy of the relationship between Keynes and Grant. While the intensity of Keynes's passion for Grant lessened within a year or two, the two remained intimate friends, sharing houses and taking trips together. Their relationship exemplified "one of the finest harmonies of Bloomsbury," according to Leon Edel. Much later, when in his forties, and after many years of active homosexuality, Keynes fell in love with the ballerina **Lydia Lopokova**. The two married in 1925 and were extremely happy together. For his part, at age thirty-five, Strachey seems to have fallen in love with the twenty-two-year-old painter **Dora Carrington** (known simply as Carrington), and the two set up house together. Bloomsbury viewed this relationship with skepticism, however. Virginia Woolf tells the story of one evening when Strachey and Carrington were entertaining guests at their country home. The couple withdrew from their company "ostensibly to copulate." One of the guests wandered upstairs and, instead of the sounds of lovemaking, overheard Strachey reading aloud to Carrington from Macaulay's *History of England*.

If E. M. Forster (1879–1970) wasn't as central to Bloomsbury as Keynes or Strachey, he was nonetheless a member of the Memoir Club and an intimate of Virginia Woolf. His liberal humanism and emphasis on personal relationships exemplified Bloomsbury thinking (as in his memorable line "If I had to choose between betraying my country and betraying my friend, I hope I should have the guts to betray my country"). Unlike Keynes or Strachey, Forster showed no hint of interest in the opposite sex.

It was a visit to the bearded Uranian sage Edward Carpenter in 1913 that Forster said provided the inspiration for his novel about homosexual love, *Maurice*. Like many others, Forster fell under the spell of Carpenter's calm and charisma. To Forster's attempts at chitchat and witticisms, Carpenter would simply answer—zen-like—"Oh do sit quiet." At one point a kind of epiphany occurred. George Merrill, Carpenter's lover, pinched Forster on his backside. "The sensation was unusual," Forster wrote later, "and I still remember it, as I remember the position of a long vanished tooth. It was as much psychological as physical. It seemed to go straight through the small of my back into my ideas, without involving my thoughts." In a state of exaltation, Forster returned to where he was staying and immediately began work on *Maurice*.

(One of Forster's biographers, Nicola Beauman, casts doubt on this account, however. She suggests the inspiration for the novel lay in the death of a homosexual friend of Forster's who killed himself a few hours after dining with Forster in June 1909. In Beauman's view, Forster's guilt and remorse over this event not only inspired *Maurice* but also led him to concoct another explanation for the novel's origins.)

In the tolerant sexual atmosphere of World War I Alexandria, where he was working tracing missing British soldiers, Forster had the first gay relationship of his life, with an Egyptian tram conductor named **Mohammed el Adl**. Forster, thirty-nine at the time, was ecstatic. "Wish I was writing the latter half of *Maurice*," he wrote to his confidant Florence Barger back in England. "I now know so much more. It is awful to think of the thousands who go through youth without ever knowing. I have known in a way before, but never like this. My luck has been amazing." Later he wrote Barger that, as a result of the relationship, he finally felt like "a grown up man. . . ." (His stay in Alexandria also marked the first time that he was freed from his mother's dominant influence for an extended period.) El Adl, who was eighteen when he met Forster, eventually married, and Forster left Egypt at the end of the War. They continued to correspond, and when el Adl was dying of tuberculosis in 1922, Forster stopped in Egypt to visit him on his way home from India.

In 1930, Forster met **Robert Buckingham**, a twenty-eight-year-old policeman who became his close companion until Forster's death in 1972. When Buckingham married, Forster developed a cordial relationship with his wife, May, eventually becoming a grandfather figure to their children. Their home even became a meeting place for Forster's circle. In the 1960s when Forster was gravely ill and spoke about his physical passion for Buckingham, Buckingham is said to have been shocked, claiming it was the first time he had known Forster was homosexual. But Beauman thinks this is nonsense: "That Morgan and Bob were definitely lovers is clear from the intimacy of their letters, from their loving pose in photographs, and from other details. . . ." In any event, his relationship with Buckingham clearly gave Forster a good deal of happiness and satisfaction over the years. In 1932, two years after he met Buckingham, Forster wrote:

> *Happiness.*
> *I have been happy for two years.*
> *It mayn't be over yet, but I want to write it down before it gets spoiled by pain. . . .*
> *Happiness can come in one's natural growth and not queerly, as religious people think. From 51 to 53 I have been happy, and would like to remind others that their turn can come too. It is the only message worth giving.*

Yet Forster remained closeted over the years. He never permitted *Maurice* to be published in his lifetime, even after it became legally possible to do so. When his friend J. R. Ackerley urged him to be more open about his homosexuality, in the manner of André Gide, Forster is said to have replied, "But Gide hasn't got a mother!"

Virginia Woolf (1882–1941), the center of Bloomsbury and the author of such admired and experimental novels as *Mrs. Dalloway* and *To the Lighthouse,* married Leonard Woolf in 1911. Although the two were totally devoted to each other, sexually their relationship was not a success. Her biographer Quentin Bell asserts that Virginia "regarded sex, not so much with horror, as with incomprehension." However, there is another way of looking at their sexual difficulties: As Vita Sackville-West wrote, Virginia "dislikes the possessiveness and love of domination in men. In fact, she dislikes the quality of masculinity. Says that women stimulate her imagination, by their grace and their art of life." Virginia was also subject to terrifying breakdowns (she drowned herself in 1941, fearing the onset of another bout of madness).

When Virginia first met Vita Sackville-West in 1922, the latter was a poet, novelist, and confirmed Sapphist, who a few years before had run off to France with the beautiful **Violet Trefusis**. Vita (1892–1962) was the wife of a gay man, the diplomat and diarist **Harold Nicolson** (1886–1969). (Their life together is related by their son, Nigel Nicolson, in his book *Portrait of a Marriage*—see "Vita and Harold," page 179.) Quentin Bell suggests that Vita could have been invented for Virginia's pleasure. She was "certainly a very beautiful woman, in a lazy, majestic, rather melancholy way," he

writes, "charming with a charm which was largely unconscious—
and the more lovable for that, intelligent and yet at the same time
in an odd way stupid, blundering through life rather, with excellent
intentions but without the acuteness, the humour, the malice, of
Virginia. . . ."

At first Virginia resisted her. But their friendship grew, taking
on an increasingly romantic character. Between 1925 and 1929,
Vita was in love with Virginia. According to Vita, they went to bed
together only twice. As she wrote her husband, Harold:

> I love Virginia, as who wouldn't? But really, my sweet, one's
> love for Virginia is a very different thing: a mental thing, a
> spiritual thing if you like, an intellectual thing, and she inspires
> a feeling of tenderness which I suppose is because of her funny
> mixture of hardness and softness—the hardness of her mind,
> and her terror of going mad again.

Bell says that for Virginia the relationship was an "affair of the
heart," but without much of a sexual component. "There may have
been—on balance I think that there probably was—some caressing,
some bedding together. But whatever may have occurred between
them of this nature, I doubt very much whether it was of a kind to
excite Virginia or to satisfy Vita," Bell wrote. (He also notes that
both husbands took their wives' intimacy with "admirable calm.")
Yet there is no doubt that Woolf was deeply engaged, as evidenced
by this diary entry:

> And Vita comes to lunch tomorrow, which will be a great amuse-
> ment and pleasure. I am amused at my relations with her: left
> so ardent in January—and now what? Also I like her presence
> and her beauty. Am I in love with her? But what is love? Her
> being "in love" (it must be comma'd thus) with me, excites and
> flatters and interests. What is this "love"?

Whatever its exact nature, their relationship did inspire great
literature—Woolf's comic novel, *Orlando,* a fictional "biography"
of Vita extending from Elizabethan times to the twentieth century,
in which the hero/heroine changes his/her sex in each new incar-
nation. Vita's son, Nigel, calls the book "the longest and most
charming love-letter in literature." It makes use of incidents and
fantasies from Vita's life—one character is based on Harold

Vita Sackville-West (left) with her childhood friend, Rosamund Grosvenor (right). *(© Bettmann Newsphotos)*

Nicolson. Nigel Nicolson, describes the making of *Orlando* in his book, *Portrait of a Marriage:*

But Orlando! *Imagine those two, seeing each other at least once a week, one writing a book about the other, swooping on Knole [Vita's ancestral home] to squeeze from it another paragraph,*

*on Long Barn [where Vita lived] to trap Vita into a new ad-
mission about her past ... dragging Vita to a London studio to
have her photographed as a Lely [a Dutch painter], tantalizing
her, hinting at the fantasy but never lifting more than a corner
of it—until on the day before publication,* Orlando *arrived in a
brown-paper parcel from the Hogarth Press, followed a few days
later by the author with the manuscript as a present. Vita wrote
to Harold: "I am in the middle of reading* Orlando, *in such a
turmoil of excitement and confusion that I scarcely know where
(or who) I am!" She loved it.*

There was no attempt on the part of Virginia or Vita to disguise
that Orlando was modeled on Vita. Three of the eight photographs
that appeared in the first edition were of Vita herself; one picture,
captioned "Orlando at the present time," showed Vita posing with
her two dogs, and dressed in a skirt, blouse, and cardigan.

By 1935, ten years after they had first become involved, their
passionate friendship began to wane. As Quentin Bell notes, "There
had been no quarrel, no outward sign of coldness, no bitterness,
but the love affair—or whatever we are to call it—had for some
time been quietly evaporating, and that particular excitement had
gone out of her life, leaving a blankness, a dullness."

Bloomsbury was neither a society of "buggers," as Virginia Woolf
would have it, nor a society of Sapphists. No Bloomsberries were
public about their sexuality (except for the "inside joke" of *Orlando*). But in the stifling atmosphere of post–Oscar Wilde England,
Bloomsbury provided an oasis of sexual ambivalence that took
Forster's dictum "Only connect" to include same-sex relationships.
When Bloomsbury became chic in the 1970s and '80s—with a flurry
of books detailing the affectional and sexual relationships of virtually every major Bloomsbury figure—Virginia Woolf and Vita
Sackville-West, Lytton Strachey and E. M. Forster became role
models for a generation of post-Stonewall gays and lesbians.

Vita and Harold

Vita Sackville-West—novelist, poet, and lover of women—and Harold Nicolson—diarist, diplomat, and gay man—were married in 1913 and remained married until Vita's death in 1962. Their homosexual relationships put their marriage under strain at the beginning—notably when Vita ran off to France with Violet Trefusis in October 1920—but they remained devoted to each other for almost fifty years. Vita's biographer Victoria Glendinning suggests that Harold was aware of his homosexuality when they married. "His generally light-hearted homosexual friendships with young men of his own background were something he took for granted but did not examine too deeply," she writes. "His instinct was not to talk about it—for psychological reasons, as well as because homosexuality was against the law—but in his heart he did not think it was wrong. Nor did it have any bearing on his love for Vita." In the case of Vita, it may have been more complicated. At the time of her marriage, she seems to have been unaware of her feelings toward women. In a letter to Harold, dated November 23, 1960, she talks about their decision to marry and reveals much about the state of public awareness about homosexuality at the time:

YOU WERE OLDER THAN I, and far better informed. I was very young, and very innocent. I knew nothing about homosexuality. I didn't even know that such a thing existed—either between men or between women. You should have told me. You should have warned me. You should have told me about yourself, and have warned me that the same sort of thing was likely to happen to myself. It would have saved us a lot of trouble and misunderstanding. But I simply didn't know.

Still, Vita and Harold found a way to live together in which they could express their homosexual feelings, as their son, Nigel Nicolson, relates in his 1973 book, Portrait of a Marriage:

Vita's elopement with Violet Trefusis was the only crisis of her marriage. Having survived it, she and Harold were able to confront with equanimity many later incidents so menacing that each separately would have broken up most homes. . . . Violet had shown them that nothing could destroy their love, which was actually enhanced by the complete freedom they allowed each other. Both were completely frank about it, in speech and letters. It no longer required argument: simpily a statement of fact and current emotion. Harold would refer to Vita's affairs as "your muddies"; she to his as "your fun." No jealousy ever arose because of them. On his side there was only a concern that she might break the heart of someone else, a rival or the woman's husband, while she was more amused than worried by what was happening to him, knowing that he had these things under greater control. To scandal, or, in his case, to the law, they seem never to have given a thought, for their intellectual friends were infinitely tolerant, and they did not mind what was said by outsiders.

An Excerpt from Virginia Woolf's *Orlando*

"Different though the sexes are, they intermix," wrote Virginia Woolf in Orlando. *"In every human being a vacillation from one sex to the other takes place, and often it is only the clothes that keep the male or female likeness. . . ." The theme of* Orlando, *Woolf's 1928 comic novel, is sexual transformation. The protagonist, based on Vita Sackville-West, moves from being man to woman, gliding in and out of the boundaries of gender. Vita's biographer Victoria Glendinning describes the book as a "phantasmagoria of images and incidents and fantasies from Vita's life and personality, spread over three centuries." The characters are meant to represent people close to Vita. The Russian princess Sasha, who is the object of Orlando's affections (as a man) in Elizabethan England, is based on Violet Trefusis, with whom Vita eloped to France after the War. Marmaduke Bonthrop Shel-*

*merdine, the explorer-sailor with whom Orlando (as a woman)
falls in love in the Victorian period, is based on Vita's husband,
Harold Nicolson. To make matters even more confusing, on their
first meeting, Orlando exclaims, "You're a woman, Shel!" while
Marmaduke Bonthrop Shelmerdine replies, "You're a man, Orlando!" Soon enough, the confusion is resolved and Woolf notes,
in a homage to Vita and Harold's relationship: "[E]ach was so
surprised at the quickness of the other's sympathy, and it was to
each such a revelation that a woman could be as tolerant and
free-spoken as a man, and a man as strange and subtle as a
woman. . . ." In the following excerpt we find Vita-Orlando at
the end of the eighteenth century in England, nominally a
woman, but moving effortlessly from one gender to another (and
running off with a woman to the Low Countries as Vita did to
France with Violet Trefusis):*

BUT TO GIVE AN EXACT AND PARTICULAR ACCOUNT of Orlando's life at this time becomes more and more out of the question. . . . [W]e seem to catch sight of her and then again to lose it.
What makes the task of identification still more difficult is that she
found it convenient at this time to change frequently from one set
of clothes to another. Thus she often occurs in contemporary memoirs as "Lord" So-and-so, who was in fact her cousin. . . . She had,
it seems, no difficulty in sustaining the different parts, for her sex
changed far more frequently than those who have worn only one
set of clothing can conceive; nor can there be any doubt that she
reaped a twofold harvest by this device; the pleasures of life were
increased and its experiences multiplied. From the probity of
breeches she turned to the seductiveness of petticoats and enjoyed
the love of both sexes equally.

So then one may sketch her spending her morning in a China
robe of ambiguous gender among her books; then receiving a client
or two (for she had many scores of suppliants) in the same garment;
then she would take a turn in the garden and clip the nut trees—
for which knee breeches were convenient; then she would change
into a flowered taffeta which best suited a drive to Richmond and
a proposal of marriage from some great nobleman; and so back
again to town, where she would don a snuff-coloured gown like a
lawyer's and visit the courts to hear how her cases were doing . . .
finally, when night came, she would more often than not become

a nobleman complete from head to toe and walk the streets in search of adventure. . . .

[T]here were many stories told at the time . . . that she fought a duel, served on one of the King's ships as a captain, was seen to dance naked on a balcony, and fled with a certain lady to the Low Countries where the lady's husband followed them.

CHAPTER 13

THE WELL OF LONELINESS

RADCLYFFE HALL (1880–1943), whose book *The Well of Loneliness* became the most influential lesbian novel of the century and the subject of the most sensational literary trial since that of Oscar Wilde, was a frequent visitor to 1920s Paris. But she never became a genuine expatriate. She was too English perhaps. Her major interests were dog breeding and spiritualism. She was staunchly Tory in her political views and a convert to Roman Catholicism; in her later years, like her close friend Natalie Barney, she became enamored of Italian fascism and flirted with anti-Semitism. Known to everyone as "John," she was famous for her "mannish" appearance—plain tailored jackets, ties and skirts; she wore a monocle and, at one point, smoked a pipe. Her lover and companion for almost three decades was Lady Una Troubridge, seven years her junior and (formerly) an admiral's wife. During virtually their entire relationship, she and Una communicated through a medium with Hall's former lover, the opera singer **Mabel Batten** (known as "Ladye"), who died in 1915. In fact, communication with Ladye was such a crucial element in both their lives that Hall dedicated all her novels to "Our Three Selves."

In 1928, when *The Well of Loneliness* was published, Hall was forty-eight and at the height of her career. Her novel *Adam's Breed,* the story of a headwaiter in an Italian restaurant in Soho who starves himself to death, had won two major British literary prizes, an achievement matched only by E. M. Forster's *A Passage to India.* She was in demand as a public speaker; the *Daily Mail* newspaper interviewed her for its series "How Other Women Run Their Homes" (she acknowledged to the *Mail* reporter that she had "a perfect mania for cleanliness"). As Michael Baker noted in his biography of Hall, *Our Three Selves,* "[L]ess than four years after the publication of her first novel, John found herself at the very peak of her profession, a writer who had acquired that enviable 'double': commercial popularity *and* critical acclaim."

By the 1920s—and to some extent even earlier—the subject of lesbianism was beginning to gain some attention in England. The

Radclyffe Hall with her dog, "Colette," in the 1930s.
(© UPI/Bettmann)

trial of the "First 47,000" in 1918, with its inference that Maud Allen, the dancer, was a lesbian, had riveted the country. In 1920, Hall herself had become involved in a scandal when a member of the Society for Psychical Research, in which Hall was active, accused her of being immoral and of breaking up Una Troubridge's marriage. Hall sued for libel. The following year, in 1921, an attempt was made to extend the penalties of the Labouchère Amendment—which criminalized oral sex between men—to women as well. The House of Commons approved the clause, but the House of Lords rejected it, and the matter was dropped. One of the major reasons the attempt failed was that many felt that silence was the best approach. As one member of the Lords, **Lord Desart**, put it during parliamentary debate, "You are going to tell the whole world that there is such an offence, to bring it to the notice of women who have never heard of it, never thought of it, never dreamed of it. I think that is a very great mischief."

Radclyffe Hall had a clear political purpose in writing *The Well of Loneliness*. "I wrote the book from a deep sense of duty," she said in a letter to her publisher. "I am proud indeed to have taken up my pen in defence of those who are utterly defenceless, who being from birth set apart in accordance with some hidden scheme of Nature, need all the help that society can give them." The hero of the *Well* is a young woman named Stephen Gordon, daughter of a landed British family much like Hall's own. The book relates her coming of age, her first affair with a woman, and above all, her relationship with Mary, the great love of her life, and their struggle to overcome social hostility and make a life for themselves. Sections of the novel are set in Paris, featuring a character based on Natalie Barney as well as a description of Paris homosexual bars. At the very end of the book, in a supreme gesture of self-sacrifice, Stephen cedes Mary to a former male lover so Mary can have a "normal" life. The book ends with the heroine's plaintive cry, "God . . . we believe; we have told You we believe. . . . We have not denied You, then rise up and defend us. Acknowledge us, oh God, before the whole world. Give us also the right to our existence!"

Hall was heavily influenced by the sexologists Krafft-Ebing and Havelock Ellis. Following Ellis's lead, she believed that homosexuality was an innate condition, not an acquired one. She modeled her characters on the case studies furnished by Ellis in *Sexual Inversion*, particularly taking up the idea of the female "invert" as masculine. Thus, Stephen, the book's heroine, has a muscular body, is "narrow-hipped and wide shouldered," excels at hunting and fencing, and favors suits from her father's tailor. The entire tone of the book—one of special pleading but with the implicit message that "inverts" can never really be happy—follows Ellis's thinking. Not surprisingly, Ellis himself wrote a commentary at the beginning of the novel, calling it a book of "notable psychological and sociological significance."

The Well of Loneliness was published on July 27, 1928. Reviews were mixed, but the book was selling well. Then, three weeks after publication, the conservative *Sunday Express* newspaper published a scathing denunciation of *The Well* headlined, A BOOK THAT MUST BE SUPRESSED. The article, signed by the paper's editor **James Douglas**, contended that *The Well* was unfit to be sold by any bookseller or borrowed from any library. Douglas wrote:

> *I have seen the plague stalking shamelessly through great social assemblies. I have heard it whispered about by young men and young women who do not and cannot grasp its unutterable putrefaction.... The contagion cannot be escaped. It pervades our social life. I would rather give a healthy boy or healthy girl a phial of prussic acid than this novel. Poison kills the body, but moral poison kills the soul.*

Hall's publisher, **Jonathan Cape** (of the firm of the same name), panicked. He agreed to send copies of the book to the Home Secretary and to the Director of Prosecutions. In a letter to the *Express,* Cape asserted that if it could be demonstrated that the best interests of the public would be served by withdrawing the book, he would do so. This offer was a miscalculation on the publisher's part, virtually inviting suppression. For the Home Secretary at the time was **Sir William Joynson-Hicks** (known as "Jix"), a moralist of the most extreme sort and treasurer of the fundamentalist Zenana Bible Mission. He was known as "the Policeman of the Lord" for his opposition to attempts to revise the Anglican prayer book. After receiving a copy of *The Well,* Jix wrote Cape, insisting he withdraw the book or face legal proceedings. Cape discontinued publication. Shortly after, the American publishing house Alfred A. Knopf, which had agreed to publish the book in the United States, abandoned plans to do so.

In England, a public letter of protest was organized by the novelist E. M. Forster (whose novel *Maurice* remained unpublished at the time) and Leonard Woolf (husband of Virginia). They both had reservations about the artistry of *The Well* but nonetheless opposed any effort to suppress it. (For her part, Virginia Woolf snootily described *The Well* in her diary as "[Hall's] meritorious dull book.") Forster met with Hall, who wanted any petition of support to attest to the novel's artistic merit. When he hinted at some misgivings on that point, Hall was offended—"screamed like a herring gull, mad with egotism & vanity," as Virginia Woolf wrote in her diary. Although Forster soon wished himself out of the affair, he and Virginia Woolf drafted a now-famous letter which appeared in the *Nation and Athenaeum:*

> *The subject-matter of the book exists as a fact among the many other facts of life. It is recognized by science and recognizable in history. It forms, of course, an extremely small fraction of the sum-total of human emotions, it enters personally into very few lives, and it is uninteresting or repellent to the majority; nevertheless it exists, and novelists in England have now been forbidden to mention it by Sir W. Joynson-Hicks. May they mention it incidentally? Although it is forbidden as a main theme, may it be alluded to, or ascribed to subsidiary characters? Perhaps the Home Secretary will issue further orders on this point. And is it the only taboo or are there others? What of the other subjects known to be more or less unpopular in Whitehall, such as birth-control, suicide, and pacifism? May we mention these? We await our instructions! . . .*

But Cape, the publisher, had his own strategy. He flew the type moulds to Paris, subleased the rights to Pegasus Press, an English-language press there, and intended to solicit orders from English booksellers and subscribers. However, just as the plan was being put into effect, British Customs officials seized 250 copies of the Paris edition on their way to Pegasus's London distributor. Customs released the seized consignments, but when the books reached the distributors, the police arrived and removed them, claiming they were acting under the Obscene Publications Act of 1857. The police then raided the Jonathan Cape offices. They arrived at lunchtime when the receptionist was alone. She directed the police to the stockroom, grabbed the only display copy of *The Well* from the showcase, and sat on it until the police left.

The obscenity trial of *The Well of Loneliness* began on November

9, 1928, at Bow Street Magistrate's court. It was standing room only. As her biographer Michael Baker relates, Radclyffe Hall sat at the solicitor's table dressed in a dark blue Spanish riding hat and a leather motor-coat with an astrakhan collar and cuffs. A newspaper described the expression in her eyes of "one of mingled pain and sadness." Una, her lover, sat in the audience, "abominably over-dressed and over-made-up," in the view of the novelist **Storm Jameson**. There were forty defense witnesses, including Virginia Woolf, E. M. Forster, **Hugh Walpole**, and others, all prepared to testify to the book's merits. (Havelock Ellis declined to take the stand, to Hall's intense disappointment.) In her diary, Woolf described the scene, in particular the appearance of the Chief Magistrate, the venerable **Sir Chartres Biron**:

> We were all packed in by 10:30: the door at the top of the court opened; in stepped the debonair distinguished magistrate; we all rose; he bowed; took his seat under the lion & the unicorn, & then proceeded. Something like a Harley St. specialist investigating a case. All black & white, tie pin, clean shaven, wax coloured, & carved, in that light, like ivory. He was ironical at first: raised his eyebrows & shrugged.

One of the first things Biron did was to rule that the testimony of Woolf and the other thirty-nine defense witnesses was not allowable. Only the magistrate himself would determine whether or not the book was obscene. During the course of the morning, **K. C. Norman Birkett**, head of the defense team, argued that in actuality the relationship between Stephen and her lover Mary in the book wasn't physical at all, merely "a schoolgirl crush transferred to adult life and innocent of sexual implications." Hall was mortified. Her novel was not "innocent of sexual implications"; that was the point. She gave Birkett a dressing-down over lunch, and he withdrew the comment at the afternoon session. The culmination of the day was a speech by the young defense lawyer **James B. Melville**, who asserted that *The Well* neither praised nor apologized for sexual inversion, but rather accepted it as "a fact of God's own creation." The book, he said, was written in a "reverent spirit," and the fact that Stephen Gordon sacrifices her lover to a man in the final chapter reflected the author's "inherent respect for the normal," her "worship for the perfect thing which she had divined in the love that existed between her parents." When he finished, the courtroom was completely still. But if Virginia Woolf was generally pleased by the proceedings (she concludes her diary entry: "then the magistrate, increasingly deliberate & courteous, said he would read the book again & give judgement next Friday at two"), the defense lawyers were less so. Once the magistrate had refused to permit their witnesses to testify, they knew that essentially the game was up.

At two in the afternoon the following Friday, Sir Chartres Biron delivered his judgment in a one-hour address to the court. *The Well of Loneliness,* he stated, expressed the view that "unnatural vice" was admirable and was not the cause of the misfortunes that befell those who practiced it. "I am asked to say that this book is not a defence of these practices?" he added. Biron described homosexuality as "these horrible practices . . . acts of the most horrible, unnatural and disgusting obscenity," and Hall's characters as "these two people living in filthy sin." When he referred to the section of the book in which Stephen Gordon and a number of other women serve as members of an ambulance corps during the War, accusing the writer of portraying "a number of women of position and admirable character" as being "addicted to this vice," Radclyffe Hall could contain herself no longer. She jumped to her feet. "I protest! I am that writer!" she said. Sir Chartres Biron replied, without referring to her by name, "I must ask people not to interrupt the court." Hall remained on her feet. "I am the authoress of this book," she insisted. The magistrate informed her that if she did not keep quiet, he would have her removed.

Biron declared the book obscene. He ordered those copies in police possession to be destroyed and imposed twenty guineas in court costs on Jonathan Cape and on Hall.

Just before the verdict was announced, her defense attorney rose and stated for the record that Radclyffe Hall would have testified if she had been permitted to do so. The conclusion of her written statement went:

> *I claim emphatically that the true invert is born and not made. I have behind me in this claim the weight of most of the finest psychological opinion. This is precisely one of the things that I wished to bring home to the thinking public. Only when this fact is fully grasped can we hope for the exercise of that charitable help and compassion that will assist inverts to give of their best and thus contribute to the good of the whole. When I wrote* The

Well of Loneliness *I had in mind the good of the whole quite as much as the good of the congenital inverts. It is not too much to say that many lives are wrecked through the lack of proper understanding of inversion. For the sake of the future generation inverts should never be encouraged to marry.*

I do not regret having written the book. All that has happened has only served to show me how badly my book was needed. I am proud to have written The Well of Loneliness *and I would not alter so much as a comma.*

The defense appealed the decision. Within a month, however, the appeal was rejected with the judge declaring *The Well* "a disgusting book . . . prejudicial to the morals of the country." In the United States, where the book was published by the firm of Covici Friede after Knopf withdrew, it was also ruled obscene. Eventually, though, the judgment was overturned. While the case was in litigation, *The Well* became a huge American best-seller, selling fifty thousand copies within a short period. In the U.S., it spawned numerous imitations but none had the staying power of *The Well,* which was the only major lesbian novel available for many years. The book was not published in England until 1949.

Like the trial of Oscar Wilde, the publication and prosecution of *The Well* had enormous consequences. For the first time, lesbianism truly entered public consciousness both in England and the United States. The publication had "all the character of a bursting dam," as one critic put it. As a result, large numbers of lesbians were able to recognize themselves and their sexuality. As one lesbian, quoted in Charlotte Wolff's book *Love Between Women,* put it, "When I read *The Well of Loneliness* it fell upon me like a revelation. I identified with every line. I wept floods of tears over it, and it confirmed my belief in my homosexuality." At the same time, the book created a public image of lesbianism that was very much in accordance with the writings of the early sexologists—one of the "mannish," doomed invert, who had to sacrifice the woman she loved to a man and who could never achieve happiness. As with the image of male homosexuality provided by the Wilde trial, *The Well of Loneliness* both created and reinforced stereotypes. Other social consequences were negative as well. In the "lesbian scare" that followed suppression of *The Well,* romantic friendships between women became increasingly equated with deviance. Writer Rosemary Auchmuty has documented how British schoolgirl romance novels that treated women's friendships effusively became far more cautious in the wake of the prosecution of The Well. Another feminist historian, Alison Oram, has described how "lesbian-baiting" of spinster schoolteachers in Britain dates from this period, as well.

Although she published other novels, Radcyffe Hall never again received the literary recognition that Adam's Breed earned her or the notoriety that The Well of Loneliness did. The entire experience of the prosecution of The Well seems to have embittered her, both against her country and against other writers whom she felt were reluctant to come to her assistance. By the late 1930s, she and Una were living in Florence, singing Mussolini's praises, and blaming the Jews for Europe's problems. (Hall did, however, later change her views about fascism.) World War II broke out when they were visiting England, and Hall died there in 1943. At the time of her death, The Well was selling a hundred thousand copies a year worldwide.

An Excerpt from Radclyffe Hall's *The Well of Loneliness*

This section describes the visit of Stephen Gordon, the novelist heroine of The Well of Loneliness, *to a gay bar in Paris. It offers a good example of the eloquence and overly melodramatic tone that characterize the book. Perhaps more than any passage in* The Well, *it gives the author's reasons for writing it in the first place.*

AS LONG AS SHE LIVED Stephen never forgot her first impression of the bar known as Alec's—that meeting-place of the most miserable of all those who comprised the miserable army. That merciless, drug-dealing, death-dealing haunt to which flocked the battered remnants of men whom their fellow men had at last stamped under; who, despised of the world, must despise themselves beyond all hope, it seemed, of salvation. There they sat, closely herded together at the tables, creatures shabby yet tawdry, timid yet defiant—and their eyes, Stephen never forgot their eyes, those haunted, tormented eyes of the invert. . . .

And now some one was making his way through the crowd, a quiet, tawny man with the eyes of the Hebrew; Adolphe Blanc, the gentle and learned Jew, sat down in Dickie's seat beside Stephen. And he patted her knee as though she were young, very young and in great need of consolation. . . .

He said: "This place—these poor men, they have shocked you. I've been watching you in between the dances. They are terrible, Miss Gordon, because they are those who have fallen but have not risen again. . . ."

He spoke softly, as though for her ears alone, and yet as a man might speak when consumed by the flame of some urgent and desperate mission. "I am glad that you have come to this place, because those who have courage have also a duty."

She nodded without comprehending his meaning.

"Yes, I am glad you have come here," he repeated. "In this little room, to-night, every night, there is so much misery, so much despair that the walls seem almost too narrow to contain it. . . . Yet outside there are happy people who sleep the sleep of the so-called just and righteous. When they wake it will be to persecute those who, through no known fault of their own, have been set apart from the day of their birth, deprived of all sympathy, all understanding. They are thoughtless, these happy people who sleep—and who is there to make them think, Miss Gordon?"

"They can read," she stammered, "there are many books. . . ."

But he shook his head. "Do you think they are students? Ah, but no, they will not read medical books; what do such people care for the doctors? And what doctor can know the entire truth? Many times they meet only the neurasthenics, those of us for whom life has proved too bitter. They are good, these doctors—some of them very good; they work hard trying to solve our problem, but half the time they must work in the dark—the whole truth is known only to the normal invert. The doctors cannot make the ignorant think, cannot hope to bring home the suffering of millions; only one of ourselves can some day do that. . . . It will need great courage but it will be done, because all things must work toward ultimate good; there is no real wastage and no destruction." He lit a cigarette and stared thoughtfully at her for a moment or two. Then he touched her hand. "Do you comprehend? There is no destruction."

She said: "When one comes to a place like this, one feels horribly sad and humiliated. One feels that the odds are too heavily against any real success, any real achievement. Where so many have failed who can hope to succeed? Perhaps this is the end."

Adolphe Blanc met her eyes. "You are wrong, very wrong—this is only the beginning. Many die, many kill their bodies and souls, but they cannot kill the justice of God, even they cannot kill the eternal spirit. From their very degradation that spirit will rise up to demand of the world compassion and justice."

Strange—this man was actually speaking her thoughts, yet again she fell silent, unable to answer.

Dickie and Pat came back to the table, and Adolphe Blanc slipped quietly away; when Stephen glanced round his place was empty, nor could she perceive him crossing the room through the press and maze of those terrible dancers.

Quentin Crisp's 1920s

Quentin Crisp, the flamboyant British wit and author of the highly praised autobiography, The Naked Civil Servant, *was born in 1908 in Surrey of a middle-class family. At eighteen, he went to study journalism at London University but soon left. As this excerpt begins, he is living at home "getting on my parents' nerves" and playing games of pontoon with a friend of his mother's named Mrs. Longhurst:*

[I]N THOSE FAR-OFF DAYS [of the 1920s] a homosexual person was never anyone that you actually knew and seldom anyone that you had met. . . . The rest of the world in which I lived was still stumbling about in search of a weapon with which to exterminate this monster whose shape and size had not yet been known or even guessed at. It was thought to be Greek in origin, smaller than socialism but more deadly—especially to children. At about this time *The Well of Loneliness* was banned. The widely reported court case, together with the extraordinary reputation that Tallulah Bankhead was painstakingly building up for herself as a delinquent, brought Lesbianism, if not into the light of day, at least into the twilight, but I do not remember ever hearing anyone discuss the subject except Mrs. Longhurst and my mother. . . .

[T]o vary the monotony of my existence, I took to wandering about the streets of the West End. . . . As I wandered along Piccadilly or Shaftesbury Avenue, I passed young men standing at the street corners who said, "Isn't it terrible tonight, dear? No men about. The Dilly's not what it used to be." Though the Indian boy at school had once amazed us all with the information that in Birmingham there were male prostitutes, I had never believed that I would actually see one. Here they were for all the world to recognize—or almost all the world. A passer-by would have to be very innocent indeed not to catch the meaning of the mannequin walk and the stance in which the hip was only prevented from total dislocation by the hand placed upon it.

The whole set of stylizations that are known as "camp" (a word that I was hearing then for the first time) was, in 1926, self-explanatory. Women moved and gesticulated in this way. Homosexuals wished for obvious reasons to copy them. The strange thing about "camp" is that it has become fossilized. The mannerisms have never changed. If I were now to see a woman sitting with her knees clamped together, one hand on her hip and the other lightly touching her back hair, I should think, "Either she scored her last social triumph in 1926 or it is a man in drag."

Perhaps "camp" is set in the twenties because after that differences between the sexes—especially visible differences—began to fade. . . . The whole structure of society was at that time much more rigid than it has ever been since, and in two main ways. The first of these was sexual. . . .

Manliness was all the rage. The men of the twenties searched themselves for vestiges of effeminacy as though for lice. They did not worry about their characters but about their hair and their clothes. Their predicament was that they must never be caught worrying about either. . . .

The sexual meaning of behavior was only sketchily understood, but the symbolism of clothes was recognized by everyone. To wear suede shoes was to be under suspicion. Anyone who had hair rather than bristle at the back of his neck was thought to be an artist, a foreigner, or worse. . . .

The other way in which society in the twenties was rigid was in its class distinctions. Doubtless to a sociologist there were many different strata merging here and there but, among the people I was now getting to know, there were only two classes. They never mingled except in bed. There was "them," who acted refined and spoke nice and whose people had pots of money, and there was "us," who were the salt of the earth.

I would still have been "them" because my slight cockney accent had been flattened out a little. But they [the group of male prostitutes he began to hang out with] forgave me for my unfair advantages because I was in the same sexual boat as they. I took to them like a duck to ducks.

Between these twin barriers of sex and class, we sat huddled together in a café called the Black Cat. . . . This was in Old Compton Street. It looked like a dozen other cafés in Soho. It had a horseshoe bar of occasionally scrubbed wood, black-and-white checked linoleum on the floor, and mirrors everywhere. . . .

Day after uneventful day, night after loveless night, we sat in this café buying each other cups of tea, combing each other's hair, and trying on each other's lipsticks. We were waited on with indulgent contempt by an elderly gentleman, who later achieved a fame that we would have then thought quite beyond him, by being involved in a murder case. Had the denizens of the Black Cat known he was such a desperate character, they would doubtless have done much more to provoke him. As it was we only bored him by making, with ladylike sips, each cup of tea last as long as a four-course meal. From time to time he threw us out. When this happened we waltzed around the neighborhood streets in search of love or money or both. If we didn't find either, we returned to the café and put on more lipstick. . . . Occasionally, while we chattered on the street corner, one of our friends would go whizzing past crying, "They're coming." At this we would scatter. It meant that, while being questioned, one of the boys had bolted and his inquisitors were after him. At such times, if a detective saw his quarry escaping, he would seize upon the nearest prey, however innocently that peson might be behaving. We treated the police as it is said you should treat wild animals. . . .

The perpetual danger in which we lived bound us together. In the café there was a lot of stylized cattiness, but this was never unkindly meant. Nothing at all was meant by it. It was a formal game of innuendoes about other people being older than they said, about their teeth being false and their hair being a wig. Such conversation was thought to be smart and so very feminine. . . . When we were not thus engaged, we talked about our sufferings, and this I greatly preferred. Soon I had learned by heart almost every argument that could be reared in the climate of that time against the persecution of homosexuals. We weren't doing any harm; we couldn't help it; and, though this was hardly watertight from a legal point of view, we had enough to bear already. Some speakers even went so far as not merely to excuse our sin but to glorify it, making it a source of national culture. The great names of history from Shakespeare onward were fingered over and over like beads on a rosary.

THE TRIUMPH OF IDEOLOGY

CHAPTER 14

CZARS AND COMMISSARS:
HOMOSEXUALITY IN RUSSIA

IN WESTERN EUROPE, as the nineteenth century progressed, a gradually liberalizing trend could be seen in legal and social attitudes toward homosexuality. In England, the last execution for sodomy took place in 1836. In France, the Code Napoléon had legalized same-sex relations. In Germany, Karl Heinrich Ulrichs and others campaigned for the abolition of the law making male homosexual relations a crime. In Russia, however, where the Czarist regime and the Russian Orthodox Church held sway, such liberalizing tendencies were slower to emerge. The persistence of traditional prohibitions against homosexuality can be seen in the fates of two of the greatest Russian cultural figures of the century.

In 1852, **Nikolai Gogol**, the classic nineteenth-century Russian author, starved himself to death at the age of forty-three. Secretive and religious, unable to resolve his attractions toward other men, Gogol came under the sway of **Father Matthew Konstantinovsky**, a fanatical Russian Orthodox priest. According to Simon Karlinsky's book *The Sexual Labyrinth of Nikolai Gogol*, Gogol confessed his homosexual feelings to Father Matthew in late January 1852, while staying at the St. Petersburg home of **Count Alexander Tolstoy**. In the midst of one of his conversations with Father Matthew, Gogol was heard to scream, "Enough! Stop it! I cannot listen any more, it is too terrifying!" Following Father Matthew's orders, Gogol attempted to purge himself of his affliction. He reduced his daily food intake to several spoonfuls of oatmeal soup or sauerkraut brine. He spent his nights in prayer, sleeping only two and three hours. Within days, he became extremely ill; his host, Count Tolstoy, called in doctors, who treated him as if he were a madman. Gogol was bled; he was plunged into icy baths; live leeches were attached to his nose. On February 21, "the strangest prose-poet Russia ever produced," as **Vladimir Nabokov** described him, was dead.

Some years later, **Tertius Filippov**, a friend of Count Tolstoy's, asked Father Matthew about Gogol's spiritual state before his death.

Father Matthew replied, "He sought inner peace and inner cleansing."

"Cleansing from what?" inquired Filippov.

"There was inner filth in him," said Father Matthew.

"What kind?"

"Inner filth, I say, and he tried to get rid of it, but could not. I helped him cleanse himself and he died a true Christian."

To his biographer Karlinsky, Gogol's death was a "ritual murder," committed in the name of God and the Russian Orthodox Church.

Almost half a century later, in 1893, another great Russian artist who was also homosexual, the composer **Peter Illych Tchaikovsky,** died at the age of fifty-three. His death, which occurred three weeks after the premiere of his Sixth Symphony (the *Symphonie pathétique*), was supposedly from cholera caused by drinking a glass of unboiled water. But there is another view of Tchaikovsky's death, one that bears a disquieting parallel to that of Gogol. In recent years, a story has circulated that Tchaikovsky did not die of cholera but in fact committed suicide. (The composer had attempted to kill himself once before, in 1877, in the midst of a short-lived marriage forced upon him by social and family pressure.) According to the respected Soviet musicologist Alexandra Orlova, Tchaikovsky was ordered to commit suicide by "a court of honor" of eight fellow alumni of the School of Jurisprudence in St. Petersburg. His death was then covered up by his doctors and by his brother **Modest** (who was also gay).

This rather extraordinary situation is said to have come about as the result of sexual advances that Tchaikovsky had allegedly made toward a nephew of the Duke Stenbok-Fermor. The duke wrote a letter of accusation to the Czar. The letter was handed to **Nicolai Borisovich Jacobi,** a high official. Jacobi feared that not only would Tchaikovsky be disgraced but that the School of Jurisprudence, which they had both attended, would be disgraced as well. Jacobi convened the "court of honor" at his home, made up of eight of Tchaikovsky's former classmates. The composer himself was present. After a meeting that lasted almost five hours, Tchaikovsky fled the house in extreme agitation. He had apparently agreed to do as he was commanded: The alternative would be family disgrace, exile in Siberia, and the revelation of his indiscretion to the Czar himself. The following day, **August Gerke**, a lawyer and former classmate of Tchaikovsky's, came to the composer's home and handed him a vial of arsenic.

The story of Tchaikovsky's alleged forced suicide is based on hearsay. It was told to Alexandra Orlova in 1966 by **Alexander Voitov**, former curator of coins at the Russian Museum in St. Petersburg. Voitov had been told this "in great secrecy," fifty years before, by Mrs. Jacobi, whose husband had convened the court of honor. There is additional evidence that at least lends credence to the claim that the composer did not die of cholera: wild discrepancies in stories told by Tchaikovsky's brothers and doctors; a letter written to the composer's brother Modest by the principal doctor in the case that can be read as an instruction manual for how to describe a death from cholera; the fact that Tchaikovsky's body was not placed in a closed casket, as was always the case with victims of the highly contagious disease. The composer's biographer David Brown writes "That he committed suicide cannot be doubted but what precipitated this suicide has not been conclusively established."

The accounts of the deaths of both Gogol and Tchaikovsky—dramatic and disturbing as they may be—are certainly open to question. No one knows for sure what Father Matthew really told Nikolai Gogol at the moment when the novelist is said to have shouted, "Enough!" The account of Tchaikovsky's supposed sentence by the "court of honor" relies on a story told eighty years ago. Simon Karlinsky, who has described the death of Gogol as a "ritual murder," dismisses the report about the forced suicide of Tchaikovsky as "a web of fantasies." But if ritual murder or the forced suicide of prominent homosexuals were not central characteristics of nineteenth-century Russian life, these accounts still reveal much about attitudes toward homosexuals at that time.

Male homosexuality was a crime in Czarist Russia under Article 995 of the legal code drafted in 1832. The code prohibited *muzhelozhstvo*, a term that the courts interpreted as meaning anal intercourse between men. Those who violated Article 995 were deprived of all rights and sent to Siberia for a period of four to five years. As in England and Germany, women were not punished for homosexual behavior.

By the turn of the century, pressure to reform the law began to surface, particularly in the period prior to the enactment of the revised legal code of 1903. The Moscow and St. Petersburg juridical societies debated whether homosexual acts should remain a criminal offense. Interest in the subject is reflected in a scene in **Leo Tolstoy's** 1899 novel, *Resurrection*, in which three senators discuss the case of a government department head accused of violating Article 995. "Where's the harm?" asks a senator named Skovorodnikov. "I can show you a book where a German writer openly puts forward the view that such acts ought not to be considered criminal, and says that marriage between men should be allowed." Tolstoy, a devout Orthodox Christian, strongly disapproved of homosexuality and opposed any change in the law. This is evident from the rather negative way he describes Skovorodnikov, a materialist and a Darwinian who "looked upon all manifestations of abstract morality or religious belief not only as despicable folly but as a personal affront to himself."

In general, the reformers' aims were limited. Their primary goal was "to reconceptualize homosexuality in secular terms as a physically or psychologically injurious practice, rather than as an act proscribed in religious writ," writes Laura Engelstein in her book *The Keys to Happiness: Sex and the Search for Modernity in Fin-de-Siècle Russia*. Nonetheless, there were those who advocated total decriminalization, most notably the jurist **V. D. Nabokov** (1870–1922), father of novelist Vladimir Nabokov. The elder Nabokov was an important liberal political figure in prerevolutionary Russia and a strong defender of individual rights. He was a supporter of Magnus Hirschfeld's campaign to repeal Germany's Paragraph 175 and translated an article he wrote on homosexuality for the 1903 edition of Hirschfeld's journal in Berlin. Although Nabokov labeled homosexuality as "deeply repugnant" to the "healthy and normal" person, he contended that homosexual acts should not be punished. If homosexuality harmed the family (as supporters of the law claimed), then why not criminalize bachelorhood as well? he asked. If the state's function was to protect the health of the citizen, then why not outlaw smoking as well? He continued his line of argument:

> From the moral point of view, satisfaction of the sexual urge is permissible only within marriage, and even then, only by natural means. Thus every *extramarital satisfaction and every unnatural one within marriage should be penalized. To claim that pederasty is more repugnant than other perversions is, in the first place, a matter of subjective judgement. In the second place, such* distinguo [sic] *are hardly possible or permissible in this particular domain. Finally, the claim that sodomy is extremely widespread is entirely doubtful. . . .*

Support for Nabokov's position came from one surprising quarter—judges from the Muslim areas of the Russian Empire who argued that it was impossible to enforce sodomy laws among peoples who did not disapprove of homosexual behavior. "The cultural relativity of moral standards in regard to sexual comportment was no secret to anyone who sat on the imperial bench," Engelstein observes.

Despite the efforts of Nabokov and others, Article 995 remained in place. However, with the reforms that followed the unrest of 1905, censorship was abolished in Russia. Works treating gay themes were published for the first time, among them **Mikhail Kuzmin**'s (1872–1936) novel *Wings,* which first appeared in a Moscow symbolist journal in 1906. *Wings* traces the sexual awakening of its young protagonist, Vanya, through his relationship with the cultivated and bisexual Stroop. A short sketch called *Thirty-Three Abominations,* written by Kuzmin's friend (and St. Petersburg salon hostess) **Lidiia Zinov'eva-Annibal** (1866–1907), explored lesbian love. *Thirty-Three Abominations* describes the romantic relationship between an actress named Vera and another young woman. When Vera permits her friend to pose for a studio of male artists, the relationship falters. The friend accompanies one of the artists on a trip abroad, and Vera commits suicide. The prose, while highly stylized, is unabashedly erotic: "She kissed my eyes and lips and breasts and caressed my body. . . . Life and death abide in the drunken juice of the rosy fruit of her fresh lips, the sacred phial of my insane love."

However, as Engelstein notes, both *Wings* and *Thirty-Three Abominations* take place on "an ethereal plane," outside of Russian social reality; they tended to confirm the widely held view that homosexuality was a product of the West and the aristocracy and had little relevance to the lives of most Russians. Engelstein also contends that while Russian modernist writers were willing to accept some exploration of the sexual spectrum, "it is clear that not even the most culturally radical cream of the creative intelligentsia, not to speak of its culturally stodgy left wing, embraced the representation of sexual deviance as an artistically appropriate liberty."

In any event, by the end of the nineteenth century, gays and lesbians were becoming visible in Russian aristocratic and artistic circles. There were at least seven gay Grand Dukes (uncles, nephews, and cousins of the last two Czars), according to Karlinsky. The most flamboyant of this group was the Grand Duke **Sergei Alexandrovich,** uncle of **Czar Nicholas II;** he regularly went to the theater and other public functions with his male lover. Vladimir Nabokov had two gay uncles—both in the diplomatic service—as well as a gay brother, **Sergei,** a dandy and an esthete who was incarcerated in a Nazi concentration camp during World War II for being gay. Probably the most well-known Russian male couple of the early twentieth century were the impresario **Sergei Diaghilev** and his lover for five years, the ballet dancer **Vaslav Nijinsky.** (See "Diaghilev, Nijinsky, and the Ballets Russes," page 208.)

As Karlinsky notes, one area of Russian life where homosexuals were quite invisible was the revolutionary movement. The German **Friedrich Engels,** leading Marxist theorist on family and sexual matters, viewed sodomy as a "gross, unnatural vice" and mocked Karl Heinrich Ulrichs's attempt to repeal Germany's sodomy law ("Really, it can only happen in Germany that such a no-good [Ulrichs] can transform lechery into a theory and invite us to 'enter,' " Engels wrote to **Karl Marx** in an 1868 letter filled with double entendres). Engels played a major role in setting the puritanical revolutionary tone. The writer **Maxim Gorky,** an early member of the Bolshevik Party (and the great exponent of "socialist realism" in art and literature), was harshly critical. Referring to the favorable depiction of homosexuality in the writings of Kuzmin and others, he noted, "They are old-fashioned slaves, people who *can't help* confusing freedom with homosexuality. For them, for example, 'personal liberation' is in some peculiar way confused with crawling from one cesspool into another and is at times reduced to freedom for the penis and nothing more."

In fact, the only Russian radicals who saw the revolution as encompassing sexual as well as economic freedom were the anarchists Emma Goldman and **Alexander Berkman;** both emigrated to the United States when they were quite young.

When the Bolsheviks took power in 1917, the revolutionary government abolished the entire criminal code of the old Russian Empire. This included Article 995. When the new Soviet criminal code was promulgated in 1922 and amended in 1926, it contained no provisions banning sexual relations between adult men, setting an age of consent of sixteen. (Such acts did remain against the law in Georgia, Azerbaijan, and the Uzbek and Turkmen socialist republics.)

Many outside of the Soviet Union have tended to idealize the

1920s as a period of gay and lesbian freedom that was quashed only in the Stalin terror of the 1930s. In some respects this is true. There were no laws on the books; nor was there censorship of works with gay themes. The Soviet Union sent representatives to meetings of Magnus Hirschfeld's World League for Sexual Reform. Hirschfeld himself was well-received on his 1926 tour of the Soviet Union, and, as already noted, the German Communist Party became an enthusiastic supporter of the abolition of Paragraph 175, Germany's antigay law. The Great Soviet Encyclopedia of 1930 writes, "In the advanced capitalist countries, the struggle for abolition of these hypocritical laws is at present far from over. In Germany, for example, Magnus Hirschfeld is leading an especially fierce and not unsuccessful struggle to abolish the law against homosexuality. Soviet law does not recognize 'crime' against morality. . . ."

Some of these policies may have been primarily part of an effort to give the Soviet regime a progressive image within liberal circles in the West. Simon Karlinsky notes that gays and lesbians who wanted careers in arts or government in the Soviet Union found it necessary to marry, something that had not been the case in the period immediately before the revolution. The new Soviet government dealt with homosexuality in two ways, he says: by regarding it as a mental disorder and by dismissing or ignoring it in literary works. Karlinsky offers as an example a book called *Sexual Life of Contemporary Youth,* published in Moscow in 1923 under the aegis of the People's Commissariat of Public Health. The book was based on an anonymous questionnaire about sexual practices. Two of the respondents were lesbians. The author of the book comments on the lesbian responses this way: "Science has now established, with precision that excludes all doubt, [that homosexuality] is not ill will or crime, but sickness. . . . The world of a female or male homosexual is perverted, it is alien to the normal sexual attraction that exists in a normal person."

Karlinsky notes that established gay writers like Kuzmin were producing some of their best work during the 1920s. Yet their books were either not reviewed in the Soviet press or dismissed as irrelevant to the new Soviet society. (This may have been due, in part, though, to the class origins of these authors or their lack of interest in towing the socialist realist line.) "In the literary and intellectual spheres it [homosexuality] was mentioned less and less, and was all but unmentionable by 1930," says Karlinsky.

The career of **Sergei M. Eisenstein** (1898–1948), the acclaimed film director (*Potemkin, Alexander Nevsky, Ivan the Terrible*) illustrates some of these negative attitudes toward homosexuality in Soviet culture. Eisenstein appears to have struggled against his sexual proclivities his entire life, even to the point of visiting Magnus Hirschfeld's Institute for Sexual Science in Berlin in order to understand his sexuality—and how to repress it. "Had it not been for Leonardo, Marx, Lenin, Freud, and the movies, I would in all probability have been another Oscar Wilde," Eisenstein told an American writer. Eisenstein was alluding to Wilde's "decadent" artistic direction, but probably to his sexuality as well. Later, he told his friend and biographer Marie Seton, "My observations led me to the conclusion that homosexuality is in all ways a retrogression. . . . It's a dead-end. A lot of people say I'm a homosexual. I never have been, and I'd tell you if it were true. I've never felt any such desire . . . though I think I must in some way have a bi-sexual tendency—like Zola and Balzac—in an intellectual way." Eisenstein showed little interest in women; in the darkening days of the Stalin purges, when his own position was uncertain, he married his devoted assistant. They never lived together, however.

By the early 1930s, as Stalin consolidated his power, the relative tolerance of the postrevolutionary period vanished. In January 1934, there were mass arrests of gays—including many actors, musicians, and artists—in Moscow and Leningrad. Two months later, a law was introduced punishing sexual acts between consenting adult males with five years' hard labor. Homosexuality was strongly denounced in the government-controlled press. In an article published in 1934 in *Pravda* and *Isvestiia*, Maxim Gorky expounded the latest twist in the party line:

> One revolts at even mentioning the horrors [anti-Semitism and homosexuality] which fascism brings to such a rich flowering. In the fascist countries, homosexuality, which ruins youth, flourishes without punishment; in the country [the Soviet Union] where the proletariat has audaciously achieved social power, homosexuality has been declared a social crime and is heavily punished. There is already a slogan in Germany, "Eradicate the homosexual and fascism will disappear."

Under the new laws, homosexuality was a crime against the state, placed in the same category as counterrevolutionary activities, sabotage, and espionage. It was now viewed as a legacy of the prerevolutionary period, a manifestation of bourgeois decadence. The much-vaunted "new Soviet man" was to be exclusively heterosexual. In 1936, the People's Commissar of Justice, **Nikolai Krylenko,** declared that there was no reason for anyone to be homosexual after two decades of socialism. Those who persisted in remaining homosexual must be "either the dregs of society, or remnants of the exploiting classes" who didn't know what to do with themselves, so they took to homosexuality. He added, "There is another kind of work that goes on in little filthy dens and hiding places, and that is the work of counterrevolution. That is why we take these disorganizers of our new social system . . . we put these gentlemen on trial and we give them sentences of up to five years."

According to Robert Conquest, in his book *The Great Terror: A Reassessment,* by the mid-to-late 1930s, some 3,000 Moscow homosexuals were incarcerated in a labor camp on the Baltic–White Sea canal, to the northeast of St. Petersburg.

Stalin protected certain gay or homosexually inclined artists. When the American radical **Upton Sinclair** wrote Stalin to accuse Eisenstein of being a "sexual pervert" (the two were quarreling about Eisenstein's film *Que Viva Mexico!,* which Eisenstein was shooting in Mexico with Sinclair's financial backing), Stalin essentially stood by the film director. Although Eisenstein's standing fluctuated during the 1930s, the internationally venerated director was too useful to the Soviets to discard entirely.

As in Nazi Germany, persecution of homosexuals was part of conservative social and sexual policies. Legal abortion was abolished in the Soviet Union in 1936, two years after passage of the antigay law. **Pierre Herbart,** who accompanied André Gide on his disillusioning trip to Russia in 1935 and '36, captured the atmosphere of an increasingly moralistic and sexually repressive Soviet Union. In his diary, he noted that conversations in Moscow were all "edifying and moral in nature." He was:

> *So sick of virtue that I could throw up. I learned that boys no longer kiss girls without first having gone before the mayor; that homosexuals are mending their ways by reading Marx in concentration camps; that taxis must be lit up at night so as not to harbor sin; that the bedsheets of Red Army soldiers are inspected in order to shame those who masturbate; that children have no need for sex education because they never think about dirty things like that; that the fee for divorce is about to be raised,*

thereby putting it out of the reach of the poor; that it is unhealthy for people to enjoy themselves sexually without reproducing. This has all been proven by science, and everybody bows down in awe before its decrees.

The numbers of gays and lesbians who were imprisoned under the new antigay laws is unknown. And exactly why Stalin moved against homosexuals with such vehemence is not entirely clear, either. Sexual conservatism had clearly been implicit in the revolutionary movement from its inception. But as Stalin's Russia moved to gain total control over both the public and private lives of its citizens, repression of sexual nonconformity became a desired end. Whether fascist or Communist, totalitarian governments viewed homosexuality and the weakening of traditional family structures as a threat to absolute state power. So, to Soviet Communists, homosexuality became a symptom of fascism that couldn't (and certainly shouldn't) exist in a workers' state; when it did exist, it was a symptom of bourgeois decadence or a holdover from the *ancien regime*. This alignment between the international proletarian movement and repressive sexual policies was to have a profound effect on the Left in general and on Communist parties as far away as China and Cuba.

Diaghilev, Nijinsky, and the Ballets Russes

WHEN MARCEL PROUST saw the Ballets Russes production of *Scheherazade* in Paris in 1910, he told a friend, "I never saw anything so beautiful." When British writer Osbert Sitwell saw the company's *Firebird* in London a year later, he said, "Now I knew where I stood. I would be, for so long as I lived, on the side of the arts." The creator of the Ballets Russes, the impresario Sergei Diaghilev (1872–1929), was more blunt. Of one of his premieres, he said, "If the theatre were to burn down to-night, the best artistic brains and the most elegant women in Europe would perish."

Diaghilev's productions, with their dazzling sets, inventive choreography, and superb dancing, took London and Paris by storm in the first two decades of the century, making him one of the leading figures of twentieth-century modernism. He transformed his lover, the dancer Vaslav Nijinsky (1890–1950), into the most famous male ballet dancer in the world; he would do the same with another protégé (and lover), **Léonide Massine.** As Martin Green writes in his book *Children of the Sun,* "Cyril Connolly has spoken of the great homosexual trail-blazers in the arts in the early twentieth century who avenged on the bourgeoisie the latter's killing of Oscar Wilde. He . . . names as the avengers Diaghilev, Proust, Cocteau, and Gide. Diaghilev was the leader, or impresario of them all."

Diaghilev came to St. Petersburg from the provinces aspiring to a career as a composer. In 1893, he inherited his mother's money and began to buy paintings. In 1895, the year of Wilde's trials, he decided to become an impresario. In his trademark flamboyant style, he wrote his stepmother:

> *I am firstly a great charlatan, though* con brio; *secondly, a great* charmeur; *thirdly, I have any amount of cheek; fourthly, I am a man with a great quantity of logic, but with very few principles; fifthly, I think I have no real gifts. All the same, I think I have just found my true vocation—being a Maecenas [a Roman patron of the arts]. I have all that is necessary save the money—*mais ça viendra.

Five years earlier, he had found a lover—his cousin **Dima Filosofov.** The expansive, exuberant Diaghilev and the aristocratic, intellectual Filosofov were inseparable for the next fifteen years. Filosofov's friends strongly influenced the development of Diaghilev's artistic ideas. Their tastes—ranging from church icons to French Impressionist painters—ran counter to the cold formalism of Russian art of the early nineteenth century and the increasingly dominant school of Russian artists who insisted that all art had to have a political or social purpose.

In 1897 Diaghilev organized his first exhibition of paintings—a show of British and German watercolors. A year later he and Filosofov founded the influential journal *The World of Art.* In its first editorial Diaghilev signaled a revolt against didactic art. "The creator must love only beauty," he wrote. "He must commune with beauty, where his divine nature is manifest."

The early issues of *The World of Art* included the serialization of a travel account called "On the Shores of the Ionian Sea" by the poet **Zinadia Gippius**. One chapter described her visit to a male homosexual colony in the town of Taormina in Sicily, centering around the photographer of male nudes, the Baron **Wilhelm von Gloeden**. After her summer in Taormina, Gippius came to believe she was a man in a woman's body. She returned to St. Petersburg looking for her ideal counterpart—a woman in a man's body. She was convinced that she had found this in Diaghilev's lover, Dima Filosofov. Thus began a long struggle with Diaghilev over Filosofov, with Gippius promising a ménage à trois with her husband, the novelist and critic **Merezhkovski**, as a means of luring Filosofov away from Diaghilev. Finally, she achieved her goal, and Filosofov moved in with her and her husband in 1904, where he remained until 1919.

The defeated Diaghilev responded by ending publication of *The World of Art,* and also by looking westward. In 1906 he organized a Russian art exhibit for the Salon d'Automne in Paris; in 1907 he sponsored concerts that presented the singer Feodor Chaliapin to the West and popularized the music of Russian composers like Mussorgsky and Borodin; in 1908 he put on a production of Mussorgsky's opera *Boris Godunov.*

That same year, as he was planning the Russian ballet season in Paris, Diaghilev met Nijinsky, a promising but relatively unknown dancer at the Imperial Ballet. Nijinsky was being "kept" by a wealthy artistocrat named **Prince Pavel Lvov**. Diaghilev and Nijinsky began a five-year relationship that "exemplified the finest features of the ancient Greek love between a teacher and his disciple," according to Simon Karlinsky. Nijinsky became his principal male dancer, and later, his choreographer. Together, they collaborated on productions of Stravinsky's *The Firebird* (1910), *Petrouchka* (1911), and *The Rite of Spring* (1913), Debussy's *Prelude to the Afternoon of a Faun* (1912) and Ravel's *Daphnis and Chloe* (1912), among others.

On a ship bound for South America, where the Ballets Russes was to perform, Nijinsky met and suddenly proposed marriage to a fellow passenger, a young Hungarian woman named **Romola**. Diaghilev dismissed him from the company. He returned to dance for Diaghilev two years later, even though by then Diaghilev had a new principal male dancer and lover—Léonide Massine. Romola Nijinsky had become her husband's manager, however, and immediately came into conflict with Diaghilev: She demanded back pay that she said Diaghilev owed Nijinsky and would threaten to call off performances unless her husband's pay was raised. These problems were exacerbated by the presence of two religious fanatics who were constantly telling Nijinsky that his relationship with Diaghilev had been a crime against God. Caught in the crossfire, Nijinsky soon went mad.

For many years, the widely held view was that Diaghilev had some kind of sinister hold on Nijinsky. Karlinsky says this impression owes its origins to Nijinsky's mad diaries and to the vindictive

Vaslav Nijinsky, dancing in the Ballets Russes production of Debussy's *Afternoon of a Faun*, 1912. (© *The Bettmann Archive*)

writings of Romola Nijinsky; he blames it on "a combination of homophobia and a popular taste for melodrama." He notes:

> *Instead of the reality of a brilliant man shaping and developing his lover's genius for the sake of the art they both loved, people find it more satisfactory to believe the version reflected, for example, in the famous 1940s film* The Red Shoes, *where the Nijinsky figure was changed into a woman (played by Moira Shearer) and the character based on Diaghilev was played as an irrationally possessive tyrant.*

Diaghilev's pattern of losing his male lovers to women continued when Léonide Massine ran off with a female English dancer after seven years with him. Only during the last decade of his life, when he was in his fifties, did Diaghilev have relationships with young men—all of them dancers or in the arts—that "did not end in loss," according to Karlinsky.

Writing in 1935 (and taking on the subject of homosexuality with great trepidation), Diaghilev biographer Arnold Haskell described Diaghilev's relationships this way:

> *It is absurd, in fact, to think of a man like Diaghileff as being blindly controlled by sex. Those who attracted him were almost without exception first-class material for the purposes of a creative artist. He may have loved them, but he selected them primarily for their mental gifts, formed them, developed them, gave them creative opportunities. . . .*
>
> *His love for the virile normal man doomed him to constant unhappiness and disappointment. It was obvious that as soon as his loved one had fully developed, he would leave Diaghileff for the first attractive woman who crossed his path. . . . Always he was saddened, surprised—and felt himself betrayed. In all these unions the mental aspect predominated. Later in his life his friendships were more paternal in spirit than anything else.*
>
> *The search for the true permanent companion was perhaps the personal tragedy of Diaghileff's life.*

Despite the unhappy conclusions to these relationships, Diaghilev's collaborations with his lovers—with Dima Filosofov on *The World of Art,* with Nijinsky and Massine—created a new movement in the world of art and dance. At the same time, he was mentor to other artistic greats. As Diaghilev's ballet master for the last period of his life, **George Balanchine**, put it, "It is because of Diaghilev that I am whatever I am." The same can be said of twentieth-century ballet.

Love Between Women in the Gulag— An Excerpt from Vasily Grossman's *Forever Flowing*

*Throughout most of the Soviet period, the subject of homosexuality was taboo in Russian literature. One of the few writers who even alluded to it was **Vasily Grossman** (1905–64), a journalist and novelist best known for his sprawling novel* Life and Fate. *In his final work,* Forever Flowing—*begun in 1955 and published in the West (but not in the Soviet Union) in 1970—the author tells the story of a Soviet political prisoner who returns home after thirty years in a labor camp. In one of the novel's flashbacks, Grossman describes a labor camp for women, where lesbian relationships are commonplace. Grossman's depiction is extremely negative, indicative of the antigay attitudes of Soviet culture. Yet, the fact that he portrays lesbianism at all is a breakthrough of sorts, and* Forever Flowing *provides some documentation of love between women in the darkest of human circumstances:*

THERE WERE SPECIAL hard-labor camps for women in which for long years no man's voice had been heard. And if it happened that some male lathe operator, truck driver, or carpenter was sent into these camps on special assignment, he might be torn apart, unimaginably tormented, killed by the women. . . . [The men criminals] were afraid to go there even with a special armed guard.

Dark, somber, grim misfortune twisted people at hard labor, transformed them into nonhumans.

In the hard-labor camps for women some women forced other women into perverted cohabitation. In the hard-labor camps for women absurd types emerged—women stud dogs, bull dykes— with deep, husky voices, a long male stride, and male gestures, dressed in britches and in soldiers' jackboots. And alongside them were those lost and pitiful beings—their "females."

The "stud dogs" drank superstrong concoctions of tea, like the men criminals, using it to get stoned; they smoked *makhorka*, and when they were drunk they beat up their cheating, light-minded girlfriends; but they also guarded them with their fists and their knives, protecting them from the insult and injury of others, and from crude passes by other women. These tragic and ugly relationships were what love turned into in hard-labor camps. It was monstrous. It provoked neither laughter nor dirty talk, but sheer horror even in the hearts of the thieves and the murderers.

CHAPTER 15

THE NAZI PERSECUTION
OF HOMOSEXUALS

O N MAY 6, 1933, three months after Hitler became chancellor of Germany, several trucks pulled up in front of Magnus Hirschfeld's Institute for Sexual Science in Berlin. A hundred students emerged, smashed down the doors of the institute, and marched into the building to the strains of a brass band. They ransacked the premises, emptying bottles of ink over manuscripts and carpets and removing books from the institute's library. In the afternoon, truckloads of storm troopers arrived to mop up the operation. A few days later, the seized books and papers—and a bust of Hirschfeld—were set aflame in front of the Opera House in Berlin before a large crowd. Hirschfeld was out of the country at the time (he had never returned to Germany after a worldwide lecture tour), and witnessed the destruction of his institute on a newsreel at a Paris cinema. Soon after, the German government deprived him of his citizenship. He died on his sixty-seventh birthday, May 15, 1935, in Nice, on the French Riviera, where he was planning to reopen the institute.

The attack on Hirschfeld's institute—while in part an act of anti-Semitism—was the first shot of the Nazi war against homosexuals. Before and during World War II, some forty thousand to sixty thousand gay men were sentenced under antigay laws; although no one knows the exact figure, thousands were incarcerated in concentration camps, where they were forced to wear a pink triangle. Nazi persecution of gays intensified throughout the 1930s, but even before Hitler took power, there had been warning signals. The destruction of Hirschfeld's institute had been preceded by accusations that it was "the international center of the white-slave trade" and "an unparalleled breeding ground of dirt and filth." In 1930, **Wilhelm Frick,** a Nazi member of the Reichstag and later Hitler's Minister of the Interior, introduced a bill calling for the castration of homosexuals, "that Jewish pestilence." Nazi newspapers advocated the death penalty for homosexual acts.

Nonetheless, many German gays, like German Jews, thought Nazi policies would moderate once they took power. Some were even infatuated with the Nazi cult of masculinity. The Nazi Party "teemed" with homosexuals, wrote gay activist Adolf Brand in a 1931 essay. What gay Nazi sympathizers failed to realize, he added, was that they were "already carrying the hangman's rope in their pockets."

Hatred of homosexuals was both the result of Nazi Party ideology and the personal obsessions of its leaders, particularly **Heinrich Himmler** (1900–45), main architect of the persecution of homosexuals. To Himmler and other Nazi ideologues, homosexuals, like Jews, were incarnations of moral degeneracy. Jews and homosexuals were viewed as "outsiders," inferiors, infecting the nation, threatening the purity of the *Volk*. As George L. Mosse points out in his book *Nationalism and Sexuality*, nationalist and Nazi typologies portrayed Jews and homosexuals in much the same way: They were aggressive, lecherous, unable to control their passions, selfish, and restless. Jews and homosexuals were accused of using their sexuality as a weapon against society: Jews supposedly pursued Christian women, while male homosexuals preyed on young Aryan men. And just as the Nazis believed in a worldwide Jewish conspiracy, they believed in a universal homosexual conspiracy as well. "Both Jews and homosexuals were regarded by their enemies as a 'state within a state,' " notes Mosse. Given these conceptualizations, it was not unsurprising that Magnus Hirschfeld's institute was near the top of the Nazi "hit list."

Yet the Nazis' supreme "warrior" and Hitler's second-in-command, **Ernst Roehm** (1887–1934), was gay and too stubborn and arrogant to hide the fact. His downfall, in the early days of the Reich, sealed the fate of homosexuals under Hitler. Defying the stereotypes propagated by his own party, Roehm was the "swashbuckling mercenary, father and drillmaster to his troops, straightforward and tactless," as Richard Plant describes him in his book *The Pink Triangle*. The son of Bavarian civil servants, Roehm was wounded during World War I and drifted into nationalist politics in the atmosphere of humiliation and recrimination following Germany's defeat. He became Hitler's greatest friend and confidant within the Nazi hierarchy—the only one the Führer addressed with the familiar "du." He was the head of the brownshirted storm troopers of the SA, a Nazi paramilitary organization that was essentially a gang of rootless ex-soldiers and assorted hooligans who

Ernst Roehm (far right) photographed with three other officers after the commutation of their sentences for participation in the abortive 1924 Munich "Beer Hall putsch." *(© UPI/Bettmann)*

spent their time terrorizing Jews and Nazi opponents. The SA's bullying tactics played a major role in paving Hitler's path to power. Roehm was known for his sexual indiscretions, for which he never apologized. "Nobody can call me a puritan . . ." he wrote. "A so-called 'immoral' man who does something competently means more to me than a so-called 'morally' clean person who is inefficient."

Hitler was willing to ignore Roehm's homosexual activities because of his organizational success in building the SA. But in 1925, the two men quarreled, and Hitler sent Roehm into exile in Bolivia, where he worked training the Bolivian army. When a mutiny broke out within the SA in 1929, Hitler ordered him home to take charge. Later when there were complaints about his sexual behavior, Hitler defended Roehm. "[The SA] is not an institute for the moral education of genteel young ladies, but a formation of seasoned fighters . . ." he insisted. "His [the SA officer's] private life cannot be an object of scrutiny unless it conflicts with the basic principles of National Socialist ideology."

In 1932, a year before the Nazis took power, some compromising letters of Roehm's were leaked to the press, providing ammunition for his enemies. Once Hitler became chancellor, he had less need of Roehm and less reason to ignore the provocation his homosexuality represented. Moreover, Roehm was a Nazi "radical" who wanted to replace the regular German army with the SA at a time when Hitler was attempting to woo industrialists and aristocrats. It became increasingly obvious that Roehm was a liability.

On June 28, 1934, the "Night of the Long Knives," the SA's rival, Himmler's SS, stormed the Pension Hanselbauer on Lake Wiessee, near Munich, where Roehm and other leaders of the Brownshirts were staying. It was part of a nationwide purge in which some three hundred people were killed. Roehm was among those arrested. Three days later, an SS officer entered his prison cell, handed him a revolver, and said, "I'll be back in fifteen minutes." Roehm reportedly replied, "Let Adolf do it himself. I'm not going to do this job." Later that day, Roehm was executed.

In *The Pink Triangle,* Plant contends that Roehm's homosexuality was essentially a "sideshow," that the major factor in Roehm's downfall was his radicalism, his insistence on replacing the regular army with the SA. If Roehm had lived, would the fate of gays in Germany have been any different? One can only speculate. But it was no coincidence that Hitler's decision to expand the provisions of Paragraph 175, the antigay law, took place exactly one year after the Roehm purge. As Plant notes, "Roehm had provided as easy a target for his enemies as had Magnus Hirschfeld. He had no respect for his superiors; he was blunt and tactless when voicing his opinions; and he rarely bothered to hide his interest in muscular young men. He was the most visible homosexual in German politics, he was a Nazi, and he was doomed."

The destruction of Roehm and the SA made Heinrich Himmler, head of the SS, the second most important man in Germany. Like other nationalists of the time, Himmler was obsessed with reproduction and with the furtherance of the German *Volk.* In a speech to SS lieutenant generals in 1937, he warned that the prevalence of homosexuality put the nation's reproductive future in jeopardy.

Homosexual clubs in Germany had two million registered members, he claimed; "experts" working on the question believed there were between two and four million male homosexuals in the country. In addition, two million German men had been killed in World War I, unbalancing the ratio between the sexes. "Our *Volk* is being destroyed by this epidemic," he said. "The *Volk* that has many children has the qualifications for world power and world mastery. A racially good *Volk* that has very few children has a certain ticket to the grave." He went on:

> We must be clear about it, if we continue to bear this burden [homosexuality] in Germany without being able to fight it, then it is the end of Germany, the end of the Germanic world. Unfortunately it is not so simple for us as for our ancestors. With them these few individual cases were of such an abnormal kind. Homosexuals, who were called Urning, were sunk in a bog. Herr Professors who find these bodies in the swamps are certainly not aware that in ninety cases out of a hundred they have a homosexual before them, who with his clothes and all was plunged in the bog. That was not a punishment, simply the extinguishing of an abnormal life . . .

Drowning people in bogs was not a feasible punishment in twentieth-century Germany, he said. But within the SS, cases of homosexuality could be taken care of easily:

> These people will obviously be publicly degraded and dismissed and handed over to the court. After the expiration of their court sentence they will by my regulations be taken into a concentration camp and in the camp they will be shot while escaping.

Himmler wished to create a *Mannerstaadt*—a state "dedicated to the worship of masculinity and to the community of men as a ruling elite," in historian Mosse's words. In a society based on strength and power, homosexuals, particularly in their guise as third sex, had no role to play.

It is less clear what Hitler himself thought about homosexuality. His concerns seem to have been primarily political: He feared homosexuals would infiltrate the political leadership and establish a kind of state-within-a-state. **Rudolf Diels,** first head of the Gestapo, recalls a conversation in which Hitler expressed the worry that homo-

sexuals in high positions would appoint subordinates simply because they were gay. According to Diels, Hitler offered an analogy:
"Look, if I have the choice between a lovely but incompetent girl
as a secretary and one who is capable but hideous, I decide all too
easily in favor of the lovely incompetent." So with homosexuals:
If they were to acquire power and influence, the Nazi state could
find itself in the hands of "these creatures and their lovers."

Whatever Hitler's personal views, the Nazis were quick to move
against homosexuals. Less than a month after Hitler took power,
a directive was issued outlawing all gay rights organizations. Kurt
Hiller, whom Hirschfeld installed as the head of his Scientific Humanitarian Committee, was sent to the concentration camp at Or-
anienburg; inexplicably, he was discharged nine months later. By
the summer of 1933, Roehm's Brownshirts were raiding gay bars
throughout the country; many were closed, although some remained
open for two more years before they were banned outright. In 1934,
the Gestapo sent a letter to police headquarters throughout Germany instructing the police to mail in lists of all "somehow homosexually active persons." (The Berlin police had a list of about thirty
thousand, which it had been accumulating for many years.) In May
1935, *Das Schwarze Korps,* the newspaper of the SS, demanded
the death penalty for gay men.

Meanwhile, the legal vise began to tighten. On June 28, 1935,
a year to the day after the Roehm purge, the language of Paragraph
175 was extended to include virtually any physical contact between
men. As a result, according to official Gestapo statistics, convictions
for violating Paragraph 175 increased dramatically, up from 853 in
1933 to 2,106 in 1935 to 8,562 in 1938. In 1936, the Federal
Security Department for Combating Abortion and Homosexuality
was established in the Berlin Gestapo headquarters. New directives
opened the way to the incarceration of large numbers of homosexuals in concentration camps. A 1938 injunction stated that a man
convicted of gross indecency with another man could be transferred
directly to a camp. A 1940 directive went further, declaring that a
man arrested for homosexual activities who had seduced more than
one partner *must* be transferred to a camp after serving his prison
sentence.

Allegations of homosexuality that had proved so useful against
Roehm were turned against the remaining institutional powers
threatening Nazi dominance. In an effort to weaken the Catholic
Church, a propaganda campaign accused priests and monks of

homosexuality. Such accusations reached their height in 1937 when **Joseph Goebbels,** Minister of Propaganda, delivered a nationwide radio speech charging that "the sacristy has become a bordello, while the monasteries are breeding places of vile homosexuality." Between 1934 and 1937, widely publicized show trials of churchmen took place, although there were only a handful of convictions. In 1938, as Plant notes, accusations of homosexuality brought down the Baron **Werner von Fritsch,** commander in chief of the armed forces. Fritsch had been critical of Hitler's plans for a general European war, on the grounds of military unpreparedness. By accusing him of homosexuality, Hitler was trying to demoralize the military leadership and prevent it from functioning as an independent force.

Even as the antigay campaign intensified, there were some exceptions to the rules. During the 1936 Berlin Olympic Games, some gay bars were permitted to reopen, and police were told not to harass visting foreign homosexuals. This respite was short-lived, however. Some gay artists and performers were protected, most notably the actor **Gustav Gründgens,** who became the director of the State Theatre. In exchange for this protection, Gründgens was required to marry the actress **Marianne Hoppe.** Berliners claimed that above their marital bed hung the epitaph on the Spartans at Thermopylae, "Here obedient to their laws we lie." (Gründgens was the model for the main character of **Klaus Mann's** satiric novel *Mephisto.*) In other cases, the reasons for exemption from persecution were less clear. For example, gay activist and editor Adolf Brand was never bothered; Brand, who was married, died in the Allied bombing of Berlin at the end of the war.

Lesbians, by and large, managed to avoid persecution. Paragraph 175 was never extended to women, and while a few lesbians did suffer in Nazi death camps, there was no systematic attempt to target them. "Most lesbians managed to survive unscathed," says Plant. "Fortunately, they fell outside the universe of Himmler's sexual obsessions." In the Nazi *Mannerstaadt,* women were simply not seen as a threat.

If there was an effort to make Germany free of homosexuals, the situation in countries occupied by Germany during World War II was more complicated. Himmler believed that homosexuality weakened the vigor of conquered peoples, so as Plant points out, in certain occupied countries, same-sex relations, if not exactly encouraged, were not penalized by law. Under Hitler's grand scheme, however, Holland was to become part of the greater Reich. As a result, Paragraph 175 was extended to the Netherlands, where there had been no antigay laws since 1811. The Dutch Scientific Humanitarian Committee (NWHK), in existence since 1911, was shut down. Although the Nazis did make a systematic attempt to persecute Dutch gay men, they had little success. The Dutch gay subculture—unlike that of Berlin during the Weimar Republic—had remained largely underground, making it less susceptible to persecution. In addition, Dutch police were generally unwilling to round up gays, and registration lists of homosexuals were apparently never handed over to the Germans.

Poland, on the other hand, was not destined to become part of the greater Reich: Its inhabitants were viewed as genetically inferior to the Germans. But the Nazis feared that the Poles, because of their proximity, might spread "degeneracy" to the Germans through seduction, and for that reason, Polish homosexuals were persecuted as well. (Poland had decriminalized homosexual acts in 1932.) In Italy, where Mussolini's sexual views were not as rigid as Hitler's, homosexuals, while subject to occasional harassment, never experienced the widespread persecution that gays in Germany and German-occupied countries did. Homosexual acts were not against the law in Italy, even during the fascist period.

In occupied Paris, gay artists were generally spared (as long as they weren't Jewish). After the 1940 armistice, the pro-Nazi Vichy government accused elements of prewar French society of a decadence that had caused the Nazi victory. Gay novelist, playwright, and film director Jean Cocteau was among those who came under attack. "Believe it or not, those worthies have decided that Gide and I are to blame for everything," Cocteau wrote to a friend. When two of Cocteau's plays were performed in occupied Paris, stink bombs were set off in the theater, and hooligans climbed onto the stage shouting obscenities against Cocteau and his lover, actor **Jean Marais,** as a couple. But Cocteau never replied to these attacks, which is one reason he may have been left alone. (Another reason may have been that he was "dangerously naive politically and flirted disgustingly with the Germans," according to Edmund White.)

Although fewer gays found their way into Nazi concentration camps than did other groups, those who wore the pink triangle had a particularly horrific time. Unlike in the case of the Jews, the Nazis' professed aim was not the extermination of homosexuals but their "reeducation." Nonetheless, death rates were high, especially compared to other groups that were also incarcerated for purposes of "reeducation." Fifty-three percent of homosexual prisoners died, as opposed to 40 percent among political prisoners and 34.7 percent among Jehovah's Witnesses. Richard Plant estimates that five to fifteen thousand gays perished in the camps, although the number may be significantly higher.

Homosexual men were "the lowest, most expendable group," writes Plant. They were often given the worst jobs, were usually rejected by other concentration camp inmates, and were denied the protection that capos (camp middlemen who headed work brigades) provided other prisoners. They had little contact with the outside world: Very few families were willing to stand by them, and friends on the outside were fearful that "guilt by association" might land them in a camp as well. Unlike other groups, any sense of solidarity among homosexual inmates was rare. As Raimund Schnabel wrote in his study of Dachau, "Among the homosexuals were exceptional people whose deviance could be called tragic; on the other hand [there were] also cheap hustlers and blackmailers. The prisoners with the pink triangle never lived long. They were exterminated by the SS quickly and systematically."

In March 1939, a year after the Nazis marched into Austria, a twenty-two-year-old Viennese student was arrested by the Nazis as a "degenerate." He had been having a relationship with a German medical student whose father was a high Nazi official. After six months in prison, he was transferred to the Sachsenhausen concentration camp, near Berlin. The anonymous student told his story to the German writer Heinz Heger, whose book, *The Men with the Pink Triangle,* provides one of the few personal accounts of the experiences of gay prisoners in Nazi concentration camps.

Although he had been treated relatively well while in prison in Austria, humiliation began immediately after the student and other new inmates arrived on the large, open parade-ground at Sachsenhausen in January 1940:

When my name was called I stepped forward, gave my name, and mentioned paragraph 175. With the words, "You filthy queer, get over here, you bum-fucker," I received several kicks from behind and was kicked over to an SS sergeant who had charge of my block.

The first thing I got from him was a violent blow on my face that threw me to the ground . . . he brought his knee up hard into my groin so I doubled up with pain . . . he grinned at me and said: "That was your entrance fee, you filthy Viennese swine . . ."

At Sachsenhausen the men who wore the pink triangle were segregated in a "queer block." The student's dormitory contained 180 prisoners or more—unskilled workers and shop assistants, skilled tradesmen and craftsmen, musicians and artists, professors and clergy, even aristocratic landowners. Homosexual prisoners were not allowed any positions of responsibility. They were forbidden to speak with prisoners from other blocks; the reason, supposedly, was concern that the Pink Triangles might try and seduce others, even though, according to the student, homosexuality was more rife in other blocks than in their own.

At night, the gay prisoners were required to sleep only in their nightshirts and had to keep their hands outside their blankets to prevent them from masturbating. "The windows had a centimeter of ice on them," the student told Heger. "Anyone found with his underclothes on in bed, or his hands under the blanket—there were several checks almost every night—was taken outside and had several bowls of water poured over him before being left standing outside for a good hour. Only a few people survived this treatment. The least result was bronchitis, and it was rare for any gay person taken into the sick-bay to come out alive."

Gays were frequently assigned to harsh special labor details in the quarries of Sachsenhausen, Buchenwald, Mathausen, and other camps; at the cement works at Sachsenhausen; and in the underground factories near Buchenwald that produced the V-2 rockets. **Rudolf Hess,** commandant at Sachsenhausen before he moved on to the same position at Auschwitz, apparently believed that hard work would turn gay men into heterosexuals; in fact, it killed most of them.

The student describes work in the clay pits of the brick works at Sachsenhausen as a factory for human destruction, until 1942 the "Auschwitz for homosexuals." No matter what the weather, inmates were forced to push a certain number of cars filled with clay from the pits uphill to the brick-making machines and their ovens. Since the clay pit was extremely deep, the path on which these carts had to be hand-pushed (on rails) was long and steep, which made it especially difficult for half-starved prisoners. Generally, five or six prisoners loaded the carts using shovels, while other groups of about the same number pushed the full carts uphill. In the process, capos and the SS would hit them repeatedly with sticks, ostensibly to hurry them up. Often carts slipped back violently on the prisoners who were pushing them. Many prisoners, the student recalled, were "already so numbed and indifferent that they didn't even bother to jump out of the way when a full cart came roaring towards them. Then human bodies would fly through the air, and limbs be crushed to a pulp, while the remaining prisoners only received more blows with the stick."

Another Sachsenhausen survivor, L. D. von Classen-Neudegg describes how a detail at the cement works turned out to be a death sentence for a group of three hundred of the camp's homosexuals. As he describes it:

> We learned that we were to be segregated in a penal command and the next morning would be transferred as a unit to the cement works. . . . We shuddered because these bone mills were more dreaded than any other work detail. . . . Guarded by staff sergeants with machine guns, we had to sprint in lines of five until we arrived. . . . They kept beating us with rifle butts and bullwhips. . . . Forced to drag along twenty corpses, the rest of us encrusted with blood, we entered the cement quarry. . . .

But that was only the beginning.

> Within two months, the special operation had lost two-thirds. . . . To shoot someone "trying to escape" was a profitable business for the guards. For everyone killed, they received five marks and three days' special furlough. . . . Whips were used more frequently each morning, when we were forced into the pits. . . . "Only fifty are still alive," whispered the man next to me. . . . When I weighed not much more than eighty-five pounds, one of the sergeants told me one morning. "Well, that's it. You want to go to the other side? It won't hurt. I'm a crack shot."

Inmates died for other reasons as well. As Sachsenhausen commandant Hess noted in his diaries, "Should one of these [Pink

Triangles] lose his 'friend' through sickness, or perhaps death, then the end could at once be foreseen. Many would commit suicide. To such natures, in such circumstances, the 'friend' meant everything. There were many instances of 'friends' committing suicide together."

It did help, however, if the "friend" was a capo, a work brigade leader. As a young and attractive man, the Viennese student became the lover of several capos, which afforded him some protection. All of these capos were "greens," which meant they were incarcerated for criminal activities, not as homosexuals. The student remembers that when he and four other Pink Triangles were transferred from Sachsenhausen to the Flossenbürg camp, in Bavaria, near the Czech border, the arriving group was scrutinized by capos as if the scene were "a slave-boy market in ancient Rome." He became the lover of a safecracker from Hamburg who saved his life "more than ten times over" and to whom he became quite attached. Although he still had to work at a granite quarry, his capo-lover was able to get him additional rations and slightly easier work. Later, when his "protector" was transferred to a different block, another capo, a Hungarian gypsy, paid off two capos to obtain him as a lover. The student relates:

> My will to survive the concentration camp was uncommonly strong, but any such survival against the brutes of the SS had a high price, the price of morality, decency, and honour. I knew this and suffered on account of it, yet without such friendships with Capos I should not be alive today. C'est la vie! Sarcastically, I turned my gypsy friend's motto "Live and let live" into my own motto "Live and let love."

The student later became a capo and foreman himself, the only Pink Triangle at Flossenbürg to achieve such a position. When an aircraft factory was established at the camp, making wings and tails for Messerschmitt planes, he was put in charge of inventory and part supplies, supervising twenty-five men.

The student's experience notwithstanding, Rüdiger Lautmann, a professor at the University of Bremen who has done a statistical study of the fate of Pink Triangles in the camps, strongly disputes the assertion that younger homosexual men enjoyed special protection as sexual partners of capos. He notes that the death rate for those under twenty wearing the pink triangle was 70 percent, one of the highest rates in any age category. The lowest death rate (30 percent) was in the twenty-six-to-thirty-year-old category. This group, he said, "manoeuvres especially cleverly in the camp ghetto. It has long grown out of the 'fancy boy age.' " Lautmann continues, "The claim that homosexuals were able to save their lives by offering pederastic services proves to be a superficial implication."

As the War progressed, the Nazis tried tactics other than simply working homosexuals to death. In one bizarre incident, the authorities established a brothel at the Flossenbürg camp, in part to "cure" homosexual inmates by compulsory visits. (The prostitutes were all Jewish and Gypsy prisoners from a nearby woman's camp.) Camp officials drilled holes in the brothel rooms so they could witness the "progress" of the homosexual inmates. Any Pink Triangle prisoners considered "cured" by their consistent "good conduct" in the brothel were supposed to be sent to become part of the Dirlewanger division—made up exclusively of prisoners—that fought against Russian partisans on the Eastern front. The Viennese student reports that he himself went three times to the brothel, then put his name down once a week and sent another prisoner in his stead.

Toward the end of 1943, a new directive from Himmler stated that homosexuals who consented to castration—and whose conduct was good—could be released from a camp. Some Pink Triangles did avail themselves of the opportunity, only to be sent to fight in the Dirlewanger penal division, virtually a death sentence in itself. Known for its brutality toward both Russian partisans and its own soldiers, the Dirlewanger brigade took heavy casualties.

Homosexual men were also subjects of medical experiments. At Buchenwald, the Danish endocrinologist **Carl Vaernet** castrated a group of homosexual inmates and injected them with large doses of male hormones. The aim of the experiment was to see whether they began to show signs of interest in the opposite sex. Although records are spotty, apparently eighteen gay men were forced to participate in this scheme. The results remain unknown, and the experiment was halted when an epidemic of yellow fever spread through the camp, a result of yet another experiment (with yellow fever microorganisms) run amuck.

When the War ended and gays were released from the camps, the survivors found themselves in a world where antigay hostility was still strong. Paragraph 175—the same law that had sent them to the camps in the first place—remained on the books until 1967 in East Germany and 1969 in West Germany. (Male homosexual relations in Austria were not legalized until 1971.) Richard Plant writes that some American and British jurists of the liberation armies ruled that a camp did not technically constitute a prison. So if someone had been sentenced to, say, eight years in prison for violating Paragraph 175, after having spent five years in jail and three in a camp, the inmate still had to finish his three years. It is not known how many people, if any, were reincarcerated for this reason. There is no doubt, however, that men who were put in camps for being homosexual were not able to take advantage of the financial restitution that the West German government offered to Jews, political prisoners, and other groups that had survived the camps.

Many gay survivors did not have the option of returning to loving families and supportive environments after the camp experience. Few traces remained of the vibrant gay culture of pre-Hitler Germany. The Viennese student returned to live with his mother in Vienna (his father had committed suicide during the War, in part because of the stigma of having a son imprisoned in a concentration camp for homosexuality). But he notes that in the early days of his homecoming, the neighbors made "a bit of a fuss" about having a "queer" concentration camp returnee in their midst. Once they realized that he led a quiet life and was never involved in any scandal, they let him alone. Given the hostility that survivors faced upon returning home and the contempt in which homosexuality continued to be held in most of Western Europe, researchers have had a difficult time locating gay survivors, especially those who would talk openly about their experiences. As Plant notes, "Although they were no longer compelled to wear the stigmatic pink triangle, they felt marked for life."

An Excerpt from Heinz Heger's
The Men with the Pink Triangle

A twenty-two-year-old Viennese student was incarcerated in the Nazi concentration camps of Sachsenhausen and Flossenbürg for his homosexuality, and remained there throughout World War II. His memoir, The Men with the Pink Triangle, *told to the German writer Heinz Heger, is one of the few personal accounts of the Nazi persecution of homosexual men:*

AT THE END of February 1941, I saw one day from the window of my office [in the building division stores office at Flossenbürg concentration camp] a police wagon drive through the camp gate and come to a halt just outside the individual cells in the bunker. These individual cells were used as arrest cells for special punishment. An *SS-Obersturmbannführer* in full uniform stepped out, dripping with silver ribbons and decorations, together with an elegant young lady in shimmering evening dress, and revealing a snow-white shoulder. She was very made-up and wore silver shoes with high heels.

At first I thought that the SS officer and his lady had had a breakdown, and had continued here with the police wagon for their inspection of the camp. But when they were both locked into individual cells in the bunker building, and the police wagon drove off again, I was eager to find out more. In the evening I immediately told my Capo friend of these strange new arrivals, and he showed great interest, particularly in the lady's jewelry. . . .

The same evening I learned from my friend, who had already found out everything about the couple, that they had been arrested in a box at the Hamburg opera, following a denunciation, and immediately brought to Flossenbürg.

The *SS-Obersturmbannführer* was an officer at the front, with many decorations, including the Knight's Cross, which I hadn't been able to see when he was brought in. His lady turned out to be a young man of 19, a soldier in the *Waffen-SS* and home on leave in

Hamburg. He was the son of one of the biggest and richest night club magnates on the Reeperbahn [the entertainment district of Hamburg].

They remained in their separate cells until the camp was liberated in April 1945, and were never allowed out the whole day long. Later I discovered that each of them was allowed out for an hour at night, separately of course, to breathe fresh air and stretch their legs. They were kept in those cells, without trial, at the express command of *SS-Reichsführer* Heinrich Himmler, cut off from the whole world, even the world of the concentration camp, for the SS didn't want such a prominent officer from the front to mix with the other prisoners and have to wear a badge. Let alone the most despised badge of all, the pink triangle of the homosexuals. They were ashamed, and certainly put out, that such a distinguished officer could be a homosexual, and offend in such a frontal way against the purity of the master race. And so they sought to keep the whole affair hushed up in their own ranks, and brush it away in the individual cells of a concentration camp. The "lady's" face was seldom seen, and that only at night. If he was allowed to go on living, and was not immediately liquidated, as the SS leadership would certainly have preferred, so as to remove any witness of this "scandal," the young man owed this to his father's influence with high-ups in the Nazi party, which certainly cost him a great deal of money.

I also learned from my Capo friend that the young man was very pretty, even for a girl, yet also had a good business sense. The gypsy Capo must have known, for he made deals with this Hamburg businessman's son via the prisoners employed on domestic work in the bunker. In return for his jewelry, which was really valuable, and which he immediately broke up into its components, diamonds, pearls and gold rings, he received substantial extra provisions, which were delivered to both him and the SS officer. I found that quite decent of the young man.

Thanks to this trade, these two prominent gays never had to suffer any real hunger, also because the young man's father immediately sent him a good deal of money. Yet they were not spared the pain of solitary confinement. When the camp was dissolved in 1945, the SS leadership wanted to have them shot, but in the general chaos they managed to escape in time in civilian clothes . . .

CHAPTER 16

THE UNITED STATES IN
WORLD WAR II

W AR CAN BRING FORWARD homosexual feelings and passions, often without naming them—witness Walt Whitman and the Civil War or Siegfried Sassoon's experiences in the trenches of the Western Front. In the aftermath of the entry of the United States into World War II in December 1941, the weak sense of American gay and lesbian identity was significantly strengthened. The mobilization of millions of people turned American society upside down, bringing young men and women from farms and small towns into sex-segregated environments, to port cities like New York and San Francisco, away from the structures provided by family, church, and hometown. This occurred at a historical point when the "medicalization" of homosexuality and the spread of the ideas of psychology had increased awareness of the subject. As a result, the War created "a substantially new 'erotic situation' conducive both to the articulation of homosexual identity and to the more rapid evolution of a gay subculture," contends historian John D'Emilio. "World War II created something of a nationwide coming out experience." Ironically, this articulation of homosexual identity—so different from previous wars—was in part the result of the military's own policies.

World War II marked the first time the U.S. military asked recruits the question "Are you homosexual?" Prior to the War, the U.S. Armed Forces had had no official policy of excluding homosexuals. Regulations had simply labeled the act of sodomy as criminal, and military personnel convicted of the offense could be sent to prison, often for years. But at an induction physical no one was asked about his sexual orientation. If homosexuals were rejected for service in World War I, it was because of physiological disorders, past prison sentences, or insane asylum records having labeled them "sex perverts." But in World War II, reflecting the growing prestige of psychiatry, the military adopted new screening procedures to weed out

(© Schlesinger Library, Radcliffe College)

gay men and lesbians. The armed forces introduced into its policies and procedures "the concept of the homosexual as a personality type unfit for military service and combat," according to Allan Berube, whose book, *Coming Out Under Fire,* remains the definitive work on the subject.

Suddenly those who were attracted to members of the same sex had an identity, at least in the eyes of the military. As personality types went, theirs was not the most desirable one to be: Throughout the War, the U.S. Armed Forces labeled homosexual men and women as "sexual psychopaths," Berube notes. The way in which the military identified such sexual psychopaths was rather limited and archaic, even by 1940s standards: Male homosexuals were to be singled out because of "feminine bodily characteristics, effeminacy in dress or manner or a 'patulous' [expanded] rectum." Most gay men couldn't be identified under these guidelines, which might explain why only four thousand to five thousand were excluded from entering military service during the entire war. Often, manpower needs took precedence over any too strenuous investigation into a potential recruit's sexual orientation. **Merle Miller,** a gay man who was editor of the University of Iowa daily newspaper (and later the biographer of **Harry Truman** and **Lyndon Johnson**), tells of his visit to his local draft board:

I was afraid I would never get into the army, but after the psychiatrist tapped me on the knee with a little hammer and asked how I felt about girls, before I really had a chance to answer, he said, "Next," and I was being sworn in. For the next four years as an editor of Yank, *first in the Pacific and then in Europe, I continued to use my deepest city-editor's-radio-announcer's voice, ordered reporters around and kept my evenings to myself, especially in Paris.*

In the early years of the War, women entering the service were not queried about their sexual orientation. It was not until October 1944 that procedures were put in place to screen out lesbians. This followed a month of secret hearings on homosexuality in the Women's Army Corps, the result of a complaint by the mother of a WAC private about goings-on at Fort Oglethorpe, Georgia. (No guidelines were issued for identifying gay women, perhaps because stereotypically lesbian characteristics were precisely those that the military looked for in female recruits.)

But, for men at least, as Berube notes, "asking and answering the homosexual question became a new military ritual that forced each selectee to make a public statement about his sexuality and to wonder privately if he might be queer."

By the middle of the War, the military had created the discharge system, in which homosexuals within the military were to be thrown out, usually with the "undesirable," or blue-colored, discharge. This could happen even if they did not participate in any gay sexual activity. (Regulations against sodomy did remain on the books, however.) It should be noted that the military viewed the "blue" discharges as reformist and enlightened: The previous way of dealing with the problem, after all, had been prison.

Despite the evolving regulations and periodic efforts to ferret out gay GIs, the military's attitude through much of the War was characterized by ambivalence—especially in view of manpower (and womanpower) needs. The U.S. military informally channeled identifiably gay GIs into a variety of stereotypically homosexual jobs—women became motor vehicle operators and mechanics; men served as clerks, medics, hospital corpsmen, chaplains' assistants, and female impersonators in musical revues and morale-boosting shows. This tended to create a sense of gay solidarity and community that many GIs—especially those from small towns—had never known before entering the service.

GIs who served as female impersonators hold a special place in gay folklore. For example, Marine Corporal **Tom Reddy** performed Carmen Miranda and Andrews Sisters drag routines during combat missions on a variety of South Pacific islands, including Guadalcanal, where GIs dressed as women were the only entertainment available. (The performers carried their rifles onto the stage during shows.) Reddy related one incident to Berube in which his group's performance was strafed by Japanese planes in the midst of the "Three Little Sisters" number. He and the two other male performers—all wearing dresses—jumped into a giant foxhole along with five hundred other marines. "The three of us stood there looking at these guys saying, 'I don't know how the hell we got into *this!*'" Later, Reddy received a Letter of Commendation from his commanding general that read, "Your ambitious and successful venture into the field of stage entertainment is an example of what may be accomplished even in adversity. I hope it will inspire others to follow your leadership."

On leave, gay soldiers and sailors discovered bars and parks where men cruised one another, particularly in port cities, such as New York, San Francisco, New Orleans, and San Diego. New York City's Astor Bar, with its slogan "Meet Me at the Astor," became the prototype of the wartime gay meeting place; one side of the bar was straight and the other side was gay. Berube quotes one GI as saying, "It would be impossible to calculate the contribution of the Astor Bar to the war effort, impossible to estimate the number of one-night romances which brought comfort to the tense fighting men and reassured them that the things worth fighting for were still with us." It was during this period, Berube argues, that bars moved to the center of gay life. As more bars opened or began to cater to gay GIs, "a process of multiplication and specialization developed," according to Berube, with different bars attracting different gay subgroups. In Washington, D.C., for instance, the novelist **John Horne Burns** found bars that catered to "the Brilliant Crowd, the Swishy Crowd, the Empire Builders, and the Drugstore Cowboys."

Men who weren't in the military were affected by the relaxation in sexual mores as well. **Donald Vining,** a young gay man who got out of the army by admitting he was homosexual, kept a diary that included descriptions of sexual encounters with military personnel during the War. Typical was a July 30, 1944, entry about two servicemen, both named Earl, whom he had brought home on separate occasions:

> *My sailor's name was Earl and I have seldom had more fun. A Texan, he was as talkative as I could wish and talked almost the whole nite away, telling me of his large family. Anecdote after anecdote tumbled out and I loved every minute of it. . . . I said of the soldier Earl, "He wanted it himself but in the morning he claimed he had just done it to oblige me." This Earl snuggled over, put his cheek closer to mine and said, "Well, I'm not doing it just to oblige you." HEADLINE: GERMANS QUELL REVOLT IN DENMARK.*

In another diary entry, Vining observed, "The war is a tragedy to my mind and soul, but to my physical being, it's a memorable experience. I can understand how Walt Whitman felt when nursing during the Civil War."

There was another way in which the War changed the face of gay life as well. "It was not until after Pearl Harbor," writes **Donald Webster Cory** in his 1951 book, *The Homosexual in America*, "that the word 'gay' became a magic byword in practically every corner of the United States where homosexuals might gather."

Meanwhile, the Women's Army Corps was attracting large numbers of lesbians—or women who discovered they were lesbians once they joined up—becoming what historian D'Emilio describes as the "almost quintessential lesbian institution." In part, this was due to the military's own restrictive criteria: Married women were not allowed to enlist, and women who became pregnant were immediately discharged. In his book *Conduct Unbecoming*, Randy Shilts says that by some "imprecise" counts, 80 percent of the women who served in World War II were lesbians. **Pat Bond,** who later became a well-known lesbian performer, tells of leading an isolated existence in Davenport, Iowa, convinced that she was forever alone—until she joined the WACs. On her first day, the recruiting sergeant gave her a taste of what was to come. The sergeant reminded her of "old gym teachers in drag," she recalled. "Stockings, little earrings, her hair slicked back and very daintily done so you couldn't tell she was a dyke, but I knew!" Bond joined up in early

1945, during the time when women, as well as men, were interrogated about their sexuality. Bond claimed that many "butch" lesbians applied to the WACs dressed in men's clothes—"wearing argyle socks and pin-striped suits and the hair cut just like a man's with sideburns shaved over the ears—the whole bit." That didn't seem to concern the examiners who "let them in like that—much to the credit of the army psychiatrists. They would say, 'Have you ever been in love with a woman?' You would say, 'Of *course* not!' sitting there in your pin-striped suit."

At Fort Oglethorpe, where Bond went through her basic training, "everyone was going with someone or had a crush on somebody or was getting ready to go with somebody," she said. During her tour of duty most of Bond's friends were lesbians. She stayed in the military after the War ended, only to be discharged in one of the military's postwar witch-hunts. (Eventually, she wound up living in San Francisco.) Despite the unfortunate finale, her military service marked the first time Bond experienced a sense of lesbian community.

But the military was quick to clamp down on any sense of solidarity when it could. For example, two gay soldiers stationed in Myrtle Beach, South Carolina, produced a mimeographed newsletter called the *Myrtle Beach Bitch,* in order to keep in touch with far-flung friends. Historian Berube believes that it was one of the first gay publications produced in the U.S. In 1944, the newsletter's two "editors"—**Woodie Wilson** and his friend **"Kate"**—were court-martialed and convicted of misusing government property in publishing their newsletter. They were sentenced to a year in the Army Disciplinary Barracks at Greenhaven Federal Prison in Stormville, New York. There, they received a glimpse of the prewar methods of dealing with homosexuals, which the new, more enlightened system of discharges was supposed to replace. Wilson described it this way to Allan Berube:

> There was a whole wing of that huge prison of declared homosexuals and convicted homosexuals. They were all isolated and they all wore "A" on the back of their uniform and it was called the "A" Block. There must have been over a hundred people in there. It's something I'll never forget, seeing some of the faces and the ages. The ages are what got me. They weren't just all young. There were old, old men with white hair. They looked like they were up there before we ever got in the war. When they

came in to eat, they ate at a separate table in the dining room. If they came to the movies, they sat in a separate section. They were ostracized like crazy. Kate and I always said, "Thank God we didn't come in here as homosexuals [convicted of sodomy]."

The new discharge system, although it appeared to be an improvement, at least on the surface, could hardly be seen as a positive development. From 1941 to 1945, some nine thousand soldiers and sailors—almost entirely men—were tossed out of the military with the incriminating "blue" discharge. By contrast, only a few hundred individuals had been convicted of sodomy under the old system from 1900 until the beginning of World War II.

Often the experiences of those discharged were humiliating in the extreme. Some soldiers were locked in psychiatric wards and gay stockades and forced to walk past thousands of jeering soldiers on their way to mess hall; others told of having to wear tags that read "Psychopathia sexualis." During the investigation into lesbianism at Fort Oglethorpe, one military investigator asked a lesbian corporal at her hearing, "Do you [and your lover] kiss long clinging kisses?" and "Do you feel various parts of one another's bodies?"

Marvin Liebman describes how, while stationed in Cairo, his homosexuality was discovered from a letter he wrote "in the style of Dorothy Parker" to a friend in Tripoli. (Liebman was later to gain notoriety as an organizer for conservative political causes and came out publicly at age sixty-nine.) "It's obvious to me, soldier," his captain informed him, "that you are a cocksucker, and that you like it, like all the other New York Jew faggots." Liebman was transferred to a psychiatric ward, essentially a long barracks with cots down each side, surrounded by barbed wire. There were forty-five men in the ward, all of them "lunatics," according to Liebman. In his autobiography, *Coming Out Conservative,* he describes his first night there:

> *I was absolutely certain that I would be killed before the night was up. I turned in my uniform for pyjamas and a maroon robe and straw slippers. I had no razor or comb or brush, or anything like that. . . . I felt really naked and alone sitting on my bunk terrified by everyone around me. . . .*
>
> *That night, after falling asleep, I was awakened by a great crash on my bed. I opened my eyes, and I saw a man who thought he was Superman leaping from my cot to the next one, and then*

on to the next, waking people up as he went. A great hue and cry arose, with people screaming and weeping. Suddenly, in the midst of the wails and moans and shrieks—with nurses and orderlies rushing about trying to calm people—I began to cry, without shame, hugging myself and rocking. That was the last time I ever cried.

After a week on the psych ward, Liebman was brought in for a hearing in which he confessed he was homosexual, although he denied that he had ever performed a sexual act with another GI. He was sent back to his former post until the orders for his discharge arrived. There, he faced more humiliation. He was forced to march in front of the entire squadron, while his commanding officer bellowed, "I would like you men to see how a New York Jew faggot drills." For the rest of his stay, every morning and every night, his captain singled him out and made him march in front of everyone:

I obeyed his orders, and with each step I lost more of my self-worth. I became numb. It was as if I had left my body and could stand outside myself, watching this miserable soldier stagger through his drill orders in the desert heat. . . .

I became a pariah, bitterly lonely and desperately unhappy. I was shunned by everyone. Not one single word of greeting or compassion or understanding or even desultory conversation was uttered.

Finally, he was given his orders, "taken to the transport plane like a prisoner," and sent home. His military papers read, "Discharged . . . for habits and traits of character not beneficial to the Armed Forces of the United States."

At the end of the War, GIs like Liebman, expelled from the military with a "blue" discharge, were banned from receiving veteran's benefits. Then the armed forces began to relent somewhat: From 1945 to 1947, many homosexual ex-servicemen who had been thrown out but had committed no known sexual acts while in the military were able to have their discharges upgraded to "honorable." In 1947, however, under pressure from hard-liners, the military promulgated a new, harsh policy, replacing the "blue" discharge with a general discharge for unsuitability.

For many gay and lesbian GIs, the "coming out" experience that was the War made it difficult to return home and face familial and social expectations. They swelled the population of port cities like New York, Chicago, and San Francisco, places where gay and lesbian subcultures were already well established. Lesbian WAC Bond was an example of this new migration. In midsize cities, such as Denver, Cleveland, and Kansas City, the number of gay bars increased noticeably by the end of the forties. Other veterans tried to fit in as best they could: Marvin Liebman married, albeit briefly. But if the War provided a chance for many gays and lesbians to recognize their sexuality and fostered at least a temporary sense of community and solidarity, a dark curtain was about to fall. A country and a culture desperately coveting "normalcy" after the uprooting effects of the War began to put great pressure on its citizens to marry and to raise families. In political terms, homosexuals, like Communists, were increasingly viewed as a potentially dangerous "enemy within." The fifties had arrived. But for many, the personal discoveries and relative freedoms of the War years could not be completely forgotten or discounted.

Homosexuals in Uniform

The American media virtually ignored the subject of the military's policies toward homosexuals during World War II. One of the few exceptions was a June 9, 1947, article that appeared in Newsweek *magazine at the time the army toughened its discharge policy regarding homosexuals:*

ALTHOUGH ARMY REGULATIONS strictly forbade the drafting of homosexuals, scores of these inverts managed to slip through induction centers during the second world war. Between 3,000 and 4,000 were discharged for this abnormality; others were released as neuropsychiatric cases. Last week, with most of the records on homosexuals tabulated, Army medical officers, for the first time, summed up their strange story.

To screen out this undesirable soldier-material, psychiatrists in induction-station interviews tried to detect them 1) by their effeminate looks or behavior and 2) by repeating certain words from the homosexual vocabulary and watching for signs of recognition. In some instances, the urinary hormone-secretion test showed a higher degree of estrogens (female hormones) than androgens (male hormones), just the opposite of a normal man. But this test was too uncertain and too expensive to try on every inductee.

Frequently, a latent homosexual, who had no knowledge of his predilection, was inducted into the service, only to develop alarming symptoms in camp and on the battlefield. Many of these men refused to admit homosexuality, even to themselves, and went to elaborate lengths to prove their masculinity. One of these ruses was regular and conspicuous absence without leave, always with female companions. Often the soldier's primary trouble was not discovered until he was haled [sic] before Army psychiatrists on an AWOL charge.

From case histories in Army files, these facts about homosexuals were gleaned:

- They topped the average soldier in intelligence, education, and rating. At least 10 percent were college graduates; more than 50 percent had finished high school. Only a handful were illiterate.
- Including all ages, there were more whites than Negroes in this group. They came mostly from the cities rather than the country.
- Although the majority had no family history of nervous or mental disease, many were from homes broken by divorce or separation. In many instances the man had been brought up by his mother as a girl, or had been an only son in a large family of girls. About half assumed a "feminine" role, the other half "masculine." Most were either unmarried or had made a failure of marriage.
- As a whole, these men were law-abiding and hard-working. In spite of nervous, unstable, and often hysterical temperaments, they performed admirably as office workers. Many tried to be good soldiers.

Once this abnormality was detected, the man was usually evacuated by the unit doctors to a general hospital where he received psychiatric treatment while a military board decided whether or not he was reclaimable. A good number begged to be cured, but doctors usually doubted their sincerity and recommended discharge. At least half of the confirmed homosexuals, one psychiatrist estimated, were well-adjusted to their condition, and neither needed nor would respond to treatment. The majority, therefore, were released.

The Blue Discharge: Early in the war, the homosexuals were sent up for court-martial, but in 1943–44, the Army decided to separate most of them quietly with a "blue" discharge (neither honorable nor dishonorable) unless some other breach of military law had been committed. Last week, however, the Army announced a stiff new policy, effective July 1.

Instead of leaving service with the vague and protective "blue" discharge, the homosexuals who had not been guilty of a definite offense would receive an "undesirable" discharge. A few of this group with outstanding combat records might receive an honorable discharge. Those found guilty of homosexual violence or of impairing the morals of minors would receive a "yellow" or dishonorable discharge.

An Excerpt from Gore Vidal's
The City and the Pillar

With the emerging sense of gay identity and community of World War II and the postwar period, a number of American novels were published that treated homosexuality sympathetically. These included John Horne Burns's The Gallery *(1947) and* Lucifer with a Book *(1949) and Gore Vidal's* The City and the Pillar *(1948). Both* Lucifer with a Book *and* The City and the Pillar *were savagely attacked by the critics. The New York Times Book Review, for example, dismissed* The City and the Pillar *as "coldly clinical," "boring," and "as sterile as its protagonist." Vidal described the reception of* The City and the Pillar *as one of "shock" and "disbelief," with people asking how he, the young war novelist once featured in* Life *magazine "posed like Jack London against a ship," could "turn into this?" According to Vidal,* The New York Times *refused to take advertising for the book.*

The City and the Pillar *is a naturalistic, coming-of-age novel, in the postwar manner. While the book is in some senses a work of "special pleading," it also pulls no punches about what the author perceived as the limitations of gay life of the period: None of the novel's gay characters finds personal happiness or fulfillment. The hero, Jim Willard, is a conventional young homosexual man from a small town who, after a stint in the navy, winds up in Hollywood, working as a tennis instructor. There, he has a relationship with Paul Sullivan, a disillusioned screenwriter (and perhaps a stand-in for Vidal himself). After Sullivan's contract is not renewed by a Hollywood studio, the two go off on a trip to New Orleans. At a gay bar there, Sullivan makes a passionate speech that anticipates the arguments of later gay rights advocates. (Curiously, Vidal removed most of the speech when the novel was republished in 1965.) The speech comes in response to a comment by the owner of the bar—"the fat man"—that living as a homosexual man in New York was tolerable because one could be relatively anonymous. An angry Sullivan replies:*

"THERE SHOULD BE NO NEED to hide, to submerge in a big city. . . . If once this great thing were declared and realized by the mass of people it would, I think, decrease. For what is hidden rapidly grows inward; it should grow outward, be what it is: a normal stage in human development. . . . [I]n America we're sick with fear. . . . We are very sick and frightened and we condemn what we don't understand. . . . We cannot even love. The men cannot love women, cannot love one another, cannot love themselves. All they have left is hate; hate of the ones who try to love; hate of the few who succeed. No, we must declare ourselves, become known; allow the world to discover this subterranean life of ours which connects kings and farm boys, artists and clerks. Let them see that the important thing is *not* the object of love but the emotion itself, and let them respect anyone, no matter how different he is, if he attempts to share himself with another. . . ."

Jim and the fat man were impressed by Sullivan's bitterness. The fat man smiled. "Do you have the courage to announce yourself to the world—in *your* profession, say?"

Paul sighed and looked at his hands. "No," he said, "I haven't the courage."

"What can one do then, since we all are frightened?"

"Live with dignity, I suppose—and try to learn to love one another..."

BEFORE STONEWALL

CHAPTER 17

THE RISE AND FALL OF THE "GAY IS SICK" SHRINKS

As THE INFLUENCE of psychiatry increased in the United States during World War II and the postwar period, the mental health profession began to take an extremely negative stance toward homosexuality. Sigmund Freud had contended that all human beings were innately bisexual. He refused to categorize homosexuality as an illness—although he believed it was the result of "arrested development"—and he expressed strong doubts about the possibility of transforming homosexuals into heterosexuals. He wouldn't agree to treat someone merely because he or she was homosexual. He readily admitted that his youthful relationship with his collaborator **Wilhelm Fleiss** contained a homosexual element. His "Letter to an American Mother" (of a gay son) is one of the most sympathetic early documents of its kind.

But many of his disciples did not share these views. One of the most influential, **Sandor Rado** (1890–1972), of Columbia University's Psychoanalytic Clinic for Research and Training in New York City, rejected Freud's notion of universal bisexuality. He attributed homosexuality to "hidden but incapacitating fears of the opposite sex" developed in early childhood. According to Rado, the heterosexual drive was present in all individuals, and homosexuals could be "changed" through psychoanalysis. To him, there was only one sexual orientation—heterosexual.

By the 1950s, the Rado view had become psychiatric dogma in the United States. **Irving Bieber** (b. 1908), professor of psychiatry at New York Medical College, assumed that homosexuality is pathological and that "every homosexual is a latent heterosexual." Bieber argued that most cases of male homosexuality are the result of a family constellation of "detached, hostile father and a close-binding, intimate, seductive mother." In such families, he insisted, during the oedipal period, the "adhesive tie" between mother and son promotes in the boy "intensely rivalrous and murderous feelings toward the father." When the father responds in a hostile manner, the boy "is not only deprived of realistic needs for paternal security and protection, but he is denied an admired, loved figure for masculine identification." Without that masculine identification, he becomes gay.

The causes of lesbianism were viewed as a variation on this theme. According to **Cornelia B. Wilbur,** an associate in psychiatry at Columbia University, a lesbian daughter is the result of a "passive, unassertive, gentle, and detached" father and a mother who is "dominant, domineering, guilt-inducing, and hostile." The daughter is hostile toward her mother but unable to turn to her father because of what she perceives as his weakness. As a result she suffers from "severe feelings of rejection and longing."

Bieber's theories were based, at least in part, on clinical data. His study of two hundred homosexual and heterosexual male patients, undertaken in the 1950s under the sponsorship of the New York Society of Medical Psychoanalysts, showed an overly close mother-son relationship in 69 percent of the homosexual cases, more than twice the number of the heterosexual "controls." However, of the 106 homosexual patients, twenty-six had been previously diagnosed as schizophrenic. Moreover, Bieber never attempted to corroborate these figures by examining homosexuals who were *not* in treatment. As Martin Duberman notes in his book *Cures,* Bieber's sample was preselected for pathology. "Looking for illness," Duberman wrote, "Bieber had found it."

Bieber was convinced that changing homosexuals into heterosexuals through psychoanalysis was conceivable in many cases. "A heterosexual shift is a possibility for all homosexuals who are strongly motivated to change," he wrote in his book *Homosexuality: A Psychoanalytic Study of Male Homosexuals,* published in 1962. Bieber cited figures that slightly more than a quarter of his patients who were homosexual at the start of treatment shifted to exclusive heterosexuality; other psychoanalysts claimed a "success rate" as high as one in two.

The new orthodoxy was taken to its furthest extreme by **Charles W. Socarides** (b. 1922), also associated with the Columbia University psychoanalysts. "Heterosexual object choice," he maintained, "is determined by two and a half billion years of human evolution." Socarides was a leading exponent of the view that homosexuality is "sick" or pathological. He insisted that almost half of those who engaged in homosexual practices also suffered from schizophrenia or paranoia or were in the throes of manic-depression. The remainder were simply neurotic, primarily of the obsessional and phobic variety. The male homosexual, he believed, was perpetually attempting to achieve some sense of missing masculinity by identifying with a male sexual partner. "They hope to achieve a 'shot' of masculinity in the homosexual act," he wrote. "Like the addict [the homosexual] must have his 'fix'."

Underlying pathology, according to Socarides, caused homosexual relationships to be doomed from the start. To him, heterosexual relationships were characterized by "cooperation, solace, stimulation, enrichment, healthy challenge and fulfillment." By contrast, gay male relationships were mere "masquerades" with qualities of "destruction, mutual defeat, exploitation of the partner and the self, oral-sadistic incorporation, aggressive onslaughts, attempts to alleviate anxiety and a pseudo solution to the aggressive and libidinal urges which dominate and torment the individual." Lesbian relationships did not fare much better, in the psychoanalytic view of the time. Cornelia Wilbur claimed they were characterized by "great ambivalence, by great longing for love, by intense elements of hostility, and by the presence of chronic anxiety." Such relationships, in her view, were "unstable and often transient" and "do not contribute to an individual's need for stability and love."

Although the views of Bieber and Socarides and their followers were the most well-known of the 1950s and '60s, various schools of psychology offered differing explanations for the origins of homosexuality. But there was near-unanimous consensus on one point: Homosexuality represented a pathology. In 1952, when the American Psychiatric Association issued its first official catalog of mental disorders, *The Diagnostic and Statistical Manual, Mental Disorders (DSM-I),* homosexuality was listed among the sociopathic personality disturbances. By the next revision, *DSM-II,* issued in 1968, homosexuality was moved to the category of "other non-psychotic mental disorders," where it was classified along with fetishism, pedophilia, transvestism, exhibitionism, voyeurism, sadism, and masochism.

In the United States, the first significant challenge to the prevailing "gay is sick" orthodoxy came in the Kinsey reports of 1948 and 1953. **Alfred C. Kinsey** (1894–1956), a University of Indiana researcher, interviewed more than ten thousand white American men and women about their sexual habits, publishing his results in two best-selling books, *Sexual Behavior in the Human Male* (1948) and *Sexual Behavior in the Human Female* (1953). By training, Kinsey was a biologist and zoologist and was the world's leading authority on the gull wasp. His approach to the study of sexual behavior—measured, dispassionate—and his refusal to take a moral position on what he found was in keeping with his scientific training. Kinsey's findings demolished conventional thinking about sex, revealing a variety of sexual practices, including homosexuality, to be far more widespread than sex researchers and the general public had ever imagined. One wag credited him with having done for sex what Columbus did for geography. A 1953 *Time* magazine cover story on him, on the date of publication of *Sexual Behavior in the Human Female,* began on a note of high drama:

> *Four men collected the information, traveling across the U.S. for fifteen years with the patient persistence of secret agents. They tried to be inconspicuous; they knew they might be misunderstood. They sought recruits in homes and prisons, saloons and parish houses, burlesque theaters and offices, then interrogated them in private. They took notes in a code which was nowhere written down, and preserved only in the memories of the four. They never traveled together, lest an accident wipe out their secret with them. Coded and catalogued, the facts were locked away, and the book written from them printed in utmost secrecy.*

Kinsey found that 83 percent of married men had had sex before marriage and that half had had extramarital affairs. Almost exactly half the women had engaged in premarital intercourse, while 25 percent had had sexual relations outside marriage. Ninety-two percent of men and 62 percent of women masturbated (the men more regularly than the women). His findings punctured the lingering myth of the "passionless" woman, showing that women were as responsive to physical stimuli as men.

It was in the area of homosexuality that Kinsey's findings were perhaps the most startling. Among his findings were:

- 37 percent of the total male population has had *at least some overt homosexual experience* to the point of orgasm, since the onset of adolescence.
- 50 percent of males who remained single until age thirty-five have had overt homosexual experience to the point of orgasm.

- 8 percent of males were *exclusively homosexual* for at least three years between the ages of sixteen and fifty-five.
- 4 percent of males were *exclusively homosexual throughout their lives.*
- 28 percent of females reported erotic responses to other females.
- 13 percent of females have achieved orgasm in homosexual relations, while 20 percent have had some homosexual experience.
- 28 percent of the women who reported homosexual activity had an experience that extended for over three years; for 25 percent of these the activity had been spread over a period of two to three years only.
- Between 2 and 6 percent of unmarried females had been more or less *exclusively* homosexual in each of the years between twenty and thirty-five years of age.

Kinsey postulated that human sexual behavior extended across a continuum, for which he constructed a seven-point rating scale, ranging from exclusive heterosexual behavior (0) to exclusive homosexual behavior (6). Interestingly, these findings tended to contradict the notion elaborated by the sexologists (and still widely held) that there is a homosexual "species" that can be somehow cordoned off from the rest of the population by their sexual proclivities. Despite the complexities of his findings, Kinsey's data on homosexuality is usually summed up by the assertion that he found homosexuals to make up 10 percent of the population.

These sensational findings made Kinsey a household word. A *New Yorker* magazine cartoon showed a woman reading the report and asking her husband, "Is there a *Mrs.* Kinsey?" (There was.) They also made him a subject of controversy. *The New York Times,* at first, refused to review *Sexual Behavior in the Human Male* or take advertising for it. Clergymen of all stripes condemned it. "It is impossible to estimate the damage this book will do to the already deteriorating morals of America," said evangelist **Billy Graham.** To **Henry Pitney Van Dusen,** head of Union Theological Seminary, Kinsey's findings revealed "a prevailing degradation in American morality approximating the worst decadence of the Roman Empire. The most disturbing thing is the absence of a spontaneous ethical revulsion from the premises of the study and the inability on the part of the readers to put their fingers on the falsity of its premises.

Alfred Kinsey's 1953 book, *Sexual Behavior in the Human Female,* stunned the American public by portraying women as sexual beings. Publication of the book was a major media event, and even the Barry Sisters, a popular singing group, expressed their shock—and fascination. *(© UPI/Bettmann)*

For the presuppositions of the Kinsey Report are strictly animalistic . . ." Eventually, in response to continuing criticism, the Rockefeller Foundation, which had bankrolled Kinsey's work, withdrew its financial support.

By demonstrating that homosexual behavior was far more widespread than previously had been assumed, Kinsey put the whole notion that homosexuality was pathological into question. Could so many Americans—who were apparently having homosexual relations with regularity, at least at some point in their lives—really be "sick"? Kinsey himself noted that, in view of his findings, it was hard to maintain the view that sexual relations between individuals of the same sex are "rare and therefore abnormal or unnatural, or that they constitute within themselves evidence of neuroses or even psychoses." Taking into account the public sentiment against homosexuality and the legal penalties placed upon male homosexual acts in England and the United States, "there seems some reason for believing that such activity would appear in the histories of a much larger portion of the population if there were no social restraints," he said. And he went on to note that the wide occurrence of homosexuality in both the ancient world and in a number of contemporary cultures where it was not stigmatized "suggests that the capacity of an individual to respond erotically to any sort of stimulus, whether it is provided by another person of the same or of the opposite sex, is basic to the species."

As he involved himself in his research, Kinsey became particularly excited about his findings about homosexuality, the "H-histories," which he described as "dynamite" in a letter to his friend and former student **Ralph Voris.** "Am trying to get [homosexual] cases in all classes, from the most cultured and socially-economically [sic] to the poorest type of professional street solicitor," he wrote Voris during a research trip to Chicago in June 1939. ". . . Have been to Hallowe'en parties, taverns, clubs, etc, which would be unbelievable if realized by the rest of the world. Always they have been most considerate and cooperative, decent, understanding, and cordial in their reception. Why has no one cracked this before? There are at least 300,000 involved in Chicago alone."

One key reason for his success was that Kinsey and his associates always interviewed his subjects face to face. Because of concern that many people would withhold information about homosexual experiences, he and his team developed particular interviewing techniques described by his colleague **Wardell B. Pomeroy** in his book *Dr. Kinsey and the Institute for Sex Research:*

> [W]e asked about a dozen questions indirectly related to a person's homosexual history before we came to the direct question: "How old were you the first time you had sexual contact with another person of your own sex?" By this time we would be fairly certain whether or not he had extensive homosexual experience. If at this point he denied an overt history of homosexuality but there were enough indicators in a positive direction to make us reasonably certain he was covering up, we learned to challenge his denials.
>
> Then it became necessary to say, with firmness, even vehemence, and yet always with kindness, "Look, I don't give a damn what you've done, but if you don't tell me the straight of it, it's

better that we stop this history right here. Now, how old were you the first time this or that happened?"

Overall, the effects of Kinsey's work on gays and lesbians were mixed. As historian John D'Emilio points out, "By revealing the wide divergence between ideals and actual behavior, he [Kinsey] informed ordinary men and women that their private 'transgressions' marked them as neither deviant nor exceptional." If this was comforting to many gays and lesbians, it did not seem to have any immediate effect on the views of the psychiatric profession, however. And Kinsey's discovery that such a high percentage of the population had had gay or lesbian experiences actually provided ammunition to those hostile to homosexuals. To them, Kinsey's numbers proved that homosexuality was a grave social threat. At the height of the McCarthy period, when witch-hunters were searching out gay men and women in the highest levels of government, Kinsey's figures were extrapolated and taken out of context as evidence that homosexuals were a national danger.

Kinsey's studies demonstrated that the numbers of individuals who were primarily homosexual or had had homosexual experiences was far greater than most Americans imagined. But it was left to **Evelyn Hooker,** a professor of psychology at UCLA in Los Angeles, to be the first member of the mental health profession to challenge the notion that homosexuals were "sick" through clinical research of her own.

Hooker became interested in the subject as a result of her friendship with one of her students, a young gay man named Sammy, and his lover. On Thanksgiving weekend 1945, Hooker and her husband joined the couple in San Francisco, where all four went to see a performance by female impersonators at a well-known club called Finocchio's. As Hooker recalled in an interview recounted in Eric Marcus's book *Making History,* after the performance Sammy turned to her and said, "We have let you see us as we are, and now it is your scientific duty to make a study of people like us. We're homosexual, but we don't need psychiatrists. We don't need psychologists. We're not insane. We're not any of those things they say we are."

Hooker hesitated, but Sammy was persistent. He could find her a hundred men to interview, he said. He stressed that the only homosexuals who had ever been studied were psychiatric patients, not average gays and lesbians. Hooker eventually consulted with her colleague **Bruno Klopfer,** one of the world's leading experts on the Rorschach psychological test. As Hooker remembers it, Klopfer virtually jumped out of his chair. "You must do it, Eee-vah-leeeen!" he told her. "You must do it! Your friend is absolutely right. We don't know anything about people like him. The only ones we know about are the people who come to us as patients. And, of course, many of those who come to us are very disturbed, pathological. You must do it!"

It wasn't until 1953, with a grant from the National Institute of Mental Health, that Hooker began her research. By then, her friend Sammy had died in a car wreck, and Hooker was on her own. She found thirty homosexual men, mostly through fledgling homophile organizations, and a control group of thirty heterosexuals—some of them firemen and policemen. The two groups were matched in terms of age, IQ, and educational background. Each of the sixty subjects was given three psychological tests widely used at the time. Test results were presented to three judges, all of them psychological experts who had no idea whether a particular subject was homosexual or heterosexual. The judges evaluated each test and gave a rating of psychological adjustment on a scale of one—superior— to five—maladjusted. On all the tests, two-thirds of the heterosexuals and two-thirds of the homosexuals scored a rating of three, which was average or better. Overall, there was no difference between gays and straights.

Hooker spent ten days with Rorschach expert Klopfer, examining the results. "At that time, the 1950s, every clinical psychologist worth his soul would tell you that if he gave those projective tests he could tell whether a person was gay or not," Hooker told Eric Marcus. "I showed that they couldn't do it. I was very pleased with that. Bruno could hardly believe his eyes. He was absolutely positive that the dynamics would be such that he would know immediately who was gay and who wasn't. But he didn't know."

Hooker delivered her paper on the study—"The Adjustment of the Male Overt Homosexual"—at a meeting of the American Psychological Association in Chicago in 1956. Her conclusion was revolutionary: Gay men could be as well adjusted as straight men and, in some cases, even better adjusted. Although her research did not make an impact on the psychiatric hardliners, it became tremendously useful to the homophile movement. Hooker became a personal hero to many gays and lesbians. She recalled a lesbian who came up to her at a gathering of homosexuals and told Hooker that when her parents found out she was lesbian, they put her in a psychiatric hospital. At the time, the standard procedure for treating homosexuals in that particular hospital was electroshock therapy. The woman's psychiatrist was familiar with Hooker's work, and he was able to save her from shock treatments. As she told the story to Hooker, tears were streaming down her face.

It was not until the emergence of the gay liberation movement in the 1970s that the American Psychiatric Association (APA) removed homosexuality from its nomenclature of disorders. The decision came amid great controversy. Gay activists "zapped" psychiatric meetings. An APA convention featured a debate between Bieber and Socarides, on one side, and a group of psychiatrists who wanted to remove homosexuality from the nomenclature, on the other. Gay activist **Ron Gold,** also on the panel, told Bieber, "You're making me sick." At another discussion, a psychiatrist on the panel created a sensation by announcing that he was gay. It marked the first time any psychiatrist in the United States had come out publicly; the drama of his revelation was heightened by the fact that he found it necessary to wear a mask and to speak through a voice-altering device. Finally, after careful consideration of the data available on the mental health of homosexuals, on December 15, 1973, the APA board of trustees made the landmark decision that "homosexuality . . . by itself does not constitute a mental disorder." In an effort to appease the Bieber-Socarides faction, the APA created a new category called "Sexual Orientation Disturbance." This classification was intended for individuals whose sexual interests were directed primarily toward members of the same sex but who "are either disturbed by, in conflict with, or wish to change their sexual orientation," as the APA put it.

Unmollified, the "gay is sick" psychiatrists led by Socarides pressed for a referendum of the entire APA membership. In April 1974, with more than ten thousand psychiatrists participating, the membership voted 58 to 37 percent to back the board's decision.

Despite the vote, many psychiatrists continued to accept the notion that homosexuality represented a pathological state (or at least one of incomplete psychological development). Three years later, a survey of 2,500 psychiatrists by the journal *Medical Aspects of*

Human Sexuality found that 69 percent still believed that homosexuality was pathological. Another 60 percent agreed that homosexual men were less capable of "mature, loving relationships" than their heterosexual counterparts. But the important thing was that the APA had removed its imprimatur from the idea that homosexuality was an illness. One of the major pillars of the stigmatization of homosexuality had fallen. Finally, in 1986, the APA removed all references to homosexuality in the *DSM-III R*.

Although gay activists assumed they had won the battle over the classification of homosexuality as a mental illness, in fact the controversy continues within the psychiatric profession to the present day. In a letter that appeared in the December 1993 issue of *Psychiatric News,* Dr. Charles Socarides lambasted the 1973 APA decision as causing "severe damage to the image of American psychiatry, eroding its scientific foundations with regard to sexual development, impeding research and therapy for homosexuals who desire help, and producing chaos in the fields of psychology, mental health, and the medical profession in general." On the same page, in the "Resident's Column," a writer still found it necessary to argue that "Homosexuality Is Not a Mental Disorder." The pathologization of homosexuality might have officially come to an end, but there remain many who are unconvinced.

CHAPTER 18

THE AGE OF MCCARTHY

ON THURSDAY, February 9, 1950, an obscure first-term senator from Wisconsin named Joseph R. McCarthy (1908–57) gave a Lincoln's Birthday dinner address to an audience of 275 Republican women in Wheeling, West Virginia. Midway through his speech, McCarthy waved a piece of paper and announced, "I have here in my hand a list of 205 that were known to the secretary of state as being members of the Communist Party and who nevertheless are still working and shaping the policy of the State Department." The following evening, in Salt Lake City, where the senator made another speech, the number of card-carrying Communist Party members employed by the U.S. State Department had fallen to fifty-seven. In Reno the following day, the senator again claimed fifty-seven but would name only four.

McCarthy was startled by the national attention that his charges gained. He later said that the scrap of paper he waved so dramatically in Wheeling was actually a laundry list. As his biographer Richard H. Rovere observed, McCarthy discovered communism "almost by inadvertence, as Columbus discovered America, as James Marshall discovered California gold."

It was the height of the Cold War. The Soviet Union had the bomb, presumably thanks to American spies; China had been "lost." Within five months, North Korean soldiers would march south across the 38th parallel, and the nation would once again find itself at war. Americans were obsessed with loyalty, with "the enemy within" as much as the enemy without. Whether it was 205 State Department Communists or fifty-seven or just four didn't particularly matter—truth and accuracy were less important than the great anti-Communist crusade. The Age of McCarthy had begun.

Less than three weeks after the Wheeling speech, Undersecretary of State **John Peurifoy** testified before a Senate committee investigating the loyalty of government workers. He was asked how many State Department employees had resigned while under investigation for being security risks since 1947. "Ninety-one persons in the shady category," Peurifoy answered. "Most of these were homo-sexuals."

Suddenly, another domestic enemy had emerged—homosexuals or "perverts" or "deviates," in the language of the fifties (even the headlines of the stately *New York Times* used the word *perverts,* just as the newspaper referred to Communists as "Reds"). The Republican opposition found another weapon to use against President Harry S Truman and his secretary of state, **Dean Acheson.** McCarthy immediately joined the fray, telling a Senate subcommittee that a "flagrantly homosexual" State Department employee, dismissed as a security risk, had had his job restored because of pressure from a high official. The chairman of the Republican National Commmittee, **Guy George Gabrielson,** warned in a letter to the party faithful that "perhaps as dangerous as the actual Communists are the sexual perverts who have infiltrated our Government in recent years. . . . It is the talk of Washington." After a Washington, D.C., vice squad officer named Lieutenant **Roy E. Blick** told the Senate that there were 5,000 perverts in Washington, 4,500 of them employed by government agencies, a Senate subcommittee launched an investigation.

Antigay hysteria became widespread. Right-wingers charged that the State Department was the target of gay "infiltration," just as it was the target of Communist infiltration. Shortly before the 1950 congressional elections, John O'Donnell, the *New York Daily News* political commentator, wrote, "The primary issue is . . . the charge that the foreign policy of the U.S., even before World War II, was dominated by an all-powerful, super-secret inner circle of highly educated, socially highly placed sexual misfits in the State Department, all easy to blackmail, all susceptible to blandishments by homosexuals in foreign nations." Rumors abounded that Adolf Hitler had compiled a list of homosexuals throughout the world who could be enlisted for espionage, sabotage, or terrorism. The alleged list bore an uncanny resemblance to the "Black Book" of 47,000 English "perverts" supposedly in possession of the Germans during World War I. Hitler's version was said to have fallen into Stalin's hands in 1945, and some believed that Communists were now updating it and using it.

In their book, *Washington Confidential,* published in 1951, Hearst reporters **Jack Lait** and **Lee Mortimer** threw all these ideas together in a highly inflammatory stew:

The good people shook their heads in disbelief with the revelation that more than 90 twisted twerps in trousers had been swished out of the State Department. . . . We pursued the subject and we found that there are at least 6,000 homosexuals on the government payroll, most of them known, and these comprise only a fraction of the total of their kind in the city. . . .

Now we have found out where the dull, dumb deviates go. . . . Nowhere else as surely as in the civil service. There, in the mediocrity and virtual anonymity of commonplace tasks, the sexes—all four of them—are equal in the robot requirements and qualifications. . . .

Foreign chancelleries long ago learned that homos were of value in espionage work. The German Roehm, and later Goering, established divisions of such in the Foreign Office. That was aped by Soviet Russia, which has a flourishing desk now in Moscow. According to Congressman [A. L.] Miller [of Nebraska], who made a comprehensive study of the subject, young students are indoctrinated and given a course in homosexuality, then taught to infiltrate in perverted circles in other countries. . . . Aware of the seriousness of the problem, the State Department has a highly hush-hush Homosexual Bureau, manned by trained investigators and former counter-espionage agents, whose duties are to ferret out pansies in Foggy Bottom.

The authors extrapolated from Kinsey's figures to make the number of gays in government appear particularly menacing:

Dr. Kinsey wasn't appalled by the 6,000 fags in government jobs. According to his calculations, 56,787 Federal workers are congenital homosexuals. He includes 21 Congressmen and says 192 others are bad behavior risks.

Despite some initial interest in the subject, Senator McCarthy didn't play a leading role in pervert-hunting. That was left to his ally, Nebraska Senator **Kenneth Wherry**, the GOP floor leader. A licensed embalmer, Wherry was dubbed "the merry mortician." He was famous for his malapropisms—referring to Vietnam as "Indigo China" and the nation's military leaders as "the Chief Joints of Staff" and prefacing his remarks with "It is my unanimous opinion." Wherry made it his personal crusade to remove homosexuals from *all* posts in government, sensitive and nonsensitive alike. Communists and homosexuals, homosexuals and Communists, they were all the same in Senator Wherry's eyes. "You can hardly separate homosexuals from subversives," he told *New York Post* columnist **Max Lerner**. "Mind you, I don't say every homosexual is a subversive, and I don't say every subversive is a homosexual. But a man of low morality is a menace in the government, whatever he is, and they are all tied together."

With Wherry as cochair, when the Senate subcommittee investigating the "employment of homosexuals and other sex perverts in government" issued its recommendations in December 1950, the results proved no surprise. The subcommittee's conclusion was unqualified: "Sex perverts" were not "proper persons" to be employed by the U.S. government. A homosexual lacked "emotional stability," according to the report, tending to have

> *a corrosive influence upon his fellow employees. These perverts will frequently attempt to entice normal individuals to engage in perverted practices. This is particularly true in the case of young and impressionable people who might come under the influence of a pervert.... One homosexual can pollute a Government office.*

The committee also addressed the issue of security risk, always the major concern of the fifties:

> *Most perverts tend to congregate at the same restaurants, night clubs, and bars, which places can be identified with comparative ease in any community, making it possible for a recruiting agent to develop clandestine relationships which can be used for espionage purposes.*

The campaign to remove homosexuals in government was effective. According to historian John D'Emilio, from 1947 through April 1, 1950, dismissals of homosexuals from civilian posts averaged five per month. But once the brouhaha about perverts in government began in the winter and spring of 1950, the numbers increased to more than sixty a month over the next year and a half. In April 1953, the newly elected president, **Dwight David Eisenhower**, issued Executive Order 10405, revising the loyalty-security program. Under the new policy, "sexual perversion" was sufficient and necessary grounds for exclusion from federal employment. In the first sixteen months of the Eisenhower directive, an average of forty homosexuals were ousted from government positions every month. (These figures do not reflect the number of job applicants who were not hired because of their homosexuality.) The civilian purge was reflected in the armed forces as well. In the late 1940s, the U.S. military was discharging homosexuals at the rate of about a thousand a year. By the early 1950s, the numbers had jumped to two thousand a year.

The Federal Bureau of Investigation was responsible for supplying the Civil Service Commission with background information on employees and applicants for employment. As D'Emilio reports, regional FBI offices compiled lists of gay bars and gathering places and entered into contact with vice-squad officers who supplied arrest records on morals charges. The Post Office monitored recipients of physique magazines, the closest the fifties came to "gay porn." Postal inspectors subscribed to gay pen pal clubs, corresponded with men who they believed to be homosexual, and put tracers on their mail in order to locate others. (Postal surveillance of magazines aimed at gay men continued until 1966, when Capitol Hill investigators probing into government invasions of privacy uncovered the practice; Postmaster General **Larry F. O'Brien** then put a stop to it.)

The effects of gay witch-hunting—and the FBI's role in it—can be seen in the experience of a man called B.D.H., who described his experiences in a statement to the American Civil Liberties Union. As D'Emilio recounts, B.D.H. had been expelled from the University of Illinois in 1942, apparently after making a pass at another student. He moved to Washington, where he worked for several years as a clerk-typist at a federal agency, and eventually returned to the Midwest. An FBI agent visited the University of Illinois and obtained his records. As a result, a friend of B.D.H.'s who worked for the State Department was charged with sexual perversion on the basis of his association with B.D.H. At three different jobs that B.D.H. held—two in St. Louis and one in Chicago—the FBI informed supervisors and coworkers of B.D.H.'s homosexuality. Fellow employees made his life miserable. In 1960, after an arm injury left him unable to type, he applied to the Illinois Divison of Vocational Rehabilitation for job retraining. He was refused because of his sexual orientation. Even in the early 1960s, B.D.H. asserts that FBI agents visited him at his home to attempt to pressure him to reveal the names of homosexual acquaintances.

Panic about homosexuals in high places spread north to Canada, where the new 1952 immigration act explicitly barred homosexuals from entering the country. At the same time, the Royal Canadian Mounted Police (the Mounties) established a special investigative unit called A-3 that concentrated exclusively on identifying and rooting out homosexuals in government jobs. Like their American counterparts, the A-3 investigators watched gay bars and public parks; they also recruited informers among gay men. The force soon had a list of three thousand names, according to Canadian journalist John Sawatsky, who investigated the Mounties' Security Service for his book *Men in the Shadows*.

In one bizarre incident, Sawatsky writes, the A-3 unit attempted to plot groupings and gathering places of homosexuals on a map of the Canadian capital of Ottawa. Every area of the city with a concentration of homosexuals was identified and marked with a red dot. Soon, the map contained so many colored dots that it became an indecipherable mass of red ink. The investigators purchased another map—the largest one available. It, too, became one great red smudge. Finally, a Mountie approached the Department of National Defence with a request that it fly over the city with high-resolution cameras in order to produce an even larger map. The Defence Department refused—it was experiencing a financial crunch at the time. At that point, the mapping of Ottawa's homosexuals came to an end.

Congressional hearings and investigations, *New York Times* headlines about "perverts," a series of (sympathetic) columns in the *New York Post* by Max Lerner, all marked the first time that homosexuality had become a public issue in the United States. But in the polarized political climate of the McCarthy years, "queer-baiting" became a weapon to be used by both McCarthyites and their enemies. Ironically, it was the inordinate concern on the part of McCarthy and his chief counsel, **Roy M. Cohn**, regarding the military service of McCarthy committee aide **G. David Schine**—a concern that may or may not have had a homosexual element to it—that was to precipitate the Army-McCarthy hearings that finally brought down the Wisconsin senator.

Was McCarthy himself gay? There were certainly widespread rumors to that effect, despite the hard-drinking bachelor senator's propensity for pawing women at parties. **Drew Pearson**, the syndicated columnist, who despised McCarthy, kept a file on the subject. In his diary entry of January 14, 1952, Pearson makes mention of a letter that a young Army lieutenant had written to Senator **William Benton** of Connecticut claiming that McCarthy had engaged in an act of sodomy with him after picking him up in a bar. But when the FBI interviewed the lieutenant, he denied everything, claiming the letter had been planted by "another homo who was jealous." None of Pearson's information ever reached print, at a time when newspapers were far less inclined to publish information about private lives of high officials than they are today.

One newspaper publisher had no such compunction, however. He was **Hank Greenspun**, the publisher of the Las Vegas *Sun*. A former press agent for a Las Vegas gambling house, Greenspun was a passionate McCarthy-hater. He had his reasons: McCarthy had once referred to Greenspun's newspaper as "the local *Daily Worker*" and charged erroneously that Greenspun was an army deserter and ex-convict. In an October 25, 1952, article in the *Sun*, Greenspun minced no words. "Joe McCarthy is a bachelor of 43 years," he noted. "He seldom dates girls and if he does he laughingly describes it as window dressing. It is common talk among homosexuals in Milwaukee who rendezvous at the White Horse Inn that Senator Joe McCarthy often engaged in homosexual activities. The persons in Nevada who listened to McCarthy's radio talk thought he had the queerest laugh. He has. He is." In another article, Greenspun wrote, "The Young Republicans held a state convention in Wausau, Wis., at which Sen. McCarthy was an honored guest. During the convention, McCarthy spent the night with William McMahon, formerly an official of the Milwaukee County Young Republicans, in a Wausau hotel room, at which time, McCarthy and McMahon engaged in illicit acts with each other." It was widely believed that Greeenspun's "information" came from Drew Pearson's files. McCarthy contemplated suing Greenspun but never did so.

All the evidence about McCarthy's alleged sexual proclivities remains circumstantial. Thomas C. Reeves, author of the most extensive biography of McCarthy, states flatly that the senator wasn't gay. But McCarthy was clearly discomfited by the accusations. In September 1953, at the age of forty-five, the Wisconsin senator married **Jean Kerr**, a member of his staff. But even marriage didn't entirely dispel the talk.

If it is unclear whether or not McCarthy was gay, there is no doubt about Roy Marcus Cohn (1927–86), who became the chief counsel to McCarthy's subcommittee in 1953 at the age of twenty-six. The son of a powerful Bronx judge, Cohn was a prodigy of sorts, with a steel-trap mind and photographic memory. He graduated from Columbia University Law School at nineteen and had to wait two years before he was eligible to take the bar exam. On the day he became a member of the bar, he was sworn in as Assistant United States Attorney for the Southern District of New York. He became a protégé of **Irving Saypol**, the U.S. Attorney, and helped send U.S. Communist leaders to prison in the Smith Act prosecution. At the spy trial of **Julius** and **Ethel Rosenberg**, he conducted the government's examination of **David Greenglass**, Ethel's brother, who had turned state's evidence. Cohn's anticommunism seems to have been genuine. He was obsessed with proving, especially in the light of the Rosenberg case, that Jews were loyal and patriotic Americans.

Cohn made useful friends outside legal circles. While assistant U.S. attorney, he leaked information on virtually a daily basis to the nation's leading gossip columnist, **Walter Winchell**. In exchange, Cohn was invited to sit at Winchell's table at the Stork Club. Sometime in 1951, he met **George Sokolsky**, the fiercely anti-Communist Hearst newspaper columnist who became his mentor. More than anyone, Sokolsky was responsible for Cohn going to Washington.

In 1953, Cohn prevailed over **Robert F. Kennedy** to become the McCarthy investigatory committee's chief counsel. Cohn brought along his friend and night-clubbing companion, G. David Schine, as "Chief Consultant" to the committee. Within a few months, the two young men were running the show. Heir to a hotel fortune, the twenty-six-year-old Schine was "a good-looking young man in the sallow, sleekly coiffed, and somnolent-eyed style that one used to associate with male orchestra singers," writes Richard H. Rovere. In fact, at one time he had been a press agent for the Vaughn Monroe orchestra and had published two or three ballads of his own, one of which was called "Please Say Yes or It's Goodbye." As an undergraduate at Harvard, Schine was known for living in a high style that featured an exquisitely furnished room, a valet, and a large black convertible equipped with a two-way telephone. Schine's anti-Communist credentials rested on a six-page pamphlet called "Definition of Communism," which, along with the Gideon Bible, was placed in every room of the Schine hotel chain.

Cohn and Schine were "a study in contrasts," notes David M.

Oshinsky in his book *A Conspiracy So Immense.* "Cohn was short, dark, intense, and abrasive; Schine was tall, fair, frivolous, and complacent." According to some observers, it was Schine who was the dominant influence. Despite Cohn's intellectual brilliance, Schine was fond of humiliating Cohn in front of strangers and acting as if Cohn was his inferior.

In April 1953, Cohn and Schine set off for Europe, ostensibly to investigate U.S.-run libraries to make sure that no left-wing literature was hiding out on their shelves. The trip was a fiasco that turned up nothing, infuriated virtually every American embassy in Western Europe, and turned the two investigators into laughing-stocks. (In one incident, Schine supposedly chased Cohn through a hotel lobby, swatting him over the head with a magazine.) Upon their arrival at a particular hotel, Cohn and Schine would ask for adjoining rooms but insist on separate accommodations, explaining, "You see, we don't work for the State Department!" The joke seems to have been primarily for the benefit of a retinue of journalists who recorded their every move; hotel reservations clerks in Rome or Vienna were unlikely to have heard very much about accusations that the U.S. State Department was a haven for homosexuals.

Nicholas von Hoffman, one of Cohn's biographers, reports that people who saw Cohn and Schine close up doubted that they were lovers or that Schine was gay. People who observed them at a distance assumed they were just two playboys. Cohn, in private conversation with friends, denied any intimate involvement with Schine. In any event, Cohn was deep in the closet. He was dating women and spending more time at the Stork Club than in Washington's gay bars. For years, he would deny that he was gay, telling journalist Ken Auletta in an interview in the 1970s, "Anyone who knows me and knows anything about me or who knows the way my mind works or knows the way I function . . . would have an awfully hard time reconciling, ah, ah, reconciling that with ah, ah, any kind of homosexuality. Every facet of my personality, of my, ah, aggressiveness, of my toughness, of everything along those lines, is just totally, I suppose, incompatible, with anything like that. . . ." As von Hoffman notes, Cohn's "embarrassed, thick-tongued denial of his sexuality" took place at a time when even high-school students had come to realize that most gay men were anything but "limp-wristed, lavender lads." Cohn's view of what constituted a gay man remained mired in stereotypical notions of the fifties. At the time of his well-publicized death from AIDS in 1986, newspapers did not hesitate to write about his homosexuality.

During Cohn's eighteen-month period of service to Senator McCarthy, the young counsel apparently had no compunction about using allegations of other people's homosexuality to destroy *them*. Whether this was an effort to hide his own homosexuality through cruelty to others, or an expression of gay self-hatred, or his own defiant pride in his own toughness and aggressiveness, or some combination of all three, is anyone's guess. The first case concerned **Samuel Reber**, the Acting High Commissioner in Germany. Cohn was convinced that Reber had deliberately trapped him and Schine into a news conference at a stop in Bonn during their European junket, in order to make them look ridiculous. According to von Hoffman's sources, the McCarthy people had dug up a story about a homosexual relationship that Reber had supposedly been involved in as an undergraduate at Harvard years before. They threatened Reber with its revelation. Reber resigned from the State Department.

Then there was the case of Senator **Lester Hunt**, a Wyoming Democrat. An opponent of McCarthy, Hunt was up for reelection the following November to a Senate that was split down the middle between Democrats and Republicans. Senator **Styles Bridges** of New Hampshire, a friend and political ally of Cohn, had a talk with Hunt. Unless Hunt withdrew from the race for reelection in November, Bridges reportedly told him, everyone in Wyoming would find out that Hunt's son had been arrested the previous October for soliciting a D.C. plainclothes policeman for "lewd and immoral purposes." Hunt withdrew from the race. Eleven days later, he shot himself to death in his Senate office.

Cohn's connection to the Hunt affair is somewhat murky. But as von Hoffman notes:

> The modus operandi was the same as that used against Samuel Reber. Hunt had been a quiet, persistent but rational foe of McCarthy's; as to Roy's relationship with [Senator] Bridges, a congressman who knew Roy well remembered that "Roy used to drop Bridges' name left and right. There was no question at all they were extremely tight. He could get him on the phone any time he wanted him; he'd brag about different things that Bridges would do. They were very, very close."

But Cohn and McCarthy soon received their comeuppance. Two months after Cohn and Schine returned from their European junket, David Schine received his draft notice. Cohn tried unsuccessfully to persuade the army to exempt Schine; when this failed, he pressured the army to grant Private Schine a commission and to assign him to some sort of duty with McCarthy's committee. McCarthy, perhaps reluctantly, went along with him. The army resisted. Military officials released a blistering report accusing McCarthy and Cohn of trying to blackmail them with threats of anti-Communist probes unless the army gave preferential treatment to Private Schine. For their part, McCarthy and Cohn claimed the army was trying to blackmail *them*, using Schine as a "hostage" to pressure the committee to turn a blind eye to accusations of communism in the armed forces. The result of all this was the Senate investigation of the charges and countercharges—known as the Army-McCarthy hearings—an investigation that would discredit McCarthy and Cohn forever. "It was Cohn's loyalty to Schine and McCarthy's to Cohn that led to decline and eventual fall," notes Rovere. Was it Cohn's loyalty to Schine that caused him to overreach? Or was it love? Infatuation? Or just blind rage and determination to assert his power over the U.S. Army? Roy Cohn was a complicated man.

The Army-McCarthy hearings of the spring of 1954 were one of the most extraordinary events in modern American history, largely because they were televised. The hearings ran for thirty-five days; twenty million Americans were estimated to have watched them. For the first time, the new medium of television brought political spectacle into American living rooms, and it gripped the nation. The hearings also featured some nasty gay-baiting, primarily aimed at Roy Cohn.

The gay-baiting began outside the hearing room when Senator **Ralph Flanders**, a Vermont Republican and foe of McCarthy, demanded in a speech on the Senate floor that the hearings get to the "real heart" of the matter. To Flanders that meant the "mystery concerning the personal relationships of the army private, the staff assistant, and the senator. There is a relationship of the staff assistant to the senator. There is a relationship of the staff assistant to the army private. It is natural that he should wish to retain the services of an able collaborator, but he seems to have an almost passionate anxiety to retain him. Why? And then there is the senator himself. Does the staff assistant have some hold on the senator? . . .

Does the committee plan to investigate the real issues at stake?"

Members of the committee were also interested in this "almost passionate anxiety" to retain Private Schine. Here was the scene in the hearing room when Roy Cohn took the witness stand:

> SEN. JOHN MCCLELLAN (D-Arkansas): *First, I will ask you if you have any special interest in Mr. Schine?*
>
> ROY COHN: *I don't know what you mean by "special interest." He's a friend of mine.*
>
> MCCLELLAN: *I mean in friendship or anything else which would bind you to him closer than to the ordinary friend.*
>
> COHN: *Nothing. He is one of a number of very good friends whom I have. I am fortunate to have a large number.*

Roy Cohn (left) and Senator Joseph McCarthy (right), photographed during the Army-McCarthy hearings, April 1954.
(© UPI/Bettmann Newsphotos)

McClellan's attempt to pin down Cohn proved unsuccessful, but the subject of Cohn's sexual proclivities soon emerged in another way that was far more damaging. This occurred when the hearings became transfixed by the celebrated case of a cropped photo. The photograph in question, introduced into evidence by the McCarthy side, pictured Private G. David Schine posing with Secretary of the Army **Robert Stevens** at an air force base. The purpose of producing the photograph was to show the secretary being friendly and considerate to Private Schine, demonstrating that there had been no attempt on McCarthy and Cohn's part to blackmail the army. But the following day, **Joseph Welch**, the genteel, bow-tied Boston lawyer who represented the army, produced an enlargement of the same photo, which showed Stevens and Schine but also included Air Force Colonel Jack T. Bradley, to say nothing of the sleeve of yet another individual. The photo had been "altered, shamefully cut down," in order to give a deceptive impression of chumminess, insisted an outraged Welch, proof that McCarthy and Cohn could not be trusted. After a series of denials by McCarthy aides as to who was responsible for the cropping, Welch faced down **James N. Juliana**, a former FBI agent who worked for McCarthy:

WELCH: *I find myself so puzzled to know why you just did not take a photostat of the picture that was delivered to you that afternoon and hand it over to Mr. [Ray] Jenkins [counsel for the committee]. Would you tell us how come you did not do this?*

JULIANA: *I just mentioned or just stated that I was under instructions to furnish a picture of only the two individuals.*

WELCH: *And who gave you these instructions?*

JULIANA: *Jenkins and—or Cohn.*

WELCH: *Did you think this came from a pixie? Where did you think that this picture I hold in my hand came from?*

JULIANA: *I have no idea.*

McCARTHY (interrupting): *Will counsel for my benefit define—I think he might well be an expert on it—what a pixie is?*

WELCH: *Yes, I should say, Mr. Senator, that a pixie is a close relative of a fairy. Shall I proceed, sir? Have I enlightened you?*

The hearing room broke up in laughter. McCarthy forced a smile. Cohn tried his best to hide any expression at all. Cohn later called Welch's parry "malicious," "wicked," and "indecent." But he had been humiliated.

In the end, the Republican and Democratic committee members offered differing reports on the hearings. But McCarthy and Cohn had seemed embattled throughout and thoroughly outclassed by Welch. For the first time, senators had openly denounced McCarthy.

McCarthy still retained intact at least some of his ability to inspire fear in his enemies, but Cohn had clearly outlived his usefulness. Part of his undoing had been his bullying tactics toward the army, but more than that, he had been an easy target for the kind of gay-baiting he himself practiced. He resigned his subcommittee post and returned to New York to practice law.

On December 2, 1954, the U.S. Senate voted by a vote of sixty-seven to twenty-two to censure Senator McCarthy. Two years later he was dead. But the fear and paranoia McCarthy and his minions inspired took longer to die.

Roy Cohn can be seen as the exemplar of the homophobia of the 1950s turned inward—and outward—with destructive force and malice. But the panicky search for "perverts" in the McCarthy era went far beyond a few homosexuals in high posts at the State Department. In a culture that was largely hostile toward and ignorant about homosexuality, dire warnings about perverts in Washington helped to create an atmosphere of persecution and purge nationwide. In the nation's capital itself, arrests of gay men numbered one thousand a year in the 1950s, with D.C. police entrapping men in Lafayette Park and downtown movie houses. In Philadelphia, during the 1950s, misdemeanor charges against gay men and lesbians numbered one hundred a month. In Baltimore, in October 1955, 162 men were arrested in a police raid on a gay bar called Pepper Hill Club; twenty-four trips by police cars and paddy wagons were required to bring all the patrons to police headquarters. And in San Francisco, thirty-six women went to jail in September 1956 when the police raided the Alamo Club, a lesbian bar. Raids on gay bars were commonplace in many cities, and those arrested often found their names and addresses printed in the newspaper the next day. A survey conducted by Kinsey's Institute for Sex Research found that 20 percent of male homosexuals surveyed had had trouble with the police.

Starting in 1955, a Florida legislative committee headed by one-time governor and state senator **Charley Johns** conducted a nine-year investigation into suspected Communists, civil rights leaders, and homosexuals, particularly in academia and public education. As a result of the probe, more than one hundred teachers lost their jobs; students dropped out of college before earning their degrees. Records of the committee, released in 1993, indicated that individuals became targets of investigation because they were seen near suspected gay haunts, including a courthouse rest room, a university library, and a bus station. Many of the interrogations took place behind closed doors in hotel rooms. A state senator at the time who was not a member of the committee said that people targeted by the committee "were scared to death. It was the most insidious form of invasion of a person's privacy."

It was in more obscure parts of the country that some of the most grievous incidents of antigay persecution took place. In Boise, Idaho, in November 1955, the arrest of three men on charges of sexual activity with teenage boys precipitated a massive witch-hunt documented in John Gerassi's book *The Boys of Boise*. An editorial in the daily *Idaho Statesman*, entitled "Crush the Monster," helped provoke the panic. "It seems almost incredible that any such cancerous growth could have taken root and developed in our midst," the newspaper wrote. "The situation is one that causes general alarm and calls for immediate and systematic cauterization." Revealingly, the person brought in by Boise officials to perform the "cauterization" was an investigator who had worked purging homosexuals in the State Department. Over a fifteen-month period, some 1,472 men were brought in for questioning, sixteen were charged (several were sentenced to long prison terms), and large numbers of gay men fled the Idaho capital.

In a less well-known incident, in Sioux City, Iowa, some twenty-nine men were committed to a mental hospital in November 1955 after the unsolved kidnapping-murder of a young boy. The men were locked up on charges of morals offenses or "conspiracy to commit morals offenses" under a new Iowa law whose terminology made little distinction between "criminal sexual psychopaths" and homosexuals. The county attorney, **Don O'Brien**, was quoted as saying, "Word is out they're not welcome in Sioux City anymore." Dr. **W. B. Brown**, the state hospital superintendent, criticized the law and the incarcerations, however, complaining of a lack of facilities. He added, "There is no specific cure or treatment for that condition. . . . The law requires me to report to the court once a year. What can I say? I can't say they are cured."

The hospital superintendent's misgivings were shared by *One* magazine, the publication closely associated with the Mattachine Society, the early homosexual rights organization. "Will homosexual acts now cease to occur among Iowa's 2,700,000?" *One* asked. "Hardly. Nor do officials like O'Brien, or the ex-mayor of Miami, or anyone else, have the right to say homosexuals are 'not welcome' in a community. [Twenty-nine] scapegoats placed, till cured, with a doctor who can't cure them. Is this due process? Can every Iowan who has committed any 'unusual' sex act, or who might be accused of having a 'mental disorder' now be held indefinitely without specific charges or trial?"

Given the forces arrayed against them, there were few ways that gays and lesbians could defend themselves through established channels. Even the American Civil Liberties Union was unwilling to come to their defense. In January 1957 the ACLU board of directors adopted a national policy statement upholding the constitutionality of state sodomy laws, as well as federal security statutes banning the employment of gay men and women. "It is not within the province of the Union [the ACLU] to evaluate the social validity of the laws aimed at the suppression or elimination of homosexuals," the board of directors affirmed.

It was clearly up to gays and lesbians themselves to fight for their own interests. No one else would do so. In the midst of the relentless drumbeat about "perverts," of government purges and bar raids and police entrapments, the earliest U.S. gay organizations of any consequence—the Mattachine Society and the Daughters of Bilitis—made their cautious appearance. Homosexuals, rarely characterized by a sense of solidarity, began to organize against common oppression. In the witch-hunting atmosphere, a feeling was emerging that something *had* to be done.

Lieutenant Blick of the Vice Squad

A few months after Lieutenant Roy E. Blick of the Washington, D.C., Police Department told a Senate committee that there were five thousand "perverts" in Washington, D.C., precipitating a Senate investigation, Max Lerner, columnist for the anti-McCarthy New York Post, *interviewed Blick. What follows is an excerpt from the article which appeared in the July 18, 1950, edition of the* Post, *and which was reprinted in Lerner's collection* The Unfinished Country:

. . . LIEUTENANT BLICK is a tough cop. When I came into his office he was in the midst of a phone conversation about homosexuals which would have been wonderful detail for a documentary except that no one would dare put it on the screen. Burly, graying, and just ungrammatical enough to match a Hollywood pattern for police lieutenants, Blick has been on the Vice Squad nineteen years, and he has pride in his job. He has four detectives on his squad who do nothing but check on homosexuals. . . .

"We would all like to know," I said, "on what basis you reached your guesses [that there are five thousand homosexuals in Washington]."

Blick seemed to grow more restless at this point. He squirmed and twisted, thrust his hands up in a helpless gesture.

"We have these police records," he finally said. "You take the list. Well, every one of these fellows has friends. You multiply the list by a certain percentage—say three percent or four percent."

"Do you mean," I asked, "that your police list is only three or four percent of the total, and you multiply it by twenty-five or thirty?"

A faltering "Yes."

"If your final estimate was five thousand, does that mean your police list was less than two hundred?"

"No," he answered doubtfully. Then he added, "I mean five percent."

"You mean that you multiplied your list by twenty?"

Again a "Yes," then a "No." Finally, "I multiply my list by five."

"You mean you started with a list of one thousand and multiplied by five to get five thousand?"

Blick shifted his gaze around the room. Again the upward thrust of the hands, as if to say "How did a good cop ever get into this sort of a situation?" But he didn't answer my question.

I made a fresh start. "You have a list of the men you arrested?" He did.

"You also have a larger list, including men you never arrested?" After hesitation—Yes, he had a larger list as well.

"Did the fellows you arrested give the names of others?"

"Yes," he answered, this time with eagerness, "every one of these fellows has five or six friends. Take Smith. We bring him in. We say to him, 'Who are your friends?' He says, 'I have none.' I say, 'Oh, come on, Smith. We know you fellows go around in gangs. We know you go to rug parties. Who are your friends?' Then he tells us—Jones, Robinson."

"So you put Jones and Robinson down on your list?" I asked.

"Yes, we put them down."

"And that's how you compiled your list?" Yes, it was. . . .

This adventure in higher mathematics had exhausted both of us. I thought back grimly to the reverent way Senators and security officers used Blick's estimate of five thousand homosexuals in Washington, with 3,750 in the government, and I reflected that this was how a statistic got to be born. . . .

I asked him how he got his figure for the number of homosexuals working for the government.

"Oh," he said, "I took the five thousand for Washington. And I figured that three out of four of them worked for the government. . . ."

I could not detect that the Senators—or, for that matter, Lieutenant Blick—were in any way shocked by the hearsay aspect of the list he had compiled. For Lieutenant Blick's importance in Washington is not only that he has become one of its statisticians, but even more that he is the Great Proscriber. In the days of Marius and Sulla, of schoolboy fame in Roman history, the prominent people in the senatorial and popular parties trembled when they found their names proscribed on a list, for it meant death. Lieutenant Blick's is the most important homosexual list distributed among government agencies. The hearsay aspect is that the names which appear on it are not only those of the Smiths who have been arrested by Blick's vice squad, but also those of the Joneses and Robinsons whom Smith under questioning had mentioned. . . .

Lieutenant Blick glows at Senator Wherry's recommendation that the District Vice Squad be strengthened with a greater appropriation. He also wishes he had a Lesbian squad.

Garden of Pansies—The Hand-On-Hip Set Wins the Battle of Washington

In the late 1940s and early 1950s, Hearst newspaper reporters Jack Lait and Lee Mortimer wrote a series of snappy and sensational books about various American cities with titles like New York Confidential, Chicago Confidential, *and, in 1951,* Washington Confidential. *The books occupied a unique territory between exposé and travel guide. "We are not reformers," wrote the authors in the introduction to* Washington Confidential. *"We are reporters. As such we will take you with us through a metropolitan area of 1,500,000, living in what should be a utopia, but which is a cesspool of drunkenness, debauchery, whoring, homosexuality, municipal corruption, and public apathy. . . . That's why we were born—to tell you what you couldn't find out without us—Confidential!"* Washington Confidential *features chapters like CHINATOWN CHIPPIES ("Washington's Chinatown offers inducements other than Chop Suey and Chow Mein"), THERE'S NOTHING LIKE A DAME ("You can say that again about those in Washington"), and IT'S A CRIME ("Murder and mayhem, rape and robbery are pastimes in Washington. Jail? Don't be naive"). It also included a "Confidential Guide" that listed everything from baby-sitting services to tattoo parlors (It also curiously listed "Drags, Costumes For, Also Wigs: Jack Mullane, 714 11th St."). In the chapter, "Garden of Pansies," Lait and Mortimer linked homosexuality with subversion (see below) and offered the following portayal of gay life in the nation's capital:*

IF YOU'RE WONDERING where your wandering semi-boy is tonight, he's probably in Washington. . . . The Washington vice squad had listed 5,000 known deviates. Dr. Ben Karpman, psychiatrist at St. Elizabeth's Hospital, believes they are in the tens of thousands.

Their chief meeting place is in leafy Lafayette Square, across

Pennsylvania Avenue from the White House. They make love under the equestrian statue of rugged Andrew Jackson, who must be whirling on his heavenly horse every time he sees what is going on around his monument. . . .

Many rich fairies and lesbians live in expensive remodeled Georgetown homes, the nearest thing to a left-bank neighborhood. This is also a left-wing center.

Some parties which take place in Washington pervert sets are orgies beyond description and imagination. Every invention of Sacher-Mosach and the Marquis de Sade has been added to and improved upon, and is in daily use. Weekends find the pansies and lady-lovers on broad, baronial estates of wealthy perverts in nearby Virginia and Maryland. Many of the third sex journey regularly to New York, where they have friends in esoteric circles. . . .

Black Washington has its share of deviates, too.

During the summer, groups of colored fairies make up "yachting" parties and cruise the Potomac on the steamer *Robert E. Lee*. One Saturday night, last summer, over 100 cops were dispatched to the docks when the "Society of Female Impersonators" was to have a midnight sail. They found one thousand seven hundred Negro men, all dressed as women, on the boat, and as many more trying to get on. A riot was in the making, but the cops busted it up and kept it quiet when they hauled away two wagon loads. The ship finally got off at 2 A.M. . . .

No one knows how many lesbians there are, because the female— or is it male—of the pervert species is seldom spoken about and is much less obvious. Psychiatrists and sociologists who have made a study of the problem in Washington think there are at least twice as many Sapphic lovers as fairies. . . .

A breakdown of occupations in one group of 543 perverts who were arrested showed some interesting sidelights. Among them was only one actor, but 92 students. There were 58 army personnel and 28 from the navy. Even the rugged Marines appeared. Among the deviates were one bartender, one barber and one baker. There were four attorneys, only two doctors and only one embalmer. This is the record:

Accountant	7	Minister	3
Actor	1	Musician	5
Airport employee	3	Navy:	
Army:		Commissioned	1
Commissioned	9	Noncommissioned	27
Noncommissioned	49	Page boy	1
Attorney	4	Pharmacist	4
Baker	1	Porter	6
Barber	1	Radio personnel	3
Bartender	1	Realtor	2
Businessman	7	Reporter	2
Butcher	1	Restaurant personnel	27
Cab driver	2	Salesman	10
Clerk	48	Sculptor	2
Diplomat	1	Servant	10
Doctor	2	Service-station operator	2
Embalmer	1	Skilled laborer	17
Embassy personnel	1	Stenographer and	
Government		secretary	4
employee	57	Student	92
Guard	9	Teacher and Professor	12
Historian	1	Technician	8
Horse breeder	1	Unemployed	50
Interior decorator	3	Unskilled laborer	31
Jeweler	1	Writer	2
Laundryman	6		
Librarian	3	Total	543
Marines, U.S.	2		

The Fruit Machine

ONE OF THE MOST BIZARRE CREATIONS of the 1950s antigay witch-hunts was an experimental device known as "the Fruit Machine." Created by the Security Panel of the Canadian government, it was a technological creation that had "shades of George Orwell and Woody Allen," as reporter John Sawatsky described it in his book *Men in the Shadows*. Its purpose was to detect homosexuals among Canadian civil servants, resulting in their dismissal. The machine was supposed to give objective evidence that someone was homosexual by measuring how the pupils of his or her eyes changed in size in response to visual sexual stimulation. In theory, a photograph of a nude male would cause a male homosexual's pupils to expand, providing ipso facto proof of his sexual proclivities (and presumed susceptibility to blackmail).

The project was top-secret. It continued for years and involved scientists and senior government officials. Funding was arranged through the Defence Research Board and office space was located in a psychology laboratory in the National Defence Medical Center. Psychiatrists and psychologists were recruited from the outside to work as consultants. With the Americans pressuring Canada to purge homosexuals in the civil service, the rationale was in part humane: Here was a way of determining who might be homosexual without resorting to the "naming names" approach with all its potential for abuse.

"The Fruit Machine" was essentially a camera suspended from a pully. As Sawatsky describes it, the subject sat in a chair similar to one found in a dentist's office, with the camera hung above him, pointed toward his pupils. In front was a black box with a fluorescent screen and a projector beaming pictures inside. The pictures ranged from boring, daily scenes to sexually explicit photographs of men and women. The subject being tested was told that it was an experiment to measure stress.

One of the participants in the experiment described the machine to Sawatsky this way: "It looked like something out of science fiction. It didn't look as if it had been built on earth. I'm not trying to be sensational about that. It was a whole bunch of girders that were small flanges to bolt equipment together, and a screen in a box containing naughty pictures."

As it turned out, "the Fruit Machine" was bedeviled with problems. First, word leaked out about the true nature of the project, and few people could be talked into volunteering. Then there were technical flaws—both in terms of lighting and measurement of the pupil—that were never solved, the major problem being that change in pupil size was so small it was difficult to measure. Finally, after four years, the project was doomed by budget cuts. By that time, the Security Panel was abandoning its previous policy of wholesale purging of gay civil servants, approaching homosexuality on a case-by-case basis instead. Fear of homosexuality as a security menace was waning in Canada. But long after its demise, "the Fruit Machine" remains one of the most bizarre legacies of the homosexual panic of the 1950s.

CHAPTER 19

THE STRUGGLE FOR BRITISH
LAW REFORM, 1950–1967

WHEN KING HENRY VIII reformed the church in England in 1533 and curtailed the power of the ecclesiastical courts, the "abominable Vice of Buggery" (anal intercourse between men) became a criminal offense, punishable by the state. It carried the death penalty. By the early nineteenth century, British courts were still pronouncing the death sentence: An average of two men were hanged each year for buggery from 1806 through 1836, the year when the last execution took place. In 1861, the death penalty was abolished for the offense. Buggery (sodomy) was now punishable by life imprisonment, while attempted buggery carried a ten-year sentence. In 1885 the Labouchère Amendment was enacted, extending the law for the first time to include oral sex between men (called "gross indecency"), punishable by two years in prison.

The casualties of Britain's laws prohibiting sexual acts between consenting adult men are legion—from the most famous casualty, Oscar Wilde, down through the years. In 1942, the writer J. R. Ackerley stumbled across a case in the Welsh border town of Abergavenny in which twenty men were put on trial for homosexual behavior. During the course of the proceedings, one nineteen-year-old defendant committed suicide by throwing himself in front of a train, and two others attempted unsuccessfully to kill themselves by hanging or poison or both. One man suffered a stroke after being arrested; paralyzed on one side, he had to be dragged to the dock and supported there by officers. Sentences in the case ranged from one to twelve years. An outraged Ackerley wrote a letter to *The Spectator,* questioning whether this was "the most enlightened method of dealing with this matter." But nothing happened. The subject remained unmentionable.

During the 1930s, prosecutions of men arrested for consensual homosexual offenses averaged about 500 a year in England and Wales. After the War, the numbers began to climb steadily—to 1,666 in 1950 and to 2,504 in 1955. By the 1950s, entrapment emerged as a common means to arrest homosexuals, particularly in public lavatories. "Chain" prosecutions became widespread as well, with the police offering immunity to witnesses who reported on other gay men. Four percent of male prisoners in British jails were said to be incarcerated for the crime of sexual relations with other men.

At least some of the increase in police activity was related to the Cold War and McCarthy period atmosphere, especially after the disappearance, in May 1951, of two senior British diplomats, Guy Burgess and Donald Maclean, accused of spying for the Soviet Union. (They turned up in Moscow in 1956.) Both were widely assumed to be gay. Two weeks after their disappearance, the *Sunday Dispatch* newspaper alluded to the event, suggesting it was time to follow the American policy of "weeding out both sexual and political perverts." According to **Peter Wildeblood**, a journalist who was to be arrested in the most famous sex scandal of the decade, the American security agencies pressured their British counterparts to do exactly that. Wildeblood asserts that it was after a meeting with FBI officials in the early fifties that the new Commissioner of Police at Scotland Yard, Sir **John Nott-Bower**, stepped up arrests of homosexual men.

The idea that the Americans were largely behind this was manifested in the popular fiction of the day. **Nancy Mitford**'s 1957 satirical novel, *The Blessing*, features a dinner party in which a senior American official, Hector Dexter, lectures the guests on the "frivolous attitude" of the British toward sexual perversion. He insists that the British have "absolutely no conception of the danger in your midst" and that "sickly, morbose, healthless, cholorotic, unbraced, flagging, peccant, vitiated, and contaminated" homosexuals were working behind the scenes for Moscow. When another guest objects that "all the old queens I know are terrific old Tories," Dexter replies:

> I am bound to contradict you. . . . We Americans, you may know, have certain very very sure and reliable, I would even say infallible, sources of information. We have our Un-American Activities Committee sections, we have our F.B.I. agents, we have countless very very brilliant newspaper men and businessmen all over the world. . . . And our sources of information inform us that nine out of every ten, and some say ninety-nine out of every hundred, of these morally sick persons are not only in the very

closest sympathy but in actual contact with Moscow. And I for one entirely believe these sources.

Contrary to what Mitford's character assumed, the crackdown had wide support in Britain. Sir **David Maxwell-Fyfe**, the Home Secretary, known for having cross-examined Goering at the Nuremberg War Crimes tribunal, told the House of Commons that homosexuals in general were "exhibitionists and proselytizers and a danger to others, especially the young." The medical journal *The Practitioner* suggested that homosexuals be sent to St. Kilda in the Outer Hebrides, an island inhabited entirely by puffins and other seabirds. Residence on St. Kilda would "strengthen their [homosexuals'] resolve" in a "natural and bracing climate," suggested the magazine. On the other side of the globe, **C. J. Delaney**, the Police Commissioner for the Australian state of New South Wales, asserted that the two greatest threats facing Australia were communism and homosexuality. The antigay hysteria of the McCarthy period met the traditional harshness of British law—and the laws that British rule had left in former colonies around the world. The results were often devastating.

In the early 1950s, a series of cases brought public attention to the growing police activity—and to the law itself. In January 1953, **William Field,** a Labour Party member of Parliament, was arrested in Piccadilly Circus and charged with importuning men for an immoral purpose; he lost his parliamentary seat. Soon after, the actor Sir **John Gielgud** was arrested in a public lavatory; he was fined ten pounds by a magistrate who suggested he seek the advice of a physician. The following year, **Lord Montagu,** who had reported a theft to the police, found himself accused of an "indecent attack" on two Boy Scouts. Montagu was acquitted. He was then immediately re-arrested, along with two of his friends—his cousin **Michael Pitt-Rivers,** and Peter Wildeblood, diplomatic correspondent for the *Daily Mail*—and accused of new charges related to improper behavior with two young airmen in the summer of 1952. During the trial, however, a number of police abuses came to light, including police tampering with Lord Montagu's passport in an effort to destroy his alibi. Nonetheless, the three men were all found guilty and sent to prison. (Wildeblood wrote an account of the trial and imprisonment called *Against the Law,* which was published in 1955.)

In the wake of the verdict, public opinion began to shift. The two airmen who testified against Montagu in exchange for immunity from prosecution were booed after they left the courtroom. In an editorial a few days after the conclusion of the trial, the influential *Sunday Times* suggested that the law was not in accord with the feelings of a large segment of the public. "The case for reform of the law as to acts committed in private between adults is very strong," the newspaper wrote. The House of Lords held a full-scale debate on the subject of homosexuality, the first in modern British history. Three months later, in August 1954, the Home Secretary asked Sir **John Wolfenden**, Vice Chancellor of Reading University, to head an inquiry into the issues of homosexuality and prostitution. The stage was set for law reform.

As Stephen Jeffery-Poulter recounts in his chronicle of the law reform struggle, *Peers, Queers, and Commons,* Wolfenden and his committee of fifteen—including three OBEs, two members of Parliament, two ministers, a judge, and a Marquess—deliberated for two years. "We read mountains of memoranda submitted to us as written evidence; and we interviewed dozens of oral witnesses," wrote Wolfenden in his autobiography. "We did honestly try to include all those who thought they had a message for us, whether they were aiming to be 'objective' or were explicately 'subjective.' "
Outside the committee hearing room, pressure for reform continued to build. E. M. Forster, commanding great respect (and still in the closet), wrote a 1955 article in the *New Statesman* urging law reform; he noted that in one police court alone six hundred cases of male solicitation had been heard. The popular novelist **Compton Mackenzie**, who had examined lesbianism back in the 1920s in his book *Extraordinary Women,* took a sympathetic look at a member of Parliament blackmailed for being gay in a new novel, *Thin Ice.* The book was in part a brief for law reform; at one point, a character states that three-quarters of the male suicides in England were the result of blackmail for homosexual activity.

On September 4, 1957, after sixty-two meetings in which it heard testimony from two hundred different individuals and organizations, the Wolfenden Committee announced its long-awaited conclusion: "We accordingly recommend that homosexual behavior between consenting adults in private should no longer be a criminal offense." The committee also recommended that the age of consent for male homosexual relations be fixed at twenty-one, putting England's laws in line with France, which had raised its age of consent after the war. The report contended that a boy of sixteen was incapable of "forming a mature judgement about actions of the kind which might have the effect of setting him apart from the rest of society." (By contrast, the age of consent for heterosexual and lesbian sex was sixteen.) The Wolfenden conclusions made front-page headlines:

VICE OFFICIAL: NO WHITEWASH, NO PRUDERY AND NO HYPOCRISY—*Daily Mirror*

RELAX THIS SEX LAW—*Evening Standard*

VICE, THE STARK FACTS—*Scottish Daily Record*

Overall, press reaction was favorable. The conservative *Daily Telegraph* called the Wolfenden Report "clear, conscientious, and courageous"; the left-wing *Guardian* described it as "a fine piece of work." Criticism came primarily from the right-wing *Daily Express* and *Evening Standard,* and from the Scottish press. The public was less than enthusiastic, however. A Gallup poll showed that 38 percent of Britons backed decriminalization, while 47 percent wanted to keep the law. In Scotland, opposition was even stronger: A poll by the *Scottish Daily Record* showed an overwhelming 85 percent against decriminalization.

In view of popular feeling, the Tory Party government was reluctant to introduce a bill in Parliament implementing the Wolfenden recommendations. In 1960, restless supporters of reform moved in the House of Commons that the government take "early action" to implement the Wolfenden recommendations. This was defeated 213 to 99. Among the few Conservative Party members who voted in favor of acting on Wolfenden was **Margaret Thatcher**, who later as prime minister was to gain the enmity of the gay community for her restrictions on government funding of gay and lesbian groups.

Despite the lack of progress on the enactment of the Wolfenden recommendations, English law and society were changing. In 1958, the Lord Chamberlain lifted the ban on plays with homosexual themes, permitting "sincere and serious" portrayals of homosexuality in the theater. This helped pave the way for the iconoclastic dramas of gay playwright **Joe Orton**, and **Frank Marcus**'s *The Killing of Sister George,* the story of a fading radio soap-opera star and her younger female lover. (The Lord Chamberlain's censorship powers were abolished altogether in 1968.) The British Board of Film Censors liberalized its policies as well. In 1960 two films about the life of Oscar Wilde were released; 1961 saw the release of a film version of **Shelagh Delaney**'s play *A Taste of Honey,* featuring a sympathetic, if pitiable, gay character; the same year came *Victim,* a movie starring **Dirk Bogarde** about a lawyer blackmailed for his homosexuality (See *"Victim,"* page 290). In 1959, Parliament approved the Obscene Publications Act, permitting the courts for the first time to take artistic merit and social importance into consideration when determining whether a book was fit to be published. The next year, Penguin Books brought out the unexpurgated version of **D. H. Lawrence**'s *Lady Chatterley's Lover.* The director of public prosecutions put the book on trial, a trial that featured a number of "expert" witnesses of the sort (E. M. Forster and Rebecca West, for example) whose testimony had been disallowed at the proceedings against *The Well of Loneliness* thirty years before. The book was judged not obscene, opening the door for all kinds of works portraying sex in a frank way. By the mid 1960s, censorship in print, on the stage, and in film—which for so long had inhibited open discussion about homosexuality—was almost dead in England.

This cultural and social liberalization reflected a generational changing of the guard as well. As Noel Annan writes:

> It also began to be recognized how much homosexuals enriched the nation's culture. Hardly surprising since by the sixties the best known English-born poet, the outstanding composer, the most famous choreographer, and the most prestigious painter— [W. H.] Auden, [Benjamin] Britten, [Frederick] Ashton, and [Francis] Bacon—were all known to be homosexuals. The generation which had admired so many dazzling performances by homosexuals on stage and screen, and the brilliance of men in academic, scientific and professional life who had remained conspicuously unmarried—this generation was now coming to power.

A year after the Wolfenden recommendations were made public, the Homosexual Law Reform Society (HLRS) and its fund-raising arm, the Albany Trust, were established. The group, whose purpose was to persuade Parliament to decriminalize homosexual acts, did not identify as a gay organization and had an honorary board of distinguished (heterosexual) figures ranging from **Bertrand Russell** to **Julian Huxley**. In May 1960, it held its first public meeting, in central London, attracting over a thousand people. Such a large meeting around the subject of gay rights was an extraordinary event in England. Otherwise, though, the HLRS was relatively cautious in its approach. It sent copies of its pamphlet "Homosexuality and the Law" to members of Parliament, met with the Home Secretary, formed branches around the country, and generally tried to educate the public about the need for a change in the law. Despite these efforts, the government was still reluctant to introduce a bill to implement Wolfenden.

In the 1964 election, the Conservative Party government was defeated, and the more sympathetic Labour Party, with reformer **Roy Jenkins** as Home Secretary, came to power. But Labour, with a majority of only four in the House of Commons, was almost as reluctant to move on law reform as the Conservatives had been. The following year, an elderly and somewhat eccentric peer, **Lord Arran**, introduced a private member's bill—that is, legislation not officially backed by the government—in the House of Lords to enact the Wolfenden recommendations. Arran's motives are unclear. He is said to have had a homosexual older brother who died tragically; some speculated that he wanted to make some reparation for his brother's death by pushing law reform. The peer himself was put under great stress in his role of leading sponsor of the bill—at one point, his office, his club, and a number of railway and subway stations in London were covered in graffiti that read, "ARRAN HOMO." "It was at this time that I began to drink, not heavily or, I like to think, noticeably," he said in a magazine article some years later. "But for over a year, I was permanently, if slightly, pickled." When the law reform bill passed the Lords, by a 94-to-49 vote in May 1965, Lord Arran pronounced the victory "the only great moment of my small life."

The most vocal opposition to the bill came from former military men such as **Viscount Montgomery**, hero of the World War II Battle of El Alamein, who told the Lords, "I regard the act of homosexuality in any form as the most abominable bestiality that any human being can take part in." Montgomery noted that some had said that such practices were allowed in France and other NATO countries. "We are not French, and we are not other nationals," Montgomery thundered. "We are British, thank God!" He suggested that the age of consent be fixed at eighty.

But a private member's bill is notoriously difficult to pass in Britain. It wasn't until July 1967—this time with behind-the-scenes government support—that decriminalization passed the House of Commons by a 101–16 vote and became law. Later that same month, Parliament approved the legalization of abortion in Britain as well.

Victory was not entirely sweet, however. The armed forces and the merchant navy were exempted from law reform, for one thing. The age of consent was set at twenty-one for all sexual acts between men. The prison sentence for an adult found guilty of committing "gross indecency" (oral sex) with another male between sixteen and twenty-one was actually *increased* from two years to five years. The new law also stated that a homosexual act would not be considered private when two or more persons took part or were present. Stephen Jeffery-Poulter notes that the approval of an age of consent five years higher than that for heterosexual or lesbian sex implied that male homosexuality was "some sort of insidious sickness which could be spread by infecting others." (It was not until 1994 that the age of consent was reduced to 18, still higher than that for heterosexual or lesbian relations.) And Lord Arran's final statement in Parliament was more of a grim reminder than anything else:

> *Homosexuals must continue to remember that while there may be nothing bad in being a homosexual, there is certainly nothing good. Lest the opponents of the Bill think that a new freedom, a new privileged class, has been created, let me remind them that no amount of legislation will prevent homosexuals from being the subject of dislike and derision or at best of pity. We shall always, I fear, resent the odd man out. That is their burden for all time, and they must shoulder it like men—for men they are.*

While the new law applied to England and Wales, consenting sexual relations between adult men remained illegal in the rest of the United Kingdom. It wasn't until thirteen years and innumerable parliamentary debates later that, in 1980, law reform was extended to Scotland. The case of Northern Ireland (Ulster) was more complicated—and more dramatic. Unlike in England, the Northern Irish campaign for law reform was largely the work of local gay activists.

As Jeffery-Poulter recounts, in 1976, the Royal Ulster Constabulary drugs squad carried out raids on the homes of a number of those involved in the campaign (they were eventually acquitted). In the wake of what appeared to be harassment toward them, Northern Ireland gays decided to submit their case to the European Court of Human Rights. Submissions to the European Court had to be made on an individual, not a group, basis. As a result, one activist, **Jeff Dudgeon**, came forth and contended that by refusing to legalize consenting homosexual behavior in Ulster, the British government was invading his privacy and discriminating against him. He officially accused the government of violating Articles 8 and 14 of the European Convention on Human Rights.

As pressure increased, the Northern Ireland Human Rights Commission recommended in July 1977 that law reform be extended to Ulster, and the British government announced it would issue a draft proposal to that effect. At that point, **Ian Paisley**, leader of Ulster's militant Protestants, intervened. He initiated a "Save Ulster from Sodomy" campaign, urging the citizenry to sign a petition opposing law reform. A cavalcade of more than sixty cars converged on Stormont, the Northern Ireland parliament, in early 1978, bearing a petition containing 70,000 names.

While this backlash caused the government in London to shelve reform, it did, however, promise not to prosecute Ulster gays for behavior that was legal in England. Meanwhile, Dudgeon's case continued to move through the torturous European judicial machinery. In September 1980, the European Commission ruled unanimously that the British government was guilty of breaching Article 8 of the European Convention on Human Rights by interfering with Dudgeon's private life. The following year, the European Court met in Strasbourg and ruled in favor of Dudgeon by a 15–4 vote. It was the first gay rights case ever decided by the European Court. On October 25, 1982, law reform in Northern Ireland passed the House of Commons and became law. Adult, consensual homosexual acts were finally legal throughout the United Kingdom.

Once the law was reformed at home, change in the former and present outposts of the Empire that had inherited the British sodomy laws was not far behind. In August 1969, Canada repealed its prohibitions on sex between consenting adults. In 1972, South Australia became the first Australian state to do so; New South Wales and Victoria followed soon after. By 1994, the island of Tasmania remained the only Australian state where the sodomy laws remained on the books. In New Zealand, after a long and arduous campaign, Parliament narrowly approved law reform in 1986. (In 1993, New Zealand passed a nationwide law banning discrimination against gays and lesbians.) And in the crown colony of Hong Kong, anticipating the Chinese Communist takeover in 1997, the Legislative Council voted in July 1990 to reform its sodomy law. Like the Northern Irish reform battle, many of these legal changes were largely due to the efforts of gay activists and gay political groups.

With the enactment of law reform—and the arrival of the 1960s—"puritanical and joyless London," as J. R. Ackerley once characterized it, began to change. The first British gay publications, *Timm, Jeremy,* and *Spartacus,* were launched. A gay political organization—the Committee for Homosexual Equality—began to agitate for a lowering of the age of consent. An initial attempt to set up a network of gay social facilities throughout the country failed, however; among the opponents were parliamentary supporters of law reform, including Lord Arran, who condemned the idea as "an open flaunting of the new and legal freedom of outlet." But a number of gay social groups eventually did emerge, to say nothing of the gay discos that began to replace the depressing and clandestine clubs that existed before reform. The relaxation of the laws concerning male homosexual sex coincided with the temper of the times. It was the era of Carnaby Street, of sexually ambiguous pop stars like **Mick Jagger** and **David Bowie,** and "swinging London." As the poet **Philip Larkin** put it in "Annus Mirabilis":

> *Sexual intercourse began*
> *In nineteen sixty-three*
> *(Which was rather late for me)*
> *Between the end of the Chatterley ban*
> *And the Beatles' first LP.*

For gay men, legal freedom would have to wait a few years beyond 1963. But for them, it was a new world, too, a world in which the international currents of gay liberation would soon flow, even in England.

Victim

THE MOST IMPORTANT BRITISH FILM on a gay theme during the period in which censorship began to relax was *Victim*, directed by **Basil Dearden** and starring Dirk Bogarde. A gritty black-and-white thriller that pleaded for tolerance for homosexuals, *Victim* was released in 1961, at a time when the Wolfenden Report had been published but the law banning sex between consenting adult males remained on the books. As a director, Dearden was known for his naturalistic approach to serious subjects. His 1959 film, *Sapphire,* was a detective story about the murder of a half-black woman who had been passing for white. In *Victim,* the subject is homosexual blackmail, rampant at the time. A married, upper-middle-class barrister named Melville Farr (Bogarde) is being black-mailed through a young working-class gay man named "Boy" Barrett (**Peter McEnery**), with whom he had a brief but platonic relationship. McEnery is arrested for stealing from his employer to ward off the blackmailer, and ends up hanging himself in jail. The Bogarde character, who had been unaware of the blackmail attempt and that McEnery was stealing in order to protect him, embarks on a quest to apprehend the blackmailers, even though it will un-questionably ruin his career—and perhaps his marriage (to the loyal **Sylvia Sims**).

Bogarde's attempt to persuade a number of frightened gay men to stand up to the blackmailers takes him on a journey through London's gay subculture. *Victim* presents a number of gay char-acters (played by superb British character actors) who are neither stereotypical nor sentimentalized—an aging hairdresser with a "weak heart" who sells his shop to flee to Canada to avoid black-mailers and the law; an actor who tries to divert Bogarde from his attempt to challenge the status quo; and the chief blackmailer him-self, a handsome but sinister type who dresses in leather, wears aviator glasses, and rides a motorcycle.

Melville Farr, the character played by Bogarde, is an early gay hero, noble, self-sacrificing, "with credentials enough to get into heaven," as Vito Russo notes in his book, *The Celluloid Closet.*

And while the film largely avoids preachiness, it doesn't fail to make its points. "As many as 90 percent of all blackmail cases have a homosexual origin," a sympathetic police inspector notes. "A law that sends homosexuals to prison offers unlimited opportunities for blackmail." Later, the same policeman tells Farr, "Someone once called this law against homosexuality the blackmailer's charter."

"Is that how you feel about it?" Farr asks.

"I'm a policeman, sir," he replies. "I don't have feelings."

Bogarde put his own career on the line to appear in *Victim,* a decision he called "the wisest" he ever made in his cinematic life. "It is extraordinary, in this over-permissive age, to believe that this modest film could have been considered courageous, daring or dangerous to make," he wrote in his autobiography, *Snakes and Ladders.* Few of the actors approached to appear in it accepted; every actress asked to play the wife turned the role down without even reading the script, except for Sylvia Sims. When production began, the set was closed to all visitors, the media kept out, and the "whole project was treated, at the beginning, with all the false reverence, dignity, and respect usually accorded to the Crucifixion or Queen Victoria," Bogarde recalled.

The film was well-received in Britain, and was the British entry in the Venice Film Festival. In America, however, *Victim* failed to gain Motion Picture Production Code approval, even though restrictions on homosexual depictions had been liberalized only two months before. The Motion Picture Association of America decided that the film violated the code through its "candid and clinical discussion of homosexuality and its overtly expressed plea for social acceptance of the homosexual." Although *Victim* was shown at a few art cinemas in the U.S., without code approval it failed to gain widespread release.

Alan Turing, Secret Hero

ONE OF THE CASUALTIES of the increase in prosecutions for homosexual acts in Britain in the early 1950s was the mathematical genius **Alan Turing** (1912–54). Turing has been described as one of the "secret heroes" of World War II. While working for the British government's Code and Cypher School, he invented the device that cracked the "Enigma," the German military code. This gave British and Allied forces advance knowledge of German land and sea maneuvers, enabling the British to win the Battle of the Atlantic. In the postwar years, Turing played a major role in the development of the modern computer, giving his name to an early facsimile called the "Turing Machine." Noel Annan, who had rooms below Turing at Cambridge University just after the War, saw him at less heroic moments. "He was a cross-country runner of international stature and enjoyed games and treasure hunts and silliness," Annan noted. "He poked fun at conventional people, enjoyed teasing the humanists by arguing that thought was made up of inputs and outputs and of storage capacity. If a machine could solve problems, could it not also think? Could it not write a sonnet?"

Turing was also a homosexual at a time when it was very dangerous to be one, especially one with a "powerful brain," as the tabloid *News of the World* put it. At Christmas 1951, while a professor at Manchester University, he met **Arnold Murray**, a nineteen-year-old working-class youth, and began a brief affair. A month later, a friend of Murray's burglarized Turing's apartment, with Murray's knowledge. Turing reported the burglary to the police. During the course of the investigation, whether out of naivete, fear, or arrogance, Turing admitted that he and Murray had had sex together. In February 1952, Britain's foremost mathematician was arrested on charges of "gross indecency," punishable by two years in prison. He and Murray were among 2,109 men against whom charges were brought that year for homosexual offenses in England and Wales.

The two men went on trial in late March 1952. They both pleaded guilty. Turing's colleagues from the university came to testify on his behalf. Murray was conditionally discharged, eventually finding his way into the world of London coffeehouses. Turing was placed on probation, on the condition that he undergo an experimental medical treatment called "organo-therapy." He was to be injected with female hormones for a year, in an effort to reduce his libido. After the treatment, he wrote a friend, he expected to return to normal. An additional problem, however, was that the injections would cause him to grow breasts.

After his trial and conviction, accounts of Turing's life become rather murky. He returned to work. He traveled to Norway on vacation and met a young Norwegian man. The Norwegian came to visit him in England but was apparently prevented from seeing Turing by the authorities. Turing's probation ended. Manchester University appointed him to a specially created position. He traveled to Greece. Then, on the evening of June 7, 1954, in his apartment in Manchester, Alan Turing killed himself, eating an apple dipped in cyanide.

Years later, gay historian **Andrew Hodges** reconstructed Turing's life, work, and death in a meticulously researched biography called *Alan Turing: The Enigma*. A play based on Turing's life, *Breaking the Code*, by Hugh Whitemore, ran successfully in London, New York, and Washington, D.C. In his book, Hodges makes a strong case that Turing was a victim of Britain's McCarthyite hysteria, that his conviction for "gross indecency" may have made his loyalty suspect. He told at least one colleague that he had been banned from cryptanalytic work because he was homosexual. His Norwegian friend, even though a national of a friendly country, was not permitted to visit him. As Hodges points out, in the mind of those concerned with national security, Turing had committed a "grave indiscretion." His brain, "filled with knowledge of the British cryptographic and cryptanalytic work of not ten years before, had been allowed to mingle with the street life of Oxford Road—and who knew where else?" Ironically, even with law reform, Turing's "crime" would still have been considered as such for the next three decades. The young man he became involved with was nineteen—two years below the age of consent that prevailed until 1994.

Piccadilly Polari

IN THE 1960S, London gays, particularly young gay men who frequented certain clubs in Soho, developed their own slang called polari (also spelled parlyaree or palare). It was a secret camp language that was never written down and was inaccessible to anyone but the initiated. Some of it originated in the backslang developed in the East End of London. The polari word *riah*, for example, meaning hair, is simply hair spelled backward. Sometimes, back-slang changed its spelling and pronunciation. For example, *ecaf,* face spelled backward, soon became *eek.* Words came from other languages, legacies of the generations of immigrants—Jews and French Huguenots, for example—who settled in the East End. *Capela,* the polari word for hat, seems to have come from the Yiddish, and *homme,* meaning men, from the French. *Naff,* the word for heterosexual man, is said to have come from the initials of the words "Normal as Fuck," but it also may be derived from the French "naif." These days, polari has died out, but one can still find traces of it, for example, in the title of the 1990 album by the pop singer **Morrissey**, called *Bona Drag,* polari for fabulous clothes. (In the song, "Piccadilly Palare" on the same album, Morrissey sings of "lovely eek" and "lovely riah)."

In his memoir of gay London in the 1960s and '70s, *Parallel Lives,* journalist **Peter Burton** recalls polari speakers who "were able to hold entire conversations which included barely a word of English." He describes those days and the evolution of a more uninhibited gay male culture than had been seen previously in Britain:

> As feely hommes *(young men), when we launched ourselves onto the gay scene, polari was all the rage. We would* zhoosh *(style) our riahs (hair), powder our eeks (faces), climb into our bona (fabulous) new drag (clothes), don our batts (shoes) and troll (go, walk) off to some bona bijou (little) bar.*
>
> *In the bar, we would stand around polarying with our sisters, varda (look at) the bona cartes (male genitals) on the butch homme (man, pronounced "o-me") ajax (nearby) who, if we fluttered our ogle riahs (eyelashes) at him sweetly, might just troll over to offer a light for the unlit vogue (cigarette) clenched between our teeth. If we had enough bona measures (money), we might buy a handful of doobs to zhoosh (throw) down our screeches (mouth or throat)—enabling us to get blocked out of our minds. . . .*
>
> *We weren't butch hommes—as anyone who has read this far will have gathered. We were hommes pollones (effeminate men), feely hommes, bona chickens living in a mixed up world, outrageous, possibly objectionable—but we didn't care. That the combination of high camp, low living, promiscuous sex, drugs,*

and cheap gin didn't kill more of us off than it did (and a lot of people from those days are dead now) is amazing. . . .

Ultimately, for us, there was something deeply reassuring about polari. This bizarre secret language gave those of us who used it an additional sense of corporate identity. We were part of a group—and that knowledge was both a comfort and a curious protection.

Canada Reforms Its Laws

IN CANADA, as in England (and in every state in the U.S.), male homosexual acts were against the law through the 1950s. "Gross indecency" (oral sex) was punishable by five years in prison. In 1953, "gross indecency" was extended to female homosexual acts as well. The laws in Canada were rarely enforced, however. As Vancouver gay activist **Doug Sanders** put it, "The problem in Canada was not persecution but the pervasive view that gays didn't exist." After the publication of the Wolfenden Report in England, and the passage of law reform there in 1967, interest in decriminalization began to grow in Canada as well.

But little happened in Canada until the shocking and controversial case of **Everett Klippert** gained national attention. Klippert was a mechanic's helper at Pine Point, in the Northwest Territories. In 1965, during a police investigation into a case of arson, Klippert told the police he was homosexual; he admitted to sexual activities with other men over a twenty-four-year period. He was sentenced to three years in prison, and there the matter might have ended. But in addition to the law outlawing sex between consenting adults, Canada also had a law on the books defining a category called "dangerous sexual offender." This was modeled after the laws of certain American states. Under the law, someone pronounced unable to "control his sexual impulses" and "likely to commit a further sexual offense" could be subject to indefinite detention, which is precisely what happened to Klippert. While in jail in Saskatchewan, he was interviewed by two psychiatrists. Although in prison for a minor sexual offense, he was labeled a dangerous sexual offender and essentially incarcerated for life.

When Klippert's attorney appealed the case to the Supreme Court of Canada in 1967, the majority of justices affirmed a decision in which they labeled virtually every sexually active homosexual in Canada a potential dangerous sexual offender. Under the existing law, the justices ruled, a person convicted of gross indecency and pronounced likely to commit this act again could be incarcerated for life. The only remedy would be to repeal the law criminalizing gross indecency. This the Supreme Court wouldn't do. "Whether the criminal l w . . . should be changed to the extent to which it had been recently in England," the court said, ". . . is obviously not for us to say; our jurisdiction is to interpret and apply laws validly enacted."

There was an immediate uproar. SUPREME COURT RULING MAKES HOMOSEXUAL LIABLE FOR LIFE, headlined the *Toronto Star*. The newspaper's editorial called the decision "A Return to the Middle Ages." In Parliament, an MP proposed that a committee similar to the Wolfenden Committee in England be established. Justice Minister **Pierre Trudeau** responded that the government would consider reforming the laws. "The state has no place in the bedrooms of the nation," Trudeau stated.

Two years later, in 1969, the government introduced a proposal for broad changes in the criminal code. In addition to reforming the laws against buggery and gross indecency, the package proposed to reform the laws on abortion, contraception, gambling, and lotteries. The country's fledgling homophile movement was dismayed that the proposal set the age of consent for homosexual acts at twenty-one, in the British manner; nevertheless, gay activists stayed out of the debate for tactical reasons. The bill was finally passed on May 14, 1969, by a vote of 149 to 55, and homosexual acts between consenting adults became legal in Canada.

CHAPTER 20

THE OTHER SIDE
OF THE 1950s

T HE FLYER for the poetry reading at a San Francisco gallery had promised: "Remarkable collection of angels all gathered at once in the same spot. Wine, music, dancing girls, serious poetry, free satori. Small collection for wine and postcards. Charming event." About a hundred people crowded around a small stage in what had once been an auto repair shop. As the lights dimmed and the second part of the program began, a little-known poet named **Allen Ginsberg** (b. 1926) ascended the stage. He was nervous and a little drunk. He read a poem that began:

> *I saw the best minds of my generation destroyed by
> madness starving hysterical naked*

As he read, Ginsberg swayed to the rhythm of the poem, "chanting like a Jewish cantor," as his biographer Barry Miles described it. His friend **Jack Kerouac** (1922–69) had bought gallon jugs of California burgundy, which were passed around the audience. Kerouac cheered Ginsberg on, shouting "Go!" at the end of each line; the rest of the audience joined in. The language of the poem was lyrical, conversational, confessional, sometimes shocking, altogether remarkable for the placid year that was 1955. The poem was called "Howl" and that first reading soon took on the stuff of legend, becoming a cultural event that one critic compared to a "detonation in a museum." The writer Ted Morgan pointed to its "absolutely compelling incantatory quality. ['Howl'] seemed to be a manifesto for all the misfits of the fifties, the rejected, the deviants, the criminals, and the insane, who could unite under this banner."

The banner was that of the Beat Generation. Amid the conformity and complacency of the "I Like Ike" years, the seeds of the sexual and social revolutions of the 1960s and '70s were being planted. With "Howl," Ginsberg gave the Beat Generation its anthem. Two years later Kerouac's exuberant novel *On the Road* was

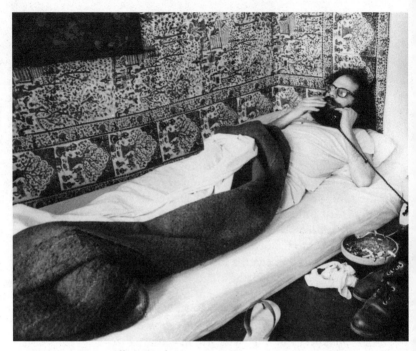

Allen Ginsberg, 1966. *(© UPI/Bettmann)*

published. And two years after that came perhaps the most auda-
cious work of the period, **William Burroughs's** *Naked Lunch*.

The Beats rejected the norms of the 1950s. As Barbara Ehrenreich
wrote, they "criss-crossed the continent between New York, Mexico, and San Francisco, hopped freight trains, talked all night over
cheap wine, had visions, coined the word "beat" (deriving it from
"beatitude,") ate peyote and smoked pot, had sex with countless
women (and men) . . ." Long before they were famous, Dr. Kinsey
had interviewed Ginsberg, Kerouac, and Burroughs as subjects
for his study of male sexual behavior. They were visionaries, ro-
mantics, who saw themselves as heirs to poets like Whitman and
Rimbaud and whose aim in life was "to heighten experience and
get out of one's usual self," in the words of sociologist **Paul
Goodman**.

Ginsberg, Kerouac, and Burroughs were the Beat founding fa-
thers. They had met in 1944 when Ginsberg was a student at Columbia University in New York City. Ginsberg had grown up in

nearby Paterson, New Jersey; his father was a high-school English teacher, while his mother had spent much of her son's youth in psychiatric hospitals, convinced that President Roosevelt himself had put wires in her head to monitor her secret thoughts. At seventeen, Ginsberg was a "spindly Jewish kid with horn-rimmed glasses and tremendous ears sticking out," as Kerouac described him. Kerouac, the French-Canadian boy from working-class Lowell, Massachusetts, had gone to Columbia on a football scholarship, dropped out, joined the navy, and been quickly discharged after flinging his rifle down on the ground one morning during drill. Burroughs, whose grandfather invented the adding machine, was slightly older and was a mentor figure to Ginsberg and Kerouac; he introduced them to writers like Kafka and Céline and also to Times Square hustlers and drug addicts.

Burroughs and Ginsberg were both gay. Kerouac was a "fellow traveller of homosexuals," as the critic Catharine R. Stimpson put it. Primarily heterosexual, he had his first gay experience while in the merchant marine, but rarely dealt with homosexuality in his novels. **Neal Cassady**, the model for the character of Dean Moriarity in *On the Road,* was the Beats' sex symbol. Cassady was handsome and charismatic and looked as if he could be Kerouac's brother. Cassady had grown up in Denver, stolen his first car when he was fourteen, and by the time he was twenty-one estimated that he had stolen over five hundred. When Kerouac arrived at his apartment for the first time, Cassady opened the door, stark naked. By his late twenties, Cassady had been married three times, fathered three children, and had had an intense love affair with Ginsberg.

But it was the Beat attitudes toward sex that were important, not who was sleeping with whom. For them, like *On the Road*'s Dean Moriarity, "sex was the one and only holy and important thing in life." As Stimpson notes, the Beats rejected the primacy of heterosexuality. They "construed an unfettered, uncensored sexuality as a good in itself. . . . They re-imagined and revised male homosexuality, and brought out of history a Whitmanesque tradition to support them." What they didn't revise and reimagine, as Stimpson points out, were gender roles: In the Beat worldview "chicks" were still "chicks" and basically didn't count for much.

Of the group, Ginsberg was the most vocal proponent of gay sexuality, although his tastes ran to men who were primarily heterosexual—Cassady and Kerouac, for example. In San Francisco, some months before the "Howl" reading, Ginsberg met a painter who invited him to his apartment to look at his work. Ginsberg was particularly taken by a large oil painting of a naked young man. He asked who the subject was and was immediately presented with the young man in question, twenty-one-year-old **Peter Orlovsky.** Orlovsky had worked at a state mental hospital and been a medic stationed in San Francisco during the Korean War; his father had been a cadet in the Czar's army before the Russian Revolution. Ginsberg and Orlovsky became lovers. In a poem called "Malest Cornifici Tuo Catullo," addressed to Kerouac, Ginsberg wrote:

> *I'm happy, Kerouac, your madman Allen's*
> *finally made it: discovered a new young cat,*
> *and my imagination of an eternal boy*
> *walks on the streets of San Francisco,*
> *handsome, and meets me in cafeterias*
> *and loves me. . .*

Shortly after the two moved in together, Ginsberg persuaded Orlovsky to take a vow of "marriage." They did so at three o'clock in the morning at a San Francisco cafeteria. As Ginsberg told biographer Barry Miles:

> *We made a vow to each other that he could own me, my mind and everything I knew, and my body, and I could own him, and all he knew, and his body; and that we would give each other ourselves, so that we possessed each other as property, to do everything we wanted to, sexually or intellectually, and in a sense explore each other until we reached the mystical "X" together, emerging two merged souls. . . .*

The relationship was to last for more than thirty years, despite Orlovsky's "dark Russian moods" and despite the fact that, like Kerouac and Cassady, Orlovsky was more heterosexual than homosexual. Over the years, Orlovsky had a number of relationships with women, some of them long-term. According to Miles, such relationships created "more than one ménage à trois of unusual complexity, which caused a great deal of tension and strain."

The Beats were not just a few iconoclasts; they fostered an entire culture, one that centered around San Francisco's North Beach neighborhood. It was a visible area of nonconformity, one that attracted media attention and hordes of weekend tourists. Although it was far from a specifically gay subculture,"homosexuality weaved its way through descriptions of the North Beach scene as a persistent, albeit minor, motif," notes historian John D'Emilio. In addition to Ginsberg, there were other openly gay San Francisco writers in the North Beach scene—**Robert Duncan** and **Jack Spicer** being the most well-known. Many of the gay bars in San Francisco were located in North Beach, so there was an overlap between the two worlds. "Through the beats' example," D'Emilio writes, "gays could perceive themselves as nonconformists rather than deviates, as rebels against stultifying norms rather than immature, unstable personalities."

Meanwhile, Ginsberg's friend William Burroughs (b. 1914) was taking Beat rebellion in still another direction. In the the early 1940s he married a young woman named **Joan Vollner Adams**. They lived in Texas and Louisiana, where Adams became addicted to Benzedrine while Burroughs shot heroin. After a police raid on their Algiers, Louisiana, house in 1949 that uncovered a cache of firearms and drugs, the two fled to Mexico. There, on December 7, 1951, in a bizarre incident, Burroughs shot his wife in the head and killed her. He had apparently placed a glass of gin on her head, fired, and missed, during a game of "William Tell." The police accepted his explanation and ruled it an accident. Eventually, Burroughs found his way to Tangier, where he lived in a male brothel owned by a gangster. Then he embarked on a brief foray into the South American jungle, looking for a drug called yage. Soon he was back in Tangier, living in a place he called the "Villa Delirium," struggling with his drug addiction, sleeping with Spanish boys, and beginning work on the book he was to call *Naked Lunch*.

With its gleaming white buildings and labyrinthine alleys, Tangier, the Moroccan port city at the northernmost tip of Africa, was the gateway to the exotic. During the 1940s and early '50s, the city was an "international zone," ruled by a polyglot Legislative Assembly that included French, Dutch, Belgians, British, Portuguese, and Moroccan Muslims and Jews. It was also a boomtown where corporations evaded foreign taxes, banking laws were nonexistent, and import duties low. "Smugglers, counterfeiters, sleight-of-hand bankers, real-estate speculators and even honest entrepreneurs found Tangier to be a postwar promised land," wrote Michelle Green in her book about the city and its expatriate subculture, *The*

Dream at the End of the World. "In Tangier's rarified climate, social climbers metamorphosed into bluebloods, bank clerks became barons, and shopgirls, grandes dames." Tangier was an uncommonly beautiful city, the diplomatic capital of Morocco, and when Woolworth heiress **Barbara Hutton** bought a house near the Casbah in 1946, it became a haunt of international cafe society as well.

For expatriates, Tangier in the late forties and fifties was attractive in many respects. For one thing, it was incredibly cheap: Four-course French meals cost the equivalent of one American dollar. It was also a city where everything was available: *Kif* (marijuana) was the drug of choice of the masses, opiates were available at the local pharmacy, and sex of all varieties could be purchased for pennies. **Truman Capote** caught the flavor of the place, noting, "Virtually every Tangerine is ensconced there for at least one, if not all, of four reasons: the easy availability of drugs, lustful adolescent prostitutes, tax loopholes, or because he is so undesirable no place north of Port Said would let him out of the airport or off the ship." Behind its veneer of decadent glamour, however, the city had a slightly sinister, if not paranoic, quality; in its *souks* and *medinas,* black magic was said to thrive. Meanwhile, conspicuous consumption by wealthy foreigners exacerbated social tensions. Native Tanjawis, as the locals were called, became influenced by the nationalism that was gaining strength in the French and Spanish protectorates that made up the rest of Morocco.

During this period, Tangier became a haven for gay and lesbian bohemia, just as did Paris, Harlem, and Greenwich Village in their heydays. At a time when male homosexuality remained against the law in England and McCarthyism dominated American life, for the wealthy, the artistic, and the rebellious, expatriation provided a solution. And the particular nature of Arab society made Tangier an appealing refuge for homosexuals especially, as there has always been a relative degree of acceptance of male homosexuality within the Arab world. In a sex-segregated society, distinctions between gay and straight have been traditionally blurred, if they existed at all. As Michelle Green notes, "Although homosexuality was still a criminal offense in England, it was eminently acceptable among Moroccans, whose male population was largely bisexual. Youngsters of eight or ten prowled the streets, propositioning visitors in French or English or German. A Spanish-run boy-brothel offered partners who would oblige the most esoteric request. . . ." In a letter to Jack Kerouac, William Burroughs insisted that the only person in town who was "neither queer nor available" was the chauffeur of one prominent expatriate. When he arrived for a visit, Kerouac came to similar conclusions. "Not too many good vibrations in Tangier," he noted. "Mostly fags abound in this sinister international hive of queens."

The gay scene in Tangier had its elegant and its seedy aspects. On the one hand, there was the "mixed" Parade bar, one of the city's smartest, that attracted a clientele ranging from William Burroughs to "diplomats, scandal-hungry journalists, nymphomaniacal heiresses, semireformed gangsters and caftaned drag queens," according to Michelle Green. In a letter to Allen Ginsberg, Burroughs gave another view of the city's nightlife:

> Arrive in the Mar Chica, all-night bar where everybody goes after midnight. With me an Irish boy who left England after a spot of trouble, and a Portuguese who can't go home again. Both queer. Both ex-junkies. Both chippying with dollies [ampules of the drug dolophine]. . . . Two Lesbians who work on a smuggling ship drunk at a table. Spanish workmen, queers, British sailors. [A drinking companion] seizes me and drags me to the bar, throwing an arm around my shoulder, and tightening his grip whenever I try to edge away. He gazes into my face, putting down a sincere routine. "Life is rotten, here, Bill. Rotten. It's the end of the world, Tanger. Don't you feel it, Bill?"

By the late forties and fifties, Tangier was attracting a cast of characters that included many of the international homosexual artistic elite: the American playwright **Tennessee Williams,** who disliked it, complaining about the rain and developing a peculiar physical condition in which vibrations ran up and down his entire body whenever he lowered his head; Truman Capote, fresh from the success of his novel *Other Voices, Other Rooms,* and who immediately busied himself with Tangier's tea-party circuit; novelist Gore Vidal, who seemed to show up mostly to annoy Capote, with whom he had a running feud; **Ned Rorem,** the composer; **Francis Bacon,** the greatest British painter of his generation, who spent three years off and on there, getting virtually no work done; and Christopher Isherwood, now settled in California. (Later, in the 1960s, British playwright Joe Orton made three visits, along with his lover **Kenneth Halliwell,** the last in late spring 1967, two months before Halliwell murdered him.) Burroughs's presence brought Kerouac, Ginsberg, and Orlovsky. **Libby Holman,** onetime torch singer and heiress (by marriage) to a tobacco fortune, married three times but known for her affairs with women, dropped by to visit her friend, the writer **Jane Bowles** (1917–73).

The Bowleses, Jane and Paul (b. 1911), were the hosts to many of these visitors. They were permanent residents (Paul had virtually *discovered* the place as an expatriate haven) and functioned as the center of the literary foreign set in Tangier. Both were Americans, and both were homosexual—in her self-deprecatory manner, Jane referred to herself as "Crippie the Kike Dyke" (she was lame and Jewish as well). They married in 1938 and settled in Tangier after the War. The only son of an affluent Long Island couple, Paul was a composer of some renown and was considered by many to be rather aloof and distant. He became known for his novels about Westerners encountering the exotic, the most famous being *The Sheltering Sky* (later turned into a movie by **Bernardo Bertolucci,** with an aging Bowles himself as narrator). Jane was the author of an eccentric novella, *Two Serious Ladies,* and a number of stories that gained a coterie of admirers. The poet **Frank O'Hara** called her play *In the Summer House,* first put on in New York in 1953, "the best American play of our time." She was also anxious and angst-ridden, drank too much, and was a fanatical believer in signs and omens. Tennessee Williams, who adored her, remembered her as

> small, piquant, darting between humor, anxiety, love and dis-
> traction. I had met nervous girls before, but her quicksilver an-
> imation, her continual cries, to me and herself: "Shall we do this
> or shall we do that? What shall we do?" showed such an extreme
> kind of excited indecision that I was skeptical of its reality—
> intrigued, certainly, but still somewhat incredulous.

The Bowles's marriage was unorthodox, to say the least. At one point, husband and wife lived in apartments next door to each other—with their homosexual lovers. Yet they had a strong dependence on each other. "I always thought of Paul and Jane as being like two twisted cypress trees that had become entwined," Michelle Green quotes one friend as saying. "Her life wouldn't have had any meaning if she hadn't had him. And perhaps his writing wouldn't have had any meaning if he hadn't had her to outshine."

Paul Bowles tended to gravitate toward mentor-protégé relationships—with a Moroccan painter named **Ahmed Ben Driss el-**

Yacoubi, and later with **Mohammed Mrabet**, a writer whose work he promoted. Jane Bowles's love life was more complicated. She fell desperately in love with **Cherifa**, an illiterate nineteen-year-old country girl who had a stall in the grain market and claimed to be descended from the patron saint of the city. Cherifa had a reputation for wildness and drinking; she wore jeans and brown golfing shoes under her red-and-white-striped Berber blanket and carried a switchblade. At first, she toyed with Jane, refusing to sleep with her but demanding a taxi as a gift and insisting that Jane pay for her twice-weekly visits to a doctor who was treating her for a skin disease. She soon began to develop a power over Jane that some ascribed to her knowledge of black magic. "I have never understood why, but I am terrified of going against [Cherifa's] orders," Jane told her friend Libby Holman.

Eventually, Jane and Cherifa did become lovers, beginning a tempestuous relationship that would continue for many years. On April 4, 1957, during the holy month of Ramadan, Jane suffered a mild stroke. Cherifa was present and doctors were sent for, but many of Jane's friends were convinced that the stroke was brought on by Cherifa; they claimed that she had used some slow-acting poison on Jane to gain control over her (Jane had promised to leave her house to Cherifa when she died). Others thought Cherifa might have used her knowledge of spells and potions to bring about Jane's stroke. Truman Capote quotes Jane as saying that Cherifa tried seriously to poison her every six months. "And don't imagine I'm being paranoid. It's quite true," were her words, according to Capote. Others dismissed the poisoning story. For example, **Edouard Roditi**, who knew Jane over a period of many years, told her biographer, Millicent Dillon, "That Cherifa poisoned Jane is part of the myth of the Tangier expatriate group. The fact is that Moroccans go in for magic, but I don't think this magic works." Jane suffered from high blood pressure.

Shortly after Jane's stroke, the political situation for Westerners, particularly Western homosexuals, began to deteriorate in Tangier. Once Morocco gained its freedom from colonial rule, it wasn't long before the International Zone's special status was eliminated and Tangier was absorbed into the newly independent country. When Paul and Jane returned there in November 1957 after a trip to England, they found Paul's lover, the painter Ahmed Yacoubi, in prison, accused of seducing a fourteen-year-old German boy. The city's new police chief launched a campaign against foreign homosexuals and pederasts, interrogating and imprisoning large numbers. As in other emerging nations where a puritanical nationalism gained political control (Egypt and Cuba, for example), the authorities made a public show of stamping out "decadent" Western influences; homosexuals were an easy target. As William Burroughs wrote Allen Ginsberg, "Tangier is finished. The Arab dogs are upon us. Many a queen has been dragged shrieking from the Parade [bar], the Socco Chico, and lodged in the local box where sixty sons of Sodom now languish. . . . The boy[s], many beaten to a pulp, have spelled a list of hundreds." Burroughs soon left; Paul and Jane Bowles fled the country as well. Within the year, the campaign against homosexuals subsided, just as suddenly as it had begun. The Bowleses returned, and Ahmed Yacoubi was acquitted of all charges and released from prison.

For Jane, however, the stroke that had occurred in 1957 marked the beginning of physical and mental decline. Cherifa moved in as companion and servant, and Jane began to view their relationship as a mother-daughter one. Jane was increasingly afflicted by anxiety and high blood pressure; she made a number of trips to England and Spain for treatment, including electroshock therapy. Eventually, she was diagnosed as a manic-depressive psychotic and spent five years in a psychiatric hospital in Spain, across the strait from Tangier. In May 1973, blind, mute, and debilitated by a series of strokes, she died in a Málaga sanitorium, and was buried in an unmarked grave.

If Tangier nourished the imagination of Paul Bowles, for other gay expatriates it was an unsatisfactory haven, personally and creatively. The isolation bred suspicion and paranoia, and the easy availability of drugs and young boys proved harmful to many. For example, when William Burroughs first arrived in Tangier, he succumbed entirely to his drug addiction, living for a year without bathing or changing his clothes. His sole ambition during this period was "to stick a needle every hour in the fibrous grey wooden flesh of terminal addiction," he wrote. Although he eventually did overcome the worst of his addiction and wrote *Naked Lunch* in Tangier, it required the arrivals of Allen Ginsberg and Jack Kerouac to get the book into some publishable shape. The diaries of British playwright Joe Orton, during his last visit to Tangier, in May and June 1967—two months before he was murdered by his lover Kenneth Halliwell—document how the ages of the boys he had sex with in Tangier became younger and younger, the longer he stayed there.

The American writer **Alfred Chester,** who lived there in the 1960s, descended into paranoia. As for Jane Bowles, she suffered from writer's block from the moment she arrived in Tangier. As she wrote in a 1967 account of her life, "From the first day, Morocco seemed more dreamlike than real. I felt cut off from what I knew. In the twenty years that I have lived here I have written only two short stories, and nothing else. It's good for Paul, but not for me."

Joe Orton in Tangier

Joe Orton, the British playwright and author of such savagely funny comedies as Loot *and* Entertaining Mr. Sloane, *visited Tangier in May and June 1967, along with his lover, Kenneth Halliwell. On August 9 of that year, in London, Halliwell bludgeoned Orton to death with a hammer and then killed himself. Orton's Tangier diary entries give a sense of his deteriorating relationship with Halliwell. They are filled with Orton's characteristic wit and sharp observation and offer a glimpse into the gay society of expatriate Tangier. The following excerpt is from* The Orton Diaries:

Saturday 20 May

DAY FINE; clear, brilliant sun. Met Stalk as arranged and, under Larbi's guidance, stood by the bus-stop. We met Mustapha. He was about fourteen. "We're going to Malabata," I said. "Would you like to come with us?" He made no objection and we waited for the bus. However, there was the prospect of fucking Mustapha in the hills outside the town and I endured all with patience and thought of the tube of KY Jelly in my haversack along with the bottles of lemonade.

At last Nigel drew up in his car. It's a four-seater and he offered to give us a lift. However, he hadn't realised that Mustapha was with us and chickened-out of taking him on the grounds that he couldn't carry six. I wanted to get out with Mustapha and wait for the bus, but Kenneth objected and said, "No, let Mustapha join us at Malabata." "But," objected Stalk, "he won't do that." "Yes, he will," said Kenneth.

By now I was in a great rage. "I'll get out and get the bus with Mustapha," I said. "No, no!" Kenneth said and, foreseeing great scenes ahead if I did get out, Nigel drove off, and before we were out of sight we saw the boy speaking to some tourist. I sat sick and glum. "It's too dangerous to take boys of that age in the car," Kenneth said. Nigel agreed. I said nothing and went into a world of my own for the rest of the day, shutting the door and refusing to speak to anyone on the ill-fated trek to Malabata. Sulking in the hot sun, refusing even to drink and thinking of the wasted KY Jelly liquefying at the bottom of the bag . . .

We met him [Nigel] again later, at dinner. He had a curious man with him, the Marquis of something or other. A man who said a pipe of opium was pure heaven, and who I suspected was wearing a toupee, though I couldn't be sure. He took us back to his house and name-dropped "I remember the Duke of Windsor saying his mother the Queen Mary never had a new dress in thirty years. And I was there when Madame de Gaulle made her famous gaffe, you know. Somebody asked her, 'What are you looking forward to when you retire?' 'I am looking forward most to a penis,' she replied. After a pause somebody said, 'Oh, *oui*, happiness, madame?' "

The Marquis' house was crammed with junk. It looked like a Chelsea antique shop. Rubbish from the rag-bag of eighteenth-century culture. Mirrors with the original glass—so cracked that to see one's self in them was to have a vision of what one's face might look like on the Day of Judgement, the marks of the grave upon it. "What shall you have to drink?" the Marquis said, leading me away from a monstrous, over-sized, headless nude statue of a man. "Coca-Cola," I said, feeling that the mere pronouncing of the word would dispel the mucky grandeur of the past. The Marquis looked put out. "You would not prefer . . . ?" and he said the name of some unsavoury and unpronounceable drink to match the furniture. "No," I said, "just a Coke." We sat drinking and he told of "the Princess Marina" and "What do you think of the Earl of Snowdon? Do you not think he's an unhappy man?" "The royal family is a noose," I said. "You don't have to put your head into it. If a man does so, he must expect to be unhappy." "Ah, *oui*," said the Marquis, shrugging his shoulders and trying to look like a character in Proust. We were sitting on the most uncomfortable chairs I have ever bummed. Near me was a table and most conspicuous on it were three photographs, a coloured one of Paul VI (unsigned), a small block of John XXIII with something written on it in the Holy Father's own fair hand, and a large, obviously forties studio portrait of the wartime Pope which said, across the white robe, "Yours very sincerely, Pius XII."

Sunday 21 May

George Greeves and Dai Rees-Davis picked us up in the car at 10:30. I told George we'd met the Marquis. "Oh, the phoney Marquis," George said. "Yes, she's a dirty bit of the South of France trade from way back. Now she's a marquis." "Well there you are," I said. "He has several portraits of the popes." I told him about the "yours very sincerely" signed one. "Oh, she probably signed that herself," George said. He took us to The Diplomatic Forest. "This is where to come if you want to get raped," he said, and then began singing in a loud bass voice, "Make way for the buggery bus. Here comes the buggery bus."

Tennessee Williams and Fifties Theater

DESPITE THE ANTIGAY ATTITUDES of the postwar period, a number of the new generation of American writers were open about their homosexuality—to varying degrees—in their life and work. Gore Vidal's 1948 novel, *The City and the Pillar*, and James Baldwin's *Giovanni's Room,* published in 1956, were bold steps. (See excerpts, pages 241 and 313.) In 1948, Truman Capote virtually announced his homosexuality with a suggestive photograph on the dust jacket of his first novel, *Other Voices, Other Rooms.* The picture attracted almost as much attention as the book itself. *Other Voices, Other Rooms* was not a gay "problem novel" like *The City and the Pillar,* but *Time* magazine's critic still complained that "the distasteful trappings of its homosexual theme overhang it like Spanish moss."

Three leading playwrights—**William Inge,** Tennessee Williams, and **Edward Albee**—were gay. Although they often treated homosexuality obliquely in their works, if at all, their sexuality was a major influence on the way they saw the world. Of the three, Inge (*Picnic, Come Back Little Sheba, The Dark at the Top of the Stairs*) was the most closeted, both personally and artistically. His characters tended to be "small people with small problems," as Michael Bronski observes, but the theme of his plays was frequently sexual repression. Tennessee Williams never hid his homosexuality. By his own admission, however, he was so afraid of rejection that in his earlier works he made sure any gay characters were dead before the action of the play began. On the other hand, he created female characters—Blanche DuBois in *A Streetcar Named Desire,* for example—that gay men readily identified with. Although Albee's groundbreaking 1962 *Who's Afraid of Virginia Woolf?,* with its blatant sexuality and coarse language, was ostensibly about two heterosexual couples, the author spent years denying they weren't really two male couples. By 1961, a backlash was developing, with *New York Times* theater critic **Howard Taubman** accusing three unnamed playwrights of "portraying marriage negatively and painting female characters as destroyers and sex maniacs," as Bronski notes. Taubman's article appeared under the headline NOT WHAT IT SEEMS: HOMOSEXUAL MOTIF GETS HETEROSEXUAL GUISE.

The most influential and successful of these playwrights was Thomas Lanier "Tennessee" Williams (1911–83). During his most prolific period, he created some of the most acclaimed works in the history of the American theater: *The Glass Menagerie* (1945); *A Streetcar Named Desire* (1947); *Summer and Smoke* (1948); *The Rose Tattoo* (1951); *Cat on a Hot Tin Roof* (1955); *Suddenly Last Summer* (1958); *Sweet Bird of Youth* (1959); and *The Night of the Iguana* (1961). He won two Pulitzer Prizes and four New York Drama Critics Circle Awards for best play.

Born in St. Louis, Williams drew many of his characters from his own family—his mother, Edwina, with her pretensions to gentility; his hard-drinking father; his sister, Rose, who went mad and was lobotomized; and Tom, himself, the devoted son. Due in part to his homosexuality, in part to his own experiences growing up,

Williams developed a strong identification with women. Despite those critics who insisted that his women were caricatures, Williams "created some of the best women characters in the moderrn theater," according to Gore Vidal. Williams himself recalled that when the Italian director **Luchino Visconti** was directing a production of *Streetcar,* Visconti turned to the playwright and announced, "Tennessee, you *are* Blanche [DuBois]." But Williams said later, "He was wrong, because I wasn't. She was mostly my Aunt Belle. Aunt Belle in Knoxville. . . . Yes. I'll admit to being other heroines. I was Alexandra del Lago [in *Sweet Bird of Youth*] from start to finish. I've probably made every speech she made. And I meant them twice as much." As Vidal wrote, "[H]is sympathies were always with those defeated by 'the squares'; or by time, once the sweet bird of youth is flown. Or by death, 'which has never been much in the way of completion.' "

If Williams identified with *Streetcar*'s Blanche DuBois and her dependence on the "kindness of strangers," it was the character of Stanley, as portrayed on stage and screen by **Marlon Brando**, that gripped audiences and completely transformed how America viewed male sexuality. Vidal analyzed it this way, in a 1985 essay:

> He [Williams] showed the male not only as sexually attractive in the flesh but as an object for something never before entirely acknowledged . . . the lust of women. In the age of Calvin Klein's steaming hunks, it must be hard for those under forty to realize that there was ever a time when a man was nothing but a suit of clothes, a shirt and tie, shined leather shoes, and a gray, felt hat. . . . In 1947, when Marlon Brando appeared on stage in a torn sweaty T-shirt, there was an earthquake; and the male as sex object is still at our culture's center stage. . . . Yet, ironically, Tennessee's auctorial sympathies were not with Stanley, but with his "victim" Blanche.

(It should be noted that two other male icons of the period— **James Dean** and **Montgomery Clift**—also played a decisive role in the cultural creation of the male as erotic object. Significantly, both were gay.)

The major relationship of Williams's life was with **Frank Merlo**, the merchant seaman whom he met in 1949 and with whom he spent the next fourteen years. Williams described Merlo as "so close to life! . . . He gave me the connection to day-to-day and night-tonight living. To reality. He tied me down to earth." Williams's friend and confidante **Maria St. Just** thought that Merlo was "the only one of Tennessee's close companions who truly loved him for what he was. He was also the only one whom Tennessee really loved." Merlo was known for his integrity and candor. The story goes that when movie mogul **Jack Warner** was entertaining Williams in his private dining room at Warner Brothers, he asked Merlo what he did for a living. Merlo looked him straight in the eye and replied, "I sleep with Mr. Williams."

Although Williams certainly never hid his relationship with Merlo and the other "secretary-companions" who followed, the playwright came out as gay publicly for the first time on **David Frost's** television show in January 1970. "I've covered the water-front," he declared, amidst applause from the studio audience. That same year, he told another interviewer, "I've never hidden my homo-sexuality, I don't think. I haven't meant to. But then, I haven't tried to flaunt it, as some have said. In many ways it has been such an integral part of my creativity, however."

Williams suffered from drinking problems and barbiturate addiction over the years and was also well-known for his hypochondria. But it was after Merlo's death in 1963 from lung cancer that he began to go downhill, his latter years characterized by what Vidal called "a most glamorous crackup." Maria St. Just describes the period this way:

> After Frank [Merlo]'s death, Tennessee felt a profound and increasing regret . . . He gradually suffered a complete breakdown, which was exacerbated by the treatment prescribed by a Dr. [Max] Jacobson, who was subsequently barred from practice.
>
> Jacobson taught his patients to inject themselves with a concoction of his own invention. Tennessee used to walk around with capsules and a syringe. I was very concerned by Tennessee's condition, and so I stole a capsule and had it analyzed by my own doctor's laboratory in London. The analysis confirmed that the capsule contained "speed," mixed with other dangerous drugs. I would throw away his pills and capsules whenever I could.

Even in his troubled final years, Williams was extremely disciplined about his writing. Vidal describes how Williams worked every morning on whatever was at hand. If he wasn't working on a play, he would open a drawer and take out a draft of a story already written and begin to rewrite it. "I once found him revising a short story that had just been published," Vidal recalled. " 'Why,' I asked, 'rewrite what's already in print?' He looked at me, vaguely; then he said, 'Well, obviously it's not finished.' And went back to his typing."

Williams died in a New York hotel room in 1983 of suffocation from inhaling a nasal-spray top. On the back of a photograph to Frank Merlo, years before, he wrote what might well serve as his epitaph: "When your candle burns low, you've got to believe that the last light shows you something besides the progress of darkness."

James Baldwin and *Giovanni's Room*

JAMES BALDWIN (1924–87) was indisputably the most influential black American writer of his time. In essays, novels, and plays, he was able to make whites understand what it felt like to be inside the skin of black Americans. During the 1960s, he became a major exponent of the civil rights movement; his essay *The Fire Next Time* spent a year on the best-seller list, and Baldwin appeared on the cover of *Time* magazine. The son of a Harlem evangelist—and himself a schoolboy preacher—Baldwin left home at age nineteen, lived in Greenwich Village, and worked as a messenger for the newspaper *PM*. He wrote book reviews for the *Nation* and *New Leader* magazines; his first essay appeared in *Commentary* in the winter of 1948. That same year, at age twenty-four, like many other black intellectuals of his generation, he exiled himself to Paris.

One of the major events of Baldwin's youth was the suicide of his friend **Eugene Worth**, "an incandescent Negro boy of twenty-four" with a "glorious future." (Worth, who served as a model for the character of Rufus in Baldwin's novel *Another Country,* leaped to his death from the George Washington Bridge.) Baldwin and Worth weren't lovers, although Baldwin wrote in his essay "The Price of the Ticket," "For what it's worth, I think I wish we had been." He recalled:

When he was dead, I remembered that he had once, obliquely, suggested this possibility. He had run down a list of his girl friends: those he liked, those he really liked, one or two with whom he might really be in love, and, then, he said, "I wondered if I might be in love with you."

I wish I had heard him more clearly: an oblique confession is always a plea. But I was to hurt a great many people by being unable to imagine that anyone could possibly be in love with an ugly boy like me. . . .

Worth's death was a factor in Baldwin's exile: He was convinced that if he stayed in the United States, he would come to a similar end. In many respects, his friend's death only toughened him. The world had despised Worth's vision and scourged him for his color. Baldwin was determined to be different: "It took me nearly no time to despise the world right back and decide that I would accomplish, in time, with patience and cunning and by becoming indestructible, what I might not, in the moment, achieve by force or persuasion."

He lived in Paris for ten years, returning to the United States in 1957. It was during this period that his first novel, *Go Tell It on the Mountain,* which described growing up in the black church, was published. Becoming an expatriate saved his life, he later wrote, confirming that "a man is not a man until he is able and willing to accept his own vision of the world, no matter how radically this vision departs from that of others." In Paris, he met **Lucien Happersberger**, a young Swiss artist who became his lover for a time and his closest and most trusted friend for forty years.

Baldwin's novel *Giovanni's Room,* published in 1956, was one of the first American works of fiction about homosexuality to gain widespread acclaim. To have written it at all was courageous for a young black writer with just one novel (*Go Tell It on the Mountain*) and one collection of essays (*Nobody Knows My Name*) to his credit. His agent supposedly told him to burn the book, and it was only after *Giovanni's Room* was published in England that an American publisher agreed to take it. Baldwin returned to the subject of homosexuality in novels like *Another Country* and *Just Above My Head.*

Although relatively open about his homosexuality from a young age, Baldwin was also ambivalent about it. He saw little possibility that shared sexuality could be the basis of community, an attitude largely formed by his experiences in the 1940s as a black gay man

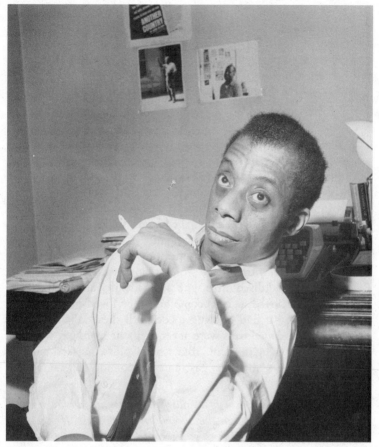

James Baldwin in his New York apartment, shortly after the publication of *The Fire Next Time, 1963. (© UPI/Bettmann)*

in New York City. In later years, he recalled a gay world of impersonal and demeaning sexual encounters, of being called "faggot" on every streetcorner, a world where his existence was "the punch line of a dirty joke."

Eager, vulnerable, and lonely, as he put it, he survived only by finding older "protectors"—a Harlem racketeer who fell in love with him when he was sixteen and, later, in Greenwich Village, an Italian man who threatened to kill anyone who touched him. In a 1954 essay on André Gide called "The Male Prison," he wrote:

> *The really horrible thing about the phenomenon of present-day homosexuality . . . is that today's unlucky deviate can only save himself by the most tremendous exertion of all his forces from falling into an underworld in which he never meets either men or women, where it is impossible to have either a lover or a friend, where the possibility of genuine human involvement has altogether ceased.*

If Baldwin saw little hope that homosexuality could lead to a sense of community, he had no faith in the transforming possibilities of the sexual revolution, either. He dismissed the notion of a world made better through "psychic and sexual health," through the "formula of more and better orgasms." "The people I had been raised among had orgasms all the time," he noted, "and still chopped each other up with razors on Saturday nights."

These attitudes persisted well into the post-Stonewall period. In a 1984 interview with *Village Voice* reporter Richard Goldstein, Baldwin expressed discomfort with a gay identity and with gay life and culture. "I loved a few people and they loved me," Baldwin told Goldstein. "It had nothing to do with these labels. . . . The people who were my lovers were never, well, the word gay wouldn't have meant anything to them." But when Goldstein asked Baldwin what advice he would give a gay man just coming out, he replied:

> *Best advice I ever got was an old friend of mine, a black friend, who said you have to go the way your blood beats. If you don't live the only life you have, you won't live some other life, you won't live any life at all. That's the only advice you can give anybody. . . .*

In the Goldstein interview, Baldwin insisted that his novel *Giovanni's Room* was not really about homosexuality. "It's about what happens to you if you're afraid to love anybody," he said. Nonetheless, with its overheated, melodramatic prose and its undercurrent of doom, *Giovanni's Room* provides a revealing look into Baldwin's feelings about homosexuality. The novel is narrated by a young white American living in Paris, caught between his American girlfriend and his love for Giovanni, an Italian waiter. The following scene begins at an early-morning restaurant in Les Halles, where Jacques, an aging and sexually promiscuous businessman,

talks to the young American narrator just before the narrator and
Giovanni make love for the first time:

> "You think," he [Jacques] persisted, "that my life is shameful
> because my encounters are. And they are. But you should ask
> yourself why they are."
>
> "Why are they shameful?" I asked him.
>
> "Because there is no affection in them, and no joy. It's like
> putting an electric plug in a dead socket. Touch, no contact. All
> touch, but no contact and no light."
>
> I asked him: "Why?"
>
> "That you must ask yourself," he told me, "and perhaps one
> day this morning will not be ashes in your mouth."
>
> I looked over at Giovanni, who now had one arm around the
> ruined looking girl, who could have once been very beautiful but
> who never would be now.
>
> Jacques followed my look. "He is very fond of you," he said,
> "already. But this doesn't make you happy or proud, as it should.
> It makes you frightened and ashamed. Why?"
>
> "I don't understand him," I said, at last. "I don't know what
> his friendship means, I don't know what he means by friend-
> ship."
>
> Jacques laughed. "You don't know what he means by friend-
> ship but you have the feeling it may not be safe. You are afraid
> it may change you. What kind of friendships have you had?"
>
> I said nothing.
>
> "Or for that matter," he continued, "what kind of love af-
> fairs?"
>
> I was silent for so long that he teased me, saying, "Come out,
> come out, wherever you are!"
>
> And I grinned, feeling chilled.
>
> "Love him," said Jacques, with vehemence, "love him and let
> him love you. Do you think anything else under heaven really
> matters? And how long, at the best, can it last? since you are
> both men and still have everywhere to go? Only five minutes, I
> assure you, only five minutes, and most of that, helas! in the
> dark. And if you think of them as dirty, then they will be dirty—
> they will be dirty because you will be giving nothing, you will
> be despising your flesh and his. But you can make your time
> together anything but dirty, you can give each other something
> which will make both of you better—forever—if you will not

be ashamed, if you will only not play it safe." He paused, watching me, and then looked down to his cognac. "You play it safe long enough," he said, in a different tone, "and you'll end up trapped in your own dirty body, forever and forever and forever—like me. . . ."

Later that morning the narrator and Giovanni go back to Giovanni's room:

His room was in the back, on the ground floor of the last building on this street. We passed the vestibule and the elevator into a short, dark corridor which led to his room. The room was small, I only made out the outlines of clutter and disorder, there was the smell of the alcohol he burned in his stove. He locked the door behind us, and then for a moment, in the gloom, we simply stared at each other—with dismay, with relief, and breathing hard. I was trembling. I thought, if I do not open the door at once and get out of here, I am lost. But I knew I could not open the door, I knew it was too late; soon it was too late to do anything but moan. He pulled me against him, putting himself into my arms as though he were giving me himself to carry, and slowly pulled me down with him to that bed. With everything in me screaming No! yet the sum of me sighed Yes.

CHAPTER 21

THE OTHER SIDE OF THE FIFTIES, PART II: LESBIAN BUTCH/FEMME CULTURE

DESPITE the repressive political and social atmosphere of the United States in the 1950s, homosexual subcultures continued to evolve. Among working-class lesbians ("gay girls," as they called themselves), bars increasingly became the center of community. Bars offered an atmosphere where young women—many of whom didn't feel comfortable entertaining lesbian friends at home—could socialize, meet potential lovers or sexual partners, and feel relatively secure. But the bars presented their own problems: alcoholism, fights, police raids, even, in some cases, infiltration by undercover police officers. In many jurisdictions, same-sex dancing was illegal, so the management had to take precautions against police raids. At bars frequented by both lesbians and gay men, a red light would flash on the dance floor at the first sign of the police, warning all-female and all-male couples to switch partners and dance with the nearest person of the opposite sex. At one lesbian bar on the outskirts of Los Angeles, the manager was said to wander about the dance floor during the course of the evening carrying a flashlight. Regulations were that there had to be sufficient distance between a couple so that a beam from the flashlight could pass between them. Otherwise, patrons could be charged with disorderly conduct.

The bars were governed by strict patterns of dress and behavior known as "butch/femme." Under the rules of butch/femme, every lesbian was forced to choose one of two ways of presenting herself: either the stereotypically masculine "butch" or the feminine "femme." Those who refused found there was no place for them in bar culture—such women were known as "kiki." **Audre Lorde,** the black poet, fell into the anomalous category when, as a young women in 1956, she went to the Bagatelle, a popular Greenwich Village bar. "I wasn't cute or passive enough to be 'femme,' and I wasn't mean or tough enough to be 'butch,' " she wrote in her autobiography, *Zami: A New Spelling of My Name.* "I was given a wide berth." In fact, the bars were so structured by roles that one Springfield, Massachusetts, establishment is said to have had two bathrooms—one marked "butch" and one marked "femme."

Butch/femme was a closed and self-contained world that "asserted difference through appearance," according to Elizabeth Lapovsky Kennedy and Madeline D. Davis, whose book, *Boots of Leather, Slippers of Gold,* examines butch/femme culture in the bars of Buffalo, New York, in the 1940s and '50s, mostly through oral histories. Styles changed, but the one constant was that butches wore men's clothing and femmes wore women's clothing. In Buffalo in the early 1950s, for example, chino pants, men's shirts, and sports jackets were *de rigeur* for white butches. By the end of the decade,

During the late 1950s and 1960s, pulp novels with lesbian themes— and lurid covers—were widely available in drug stores and on newsstands in the U.S. By 1964–65, some 348 such novels had been published. Although many perpetuated stereotypes, others of the genre—written by lesbian novelists such as Ann Bannon and Valerie Taylor—offered positive portraits of lesbian life (although usually featuring obligatory unhappy endings). The novels were primarily aimed at a heterosexual male audience, but for many lesbians they became prized possessions. Feminist theorist Kate Millett said she treasured her collection of pulps because "they were the only books where one woman kissed another." *(Robert D. Rubic, New York Public Library: International Gay Information Center Archives, Rare Books Division)*

sports jackets were "out" and cardigan and V-neck sweaters "in," a development that one bar-goer of the time ascribed to the "growing influence of the Perry Como look." Short hair was mandatory for butches; slicked-back DA (ducktail) haircuts were popular among some of the "tougher" women. Black butch women preferred a dressier look: three-piece suits or dark pants with starched white shirts and formal collars. Femmes, white and black, followed the women's fashions of the day: In the 1950s, they cultivated the "sweater girl" look made popular by actresses like Lana Turner, Jane Russell, and Marilyn Monroe. Long hair and makeup—and often high heels—were essential components of the femme image.

But it wasn't just the dress that distinguished butch and femme. One had to behave one's part as well. In an interview in the documentary film *Word Is Out*, comedian Pat Bond, who came out as a lesbian and a butch when she joined the Women's Army Corps during World War II, describes the mores of a slightly earlier period:

> *Yeah, there was a lot of pressure to look butch if you were. . . . I was never too good at it. . . . I looked really funny trying to look like a man. Men's pants look funny because I'm very short-waisted and big-busted. Trying to wear the short haircut with sideburns shaved over the ears, I looked like the missing link. So I would affect how I stood, and you learned to walk like a man* (gets up and demonstrates) *with a grim look on your face— that suggested maleness, somehow, being grim. Stomp, stomp, stomp. You always stood, if possible, with one foot up like this* (foot on chair and arm resting on knee), *and when you sat you'd cross your legs like that, not like a woman crosses her legs. . . . I remember sneaking into the bathroom and putting on cologne— 'cause you were only allowed to wear Old Spice aftershave lotion. And you had to wear men's jockey shorts, which never fit me. It was terrible. You were always adjusting the damn things. . . .*

Butch and femme behaviors were manifested in other ways, too. Butch women were sexually aggressive; they always made the first move. They lit their femme's cigarettes and opened car doors for her. Two butches could never be lovers, nor could two femmes. It was acceptable, however, for someone to be femme in one relationship and butch in the next or vice versa. There was solidarity among butches—they were friends and allies. But that apparently wasn't true among femmes, who tended to be competitors, at least according to Kennedy and Davis's Buffalo sources. Butches protected their femmes, both from other butches and from the hostility of the straight world. Butches fought and drank hard and generally comported themselves in ways that would make any Hollywood tough guy proud.

The origins of butch/femme are murky. It may be derived in part from the tradition of "passing" women of the nineteenth and early twentieth centuries. Certainly, there was a historical tradition of lesbians dressing in male garb—the Parisian women of the Belle Époque, for instance, and novelist Radclyffe Hall of a later generation. Historian Lillian Faderman suggests that Hall's novel *The Well of Loneliness*—in which the heroine, Stephen Gordon, was "butch" and her lover, Mary, the counterpart of "femme"—may have been influential in setting the tone as well. Faderman also hypothesizes that fear of undercover police may have encouraged the adoption of the mandatory butch/femme style: A policewoman would automatically stand out because, in theory, she wouldn't be sufficiently knowledgeable of the local folkways to dress properly.

It should be emphasized that in the 1950s, butch/femme was primarily a working-class phenomenon. Although some middle-class lesbians were influenced by butch/femme roles, many were critical of what they considered the negative image created by working-class butches. The playwright **Lorraine Hansberry** (author of the Pulitzer Prize–winning play *A Raisin in the Sun*; see also "Lorraine Hansberry," page 328) wrote a letter to *The Ladder*, the magazine of the homophile group the Daughters of Bilitis, saying, "Someday I expect the 'discrete' lesbian will not turn her head on the streets at the sight of the 'butch' strolling hand in hand with her friend in their trousers and definitive haircuts. But for the moment it still disturbs. It creates an impossible area for discussion with one's most enlightened (to use a hopeful term) heterosexual friends." From 1957 to 1967, each issue of *The Ladder* listed among the organization's goals "advocating a mode of behavior and dress acceptable to society."

Was butch/femme merely an aping of the sexist mores of fifties culture? Audre Lorde believed so. In *Zami*, she wrote, "For some of us, role-playing reflected all the deprecating attitudes towards women which we loathed in straight society. It was a rejection of these roles that had drawn us to 'the life' in the first place. Instinctively, without particular theory or political position or dialectic, we recognized oppression as oppression, no matter where it came from." Others take a very different view. **Joan Nestle,** a self-described femme who came out in New York City bars in the late 1950s and later became an exponent of butch/femme culture, contends that butch/femme relationships were "complex erotic statements, not phony heterosexual replicas." As Nestle writes in her book, *A Restricted Country:*

> *[Butch/femme relationships] were filled with a deeply Lesbian language of stance, dress, gesture, loving, courage, and autonomy. None of the butch women I was with, and this included a passing woman, ever presented themselves to me as men: they did announce themselves as tabooed women who were willing to identify their passion for other women by wearing clothes that symbolized the taking of responsibility. Part of this responsibility was sexual expertise. In the 1950s this courage to feel comfortable with arousing another woman became a political act.*

Nestle claims that the questions "Are you butch?" or "Are you femme?" really meant "Are you sexual" and "Are you safe?" However one views butch/femme, there can be no doubt that its highly defined patterns of dress and behavior offered many women a sense of security during a period when hostility against gays and lesbians was at its height.

In the postwar period, Buffalo was a prosperous industrial and commercial center of almost six hundred thousand people, featuring several bars frequented by homosexuals, with names like the Carousel (a mixed gay and lesbian bar) and Bingo's (entirely lesbian) and the Mardi Gras (mixed gay and straight). Gays and lesbians from nearby cities like Rochester and Toronto flocked to the Buffalo bar scene. Because of a famously corrupt city government and police force, there were virtually no raids on gay bars in the fifties; bar culture was able to flourish undisturbed.

The lesbian community that Kennedy and Davis describe was one rigidly divided by social class. Working-class and middle-class lesbians rarely socialized together. Middle-class lesbians usually didn't go to bars, anyway; those who did so tended to go to the same bars as gay men, instead of those frequented by their working-class sisters. Working-class gay women, white and black, went to the same bars, mostly seedy and run-down. There, butch/femme reigned supreme.

But it was a dangerous, often violent world. The butch/femme couples were far more obvious than their more closeted, respectable middle-class counterparts. To Joan Nestle, they represented women's "erotic autonomy," the sexual implications of two women together. This made them susceptible to harassment on the streets. Or as one Buffalo lesbian told Kennedy and Davis, "You were there, you were gay, you were queer and you were masculine. Men hated it."

In Buffalo, the violence and harassment that butch/femme couples experienced on the streets spilled over into the bars. In an atmosphere exacerbated by alcohol and social hostility, butches battled over femmes with straight men—and sometimes with other butches, too. "A weekend wasn't a weekend if there wasn't a fight," one Buffalo lesbian said. "They threw chairs, they threw tables." Another described a fight that broke out during her first visit to one of the city's rougher bars: "Glasses were flying and everything. I remember I went under a table and thought, 'Oh God! What is this?' But I kept going back because this was the only way I could get to know people that were like me." There were usually no bouncers in such bars, and the owners did little to protect their clientele. But not all the fighting was defensive in nature. Butches sometimes attempted to "expand" their territory, by gaining a foothold in bars frequented by straights; this usually resulted in more fights.

The macho atmosphere in the bars was reflected in the way butches often treated femmes. In Buffalo bars of the 1950s, it was customary for butches to accompany their femmes to the bathroom. This originally seems to have evolved in order to protect femmes in rough street bars, but it also reflected the controlling nature of many of these relationships. For example, a femme was not permitted to move freely around the bar or talk or dance with others without her butch's consent. Butches would frequently test a femme's loyalty through various tricks. One Buffalo lesbian described it this way:

> The big thing was they used to leave notes, "Meet me at the juke box at 10:15." Butches used to have somebody give their fem notes to see if they would get up and do it. And everybody would sit and [wait]. . . . Say like I was a pal of D.J.'s right? I'd walk over to her fem and say, "Here, somebody told me to give you

this." And [it] would say, "Meet me at the juke box at 10:15"
or something. And then everybody'd sit back and say, "Oh, God,
she's not gonna do it. 'Cause she's gonna get a beating if she
does." And a lot them did, they got right up and went to the
juke box....

In such a situation, what the loyal femme should have done was to
hand over the note to her butch.

The rules of butch/femme interaction often extended from bar-
room to bedroom. The cornerstone of butch/femme sexuality was
that the butch pleased the femme sexually. But this had its ex-
tremes—in particular, the sexual rituals of the "stone butch," or
the "untouchable," as she was called. "Untouchables" insisted on
wearing their clothes in bed and would not let their partner touch
them during sexual acts. As one woman told Kennedy and Davis,
"I feel that if we're in bed and she does the same thing to me that
I do to her, we're the same thing." For the "stone butch," the most
unacceptable thing was to "roll over," in the slang of the time, and
allow the femme to make love to her.

In Buffalo at least, relations between black and white lesbians
were apparently quite good. The bars desegregated during the mid-
fifties. Black lesbians, previously relegated to socializing at house
parties, could now go to previously all-white establishments. Although the number of black women who went to the bars was not
large, there were several interrracial couples well-known in the community. Some of the women Kennedy and Davis interviewed suggested that relations between black and white women were better
in the fifties than they are today. As one Buffalo lesbian noted, "You
had to be more friendly with other people. . . . Times were harder."
In New York City, black poet Audre Lorde found a similar situation.
"Lesbians were probably the only Black and white women in New
York City in the fifties who were making any real attempt to communicate with each other," she wrote.

The authors of *Boots of Leather, Slippers of Gold* contend that
butch/femme culture represented a transition stage in the evolution
of lesbian identity. Earlier in the century—under the influence of
the sexologists—homosexuality had been viewed as a matter of
gender inversion, they note. Homosexuality was assumed to mean
taking on the characteristics of the opposite sex. For women, a
desire for automony or independence or erotic attraction to other
women was associated with masculinity, but the "feminine" part-

ners of these women were not considered to be homosexual. So in Buffalo, as late as the 1940s, butches were assumed to be gay but their femme partners were not. As time went on, however, homosexuality was increasingly defined as being attracted to members of the same sex, without necessarily taking on particularly masculine or feminine characteristics. Thus, in 1950s Buffalo, both butch and femme were seen to be "gay girls." Still, the legacy of an earlier era when lesbianism was thought to involve a masculine identification was retained in butch/femme culture.

By the 1970s, with the emergence of lesbian liberation and feminism, butch/femme was widely condemned, seen as retrograde, as a mere imitation of sexist patterns. It persisted in small towns, in some working-class communities, and in some ethnic and racial subcultures, but among the mainstream lesbian-feminist movement it was viewed as an embarrassing legacy of an oppressive past. By the 1980s, there was renewed interest in butch/femme. This was the result of increasing lesbian sexual experimentation and the writings of women like Joan Nestle who took an unapologetic view of butch/femme culture. In their book, Kennedy and Davis take this one step further, arguing that the gay and lesbian liberation movement of the 1970s had its roots in the fighting spirit of the butch/femme bars.

Black Poet in a White Butch/Femme World

Audre Lorde came out as a lesbian while a student at Hunter College in New York City in the mid-1950s. Eventually, she became America's most well-known black lesbian poet. One of her books of poetry, From a Land Where Other People Live, *was nominated for a National Book Award in 1974. At the time of her death from cancer in 1992, Lorde was the poet laureate of New York State. In her autobiography,* Zami: A New Spelling of My Name, *Lorde describes being a young black lesbian in New York City in the fifties:*

I REMEMBER how being young and Black and gay and lonely felt. A lot of it was fine, feeling I had the truth and the light and the key, but a lot of it was purely hell.

We had no mothers, no sisters, no heroes. We had to do it alone, like our sister Amazons, the riders on the loneliest outposts of the kingdom of Dahomey. We, young and Black and fine and gay, sweated our first heartbreaks with no school nor office chums to share that confidence over lunch hour. Just as there were no rings to make tangible the reason for our happy secret smiles, there were no names nor reason given or shared for the tears that messed up the lab reports or the library bills.

We were good listeners, and never asked for double dates, *but didn't we know the rules?* Why did we always seem to think friendships between women were important enough to *care* about? Always we moved in a necessary remoteness that made "What did you do this weekend?" seem like an impertinent question. We discovered and explored our attention to women alone, sometimes in secret, sometimes in defiance, sometimes in little pockets that almost touched ("Why are those little Black girls always either whispering together or fighting?") but always alone, against a greater aloneness. We did it cold turkey, and although it resulted in some pretty imaginative tough women when we survived, too many of us did not survive at all. . . .

During the fifties in the Village, I didn't know the few other Black women who were visibly gay at all well. Too often we found ourselves sleeping with the same white women. We recognized ourselves as exotic sister-outsiders who might gain little from banding together. Perhaps our strength might lay in our fewness, our rarity. That was the way it was Downtown. And Uptown, meaning the land of Black people, seemed very far away and hostile territory. . . .

Most Black lesbians were closeted, correctly recognizing the Black community's lack of interest in our position, as well as the many more immediate threats to our survival as Black people in a racist society. It was hard enough to be Black, to be Black and female, to be Black female, and gay. To be Black, female, gay, and out of the closet in a white environment, even to the extent of dancing in the Bagatelle [a lesbian bar in Greenwich Village], was considered by many Black lesbians to be simply suicidal. And if you were fool enough to do it, you'd better come on so tough that nobody messed with you. I often felt put down by their sophistication, their clothes, their manners, their cars, and their femmes.

The Black women I usually saw around the Bag were into heavy roles, and it frightened me. . . . They were tough in a way I felt I could never be. Even if they were not, their self-protective instincts warned them to appear that way. By white america's racist distortions of beauty, Black women playing "femme" had very little chance in the Bag. There was constant competition among butches to have the most "gorgeous femme" on their arm. "And "gorgeous" was defined by a white male world's standards. . . .

The other Black women in the Bag came protected by a show of all the power symbols they could muster. . . . They were well-heeled, superbly dressed, self-controlled high-steppers who drove convertibles, bought rounds of drinks for their friends, and generally took care of business.

But sometimes, even *they* couldn't get in unless they were recognized by the bouncer. . . .

The Black gay-girls in the Village gay bars of the fifties knew each other's names, but we seldom looked into each other's Black eyes, lest we see our own aloneness and our own blunted power mirrored in the pursuit of darkness. . . .

Lorraine Hansberry

WHEN LORRAINE HANSBERRY'S play *A Raisin in the Sun* opened on Broadway on March 11, 1959, it was an immediate success. The story of a black family living on Chicago's South Side, *A Raisin in the Sun* ran for two years, winning the New York Drama Critics Circle Award for Best Play of the Year. At age twenty-nine, Hansberry (1930–65) was the youngest American and the first black dramatist to win the coveted award. Later, *A Raisin in the Sun* became a Hollywood movie and a Tony Award–winning musical (called simply *Raisin*). As James Baldwin wrote of Hansberry's play, "Never before, in the entire history of the American theatre, had so much of the truth of black people's lives been seen on the stage." Five years later, as Hansberry was dying of cancer at age

Lorraine Hansberry. (© *The Bettmann Archive*)

thirty-four, an extraordinary outpouring of support kept her play *The Sign in Sidney Brustein's Window* running for more than one hundred performances after unenthusiastic reviews seemed to doom it in its opening week. The campaign to keep *Sidney Brustein* alive became a Broadway legend. (It closed permanently on the day Hansberry died.)

What is less well-known is that Lorraine Hansberry was a lesbian. In fact, throughout the 1950s, she wrote a series of anonymous letters to *One* magazine and *The Ladder,* publications of the early homophile organizations. The letters were signed only with the initials L.H. or L.H.N. *The Sign in Sidney Brustein's Window* features a male homosexual character, and her unfinished play *Les Blancs* includes a gay couple. Her husband, **Robert Nemiroff,** noted that Hansberry's homosexuality "was not a peripheral or casual part of her life but contributed significantly on many levels to the sensitivity and complexity of her view of human beings and of the world." (Hansberry and Nemiroff were divorced in 1964 but remained close collaborators; after her death, Nemiroff arranged her unpublished material into the stage work *To Be Young, Gifted and Black*.)

Hansberry was born in Chicago to a family deeply involved in black politics and culture. Her father, **Carl Hansberry,** built up a successful real-estate business, ran for Congress, and was active in the NAACP and the Urban League. In 1938, he moved his family to an all-white neighborhood near the University of Chicago in an effort to challenge the city's real-estate covenants, which legally enforced housing discrimination against blacks. Carl Hansberry fought the issue all the way to the U.S. Supreme Court and won. (At one point, while he was in court, his family faced a hostile white mob that had gathered in front of the house; a concrete slab was thrown through the window, narrowly missing Lorraine, who later used the incident as the basis of a scene in *A Raisin in the Sun*.)

In 1950, Lorraine Hansberry moved to New York City, where she worked on Paul Robeson's radical black newspaper, *Freedom*. She met Nemiroff, a graduate student at New York University and an aspiring writer, on a picket line, and they married in 1953. After the success of *A Raisin in the Sun,* she continued to be involved in the black civil rights movement, on one occasion tangling with then—Attorney General Robert F. Kennedy at a stormy meeting. James Baldwin recalled Hansberry in those years, when the two black (and gay) writers spent hours together arguing about "history and tremendously related subjects" at Hansberry's Greenwich Village apartment:

> *Often, just when I was certain that she was about to throw me out, as being altogether too rowdy a type, she would stand up, her hands on her hips . . . and pick up my empty glass as though she intended to throw it at me. Then she would walk in to the kitchen, saying, with a haughty toss of her head, "Really, Jimmy. You ain't right child." With which stern put-down, she would hand me another drink and launch into a brilliant analysis of just why I wasn't "right." I would often stagger down her stairs as the sun came up, usually in the middle of a paragraph and always in the middle of a laugh. . . .*

Hansberry's letters to *The Ladder* and *One* magazine ranged in subject matter from butch/femme role-playing (which made her uncomfortable) to the links between the oppression of women and that of homosexuals. In a 1957 letter to *The Ladder*, the publication of the Daughters of Bilitis, she wrote, "I'm glad as heck that you exist. You are obviously serious people and I feel that women, without wishing to foster any strict *separatist* notions, homo or hetero, indeed have a need for their own publications and organizations." In another letter to *The Ladder* that same year, she added,

> I think it is about time that equipped women began to take on some of the ethical questions which a male-dominated culture has produced and dissect and analyze them quite to pieces in a serious fashion. . . . In this kind of work there may be women to emerge who will be able to formulate a new and possible concept that homosexual persecution and condemnation has at its roots not only social ignorance, but a philosophically active anti-feminist dogma.

Four years later, in an unpublished (and unmailed) letter to *One,* she explored the differences in the social attitudes toward male and female homosexuals: Gay men, she thought, were viewed as "tantamount to the criminal," while lesbians were "naughty, neurotic, adventurous, titillatingly wicked or rebellious." No one particularly wanted to put lesbians in jail: "They more want to read about it or hear it described so they can cluck their tongues and roll their eyes. The fact is that women are not held as responsible for themselves as men are because they are not held as definitely human."

In *The Sign in Sidney Brustein's Window,* the abrasive, intellectual protagonist, in a conversation with a gay playwright named David, launches into a critique of fifties homosexuals that reflects Hansberry's own viewpoint:

> If somebody insults you—sock 'em in the jaw. If you don't like the sex laws, attack 'em, I think they're silly. You wanna get up a petition? I'll sign one. Love little fishes if you want. But, *David,* please get over the notion that your particular "thing" is something that only the deepest, saddest, the most nobly tortured can know about. It ain't— (Spearing into the salad) *it's just one kind of sex—that's all. And, in my opinion—*(Revolving his fork) *the universe turns regardless.*

In her attempts to link sexism and gay oppression and in her rejection of the self-pitying homosexual of the fifties, Hansberry anticipated some of the ideas of gay liberation. But she never lived long enough to become one of those women she spoke of, who would attempt to formulate a new concept of "homosexual persecution and condemnation." Her death in 1965—four years before Stonewall and the beginnings of the lesbian-feminist movement—may have deprived the gay movement of an eloquent thinker and spokesperson. It unquestionably deprived American culture of a great artist.

CHAPTER 22

THE HOMOPHILES

IN 1948, Communist Party organizer and cultural worker **Harry Hay** (b. 1912) was teaching a course on the "Historical Materialist Development of Music" at the People's Educational Center in Los Angeles. Hay had been a member of the Communist Party for fifteen years, and had married another Party member, on the suggestion of a Party higher-up to whom Hay had confided his homosexuality. One evening in 1948, Hay found himself at a "beer bust" at the University of Southern California, hosted by some gay men. By the end of the evening, Hay and those present—with the help of a couple of quarts of beer—had conceived of the idea of a homosexual organization to support the presidential bid of third-party candidate **Henry Wallace.** The group was to be called "Bachelors for Wallace." But the following morning, when Hay called up the enthusiasts of the night before, they could remember little except their hangovers.

It took two more years, until 1950, for Hay's thinking to come to fruition. That was the year that Senator Joseph McCarthy gave his famous Wheeling speech; gays were being purged in large numbers from the U.S. State Department. Hay was convinced that the anti-Communist forces were looking for a new scapegoat and that the scapegoat would be homosexuals. So along with some gay students in his music class, mostly Communists and former Communists, he began to talk seriously about forming a homosexual rights organization. They would call it the Mattachine Society.

Unlike in Germany, there had never really been a gay rights movement in the United States. The sole attempt came in 1924 when a Chicago postal employee, **Henry Gerber,** founded the Society for Human Rights to work for public education and law reform. Gerber had served in the U.S. Army of Occupation in Germany after World War I and had been influenced by the German homosexual rights movement. His new organization obtained a state charter and published the first issue of a newspaper. But after Gerber and other members were arrested (the wife of the group's vice president had contacted a social worker who went to the police), the Society for Human Rights disbanded and was never heard from again.

In the spring and summer of 1951, Mattachine put its "missions and purposes" into writing. Its aims included unifying isolated homosexuals and creating "an ethical homosexual culture . . . paralleling the emerging cultures of our fellow-minorities—the Negro, Mexican, and Jewish Peoples." The statement asserted that homosexuals constituted "one of the largest minorities in America today," a group "victimized daily as a result of our oppression." This characterization of homosexuals as an oppressed minority was influenced by Communist social and political analysis. (The American Communists themselves, following the Stalinist line, strongly opposed homosexuality.) It was a radical, almost revolutionary, view, in an era when even the most advanced thinking portrayed homosexuals as "sick" individuals who had little in common beyond their illness.

According to Hay, the name Mattachine derived from a medieval French society of unmarried townsmen who conducted dances and rituals in the countryside during the Feast of Fools at the vernal equinox. The original Mattachines always performed wearing masks; their dance rituals sometimes turned into peasant protests against the aristocracy. Hay chose this name for his new society because he saw the homosexuals of the 1950s as a "masked people, unknown and anonymous, who might become engaged in morale building and helping ourselves and others."

The Mattachine Society had a "secret, cell-like hierarchical structure," according to historian John D'Emilio, whose book *Sexual Politics, Sexual Communities* provides the most comprehensive account of U.S. gay and lesbian organizing before Stonewall. There were five "orders" of membership, arranged in a pyramid; as Mattachine grew, each order was supposed to subdivide into separate cells. The fifth order—the founders—provided the organization with a centralized leadership. Many of the first- and second-order members had no idea who the leadership was. In part, this organizational structure may have been set up to disguise the fact that Communists and ex-Communists were among the founders, but Hay was also convinced that America was on the road to fascism and that the new organization needed to be as impenetrable as possible.

Mattachine's earliest activities were discussion groups, held in private homes, whose time and place were spread by word of mouth.

Jim Kepner, later to be a writer for the Mattachine-affiliated magazine, *One,* recalled that at the first gathering he attended there were about 180 people present—mostly men, but some women, too. He also observed that the format of the discussion was such that a visitor couldn't tell who was running it. By the time he went to his second or third meeting, Kepner began to hear rumors that some of the people in charge were Communists. "That was very disturbing in this period in history," he noted, "because almost all the people who came to the discussion groups were very conformist, and they loved nothing better than to say, 'We're just like everybody else except for what we do in bed. . . .' "

In February 1952 one of Mattachine's founders, **Dale Jennings,** was arrested in a Los Angeles park on charges of soliciting an undercover police officer. Mattachine created a Citizens Committee to Outlaw Entrapment, circulating leaflets publicizing the case in gay bars in Los Angeles and at gay beaches in Santa Monica. At his trial, Jennings denied all guilt but admitted to being a homosexual (an almost unheard-of thing to do at a time when gay men arrested in such cases invariably pleaded guilty, to avoid public exposure). The jury deadlocked, and the case was dropped. The Mattachine Society proclaimed victory and thereafter began to grow rapidly. Discussion groups extended south to San Diego and north to the San Francisco Bay Area. John D'Emilio reports that by May 1953, total participation in the society was estimated at more than two thousand people.

During 1953, Mattachine decided to start a monthly magazine. Called *One,* it was the first homosexual publication of any consequence published in the United States. *One* combined "scientific" articles about homosexuality from doctors, psychologists, and the like (mostly in its earlier years), with more personal and sociological pieces (in the late fifties and sixties). Although *One* was formally independent of Mattachine, most of its editorial board was made up of Mattachine members. Within a few months, it was selling two thousand copies a month. *One* also began to circulate outside California, spreading word about the new homosexual organizing to other parts of the country. (When the U.S. Post Office prevented mailing of the November 1954 issue, claiming it was obscene, *One* fought it all the way to the U.S. Supreme Court, which ruled in *One*'s favor. The magazine continued publication until 1967.)

In March 1953, Mattachine mailed out a questionnaire to candidates for the Los Angeles city council and school board asking their views on police harassment of homosexuals and on sex education in the schools. **Paul Coates,** a columnist for the *Los Angeles Mirror,* obtained a copy of the questionnaire and researched the "strange new pressure group," as he put it. In a column, he revealed that the organization's legal adviser, **Fred Snider,** had been an "unfriendly witness" before the House Un-American Activities Committee. Coates observed that homosexuals had been "found to be bad security risks in our State Department" and suggested there might be as many as two hundred thousand "sex deviates" in the Los Angeles area. "A well-trained subversive could move in and forge that power into a dangerous political weapon," he warned. "To damn this organization, before its aims and direction are more clearly established, would be vicious and irresponsible. Maybe the people who founded it are sincere. It would be interesting to see."

Harry Hay was exultant. He sent out twenty thousand copies of Coates's column. But others within Mattachine began to wonder exactly who the leaders of their organization really were. Pressure mounted on Mattachine's ruling Fifth Order to reveal themselves. **Marilyn Rieger,** a Los Angeles member, noted that "many members of the meetings . . . feel that Mr. Coates asked legitimate questions . . . and that explanations are definitely in order." The founders responded by calling a convention to restructure the organization in an open, democratic manner. A hundred or so members came together the following month at a Los Angeles Unitarian church. The founders, notably Hay and **Chuck Rowland,** defended their leadership—and the actions of Fred Snider before the Un-American Activities Committee. Hay (who by then had left the Communist Party) reminded those assembled that with the federal government purging gays and lesbians, *everyone* had something to hide from investigators.

Nonetheless, opposition and charges of Communist infiltration of Mattachine grew. At another large meeting the following month, the San Francisco delegation, led by **Hal Call,** asked the organization to make "a very strong statement concerning our stand on subversive elements." Call's proposal failed. But the Mattachine founders knew their days were numbered. They announced they would not seek office in the newly structured Mattachine. Soon, almost all dropped out of the organization.

With the resignation of the founders, a new breed of leaders with a very different outlook took over Mattachine. They rejected the notion of gays and lesbians as a minority group, stressing that homosexuals were really no different than heterosexuals. The new leadership also rejected activist tactics, such as taking on entrapment cases and working for repeal of sodomy laws. A San Francisco Mattachine pamphlet reflected this thinking: "Any organized pressure on lawmakers by members of the Mattachine Society as a group would only serve to prejudice the position of the Society. . . . It would provide an abundant source of hysterical propaganda with which to foment an ignorant, fear-inspired anti-homosexual campaign."

The Mattachine focus would now be on public education, not political activism, in particular relying on (heterosexual) "experts"—sociologists, psychologists, legal and medical figures, and the like—who could provide support to the cause. Alfred Kinsey was one who approved of this approach. He advised Mattachine to avoid "special pleas for a minority group" and to restrict itself to helping "qualified research experts." The flavor of the earlier, more activist days was retained only in One, which became increasingly independent of the revamped Mattachine. (In January 1955, the society established its own magazine, Mattachine Review, published out of San Francisco.)

Mattachine's cautious approach signaled the emergence of what is known as the homophile movement—characterized by a deliberately low profile and an emphasis on education and the backing of "experts." In later years, Mattachine founder Harry Hay has tried to portray the battle for control of the early Mattachine as one of courageous leftist activists against unimaginative "status quo" types. "The people who remained [after the founders left] were interested in being middle class," he asserted. But it is highly questionable whether a gay group led by Communists and former Communists could ever have survived in the midst of the McCarthy period. (Hay himself was called before the House Un-American Activities Committee in 1955 for his Communist activities.) John D'Emilio observes that although a gay subculture was emerging during this period in the United States, it was still relatively undeveloped:

> The [early Mattachine] claim that homosexuals were a minority with a distinctive culture was still too much at odds with the situation of gay men and women. The dominant view of homosexuality, with its emphasis on the individual nature of the phenomenon, more accurately described gay existence. Moreover,

*by 1953 the right-wing attacks upon "sexual perverts" had gath-
ered full force, and police harassment was on the rise. Both of
these seemed to magnify the risks of joining a gay organization
and discouraged individuals from espousing anything that
smacked of radicalism. For a gay emancipation movement to
grow and become strong, the conditions of gay life and the
political climate in America would have to change.*

With the coming to power of the more "moderate" elements,
Mattachine membership went into decline. Some discussion groups
shut down altogether. By 1955, however, the organization was
slowly growing again, with new chapters in New York and Chicago.
That same year, the Daughters of Bilitis (DOB), the nation's first
lesbian organization, was established in San Francisco. The founders
of DOB were **Del Martin** (b. 1921) and **Phyllis Lyon** (b. 1924).
Martin, a San Francisco native, had been married and later divorced
after falling in love with a woman. In 1949, she moved to Seattle
to work for a firm that published trade journals. There she met
Lyon, who had studied journalism at Berkeley and had worked as
a crime reporter for a small-town newspaper. The two became close
friends and eventually lovers. In 1953, they moved back to San
Francisco together.

Martin and Lyon felt uncomfortable in the city's lesbian bars,
and in an attempt to make friends, they decided to form a lesbian
social club. The club, called the Daughters of Bilitis, took its name
from French author Pierre Louys's turn-of-the-century literary work
that included love poems between women. As Martin and Lyon
described it in their book, *Lesbian Woman,* "We thought that
'Daughters of Bilitis' would sound like any other women's lodge—
you know, like the Daughters of the Nile or the DAR. . . . If anyone
asked us, we could always say we belonged to a poetry club."

Soon, Lyon and Martin became familiar with the Mattachine
Society and *One,* and decided DOB should be more than just a
social club. Its aim would be to promote the "integration of the
homosexual into society" through "education of the variant" and
of "the public at large." (Its statement of purpose avoided the words
lesbian or *gay woman,* preferring *variant* instead.) DOB differed
from Mattachine in that its primary focus was on their members'
personal needs. This was in part an awareness of the isolation and
invisibility of gay women. "DOB existed as a self-help effort for
women, a haven where they could experience a sense of belonging,

put their lives in order, and then, strengthened and regenerated, venture forth into society," wrote D'Emilio. The organization was known for its "gabs 'n javas" sessions—literally "talk and coffee." The sensitivity toward lesbian isolation was reflected in *The Ladder*, the organization's publication (launched in 1956), which was particularly directed toward women living far from the major urban centers.

Shirley Willer, a nurse who was to become a president of DOB New York in the 1960s, gave some of the flavor of the organization when she described her first meeting to Eric Marcus:

> *My introduction to the Daughters was wild. I was told that the meeting was going to be at this particular lady's house and I could distinguish it by the barking dog. So I went to the address and went up the steps to the second or third floor, and sure enough there was this barking dog. I knocked at the door, and a young lady answered and said, "What do you want?" I said, "Well, there's going to be a meeting here tonight, isn't there?" She said, "Oh my God, no!" She had a sink full of dirty dishes, an accumulation of at least a week, and her house was a total disaster . . . So I washed dishes and helped clean her apartment. That was my introduction to the Daughters.*

The leaders of DOB saw male homosexuals as their primary allies; they cosponsored public events with the Mattachine Society and attended Mattachine conventions. No organized feminist movement existed in the United States at that point, and if one had, it isn't clear that DOB would have gravitated in that direction, anyway. But the Daughters often felt condescended to by the male side of the movement, perceived as a mere "women's auxiliary." They became particularly angered when they were accused of "competing" with Mattachine by insisting upon a separate organization. As Del Martin put it in a speech at a 1959 Mattachine convention:

> *At every one of these conventions I attend, year after year, I find I must defend the Daughters of Bilitis as a separate and distinct women's organization . . . What do you men know about Lesbians? In all of your programs and your "[Mattachine] Review," you speak of the male homosexual and follow this with—oh, yes, and incidentally there are some female homosexuals, too. . . . One [magazine] has done little better. For years they*

have relegated the lesbian interest to the column called "Feminine Viewpoint." So it would appear to me that quite obviously neither organization has recognized the fact that lesbians are women and that this twentieth century is the era of emancipation of women. . . .

There was an element of condescension to DOB itself, however, a "scolding-teacher attitude," in the words of two other early DOB activists, **Kay Tobin** and **Barbara Gittings.** The organization had been originally conceived as an alternative to the bars and placed itself in opposition to bar culture. It saw itself as encouraging lesbians to be respectable. Tobin noted that the title itself of *The Ladder* implied that "the little lesbian was beginning to climb the ladder, upgrading herself so that she would become an OK person instead a 'variant,' who had a poor self-image, who didn't hold a regular job, who wasn't a participating member of society." The organization put particular store in lesbians dressing in an appropriately feminine manner. Gittings, the first president of New York's DOB and later the editor of *The Ladder,* relates the story of a woman who had been living "pretty much as a transvestite most of her life" and who was persuaded to attend a DOB convention wearing female clothing. "Everybody rejoiced over this as though some great victory had been accomplished—the 'feminizing of this woman.' "

For these early gay organizations, simply keeping alive was a difficult task. Membership remained small—especially in the case of DOB, which had difficulty attracting middle-class, professional women. The attempt by both Mattachine and DOB to ally themselves with medical and psychiatric "experts" created major dilemmas because there were few Evelyn Hookers or Alfred Kinseys, who held sympathetic views of homosexuals. As a result, both Mattachine and DOB sometimes wound up inviting to their meetings speakers who were exponents of the "gay is sick" theory—the same kind of people who would be zapped by gay militants a decade later. As DOB's Barbara Gittings explained in an interview with historian Jonathan Ned Katz:

At first we were grateful just to have people—anybody—pay attention to us that we listened to and accepted everything they said, no matter how bad it was. . . . When somebody with professional credentials came to address your meetings, that legitimized the existence of your organization. And then when you went out

*and approached other people, you could say that Dr. So and So
or the Rev. So and So had addressed you; that made you less
pariahlike to these other people whom you needed.*

The greatest obstacle these organizations faced was fear. The
leaders of Mattachine always used pseudonyms, and understand-
ably so. FBI agents tape-recorded Mattachine lectures; FBI and
police informants regularly attended Mattachine meetings and conventions and collected the names of those in attendance. Police
surveillance could have disastrous consequences, as was the case at
the 1959 Mattachine convention in Denver. As John D'Emilio relates
in his book, the city's Mattachine leader, known as **Carl Harding,**
decided to break with the low profile of previous Mattachine conventions. He invited **Robert Allen,** the majority leader of the Colorado state assembly, and **William Reynard,** a member of the board
of directors of the Colorado Civil Liberties Union, to address the
delegates. A press conference would be held at which Mattachine
officers would be photographed and interviewed, using their real
names. All this went smoothly. The *Denver Post* covered the convention fairly and respectfully; Mattachine membership increased
dramatically; new faces appeared at the convention. But among the
new faces were "two burly gentlemen" who were apparently morals
officers. A few weeks after the convention, the police raided the
homes of conference organizers, and in the home of **Bill Matson,**
the chapter's librarian, they discovered photographs of male nudes;
Matson was arrested for violating an antipornography statute. The
police also found (and confiscated) the chapter's mailing list. Panic
swept the organization, and the Denver chapter fell into a decline
from which it never recovered.

With the advent of the 1960s, the climate in America began to shift,
gradually at first, and then dramatically by the end of the decade.
The election of **John F. Kennedy** as president raised expectations
for social and political change. The ability of the black civil rights
movement to mobilize large numbers of people—and its successful
use of confrontational tactics—moved social protest to the center
of American politics. Meanwhile, the availability of the birth-
control pill paved the way for the sexual revolution that would
radically change American mores.

Although social attitudes toward homosexuality didn't change overnight—far from it—there was an increasing frankness about the subject. A number of obscenity law decisions in the late 1950s and '60s made it much easier to treat the subject in fiction without fear of prosecution. Some of the critically acclaimed books of the decade—James Baldwin's *Another Country* and **Mary McCarthy's** *The Group,* for example—featured gay characters. Grove Press published avant-garde works with explicit treatments of homosexuality by gay authors such as William Burroughs, **John Rechy,** and Jean Genet. The Supreme Court cleared male physique magazines of obscenity charges; by the middle of the decade, total monthly sales of these magazines topped 750,000. In 1961, under strong pressure from filmmaker **Otto Preminger,** who wanted to make a movie version of the best-selling novel *Advise and Consent,* Hollywood's Production Code was changed to permit the protrayal of homosexuality on the screen on the proviso that it was treated with "care, discretion, and restraint." Although, as Vito Russo noted, lesbians and gay men in American films of the 1960s were almost always portrayed as "pathological, predatory, and dangerous," the fact that they were represented at all signaled an advance. Later in the decade, on the stage, **Mart Crowley's** highly successful *The Boys in the Band* provided a bitterly funny, if stereotypical, look at gay life. (It ran for 1,001 performances off-Broadway.)

The new climate was not only a cultural one. In 1962, the American Law Institute formulated a model penal code that proposed the abolition of state laws outlawing homosexual acts. Illinois, in 1961, and Connecticut, in 1969, became the first states to decriminalize same-sex relations between consenting adults. And, on the medical front, although the "gay is sick" dogma of psychiatrists like Bieber and Socarides remained dominant, by the end of the decade psychiatric thinking was facing opposition from inside and outside the profession.

In this atmosphere, militants began to challenge the cautious leadership of the two dominant gay organizations, Mattachine and DOB. The most significant early militant figure was **Franklin Kameny** (b. 1925). An astronomer with a Ph.D. from Harvard, Kameny was fired from the U.S. Army Map Service in Washington, D.C., in 1957 after investigators discovered that he had been previously arrested on a lewd conduct charge. Kameny unsuccessfully appealed his case to the Civil Service Commission and to the courts. Unable to find another job, he became a professional activist, devoting his life to overturning the U.S. government ban against the hiring of gay men and women. "My dismissal amounted to a declaration of war against me by my government," said Kameny. It was an eighteen-year war that only ended when the U.S. Civil Service Commission announced in 1975 that it would no longer exclude homosexuals from government jobs.

In 1961 Kameny and his friend **Jack Nichols** established a chapter of the Mattachine Society in the nation's capital. Kameny's approach was significantly different from that of other Mattachine leaders. He argued that gay activists should embrace a direct-action strategy similar to that of the black civil rights movement. In a major departure from homophile doctrine, he insisted that gay people themselves, not medical and legal professionals, were the experts on homosexuality. He also broke with the homophile movement in another way, rejecting the "gay is sick" model that homophile leaders had been reluctant to condemn, lest they lose their carefully cultivated contacts with the professionals. "The entire movement is going to stand or fall upon the question of whether homosexuality is a sickness, and upon our taking a firm stand on it," he told New York Mattachine in a 1964 speech.

Kameny was influential in changing the entire tone of the homophile movement. DOB activist Barbara Gittings described him as someone who had "a clear and compelling vision of what the movement should be doing and what was just. He believed that we should be standing up on our hind legs and demanding full equality, and to hell with the sickness issue. *They* put that label on us! *They* were the ones that needed to justify it! Let *them* do their justification! We were not going to help them!"

It was Kameny who was later to coin the slogan "Gay Is Good."

Under Kameny's leadership, Washington Mattachine focused on discriminatory U.S. government policies, taking aim at the Civil Service Commission and the armed forces, as well as the blanket denial of security clearances to all homosexuals. Kameny's tactics primarily involved letter-writing campaigns and meetings with government officials—the homophile movement hadn't reached the point of public demonstrations yet. Nonetheless, his approach was still far more aggressive than anything seen since the radical beginnings of the movement. When Washington, D.C., police raided a gay restaurant in 1963, arresting several patrons and subjecting them to verbal abuse, Kameny got the arrested men to sign affidavits complaining of police maltreatment and lodged a formal complaint with the police department and the D.C. board of commissioners.

The activities of Washington Mattachine were beginning to attract notice in various quarters. In May 1963, Rep. **John Dowdy,** a Texas Democrat who was the chairman of a House subcommittee that dealt with the District of Columbia, introduced a bill revoking Mattachine's permit to raise funds. Kameny testified for four and a half hours at subcommittee hearings. The bill passed the House but died in the Senate. The failure of the legislation was a publicity bonanza and a boost for the fledgling movement; a gleeful Kameny suggested that Dowdy should be given an award as "the man who contributed the most to the homophile movement in 1963." (Dowdy was later indicted by a federal grand jury on bribery charges.)

Kameny's influence was felt beyond Washington Mattachine. Echoing Kameny, Barbara Gittings, editor of *The Ladder,* DOB's newspaper, criticized DOB's dependence on "experts" at their 1964 convention. A year later, she printed a long article by Kameny in *The Ladder,* urging readers to "move away from the comfortingly detached respectability of research into the often less pleasant rough-and-tumble of political and social activism." Gittings's positions antagonized the Daughters' conservative leadership. In 1965, she was replaced as editor of *The Ladder,* and although like-minded militants captured control of DOB New York, the old guard quickly reasserted control.

That same year, Kameny's tactics reached a new stage when a group of ten homosexuals—the men dressed in coats and ties, and the women in dresses—picketed the White House carrying signs like SEXUAL PREFERENCE IS IRRELEVANT TO FEDERAL EMPLOYMENT and CIVIL SERVICE COMMISSION IS UN-AMERICAN. In a repeat action a few months later, forty-five people marched. Similar demonstrations were held at the Pentagon, the State Department, the Civil Service Commission building, and at Independence Hall in Philadelphia. It was nothing compared to the large numbers that had marched on Washington for black civil rights and who were beginning to march against the Vietnam war, but for the homophile movement, it was a giant step forward.

Despite Frank Kameny's more confrontational strategy, the numbers of people involved in Mattachine Washington and the East Coast homophile organizations remained small. It was in San Francisco,

Members of early homophile groups picket the White House in a 1965 demonstration organized by Washington, D.C., Mattachine leader Frank Kameny. *(© UPI/Bettmann)*

as John D'Emilio points out, that the movement began to enlist larger numbers of gays and lesbians to fight for their rights.

During the war and postwar period, San Francisco had experienced a surge in population growth. The city functioned as a point of departure for the war in the Pacific and was a key center of the war industry. Many GIs exposed to its charms remained there after the War, and between 1940 and 1950, the city's population grew by over 125,000. A large number of these new residents were homosexuals. D'Emilio notes that purges from the armed forces during World War II had deposited lesbians and gay men in San Francisco with dishonorable discharges, sometimes hundreds at a time. Many were reluctant to go home. Moreover, California was the one state where courts upheld the right of homosexuals to congregate in bars and public establishments. By the late 1950s, the city had some thirty gay bars, perhaps more than New York City, according to D'Emilio. Gay migration continued into the 1950s; during that decade, the number of single-person households in the city doubled, representing 38 percent of San Francisco's residence units.

Nonetheless, following the 1959 mayoral campaign, San Francisco police initiated a three-year crackdown against the city's gay bars. In that election, the challenger, city assessor **Russell Wolden,** charged that the incumbent mayor, **George Christopher,** had transformed the city into "the national headquarters of the organized homosexuals in the United States." The charges backfired, with the city's major newspapers accusing the candidate of insulting and degrading San Francisco. Wolden lost at the polls. But once the election was over, the Christopher administration responded with a massive campaign of harassment of the city's gay bars. No one would ever accuse the mayor again of being "soft" on "sex deviates." By October 1961, the state Alcohol Beverage Commission had revoked the liquor licenses of twelve of the city's gay bars; misdemeanor charges against men and women resulting from raids on gay bars were running at an estimated forty to sixty a week. (In August of that year, in the biggest bar raid in the city's history, 103 patrons were arrested at the Tay-Bush Inn, a gay bar in the Tenderloin.)

Revealingly, it was a bar—not organizations like Mattachine or DOB—that provided the center of resistance to the police crackdown. The bar was the Black Cat, located on Montgomery Street a few blocks from the center of North Beach, the Beat (and also gay) section of San Francisco. The Black Cat had been a bohemian hangout and the setting for a section of Kerouac's *On the Road;* writers like **William Saroyan** and **John Steinbeck** frequented the place. By the 1950s, it had a large gay clientele. To Allen Ginsberg, the Black Cat was

> *the greatest gay bar in America. It was really totally open, bohemian, San Francisco . . . and everybody went there, heterosexual and homosexual. It was lit up, there was a honky-tonk piano; it was enormous. All the gay screaming queens would come, the heterosexual gray flannel suit types, longshoremen. All the poets went there.*

One of the more colorful characters associated with the Black Cat was **José Sarria,** known for wearing red high heels as he waited on tables. One Sunday afternoon, taking his cue from the bar's pianist, who was playing music from *Carmen,* Sarria began singing arias as he brought drinks to his customers. Within a few months, Sarria—wearing a woman's hat and a red dress—was putting on one-man Sunday-afternoon operatic productions. His performances attracted large numbers of gay men. Soon, Sarria was turning his performances into camp agitprop. He would set *Carmen* in a San Francisco park, turning the heroine into a gay man trying to hide from the vice squad. In his book *The Mayor of Castro Street,* Randy Shilts contends that Sarria's weekly operas provided the equivalent of the first gay news service. During one police crackdown on gay cruising areas, for example, Sarria told his audience, "A blue fungus has hit the parks. It does not appear until about 2 A.M. It twinkles like a star. Until this fungus dies, it's best to stay out of our parks at 2 A.M." At the end of every night at the Black Cat, Sarria would ask patrons to join hands and all sing "God Save Us Nelly Queens."

Sarria's performances made many aware for the first time of their rights as gay people. **George Mendenhall,** later a well-known San Francisco gay journalist, was among them. He commented in the film *Word Is Out:*

> It sounds silly, but if you lived at that time and had the oppression coming down from the police department and from society, there was nowhere to turn . . . and to be able to put your arms around other gay men and to be able to stand up and sing, "God Save Us Nelly Queens" . . . We were really not saying, "God Save Us Nelly Queens." We were saying, "We have our rights, too."

In 1961, as bar and street harassment increased, Sarria ran for a seat on the San Francisco Board of Supervisors. His candidacy made him the first openly gay person in the United States to run for public office. Although he was never a serious contender, on Election Day he polled more than 6,000 votes. But even Sarria's electoral showing could not save the Black Cat; under continued police pressure, the bar shut down in 1963.

As a result of the police raids, Sarria's campaign, and the virtual invisibility of the existing homophile groups, several new gay organizations emerged in San Francisco. The owners of the city's embattled gay bars joined together to form a Tavern Guild. In 1964 came the Society for Individual Rights (SIR), an organization that combined social events and political action. SIR sponsored a variety of activities, from bowling leagues to bridge clubs. Its magazine, *Vector,* was available throughout the city. It sponsored voter registration drives and "Candidates' Nights," in an effort to get politicians to view the gay community as a political force.

Gay activists also allied themselves with liberal church leaders in an organization called the Council on Religion and the Homosexual (CRH). On the eve of January 1, 1965, the Council, along with SIR, Mattachine, and DOB, sponsored a fund-raising ball at California Hall. When the sponsoring ministers met with the police before the ball, the police first tried to get them to cancel the event; after the ministers refused, the police then promised not to interfere. There was the possibility of trouble, but no one quite expected the intensity of the police response, which turned the area around California Hall that night into a virtual war zone. The police lit up the entrance with kleig lights and photographed each one of the six hundred people who entered, many of whom were in costume. Police wagons were parked just outside, and officers made a number of forays into the hall, allegedly to inspect the premises. "They could not have been any better prepared if they had gone there to face gangsters with machine guns," Evander Smith, a lawyer for the sponsoring organizations, told Eric Marcus. When Smith and another gay lawyer, Herb Donaldson, tried to block the police from doing their fourth "inspection," they were arrested. So were two others, both heterosexuals: another lawyer who was Smith and Donaldson's backup that night, and a woman who was working the door. When Smith and Donaldson were released from custody, they returned to the hall and found the place in chaos. "For all intents and purposes, the police were just running roughshod, walking in and out across the dance floor like they had taken over the place," recalled Donaldson. "Some of the people were just terrified."

On January 2, a group of ministers associated with the Council on Religion and the Homosexual held an angry news conference, denouncing the police for "deliberate harassment and bad faith." The American Civil Liberties Union agreed to defend those arrested. The local media, not known for their sympathy toward gays, blasted the police as well. When the case came to court, the defense listed twenty-five of the most prominent lawyers in San Francisco as "counsel." The judge directed the jury to come up with a not-guilty verdict before the defense had even presented its case.

The event became known as "San Francisco's Stonewall," and, indeed, the citywide revulsion at police tactics marked a turning point. In the aftermath, the police department halted its crackdown on gay bars; henceforth a member of the police-community relations board would function as a liaison to the gay community. The gay community emerged from the debacle as a political force as well: By the year's end, **Jack Morrison,** the first incumbent supervisor ever to seek the gay vote, appeared at the SIR "Candidates' Night," along with a number of insurgent candidates. In 1969, when **Dianne Feinstein** ran for city supervisor, she credited the gay community with her margin of victory. Meanwhile, SIR began holding regular gay dances; by 1967, its membership had swelled to twelve hundred, making it the largest gay organization in the United States.

Lawyer Herb Donaldson credited the police response to the ball and the trial that followed with setting the stage for the city's emergence as a gay "mecca." He noted that, in an attempt to inflame public opinion, the police estimated that there were seventy thousand homosexuals in San Francisco. "There weren't," said Donaldson, "but when they carry it on the wire services that there are 70,000, you've got 70,000 others out in the country who want to come and join that 70,000 here! They're still coming!" Eighteen years to the day of his arrest at California Hall, Donaldson was sworn in as California's first openly gay judge.

While the social and political atmosphere for homosexuals was being transformed in San Francisco, those who favored a more militant approach were gaining ascendency in the New York branch of the Mattachine Society. **Randy Wicker** and **Craig Rodwell,** both stirred by the black civil rights movement, tried to add political action to the Mattachine agenda. Wicker, in particular, was influential in gaining the first media coverage of the the city's homosexual community. He persuaded the listener-supported radio station WBAI to broadcast a program in which seven homosexuals talked about their lives. Wicker took reporters for *Harpers, The New York Times,* the *New York Post,* and the *Village Voice* on "field trips" to visit the gay subculture; the result was a spate of favorable press coverage. He persuaded the *Voice* and the *Times* to permit advertisements for homophile events. In the fall of 1964, despite the opposition of the Mattachine leadership, Wicker, Rodwell, and nine others picketed the Whitehall Street Induction Center to protest the armed forces' ban on homosexuals and the release of draft records to employers.

In May 1965, the militant faction wrested control of New York Mattachine from the old guard, electing **Julian Hodges** as the organization's president and Rodwell's lover, **Dick Leitsch,** as vice-president. The militants quickly moved to put their stamp on Mattachine: They issued a policy statement asserting that homosexuality was not a sickness (something the old leadership refused to take a stand on), picketed the United Nations to protest Cuba's policy of putting homosexuals in internment camps, and marched alongside Washington Mattachine in its protest outside the White House and other government agencies.

Mattachine's next focus was to make the entrapment of gay men by police officers a public issue. Shortly after the election of the liberal **John Lindsay** as New York's mayor in November 1965, the police began a cleanup of Times Square and Greenwich Village. Street arrests of homosexuals rose sharply, particularly in the gay cruising area on the western side of Washington Square Park. At a meeting at a Greenwich Village church, Police Inspector **Sanford Garelik** was strongly criticized by Mattachine members and other gay Villagers for the crackdown. He denied that the police engaged in entrapment, but that very night, police officers entrapped two men at Julius, a Village gay bar; the men were charged with solicitation. Garelik's statement and the ensuing arrests were highlighted in the press, embarrassing the Lindsay administration. After a meeting between Lindsay and representatives from Mattachine, the ACLU, and other groups, the city's police commissioner announced that he opposed the practice of entrapment and would limit its use.

An emboldened Mattachine turned to the vulnerability of gay bars to police raids. Officially, in New York State, the State Liquor Authority was authorized to close bars and taverns that served homosexuals. To test the regulations, in April 1966, Mattachine members, including Dick Leitsch and Craig Rodwell, took reporters and photographers on a "sip-in" of Greenwich Village drinking spots. The investigation got off to a rocky start: A Ukrainian bar on St. Mark's Place that supposedly had a hand-lettered sign above the bar reading, IF YOU ARE GAY, PLEASE STAY AWAY, was closed, apparently tipped off in advance. At a Howard Johnson's restaurant on Sixth Avenue and Eighth Street, the manager greeted the group's announcement that they were gay and wanted to be served with, "How do I know you're homosexuals?" Informing the reporters that the men looked like "perfect gentlemen," the manager ordered the waiter to bring them drinks. Ironically, it was at the gay bar, Julius, that they finally found a bartender who refused to serve them once they had stated they were homosexuals. Mattachine announced that it was filing a complaint with the State Liquor Authority against Julius for discriminating against homosexuals. (The organization also announced it would pay Julius's legal costs.)

For a time, it appeared that Mattachine's action had merely resulted in a standoff. The State Liquor Authority chairman told the media that his agency never told bars *not* to serve homosexuals, although it took no action against owners or bartenders who refused to do so. This statement essentially defused the issue. It wasn't until the following year that the state appellate court finally settled the controversy, ruling that the SLA could only revoke a bar's license if there was substantial evidence of indecent behavior, not just for serving a drink to a lesbian or a gay man.

Activism and the shift in the social climate brought about other changes as well. In November 1967, Mattachine activist Craig Rodwell opened America's first gay bookshop, the Oscar Wilde Memorial Bookshop, on Mercer Street in Greenwich Village. That same year, Columbia University's Student Homophile League became the first gay and lesbian campus group in the nation to gain official recognition. Similar groups were soon established at Cornell, Stanford, and New York University (where author-to-be **Rita Mae Brown** was among the first members). Across the country, the *Los Angeles Advocate,* a gay paper with a hard-hitting, unapologetic approach to the news, began publication. Also in Los Angeles, the Reverend **Troy Perry** established the Fellowship of Metropolitan Community Churches, the first gay and lesbian religous denomination. Meanwhile, the homophile movement had spread north across the border to Canada with the formation of Vancouver's Association for Social Knowledge (ASK) in 1964. Two years later, ASK established a gay and lesbian community center that held regular Saturday-night dances, attracting as many as two hundred people. It is believed to be the first such community center in North America.

As the sixties came to an end, a new world beckoned, one in which the older homophile organizations just didn't fit. Their numbers remained tiny, despite their now more aggressive strategies. The assassinations of Robert F. Kennedy and **Martin Luther King, Jr.,** the mass demonstrations against the Vietnam war, the growth on college campuses of the radical Students for a Democratic Society, and the emergence of the feminist movement all transformed the social and political landscape. The values of the homophile movement—respectability, conciliation, coats and ties at Washington pickets—seemed out of another era. It was the age of the culture of protest, of sex, drugs, and rock 'n' roll, and of the battle cry

"Don't Trust Anyone Over Thirty." The problem was that many of the leaders of Mattachine and DOB *were* over thirty, and even if they weren't, they might as well have been.

The emergence of the women's movement put the Daughters of Bilitis in a particularly difficult spot. A debate broke out within the organization's ranks as to whether to continue to ally themselves with gay male activists in Mattachine or with the emerging feminist movement. Del Martin, DOB's founder, favored the latter course. In a 1967 issue of *The Ladder,* she wrote, "The Lesbian, after all, is first of all a *woman.* . . . It is time that the Daughters of Bilitis and the Lesbian find and establish a much broader identification than that of the homosexual community or the homophile movement." Martin and her lover and DOB cofounder, Phyllis Lyon, did join the National Association for Women—the first openly lesbian couple to do so. Eventually, those who shared their views took over the leadership of DOB. But many of the old-line members found the desertion of their fellow homophiles and the attempts to ally with the women's movement intolerable. By 1970, DOB was dead as a national organization, and Mattachine followed shortly after.

Until historians like John D'Emilio, Jonathan Katz, and others resurrected it, the homophile movement was virtually forgotten. Still, the pre-Stonewall movement made important gains that opened the doors to what came afterward—it strengthened the legal status of gay bars in many states, pressured city officials in New York to end entrapment of gay men, brought about an end to bar harassment in San Francisco, and prompted the first sympathetic media coverage of the gay community. Above all, these organizations enabled many gays and lesbians to survive in the midst of a period in which the most powerful forces of society appeared arrayed against them.

In June of 1969, three nights of rioting at a Greenwich Village bar were to eclipse all that went before and to put the gay movement in line with the mass movements of the 1960s. The era of gay and lesbian liberation was about to begin.

"The Raid"—An Excerpt from *One* Magazine

This excerpt from the July 1960 issue of the homosexual magazine One *is a report on a bar raid in Miami, written by Chas. K. Robinson. In its description of the response to the raid, the article indicates a new militancy on the part of the gay community, perhaps signaling the shift from the 1950s to the '60s:*

IT WAS A TYPICAL FRIDAY NIGHT at the "E" Club in Miami. From the juke-box Johnny Mathis was singing "Misty," and the bar was half empty since it was known as a late place. About 35 people were scattered around the U-shaped bar—the usual grand piano that doubles as a table—and the long booths that run from one end of the room to the other.

Cocktail glasses hung from the red ribbons over the cash register and water flowed from a small indoor fountain behind the bar. . . . Things were quiet and going as usual this particular Friday night. One bartender had just finished saying to the other, as they met at the cash register to ring up their sales, "Gee, I hope business doesn't drop off now that the season is over," when a man in a black suit walked in and stood near the door. Quickly five others moved to strategic positions around the bar. It happened so fast that no one really took notice. Once the men were scattered around the bar, the "leader" said over the voice of Mr. Mathis, "OK, all drinks off the bar. Everyone in here is under arrest." Several quiet curses were heard, and someone with bleached hair said to a friend, "Damn, not only is my life ruined, but the whole evening is spoiled." It was the last joke of the evening: the "E" club had just been raided.

The following Sunday, April 17th, *The Miami News* was caught with its yellow jounalism streak showing when it published a lengthy article written in the typically juicy style of that paper under the heading, "Trail Bar Raided as Deviates' Den." Then article began, "A raid by Metro officials on a Tamiami Trail bar described as a homosexual hangout resulted in the arrest of 22 men on disorderly conduct charges. . . .

"The manager of the place also was arrested and charged with operating an establishment for deviates. . . ."

" 'Habitues of the place were reported to embrace each other, wear tight-fitting women's pants and bleach their hair,' " [Metro Capt. Patrick] Gallagher said.

"When Gallagher and six other officers descended on the place last Friday night they found the dim-lit bar full of men, some of them paired off in 'couples,' he said. . . .

"Officers took all the men in the place to headquarters. Several were released after screening and 22 were booked."

The article goes on to say that of the 22 booked "for being in a place frequented by homosexuals," all were later released on $250 bond, except for the manager, who was released on $750 bond.

Wm. J. Tucker, Jr., the *Miami News* reporter who wrote the story, then went on to list the name, age, address and occupation of all 22 persons. He rationalized his listing of the names to this writer as being "both news and in the public interest. Anyway, the public should know who these people are." Tucker also added that he hadn't even considered withholding the names until after conviction. "If people are cleared or the charges dropped, we'll run the usual 'Follow-up' story." He declined to speculate on the damage to careers or families in the meantime, however. . . .

James Bellows, Managing Editor of the *News*, defended the story along the same lines as Tucker. When asked why the *News* was the only paper in Miami to run the story, Bellows bellowed, "I run the *News* the way I see fit!" . . .

An interesting side-effect to this whole mess down here has been the ire raised among homosexuals. The main complaint is directed toward the *Miami News* for its unwarranted April 17th publicity, and also to the police for starting the whole thing. Approximately 10 people I've talked to since the raid say they've called the *News*, identified themselves as either being in the raid or as an interested party, and protested the ugly story printed. . . . The upshot of the whole business is that the homosexuals down here in Miami are at last getting tired of having their careers and personal lives ruined by unwarranted police raids.

The Secret Life of J. Edgar Hoover

WHEN AN ARTICLE in the November 1955 issue of *One* magazine claimed that homosexuals occupied "key positions" within the Federal Bureau of Investigation, there was anger, if not consternation, in the upper reaches of the bureau. "I think we should take this crowd on and make them 'put up or shut up,' " said associate FBI director **Clyde Tolson**. FBI director **J. Edgar Hoover** responded, "I concur." In this manner, according to an FBI memoranda quoted in Randy Shilts's book *Conduct Unbecoming,* Hoover and Tolson initiated the FBI's campaign of surveillance and harassment of homophile organizations.

Today, it is widely believed that J. Edgar Hoover (1895–1972) was gay himself and the lover for more than forty years of his deputy, Clyde Tolson. The evidence, much of it reported in Anthony Summers's 1993 book, *Official and Confidential: The Secret Life of J. Edgar Hoover* (and repeated on the PBS-TV show "Frontline"), is circumstantial. For example, Summers quotes a former model, **Luisa Stuart,** who insists that she saw Hoover and Tolson holding hands in the backseat of a limousine in which all three were riding on their way to the Cotton Club on New Year's Eve, 1936. "I didn't really understand anything about homosexuality in those days," said Stuart. "I was so young, and those were different times. But I'd never seen two men holding hands." Then there is the seemingly ingenuous statement by singer **Ethel Merman,** who, when asked in 1978 about **Anita Bryant's** antigay campaign, replied, "Some of my best friends are homosexual. Everybody knew about J. Edgar but he was the best chief the FBI ever had." Probably the most bizarre claim is offered by **Susan Rosensteil,** wife of the Mafia-linked owner of Schenley distilleries. She says she saw Hoover in a suite at the Plaza Hotel in New York in 1958 wearing a fluffy black dress, lace stockings, high heels, and a black curly wig. Roy Cohn, allegedly present at the time, was said to have introduced the FBI director to Mrs. Rosensteil as "Mary." (Less sensational but more disturbing in their implications are reports, repeated by Summers, that the

Mafia possessed compromising photos of Hoover and Tolson that they used to pressure the FBI to go easy on organized crime.)

This flood of accusations and recollections is as much a function of Hoover's fall from fashion as anything else. The time has long since passed when Hoover made presidents tremble, possessed files on everyone who mattered in public life, and, in the eyes of the American public, could make "water run uphill," as **James Stewart** put it in the film *The FBI Story*. By 1993, after the Summers revelations, Hoover was remembered primarily as the man who had bugged Martin Luther King, Jr.'s, telephone; he was mocked by **Jay Leno** and ridiculed in *New Yorker* cartoons; Senator **Howard Metzenbaum** proposed removing his name from the FBI building in Washington. (*The New Yorker* suggested instead that the name be changed to the Jaye Edgar Hoover building, a reference to the transvestite character played by **Jaye Davidson** in the film *The Crying Game*.) As a *Washington Post* headline writer noted, "It's been a long slide from national hero to devil in a black dress."

Despite the questionable veracity of the stories about him, what can be said definitively is that Hoover and Tolson were inseparable companions for over forty years after they met in 1928. Tolson's rise from a lowly FBI special agent to assistant director of the bureau took a grand total of two years. Hoover and Tolson lunched together at the Mayflower Hotel in Washington five times a week for forty years and had dinner at Harvey's Restaurant five nights a week over the same period of time. Hoover's photo albums, found after his death, consisted almost entirely of pictures of Tolson in front of various backdrops at resorts where the two vacationed together.

Yet, as with the romantic friendships of the nineteenth century, we may never know for sure if Hoover and Tolson had a sexual relationship. In fact, the zeal of so many to "prove" that Hoover was homosexual or a drag queen or both smacks of gay-baiting, an effort to make an evil man appear even more evil by hurling the accusation that he was homosexual. **G. Gordon Liddy,** talk-show host and former FBI agent himself, was not altogether wrong when he wrote, "It is curious that, at a time when the Left is marshaling all the forces of political correctness in an effort to win for homosexuality equivalency of place with heterosexuality, both culturally and legally, it nevertheless hurls the accusation of homosexuality (upon no evidence whatsoever) at its enemy, the late director of the FBI."

But, if Hoover has been unfairly "outed" (and gay-baited), how does one explain his overly zealous persecution of the homophile movement? His campaign against a tiny handful of relatively ineffectual gay activists was obviously far out of proportion to the danger they represented to national security. It is certainly fair to question whether it was really necessary for FBI agents to record the license-plate numbers of every participant in the homophile picketing of the Pentagon in 1965—or whether the 1959 Mattachine Society convention in Denver presented such a threat that it required a twenty-two-page file that included conference minutes, financial reports, and lunch and dinner menus.

Was Hoover a homophobe or was he a self-loathing homosexual, a classic case of someone who attempted to deflect attention from his own homosexuality by pointing out that of others, even to the extent of destroying lives and careers? *One* magazine may have been on the right track in that November 1955 article that so disturbed Hoover and Tolson when it described a segment of gay male society—the "Tories," as the magazine referred to them—as "the elegant ones who have decided to express their social hostility by being more correct than the foremost representatives of the dominant (and dominating) culture." In his relentless crusade against the homophile organizations of the 1950s and '60s, Hoover, like his friend Roy Cohn, seems to have taken all this to a new and vicious extreme.

In any event, it is clear that Hoover was extraordinarily sensitive about the subject of homosexuality. Activist Frank Kameny recalls how, in the 1960s, Washington Mattachine put selected government officials on its list to receive copies of their newsletter, *The Gazette*. Among them were the president, justices of the Supreme Court, and J. Edgar Hoover. One day, in the summer of 1963 or '64, after mailing out an issue of *The Gazette,* Kameny received a phone call from a man identifying himself as FBI agent John A. O'Beirne. At O'Beirne's request, Kameny went to see him at the Justice Department the next day.

The agent wanted to know why Hoover was receiving *The Gazette*. Kameny explained that Mattachine had sent subscriptions to a number of government officials. "Mr. Hoover would like to be taken off your mailing list," O'Beirne informed him. Kameny said he would check with his executive board. "It was rather hilarious," Kameny recalled. "Here the members of the Mattachine Society were concerned that they might be on lists maintained by J. Edgar Hoover . . . and J. Edgar Hoover was even more concerned that he was on a list maintained by the Mattachine Society of Washington!" In the end, Mattachine never did take Hoover off its list.

The Word *Gay*

Most of the terms used to describe homosexuals and homosexuality have had biblical, legal, or clinical origins, none very positive: invert, pervert, deviate, pederast, sodomist, sodomite, homosexual. Other terms, derived from ancient Greece, such as Uranian *and* Sapphist, *never caught on. Even the word* lesbian *developed negative connotations over the years. As Donald Webster Cory pointed out in his book* The Homosexual in America, *first published in 1951, "Needed for years was an ordinary, everyday, matter-of-fact word that could express the concept of homosexuality without glorification or condemnation." Such a word was gaining in popularity, he noted. The word was* gay. *But even when Cory was writing,* gay *still had a "secret and code-like character." In fact, as he pointed out,* The American Dictionary of Slang *offered 174 synonyms for homosexual, but did not mention the word. In his book, Cory makes the following observations about the use of* gay, *from the vantage point of the early 1950s:*

How, when, and where this word originated, I am unable to say. I have been told by experts that it came from the French, and that in France as early as the sixteenth century the homosexual was called *gaie;* significantly enough, the feminine form was used to describe the male. The word made its way to England and America, and was used in print in some of the more pornographic literature soon after the First World War. Psychoanalysts have informed me that their homosexual patients were calling themselves *gay* in the nineteen-twenties, and certainly by the nineteen-thirties it was the most common word in use among homosexuals themselves. It was not until after Pearl Harbor that it became a magic by-word in practically every corner of the United States where homosexuals might gather. . . . And yet, even to this day, despite its decades (if not centuries) of use, it is practically unknown outside of homosexual circles, except for police officers, theatrical groups, and a few others. . . .

Gay! The word serves many purposes. It is like the Z. of Tchaikowsky's diaries and letters, a secret code that will always be understood by some, never by others. "There was much Z.," Tchaikowsky wrote in his diary about a party he attended on April 23, 1884, and the diarist of today would express it in almost the same words: "The party was so very gay!" Not only is correspondence quite safe from being understood in the event of interception, but even conversation can be held in which the homosexuals in a room use a language which they alone understand, but, unlike the situation prevailing were a foreign tongue being spoken, the others present are unaware of their ignorance. . . .

Within homosexual circles, the use of the word is almost universal, but its acceptance is often with reluctance. Some object to its ambiguous meaning, which is precisely what the group has found most advantageous about it. An advertisement for a roommate can actually ask for a gay youth, but could not possibly call for a homosexual. Even *Lesbian* would be an impossible word to use in this connection, and hence the female inverts are beginning to use the word *gay,* although less frequently than the males. . . .

Some of the usefulness of *gay* diminishes as its meaning becomes more widely understood. . . . As it becomes better known, its secret character, and the advantages derived therefrom, are to a certain extent vitiated. . . .

The homosexual society requires a word like *gay* so that conversation can be free and unhampered; the fetters of conventional condemnation have not yet relegated this word to the realm of the outlawed nor associated it with a stereotype. . . . The secret and code-like character of *the gay* and *the straight,* so reminiscent of words and signs of fraternal orders, will be needed so long as there is a submerged and semi-legal society of homosexuals, and new words to meet new exigencies will have to be found.

Bayard Rustin, "Outside Agitator"

IT WAS 1956, the height of Dr. Martin Luther King, Jr.'s, campaign to end segregation on the buses in Montgomery, Alabama, and things were going badly. A grand jury had returned the largest wholesale indictment in the history of the county; the police were about to arrest the leaders of the boycott. Martin Luther King was out of town. Then, seemingly out of nowhere, a Quaker pacifist from New York named **Bayard Rustin** (1910–87) arrived in Montgomery. He immediately met with the Reverend **Ralph Abernathy** and **E. D. Nixon,** two of the embattled boycott's leaders. Why wait for the police deputies to come after them? Rustin asked Nixon. He suggested a more imaginative strategy, based on his many years as a proponent of Gandhian nonviolence: The leaders of the boycott should go down to the courthouse and present themselves for arrest instead of waiting for the police to come and get them.

Nixon took Rustin's advice. He was booked, fingerprinted, and released on bond. Other boycott leaders did the same. Crowds began to form around the courthouse cheering them on. The jail-house door was suddenly turning into "a glorious passage," and the "arriving criminals were being celebrated like stars at a Hollywood premiere," as Taylor Branch describes the scene in his book *Parting the Waters.* When King returned to Montgomery, the movement had been transformed. But overnight, Rustin had become a controversial figure in Montgomery—an "outside agitator." He had to be smuggled out of town in the back of a car.

Bayard Rustin rapidly emerged as one of Martin Luther King's most trusted advisers, the link between the fledgling civil rights movement and a wider world of tacticians of pacifism and non-violence. He brought to the civil rights movement the experience of his years as the youth secretary for the pacifist **A. J. Muste's** Fellowship of Reconciliation and as an aide to the black labor leader **A. Philip Randolph.** But Rustin had two liabilities: He had been a member of the Communist Youth League in the 1930s, and he was gay.

The youngest of nine children in a family of Negro caterers in

West Chester, Pennsylvania, Rustin lived a thoroughly unconventional life: "a vagabond minstrel, penniless world traveler, sophisticated collector of African and pre-Columbian art, and a bohemian Greenwich Village philosopher," as Branch describes him. In the 1930s, he worked singing backup for the folksinger **Leadbelly,** and traveled for nearly two years with **Josh White.** He was tall, handsome, and spoke with a West Indian accent, despite his Pennsylvania roots; he never made more than twenty-five dollars a week in his life. Rustin spent part of World War II in Lewisburg Penitentiary because of his pacifist views. After the War, he participated in a Congress of Racial Equality–sponsored bus ride through the South to test a new Supreme Court ruling that black passengers on interstate routes could not be forced to sit in the back of the bus. Convicted under local segregation laws, he wound up on a chain gang. Later, he went to India at the invitation of Gandhi's Congress Party, and to Africa, where he advised independence leaders like Ghana's **Kwame Nkrumah.**

In his early days, fellow activists in the pacifist movement were aware of Rustin's homosexuality but it never became public knowledge. Then in January 1953, he was arrested with two other men in the back of a parked car in Pasadena, California, and served thirty days in jail on a morals charge. He was forced to resign his position in the Fellowship for Reconciliation. When the Montgomery bus boycott began two years later, Rustin saw his chance at rehabilitation.

Rustin remained an important strategist and aide to Dr. King throughout the years of the civil rights movement. Although King was not personally bothered by Rustin's homosexuality, it was clearly something that could be used against both men. When King and A. Philip Randolph were planning a demonstration at the 1960 Democratic Party convention, King received a phone call from the black New York Congressman **Adam Clayton Powell, Jr.,** demanding that he call off the protest. If King didn't do so, Powell said, he would announce to the press that King and Rustin were having an affair. In the end, King defied Powell, but his relationship with Rustin became strained.

In 1963, black leaders decided to organize a historic March on Washington. A. Philip Randolph proposed that Rustin be in charge of putting it together, but there was division in the ranks of the movement leaders; Rustin was viewed as too vulnerable to rumor and innuendo. Finally a compromise was reached: Randolph would lead the march and Rustin would be his deputy. That meant, for all intents and purposes, that Rustin would really run the event. He immediately set up an office in a crumbling Harlem building and unfurled a giant banner from a third-story window. He had less than two months to make the march a reality.

Meanwhile, FBI director J. Edgar Hoover was busily wire-tapping Martin Luther King's telephone coversations. In one conversation overheard by the FBI, King and a friend expressed concern that Rustin might get drunk before the march and "grab one little brother." Hoover immediately disseminated the "little brother" remark to his friends in Congress. The following day, South Carolina Senator **Strom Thurmond** got up on the Senate floor and denounced Rustin for sexual perversion; he placed a copy of Rustin's police booking slip from the 1953 morals arrest in the *Congressional Record*.

Despite this attempt to discredit him, Rustin put together the greatest march for civil rights in the nation's history, culminating in Dr. King's "I Have a Dream" speech. Within a year, the Civil Rights Act of 1964 and the Voting Rights Act of 1965 were law. Rustin and the other organizers of the march became almost legendary figures. But like many others of the time, his sexuality—and his radical political past—meant that everything he did had to be behind the scenes. Rustin "was not someone who ever concealed his identity," said **Walter Neagle,** his lover in his latter years. But it was only in the 1980s, when Rustin gave interviews to Boston's *Gay Community News* and to the *Village Voice,* that his homosexuality become known to a wider public.

THE GAY LIBERATION DECADES

CHAPTER 23

STONEWALL AND THE BIRTH OF GAY AND LESBIAN LIBERATION

AT 1:20 A.M. on the night of June 17, 1969, eight officers from the Public Morals Section of the First Division of the New York City Police Department raided the Stonewall Inn, a gay bar located on Christopher Street, just off Seventh Avenue, in Greenwich Village. The Stonewall was a less-than-respectable establishment, even by the standards of gay bars of the time. It was owned by the Mafia. It was a hangout for drag queens and teenage hustlers, and on weekend nights, a go-go boy danced on top of the bar. Gay activist Craig Rodwell blamed unwashed drinking glasses at the Stonewall for a 1969 outbreak of hepatitis among gay men in New York. In less than two and a half years after it first opened, however, the Stonewall had become the most popular bar for gay men in Greenwich Village. As historian **Martin Duberman** described it in his book *Stonewall*, "Many saw it as an oasis, a safe retreat from the harassment of everyday life, a place less susceptible to police raids than other gay bars and one that drew a magical mix of patrons ranging from tweedy East Siders to street queens." It was said to be the only gay male bar in New York City where dancing was allowed.

The raid on the Stonewall that evening followed the usual pattern of police harassment of gay bars in New York. The manager was served with a warrant for selling liquor without a license. Police ordered patrons to leave the bar; those who had no identification or who were wearing clothes of the opposite sex were to be taken to police headquarters. Usually, in such raids (four Village gay bars had been raided in the preceding few weeks), those given permission to leave would file out docilely, to avoid further tempting arrest or exposure. However, this evening, instead of going home, the patrons began to congregate outside the bar. The mood was festive. As those "released" emerged one by one from the Stonewall—often striking poses and making campy comments—the crowd greeted them with cheers. *Village Voice* reporter Lucian Truscott IV, who described the events in a front-page article headlined "Gay Power Comes to Sheridan Square," takes up the story:

> Suddenly, the paddywagon arrived and the mood of the crowd changed. Three of the more blatant queens—in full drag—were loaded inside, along with the bartender and doorman, to a chorus of catcalls and boos from the crowd. A cry went up to push the paddywagon over, but it drove away before anything could happen. . . . The next person to come out was a dyke, and she put up a struggle—from car to door to car again. It was at that moment that the scene became explosive. Limp wrists were forgotten. Beer cans and bottles were heaved at the windows, and a rain of coins descended on the cops. . . .

The police took refuge within the bar. Outside, someone uprooted a parking meter and tried to break down the Stonewall's front door. Someone else squirted lighter fluid through the window, followed by a few matches. From inside the bar, the police—clearly rattled—turned a fire hose on the crowd. A few minutes later several carloads of police reinforcements arrived and attempted to clear the street, but just when they thought they had succeeded in dispersing the crowd, people would re-form behind them—yelling, throwing bricks and bottles, and setting fires to trash cans. According to Duberman's account (although the *Voice*'s Truscott claims this took place the following evening), the police found themselves face to face with a chorus line of mocking queens, kicking their heels in the air and singing:

> We are the Stonewall girls
> We wear our hair in curls
> We wear no underwear
> We show our pubic hair . . .
> We wear our dungarees
> Above our nelly knees!

By the time order was restored, thirteen people had been arrested.

The next night, Saturday, the police were back, but so were the crowds, and the events were already beginning to take on a more political character. Signs had been scrawled on the boarded-up front window of the bar: THEY INVADED OUR RIGHTS; LEGALIZE GAY BARS; SUPPORT GAY POWER. As the crowds faced off against the police, there were shouts of "Gay power" and "Christopher Street belongs to the queens." Like the night before, the rioters threw bottles and bricks; the police charged into the crowd on two occasions, attacking the rioters with nightsticks. On Sunday night, things had calmed down somewhat. The Stonewall was open again; employees had managed to clear away the debris. Among the patrons was Allen Ginsberg, who was making his first visit to the Stonewall. That night, Ginsberg uttered his oft-quoted remark "You know the guys there were so beautiful—they've lost that wounded look that fags all had ten years ago."

It was the "Boston Tea Party of the gay movement," as the writer **Dennis Altman** put it. It was "the hairpin drop heard around the world," as a Mattachine Society leaflet described it. In just three nights, something had changed. And **Judy Garland** was dead. It was uncannily symbolic that the Friday the riots began was also the day of the funeral of the most beloved icon of the *Boys in the Band* gay culture that worshiped the tenacity of female entertainers like Garland but mirrored their helplessness as well. Twenty thousand people had stood in line to view Garland's body at an uptown funeral parlor. On the streets outside the Stonewall that weekend and in the days and months that followed, the "old" gay culture and the homosexual male that sustained it was (mostly) laid to rest as well. From now on, everything would be described as "pre-Stonewall" or "post-Stonewall." As Tom Burke put it in an article in the December 1969 issue of *Esquire*:

> Pity: just when Middle America finally discovered the homosexual, he died . . . he has expired, with a whimper, to make way for the new homosexual of the Seventies, an unfettered, guiltless male child of the new morality in a Zapata mustache and an outlaw hat, who couldn't care less for Establishment approval, would as soon sleep with boys as girls, and thinks "Over the Rainbow" is a place to fly on 200 micrograms of lysergic acid diethylamide [LSD].

On July 16, a little more than two weeks after the events outside the Stonewall, Burke had the opportunity to glimpse that "new homosexual" close-up for the first time. New York Mattachine had called a public meeting at St. John's in the Village Episcopal Church, on Waverly Place. Dick Leitsch, the Mattachine president, dressed in a brown suit and looking to Burke like "a dependable, fortyish

Cartier salesclerk," presided over the meeting. In his opening remarks, Leitsch declared that although police brutality should be protested, it was important for the gay community to remain on good terms with the Establishment. Acceptance of homosexuals would come slowly, primarily through educating the straight population. At that point, according to Burke's account:

> *A tense boy with leonine hair is suddenly on his feet. "We don't want acceptance, goddamn it! We want respect! Demand it! We're through hiding in dark bars behind Mafia doormen. We're going to go where straights go and do anything with each other they do and if they don't like it, well fuck them!"* . . .
>
> *"Well, now I think," says Mrs. Cervantes [Mattachine assistant], "that what we ought to have is a gay vigil, in a park. Carry candles, perhaps. . . . I think we should be firm, but just as amicable and sweet as . . ."*
>
> *"Sweet!" The new speaker resembles Billy the Kid. He is James Fouratt, New Left celebrity, seminarian manqué. . . .*
>
> *"Sweet! Bullshit! There's the stereotype homo again, man. . . . Be proud of what you are, man! And if it takes riots or even guns to show them what we are, well, that's the only language that the pigs understand!"*
>
> *Wild applause. . . .*
>
> *Dick Leitsch tries to reply but Fouratt shouts him down. . . .*
>
> *A dozen impassioned boys are on their feet, cheering. . . .*
>
> *Again and again, Dick Leitsch tugs at his clean white tie, shouting for the floor, screaming for order. He is firmly ignored.*

Within days, at a meeting at nearby Alternate U., a radical evening school that offered classes ranging from organic foods to the Cuban Revolution, the first meeting of what was to become the Gay Liberation Front (GLF) took place. Then, exactly one month after the events at Stonewall, three to four hundred gays and lesbians gathered at Washington Square and marched to the site of the riots, chanting, "Gay power!" and singing "We Shall Overcome." The gay revolution—the last of the revolutions of the 1960s—had finally arrived.

The gay and lesbian revolution was the stepchild of all the radical social and political movements of the decade—the student movement and the New Left, the anti-Vietnam movement, radical feminism, the Black Panthers, hippies and yippies. It began in New York but became international in scope. Soon London and Paris and Rome, Sydney and Melbourne, even Buenos Aires, would follow. Gay liberation's ideology and tactics bore little resemblance to the cautious, well-behaved liberalism of the homophiles. In the United States, many of its leaders emerged not from the homophile movement but from the New Left and the social movements of the period. For example, Gay Liberation Front radical **James Fouratt,** the Billy the Kid look-alike who shouted down Dick Leitsch at the Mattachine meeting, had been a member of Abbie Hoffman's Yippies. **Carl Wittman,** author of "A Gay Manifesto," which was influential both in the United States and in Europe, had been a Students for a Democratic Society (SDS) organizer and theoretician. **Allen Young,** who coedited two early gay liberation anthologies, had worked for the leftist Liberation News Service and had gone to Castro's Cuba with the Venceremos Brigades to help with the sugar harvest. **Lois Hart,** an early Gay Liberation Front women's leader, had spent time at **Timothy Leary's** estate in Millbrook, New York. They were young, alienated, radicalized by the war and the culture of protest of the 1960s, dismissive of mainstream values and politics-as-usual. When their revolution arrived, it was incredible how quickly it swept all before it, leaving the tortured and apologetic past far behind.

More than anything, the gay revolution represented a change in consciousness. It advocated nothing less than the complete transformation of society. What distinguished the new generation of gay liberationists from the homophiles was more than just an increased degree of militancy. As Dennis Altman, the Australian writer who was the most perceptive chronicler of the ideas behind the early gay liberation movement, observed, "No longer is the claim made that gay people can fit into American society, that they are as decent, as patriotic, as clean-living as anyone else. Rather, it is argued, it is American society itself that needs to change." To the young radicals, there was no need to create a "favorable" public image, as the homophiles had tried so hard to do. Now, Blatant was Beautiful.

A proud (and often public) declaration of one's homosexuality became the first act of joining the new movement—a marked change from the use of pseudonyms by many homophile leaders. As *Village Voice* writer **Jill Johnston** put it, "The key phrase is COME OUT. Come out of hiding. Identify yourself. Make it clear. Celebrate your sexuality." (Johnston herself "came out" in the pages of the *Voice,* where she was the dance critic.) In the new world, nothing was sacrosanct: The nuclear family, monogamy, marriage, everything had to go. Sex and gender roles and the sexual objectification of others were to be obliterated. Monogamy would be replaced by open relationships (although not necessarily by promiscuity), and traditional family structures by communal living. There would be a revitalized sense of community. The young movement's allies were not compassionate psychologists or liberal churchmen but other downtrodden groups. Gay liberation looked to student radicals at home, to revolutionary movements abroad, and above all, to the potential for revolutionary change *within* each gay and lesbian person.

Just as African-Americans took on the term *black* to describe their newfound sense of pride and self-assertion, the word *gay* supplanted the clinical *homosexual* and the derogatory *queer.* (A decade and a half later, a new generation would take back the word "queer.") In the keynote speech at the National Gay Liberation Front Student Conference in San Francisco, in August 1970, **Charles P. Thorp,** the youthful head of the gay group at San Francisco State College, explained the difference. "Those who say they like the word Homosexual better than Gay say in essence they accept our sick-psychiatrist friends' definition of us. . . ." he said. "Homosexual is a straight concept of us as sexual. Therefore, we are in a sexual category and become a sexual minority . . . rather than an ethnic group, a people! But the word Gay has come to mean (by street usage) a life style in which we are not just sex machines. . . . We are whole entities. . . . Gay is a life-style. It is how we live. It is our oppression. It is our Tiffany lamps and our guns. Gay is our history and the history we are just beginning to become."

Much of the early gay liberation thinking was hostile to the bars and the baths that had increasingly come to dominate homosexual life in the 1950s and '60s. Movement rhetoric featured attacks on Mafia bars (especially in New York City); they were viewed as exploiting the community financially, ghettoizing gays and lesbians, and creating an environment where patrons were "so busy playing hunter or game that they can perceive no other reality, including the deeper reality of their own existence as Gay people," as one early liberationist put it. The sexual encounters of bathhouses came in for criticism as well—not because they spread disease (that criticism would come later), but because they encouraged sexual objectification and discouraged individuals from integrating their sexuality with the rest of their lives.

In the view of the early liberationists, new community institutions and a distinctive gay culture were what was required. In his "Gay Manifesto," Carl Wittman drew a contrast between San Francisco as "ghetto"—a kind of refugee camp for homosexuals where "straight cops patrol us, straight legislators govern us, straight employers keep us in line, straight money exploits us"—and San Francisco as "free territory":

> To be a free territory, we must govern ourselves, set up our own institutions, defend ourselves, and use our own energies to improve our lives. The emergence of gay liberation communes and our own paper is a good start. The talk about a gay liberation coffee shop/dance hall should be acted upon. Rural retreats, political action offices, food cooperatives, a free school, unalienating bars and after hours places—they must be developed if we are to have even the shadow of a free territory.

This vision of homosexuals as a group oppressed by an evil and exploitive system and who had to create their own institutions was very different from the view of the homophile activists, who contended that there was little difference between heterosexuals and homosexuals. The new gay liberationists also differed from the older generation in that they saw themselves as contributing to the overall world revolutionary struggle. For example, at a meeting of the North American Conference of Homophile Organizations (NACHO), held in Kansas City in late August 1969—just two months after Stonewall—radicals drew up a twelve-point program, denouncing the "insane war in Vietnam" and declaring support for a variety of struggles of other groups—"the black, the feminist, the Spanish-American, the Indian, the Hippie, the Young, the Student, and other victims of oppression and prejudice." They even went so far as to reject the traditional approach of fighting for civil rights for homosexuals, declaring, "We regard established heterosexual standards of morality as immoral and refuse to condone them by demanding an equality which is merely the common yoke of sexual repression." All twelve points pushed by the radicals were defeated by the more mainstream forces who controlled the convention, but the fact that such ideas were seriously debated by the conference was indicative of how swiftly things were changing.

The building block of gay liberation—following the example of the feminist movement—was the consciousness-raising group. The idea was that as participants shared experiences, they would come to see their problems not as individual ones but as a part of shared oppression. In the jargon of the time, the personal would become the political.

In New York City, the weekly Sunday-night meetings of the Gay Liberation Front (GLF) tended to be larger and noisier variations on the consciousness-raising model. They were unstructured and chaotic, "a cross between a Quaker meeting and an informal rap session," as Dennis Altman put it. Personal declarations and revolutionary rhetoric flourished. Writer and activist **Arthur Bell** captured the flavor of the early meetings in his book *Dancing the Gay Lib Blues:* "Characters were defined and established: the gay witch who chaired the meetings, the blond-maned cowardly-lion-looking moppet who tore up money at the New York Stock Exchange, the radical lesbian who purred hatred, the six-foot-six transvestite who played basketball before each meeting. . . ." But the unruliness of the meetings—and the predilection of GLF to support the issues of every minority group (all struggles were one, after all!), sometimes to the point of ignoring gay issues—gave Bell and others pause. Bell described one meeting when "a crazy" interrupted the proceedings to report that women were being discriminated against at the Electric Circus, a club on St. Mark's Place in the East Village. The meeting broke up in chaos, with half the participants rushing off to demonstrate outside the Circus, while the other half remained to discuss business. (Bell was one of a group of men who left GLF six months after its inception to found the Gay Activists Alliance; he later became a writer for the *Village Voice*.)

In its efforts at community-building, New York GLF sponsored a series of activities ranging from encounter groups to spaghetti dinners. Perhaps most important were the series of dances that GLF sponsored at Alternate U., starting in August 1969. A gay and lesbian dance was something unheard of in New York at the time, where the only gay dancing took place at the Mafia-run Stonewall Inn. By October of 1969, GLF dances were attracting 450 people, providing the alternative to the bars that the theoreticians advocated. Gay dances spread to universities across the country, and by the end of the year, were a monthly staple of social activities at the University of California at Berkeley. In January 1970, the University of Minnesota held its first dance (and, soon after, elected **Jack Baker,** an openly gay man whose campaign poster featured him wearing high-heeled shoes, as student association president).

As a political organization that took its cues from the New Left, members of New York GLF initiated a number of protest actions. Members picketed the *Village Voice* to protest the newspaper's refusal to permit the use of the word *gay* in classified advertising; the *Voice* capitulated. GLFers protested the cutting down of trees at a gay cruising area in a Queens park. They also took part in expressions of solidarity with other radical groups—picketing the Women's House of Detention in Greenwich Village to protest the incarceration of Black Panther Party members, for example.

GLF groups quickly established themselves in the San Francisco Bay Area. There, in keeping with the spirit of the center of the counterculture, the early emphasis was on political theater. Gay guerillas performed in Berkeley's Sproul Plaza before a crowd of two thousand during the university's 1969 "disorientation week"; gay liberationists took over a meeting of San Francisco's establishment gay organization, the Society for Individual Rights (SIR), putting on a theater piece called *No Vietnamese Ever Called Me Queer.*

The GLF's keenness to align itself with revolutionary movements pointed up some of the contradictions within its ideology. When New York GLF members took part in an antiwar demonstration marking Hiroshima-Nagasaki Day during the first summer of the group's existence, they received a distinctly chilly reception. Black radicals, in particular, were hostile. The playwright **Leroi Jones** denounced homosexuality as a "white man's weakness," and **Eldridge Cleaver,** in his book *Soul on Ice,* wrote, "Homosexuality is a sickness, just as are baby-rape or wanting to be head of General Motors." Black Panther Party head **Huey Newton** did take the bold step of announcing he was willing to work with the gay and women's movement, however. At the Panthers' invitation, some thirty GLFers attended a Panther-sponsored Revolutionary People's Constitutional Convention, but many returned disillusioned by the sexism of the gathering. And when gays participated in the Venceremos brigades to help with the sugar harvest in Cuba—the same country that just a few years before had rounded up homosexuals and put them in internment camps—they discovered that the enthusiasm of other *brigadistas* for the Cuban revolution prevented them from challenging the revolution's antigay policies.

. . . .

Meanwhile, New York's Gay Liberation Front was experiencing other problems: Its lesbian members were getting restless. They became increasingly convinced that the organization was male-dominated. Although a number of the men did try their best, the women felt that GLF gay men were just not sufficiently sensitive to sexism and issues of particular concern to lesbians. Starting in the spring of 1970, GLF lesbians sponsored a series of all-women dances. And GLF lesbians could not remain aloof from the currents of feminism. At about the same time, Rita Mae Brown, who had been active in the New York chapter of the National Organization for Women (NOW), showed up at a Gay Liberation Front meeting. Brown's visit to GLF was a catalyst; from that moment, women's consciousness-raising groups within GLF began to explore the relationships between lesbianism and feminism, a development that was to fundamentally alter the course of the gay and lesbian movement.

The feminist movement itself had not been exactly congenial to lesbianism ever since feminist pioneer **Betty Friedan** had warned in the early days of the movement of a "lavender menace." For the women's movement, the issue was a particularly delicate one: Friedan and others were fearful that a fragile movement promoting the independence of women could be destroyed by accusations that it was dominated by lesbians. "Lesbian is the one word that can cause the Executive Committee [of New York NOW] a collective heart attack," wrote Rita Mae Brown and two friends in a letter in which they resigned from NOW to protest its antilesbian attitudes.

Brown's experience in the women's movement was typical of other lesbians' experience. Her involvement in politics began in 1968 when she helped found the Student Homophile League at New York University, where she was an undergraduate. She was quickly disillusioned, finding the men in the group indifferent to the concerns of lesbians, so she joined the National Organization for Women. At her first meetings, Brown felt alienated and ignored by the "bejewelled and well-dressed women" in attendance. Finally someone spoke to her. "I questioned her on the lesbian issue," Brown wrote in her essay "Take a Lesbian to Lunch," "and she bluntly told me that the word 'lesbian' was never to be uttered. 'After all, that is exactly what the press wants to say we are, a bunch of lesbians.' She then went on to say patronizingly: 'What are you doing worrying about lesbians; you must have lots of boy-friends.' "

But Brown felt she had nowhere else to go. She stayed at NOW, eventually becoming editor of New York NOW's newsletter and the administrative coordinator for the national organization. As long as she didn't bring up the lesbian issue, everything was fine. She also found that there were women at NOW who were interested in going to bed with her in order to pass themselves off as "new-wave feminists." Such women viewed lesbianism only as a sexual activity, not "a different way of living," Brown noted critically. Eventually, in November 1969, when the name of the Daughters of Bilitis was left off a NOW press release listing the sponsors for the first Congress to Unite Women, Brown's patience reached the limit. Two months later, she left the organization.

When she found her way to the Gay Liberation Front in the spring of 1970, a new phase both for Brown and for the GLF women began. Gradually, the GLF women began to conclude that lesbian oppression and gay male oppression had less in common than they had originally believed. Some of the women in GLF, particularly those in Brown's study group, began to move away from the men; the idea of an autonomous organization beckoned. As Brown put it, "We are no longer willing to be token lesbians in the women's liberation movement nor are we willing to be the token women in the Gay Liberation Front."

Newly emboldened, members of Brown's study group made a surprise appearance in May 1970 at the second annual Congress to Unite Women, held at a Manhattan school. On the opening night of the congress, some three hundred women were sitting in a large auditorium, waiting for a panel discussion to begin. Suddenly, the lights went out. When they came on again, the walls were covered with posters: TAKE A LESBIAN TO LUNCH; SUPERDYKE LOVES YOU; THE WOMEN'S MOVEMENT IS A LESBIAN PLOT. Meanwhile, seventeen women, all wearing T-shirts that said "Lavender Menace" in a mockery of Betty Friedan's phrase, had taken control of the stage. For the rest of the evening, the "Menaces" held forth, talking about their lives as lesbians and inviting members of the audience to speak as well. By the last session, the congress voted to adopt a set of resolutions put forth by the Lavender Menaces. They went:

1. Be it resolved that Women's Liberation is a Lesbian plot.
2. Resolved that whenever the label "Lesbian" is used against

the movement collectively, or against women individually, it is to be affirmed, not denied.

3. In all discussions on birth control, homosexuality must be included as a legitimate method of contraception.

4. All sex education curricula must include Lesbianism as a valid, legitimate form of sexual expression of love.

At the close of the conference several Lavender Menaces announced the formation of consciousness-raising groups for women interested in exploring lesbianism and feminism. The eventual result was an organization called Radicalesbians, the first East Coast lesbian group since DOB was established years before. In its statement, called "The Woman-Identified Woman," Radicalesbians began with the memorable lines "What is a lesbian? A lesbian is the rage of all women condensed to the point of explosion. . . ."

From this point, many lesbians began to move away from the "mixed" gay liberation movement toward the formation of all-women groups committed to lesbian-feminism. In San Francisco, lesbians active in women's liberation groups had already formed an organization called Gay Women's Liberation. The New York chapter of the Daughters of Bilitis, while not specifically lesbian-feminist in orientation, sponsored a series of feminist speakers. Gradually, lesbians began to see themselves not merely as a distinct group with issues that were different from gay men, but as a feminist vanguard that *all* women could join. As lesbian-feminist theoretician **Charlotte Bunch** put it, "Lesbians must become feminists and fight against woman oppression, just as feminists must become Lesbians if they hope to end male supremacy." (For a more detailed exposition of the lesbian-feminist point of view, see the excerpt from Rita Mae Brown's "The Shape of Things to Come," p. 387.)

But the lesbian movement continued to encounter some of the same problems with straight feminists that the Gay Liberation Front encountered with the radical left: It identified with the women's movement, but there were at least some factions in the women's movement that wanted nothing to do with them. Betty Friedan, for one, was still fearful of the "lavender menace," even as the term was being ridiculed on the stage of the Congress to Unite Women. She led a successful effort to keep lesbians from being elected or reelected to posts in New York NOW. As late as 1973, she was telling *The New York Times* that lesbians had been sent to infiltrate the women's movement as part of a CIA plot.

For certain prominent feminists, "coming out" as a lesbian remained a frightening, if not traumatic, event. This was particularly true for **Kate Millett,** author of the influential book *Sexual Politics.* Millett had been lionized by *Time* magazine, which put her picture on its cover (and also featured a photograph of her kissing her husband). But Millett was a lesbian, and although she had said so at a Daughters of Bilitis meeting, she had never declared it publicly. At a meeting before five hundred people at Columbia University in the fall of 1970, she was confronted by a young woman named **Teresa Juarez,** who demanded from the audience, "Are you a lesbian? Say it. Are you?" Millett described the event in her autobiographical work, *Flying*:

> *Everything pauses, faces look up in terrible silence. I hear them not breathe. That word in public, the word I waited half a lifetime to hear. Finally I am accused. "Say it! Say you are a Lesbian." Yes I said. Yes. Because I know what she means. The line goes, inflexible as a fascist edict, that bisexuality is a cop-out. Yes I said yes I am a Lesbian.*

As lesbians increasingly moved toward an identification with feminist issues, straight women and some sectors of the women's movement moved toward them. San Francisco NOW was quite accepting of lesbians. Feminist leader **Ti-Grace Atkinson** proclaimed that "feminism is the theory and lesbianism is the practice." The "political lesbian" emerged—the woman who didn't have sexual relations with other women but made a total commitment to the lesbian movement out of solidarity with other women and opposition to male power and control. When Kate Millett revealed publicly that she was a lesbian and *Time* published a second article on her, contending that her disclosure "is bound to discredit her as a spokesman for her cause, cast further doubt on her theories, and reinforce the views of those skeptics who routinely dismiss all liberationists as lesbians," prominent heterosexual feminists rallied around her. At a news conference a few days after the article was published, feminists like **Gloria Steinem, Susan Brownmiller,** and **Flo Kennedy** staunchly defended Millett and expressed their support of homosexual liberation.

Finally, at the September 1971 national NOW convention, the organization passed a resolution that stated:

> *Be it resolved that N.O.W. recognizes the double oppression of lesbians;*
>
> *Be it resolved that a woman's right to her own person includes the right to define and express her own sexuality and to choose her own life-style; and*
>
> *Be it resolved that N.O.W. acknowledges the oppression of lesbians as a legitimate concern of feminism.*

The convention decision—approved almost unanimously—was a "complete turnabout," as Sidney Abbot and Barbara Love noted in their book, *Sappho Was a Right-On Woman*. Although the issue would continue to be divisive at different points throughout the next decade, for the first time NOW had expressed a strong sense of solidarity with lesbians. For lesbians, it was an important step as well, as they moved away from gay men and toward a more women-identified political and social stance.

Lesbians were not the only restless members of the Gay Liberation Front. In December 1969, a group of men left the organization to found the Gay Activists Alliance (GAA), which rapidly became the most visible and largest gay organization in New York. The founders included **Jim Owles,** an ex-GI from Chicago who had been discharged from the air force for antiwar agitation and became GAA's president at the ripe old age of twenty-three; **Marty Robinson,** twenty-seven, a carpenter (and son of well-to-do Jewish parents) who had been involved in the Mattachine Society and radicalized by the Stonewall riots; and **Arthur Evans,** slightly older, a former Columbia Ph.D. candidate considered the "brains" behind the new group. They represented a reform-oriented faction that was determined to work exclusively on gay issues—as opposed to GLF's multi-issue orientation—and whose interest in raising gay issues in mainstream politics was more akin to the old Mattachine approach. They also favored a less chaotic atmosphere than the one that prevailed at the Gay Liberation Front: The new organization's bylaws stated firmly that "meetings shall be conducted according to *Roberts Rules of Order*."

Watching a GAA meeting in progress, Dennis Altman observed that "the leadership would, in other circumstances, have all been president of their student councils." Nonetheless, GAA had its own less-than-conventional members, like street transvestite **Ray "Syl-**

via" **Rivera,** and others who were more interested in developing a new gay culture rather than in political action. It also had a "pleasure committee" that sponsored popular dances.

If GAA ressembled Mattachine in its civil rights orientation, it was radical in its own way. The organization saw its primary goal as rallying homosexuals through direct action. It perfected the fine art of the "zap," in which GAA members confronted politicians, the media, and other individuals and institutions. Early targets of "zaps" included New York mayoral and gubernatorial candidates, *Harper's* magazine (a sit-in), and the New York City Clerk's Office (a mock engagement party for two gay male couples). Just the threat of a zap was enough to convince the producers of **Dick Cavett**'s television show to invite two GAA members as guests (along with **Phyllis Diller, James Earl Jones,** and **Nora Ephron**). Then there was the famous "quack-in" at Fidelifacts of Greater New York, a credit agency on Forty-second Street. GAA accused Fidelifacts of gathering information about the sex lives of individuals and selling its findings to client companies and other investigatory agencies. Fidelifact's president was quoted as saying, "If one looks like a duck, walks like a duck, associates only with ducks, and quacks like a duck, he is probably a duck." In response, twelve GAA members— dressed in duck costumes—were seen waddling at the entrance to Fidelifacts, quacking and carrying picket signs.

The zap had a psychological as well as a political purpose. "The real significance of zapping a political figure like [New York City Mayor] John Lindsay," wrote Dennis Altman, "may lie less in its effect on the policies being challenged than in the new self-confidence and identity the activity provides those who participate and the new model of gayness it offers to those as yet too scared to come out."

Often, while the zap antagonized politicians in the short run, it could be enormously successful in the long run. The tactic also forced politicians to confront the gay issue for the first time. For example, about three dozen GAA members zapped **Arthur Goldberg,** the former U.S. ambassador to the United Nations who was a candidate for the Democratic nomination for governor in 1970. As Goldberg emerged from his limousine at a busy intersection on Manhattan's Upper West Side, GAA members approached him and asked politely if he favored sodomy law repeal and an end to police harassment. Taken aback, Goldberg responded, "I think there are more important things to talk about," and went off to shake some hands. Soon enough, GAA protesters were shouting, "Answer homosexuals! Answer homosexuals!" After a few more hand-shakes, Goldberg thought it wise to make a speedy exit. Protesters followed him to his limousine, shouting "Gay power!" and "Sur-round the car, surround the car!" Still another GAA protester began chanting, "Crime of silence, crime of silence, crime of silence." Such tactics could not have endeared the GAAers to Goldberg, but they did indicate that gays were a force to be reckoned with. Gold-berg won the Democratic primary to oppose incumbent **Nelson Rockefeller.** Two weeks before the November election, he became the first New York gubernatorial candidate ever to announce his support for gay rights.

A GAA attempt to sit in at the Republican state headquarters proved less successful, however, when five GAA leaders were ar-rested, marking the first time members of a gay political group were arrested for protests regarding gay issues. But the "Rockefeller Five," as they were known, became a movement rallying point.

Not every politician required a zap in order to see the wisdom of supporting gay rights. **Bella Abzug,** running for Congress in 1970, became the first candidate for major office to speak at a GAA meeting and she soon became the darling of the organization (and of gay voters in general). Soon all manner of politicians were vying for GAA endorsements. A GAA Elections Committee sent out ques-tionnaires to candidates, invited them to speak at membership meet-ings, and sponsored voter registration drives. The Mattachine Society had tried to do some of the same in earlier days, but with the enhanced visibility afforded by zaps and candidate forums, GAA was beginning to show that homosexuals were an active and im-portant voting bloc. Once again, the psychological effect on gays and lesbians themselves was as important as any political gains: If a handful of activists could convince politicians that gays were a key political constituency, then they *were* a key political constitu-ency, not just a marginalized group of people.

The next phase of GAA's political involvement was its effort to introduce a bill into the New York City Council that would ban discrimination against gays and lesbians in employment and hous-ing. This was another way that Owles, Robinson, and other GAA leaders thought that gays could establish themselves as a legitimate minority group. The organization launched a petition drive to prod **Carol Greitzer,** a member of the city council representing the Village and the Upper West Side, and no friend of gay rights, to introduce the bill. Greitzer remained wary, but in early January 1971, two other Council members, **Eldon Clingan** and **Carter Burden,** held a news conference to announce that they were introducing Intro 475, which would add the words "sexual orientation" to the provisions of New York City's Human Rights law.

Introducing legislation was one thing; passing it was another. Just getting hearings on the bill proved difficult, requiring still another zap, this time at the apartment building of reluctant city councillor **Saul Sharison.** But once committee hearings did occur, in the fall of 1971, they exposed conflicts within GAA between those who were serious about getting a bill enacted and those who wanted to use the hearings as an occasion for political theater. The issue reached a dramatic point during the questioning of **Richard Amato,** a GAA member who had conducted extensive research into employment discrimination against homosexuals. In the course of questioning by Councillor **Michael De Marco,** an opponent of the measure, Amato was asked, "What if we employ a Mr. Schultz on Monday and Tuesday we get a Miss Schultz? That's the problem. I just saw two people in dresses trying to get into the men's room. . . ."

At that moment, the two cross-dressers in question (including GAA's Ray "Sylvia" Rivera) screamed from the back of the council chambers that the only reason they had gone to the men's room was because they had been refused entry to the ladies' room. Councillor De Marco—sensing a golden opportunity—urged them to come forward. They were soon joined by other GAA members who began shouting "Heterosexual bastards" in front of the council chambers. From that point on, the hearings turned rowdy, as witnesses were cheered and jeered by members of the audience. On the third day, when Councillor Sharison threatened to adjourn the hearings after one outburst, a group of GAAers rushed to his desk shouting, "Justice! Justice! Justice!" and "Bigot! Bigot! Bigot!" The committee finally voted seven to five *not* to bring the bill to the full Council for a vote.

In an article in the *Village Voice,* the GAA's Marty Robinson tried to justify the seemingly self-defeating tactics that led to the defeat of Intro 475:

> . . . *when GAA undertook Intro 475, it was not advocated as the goal for the movement but as a tactic, a tool toward liberation. It was called anti-closet legislation, to underline how the*

threat of loss of employment had been used to keep Gays in silent submission. Intro 475 does have much value in itself, but Gay Liberationists . . . saw Intro 475 as the best way of getting the message to the community: the closet is built in fear, not shame. In that very real sense, Intro 475 never was and never could be defeated. Many gays came out of the closet for the struggle and many more will join them as that struggle continues.

It was not until 1986 that a gay rights bill would pass the New York City Council.

GAA itself soon faded from the scene, as conflicts between reformist and radical factions within the organization intensified. In 1973 one group, under the leadership of GAA's president, **Bruce Voeller,** a professor of biology at Rockefeller University, left the organization, forming the National Gay Task Force (NGTF). The new organization's aim was to be a gay version of the NAACP or the ACLU, establishing gays and lesbians as a political force, and synthesizing "the old homophile and the reformist gay and lesbian liberationist approaches into a new hybrid with broader appeal," according to gay historian Toby Marotta. Voeller became the organization's first executive director. NGTF's board of directors attracted a variety of gay luminaries, ranging from homophile veterans Frank Kameny and Barbara Gittings to historian Martin Duberman and **Howard Brown,** who had been John Lindsay's health services administrator and who had "come out" on the front page of *The New York Times*. The future shape of American gay politics was emerging.

It had been an exhilarating first few years for the new gay and lesbian liberation movement. The events of that early period would set the stage for much that would happen in the next twenty-five years throughout the United States: the emphasis on "coming out"; the use of political theater, zaps, and similar tactics to achieve visibility and publicity; the drive to pass gay rights legislation as a way of gaining legal protections *and* rallying the gay community; and, with the National Gay Task Force, the establishment of the first national group. In their adoption of freewheeling organizational formats, later organizations like ACT UP and Queer Nation could be said to be the "children" of the Gay Liberation Front; in their fondness for zaps, they were descendants of the Gay Activists

Alliance. The attempt to build a separate lesbian culture of the mid-seventies and early eighties was the logical extension of the movement of lesbians away from "mixed" organizations in the first two years of gay liberation. The early years also offered a glimpse of some of the divisions that continue to divide the gay and lesbian movement to this day: conflicts between radicals and reformers; between lesbians and gay men; between those who favor supporting the struggles of other groups and those who want to focus exclusively on gay issues.

In just the first year, the movement's progress was amazing. Nothing illustrated it better than the gay pride march that took place in New York City on June 28, 1970, the first anniversary of Stonewall. Somewhere between five thousand and twenty thousand people marched from New York's Greenwich Village to Central Park. Two hundred members of the Gay Activists Alliance, an organization that had barely existed six months before, led the way. GLF and the Lavender Menaces marched; so did the New York chapters of the Mattachine Society and the Daughters of Bilitis. Participants came from Philadelphia and Washington and Baltimore. *The New York Times,* which had virtually ignored the original Stonewall riots, put the event on page one; *The New Yorker* wrote about it in "The Talk of the Town." But it was the *Village Voice,* as usual, that best caught the spirit of the event:

> *They stretched in a line, from Gimbels to Times Square, thousands and thousands and thousands, chanting, waving, screaming—the outrageous and the outraged, splendid in their flaming colors, splendid in their delirious up-front birthday celebration of liberation. . . .*
> *They swept up Sixth Avenue, from Sheridan Square to Central Park, astonishing everything in their way. No one could quite believe it, eyes rolled back in heads, Sunday tourists traded incredulous looks, wondrous faces poked out of air-conditioned cars.* My God, are those really homosexuals? Marching? Up Sixth Avenue? . . .

That same day, twelve hundred marched down Hollywood Boulevard in Los Angeles, in a celebration calling itself Christopher Street West. The *Los Angeles Advocate,* the gay newspaper, reported that crowds ten deep lined both sides of the street; estimates of the number of spectators were as high as fifteen thousand to twenty thousand. The newspaper couldn't resist observing that "sensation-sated Hollywood had never seen anything like it. Probably the world had never seen anything like it since the gay days of Ancient Greece." Meanwhile, in Chicago, several hundred marched—with six police squad cars and three paddy wagons following behind. The *Advocate*'s Chicago correspondent reported that a postmarch communal dinner was attended by about two hundred, including Men Against Cool, a coalition of straight and gay men who supported women's liberation. After the dinner, the newspaper reported, "A group went to the Playboy Club and had a demonstration in support of Women's Liberation, with slogans like 'Gay Brother Support for Sister Power' . . ."

The movement was sweeping from coast to coast, and Stonewall was to remain a rallying point. It would be years before there were gay pride marches in places like Louisville, Kentucky, and Worcester, Massachusetts, and Des Moines, Iowa. But that would happen, too. "Are we trying to invent a new existence, whizzing through decades of social evolution in an afternoon? Or only joyriding?" Kate Millett wanted to know. The next twenty-five years would offer some clues.

"A Gay Manifesto"

*Carl Wittman's "A Gay Manifesto" was one of the most important documents of the gay liberation period. Wittman (1943–86) graduated from Swarthmore College, outside Philadelphia, and played a prominent role in the early days of Students for a Democratic Society (SDS), the radical student group. He was one of the authors—along with **Tom Hayden**—of the SDS strategy for organizing poor whites. At age twenty-three, Wittman moved to San Francisco, where he continued the union organizing work that he had begun on the East Coast and became active in co-op movements there. It was in San Francisco that Wittman came out as a gay man; from that point, his interests began to move from labor to more broad-based social concerns. According to his* *friend Michael Bronski, Wittman said that he wrote his manifesto in the spring of 1969, before Stonewall. In fact, the document makes no mention of Stonewall. The manifesto was reprinted in the underground and leftist press, where gay radicals would have encountered it for the first time. Wittman later founded a gay commune in Wolf Creek, Oregon, that published the magazine RFD, "a journal for country faggots," as it called itself. He died of AIDS in 1986. Wittman emphasizes that his manifesto was written from the point of view of a white, middle-class man and for gay men. In it one can see a working out of many of the early gay liberation ideas:*

IN THE PAST YEAR there has been an awakening of gay liberation ideas and energy. How it began we don't know; maybe we were inspired by black people and their freedom movement; we learned how to stop pretending from the hip revolution. . . .

Where once there was frustration, alienation, and cynicism, there are new characteristics among us. We are full of love for each other and are showing it; we are full of anger at what has been done to us. And as we recall all the self-censorship and repression for so many years, a reservoir of tears pours out of our eyes. And we are euphoric, high, with the initial flourish of a movement. . . .

We want to make ourselves clear: our first job is to free ourselves; that means clearing our heads of the garbage that's been poured into them. . . .

Male chauvinism: All men are infected with male chauvinism—we were brought up that way. . . . Male chauvinism, however, is not central to us. We can junk it much more easily than straight men can. For we understand oppression. We have largely opted out of a system which oppresses women daily—our egos are not built on putting women down and having them build us up. Also, living in a mostly male world we have become used to playing different roles, doing our own shit-work. And finally, we have a common enemy: the big male chauvinists are also the big anti-gays.

But we need to purge male chauvinism, both in behavior and in thought among us. Chick equals nigger equals queer. Think it over. . . .

"Gay stereotypes": The straights' image of the gay world is defined largely by those of us who have violated straight roles. There is a tendency among "homophile" groups to deplore gays who play

visible roles—the queens and the nellies. As liberated gays, we must take a clear stand. 1) Gays who stand out have become our first martyrs. They came out and withstood disapproval before the rest of us did. 2) If they have suffered from being open, it is straight society whom we must indict, not the queen.

Closet queens: This phrase is becoming analogous to "Uncle Tom." To pretend to be straight sexually, or to pretend to be straight socially, is probably the most harmful pattern of behavior in the ghetto. . . .

If we are liberated, we are open with our sexuality. Closet queen-ery must end. Come out.

But saying come out, we have to have our heads clear about a few things: 1) Closet queens are our brothers, and must be defended against attacks by straight people. . . . Each of us must make the steps toward openness at our own speed and on our own impulses. Being open is the foundation of freedom; it has to be built solidly. . . .

On *Positions and Roles:* Much of our sexuality has been perverted through mimicry of straights, and warped from self-hatred. These sexual perversions are basically anti-gay:

"I like to make it with straight guys."
"I'm not gay, but I like to be 'done.'"
"I like to fuck, but don't want to be fucked."
"I don't like to be touched above the neck."

This is role-playing at its worst; we must transcend these roles. We strive for democratic, mutual, reciprocal sex. This does not mean that we are all mirror images of each other in bed, but that we break away from roles which enslave us. . . .

Perversion: We've been called perverts enough to be suspect of any usage of the word. Still many of us shrink from the idea of certain kinds of sex: with animals, sado/masochism, dirty sex (involving piss or shit). Right off, even before we take the time to learn any more, there are some things to get straight:

1. We shouldn't be apologetic to straights about gays whose sex lives we don't understand or share.
2. It's not particularly a gay issue, except that gay people probably are less hung up about sexual experimentation.
3. Let's get perspective: even if we were to get into the game of

deciding what's good for someone else, the harm done in these "perversions" is undoubtedly less dangerous or unhealthy than is tobacco or alcohol. . . .

Black liberation: This is tenuous right now because of the up-tightness and supermasculinity of many black men (which is understandable). Despite that, we must support their movement, particularly when they are under attack from the establishment; we must show them that we mean business; and we must figure out who our common enemies are: police, city hall, capitalism.

Homophile groups: Reformist or pokey as they sometimes are, they are our brothers. They'll grow as we have grown and grow. . . .

Conclusion: An Outline of Imperatives for Gay Liberation:

1. Free ourselves: come out everywhere; initiate self-defense and political activity; initiate counter community institutions.
2. Turn other gay people on; talk all the time; understand, forgive, accept.
3. Free the homosexual in everyone: we'll be getting a good bit of shit from threatened latents: be gentle, and keep talking and acting free.
4. We've been playing an act for a long time, so we're consummate actors. Now we can begin to be, and it'll be a good show!

Lesbianism and the Women's Movement

In 1972, a collective of lesbians living and working in Washington, D.C., called the Furies published a series of essays on the subject of lesbianism and the women's movement. In her essay, called "The Shape of Things to Come," Rita Mae Brown expressed the lesbian-feminist point of view that saw lesbians as the vanguard of the women's movement:

LESBIANISM, politically organized, is the greatest threat that exists to male supremacy. How can men remain supreme, how can they oppress women if women reject them and fight the entire world men have built to contain us? The beginning rejection is to put women first in your life, put yourself first. . . .

Committing yourself to women is the first concrete step toward ending that common oppression. If you cannot find it in yourself to love another woman, and that includes physical love, then how can you truly say you care about women's liberation? . . . Relationships between men and women involve power, dominance, role play, and oppression. A man has the entire system of male privilege to back him up. Another woman has nothing but her own self. Which relationship is better for you? It's obvious.

If women still give primary committment and energy to the oppressors how can we build a strong movement to free ourselves? Did the Chinese love and support the capitalists? Do the Viet Cong cook supper for the Yankees? Are Blacks supposed to disperse their communities and each live in a white home? The answer, again, is obvious. Only if women give their time to women, to a women's movement, will they be free. You do not free yourself by polishing your chains, yet that is what heterosexual women do. . . .

Why would any heterosexual woman give up the privileges men grant her for being heterosexual? Most often she will only give them up if she sees there is something better than the crumbs thrown to her from men. What can Lesbianism offer? It offers double oppression. It offers the threat of getting fired from your job, estranged from your family and old straight friends, it offers getting your throat slit by straight women in the service of men, it offers constant struggle against an inhumane and diseased world where violence is the key to power and love is a word found in poetry but not on the streets. Why take on those burdens?

Because Lesbianism also offers you the freedom to be yourself. It offers you potential equal relationships with your sisters. It offers escape from the silly, stupid, harmful games that men and women play, having the nerve to call them "relationships." It offers change. You will change yourself by discovering your woman-identified self, by discovering other women. No one, not even another Lesbian, can tell you who that self is. It is your individual challenge, your life. You will be on unfamiliar ground with no old patterns to guide you. As you change yourself, you will begin to change your society also. A free, strong self cannot live in the muck that men have made. You will make mistakes and suffer from them. You will hurt and be hurt trying to find new ways. But you will learn and push on. You will discover the thousand subtle ways that heterosexuality destroyed your true power; you will discover how male supremacy destroys all women and eventually the creators of it, men. You will find once your consciousness is raised it cannot be unraised. Once you have a vision of the new world you can no longer accept the old one. You will become a fighter. You will find love and that you are beautiful, strong and that you care. You will build communities with other women from all classes and races, those communities will change the material parts of our lives. You will share what you have with others and they with you. You will revolt against this whole filthy world that tried to cover you and your beauty under a ton of male supremacist slime. That is what Lesbianism offers you.

Gay Liberation Comes to London

IN JULY 1970, Jeffrey Weeks, the British gay historian, read about the first gay pride march in New York. He was sure that something like that "could never happen in London—and a good thing too." Five months later, in November of the same year, Weeks was enthusiastically attending meetings of London's Gay Liberation Front, "feeling that my whole outlook and life were being transformed."

The gay liberation movement was quickly spreading throughout the English-speaking world. In Canada, gay liberation groups were formed in Vancouver, Toronto, and Montreal; in 1971 the first issue of *The Body Politic,* the Canadian gay newspaper, appeared. In Australia, the country's first gay organization, CAMP Inc. (The Campaign Against Moral Persecution), was founded in Sydney in 1970. CAMP Inc. took a homophile-oriented approach; two years later Sydney Gay Liberation emerged, along with campus groups in Sydney and Melbourne, and a lively gay press.

In England, gay liberation was imported by two young men who returned from a visit to the United States. The first meeting of London's Gay Liberation Front (GLF) took place in November 1970 in a basement room at the London School of Economics. By early the following year, weekly GLF meetings were attracting between four and five hundred people. As in the U.S., the British version of gay liberation was strongly influenced by the international student movement and the counterculture. Coming out was viewed as crucial. Jeffrey Weeks notes that everyone was encouraged to wear badges with slogans like "Gay Power" and "Gay Is Good" and later "Lesbians Ignite" and "Avenge Oscar Wilde." GLF sold some eight thousand badges in its first year. The early British gay liberationists attacked gay bars as exploitive and public lavatories (know as "cottages") as dehumanizing, the latter being places where a good deal of sexual activity among gay men took place. The gay liberation newspaper *Come Together* wrote: "The cottage is the coffin—come out and live. The meat market smells! Drink up and leave the racketeering bars. Pull the flush in the cottage. Have a revolution in your life." GLF dances were soon drawing huge crowds (the first dance at the Kensington Town Hall was attended by seven hundred people, with another five hundred turned away).

Meanwhile, GLF was engaged in demonstrations, zaps, and street theater. During the trial of some members of a women's group for a protest at the Miss World pageant, GLFers held a mock "Miss Trial" competition outside the court. In spring and summer, "Gay Days"—open, large-scale picnics and celebrations—were held in public parks. Then, in June 1972, on the third anniversary of Stonewall, some two thousand gays and lesbians marched down Oxford Street, the first time a gay march of that magnitude had taken place in Britain.

Weeks described a typical "week in the life of GLF" in the summer of 1972, which included a Vietnam vigil and a picket at Pentonville Jail (in solidarity with striking dockers), an "End of Season" dance at Fulham Town Hall, a "Gay Day" on Clapham Common, a disco in a pub in Putney, and a meeting of South London Lesbian Liberation. Then there were the regular meetings of various CR groups and other GLF groups—the Counter Psychiatry Group (to challenge the "gay is sick" psychiatrists), the Church Research Group, the Youth Education Group, and the like.

In early 1972, the women in London GLF decided to withdraw and set up their own organization. At about the same time, other disagreements within GLF began to surface as well—between a leftist faction oriented toward the trade union movement and another group that was primarily interested in life-style and cultural issues like communal living and drag.

By the summer of 1972, gay liberation was essentially collapsing. In part, this reflected the changing cultural climate in England at that time; the counterculture was on the wane. "The essence of GLF was to change consciousness," wrote Jeffrey Weeks in his book *Coming Out.* "But once it had begun to change it—and without a revolution!—it seemed less necessary to build the sort of radical movement that GLF claimed as essential to carry it through."

Even as GLF broke up, though, an expanded sense of gay community was taking root in England. A variety of organizations had established themselves and continued to do so—telephone counseling services and social organizations; gay and lesbian religious groups and groups for gay professionals; gay and lesbian groupings within all three major political parties; a theater group called Gay Sweatshop. A growing male commercial scene—clubs, discos, travel agencies—took advantage of the new openness. The biweekly *Gay News* was launched in June 1972, promising articles on "such differing aspects of our society as Marlene Dietrich and queer bashing." It soon boasted a circulation of twenty thousand and was sold on major newsstands. Meanwhile, a lesbian magazine called *Sappho* provided a center for lesbian community. The cultural openness about the subject of homosexuality that had begun in the sixties intensified in the early seventies. Even E. M. Forster's Edwardian gay novel, *Maurice,* was finally published after the author's death in 1972.

After the passage of law reform, Lord Arran, the chief sponsor, had said in a 1967 speech in the House of Lords, "Any form of ostentatious behavior, now or in the future, any form of public flaunting, would be utterly distasteful and would, I believe, make the sponsors of this Bill regret that they have done what they have done." He could not have possibly foreseen how much Britain would change in just a few short years.

Gay Liberation Comes to Paris

DESPITE A REPUTATION for sexual tolerance, France in the post–World War II period was as repressive regarding homosexuality as any country in Europe. Although no laws punished homosexual activity between consenting adults, in 1942 the fascist Vichy government had raised the age of consent to twenty-one. This remained unchanged after the War, and new restrictions were added. A 1946 law stated that only persons of "good morality" could be employed in civil service positions; this regulation covered teachers, including university teachers. A 1949 decree issued by the Préfet de Paris forbade men from dancing together in a public place. In July 1960, under President **Charles de Gaulle,** the National Assembly passed the Mirguet Amendment, defining homosexuality as a "social scourge," along with prostitution and alcoholism, and urging the government to take action to combat it.

In this atmosphere, the first homophile organization, Arcadie, took a very cautious line. Established in the early 1950s by an ex-seminarian and philosophy professor, **André Baudry,** it was Roman Catholic in orientation and emphasized homosexuality as a consciousness, not as a sexuality. Arcadie was essentially nonpolitical, seeking to foster the impression that homosexuals were conventional people with conventional desires. It attracted a number of intellectual figures and, beginning in 1954, published a literary review (that included drawings by Jean Cocteau). In 1957, it opened a clubhouse in Paris but forbade kissing on the dance floor.

But the period of homosexual "apologetics," as Edmund White characterized it, ended with the May Days of 1968. In the aftermath of the student revolt, which almost toppled the government, the first "pederastic committee" was established. Then, in 1971 came the Front Homosexuel d'Action Révolutionnaire (FHAR), established by a group of lesbians who split off from Arcadie. **Guy Hocquenghem,** French gay activist and theorist, recalled his first FHAR meeting:

I arrived at a small room where there were about thirty peo-
ple. . . . Everyone told their life story, their dreams, their desires,
with whom, how, and why'd they'd slept with the people they'd
slept with. And how they'd been living. . . . Some of them had
been to the States and had seen what had become the Gay Lib-
eration Front there. They dreamed of doing something like it in
France.

In a manifesto published in *Tout,* a Maoist newspaper edited by
Jean-Paul Sartre, the FHAR put forth its demands: "Abortion and
contraception on demand and free of charge; Homosexual rights
and rights to all sexualities; Rights of minors to freedom of desire
and its fulfillment." Later that year, it issued a *Report Against
Normality,* proclaiming the enemy to be *"le sexisme, le phallocratisme, et l'hétérofliqµisme."* The FHAR soon spread to French cities
outside Paris, to Belgium, and to northern Italy.

The French gay liberation movement shared many characteristics
with the movement in the U.S. and England—a propensity to revolutionary rhetoric, a flamboyant style, an identification with other
marginalized social groups. The French situation was distinctive,
however. Dennis Altman, the Australian gay liberation chronicler,
noted that organizing a homosexual movement was difficult in
France because on one hand there was "a large, if very alienating,
commercial gay world" (which encouraged apathy), while on the
other hand there was a "lack of such a clear symbol to rally around
as is provided by the anti-homosexual laws of the Anglo-Saxon
world." The conservative wing of the French movement (Arcadie)
was "virtually invisible," while the radical wing seemed "quite dis-
interested in identifying concrete examples of discrimination."

Altman observed that the French gay movement—like its Italian
spin-off—was preoccupied with its relations with the political Left
in a way that wasn't true in England, the U.S., and Australia. There
was no possibility in France or Italy that a movement, even a conference, could bring together homosexuals of varying political
views. "The gay militants of the Latin world are not interested in
the sorts of Gay Pride manifestations that now exist in New York
and San Francisco, financed by gay bars and including mainstream
politicians who have begun to discover the possibility of a gay vote,"
Altman wrote.

Nonetheless, when Altman visited France in 1977, he found an "explosion of energy" reminiscent of the early seventies in the United States; there were gay film festivals in Paris and Lyons, several large demonstrations, the opening of a gay center near Montparnasse. At demonstrations, members of GLH-PQ (successor organization to the FHAR) shouted, *"Travail, famille, phallus: on a marre"* ("We're sick of work, the family, and the phallus"). There was a fascination with transvestism and pederasty.

Altman experienced the flavor of French gay liberation when he attended an outdoor Socialist Party gathering one Saturday afternoon in a working-class suburb of Paris. The gay liberation group GLH-PQ had a stall. Twenty men and women, their attire ranging from drag to jeans, were chanting GLH songs, largely parodies of French popular music. No one could follow the words—including many of the singers—but the audience applauded, anyway. Others lay on the grass, smoking pot, talking, and embracing. It was "a little bit of Gay Pride Week amid the French left," suggested Altman. At a certain point, members of GLH marched through the grounds, only to be accosted by a group of young toughs in leather jackets and tattoos. Before the scene turned violent, both sides backed off.

Altman was somewhat disillusioned. The GLH, he thought, was no longer aiming at the creation of a new society but rather "a new life style for marginal homosexuals." For the majority of homosexuals, especially working-class kids from the suburbs, "the GLH must seem as alienating as the chic bars of St. Germain."

Yet as gay liberation, despite its drawbacks, took root in France, the political parties of the Left were becoming increasingly responsive to homosexuals. The Socialist Party, led by **François Mitterrand,** was promising to lower the age of consent, if elected. Altman suspected that a victory of the Socialist-Communist alliance could significantly alter the atmosphere for gays and lesbians, for France, he noted, "is a society where the possibilities of major political change are taken seriously."

CHAPTER 24

THE 1970S: THE TIMES OF HARVEY MILK AND ANITA BRYANT

NINETEEN SEVENTY-FIVE was a very good year for the burgeoning gay and lesbian movement in the United States. After Frank Kameny's eighteen-year crusade, the U.S. Civil Service Commission announced it would no longer exclude homosexuals from federal employment. **Elaine Noble** took her seat in the Massachusetts House of Representatives as the nation's first openly gay legislator. In Minnesota, first-term State Senator **Allen Spear,** a former history professor, announced his homosexuality in a newspaper interview. Air Force Technical Sergeant **Leonard Matlovich** handed a letter to his captain announcing that he was gay and launching the effort to overturn the ban on homosexuals in the U.S. military. (See "In the Statehouse: Representative Elaine Noble and Senator Allen Spear," p. 415, and "Leonard Matlovich," page 411.) And former National Football League running back **Dave Kopay** revealed his homosexuality, confounding stereotypes.

It was a particularly good year in the state of California. The state legislature voted to repeal the hundred-year-old statute that made "crimes against nature" a felony offense (although the lieutenant governor, **Mervyn Dymally,** had to be called in to break a 20–20 tie in the state senate). In the San Francisco municipal elections, Senate Majority Leader **George Moscone,** who had been instrumental in the repeal of the "crimes against nature" law, won the post of mayor; pro-gay candidates were elected sheriff and district attorney in a city where law enforcement officials had traditionally been implacable foes of gays and lesbians. Meanwhile, a Castro Street camera store owner and openly gay newcomer named **Harvey Milk** ran a strong seventh in the race for six seats on the board of supervisors (the city council). Throughout the country, progress on gay and lesbian rights looked unstoppable; no meaningful organized opposition had yet emerged. And nowhere did it seem more unstoppable than in San Francisco.

Within a few short years, San Francisco had become the un-questioned gay capital of the United States. In the post-Stonewall atmosphere, increasing numbers of gays and lesbians felt comfort-able coming out, although often not in their hometowns. The tra-ditional pattern of gay migration out of uncongenial smaller cities and towns into large urban areas was becoming a flood. By the middle of the decade, police estimated that there were 140,000 gays in San Francisco—one-fifth of the population—and that the num-bers were growing by some eighty a week.

This second wave of gay migration (the first one had followed World War II) was not entirely surprising. In the 1960s, the lead-ership of Mayor **Joseph Alioto** had transformed a blue-collar man-ufacturing city into a tourist center and a headquarters for banks and corporations. The new San Francisco needed mobile young people with college educations, and white middle-class gay men fit the bill perfectly. As previously noted, mainstream gay political activity had deeper roots in San Francisco than in any American city, including New York, starting with the establishment of the Society for Individual Rights (SIR) in the early 1960s.

In 1971, gay activist **Jim Foster** organized SIR's political com-mittee into the Alice B. Toklas Memorial Democratic Club. The following year was a presidential election year, and Senator **George McGovern** was running for the Democratic Party's nomination. The liberal South Dakota senator issued a seven-point plank supporting gay rights. California, with its large block of delegates and tradition of progressive politics, would be a key primary for McGovern. In California, the candidate who was first in delivering all his nomi-nating petitions to the Secretary of State's office had his name listed first on the ballot—a major advantage. In a well-organized lightning strike, Foster's gay legions were able to gather one-third of all the Northern California signatures that McGovern needed, ensuring that the senator's name would be the first that voters saw when they entered the polling booth.

At the Democratic Party's national convention in Miami Beach, Foster received his reward: permission to give a nationally televised speech to the convention on the same night that McGovern would accept his party's nomination. "We do not come to you pleading your understanding or begging your tolerance," Foster began. "We come to you affirming our pride in our life-style, affirming the validity to seek and maintain meaningful emotional relationships and affirming our right to participate in the life of this country on an equal basis with every citizen." It was an astounding moment, although one that may not have helped a nominee already disparagingly dubbed the candidate of "acid, amnesty, and abortion."

Among the new migrants to San Francisco in those years was Harvey Milk (1930–77). Milk was older than most of the other gay newcomers—by the time he settled permanently in San Francisco, he was in his forties. He had grown up in a middle-class, Jewish family in Woodmere, New York, one of the affluent "five towns" of Long Island. As Randy Shilts relates in his biography, *The Mayor of Castro Street*, Milk lived a comfortable if closeted life in New York City in the 1950s and '60s: He worked as a financial analyst, went to the opera, and supported **Barry Goldwater** for president. Among his gay relationships was one with activist Craig Rodwell, although it seemed to have had little impact on the then-apolitical Milk. By the end of the 1960s, he was moving in avant-garde theater circles, and had become a friend of **Tom O'Horgan**, director of the musical *Hair*. Eventually, the counterculture worked its effect on him: He grew his hair long, burned his Bank Americard, and, with his boyfriend of the time, lit out in 1972 for the West Coast.

When he arrived in San Francisco, Milk settled in the Castro neighborhood, at that time a run-down, largely Irish part of town, with a couple of gay bars that catered to hippies from the nearby Haight-Ashbury. After a roll of film he brought in to be developed was ruined, the impulsive Milk decided to open a camera store. According to Shilts, it was after a state bureaucrat arrived at his store demanding a one-hundred-dollar deposit against sales taxes that Milk decided to run for the board of supervisors. He announced his candidacy in the summer of 1973 from a soapbox in a small plaza on Castro Street. (A friend had painted the word *soap* on the side of a crate.)

It didn't take long before the ponytailed political novice ran smack into the opposition of the city's gay establishment, led by Jim Foster, fresh from his triumph at the Democratic National Convention the year before. "We're like the Catholic Church," Foster informed Milk. "We take converts, but we don't make them Pope the same day." Foster believed that San Francisco wasn't ready for a gay supervisor. Characteristically, Milk wouldn't defer to Foster's wisdom—or seniority. Despite the opposition of Foster and the rest of the city's gay political leadership, he ran a surprisingly strong campaign, coming in tenth out of a field of thirty-two and polling seventeen thousand votes. Milk spent the next two years forging political alliances. Endorsing a boycott of Coors beer, he made friends with a Teamster leader (who in exchange promised him slots for gay men as beer truck drivers). He established the Castro Village Association, a group of gay merchants that in the summer of 1974 organized the area's first street fair. His camera shop on the Castro quickly became what Shilts called a "vest-pocket city hall." He had become the mayor of Castro Street.

When the 1975 elections came along, Milk was in a much improved position. But he still faced a major hurdle: All six incumbent supervisors were running for the six at-large seats. He cut off his ponytail and ran a populist campaign, casting himself as the neighborhood candidate in opposition to downtown corporate interests.

San Francisco city supervisor Harvey Milk (left) and journalist Randy Shilts (right) celebrate on election night 1978, a few weeks before Milk's assassination. (© *Steve Savage*)

He gained the endorsements of three of the toughest unions in the city—the Teamsters, firemen, and hard hats. The cigar-chomping labor boss **George Evankovich** became one of his biggest boosters. "That guy has charisma," Shilts quoted Evankovich as saying. "A lot of our guys think gays are little leprechauns tip-toeing to florist shops, but Harvey can sit on a steel beam and talk to some iron-worker who is a mean sonuvabitch and probably beats his wife when he has a few too many beers, but who would sit there and talk to Harvey like they knew each other for years." When the election results were tallied, Milk came close, finishing just behind the six incumbents.

In recognition of Milk's strong showing, Mayor Moscone named him to the Board of Permit Appeals. The mayor also broke new ground, naming lesbian activists **Jo Daly** and Phyllis Lyon to the city's Human Rights Commission and Del Martin to the Commission on the Status of Women. (Lyon and Martin cofounded the Daughters of Bilitis.)

By the time Milk ran for supervisor a second time, the dilapidated Castro neighborhood that he and a few other gay hippies had "discovered" three years before was transforming itself into Gay Main Street, U.S.A. As gay refugees poured into San Francisco, street after street of genteel Victorian houses were gentrified, a pattern that was to repeat itself across the country in cities from Boston to Louisville to Key West. Property values increased five-fold in some cases, and many of the older people in the neighborhood couldn't afford *not* to sell. The Castro was fast becoming a ghetto of white middle-class gay men.

With the gay influx a new type of male homosexual emerged, dubbed the "Castro Street clone." The gentle, long-haired gay hippie of the early seventies was mostly a thing of the past. Another kind of conformity was "in": It was the era of the flannel shirt, tight jeans, hair cut short, the clipped mustache, and the muscular body. A gym membership was as essential in the new gay culture as a collection of Judy Garland records had been a decade earlier. Almost everyone looked like a cowboy or a construction worker—or tried to. In the process, the Castro was becoming a sexual supermarket, the most active cruising strip west of Christopher Street. In its public face, the Castro was an all-male world: The new lesbian migrants— eager to create their own institutions and influenced by the currents of separatism—frequently bypassed San Francisco altogether, preferring nearby Oakland or Berkeley or communes in northern California and southern Oregon. Those who did settle in San Francisco were relatively invisible.

A gay community with its own businesses and institutions was coming to the fore in the Castro. Increasingly, it was no longer a poor neighborhood. While Milk emphasized populism and presented homosexuals as another of San Francisco's downtrodden minorities, in fact the majority weren't poor and didn't have much in common with other oppressed groups. Frances FitzGerald caught the contradictions in her essay on the Castro in her book *Cities on a Hill*:

> *[The new gay migrants] might be refugees from oppression, but they were also, by and large, young white men who had arrived in town at the very moment to begin careers. In practice they were taking professional and managerial jobs, or they were staffing the numerous new service industries, or they were starting businesses of their own. In many ways they were proving a boon to the city. . . . But in settling the poor neighborhoods, they were pushing up real-estate prices and pushing out black and Hispanic families.*

After an abortive run for the state assembly, Milk ran for city supervisor a third time in 1977. The year before, the method of choosing the board of supervisors had been changed to reflect the concerns of San Francisco's neighborhoods: Elections were now on a district, as opposed to a citywide, basis. This made Milk's task easier. But he still had to vanquish **Rick Stokes,** the candidate of the city's gay establishment. Milk ran first in a sixteen-person field, winning 30 percent of the vote. It was in that race that Milk developed what his aides called "The Hope Speech," one that he gave repeatedly during the campaign:

> *And the young gay people in the Altoona, Pennsylvanias and the Richmond, Minnesotas who are coming out and hear [antigay crusader] Anita Bryant on television. . . . The only thing they have to look forward to is hope. And you have to give them hope. . . . Hope that all will be all right. Without hope, not only gays, but the black[s], the seniors, the handicapped, the us'es, the us'es will give up.*

In the same election, a police officer and firefighter named **Dan White,** representing a conservative, largely Irish working-class district, was elected as city supervisor along with Milk, also for the first time. In a mimeographed sheet distributed at a campaign rally, White declared, "You must realize that there are thousands upon thousands of frustrated, angry people such as yourselves waiting to unleash a fury that can and will eradicate the malignancies which blight our beautiful city. . . . I am not going to be forced out of San Francisco by splinter groups of radicals, social deviates and incorrigibles." His campaign slogan was "Unite and Fight with Dan White." The backlash was beginning in San Francisco.

Milk's election aside, 1977 (and 1978) were not particularly good years for gays and lesbians. The political atmosphere in America was changing. Growing opposition to issues like abortion and the Equal Rights Amendment and increased agitation in favor of school prayer indicated a shift to the right. Television evangelists, tapping into worries about moral decline, were gaining increasing numbers of viewers (and financial contributions) and becoming a social and political force. With the election of **Jimmy Carter** in 1976, America had its first "born again" president, a moderate to liberal one, to be sure, but one whose election underscored the clout of evangelical voters.

Nineteen seventy-seven did get off to an auspicious start, at least. Carter aide **Margaret (Midge) Costanza** welcomed representatives of national gay and lesbian groups at a meeting at the White House, the first time that had ever happened. A national gay rights bill had already been introduced into the House of Representatives with thirty-nine cosponsors. Carter had pledged during the campaign to sign it, and the Costanza meeting raised hopes that the new president could be held to his promise. The antigay governor of New Hampshire, **Meldrim Thomson,** discovered that in signing a package to reform that state's rape laws, he had inadvertently agreed to the elimination of penalties against homosexual acts. Thomson decided not to revive the law, and New Hampshire became one of eighteen states that, by then, had repealed their sodomy statutes. Meanwhile, in January 1977, Miami joined some forty U.S. cities—including Los Angeles, Washington, D.C., Minneapolis, and Seattle—in enacting gay rights protections. The vote by the Dade County Commission was 5–3.

In the wake of the commission's vote, Anita Bryant—pop singer, former Miss Oklahoma, publicist for Florida orange juice, and

Anita Bryant pours orange juice for board members of her group "Save Our Children" at her Miami Beach home, in May 1977. (© UPI/Bettmann)

born-again Christian—announced that she would lead a campaign to repeal the ordinance. Bryant had testified at commission hearings, claiming that gay rights protections would "violate my rights and the rights of all decent and morally upstanding citizens." (**Alvin Dark,** manager of the San Diego Padres baseball team, also testified against the proposal.) Within six weeks, Bryant's organization, Save Our Children, Inc., had collected sixty-five thousand signatures on a petition to force a county-wide referendum on the ordinance. Suddenly, organized opposition to the gay rights movement had emerged.

The issue quickly gained national attention. As the *Miami Herald* reported, "The campaign is over Gay Rights, and it has all the ingredients—from sex to religion to Anita Bryant bursting into the 'Battle Hymn of the Republic'—for a national media spectacular." Bryant based her campaign on the slogan "Homosexuals cannot reproduce, so they must recruit." If the ordinance remained on the books, she warned, "militant homosexuals" would "influence children to their abnormal way of life." Her support was wide-ranging—from evangelical Christians to the president of the local B'nai Brith. A state legislator read sections of the book of *Leviticus* aloud on the senate floor in Tallahassee. The moderate Democratic Governor **Reuben Askew** declared that he would not want an open homosexual teaching his children and that he had "never viewed the homosexual lifestyle as something that approached a constitutional right." A letter from the Roman Catholic archbishop calling for repeal was read aloud in Catholic churches on the Sunday preceding the vote. The gay side, led by **Jack Campbell,** head of a national bathhouse chain, centered its strategy on a media campaign that eschewed door-to-door canvasing. Although Bryant talked about a "well-organized, highly financed, and politically militant group of homosexual activists," in an atmosphere inflamed by anxiety about gay men "recruiting" children, supporters of the ordinance never had a chance. On June 7, 1977, Dade County voters repealed the gay rights law by a vote of 202,319 to 89,562. In her victory statement Bryant said, "Tonight the laws of God and the cultural values of man have been vindicated. The people of Dade County—the normal majority—have said, 'Enough, Enough, Enough.' "

The lopsided result in Miami shook gays and lesbians out of their complacency. There were large and angry demonstrations in New York, San Francisco, Boston, and other cities. A campaign was launched to hound Bryant off the stage of American political life through a boycott of Florida citrus products—and through personal ridicule. Two weeks after the Miami vote, a thirty-three-year-old San Francisco gardener, **Robert Hillsborough,** was stabbed fifteen times in the chest and face by a youth shouting, "Faggot, faggot, faggot!" Hillsborough's murder made the front pages of the San Francisco newspapers and the gay press nationwide. Gays and their allies seized upon the death as a symbol of the new and dangerous atmosphere created by Bryant. As Hillsborough's seventy-eight-year-old mother put it, "My son's blood is on her [Bryant's] hands." At the annual San Francisco Gay Freedom Day parade—held five days after Hillsborough's murder—250,000 marched down Market Street. It was the largest crowd ever for a gay and lesbian parade. Marchers carried pictures of Hitler, Stalin, Ugandan dictator Idi Amin—and Anita Bryant.

Despite the crowds on Market Street, opponents of gay rights now had the momentum. The following April, St. Paul, Minnesota, voters repealed that city's gay rights law by a 54,090–31,690 vote.

"Like the Union Army at the second Manassas, the gay-rights movement has been routed anew in its second collision with Christian
fundamentalists," exulted columnist **Pat Buchanan**. Voters in Wich-
ita, Kansas, and the liberal college town of Eugene, Oregon, followed suit the following month. The Oklahoma state legislature
passed a law dismissing teachers who advocated or "practiced"
homosexuality. The argument of the opponents of homosexual
rights was always the same: Gay and lesbian civil rights protections
meant molestation of children, homosexual "recruitment," and a
threat to the already-embattled American family. In California, **John
Briggs,** a state senator with aspirations for higher office, garnered
enough signatures to put a referendum on the 1978 statewide ballot
seeking to bar open homosexuals from teaching in the state's public
schools.

The Briggs Initiative—Proposition 6—was the first attempt during this period not merely to roll back gay rights laws but to legally
discriminate against homosexuals. If California were to pass such
a law statewide, it would be calamitous for the new movement.
Two months before the November election, the polls showed Briggs
headed for an overwhelming victory. In each discussion on the issue,
Briggs would bring up the same dubious (but presumably frightening) statistics—that homosexuals comprised a third of the teachers in San Francisco and 20 percent in Los Angeles. "Most of them
are in the closet," he would say, "and frankly, that's where I think
they should remain." Briggs's leaflets featured inflammatory newspaper clippings with headlines like TEACHER ACCUSED OF SEX ACTS
WITH BOY STUDENTS and FORMER SCOUTMASTER CONVICTED OF
HOMOSEXUAL ACTS WITH BOYS. In one speech, the state senator
warned, "If you let one homosexual teacher stay, soon there'll be
two, then four, then eight, then twenty-five—and before long, the
entire school will be taught by homosexuals."

But as the state's political, labor, and religious establishment lined
up against Briggs, his early lead began to evaporate. Perhaps the
most important endorsement that the anti-Briggs forces received
came from former California Governor **Ronald Reagan.** "Whatever
else it is, homosexuality is not a contagious disease like measles,"
said the future pr. '~nt. Former president **Gerald Ford** urged a
"no" vote. President .nmy Carter also came out against Briggs at
a rally for Governor **Jerry Brown**—although only after Brown assured him it was "perfectly safe" to do so. In November, Proposition
6 was defeated by a three-to-two margin.

That same day, gay rights forces won another badly needed victory as Seattle voters rejected an attempt to repeal that city's gay rights law by 63 to 37 percent. (Supporters of the Seattle ordinance defined the issue early and successfully as one of privacy, and their campaign poster featured a huge keyhole with an eye peering through it.) The Seattle vote marked the first time a gay rights ordinance had been upheld in a popular vote.

The newly elected San Francisco supervisor Harvey Milk had campaigned hard against the Briggs Initiative. He and Briggs engaged in a number of debates together throughout the state. Shilts relates how, late in the campaign, Briggs invited Milk to a debate on his home turf of conservative Orange County. At the Orange County airport, Milk and campaign aide **Dick Pabich** ran into none other than Briggs himself, his wife, and a state police bodyguard. The five went off to have a cup of coffee in the airport lounge. For half an hour Milk and Briggs swapped stories about the campaign "like two World War II buddies reminiscing about their days in the trenches," Shilts writes. When Briggs departed, Milk said to Pabich, "This really is a big joke to him." But during the debate itself the two men relentlessly attacked each other.

Another opponent of gay rights whom Milk tried to win over was his fellow supervisor Dan White. When Milk and White were both elected to their first terms on the board of supervisors in the fall of 1977, the San Francisco media found these political outsiders and polar opposites—the outspokenly gay Milk and the deeply conservative White—objects of fascination. The two made a number of joint appearances on local talk shows. In conversation with a friend, Milk said, "Dan White is just stupid. He's working class, a Catholic, been brought up with all those prejudices. I'm gonna sit next to him every day and let him know we're not all those bad things he thinks we are."

Initially, Milk's courting of White seemed to have some effect. When Milk introduced a bill banning discrimination against homosexuals in housing and employment, White supported it in committee, relating how his experiences as a paratrooper in Vietnam had taught him that qualities attributed to different groups— whites, blacks, Asians, gays—"just didn't hold up under fire." "It doesn't matter what a person is, what his preferences are," said White. "As long as they respect other people and they abide by courtesies and values, I think we can all get along." He also backed a resolution honoring Daughters of Bilitis founders Del Martin and Phyllis Lyon on the occasion of their twenty-fifth anniversary. And White did some courting of his own, persuading board of supervisors president Dianne Feinstein to make Milk the chairman of the Streets and Transportation Committee, a position Milk coveted.

Still, their relationship remained uneasy, and when Milk cast the deciding vote in favor of setting up a facility for juvenile offenders in White's district—something that White vehemently opposed—White felt betrayed. The very next week he changed his position on the gay rights bill, becoming the only supervisor to oppose it. White refused to talk to Milk for months; at the same time, Milk became disillusioned by White, increasingly seeing him as a tool of downtown real-estate interests and the police.

In the fall of 1978, White abruptly resigned from the board of supervisors, citing financial pressures. Ten days later, after a meeting with the leaders of the Board of Realtors and the Police Officers' Association, he asked Mayor George Moscone to reinstate him. At first, Moscone was disposed to do so, but under pressure from White's political opponents, including Milk, he changed his mind. On the morning of Monday, November 27, 1978, the day that Moscone was to name someone else to fill White's seat, White packed his .38 caliber Smith & Wesson and headed for City Hall. He walked into Moscone's office and, after the mayor informed him he wasn't going to reappoint him to his seat, shot him four times, including twice in the head. Apparently, no one heard the shots. Then he found Milk, whom he was convinced was the mastermind behind the mayor's failure to reappoint him. He took his fellow supervisor into his recently vacated office—empty save for a desk, two chairs, and a bare metal bookshelf—and closed the door behind them. There, he shot Milk four times as well. After Milk had fallen to the floor, White put his gun almost against Milk's skull and fired off a fifth round.

Dan White went on trial six months later for murder. Defense challenges assured that there were no blacks, Asians, or gays on the jury, which turned out be comprised mostly of white working-class Catholics. "If you had to guess you'd say that only one or two at most might have voted for George Moscone," writer Mike Weiss observed in his book about the assassinations, *Double Play: The*

San Francisco City Hall Killings. "They were a pretty representative sample of the new San Francisco working class, a pretty good cross section of the kind of people who felt oppressed and neglected by the political system." Randy Shilts noted ruefully, "Dan White would truly be judged by a jury of his peers."

The defense painted White as the victim of "diminished capacity," a family man who somehow had gone off the rails. "Good people, fine people, with fine backgrounds, simply don't kill people in cold blood," defense lawyer **Doug Schmidt** told the jury in his opening statement. He blamed stress, plus a depressive episode triggered by a chemical change in the body. White was "an idealistic young man, a *working-class* young man," Schmidt declared. "He was deeply endowed with and believed strongly in traditional American values, family and home. . . . Above all else, he was fair, perhaps too fair, for politics in San Francisco. He trusted people. . . ."

During the course of the trial, White's sister—a nurse—and a psychiatrist testified that White had been depressed throughout the summer before the assassinations and had been consuming inordinate quantities of junk food. According to Dr. **Marty Blinder,** junk food could cause extreme variations in blood sugar levels resulting in antisocial behavior—what would later be known as the "Twinkie defense."

For its part, the prosecution's case was poorly argued. Prosecutor **Tom Norman** failed to challenge the defense picture of White's exemplary life; he made no effort to explore the defendant's motivations, neglecting to point out his increasingly rancorous relationship with Milk, for example. Only when City Supervisor **Carol Ruth Silver** took the stand was it revealed that White and Milk's relationship had been less than friendly; and it was Silver who late in the trial had contacted the prosecution, asking that she be allowed to testify, not the prosecution who contacted her. "Without a believable motive, without a demonstration of malice, they could not find Dan White guilty of murder," noted Weiss. "Never once in four hours [of summation] had Tommy Norman said: revenge." When Norman played a tape of White's confession, it wound up creating sympathy for the defendant:

> *I wanted to talk to him [Milk], and, and, and just try to explain to him, you know, I, I didn't agree with him on a lot of things, but I was always honest, you know, and here they were devious and then he started kind of smirking 'cause he knew, he knew*

that I wasn't going to be reappointed. And ah . . . it just didn't make any impression on him. I started to say you know how hard I worked for it and what it meant to me and my family and then my reputation as a hard worker, a good honest person and he just kind of smirked at me as if to say, too bad and then and then I just got all flushed and, and hot and I shot him.

At least three jurors wept openly as they listened to the tape recording.

On Monday, May 21, 1979, the jury announced its verdict: It found White guilty on two counts of voluntary manslaughter. He would receive seven years and eight months in prison, which meant he would most likely be out in five years. Acting Mayor Dianne Feinstein, who was present at City Hall at the time of the shootings, expressed the popular feeling. "As I look at the law," she said, "it was two murders." In the aftermath of the verdict, a large and angry crowd marched on City Hall and virtually besieged the building for three hours, burning a dozen police cars. Later, the police rampaged through the Castro, bursting into one gay bar and attacking virtually everyone in sight. Sixty-one police officers and one hundred gays were hospitalized in what came to be known as the "White Night Riots."

No contemporary American gay leader has yet to achieve in life the stature Milk found in death. A 1984 biographical film, **Robert Epstein's** *The Life and Times of Harvey Milk,* won an Academy Award for best documentary; the assassination and trial inspired a Broadway play and, later, an opera. Mayor Feinstein picked former minister **Harry Britt** to take Milk's place on the board of supervisors, therefore establishing a "gay seat" on the board. However, as Frances FitzGerald wrote, Britt lacked Milk's "extraordinary political energy and his sheer chutzpah." FitzGerald wrote:

The Castro mourned Harvey Milk, and yet it could not seem to make him into a living legend—that is, into a legend that would nourish and sustain it. The Castro saw him as martyr but understood his martyrdom as an end rather than a beginning. He had died, and with him a great deal of the Castro's optimism, idealism, and ambition seemed to die as well. The Castro could find no one to take his place in its affections, and possibly it wanted no one.

In early 1985, Dan White was released from prison. He returned to San Francisco but was unable to find a job and lived in relative obscurity. Before the year was out, he committed suicide by inhaling carbon monoxide fumes in his garage.

Although the assassinations of Moscone and Milk were obviously the acts of a very troubled man, they cannot be understood outside the backlash in American society regarding the new visibility and perceived power of gays and lesbians. In San Francisco, White clearly articulated the feelings of many traditionally minded ethnic groups, of the police, of social and religious conservatives. (His own district was the only one in the city to vote in favor of the Briggs Initiative.) He saw himself as defending his values and his community against social forces he feared and could not understand. Despite the horror of his crimes, White had more support than many in San Francisco wanted to admit.

In much of the rest of the country, the battle lines were drawn somewhat differently: with gays and lesbians on one side and the resurgent Religious Right, typified by Jerry Falwell's Moral Majority, on the other. The antigay forces were helped considerably by the election of their ally, Ronald Reagan, as president in 1980. (Despite Reagan's opposition to the Briggs Initiative, he was strongly against gay civil rights protections.) Homosexuality was not the only issue that concerned the Religious Right—abortion, the Equal Rights Amendment, and prayer in the schools were even more important, particularly during this period. But homosexuality could be made to stand for everything that many heterosexual Americans felt was wrong with the country—an increasing sense of social breakdown, growing sexual permissiveness, and the weakening of family and authority structures. The migration of gays into urban centers made them "invisible" in much of the U.S.—and easier to be used as scapegoats. If the gay issue was not *the* major issue for the Religious Right, it did provide a useful "cash cow" for the coffers of various groups. In order to raise money, they didn't hesitate to portray homosexuals and homosexuality in the most inflammatory terms. A 1981 fund-raising letter from Jerry Falwell, echoing Anita Bryant, went, "Please remember, homosexuals do not reproduce! They recruit! And, many of them are out after my children and your children." The Christian Voice organization put it even more starkly: "Can't let militant gays, ultra liberals, atheists, porno pushers, pressure Congress into passing Satan's agenda instead of God's."

The conflicts between newly visible gay communities and the Religious Right extended to other parts of the English-speaking world as well. In England, in 1976, morality crusader **Mary White-house** managed to get *Gay News*, the British homosexual paper, charged with blasphemy for publishing a poem about Christ. Although no one had been successfully prosecuted under the blasphemy law since 1921, the *Gay News* editor was found guilty, receiving an eighteen-month suspended sentence and a fine of five hundred pounds. (The fine, as well as legal costs to fight the case, marked the beginning of financial problems that were eventually to lead to the newspaper's demise in 1983.) In Canada, evangelicals sponsored Anita Bryant on a national tour in 1978. Two years later, with the defeat of progay candidates in municipal elections and the rise of vocal antigay forces, Toronto police began a series of raids on gay bathhouses, in which more than three hundred people were arrested. In New Zealand, in the mid-1980s, fundamentalist ministers from the United States took part in an unsuccessful effort to oppose repeal of the country's sodomy law. In Australia, the Reverend **Fred Nile,** a fundamentalist minister, became the leading opponent of Sydney's annual gay and lesbian Mardi Gras parade, on one occasion publicly praying for rain to halt the proceedings.

By the end of the 1970s, the backlash had slowed the advance of gay and lesbian rights but had failed to stop it. Interestingly, as Randy Shilts observed in *The Mayor of Castro Street,* the two groups—gays and lesbians and evangelical Christians—seemed well-matched adversaries, with striking similarities. Both gays and evangelicals shared their own particular versions of the "born-again" experience, Shilts noted. For evangelical Christians, it was a theological experience—finding God in a sinful world; for gays it was a social one, "coming out" in a generally hostile heterosexual environment. For both, their new identities frequently meant breaking with the past and starting a new life and a new social network. Both groups, Shilts pointed out, put great emphasis on "testifying" to their experiences—born-again Christians in their rounds of testimony for the Lord, and gays and lesbians by announcing their homosexuality to friends and relatives. Finally, both saw themselves in what they perceived to be an ultimate struggle. The war between gays and the Religious Right was to continue throughout the 1980s, culminating in the referendum campaigns in Oregon and Colorado in 1992 and the battle over gays in the military.

By the end of the 1970s, gays had begun to establish themselves as a force in mainstream American politics, particularly in large urban areas and in key states like California. But the progress that had seemed so unstoppable just a few years before now faced fierce and committed opponents.

Leonard Matlovich: A Soldier's Story

ON MARCH 6, 1975, Air Force Technical Sergeant Leonard Matlovich (1943–88) walked into the office of his superior, Captain **Dennis Collins,** the officer in charge of race-relations instruction at Langley Air Force Base in Hampton, Virginia. "I have a letter I'd like for you to read," said Matlovich. After Collins looked over the first few sentences, he slumped into a chair and demanded, "What does this mean?" Matlovich replied, "This means *Brown* versus *The Board of Education.*"

The letter, addressed to the Secretary of the Air Force, began:

> *After some years of uncertainty, I have arrived at the conclusion that my sexual preferences are homosexual as opposed to heterosexual. I have also concluded that my sexual preferences will in no way interfere with my Air Force duties, as my preferences are now open. It is therefore requested that those provisions in AFM-39-12 relating to the discharge of homosexuals be waived in my case. . . .*

It ended:

> *In sum, I consider myself to be a homosexual and fully qualified for military service. My almost twelve years of unblemished service supports this position.*

With Matlovich's letter, the battle to overturn the U.S. military's policy barring gays and lesbians began. The thirty-one-year-old air force technical sergeant was in many respects the "perfect" test case. He had volunteered for three tours in Vietnam, where he had been awarded a Purple Heart and a Bronze Star. He had been awarded the Air Force Meritorious Service Medal for his work as a race-relations instructor—his job at the time he wrote his letter to the Secretary of the Air Force.

Matlovich was the ultimate "straight arrow." His father was a career air force officer, and young Matlovich had grown up on military bases. He enlisted in the air force just out of high school. He had been president of his county's chapter of Young Republicans and had campaigned for Barry Goldwater for president in 1964. Raised as a Roman Catholic, he left the Church because he believed that the reforms of Vatican II were too radical. In the summer of 1968 he became a Mormon, a religion more suited to a worldview that venerated authority and tradition above everything.

"I've always been very conservative," Matlovich told his biographer, Mike Hippler. "And I've always had a military mind. When I graduated from high school, I was reading about the U.S. involvement in Vietnam, and I was so afraid that if I didn't hurry up and get over there, it would be over before I had an opportunity to prove my manhood. You see, I had to prove that even though I had strong attractions to other men, I could go to war just like anyone else."

Matlovich was aware of his homosexuality early on but he tried to fight it. His work as a race-relations instructor helped him come to terms with his sexual orientation. It was, in fact, from one of his students that he learned of the existence of the first gay place he ever stepped inside, a restaurant called the Yum Yum Room in Pensacola, Florida. There, at age thirty-one, he met a man with whom he had the first sexual experience of his life. But his race-relations classes had a profound effect on him in other ways. As Randy Shilts notes in his book *Conduct Unbecoming*, "Every day, he reminded his classes of the plea of his new hero, Dr. Martin Luther King, Jr., that they judge people by the 'content of their character,' not by the color of their skin. Slowly, week after week, the words sank in, not only to his students but to Matlovich himself." From there, it was a short distance to confronting the military ban on homosexuals. As it turned out, Matlovich's strongest supporters when he came out were the black airmen at Langley.

Matlovich's was only one of a number of challenges to the military ban that began to advance through the legal system in the late 1970s. Another was that of **Vernon "Copy" Berg III,** a naval ensign who decided to fight the navy's decision to discharge him after it was discovered that he was having an affair with a navy civilian instructor. There was Air Force Staff Sergeant **Rudolf "Skip" Keith,** a black man who came out of the closet during a race-relations class at Dover Air Force Base, near Washington. Private First Class **Barbara Randolph** and Private **Debbie Watson** of the Women's Army Corps at Fort Devens, Massachusetts, announced to their commanding officer that they would fight the military exclusion right up to the Supreme Court. Yet another case was that of **Miriam Ben-Shalom,** a single mother and army reserve drill instructor in Milwaukee. When, after reading about Matlovich, Ben-Shalom asked her commander, "Why don't they kick *me* out?" he supposedly replied, "Because you're a good NCO."

Of all these cases, Matlovich's had the highest profile. Six months after his letter to the Secretary of the Air Force, he appeared on the cover of *Time* magazine in uniform—medals and all—with the caption "I Am Homosexual." On the inside pages were photos of him dancing in a gay bar and recovering from wounds in Danang, South Vietnam. It was the *Time* cover that encouraged Ensign "Copy" Berg to fight his discharge from the navy and Miriam Ben-Shalom to tell her commanding officer that she was a lesbian.

In November 1975, the air force discharged Matlovich, and Federal District Court Judge **Gerhard Gesell** refused to overturn his ouster. (Three weeks later, the Mormon Church excommunicated him.) Yet the legal momentum seemed to be working in Matlovich's favor. In December 1978, the U.S. Court of Appeals ruled that the discharges of both Matlovich and Ensign Berg were illegal, although it did not order the reinstatement of either man. The court ordered Judge Gesell to reexamine the case. He did. In September 1980, Gesell ordered the air force to reinstate Matlovich by December 5 of that year. Victory, at last, seemed at hand.

In a last-ditch effort to avoid having to take him back, the air force offered Matlovich a cash settlement. No one really expected he would take it. It was clear, however, that whatever Matlovich decided, the air force would appeal the case to the Supreme Court. There, it was also clear that Matlovich would lose, especially now that Ronald Reagan had just been elected president, ensuring a more conservative court for years to come. If he didn't accept a settlement from the air force now, chances were good that he would eventually lose his case and wind up with nothing. Meanwhile, Matlovich was earning his living at the time selling used cars at a Ford dealership in San Francisco, where he had moved in 1979. (That same year, he had been handed a humiliating defeat in his run for a seat on the San Francisco Board of Supervisors, polling only 2 percent in a race won by Harvey Milk's successor, Harry Britt.) So Leonard Matlovich, within days of being reinstated in the air force, agreed to take the tax-free $160,000 offered by the air force and drop his case.

Despite occasionally sympathetic lower-court decisions, the military ban remained in place. Restrictions were toughened during the Reagan-Bush years, a decade when seventeen thousand gays and lesbians were discharged from the U.S. Armed Forces for their sexual orientation. As for Matlovich, he was never quite able to get his life back together. He opened a pizza parlor in the Russian River resort town of Guerneville that soon went out of business; then he moved back East to form a group of gay conservatives (Concerned Americans for Individuals Rights, or CAIR) that never got off the ground due to internal bickering.

In September 1986, Matlovich was diagnosed with AIDS. With his diagnosis, his activism was reborn. Wearing his air force jacket, covered with medals, and carrying an American flag, he was among those arrested blocking traffic in front of the White House at a major AIDS protest in the spring of 1987. He made headlines in October of that year when a Northwest Airlines ticket agent informed him he couldn't fly on the airline to the gay rights march on Washington because he had AIDS. Matlovich summoned the media. After a spate of unfavorable publicity, Northwest revised its policy.

On June 22, 1988, Leonard Matlovich, "arguably the most influential gay activist of his generation," in Randy Shilts's words, died in West Hollywood, California, at age forty-four. He was buried in Arlington National Cemetery. The inscription on his gravestone reads, "When I was in the military, they gave me a medal for killing two men, and a discharge for loving one."

In the Statehouse: Representative Elaine Noble and Senator Allen Spear

IN 1974, a little-known Boston feminist and community activist named Elaine Noble confounded the political pundits by being elected to the Massachusetts House of Representatives as the nation's first openly gay state legislator. Shortly after Noble's election, Allen Spear, a former history professor who had been elected to the Minnesota State Senate in 1972, representing a Minneapolis district, told a newspaper interviewer that he was gay. The fact that two state legislators would voluntarily announce their homosexuality—with Noble doing so *before* she was even elected—was a remarkable development. Soon, Spear and Noble were joined by other openly gay colleagues: **Karen Clark,** in the Minnesota House of Representatives, and **Brian Coyle** and **David Scondras,** in the Minneapolis and Boston city councils, respectively.

While Noble and Spear both came from politically liberal districts with large numbers of gay voters, neither represented their city's "gay ghettos." Spear's Minneapolis district comprised the area around the University of Minnesota campus, as well as some senior-citizen high-rises and ethnic pockets. Noble's district in Boston's Fenway neighborhood was largely composed of elderly and low-income constituents. The legislators' affirmations of their homosexuality did not seem to scare off these voters; Noble easily won a second term, and, a year after he came out, Spear was reelected with a whopping 68 percent of the vote.

Both Spear and Noble worked hard—and unsuccessfully—to get gay rights bills passed in their states. (In 1989, Massachusetts finally became the second state, after Wisconsin, to enact gay rights; Minnesota remains without statewide gay antidiscrimination protections.) But the two didn't spend a majority of their time focusing on gay and lesbian issues. Noble lobbied hard for her elderly constituents. Spear, a member (and later chair) of the Senate Judiciary Committee, spent much of his time on issues such as criminal law, DWI (driving-while-intoxicated), due process for people committed to mental hospitals, and child abuse.

Both legislators eschewed the role of maverick, working hard to be "inside" players. Noble cultivated good relations with the old-time, Irish politicians who dominated the Massachusetts House, gaining the enmity of some in the gay community, who felt that she was "selling out" to the establishment. Spear rose swiftly through the ranks of the Democratic Senate hierarchy. Yet Spear, in particular, stayed close to his progressive roots. One of his proudest moments in politics came when he was chosen to give the eulogy on the floor of the Minnesota Senate for **Elmer Benson,** the populist Farmer Labor party governor of Minnesota in the 1930s.

As much as these politicians tried to be representatives of their district first and gay representatives second, it was difficult. This was especially true for Noble, for whom, as a woman and a lesbian, expectations were extremely high. On the one hand, she faced abuse and threats from homophobes; on the other hand, every gay man and lesbian in Massachusetts—and sometimes, it seemed, in the entire nation—viewed her as their personal legislator. When the Massachusetts House was redistricted in 1978, Noble found herself having to face off in the same district with her political ally, then–State Representative **Barney Frank.** (Frank, who was then in the closet, came out as gay in 1987 during his third term in the U.S. Congress.) Rather than risk an "inter-family" battle with the extremely popular Frank, Noble did not seek a third term. She ran unsuccessfully for the Democratic nomination for U.S. Senate and then served Boston Mayor **Kevin White** as the city's liaison to the state legislature and as head of the Democratic City Committee. She was later defeated twice in elections for city councillor in Cambridge, Massachusetts. Being the "first" had taken its toll on Noble: She never regained her political footing.

Spear, on the other hand, has been able to thrive in the Minnesota legislature, where he still serves today. He has been reelected five times and, in January 1993, was elected president of the Minnesota Senate, the highest position an openly gay person has ever achieved in state government in the United States.

The Man Who Saved the President

ON SEPTEMBER 22, 1975, President Gerald Ford was speaking at a luncheon of the World Affairs Council at the St. Francis Hotel in downtown San Francisco. As the president walked out of the hotel to his limousine, a large crowd began to applaud. In the midst of the crowd, a gray-haired woman in a blue raincoat named **Sara Jane Moore** raised her arm in the direction of the president. A man grabbed Moore's arm and wrestled her to the ground. The gun she was carrying went off and missed Ford by only a few feet.

Oliver W. "Bill" Sipple, a thirty-three-year-old ex-marine who had happened by the St. Francis on his afternoon stroll and found himself standing next to Sara Jane Moore, had saved the president's life. But when the Secret Service and police interviewed Sipple following the assassination attempt, he pleaded with them not to release his name. The police were incredulous. Of course, his name made the papers anyway.

Two days later, **Herb Caen,** the gossip columnist for the *San Francisco Chronicle,* offered a different slant on the story:

> *One of the heroes of the day, Oliver "Bill" Sipple, the ex-Marine who grabbed Sara Jane Moore's arm just as her gun was fired and thereby may have saved the President's life, was the center of midnight attention at the Red Lantern, a Golden Gate Ave. bar he favors. The Rev. Ray Broshears, head of the Helping Hands center and Gay Politico Harvey Milk, who claim to be among Sipple's close friends, describe themselves as "proud— maybe this will help break the stereotype." Sipple is among the workers in Milk's campaign for supe [city supervisor].*

Soon enough a number of other newspapers picked up the story, with the *Chicago Sun Times* headlining its article "Homosexual Hero." In *The Mayor of Castro Street,* Randy Shilts claims that it was Harvey Milk who leaked the report of Sipple's homosexuality to the *Chronicle.* Milk had met Sipple ten years before, just after Sipple had left the marines and was hanging out in gay bars in Greenwich Village.

The reason for Sipple's initial reticence was obvious: He wasn't prepared for his homosexuality to be known to millions of people. He was furious at what he considered an invasion of his privacy. A few days later, after a telephone conversation with his mother, he told reporters, "I want you to know that my mother told me today that she can't walk out of her front door, or even go to church, because of the pressures she feels because of the press stories concerning my sexual orientation. My sexual orientation has nothing to do with saving the President's life."

It was a complicated matter. Sipple was living proof that a gay person could perform heroic deeds in a country that wouldn't allow gays and lesbians to serve in its armed forces. In that sense, his sexuality was a legitimate news story, and important in terms of the public image of homosexuals, especially in those early days of the gay rights movement. On the other hand, Sipple certainly had the right to keep his sexuality private, if he wished. He was simply a citizen who had done an exemplary deed—saved the life of the president of the United States—and shouldn't be made to suffer in any way because of it. In this clash of two values, the Sipple case anticipated by more than a decade the controversies of the late 1980s surrounding "outing."

It was weeks before Sipple got even the briefest note of thanks from a pusillanimous White House. He later sued seven newspapers, including the *San Francisco Chronicle,* for $15 million, charging them with invasion of privacy. The judge threw out the case; in his view, once Sipple had thrust himself into the limelight that afternoon in front of the St. Francis, he had become a public figure and thus journalistic "fair game." Oliver W. Sipple died in February 1989 at age forty-seven.

The Rise of the Gay Press

"WHO IS ANITA BRYANT and Why Does She Hate Us?" asked the headline in the *Gay Community News (GCN)* shortly after the singer announced her antigay crusade in Miami in early 1977. The Boston weekly, the closest the early movement came to a newspaper of record, was one of a number of gay and lesbian publications that established themselves across the United States in the post-Stonewall period. By the middle of the 1970s, virtually every major city boasted its own gay newspaper—the *Washington Blade,* the *Philadelphia Gay News,* San Francisco's *Bay Area Reporter,* Chicago's *Gay Life,* Cleveland's *High Gear.* Even off-the-beaten-path Rochester, New York, had a newsy monthly called *The Empty Closet.* (Curiously, New York City was unable to sustain a gay newspaper during this period, though the *Village Voice* was able to fill the void to some extent; this situation persisted until the *New York Native* came along at the beginning of the eighties.) Most successful of all these publications was the West Coast–based *Advocate,* founded in 1967. *Christopher Street,* a monthly magazine that emphasized fiction and social and cultural criticism, also achieved wide national readership.

The pre-Stonewall gay press—*One, The Ladder, Mattachine Review*—had been characterized by a somewhat apologetic tone, particularly in its early days, sometimes even opening its pages to antigay psychiatric "experts." After Stonewall, broadsheets like New York's *Gay and Come Out!* reflected the euphoria and militancy of the time; in the early seventies, Boston's *Fag Rag* and San Francisco's *Gay Sunshine* offered a sexual liberationist perspective. (*Fag Rag* was famous for treatises like **Charley Shively**'s "Cock-Sucking as an Act of Liberation.") The gay press that emerged toward the middle of the decade tended to reflect the shift of the gay movement toward a more mainstream, civil rights perspective. With the "straight press" still wary of covering gay issues, gay newspapers offered a blend of news, interviews, and book and movie reviews, spiced with advice columns and listings of bar happenings. They were also sold openly on newsstands, a major change from the days before Stonewall.

The gay press reflected the absence of lesbians in the gay political movement of the time. While most publications claimed to provide coverage of both lesbians and gay men, in fact they were largely oriented toward men. Boston's collectively run *Gay Community News* was an exception: It tried to present a balance of gay male and lesbian news and features, and, from its inception, its staff included both men and women. There were few specifically lesbian publications; probably as many lesbians could be found reading feminist newspapers like *Off Our Backs* as the gay press.

Many of these fledgling publications had difficulty supporting themselves financially, often relying on advertisements from gay bars and marginal gay businesses, as well as personal ads. Nonetheless, the gay media, particularly the nationally circulated *Advocate,* provided an outlet for the marketing of the emerging gay consumer culture. *The Advocate*'s motto was "Touching Your Lifestyle," and its pages were filled with advertisements targeted at gay men; by the end of the decade this had expanded from bars and baths to record and liquor companies. The idea that homosexuals *had* a life-style, one that was both enjoyable and appealing, represented an important development in itself.

This approach had its critics, however. In portraying the homosexual as a "good consumer," Michael Bronski contended *The Advocate* promoted an ethic of "liberation by accumulation" in which "social acceptance and mobility could be achieved by buying the correct accessories." *Advocate* publisher **David B. Goodstein** saw it differently: "I'm trying to reach the gays we don't ordinarily see. I'm convinced that 85 percent of the gays in the United States lead very private lives, don't care about the gay scene and go to bars no more than four times a year. They're just like other suburban couples. *The Advocate* is for middle-class readers—radicals don't read, they don't have the time."

Indeed, gay "radicals" increasingly emerged as Goodstein's bête noire. The *Advocate* publisher became increasingly outspoken (and controversial), criticizing the movement's sexual liberationist wing for allegedly impeding political progress. (*The Advocate* had coined the term "gay destroyers" back in 1973.) By the end of the decade, Goodstein became a disciple of **Werner Erhard's** self-help program, est, which emphasized individual responsibility. Goodstein eventually started his own version of est, called The Advocate Experience, which he marketed around the country (and required his own staff to participate in).

Beyond its role in creating the new gay consumer culture, the gay media played an important role in disseminating the ideas of the movement to a wider homosexual public. A number of gay and lesbian journalists and political leaders got their start in the gay press: author Randy Shilts began his career as a reporter for *The Advocate;* the *Gay Community News* was the starting point for a number of movement leaders, including **Urvashi Vaid,** later head of the National Gay and Lesbian Task Force; **Kevin Cathcart,** who became the executive director of the Lambda Legal Defense and Education Fund, the national gay legal organization; **Richard Burns,** executive director of New York City's Gay and Lesbian Community

Center; and **Eric Rofes,** former head of San Francisco's Shanti Project.

The gay press was not just an American phenomenon. The Canadian monthly *The Body Politic,* perhaps the most respected of the gay publications, continued to publish throughout the 1970s and '80s (although the Canadian government tried to shut it down after it ran an article on intergenerational sex). The British newspaper *Gay News* started in 1972; in Paris, *Gai Pied* was founded in 1979 and soon became the largest-selling gay newspaper in Europe. (Philosopher Michel Foucault, a founder and contributor, provided the title, a sexual pun.) And the role of the gay media in creating community was underscored when a *Gay Pravda* was published in Amsterdam and circulated in the Soviet Union during the Gorbachev years of *glasnost* and *perestroika.*

CHAPTER 25

SEX AND MUSIC IN
THE SEVENTIES

"**I** HAVE CRUISED rich, poor, middle class, and petit bourgeois; black, white, yellow, and brown; scholars, jocks, Gentlemanly Cs, and dropouts; farmers, seamen, railroad men, heavy industry, light manufacturing, communications, business, and finance; civilians, soldiers and sailors, and once or twice cops." So wrote the sociologist Paul Goodman in his 1969 essay "The Politics of Being Queer."

The early gay liberation theorists had preached a revolutionary gospel that was political, social, and sexual. They criticized what they viewed as the exploitation of the bars and the depersonalization of the baths, advocating the formation of a more humanistic gay culture—the coffee shop/dance halls, rural retreats, food cooperatives, and free schools of Carl Wittman's "Gay Manifesto." They also asserted that monogamy was an imitation of all that was wrong with heterosexual relationships, that gay sexual encounters were "acts of liberation" that broke down barriers of race and social class. Goodman, for example, argued in his essay that "queer life" can be "profoundly democratizing, throwing together every class and group. . . . Given the usual coldness and fragmentation of community life at present, my hunch is that homosexual promiscuity enriches more lives than it desensitizes."

But as the political ideology of early gay liberation evolved into the reformist approach of the gay rights movement, of Harvey Milk and Allen Spear and Elaine Noble, many of the radical social notions began to fade as well. The countercultural visions of the gay liberation prophets gave way to a more mundane and middle-class gay world—the restaurants, discos, boutiques, softball and bowling leagues, marching bands and choral groups, churches and synagogues of the urban gay ghettos. While these institutions did create a strong sense of community, to many they seemed a pale version of the larger society, not the brave, new egalitarian world that the early gay liberationists had in mind.

For many urban gay men, what remained of the original gay liberation dream was the sexual component. The fears of previous decades were vanishing: In many American cities, police entrapment had diminished; in the new atmosphere of openness, there was less concern about having one's homosexuality exposed. It was as if years of repression had suddenly shed its skin, as if every gay man were sixteen again and all the men about whom he had ever fantasized—those cowboy and construction worker wannabes cruising in front of Harvey Milk's camera store, for example—were suddenly available for a smile. Promiscuity was "the *lingua franca,* the Esperanto of the male homosexual community," in the words of the novelist **Andrew Holleran.** Paul Goodman's pre-Stonewall cruising of "sailors and Gentlemanly Cs" seemed quaint compared to the character in **Larry Kramer's** 1978 novel, *Faggots,* who summed up a year of sexual activity in his Seven Star Mini Diary:

> *Dates leading to orgasm: 87 (not counting street tricks, the tubs, or Fire Island; definitely not counting The Meat Rack).*
> *Dates interesting enough to want to see again: 2*
> *Dates seen again: 23*
> *Refusals: 23*
> *Tubs attended how many times: 34*
> *Discos danced at how many nights: 47 (not counting Fire Island)*

There were still plenty of men who lived in monogamous gay couplings—and an even greater number who were married to women and took their gay sex where they could find it, if at all. But, especially in the large metropolitan areas, gay male couple relationships were frequently open ones, with plenty of room for outside sexual adventures. The novelist Edmund White, in his 1980 book of nonfiction, *States of Desire: Travels in Gay America,* described the prevailing mores in trendsetting New York City this way: "Sex is casual, romance short-lived; the real continuity in many people's lives comes from their friends."

In those days, no one worried much about sexually transmitted diseases. Syphilis and gonorrhea could be cured by a quick visit to the doctor. Hepatitis B was a little scarier—a harbinger of things to come—but not scary enough to spoil the fun.

The new openness about homosexuality and the diminishing police harassment contributed to the establishment of a commercial world surrounding gay male sexual activity. Bathhouses, porno theaters, and "backroom" bars proliferated, estimated to represent a $100 million industry in the United States and Canada. Sex could be experienced in surroundings of bourgeois comfort—the Australian writer Dennis Altman observed that one Chicago bathhouse offered six types of Twining's tea—or in the self-conscious squalor of S&M backroom bars, like New York's Anvil and the Mineshaft.

The most famous of the early sex palaces was the Continental Baths, located on Manhattan's Upper West Side. In the early seventies, the Continental Baths became a haunt of the beautiful (mostly heterosexual) people. The Continental wasn't just a gay bathhouse—its basement level featured a dance floor and live entertainment. **Bette Midler** got her start there (another unknown named **Barry Manilow** accompanied her on the piano). On weekends, well-dressed heterosexual couples would watch the floor show, surrounded by homosexual men who drifted down from upstairs in towels. (Nongay patrons were forbidden entrance to the upper three floors.) Dennis Altman noted the contradictions—the bright lights and glitter of the basement entertainment area contrasting with the half-lit complex of lockers and cubicles on the upper floors. He marveled that a bathhouse designed for sodomy, fellatio, and other sex acts that were illegal in New York State had become the latest "in-spot." The gay sex upstairs provided a "particular frisson of excitement" to the straight patrons downstairs, Altman thought. And he couldn't resist pointing out the limits of liberation, bathhouse-style: "A gay man with $15 can get both sex and entertainment at the Continental and know he is mixing with the beautiful people. He might still turn up to work on Monday and be fired for being a fag."

As the seventies wore on, gay male sex, which in previous decades had often been quick and anonymous out of anxiety or necessity, was increasingly becoming quick and anonymous out of choice. The joy of cruising, of chatting up those "sailors and Gentlemanly Cs," the egalitarian, barrier-breaking qualities of promiscuity that Paul Goodman had touted, were being lost amid the ease and availability of it all. In the gay ghettos, particularly in New York City, a certain decay was setting in. In his New York chapter in *States of Desire*, Edmund White caught the flavor of the changing mores:

Street cruising gave way to half-clothed quickies; recently I overheard someone saying, "It's been months since I've had sex in bed." Because back rooms exist, everyone can parade the streets, exchanging glances but not submitting to the uncertainty of negotiating terms ("Your place or mine?" "What are you into?"); everyone knows that after all (or nothing) is said and done, there's a free blow-job waiting for him at the back of the Strap. . . .

At the same time, gay male culture began to take on an orgiastic quality, fusing sex and public spectacle. White's travels in gay America took him to the "Black Party" at Flamingo, the most popular dance bar in New York City. Only members and their guests were admitted; "black" meant mostly leather. The inner room was full of shirtless men casually watching the entertainment, which turned out to be "hired musclemen garbed as centurions or deep sea divers or motorcylists," striking poses on raised trestles along one wall. Everyone in the audience could have been put on professional display themselves, White thought, "since the crowd was extraordinarily muscular." On the dance floor, the crowd was packed so tightly that "we were forced to slither across each other's wet bodies and arms. . . . Freed of my shirt and my touchiness, I surrendered myself to the idea that I was just like everyone else. A body among bodies."

The trends of "fast lane" urban gay male culture of the seventies—the anonymity of the sexual encounter, the merger of sex and spectacle—reached their high point at the most famous (or infamous) bar of the period, the Mineshaft. The Mineshaft was an S&M backroom bar located on two windowless floors in New York's meatpacking district, just a few blocks from the Hudson River. (A version of the bar's interior was featured in a scene in **William Friedkin's** murder mystery *Cruising,* a film whose dark and violent portrait of gay life made it the target of protests in the late seventies.) The Mineshaft had its own dress code—designer clothes of any kind were forbidden; so were suits, ties, dress shoes, drag, and cologne. Except for the bar's front room, talking out loud was discouraged. That would spoil the mood. For the Mineshaft was a stage on which almost every imaginable fantasy was acted out in ritual fashion. There were no live sex shows as at another famous bar of the period, the Anvil. Here, the spectators themselves were the performers.

In his article "The Mineshaft: A Retrospective Ethnography," University of Nebraska sociology professor Joel I. Brodsky described the bar in detail. The main upstairs room, called the "playground," featured slings from which men who wanted to be fist-fucked were suspended. The bartender provided paper cups of Crisco and handfuls of paper towels to those performing the fisting. Two flights down was still another large room, whose darkened corners were the setting for more run-of-the-mill sex, between pairs or in groups. There was a section with wooden stalls, featuring glory holes, and in another section stood several bathtubs, where men sat—sometimes naked, sometimes clothed—waiting for others to urinate on them.

Edmund White, another visitor, viewed all this self-conscious decadence with a sense of humor. He emphasized the hazy, unfocused quality of the place. You would see a friend at the front bar and gossip with him for a few minutes. Then you'd enter the back rooms and wait for your eyes to adjust to the darkness. White went on, "You touch, with your blind hand, something that feels like a—could it be? Yes, it is—a shoeshine stand. A man dressed as a cop is having his shoes polished."

But White also recalled one night standing in a crowd at the Mineshaft and "watching something unspeakable" when a man next to him suddenly crashed forward, landing on his face. He was unconscious and bleeding profusely. White dragged him out to the cloakroom. "A treacherous combination of booze and downs," he concluded. The man was eventually revived and sent by cab to the emergency room at St. Vincent's Hospital.

The Mineshaft was closed down by the New York Department of Health in 1985, at the height of the AIDS epidemic.

The emphasis on sex that characterized life for many gay men in the seventies had its critics, even at the time. But criticism was difficult because almost everyone participated to some extent in the new sexual culture. As early as 1974, Dennis Altman was expressing the concern that the explosion of the gay commercial scene was giving many men the illusion that oppression was a thing of the past. "Growing hedonism does not mean a resolution of the guilt and self-hate so deeply imbued in us," he wrote in an essay called "Fear and Loathing and Hepatitis." Altman suggested that the persistence of such negative feelings might explain the upsurge in interest in S&M, bondage, "water sports," and humiliation. He added:

> *If I were persuaded that these represented a working out of aggression and frustration, leaving the participants better able*

to cope with the violence of modern society, I could join those who see shit, fist-fucking, and leather as a further stage in liberation. I can only view it as evidence of the enormous ambivalence, and perhaps, boredom that has accompanied growing "freedom."

For his part, David Goodstein, publisher of *The Advocate*, was critical of the young gay men who hung out on Castro Street and showed no interest in improving the community. "I oppose the gay obsession with sex," Goodstein told Edmund White. "Most gay men have their lives led for them by their cocks. In return for ten minutes of pleasure they design the rest of the day." White couldn't help but note that Goodstein's magazine represented one "of the largest emporia for gay sex through its advertisements." In White's view, the irony of the publisher of *The Advocate* complaining about promiscuity to White, the coauthor of the book *The Joy of Gay Sex*, was just too exquisite for words.

In *Dancer from the Dance*, the most celebrated gay novel of the decade, Andrew Holleran created a world of mythic glamour that focused around a group of characters who "could not stop dancing." They moved with "the regularity of the Pope from the city to Fire Island in the summer, where we danced until fall and then . . . we found some new place in Manhattan and danced all winter there." Among the group were assorted souls who had "no idea what they were doing on earth" and had a "crazy look in their eyes because their real happiness was only in music and sex."

For many gay men, it wasn't just sex that summed up the seventies; it was dancing and disco music as well. As a musical form, disco began in small black gay clubs in New York City. There, deejays "overlapped soul and Philly (Philadelphia International) records, phasing them in and out to form uninterrupted soundtracks for non-stop dancing," according to Anthony Thomas, who wrote about the roots of house music in the gay magazine *OUT/LOOK*. The result was a continuous fabric of pulsating rhythm that completely dominated the dance floor. White gay bars had traditionally featured black music, ignoring the rock 'n' roll played in white straight bars. By 1974 or so, disco had come to dominate white gay bars. The music was truly underground: Gay bars and a few black clubs were the only places you could encounter it. The first disco hits of the mid-1970s that "crossed over" to a mainstream audience—songs by black singers **Gloria Gaynor** and **Donna Summer**—received their first major exposure in gay clubs.

Disco was, above all, dance music. The lyrics were largely unimportant. In fact, in some cases, lyrics barely existed at all—Donna Summer's hit song "Love to Love You Baby" was made up of not much more than repetitions of the title lyric to the sound of a pulsating synthesizer. Disco lyrics rarely, if ever, addressed social issues, nor did they have any overt gay content (the closest they came to gay content were Gloria Gaynor's "I Will Survive" or the **Village People's** campy "YMCA"). There were few gay performers, either—the black gay singer **Sylvester** ("Disco Heat" and "Fever") was an exception.

But disco's lyrics couldn't be dismissed altogether. They glorified sex and sensuality, themes that were perfectly in tune with an evolving culture in which there was perhaps little more to be said than "Love to Love You Baby." Gay men had always identified with female vocalists—particularly black female vocalists from **Billie Holiday** to **Diana Ross**—pouring out songs of unrequited love. Disco carried on that tradition. The new musical form also offered up its own divas for veneration, such as Donna Summer, the quintessence of disco glamour. (Summer's gay public deserted her later in her career, however, when she became a born-again Christian and was quoted as saying that AIDS had been sent by God to punish homosexuals.)

Disco was pop music in Cinemascope. As such, it required an outsize setting—the discotheque. By the middle of the decade, gay bars were becoming larger and more visible. If, in the past, most gay bars had been dark and furtive places, now there were spacious, bright discos with high-tech light shows, mirrors and mirror balls, and an air of glamour and celebration. The new gay discos became associated with upward mobility: They were places to see and be seen and to show off one's body, one's clothes, one's dancing. The "disco bunny," who, like Holleran's characters, lived only to dance, became a fixture of gay culture. And because the only white bars where disco could be heard were gay bars, heterosexuals began to patronize gay clubs, sometimes taking them over. Gay nightlife became part of the larger culture. Gays were the trendsetters in music, in dress, and on the dance floor. You could bring your straight friends to a gay disco, something unheard of in homosexual bars in the past.

The emergence of disco also demonstrated the power of the gay consumer for the first time. In the mid-to-late seventies, **Neil Bogart,** president of Casablanca Records, was estimating that gays represented 25 percent of disco record sales in the United States. It took a while before record companies began to advertise in the burgeoning gay media. But in 1980, when disco had given way to the more mainstream (and less gay-oriented) "dance music," Warner Brothers' dance music department was spending 10 to 15 percent of its print-advertising budget in publications like *The Advocate* and *Christopher Street.* "If I can get the blacks, the Hispanics, and the gays to agree on something, do you think I can create a trend musically?" **Ray Caviano,** executive director of dance music for Warner Brothers, asked a reporter at the time. "You bet I can. There is some hot blood running through all these three."

By 1976, with the crossover success of performers like Gaynor and Summer, purists were already muttering that disco was dead. Heterosexual discos began to open. It wasn't "our music" anymore. The film *Saturday Night Fever,* starring **John Travolta,** represented the apex of disco's move into mainstream culture. If disco wasn't the exclusive province of gay clubs anymore, its performers were no longer almost exclusively black, either; on the heels of the success of *Saturday Night Fever,* the **Bee Gees,** a white Australian group, became the hottest disco property. The (racially mixed) Village People, which played with macho gay fantasy stereotypes—the cop, the construction worker—gained popularity toward the end of the decade, but it was a last gasp.

Within gay culture, disco didn't die as much as simply play itself out. (By 1977, its successor, "house music," with its emphasis on drums and percussion, was making its debut at Chicago clubs.) Disco had moved gay culture out of the shadows and into the light, an important development at the time. Yet as Holleran wrote in *Dancer from the Dance:*

> For that is the curious quality of the discotheque after you have gone there a long time: In the midst of all the lights, and music, the bodies, the dancing, the drugs, you are stiller than still within, and though you go through the motions of dancing you are thinking a thousand disparate things. . . . You stand there on the floor moving your hips, wondering if there is such a thing as love, and conscious for the very first time that it is three-twenty-five and the night only half-over. You put the popper to your

nostril, you put a hand out to lightly touch the sweaty, rigid stomach of the man dancing next to you, your own chest is streaming with sweat in that hot room, and you are thinking, as grave as a judge: What will I do with my life? . . .

If, as Holleran suggests, a sense of disillusion was slowing setting in with the culture of sex and disco, it wasn't allowed to take its natural course. Many were forced to ask Holleran's question, "What will I do with my life?" long before they were emotionally and psychologically prepared to do so. As the eighties arrived, AIDS would show the limits of the world that gay men had created in the euphoric decade after Stonewall, pointing the way to a very different kind of community.

CHAPTER 26

LESBIAN NATION AND WOMEN'S MUSIC

THE LESBIAN-FEMINIST CULTURE that emerged in the United States in the 1970s took a very different direction from that of gay men. If gay men celebrated sex, lesbians honored a more abstract idea of woman-loving. If gay men created a community that seemed to mirror mainstream society, lesbians tried to forge one that was more utopian, more in line with countercultural values.

Interestingly, music—disco for the men and "women's music" for lesbians—played a formative role in both cultures. The "Black Party" at New York's Flamingo disco had its equivalent in women's concerts and music festivals. Both offered particular kinds of affirmations—the shirtless, sweating men exulting in a long-repressed sexuality; the women standing together, locking arms, and singing in unison at the end of a concert by **Holly Near** or **Cris Williamson.** Until the political backlash toward the end of the seventies, lesbian-feminists and gay men rarely socialized or worked together politically. Both groups were too busy creating their own cultures; neither necessarily saw the other as an ally.

The increasing identification with feminism created a political agenda for lesbians that went far beyond equal rights. The leading lesbian-feminist theorists of the period, such as Rita Mae Brown and Charlotte Bunch, argued that, in order to overthrow the patriarchy, *all* women should become lesbians. Not to do so was to collaborate with the enemy, i.e., men; by remaining heterosexual, women were simply "polishing their chains," in Brown's words. While some women were clearly lesbian in their orientation—having had sexual feelings for women for as long as they could remember—for others, becoming involved in a relationship with another woman or identifying as lesbian was genuinely a "choice." That choice was a political one—opposing the male-dominated system. "When I came out [in the seventies], I didn't even get that you were a lesbian for sexual reasons," said **Susie Bright,** sexual rebel of a later era. "It was almost like another political challenge."

In fact, sometimes lesbian relationships of the period were hardly sexual at all. Lillian Faderman suggests that in some cases they were not very different from the romantic friendships between women toward the end of the last century. In a 1978 essay, the poet and essayist **Adrienne Rich** would contend that all women lived within a "lesbian continuum," which included a range of "women-identified experience," not simply "the fact that a woman has had or consciously desired genital sexual experience with another woman."

Women adopted their own terminology to distinguish themselves from homosexual men—and from lesbians of the pre-feminist period. They were no longer "gay girls"; the word *gay* was too male. They took pejorative expressions from the past such as "lesbian" and "dyke" and made them their own. Many women who had come out in an earlier period still couldn't stomach the words *dyke* or *lesbian,* which had too many ugly and unpleasant connotations. They stuck doggedly to the term "gay woman" to define themselves.

The aim of post-Stonewall lesbians was to establish an alternative, egalitarian, women-centered culture—a Lesbian Nation, to use the term coined by *Village Voice* critic Jill Johnston. There was no attempt to transform patriarchal institutions, to make them more humane: These were viewed as a lost cause. Some women took the path of total lesbian separatism, determined to have no interactions with men whatsoever. Although separatists were always a minority, they had a profound influence on lesbian-feminist culture in general.

Lesbian-feminism was predominately a white middle-class movement. To a large extent, it also was a nonurban movement, in constrast to that of gay men, who tended to flock to the "liberated zones" of the big cities. Rural communes proliferated: Rita Mae Brown and other Radicalesbians led the way when they left New York City in the early 1970s to settle in rural Vermont. College towns, like Northampton, Massachusetts, and Boulder, Colorado, became lesbian havens. Lesbians who did live in large metropolitan areas often didn't live in the gay male ghettos (they were too expensive, for one thing), but settled on the fringes—in Berkeley and Oakland, instead of San Francisco's Castro; in Boston's Jamaica Plain and Somerville instead of the South End.

In the 1970s a variety of "women's" institutions were established that were largely—although not entirely—run by lesbians and were part of the construction of a Lesbian Nation. There were women's bookstores, credit unions and health clinics, food co-ops and child-care centers. Women's publishing companies started up: Naiad Press, established in 1974, which became the longest-lasting of the lesbian small presses, and Daughter's Press, which brought out Rita Mae Brown's coming-of-age novel, *Rubyfruit Jungle* (later published in a mass-market edition by Bantam in 1977). Faderman notes that, at one point, lesbian-feminists actually explored the possibility of setting up their own quasi-legal system, like the independent Jewish courts of pre–World War II Eastern Europe.

The lesbian-feminist value system was a rigid one, strongly influenced by the counterculture. As Faderman wrote, "In their youthful enthusiasm, lesbian-feminists believed that they had discovered not just a path but the only path." The terms "politically correct" and "politically incorrect" came into wide use. In *Odd Girls and Twilight Lovers,* Faderman listed a number of the "dogmas" of lesbian-feminism. Among them were:

- Nonhierarchy. Collective decisions should govern the running of all lesbian and women's institutions and businesses.
- There should be no leaders. "Star tripping" was strongly frowned upon. Women like Rita Mae Brown, Kate Millett, and Elaine Noble, who received a great deal of media attention, were viewed with suspicion.
- Downward mobility was prized. Making money—unless it was "purely" obtained—was politically incorrect.
- Women who worked at nontraditional jobs were widely admired. Middle-class professionals were, with a few exceptions, seen as "selling out."
- The working class was generally "superior" to the middle class.
- Stylish clothing, high heels, skirts, dresses, and makeup were frowned upon.

Sexual lives were not exempt from dogmas of political correctness. In a culture that encouraged women to "choose" to become lesbians, bisexuality was viewed as particularly threatening. The "butch/femme" culture, which had dominated the lesbian social order for so many years, was dismissed as politically retrograde, as a replication of male-female coupling, a sign that you "had a prick in your head." Anything that smacked of roles or objectification or nonegalitarian sex was strongly criticized. As Faderman noted, women were supposed to look butch and to have sex with other women who looked butch.

Writer Joan Nestle, who a decade later became a strong proponent of the revival of butch/femme culture, described how in the post-Stonewall period, femmes in particular were objects of scorn. "At gatherings of the seventies, if a woman walked in wearing makeup, lipstick, nail polish, even heels, she would not be spoken to, or asked to leave," Nestle recalled. "She was viewed as the enemy." The result was the "exclusion of a whole community of women."

Some of the old butches and femmes adapted to the new orthodoxy as best they could. Others faded from sight. A butch/femme "underground" persisted in working-class and black and Latino communities, and among women in prison. One study of "lower-lower-class" black lesbians in central Harlem during the mid-1970s showed that only 17 percent of those surveyed would *not* identify themselves as either butch or femme. The butch lesbian was "a fixture on the [black] ghetto scene," the study found. Faderman quotes a Boston woman who, in relating battles between different factions at the Cambridge Women's Center, emphasized the class divisions that divided the lesbian-feminists from the butch/femme women. "Who were these people to come out of their middle class and tell us what being lesbian was supposed to mean?" she demanded. "They even took over the term 'dyke.' Here they were from their rich, sheltered backgrounds wearing their dyke buttons. They didn't have to go through the name-calling we suffered through. Their version of being a lesbian was 'fashionable.' How could they understand what butch meant to those of us who had lived it?"

Despite the determination of many women to create a separate culture, there were some institutions where lesbians and gay men continued to work together. The National Gay Task Force (later renamed the National Gay and Lesbian Task Force) always had male and female co-executive directors and worked on issues of concern to both communities. Lesbians who held leadership posts in NGTF's early days included the first codirector, **Jean O'Leary,** a former nun, and **Ginny Vida,** who served as media director. As previously noted, *The Gay Community News (GCN),* the Boston-based weekly newspaper founded in 1973 (and for many years the only gay weekly in the United States), was one of the few gay publications where lesbians and gay men successfully worked together. The Fellowship of Metropolitan Community Churches (MCC) was another place where lesbians and gay men worked (and worshiped) together; many of the ministers were women. In smaller communities, gay bars and political organizations tended to be more mixed, because neither gay men nor lesbians had sufficient numbers to function on their own.

Yet these mixed groups were exceptions rather than the rule. For a large number of women, it was the ideals of lesbian-feminism, of creating a world according to a whole new set of values, that provided a tremendous sense of exhilaration in the post-Stonewall era. As the singer Holly Near put it, referring to women's music, "We were going to change the world. It was not unlike how the Black Panthers or the hippies felt. Women experienced the same kind of surge of self-discovery and self-love and purpose and vision. Revolution has to come from a state of profound excitement. We were in a state of profound excitement!"

"Women's music" was a major glue that held the lesbian-feminist culture together in the 1970s. Unlike disco—which was performed primarily by heterosexual musicians and recorded by mainstream record companies—women's music was recorded and distributed by women and performed at women's coffee houses, concerts, and music festivals. Women's music started off as folk music but soon encompassed a variety of styles, including blues, salsa, and soul. Lyrics were sometimes overtly lesbian—**Meg Christian's** "Ode to a Gym Teacher," for example, or Cris Williamson's "Sweet Women." In other cases, they involved genderless love ballads.

Although it was called "women's music," in reality, as Holly Near pointed out, it was essentially lesbian music. To have used that term, however, would have scared off too many women. "There was an inherent understanding on the part of lesbians," said Near, "that not all women knew if they were lesbians or not." One purpose of the new music was—very gently, in a nonthreatening manner—to coax women out of the closet, to make them aware of feelings toward other women, feelings that might not always be sexual, but often were.

In the earliest days, women's music was synonymous with Olivia Records, a recording collective first established by a group of five lesbians who lived in Washington, D.C. Eventually the women all quit their jobs and moved to the West Coast, living in a collective household in Los Angeles. Olivia's first recording was a single with a song by Meg Christian on one side and a song by Cris Williamson on the other. Olivia's first LP soon followed—*I Know You Know*, by Christian. The collective initially hoped to sell 5,000 albums; the record sold 75,000. In 1975, Cris Williamson's *The Changer and the Changed* was released. It sold 250,000 copies and remained for many years the biggest seller in the history of women's music.

When no company would agree to distribute Olivia's recordings, the collective recruited women around the country to function as its own distribution network. Producers were reluctant to produce concerts by its artists, so Olivia found women in different cities to do the job instead. As a result, women's production companies sprung up nationwide. "In a big city, the first concert would draw two hundred people, then a thousand," recalled **Judy Dlugacz**, Olivia's president. By 1977 and '78, Olivia had moved its headquarters to the San Francisco Bay Area and had released ten albums, featuring new performers like **Teresa Trull, Linda Tillery,** and **Mary Watkins.**

Soon, however, Olivia was not the only company producing women's music. During this same period, Holly Near, a Bay Area singer best known for her opposition to the Vietnam war, was attempting to land a mainstream record contract. When she failed, she established her own company, Redwood Records. In 1976, Near came out as a lesbian.

Perhaps the most controversial thing that women's recording and production companies did was to produce "women-only" concerts. This immediately caused a great stir. "What we were saying was that there had never been a place for women to see each other in such a positive way and to know each other in such numbers," said Olivia's Judy Dlugacz. "For the first two years, we tried to create these spaces. By doing so, we were able to create community. We enabled more women to come out than anything did." Olivia abandoned the practice after two years. However, women's music festivals, which proliferated around the country, continued to exclude men (and sometimes kept out the male children of festival-goers as well). The first women's music festival was held in Champagne, Illinois, in 1974.

Recording stars like Holly Near, Meg Christian, Cris Williamson, and **Margie Adam** became important role models to young lesbians. They were as close to "leaders"—if not idols—as the deliberately leaderless movement of the 1970s was willing to accept. A Birmingham, Alabama, musician of a later period, **Lissa LeGrand,** described how the personal lives of these performers affected other women. She pointed out, for example, that alcoholism was an issue for many lesbians and that some performers were vocal about being recovering alcoholics: "People could say, 'Margie Adam, I know her story. She is a recovering alcoholic.' Or Meg Christian. So a lot of people were not just drawn to the music. They could see the performers as women who had gone through hard times, who had been addicted to something harmful. 'She got over it. Maybe I can, too.' It has not been just the music but also the philosophy and politics exemplified in the lives of entertainers that have been an important focus for women." (Within a few years, Holly Near became less of a role model, however, when it became known that she was dating men.)

By the early 1980s, however, the popularity of women's music had peaked. The euphoria of the early years faded. Ronald Reagan was in the White House; the postfeminist era had arrived. In addition, female performers were starting to be more accepted in the recording industry than in the past. Mainstream artists like **Cyndi Lauper, Tina Turner, Patti LaBelle,** and, later, **Tracy Chapman** and **k.d. lang** began to compete for the female dollars. "You'd find more dykes at a Tina Turner concert than you would at a Holly Near concert," Near herself observed. And as the eighties wore on, more and more lesbian singers attempted to achieve success through more traditional channels, although in most cases they had to remain in the closet. Among younger lesbians, women's music was viewed as passé: There was a widespread feeling that shared sexual orientation did not require a uniformity of cultural tastes. Yet no one could deny the role that women's music had played in creating community in the seventies, which made it significantly easier for lesbians to come out in the years that followed.

During the Reagan years, some of the more utopian aspects of lesbian-feminist culture began to fade as well. Women were becoming more upwardly mobile and career-oriented, especially as economic opportunities widened. Particularly among younger lesbians, a reaction set in against lesbian-feminist dogmas regarding appearance, sex, and money. Creating a separate culture seemed increasingly unrealistic and perhaps not even desirable. And as the political backlash intensified, it became clear that it was essential to work alongside gay men to oppose the growing power of the Religious Right; AIDS drew lesbians and gay men together, too. Pockets of separatism and political purism remained, of course. But there was a greater sense of self-confidence and of options—and a feeling that there wasn't just one way to be a lesbian.

CHAPTER 27

THE 1980S: THE AGE OF AIDS

T HE FIRST INDICATIONS that something was wrong came in January 1981, when a thirty-one-year-old gay man arrived at the emergency room at UCLA Medical Center in Los Angeles with a fungal infection in his throat that almost completely blocked his esophagus. Two weeks later he developed *Pneumocystis carinii* pneumonia (PCP), a lung infection previously seen almost exclusively in cancer or transplant patients. Immunologist Dr. **Michael Gottlieb** was mystified. At about the same time, Dr. **Alvin Friedman-Kien,** a New York University dermatologist, was examining a gay man for Hodgkin's disease and noted some unusual purplish-red spots on the man's legs. Other physicians dismissed them as bruises, but to Friedman-Kien, they appeared to be Kaposi's sarcoma (KS), a rare form of skin cancer usually found in older men of Mediterranean ancestry. Two weeks later, Friedman-Kien saw another similar case, again in a gay man. He telephoned a colleague in San Francisco, who reported that he had encountered two such cases among gay men there. In the summer of 1981, Gottlieb and Friedman-Kien detailed their findings in an article in the Centers for Disease Control's *Morbidity and Mortality Weekly Report.* Whether the patients in question had PCP or Kaposi's sarcoma or both, the physicians noted that they all showed an unexplained lowering of immune function.

At first no one quite knew what to make of the new disease—or even what to call it. Was it perhaps, as some physicians suggested, the result of using amyl nitrates ("poppers"), the sexually stimulating inhalants popular among many gay men? Or was the new disease the result of "immune overload," in which the body was exposed to so many kinds of diseases—syphilis, gonorrhea, hepatitis, for example—that the immune system simply collapsed? Was it caused by a virus? And if so, were there perhaps one or more cofactors needed to trigger its effects? Was it transmitted sexually or could it be spread by casual contact as well? How long was the incubation period? And was it always fatal?

The new disease was dubbed the "gay cancer"; it was called

"Saint's disease," a reference to the popular New York gay club frequented by many of the group first diagnosed; it was also referred to as Gay-Related Immune Deficiency (GRID). When it was revealed that members of other groups—hemophiliacs, Haitian immigrants, recipients of blood transfusions, intravenous drug users, the sex partners (and sometimes children) of those carrying the virus, and millions of heterosexual men and women in Asia, Africa, and Latin America—were also infected, it was clear that the disease wasn't necessarily "gay" after all. It was given a new name—Acquired Immune Deficiency Syndrome, or AIDS.

In January 1983, two years after the first cases were seen in the United States, researchers at the Pasteur Institute in Paris isolated what they believed to be the virus that caused the disease. A year later, Dr. **Robert Gallo** in the United States announced that he had done the same. The French called it LAV; the Americans called it HTLV-III; eventually the nomenclature settled on was HIV (Human Immunodeficiency Virus). Two more years later, in March 1985, the U.S. Food and Drug Administration licensed the first test to detect the antibody to the virus.

In the intervening period, scientists had learned a great deal about AIDS. They learned it was spread through blood or blood products, through sharing of hypodermic needles, and through sexual contact involving an exchange of body fluids. They determined that it could not be spread through casual contact and that unprotected anal sex was the most "efficient" way to transmit the virus, with the receptive partner most at risk. They estimated that the incubation period for full-blown manifestations of the disease could be many years—five, ten, even fifteen. But although scientists learned all this, in a relatively short period of time, they still couldn't find a way to prevent AIDS or treat it.

Soon, the numbers in the United States began to grow alarmingly: 1,300 infected as of April 1983, by official count: 8,797 by the middle of 1985, with half of them already dead. Of the number of recorded cases, more than 70 percent were gay and bisexual men. By 1985, surveys indicated that extremely high percentages of sexually active gay men had tested positive for HIV: 50 to 60 percent in some studies in New York City and San Francisco, 25 percent in Pittsburgh and Boston.

· · ·

The first reaction in the gay community came in an article in the August 24, 1981, issue of the *New York Native,* the city's gay newspaper, written by the novelist and screenwriter Larry Kramer. Headlined "A Personal Appeal," the article began, "It's difficult to write this without sounding alarmist or too emotional or just plain scared." Kramer went on:

> Today I must tell you that 120 gay men in the United States—most of them here in New York—are suffering from an often lethal form of cancer called Kaposi's sarcoma or from a virulent form of pneumonia that may be associated with it. More than thirty have died.
>
> By the time you read this, the necessary figures may be much higher.
>
> The men who have been stricken don't appear to have done anything that many New York gay men haven't done at one time or another. We're appalled that this is happening to them and terrified that it could happen to us. It's easy to become frightened that one of the many things we've done or taken over the past years may be all it takes for a cancer to grow from a tiny some-thing-or-other that got in there who knows when from doing who knows what.

Within the gay community early reactions varied—from the urgency of Kramer's appeal to confusion to outright denial. Toward the middle of the decade, once the antibody test was in place and more was known about transmission, a numbed kind of adjustment to living with the disease had taken hold. Then, by 1987 and '88, with so little progress being made and the Reagan administration seeming so uncaring, the accommodation to the dailiness of AIDS gave way to a wave of anger and protest.

It was obvious from the beginning that some of the sexual practices of gay men played a crucial role in the transmission of AIDS within the gay community. But because, for so many homosexual men in the post-Stonewall period, gay identity and culture had been expressed almost entirely in sexual terms, the new disease cut to the very heart of gay liberation. It threatened an entire way of life. Within the gay community (and without), the struggle to stop the spread of AIDS became a struggle over sex.

In New York City, Larry Kramer found himself at the center of this struggle. Kramer had written the screenplay for **Ken Russell's** highly successful film version of D. H. Lawrence's novel *Women in Love*. He was also the author of *Faggots,* a novel whose portrait of the New York–Fire Island world of "fast-lane" gay men had been harshly criticized in the American gay press as moralistic and self-loathing. (The Oscar Wilde Memorial Bookshop in New York City refused to stock the book for that reason.) Three of Kramer's friends had been among the early casualties of the disease. So in August 1981, shortly after Drs. Gottlieb and Friedman-Kien had published that first article about AIDS in the CDC's *Morbidity and Mortality Report,* Kramer brought Friedman-Kien and some eighty gay men together for a meeting at his New York apartment. There they raised $6,635 for Friedman-Kien's research. On Labor Day weekend, members of the same group canvased Fire Island. They staffed tables on the docks of the resort communities of the Pines and Cherry Grove, handing out brochures to arriving vacationers and trying to raise more money.

Six months later, Kramer brought a smaller group of gay men together at his apartment. Virtually nothing was being done about the disease, he told them. It was time to start an organization that would educate the gay community, take care of the sick, and fight for the rights of people with AIDS. The result was the organization to be known as Gay Men's Health Crisis (GMHC).

His reputation as a critic of gay male sexual mores, however, had made Kramer a controversial figure. He quickly came under attack for his suggestion in the *New York Native* that there might be a connection between the new disease and "one of the many things we've done or taken over the past years." To some sexual liberationists, this was heresy. In a December 21, 1981, letter to the *Native,* playwright **Robert Chesley** warned darkly:

> *Read anything by Kramer closely. I think you'll find that the subtext is always: the wages of gay sin are death. I ask you to look closely at Kramer's writing because I think it's important for gay people to know whether or not they agree with him. I am not downplaying the seriousness of Kaposi's sarcoma. But something else is happening here, which is also serious: gay homophobia and anti-eroticism.*

Despite the personal attacks on Kramer, within a year Gay Men's Health Crisis had established itself as the nation's premiere AIDS-service oganization. It gave out some three hundred thousand "Health Recommendation" brochures and set up an AIDS hotline; its programs offered legal and financial assistance, crisis intervention counselors, and individual and group therapy. It also set up a program of volunteer "buddies" to visit, do chores for, and provide emotional support for those who were sick. These programs became a model for AIDS-services organizations that sprung up in large cities around the country, largely started by gay men and lesbians. In that first year, GMHC had raised $150,000, in a community previously characterized by great reluctance to fund gay organizations and institutions. In its second newsletter, GMHC's board wrote, "We have never encountered so much love between men as we have felt in GMHC, and watching this organization grow in response to our community's terrible new needs has been one of the most moving experiences we have ever been privileged to share."

But there were things that GMHC was not doing that Larry Kramer believed it should be doing. Right from the start, Dr. Friedman-Kien had told Kramer that it was essential that gay men stop having sex or at least use condoms. Kramer wanted GMHC to take this public stance, but the GMHC board—on which Kramer served—was reluctant to do so. Kramer also wanted GMHC to be more confrontational in pressing the city of New York to provide funding for AIDS services (the city was doing nothing); again, GMHC's board hesitated. Kramer found himself in the midst of ongoing battles with other board members, notably **Paul Popham,** the closeted executive at McGraw-Hill who served as board president. In these confrontations, the popular, consensus-oriented Popham prevailed over the tempestuous Kramer. As Bruce Nussbaum wrote in his investigative account of the AIDS epidemic, *Good Intentions,* Kramer was someone who "lived with furies inside him. Every few minutes they rose up, and Kramer spiked into a hot, blistering anger. A calm would then settle on him, only to be replaced with yet another outburst . . . Larry Kramer was the Vesuvius of anger. He was one of the angriest men on earth. Kramer saw injustice everywhere. It was almost like an affliction."

The battles with Popham and other board members reached their culmination when New York Mayor **Ed Koch** finally consented to meet with two GMHC board members. Kramer assumed that he and Popham were the obvious choices to talk to the mayor, but Popham worried that Kramer might harangue the mayor and sabotage the meeting. Another board member was chosen to go in

Kramer's stead, and a miffed Kramer quit the board. (He would write his own version of these conflicts in his play *The Normal Heart*.)

Exasperating as he could be on any number of occasions, Kramer's "furies" served the gay community well, especially when his essay "1,112 and Counting" appeared in the *New York Native* in March 1983. The five-thousand-word article, the longest the *Native* had ever run, was a passionate call to action against AIDS. It began: "If this article doesn't scare the shit out of you, we're in real trouble. If this article doesn't rouse you to anger, fury, rage, and action, gay men may have no future on this earth. Our continued existence depends on just how angry you can get." The article concluded with the names of twenty dead men whom Kramer knew personally.

In his book *And the Band Played On*, Randy Shilts describes "1,112 and Counting" as "inarguably one of the most influential works of advocacy journalism of the decade." Even the city government of New York took notice: Two days after the article was published, Mayor Koch and Health Commissioner **David Sencer** announced the formation of an Office of Gay and Lesbian Health Concerns. In some respects, the new office was merely a bureaucratic sop, but it showed the power of Kramer's rhetoric.

The influence of "1,112 and Counting" was felt as far away as San Francisco. It was there that the apocalyptic political battle of the early AIDS years took place—the conflict over closing the gay bathhouses. The lines were drawn in early 1983 in a controversy over whether information about the prevalence of AIDS in San Francisco's gay community should be released at all. In January of that year, two researchers from the University of California Medical Center prepared to release findings that showed that one out of every 333 gay men in the Castro had been diagnosed with AIDS. But, according to Randy Shilts's account, when the researchers held meetings with a group of gay physicians and representatives of the city's three gay Democratic clubs, the consensus was against publishing the findings; they feared publication would cause an antigay backlash. Nonetheless, the study was leaked to Shilts, a reporter at *The San Francisco Chronicle*, who ran the story.

Soon after, the Harvey Milk Democratic Club voted to publish a pamphlet warning about sexual transmission of AIDS. The club also tried to convince bathhouse owners to post warnings about high-risk sex. The bathhouse owners refused. Meanwhile, the Milk club's **Bill Kraus** had written a letter to the *Bay Area Reporter*, the local gay newspaper, that echoed Kramer's "1,112 and Counting." Kraus wrote: "We believe it is time to speak the simple truth. . . . Unsafe sex is—quite literally—killing us. . . . When a terrible disease means that we purchase our sexual freedom at the price of thousands of our lives, self-respect dictates it is time to stop until it once again is safe." (An aide to California Congressman **Philip Burton** until Burton's death in 1983, Kraus emerges as one of the heroes of *And the Band Played On*.)

In March 1984, gay activist **Larry Littlejohn** announced that he planned to file an initiative petition to ban all sexual activity in San Francisco's gay bathhouses. Only 7,332 signatures were needed to put the proposition on a citywide ballot; once that happened, there was no doubt that it would pass. All eyes turned toward **Mervyn Silverman**, the city's public health director. One side of the gay community, specifically the Harvey Milk Democratic Club, vehemently wanted him to shut down the baths; the other side, including the Alice B. Toklas Democratic Club and the city's gay press, were just as vehement in insisting that the bathhouses remain open.

There were approximately thirty publicly licensed bathhouses, bookstores, and clubs in San Francisco where gay sex took place. Only 5 to 10 percent of gay men went to the baths, according to surveys. Yet the fate of the bathhouses quickly became the overriding issue in the gay community. Those who favored shutting the bathhouses saw it simply as an issue of saving lives, compared to which all other considerations were secondary. Those who wanted to keep them open believed that the bathhouses represented sexual freedom and gay liberation—everything gay people had been fighting for since Stonewall and before. Once the baths went, the bars could be next and after that, who knew? There were also individuals and institutions with an economic interest in keeping the baths open— the bathhouse owners, obviously, but also San Francisco's gay newspapers, which were heavily dependent on bathhouse advertising.

The rhetoric, particularly on the pro-bathhouse side, reached extraordinary heights. At a public meeting, one opponent of bathhouse closing screamed at Larry Littlejohn, "You have given the Moral Majority and the right wing the gasoline they have been waiting for to fuel the flames that will annihilate us!" Another accused Littlejohn of "genocide." Shortly after a group of proponents of closing the baths officially requested Public Health Director Silverman to do so, the *Bay Area Reporter* editorialized, "The Gay Liberation movement in San Francisco almost died last Friday morning at 11 A.M. No, that's not quite it. The Gay Liberation Movement here and then everywhere else was almost killed off by sixteen gay men and lesbians last Friday morning. The group, whose number changed by the hour . . . signed a request or gave their names to give the green light to the annihilation of gay life." The newspaper then published a "traitor's list" that included Harry Britt, the city supervisor who was Harvey Milk's successor; Bill Kraus; and Larry Littlejohn, "father" of the initiative.

In early October 1984, after a series of delays, Dr. Silverman finally ordered the closing of the baths, comparing them to "Russian Roulette parlors." "These fourteen establishments are not fostering gay liberation," he said. "They are fostering disease and death." Much legal wrangling followed this decision—at one point, a Superior Court judge told the bathhouse owners they could reopen if they hired monitors and removed patrons who engaged in high-risk sex. But once Silverman made his decision, the bathhouse fight was essentially over. The baths never reopened. Eventually the issue just faded away.

Beyond the merits of the arguments on both sides, the bathhouse controversy signified whether San Francisco's gay community was ready to face up to AIDS; as such, it was a turning point. (New York and Los Angeles closed their bathhouses a year later.)

Meanwhile, other important developments were taking place. In the midst of the controversy over the bathhouses, in April 1984, Dr. Robert Gallo announced his finding that HIV was the cause of AIDS. A year later, **Margaret Heckler,** the Secretary of Health and Human Services, announced the licensing of the antibody test. It was now evident what caused AIDS and how the disease was transmitted; no one could claim anymore, as some had done right up to the end of the bathhouse battle, that HIV was not spread by unsafe sex. Despite its imperfections, the antibody test meant that gay men could now find out whether or not they were HIV-positive. The hysteria surrounding the epidemic began to abate somewhat. Gay men in San Francisco—and in other cities around the country—now had to live with AIDS as an everyday fact and adjust their lives accordingly. In an interview with author Frances FitzGerald in *Cities on a Hill,* San Francisco psychotherapist **Leon McKusick** suggested that the gay community was going through the same stages many individuals did when they were confronted with a life-threatening illness—denial, bargaining, and, finally, acceptance.

"The community has now accepted AIDS," he said. The personal began to overtake the political—at least for a while.

In April 1985, when she returned to the Castro after covering the bathhouse controversy the year before, FitzGerald found a very different place. The tourists had vanished, as well as a number of the most expensive gift stores and boutiques. Among the gay men she had known the year before, dogmatism (about issues like the closing of the baths) had disappeared, and denial had been replaced by an "extraordinary stoicism." She wrote:

> The gay bars were still there, and on Saturday mornings the street would fill up with young men ... Most looked like all other men of their age, and most were clearly doing Saturday errands, having been at work all week. The Castro was still a gay neighborhood, but it had lost its "gender eccentricities." It was a neighborhood much like the other white, middle-class neighborhoods surrounding the downtown ... [It was] stable and domesticated.

When novelist Andrew Holleran returned to New York City for periodic visits during the 1980s, he found the city "shrunk to a single fact." It was a cemetery. At the end of a day spent visiting friends in hospital rooms—"intelligent, brave, accomplished men breathing oxygen through tubes, staring at a brick wall," Holleran would run, not walk, straight to a porno theater on Fourteenth Street and Second Avenue called the Metropolitan. Nothing else quite provided the same degree of comfort. It was like crawling back into the womb—"dark and quiet and calm." To Holleran, the Metropolitan and places like it were all that he felt were left of male homosexuality, or at least the central—sexual—aspect of male homosexuality. By 1987, the bright lightbulbs of safe sex had replaced the legendary darkness of the place: There were mostly black and Puerto Rican men watching heterosexual porn movies and a few desultory sexual acts going on in corners—"no clumps, no orgies; none of the feeding frenzies that, even before the plague, made one wonder what it all meant." For Holleran, the Metropolitan provided an escape from the reality of gay New York in the eighties; it was also home.

AIDS presented an enormous personal challenge to gay men, both the sick and the well. Those who had made sex and sexual encounters the key ingredients of who they were and how they thought about themselves were compelled to refashion their lives, to find new areas of meaning. For a long time, confusion reigned. There were those like Holleran who would obsessively visit old haunts and cruising spots, go through the old motions, but with the excitement and the sense of conviction gone out of it all. There were those who denied anything was happening and risked their lives to prove it. Others retreated into celibacy; still others grabbed on to the first monogamous relationship in sight.

The thirtyish owner of a small Boston computer firm exemplified many of the dilemmas of gay men of the period—and some of the solutions. Until AIDS arrived, this man had led a comfortable life. He didn't have a lover, but he and his closest friend spent many an evening at the Bird Sanctuary along the Charles River, where anonymous sex with other men was easily available. But when, within a period of two months, his two closest friends were both diagnosed with AIDS, he realized he couldn't lead his life as before. He stopped frequenting his cruising haunts and eventually became involved in a relationship. He started playing volleyball in a gay sports league. He began to question his life. Before AIDS, he said, "the future was always bright. Things were always looking up." Now he was asking the question "How should a man live?" Should he push to build up his company? Just enjoy himself? Try and create something more lasting in terms of community organizations or institutions? If AIDS hadn't come on the scene, if he hadn't seen two close friends cut down in the prime of their lives, he would never have asked those questions. He marched in his first gay pride march. He started volunteering at the AIDS Action Committee—Boston's version of Gay Men's Health Crisis. It marked the first time he had gotten involved in any kind of gay-oriented community organization.

Still, the foundation of his life had changed. For people his age, he noted, "Sex was such a big part of our identity. You have to redefine things. I had a fairly comfortable self-image and lifestyle that has been radically altered. As it turns out, the things I have changed to are a lot more enjoyable." Still, he said, "I am in mourning. Those days seem fun in retrospect. I am not so sure they actually were. But I hate having things taken away from me."

By the middle of the decade, safe sex had established itself as the norm for most gay men. There was a growing sense that a sexual middle ground was possible—that one could reduce the number of sexual partners, forgo high-risk sexual practices, and still lead a relatively satisfying sex life. For those who still wanted an updated version of seventies gay mores, "jerk-off parties" and commercial JO clubs came into fashion. At one New York JO club, the public-address system blared, "No Unsafe Sex, No Drugs," and an employee walked around conspicuously making sure people obeyed the rules. AIDS-service organizations around the country began offering "Eroticizing Safer Sex" workshops.

Even if sex became more secure than it had seemed at the beginning of the epidemic, a different kind of community began to emerge, one that didn't revolve primarily around sexual pickups and cruising. Becoming an AIDS "buddy" replaced being a disco bunny as a rite of passage for many gay men. As the bars and cruising areas declined in importance, new kinds of organizations and institutions rose to take their place: Twelve-step groups, sports leagues, and gay churches and synagogues. A sense of social conservatism set in. With less need to be at the center of the action, gay men began to settle outside the confines of the gay ghettos. In Boston, for example, gay social and political groups were formed in a number of the city's outer neighborhoods, such as Dorchester, Jamaica Plain, and Allston-Brighton.

The interest in gay sports was reflected in the establishment of the Gay Games. The creation of **Tom Waddell**, a San Francisco physician and former Olympic decathlete, the first Gay Games took place in San Francisco in 1982. (The U.S. Olympic Committee successfully sued to bar the use of the name "Gay Olympics.") Gay Games II, held in San Francisco in 1986, featured some 3,500 athletes from 37 states and 17 countries. Later Gay Games were held in Vancouver in 1990 and New York City in 1994. The New York Games, coinciding with the twenty-fifth anniversary of Stonewall, attracted 11,000 participants and were among the gay "mega-events" of the nineties.

The prominence on the scene of gay and lesbian religious groups went beyond the already-established MCC churches (270 congregations in ten countries by the late 1980s). An association of gay Pentecostal churches was established, with congregations in Oklahoma City, Houston, and Dayton, Ohio. There was a black gay evangelical church in Washington, D.C., that in many ways seemed indistinguishable from black churches anywhere. Gay and lesbian synagogues started up in a number of cities. The San Francisco synagogue even featured a religious school for the children of its members.

Another striking development was the forging of closer bonds between lesbians and gay men. Lesbian separatism was proving increasingly less viable; gay male culture didn't appear as sex-focused and thus as alien to women as in the past (some lesbians were experiencing a sexual revolution themselves—see "The Great Lesbian Sex Debates," page 467); and the AIDS crisis underscored the need for mutual caring. So the two communities—so divided in the 1970s—began to move closer together. Moreover, the "lesbian baby boom" of the late 1980s—with many women having children through artificial insemination—brought growing numbers of lesbians and gay men into coparenting arrangements.

Many of the social changes in the lives of gay men might have occurred anyway if AIDS hadn't come along. The aging of the "baby boom" generation, the more conservative social climate, the gradual lessening of social hostility toward homosexuals, an increasing sense of self-confidence and self-esteem, were all factors in pushing gay values more toward the "stability and domesticity" that Frances FitzGerald had seen in the Castro. But the arrival of AIDS unquestionably accelerated the process, individually and collectively.

In his book *States of Desire,* written before the onset of AIDS, Edmund White seemed to anticipate the shift. He wrote:

> I can picture wiser people in the next century regarding our sexual mania as akin to the religious madness of the Middle Ages—a cooperative delusion. I feel that homosexuals, now identified as the element of our society most obsessed with sex, will in fact be the agents to cure the mania. Sex will be restored to its appropriate place as pleasure, a communication, an appetite, an art; it will no longer pose as a religion, a reason for being. In our present isolation we have few ways besides sex to feel connected to one another; in the future there might be surer modes for achieving a sense of community.

As the eighties began, the combination of the AIDS epidemic, right-wing backlash, and the election of Ronald Reagan (allied to the Religious Right) as president threatened to halt the political gains the gay and lesbian movement had made in the previous decade. Antigay forces were quick to take advantage of public concern with AIDS, equating homosexuality and disease. Syndicated columnist (and later, presidential candidate) Pat Buchanan was in the forefront. "The sexual revolution has begun to devour its children," he wrote in a May 1983 column. Homosexuals, he said, were "a community that is a common carrier of dangerous, communicable, and sometimes fatal diseases." Buchanan pronounced AIDS to be "nature's revenge. . . . The poor homosexuals: they have declared war on nature and nature is exacting an awful retribution." The July 1983 issue of *Moral Majority Report* featured a cover with a typical white American family—Mom, Dad and two children— wearing surgical masks. The headline read: AIDS: HOMOSEXUAL DISEASES THREATEN AMERICAN FAMILIES.

Meanwhile, *Human Events,* the right-wing weekly, was taking an even more incendiary path, reporting that "there has even been speculation that AIDS victims could deliberately contaminate the blood supply, thus spreading the condition into the general population, as a way to make certain that there is increased pressure on the federal government to find a cure." In Texas, a group called Dallas Doctors Against AIDS was working toward reinstating the state sodomy laws, with public-health concerns as its rationale. In Nevada, in the summer of 1983, the Pro-Family Christian Coalition attempted to cancel the annual Gay Rodeo on the basis that it was a health hazard.

The newest version of the disease model of homosexuality— combined with public fears about the spread of AIDS through blood transfusions and food handling—led many gay men to fear a national witch-hunt, even quarantine. That never happened, of course. In fact, a surprising degree of gay political and social progress continued in many parts of the country. In 1983, at the height of public AIDS hysteria, Boston and Minneapolis elected their first openly gay city councillors—David Scondras and Brian Coyle. That same year, Key West, Florida, a resort town that was experiencing an influx of homosexual migrants, elected an openly gay man, **Richard Heyman,** as mayor. Despite the negative social impact of the epidemic—the increase in violence against homosexuals, for example—AIDS helped give the gay community increased visibility. It seemed to create as much sympathy as it did fear, giving homosexuals a human face. When actor **Rock Hudson** died of AIDS in 1985, there was a shift in the national attitude toward the disease. At least in terms of public rhetoric, AIDS became the nation's "number-one health priority." In many segments of society, support for AIDS causes became chic, especially when actress **Elizabeth**

Taylor began associating herself with efforts toward finding a cure as a board member of the American Foundation for AIDS Research (AmFAR).

It was only after the death of Hudson—five years into the epidemic—that President Ronald Reagan delivered his first policy speech on AIDS. Afraid to antagonize its supporters on the Religious Right, unwilling to marshal federal resources on social issues, the Reagan administration stubbornly refused to allocate any significant research or education money toward AIDS. Year after year through the 1980s, the Reagan administration would propose a niggling amount of money to fight the disease; Congress would then significantly increase AIDS funding over administration objections. In its proposed 1986 budget, made public just before Hudson's death, the Reagan administration proposed *reducing* AIDS funding by 10 percent, at a time when the numbers of cases of AIDS in the United States were doubling every six months.

The twin effects of the epidemic and the Reagan administration's neglect strengthened the gay community as a political force during this period. Before AIDS, few gays and lesbians had participated in their own civil rights struggle. The emphasis placed by activists on repeal of the sodomy laws and passage of antidiscrimination legislation failed to galvanize most homosexuals. The issues were too abstract. The gay middle class tended to look down on the movement as too "radical" and were loathe to support it, financially or otherwise. Lesbians, in many cases, identified more with women's issues than gay issues. National gay organizations were weak; over the years no visible national leaders had emerged (Harvey Milk came closest). Only when there was an external threat—Anita Bryant's "Save Our Children" campaign or the Briggs Initiative in California—did the community mobilize to any significant extent.

But AIDS changed all that, bringing into the movement many gay men—and lesbians, too—who had never participated in any gay political activity before. It was literally a matter of life and death. The involvement of many middle-class gay men in AIDS-services organizations around the nation led inexorably to political activity once it became evident that the Reagan administration was unwilling to commit significant resources to fight AIDS. Wealthy gay men who had never taken gay organizations seriously in the past opened their checkbooks when their friends started dying. Lesbians who had worked on women's health issues and could identify with government neglect regarding AIDS began to feel they might have a place in the mainstream gay rights movement. The death of so many gay male activists created a void that lesbians began to fill. In San Francisco, for example, where gay politics had been entirely a male preserve, lesbian rights lawyer **Roberta Achtenberg** ran a strong but unsuccessful campaign for a state assembly seat in 1989. The following year she was elected to the San Francisco Board of Supervisors, along with another lesbian activist, **Carole Migden**. In 1990, civil rights attorney **Donna Hitchens**, also a lesbian, was elected to the San Francisco Superior Court, defeating a sitting judge.

The two main national organizations—the National Gay and Lesbian Task Force and the Human Rights Campaign Fund—benefited from the new concern about political issues. By 1988, the Human Rights Campaign Fund (HRCF), which gives money to political candidates who support gay rights and AIDS issues, became the ninth largest PAC in the country. In 1983, the organization had raised $325,000; in 1988, its budget was $2.1 million. In the 1988 campaign, nearly 125 senators and congressmen accepted HRCF contributions. As they pushed for AIDS funding, the epidemic provided both national gay organizations visibility and credibility they had never had before. Suddenly, Congress and government departments were paying attention, even if the White House wasn't.

The changing situation brought new issues to the fore, notably parenting and family issues. This was due in part to the "lesbian baby boom." But AIDS was a major factor as well: As more and more gay men became sick, recognized ties became important to prevent a dying man's assets and possessions from reverting to his parents or other members of his "family of origin." Issues like domestic partner legislation and bereavement leave became new priorities for the movement. As early as 1982, the San Francisco Board of Supervisors voted to mandate that "domestic partners" of city employees be treated the same as spouses of married workers in terms of health insurance and bereavement leave (The bill was vetoed by Mayor Dianne Feinstein.) By the 1990s, a number of cities ranging from Seattle to Minneapolis to New York City permitted gay and lesbian couples to register their partnerships. In its last days, the administration of New York City Mayor **David Dinkins** offered gay and lesbian city employees health benefits for their domestic partners. And, in 1994, Vermont extended health and dental coverage to unmarried heterosexual and homosexual partners of state workers, becoming the first state to do so.

Overall, the 1980s were mixed in terms of gay political progress. In 1986, after fifteen years of trying, New York City passed its first gay civil rights bill, 21–14, a major victory for the movement. On the other hand, Houston repealed its law, in part due to public apprehension about AIDS. In 1989, Massachusetts became the sec-

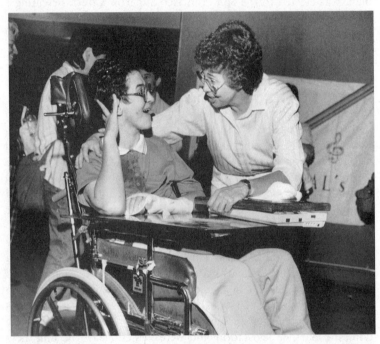

The struggle of Karen Thompson (right) to become the legal guardian of her lover, Sharon Kowalski (in wheelchair), emerged as a major lesbian cause célèbre in the 1980s. Kowalski, of St. Cloud, Minnesota, had become a quadriplegic and had suffered brain damage as the result of an automobile accident. After the accident, Kowalski's parents prevented Thompson, her lover of four years, from having any contact with her. Eventually, Thompson prevailed in a court decision that highlighted the growing importance of "family issues" among lesbians and gay men. The two women are pictured together in San Francisco in June 1990. (© *Rick Gerharter, Impact Visuals*)

ond state in the U.S. (after Wisconsin) to enact a gay rights bill. But the state's governor, **Michael Dukakis**, also promulgated the state's first executive policy to discriminate actively against homosexuals, by barring gays from being foster parents. Representative Barney Frank of Massachusetts became the first member of the U.S. House of Representatives to come out of the closet of his own free will. (His colleague Representative **Gerry Studds** had revealed his homosexuality a few years before, after being censured for having sexual relations with a House page.) But no one else in Congress was rushing to follow their examples.

One area where AIDS had a particularly negative effect was in attempts to repeal sodomy laws, still on the books in almost half the states. Progress was stalled because legislators in few of these states were disposed to vote for sodomy law repeal, lest they be accused of contributing to the spread of AIDS. Given the situation, activists had hoped that the Supreme Court would overturn the remainder of these laws, providing a "quick fix." In 1986, however, an increasingly conservative Court upheld the Georgia sodomy statute in the case of *Bowers* v. *Hardwick,* affirming that individual states had the right to make laws declaring private sexual activity by consenting adults a crime. Justice **Lewis Powell** provided the decisive vote in the Court's 5–4 decision, unquestionably the major gay legal setback of the decade.

On Columbus Day weekend, 1987, hundreds of thousands of gay people marched on the nation's capital in a dramatic show of strength. Although it did not receive the publicity that a similar march would receive in 1993, the U.S. Park Police estimated that two hundred thousand people were in attendance; march organizers claimed six hundred thousand. Presidential candidate **Jesse Jackson** was among the speakers. The event featured the unveiling of the Names Project Quilt, composed of almost two thousand panels commemorating people who had died of AIDS. It was the size of two football fields, crisscrossed by pathways of canvas that enabled visitors to view each panel. (Roy Cohn, **Liberace,** and Rock Hudson each had their own panels.) The brainchild of San Francisco politico **Cleve Jones,** the quilt was an impressive symbol of the community pulling together. The weekend's activities were an expression of collective exhilaration and sadness. But the number of marchers and the emotions of the event failed to translate into national political clout: Three days later, both houses of Congress voted over-

The unveiling of the Names Project AIDS Memorial Quilt provided the most emotional moments of the 1987 lesbian and gay march on Washington. *(© Donna Binder, Impact Visuals)*

whelmingly to support an amendment by North Carolina Senator **Jesse Helms** to ban the use of federal funds for educational projects or programs that "promote or encourage, directly or indirectly, homosexual activity."

On a Tuesday night in March 1987, six months before the March on Washington, the decade entered a new phase. The setting was the monthly speaker's series at New York's Lesbian and Gay Community Center. Onstage, once again, was Larry Kramer, who started off by asking everyone on one side of the audience to stand up. "At the rate we are going, you could be dead in less than five years," he informed them. "Two-thirds of this room could be dead in less than five years." He went on to excoriate the Food and Drug Administration for its slowness in testing and approving experimental AIDS drugs. A billion dollars was being thrown at AIDS, but it was not buying anything that could save the two-thirds of the people in that room, Kramer said. There were now thirty-two thousand cases of AIDS in the United States. Something had to be done. He went on:

Today's front page of The New York Times *has an article about two thousand Catholics marching through the halls of Albany today. . . . That's advocacy! . . . Why are we so invisible, constantly and forever! . . .*

Did you notice what got the most attention at the recent CDC conference in Atlanta? It was a bunch called the Lavender Hill Mob. . . . They protested. They yelled and screamed and demanded and were blissfully rude to all those arrogant epidemiologists who are ruining our lives.

The speech was vintage Kramer—emotional, impolitic, always somehow on target. But this time it seemed to have caught the popular mood. The audience proposed following up Kramer's rhetoric with action. Two days later, three hundred people met and established a new organization—the AIDS Coalition to Unleash Power (ACT UP). The group decided to focus on one issue—to fight for the early release of all experimental drugs that could treat AIDS. Its motto would be "United in anger and committed to direct action to end the AIDS crisis." It was time for action—for screaming and yelling and being "blissfully rude," as Kramer would have it. The politics of anger had arrived.

Soon after ACT UP's founding, the new organization got the opportunity to show its mettle. Burroughs Wellcome, manufacturers of AZT, the only drug licensed to treat AIDS, announced that it was pricing AZT at ten thousand dollars for a year's supply. To ACT UP members, that price tag smacked of profiteering. So 250 people marched on Wall Street. They hung an effigy of FDA Commissioner **Frank Young** in front of a church in the heart of the Financial District. They passed out leaflets condemning Burroughs Wellcome for its pricing of AZT. Then they did something that hadn't been done before at gay rights or AIDS demonstrations— they sat down in traffic in the middle of rush hour, completely tying up lower Manhattan.

The Wall Street demonstration was a turning point. In June, sixty-three gay activists were arrested in front of the White House, protesting Reagan's AIDS policies. ACT UP chapters were established in Los Angeles, Boston, and Philadephia. Civil disobedience tactics began to spread from AIDS issues to gay issues that weren't directly related to AIDS. The day after the March on Washington, some 650 gays and lesbians were arrested on the steps of the U.S. Supreme Court, protesting the *Bowers* v. *Hardwick* decision upholding the state sodomy laws. (Interestingly, the majority of those arrested were women, a sign that lesbians were increasingly a force in gay politics—and a particularly militant force.) A few months later, in Boston, four hundred members of a group called Mass Act Out disrupted Massachusetts State House proceedings for several hours to protest the state senate's refusal to pass a gay rights bill. Fourteen demonstrators were arrested, including eight who handcuffed themselves to chairs in the visitors' gallery.

ACT UP represented a new generation in gay politics. Many of its members were gay men in their twenties who had never been involved in gay political activity before. A large number were HIV-positive. As **Andrew Sullivan** noted in an article in *The New Republic,* "The combination of nearing death and political activism makes for a unique phenomenon. ACT UP is not merely a brigade of gay rights activists. It is not even a countercultural crusade for the rights of others. It is a movement primarily designed to prevent the demise of its own." Not everyone in ACT UP was HIV-positive, to be sure. Large numbers of lesbians joined in, especially in the vanguard New York City chapter; many of the women were veterans of feminist and left-wing organizing and brought a political savvy that the male neophytes lacked. ACT UP meetings tended to have the flavor of those of the old Gay Liberation Front—they were long, anarchic, with decisions made by a laborious consensus process. The movement created a distinctive visual style, a kind of AIDS aesthetic, from its SILENCE = DEATH logo featuring a pink triangle against a black background to the "uniform" of short hair, white T-shirt, jeans, and boots favored by many of its male participants.

ACT UP "demos" were known for their keen sense of political theater and an ability to attract media coverage. Most famous was its October 1988 effort to shut down the Rockville, Maryland, headquarters of the U.S. Food and Drug Administration, where over a thousand people participated in a series of minidemonstrations over a nine-hour period. At one of the day's protests targeting the FDA's refusal to release sixty experimental drugs to people with AIDS, ACT UP members held a "die-in" in front of the agency. They lay down on the street and held paper "tombstones" over their heads that read: I DIED FOR THE SINS OF THE FDA; DEAD— AZT WASN'T ENOUGH; DEAD—AS A PERSON OF COLOR I WAS EXEMPT FROM DRUG TRIALS; I GOT THE PLACEBO—RIP. By the end of the day, 176 people had been arrested. And if ACT UP didn't exactly shut down the FDA, they came close. A quarter of the agency's employees failed to show up that day; those who did come to work spent much of their time staring out the window to catch a glimpse of the demonstration taking place outside.

Within a few years, the combination of ACT UP protest activities and the analytical work of the organization's Treatment and Data Committee produced major changes in the FDA approach to experimental drugs. Drug regulation was eased; drugs proven safe but not yet proven effective were made available to AIDS patients on a "parallel track." **Anthony Fauci,** head of the National Institute of Allergy and Infectious Diseases, actually began attending ACT UP meetings. Grass-roots organizations, like the Community Research Initiative, put further pressure on the FDA by doing their own drug research; drug undergrounds called "buyers' clubs" provided people with AIDS access to drugs they wouldn't have otherwise been able to obtain if they relied strictly on government protocols.

But if ACT UP could claim success on issues like drug policy, in other areas the organization's activities frequently seemed self-

Members of the ACT UP protest in front of the U.S. Food and Drug Administration headquarters in Rockville, Maryland, October 1988. (© *Marilyn Humphries, Impact Visuals*)

indulgent and counterproductive. Andrew Sullivan noted the organization's "Manichean vision," which made it an article of faith that there existed "no moral difference between negligent complicity in the AIDS crisis and the act of murder." This was particularly true regarding ACT UP zaps of the Roman Catholic Church. Journalist **Michelangelo Signorile** describes a zap of **Joseph Cardinal Ratzinger,** the German prelate, who was in New York for a speaking engagement at the invitation of that city's **John Cardinal O'Connor.** Ratzinger had written a paper for the Vatican that described homosexuality as a moral evil. As Ratzinger rose to speak at St. Peter's Church, a group of eight people in the crowd leaped to their feet and began to chant, "Stop the Inquisition!" Someone else yelled, "Antichrist!" and "Nazi!" Signorile himself jumped onto a marble platform, pointed at Ratzinger, and shouted, "He is no man of God—he is the Devil." Then there was the December 1989 zap at St. Patrick's Cathedral that featured ACT UP members stomping on communion wafers. Such behavior might have brought ACT UP media coverage, but it antagonized the public and turned strained relations between the gay community and the Roman Catholic Church in New York City into permanent enmity.

By the end of the decade, ACT UP radicalism spawned a new organization called Queer Nation that, through street theater and confrontation tactics, took gay visibility to dizzying new heights. Queer Nationals invaded shopping malls, singing "It's a Queer World, After All"; held "kiss-ins" at predominately straight bars and restaurants; marched through hostile neighborhoods, like Brooklyn's Bensonhurst, to protest gay-bashing. Queer Nation reveled in making use of parody and humor to make its points. In her book *Family Values,* San Francisco Queer National **Phyllis Burke** describes a "Heterosexual Questionnaire" that she and other Queer Nation members distributed to shoppers in one "action" at a suburban mall:

> *What do you think caused your heterosexuality?*
>
> *Most child molesters are heterosexual. Do you consider it safe to expose your children to heterosexuals? Heterosexual teachers, particularly?*
>
> *Is it possible that your heterosexuality stems from a neurotic fear of people of the same sex? Maybe you just need a positive gay experience.*

In line with its emphasis on gay visibility, Queer Nation pioneered the use of "outing" in an effort to push prominent gay people out of the closet, plastering New York City with pictures of closeted celebrities that read "Absolutely Queer." Outing violated the long-standing gay liberation tenet that held that although it was desirable for people to come out, they should do so at their own pace and their privacy should be respected. The major gay and lesbian organizations condemned the tactic, and the mainstream media was queasy. Washington Queer National **Michael Petrelis** held a news conference in which he attempted to "out" a number of senators and congressmen. The media showed up, but no one printed Petrelis's list. The New York gay magazine, *OutWeek*, edited by Michelangelo Signorile, was a major proponent of outing. *OutWeek*'s revelation of millionaire businessman **Malcolm Forbes's** homosexuality shortly after Forbes's death brought notoriety to the magazine and to Signorile. Signorile stated that one reason he wanted to "out" Forbes so soon after his death was "I felt that the historical record had to be corrected quickly, before a slew of biographies came out falsely saying that Elizabeth Taylor had been Forbes' lover." After *OutWeek* folded, *The Advocate* printed Signorile's article revealing that Pentagon spokesperson **Pete Williams** was gay. *The Advocate*'s editor, **Richard Rouilard,** was opposed to outing but claimed that Williams's situation was a "singular case" in view of the U.S. armed forces' policy of discrimination against gays and lesbians. In 1992, *The Advocate* found yet another exception, outing a Louisiana congressman with an antigay voting record; the congressman was easily reelected, however.

As with ACT UP, there was a sense of exhilaration and theatricality about Queer Nation that captured the imagination of many gays and lesbians, particularly the younger generation. The social conservatism that characterized the middle of the decade was fading, and Queer Nation encapsulated the new mood. But the organization's "in your face" tactics antagonized many others. Randy Shilts called Queer Nationals "brownshirts" and "lavender fascists." Some AIDS activists disparaged them as an "ACT UP for Negatives," who didn't know quite what to do with themselves. The increasing use of the word *queer* in place of "gay and lesbian" among the younger activists rankled many who remembered the term as an epithet. And outing divided the community. Yet as the decade ended, it was groups like ACT UP and Queer Nation that seemed to have the initiative. As the queer rap went:

> *We're here.*
> *We're queer.*
> *Get used to it.*
> *We're here.*
> *We're queer.*
> *We're fabulous.*

The AIDS decade had brought about extraordinary changes within gay and lesbian life—creating a deeper sense of community, putting gays in the public eye, restoring the fractured coalition between gays and lesbians. The community's response to the AIDS epidemic impressed the general public (and gays themselves) with a sense of homosexual men as courageous, caring individuals, not the frivolous pleasure-seekers that had been the image of the decade before. The Reagan and Bush administrations' appalling neglect of AIDS strengthened homosexuals as a political force and pushed certain sectors of the community into a militancy that hadn't been seen since the earliest days of gay liberation. ACT UP and Queer Nation tactics may have antagonized many, but they were symptomatic of gays' and lesbians' growing self-confidence and determination to stick up for themselves. There was no doubt that as the nineties dawned there was now a stronger, more committed gay community, hardened by adversity, that was poised to play a greater role in American life.

An Excerpt from Randy Shilts's
And the Band Played On

Randy Shilts's And the Band Played On, *published in 1987, remains the most influential book written about AIDS. It is a sweeping history of the early years of the epidemic, from the*

*first reported cases of the disease to the death of actor Rock
Hudson. The book is also an investigative account that indicts
the U.S. government, the scientific establishment, the blood
banks, and some of the leaders of the gay community for their
inaction in the early years of the epidemic. Shilts (1951–94)
was a reporter for the daily* San Francisco Chronicle *(the first
openly gay reporter for a major U.S. daily newspaper) and
covered the AIDS crisis almost from the beginning; his massively
documented* Conduct Unbecoming, *a portrait of the experience
of gays and lesbians in the U.S. military over three decades,
was published in 1993. He himself was diagnosed with HIV,
just as he finished writing* And the Band Played On. *The following excerpt from that book represents his tribute to the courage and fortitude of San Francisco's gay community during the
1980s:*

THE LOUDEST OVATIONS of the day [the 1985 San Francisco
Gay Freedom Day Parade] came not for politicians or entertainers,
but when the rally's master of ceremonies announced the release
of two San Francisco gay men who had been among the twenty-
nine Americans held hostage by terrorists in Lebanon. The two
men, who had been aboard TWA Flight 847 on an Athens-to-Rome
leg of a world tour, had spent most of their captivity living with
the terror that their fundamentalist Moslem captors would learn
that they were gay and kill them, as they had killed an American
serviceman on the flight.

Early in their captivity, San Francisco news organizations learned
that hostage Jack McCarty had worked as a chef for the Elephant
Walk on 18th and Castro streets, one of the city's most famous gay
bars, before embarking on the tour with his lover, postman Victor
Amburgy. With unprecedented restraint, local news organizations
withheld reporting on this angle of the story, fearing the gay story
would result in the two hostages' deaths.

In the long days of captivity, McCarty and Amburgy were kept
in dark, rat-infested basements while the terrorists played Russian
roulette with the hostages, again and again. When other hostages
began to crack, some of the Americans turned to McCarty, who
had seemed preternaturally calm. McCarty could not tell them the
reason he could handle the prospect of imminent death—that he
was a gay man from San Francisco. Instead, he adopted the role of

unofficial counselor to the other hostages. It was a role to which McCarty was accustomed; he had been a Shanti Project [a San Francisco AIDS-services organization] volunteer.

Throughout the ordeal, the forty-year-old chef recalled Scott Cleaver, a twenty-seven-year-old whom he had counseled as part of his Shanti work. McCarty had watched Cleaver muster incredible strength and courage to fight his terminal disease, and McCarty promised himself he would be as brave in the hands of these terrorists. The fortitude was something he shared with the other hostages, and it helped them all survive.

When Amburgy and McCarty stepped off the Air Force plane after their release, while a quarter-million lesbians and gay men celebrated Gay Freedom Day in San Francisco, they walked down the ramp arm-in-arm. They loved each other, and they were proud they loved each other, and they had survived in part because of the strength they had developed as gay men in San Francisco.

The Vatican Cracks Down

THE 1980s were a time of turmoil within American churches over the issue of homosexuality, as institutions traditionally condemnatory of same-sex relationships attempted to come to terms with changing social mores. The liberal Unitarian Universalists were offering church blessings to gay and lesbian couples. The Episcopal bishop of Newark, **John Shelby Spong,** called on his church to "open its eyes to reality" and do the same. The United Church of Christ formally ordained as a minister an openly gay man who was involved in a three-year relationship with another man. On the other hand, in the United Methodist Church, considered progressive on most social issues, a lesbian minister was put on trial in 1987 before a jury of thirteen Methodist clergy, charged with being a "self-avowed, practicing homosexual." Thirty-five Presbyterian churches around the U.S. declared themselves "More Light" churches, and in defiance of church rules barring homosexuals as church officers, were ordaining openly gay and lesbian ministers, elders, and deacons. Within a number of religious denominations, gay and lesbian groups—Dignity (Roman Catholic), Integrity (Episcopal), Affirmation (Methodist), Lutherans Concerned, and Presbyterians Concerned, among others—were pushing hard for their denominations to support gay rights and ordain gay and lesbian clergy.

But it was within the Roman Catholic Church that the debate was the fiercest. Under the stern leadership of **Pope John Paul II**, the Vatican was cracking down on dissent in a wide variety of areas, including homosexuality. The Reverend **John J. McNeill**, a Jesuit who, in his 1979 book, *The Church and the Homosexual*, had argued that monogamous and stable homosexual relationships could be morally good, was forbidden from writing or speaking publicly on the subject, and was later expelled from his order. Vatican curial officials stripped Father **Charles E. Curran** of his license to teach theology at Catholic University in Washington, D.C. Archbishop **Raymond Hunthausen** of Seattle lost his prerogatives in five key administrative areas. Both Curran and Hunthausen had dissented from Vatican views on sexual morality, including homosexuality. In St. Cloud, Minnesota, the Reverend **Bill Dorn** was dismissed from his post as the co-pastor of the Newman Center at St. Cloud University after writing in the diocesan newspaper that the Church has "a responsibility to develop a theology of sexuality that sees sexuality as a blessing and understands homosexuality as being part of a gift." Shortly after, Father Dorn publicly announced that he was gay and was ordered to take an indefinite leave of absence from the priesthood.

In the past, the Vatican had made a distinction between homosexual *inclinations,* which it regarded as "morally neutral," and homosexual *acts,* which were viewed as sinful. But in an October 30, 1986, document issued by the Congregation for the Doctrine of the Faith, the office charged with preserving the orthodoxy of Catholic belief, Rome significantly toughened its position, declaring that even an inclination toward homosexuality was "an objective disorder." The document stated:

> *Therefore special concern and pastoral attention should be directed towards those who have this condition, lest they be led to believe that living out this orientation in homosexual activity is a morally acceptable option. It is not. . . . It is only in the marital relationship that the use of the sexual faculty can be morally good. A person engaging in homosexual acts therefore acts immorally.*

The declaration also included an allusion to AIDS. It noted that advocates of gay rights did not appear to be concerned that "homosexuality may seriously threaten the lives and well-being of a large number of people." Although AIDS was not mentioned by name, a senior Vatican official told *The New York Times* that the document's language was "certainly" referring to the epidemic.

But the passage in the document that most affected the lives of gay and lesbian Catholics was the one that stated that all support should be withdrawn from any organization that undermines the teaching of the church on homosexuality, "which are ambiguous about it or which neglect it entirely." The group to which the Vatican referred was Dignity, the organization of gay Catholics that had one hundred chapters nationwide with five thousand members. Among other support activities for homosexuals, Dignity celebrated special masses in Catholic churches throughout the United States and Canada.

Quickly, bishops across North America moved to bar Dignity from celebrating mass on church property. Dioceses that rescinded permission for Dignity masses included Atlanta, Minneapolis, Buffalo, Brooklyn, Pensacola, and Vancouver. In Washington, D.C., Archbishop **James A. Hickey** ordered that Dignity no longer be permitted to use a chapel on the Georgetown University campus for weekly mass; Dignity had been holding mass at the chapel for the previous eleven years. In New York City, the archdiocese pressured the Church of St. Francis Xavier in Greenwich Village to discontinue Dignity masses, which had been taking place for eight years and drawing two hundred to three hundred people. "I would see no other way to interpret the decree from the Congregation for the Doctrine of the Faith," said New York's John Cardinal O'Connor. O'Connor gave the sanction of the archdiocese to a small group for homosexuals called Courage, which, unlike Dignity, insisted on celibacy for gay men and women.

In New York City, Dignity New York's president, **Timothy J. Coughlin,** described himself as "angry and hurt" at O'Connor's action. "We've done what the Archdiocese has failed miserably to do—give gay and lesbian Catholics a sacramental life, a sense of community, pastoral care, and a ministry to persons with AIDS," he said. In New York and other cities, Dignity simply moved its services somewhere else. The last Dignity masses were often emotional occasions. In Minneapolis, for example, at the final Dignity service at the Newman Center at the University of Minnesota, Dignity members stripped the altar and took down the chalice and banners and Easter candles. Carrying ceremonial ornaments in their arms and singing, Dignity members marched out of the church and across the street to the Episcopal university center, where they had been granted approval to hold services. In Manhattan, the last Dignity mass at the Church of St. Francis Xavier was similarly emotional and surprisingly euphoric.

But despite the gestures of defiance, the Vatican had succeeded in its aim: expelling gay groups from Roman Catholic churches. It just wasn't the same to celebrate mass in the chapel of an Episcopal church. The Vatican had created a new diaspora—a diaspora of gay and lesbian Catholics.

The Great Lesbian Sex Debates

IT WAS RITA MAE BROWN who back in 1975 first called attention to the lack of sexual options for lesbians when, disguised as a man (fake mustache and all), she snuck into a gay male bathhouse in New York City called Xanadu. There was no such thing as a lesbian bathhouse, and Brown thought that was a pity. She wrote in the Boston weekly *The Real Paper*:

> *I do want a Xanadu. I want the option of random sex with no emotional commitment when I need sheer physical relief. . . . It is in our interest to build places where we have relief, refuge, release. Xanadu is not a lurid dream; it's the desire of a woman to have options. Like men we should have choices: deep, long-term relationships, the baths, short-term affairs.*

Brown's was a voice in the wilderness of the 1970s, when sex was viewed as almost extraneous to the task of building a Lesbian Nation. Many lesbians were involved in political activities and institutions—the antiporn movement, Take Back the Night marches, rape crisis centers—that attempted to combat the sexualization of American culture and the abuses of sex. But by the early 1980s, some lesbians were beginning to reevaluate prevailing lesbian mores concerning sex and relationships—mores that dictated serial monogamy and frowned upon butch/femme role-playing, sado-masochism, and anything that smacked of the inequalities of heterosexual relations.

There seemed to be good reason for a reevaluation, for lesbian couples, by all accounts, weren't having sex very often. In the book *American Couples,* published in 1983, University of Washington psychologists Philip Blumstein and Pepper Schwartz found the frequency of sexual relations among the 788 lesbian couples they surveyed to be far less than it was for heterosexual or gay male couples. Among lesbian couples who had been together for between two to ten years, they found that 37 percent had sex once a week or more, compared to 73 percent for their gay male and married heterosexual counterparts. In part, such findings may have reflected differences in socialization between men and women, in particular cultual messages that discouraged women from viewing themselves as sexual beings. But some were convinced that the lesbian-feminist insistence on sameness and equality between sexual partners may have played a part in diminishing erotic feeling and sexual pleasure.

The subject came to the forefront in April 1982 at a lesbian conference called "Towards a Politics of Sexuality," held at Barnard College in New York City. Instead of presenting women as victims of sexual abuse and violence, conference participants portrayed various kinds of sex as enjoyable and affirming—including butch/femme and S&M. To some women, even to suggest this was heresy. The conference was picketed by members of the organization Women Against Pornography (WAP), who passed out flyers denouncing several speakers as "perverts."

Soon, the new lesbian sex radicalism turned into a full-scale movement. In 1984, two lesbian porn magazines were launched: *Bad Attitude,* published in Boston, and *On Our Backs,* based in San Francisco. (Two lesbian S&M magazines emerged as well.) Both *Bad Attitude* and *On Our Backs* featured erotic stories and illustrations; one issue of *On Our Backs* even offered a parody of a *Playboy* centerfold called "Bulldagger of the Season," a reference to a slang term for a butch woman. Boston and San Francisco—two cities where lesbians and gay men tended to work together politically—became the centers of the new movement, perhaps indicating the influence of gay men on their lesbian counterparts. Lesbian bars in San Francisco began featuring burlesque shows, something unheard of in the past. By the middle of the decade, the first porn videos made by women for women were produced.

Susie Bright, the *On Our Backs* editor, whom the *San Francisco Chronicle* described as an "X-rated intellectual," emerged as the ideologue of the new sex radicalism. She stressed the importance of lesbians freeing themselves from the antisexual "yoke"—the *Well of Loneliness* depiction of the lesbian as "the noble soul who will always put her principles above her sexuality." Exploring sex was akin to women breaking into a nontraditional job, she argued: "There is the sense of confidence, the sense of accomplishment, the power." Many lesbian-feminists didn't see it that way, however. They believed that efforts to "spice up" lesbian sex through butch/femme and S&M "validated the system of patriarchy, in which one person has power over another or objectifies her," as Lillian Faderman characterized their viewpoint. And they argued that sex radicals like Susie Bright were "deluding themselves and other women into believing that male images, fantasies, and habits were desirable for women, too."

Passions on both sides of the debate ran high. Joan Nestle, exponent of the butch/femme revival, claims that one member of Women Against Pornography went to Queens College, where Nestle worked, and warned students and faculty that Nestle was into S&M and "unequal patriarchal power sex." The popular women's music festivals were scenes of bitter confrontations over S&M workshops. Even the National Organization for Women joined the fray, reaffirming its support of lesbian rights but condemning issues like pornography, public sex, and sadomasochism, "which have mistakenly been correlated with Lesbian/Gay rights by some gay organizations."

By the late 1980s, however, the lesbian sexual revolution seemed to have peaked. Lesbian burlesque lost its audience; most of the sex magazines folded. A San Francisco bathhouse that had featured a lesbian night soon dropped it for lack of interest. The impact of AIDS put a brake on lesbian sexual experimentation, too, even though few, if any, cases of AIDS were believed to have been transmitted through sex between women.

As a result of the sex debates, however, many lesbians felt less constrained to follow the dictates of political correctness, and there was a greater freedom to talk about sex. The breakdown in conformity in sexual matters was another sign of self-confidence in lesbian community-building; it also was an indication that lesbians and gay men were drawing closer together. But Rita Mae Brown's "dream" that lesbians would abandon serial monogamy and take a much more uninhibited approach to sex went unrealized. "The encouragement of the sexual radicals was not sufficient to counter the greater forces of their female socialization," writes Lillian Faderman. "Thus lesbian sex radicals have remained a tiny minority within a minority."

Michel Foucault

WHEN THE AMERICAN NOVELIST EDMUND WHITE asked French philosopher and historian Michel Foucault (1926–84) how he got to be so smart, Foucault ascribed it, rather modestly, to his attraction to other boys. "I wasn't always smart, I was actually very stupid in school," Foucault told White. As a result, he was sent to a new school where "there was a boy who was very attractive who was even stupider than I was. And in order to ingratiate myself with this boy who was very beautiful, I began to do his homework for him—and that's how I became smart, I had to do all his work to just keep ahead of him a little bit, in order to help him. In a sense, all the rest of my life I've been trying to do intellectual things that would attract beautiful boys."

At the time of his death from AIDS in June 1984, Foucault was the most famous intellectual figure in France, perhaps in the world. He had written more than twenty books and had a profound impact on a number of disciplines—philosophy, history, criticism, political theory, and the history of sexuality. In his book *Madness and Civilization* (published in France in 1961), he examined Western attitudes toward insanity since the Middle Ages; in *Discipline and Punish* (1975), he took a critical look at the emergence of the "enlightened" modern prison; in the first volume of *The History of Sexuality* (1976), he questioned the accepted notion that the period between the sixteenth and nineteenth centuries had been characterized by sexual repression. He was engaged in many of the political issues of his time: At various points, he was a Maoist, a crusader for the rights of prisoners, and a gay liberationist. "In the eyes of his admirers, he had replaced Jean-Paul Sartre as the personification of what an intellectual ought to be: quick to condemn, determined to expose abuses of power, unafraid to echo Émile Zola's old battle cry, 'J'accuse!'," noted James Miller in his biography *The Passion of Michel Foucault*.

Associated with the poststructuralist French philosophers, Foucault rejected the liberal, humanistic view that saw history as an unending march of progress. He contended that human beings, instead of being "free," as Sartre believed, were at the mercy of historical forces. Power was the decisive factor in human relations, and attempts to improve or replace institutions were futile, only perpetuating them in different forms. As Foucault scholar Alexander Nehamas notes, the cornerstone of the philosopher's thinking (and what was particularly revolutionary about it) was his insistence that all human situations—as well as our opinions, habits, and institutions—are products of history, though we may be convinced that they are natural facts. "No philosopher has ever matched his ability to find history where others find nature, to see contingency where others see necessity," writes Nehamas. "He was the master at revealing the emergence of radically new objects—insanity, illness, even the human individual—where others had detected only a difference in the treatment of unchanging realities."

Foucault applied these ideas to sexuality, arguing once again that it was historical forces that created or "constructed" homosexuality as a concept and an identity. As noted earlier, he argued that the nineteenth century—with its relentless categorization of sexual "perversions"—had, instead of repressing sexuality, actually done the opposite. In the case of homosexuality, the early sexologists had transformed the sin of sodomy into the "personage," the "species" of the modern homosexual. Although Foucault noted that this development brought about increased social controls, the new categorization had another, more encouraging, effect:

> It also made possible the formation of a "reverse" discourse: homosexuality began to speak in its own behalf, to demand that its legitimacy or "naturality" be acknowledged, often in the same vocabulary, using the same categories by which it was medically disqualified.

Foucault's depiction of homosexuality as a social construct challenged assumptions that homosexuality and homosexuals had always existed as concepts from antiquity down to the present day. Although his work did not create the debate between "essentialists" and "social constructivists" among gay historians, Foucault's arguments made the constructivist view irresistible to many.

Although he resisted being known as a "gay" philosopher, in his later years Foucault became increasingly open about his homosexuality. He was one of the founders of the French magazine *Gai Pied* and contributed an essay to its first issue. He publicly campaigned for the enactment of a uniform age of sexual consent in France for heterosexuals and homosexuals, which was finally achieved under the Mitterrand government in 1981. In the early 1980s, he granted interviews to American gay publications, in which he argued that homosexuals had to create their own cultural forms. In a 1982 interview with *Christopher Street*, he said:

> It's not enough as a part of a more general way of life, or in addition to it, to be permitted to make love with someone of the same sex. The fact of making love with someone of the same sex can very naturally involve a whole series of choices, a whole series of other values and choices for which there are not yet real possibilities. It's not only a matter of integrating this strange little practice of making love with someone of the same sex into pre-existing cultures; it's a matter of constructing cultural forms.

The lover and companion of most of his adult life was **Daniel Defert,** political activist and (later) sociology professor, whom he met in 1960 when Defert was a philosophy student. "I have lived for eighteen years in a state of passion towards someone," Foucault said, referring to Defert, in a 1981 interview. "At some moments, this passion has taken the form of love. But in truth, it is a matter of a state of passion between the two of us."

If Foucault broke down barriers and challenged received ideas in his intellectual work, he did so in his personal life as well. He experimented with drugs, such as LSD. In the mid-1970s, while a visiting professor at Berkeley, Foucault became intrigued by San Francisco's gay S&M and leather subculture. James Miller suggests that Foucault's experiences in the S&M scene helped him develop his ideas about sexuality. In the bars and bathhouses of San Francisco's Folsom Street he saw new forms of sex (like fisting) evolve and older forms reinterpreted; this may have led him to the view that sex is socially constructed. Miller also claims that Foucault, long fascinated with death, sought it, perhaps welcomed it, in the bathhouses of San Francisco in the early years of the AIDS epidemic. He also suggests, with little substantiation, that Foucault may have deliberately spread AIDS to other men in those bathhouses.

Foucault's friend **Hervé Guibert** wrote a novel called *To a Friend Who Did Not Save My Life*, which features a character based on Foucault. The character returns to Paris from San Francisco with a hacking cough, extolling the virtues of the city's bathhouses:

> *That day, I said to him: "There mustn't be a soul left in those places, because of AIDS." "That's what you think. On the contrary, there have never been more people in the bath-houses, and it's become extraordinary. That hovering threat has created new complicities, a new tenderness, new solidarities. Before, no one exchanged a word; now people talk to each other. Everybody knows exactly why he is there."*

When Foucault died in June 1984, it was front-page news in every major French newspaper; one newspaper, *Libération*, even put out a special twelve-page supplement devoted to Foucault's achievements. The word *AIDS* was never mentioned, however. After his death, Daniel Defert established France's first national AIDS organization.

The Contradictions of the Gay Conservative: Terry Dolan

WHEN CONSERVATIVE POLITICAL ACTIVIST **John Terrence "Terry" Dolan** (1950–86) died of AIDS in December 1986, two memorial services took place. At one, held at Washington, D.C.'s, Dominican House of Studies, his family and political associates—including Senator **Orrin Hatch** (R-Utah) and syndicated columnist **Pat Buchanan**—paid their last respects. At the other, at St. Matthew's Cathedral, mourners included the openly gay former congressman **Robert Bauman** and fifty of Dolan's (mostly gay) friends; the Reverend **John Gingrich**, the cathedral's liaison with the gay community and Dolan's priest for the last six months of his life, celebrated mass.

The separate services pointed up the dilemma of being a gay political conservative in the United States, especially at a time when the Republican Party had allied itself closely with the Religious Right. Dolan had played a crucial role in the Reaganite ascendancy of the 1980s. As the founder and director of the National Conservative Political Action Committee (NCPAC), he was among the first people to take advantage of post-Watergate campaign finance laws that put no limitations on the amount of money an independent organization could spend to support a political candidate. In the 1980 election campaign, NCPAC targeted for defeat six of the most liberal Democratic members of the Senate. The organization spent $1.2 million, using a new and shocking strategy at the time—negative advertising. Four of the targeted senators—George McGovern, **Frank Church, Birch Bayh,** and **John Culver**—were defeated, tipping control of the Senate to the Republicans for the first time in twenty-five years. (Only **Alan Cranston** and **Thomas Eagleton** survived.) NCPAC also contributed $2 million to Reagan's presidential bid that year.

The 1980 campaign victories made the young Dolan a hero to the political Right—and anathema to many fellow gays and lesbians. (All the defeated senators were far more likely to support gay rights issues than those who replaced them.) Larry Kramer claims to have thrown a drink in his face at a cocktail party. But Dolan can't be dismissed as just another self-loathing gay-baiter of the Roy Cohn–J. Edgar Hoover school. It is true that he publicly denied being gay, even after a young federal employee named **Richard Anderson** signed an affidavit stating that he had had sexual relations with Dolan. But Dolan called himself "a constitutional conservative" and, in a 1982 interview with *The Advocate,* he said that "some of the rhetoric that some of my friends on the right have used on gay activism has been excessive" and "sexual preference is irrelevant to political philosophy."

Despite his organization's ties to the Religious Right, Dolan insisted that NCPAC itself never engaged in attacks on homosexuals. And yet the group did send out a fund-raising letter over the signature of Representative **Phil Crane,** which said, "Our nation's moral fiber is being weakened by the growing homosexual movement and the fanatical ERA pushers (many of whom publicly brag they are lesbians)." Dolan later apologized for the letter and claimed that it had been written without his knowledge or approval.

It was a difficult balancing act. In his last years, Dolan was said to be one of the prime movers behind the formation of a group of gay conservatives called Concerned Americans for Individual Rights (CAIR). Friends argued that he was moving increasingly toward the closet door. In an interview with the *Washington Post* after Dolan's death, Leonard Matlovich, gay military activist, said, "Terry was beginning—it's a long process. I can't condemn him for that. He was having more and more courage all the time...." But it is difficult to imagine that he could have kept his position at NCPAC if he came out.

Rumors about Dolan's private life did make it into the newspapers, and this unquestionably hurt his political standing within the conservative movement. Until his death, he denied having AIDS, claiming he was suffering from anemia and diabetes. (His family continued to deny it.) However, newspaper obituaries in *The New York Times* and *Washington Post* listed AIDS as the cause of death.

Dolan was not the only prominent gay right-winger of the Reagan period. Another was **Carl "Spitz" Channell,** whom White House aide Lieutenant Colonel **Oliver North** used to solicit contributions from wealthy conservatives to finance military assistance to the Nicaraguan contras. National Public Radio reported that some of the $10 million that Channell raised was paid to male companions of his organization's executives, including Channell himself, for unspecified services. Channell was indicted in the Iran-Contra scandal and pleaded guilty of conspiring to defraud the government. He later died after he was hit by a car while crossing a Washington street. Still another prominent conservative, Representative Robert Bauman, lost his bid for reelection after receiving a suspended sentence in 1980 for soliciting sex from a teenage male prostitute. Bauman then came out of the closet. The American Conservative Union, the organization he had founded, attempted to remove him from its board after he spoke out in support of gay rights.

Dolan's life and death indicate how much being a gay conservative had changed from previous decades. Dolan was clearly under pressure from other gays to come out. There was a supportive network of like-minded people ready to back him up. He felt he had to apologize for any appearance of "gay-baiting." And the media was less willing to cover up for him as it had done for homosexuals in prominent positions in the past. Death from AIDS provided the ultimate "outing."

Still, to be an American conservative and a Reagan supporter in the 1980s meant living in the midst of contradictions, especially as the Republican Party became increasingly identified with the Religious Right. It meant supporting an administration whose policies might actually kill you. Dolan died before he could find a way out of these contradictions—as those two memorial services showed.

The Gay Fiction Boom of the 1980s

IN THE 1970S, mainstream book publishers in the United States remained cautious about crowding their lists with books on gay themes. Still, the few gay novels that were published during the decade had an enormous impact on gay and lesbian audiences: **Patricia Nell Warren's** *The Front Runner* (the 1974 best-seller about a love affair between a gay track coach and his star runner); Rita Mae Brown's lesbian coming-of-age novel, *Rubyfruit Jungle* (originally published by a small women's press before it was released as a mass-market paperback in 1977); and Andrew Holleran's haunting 1978 portrait of "fast lane" gay culture, *Dancer from the Dance.* The success of these novels (and that of Edmund White's *A Boy's Own Story,* published in 1982) was an early indication that books aimed at a gay and lesbian audience could sell—and find some straight "crossover" audience, too.

Hungry for reflections of themselves and their lives that they couldn't find at the movies or on TV, gays and lesbians continued to take their images from fiction, as they had since *The Well of Loneliness.* At the same time, small gay and lesbian presses began to thrive, in the manner of women's record companies. By the early 1980s, virtually every gay community of significant size had its own bookstore, which often functioned as a community center as much as anything else.

By the mid-1980s, publishers were discovering a large gay male book-buying audience, particularly for fiction. St. Martin's Press was the pioneer in the area, thanks to openly gay editor **Michael**

Denneny; he later started St. Martin's own gay paperback line, Stonewall Editions. **Bill Whitehead,** an editor at Dutton, published Edmund White. (White was in a class by himself, particularly once Vladimir Nabokov named him the American writer he most admired.) Under the editorial guidance of gay literary "talent scout" **George Stambolian,** a series of anthologies called *Men on Men* showcased the works of less-established gay male writers. *Christopher Street* magazine excerpted new works of fiction, promoting prepublication interest. There was suddenly an enormous number of titles to choose from, including all kinds of gay genre novels—mysteries, gothics, Regencies, science fiction.

Despite the earlier success of *Rubyfruit Jungle* (and the continuing popularity of Rita Mae Brown's novels), major publishers remained leery of lesbian fiction—the lesbian book-buying audience was not thought to be as large or as affluent as that of gay men. As a result, small presses, like Florida's Naiad Press, remained in the forefront of lesbian publishing. (Genre novels were particularly popular among lesbian readers.) But change was in the offing there as well, as when Naiad author **Sarah Schulman** "jumped" from the small press to the mainstream with a gritty and slang-filled lesbian detective novel, *After Delores,* published in 1988. Moreover, older, more established lesbian writers like **May Sarton,** who hadn't written about lesbian subjects in the past, began to do so.

As all this was happening, the kinds of gay fiction being written were changing, too. The homosexual "problem" novel, in the manner of *The City and the Pillar* or *Giovanni's Room,* was no longer dominant. As the novelist and short-story writer **Richard Hall** noted in a 1988 essay in *The New York Times Book Review,* gay writing had evolved since World War II from "a literature of guilt and apology to one of political defiance and celebration of sexual difference." In fact, by the late eighties, a number of gay writers had gone even further, taking characters' homosexuality as a given and leaving it at that. The "high art" tradition of much of the earlier gay writing (Proust, Gertrude Stein, Djuna Barnes) was fading, replaced by more personal, smaller-scale realism. Gay novels didn't necessarily have to be artistic or experimental anymore to get published or to be taken seriously.

The kinds of characters that previously had been the norm in fiction about male homosexuals—the doomed heroes of *Dancer from the Dance,* the hustlers of **John Rechy's** *City of Night,* the romanticized criminals of French writer Jean Genet's works—were found less frequently as well. Writers like **David Leavitt, Peter Cameron, Armistead Maupin, Stephen McCauley,** and **Christopher Bram** mixed gay and straight characters, wrote about "ordinary" gay people, domestic life, and, increasingly, unusual family configurations. These themes reflected the "normalization" of gay life in the 1980s. Novels with lesbian heroines appeared on the lists of mainstream publishing houses: **Meg Wolitzer's** 1986 novel, *Hidden Pictures,* concerned two lesbians who move to the suburbs. British writer **Jeanette Winterson's** novel *Oranges Are Not the Only Fruit,* published in 1985, concerned a young girl growing up in an evangelical Christian family in the industrial Midlands. As Richard Hall wrote in his essay:

> *Finding a family of sorts has become the chief interest of characters in much gay fiction. Protagonists are settling down with relatives, heterosexual women, buddies, lesbians, lovers. Children, the final imprimatur to family life, are being borrowed, adopted, created by artificial insemination. Everyone is trying to get along under one roof. The sexual outlaw, long a staple of gay fiction . . . is giving way to the sexual in-law.*

By the end of the decade, AIDS became a central preoccupation of gay novelists. For some the subject remained almost too raw and painful to write about, yet few if any gay novels appeared without some reference to the epidemic. (Even lesbian writers like Sarah Schulman have tackled the subject.) Books that focused on AIDS often confronted the pain through humor. New York writer **David B. Feinberg's** *Eighty-Sixed* was characterized by an in-your-face, lacerating wit that was very much in the spirit of ACT UP; **John Weir's** *The Irreversible Decline of Eddie Socket* masked the pain with a humor that was sweeter and self-deprecating. British writer **Adam Mars-Jones** took a more minimalist approach.

Some older writers were uncomfortable with the perceived limitations of becoming known as a "gay writer." Gore Vidal mostly stayed away from the subject, insisting he wasn't gay but "homosexualist," anyway. And not all the "gay" writers reflected the trends of the decade. Two of the most admired English-language gay novelists of the 1980s, Edmund White and British writer **Alan Hollinghurst** *(The Swimming Pool Library)* carried forth more traditional homosexual artistic traditions. Australian Nobel laureate **Patrick White's** *The Twyborn Affair* and Jeanette Winterson's *Oranges Are*

Not the Only Fruit explored territories outside the prevailing "domestic" realism. What could be said, however, was that by the 1980s, gay and lesbian fiction was earning itself the right to be whatever its authors wanted: They could adopt different styles, tackle various genres, treat all kinds of subject matter. The only question was if—and when—the movies were going to catch up.

THE INTERNATIONAL SCENE

CHAPTER 28

COMMUNISM AND FASCISM

I̲N THE TWENTIETH CENTURY, the emergence of totalitarian regimes governed by ideologies that viewed homosexuality as a threat to state power put gays and lesbians under great pressure. This was true on both the political Left—in the case of the Soviet Union—and on the political Right—in Nazi Germany. Before World War II, the Soviet Union was the world's only Communist state; after the war, Eastern Europe fell under Soviet domination, and more home-grown Communists took power in China and, eventually, in Cuba. With the exception of East Germany, all these Communist regimes parroted the 1930s Soviet line that homosexuality represented a form of "bourgeois decadence" that had to be eradicated in the process of creating the new Socialist man and woman. In Fidel Castro's Cuba, a combination of Latin machismo and Communist ideology brought the force of the state down against gay men. And in Argentina, during the period of military rule in the 1970s and '80s known as the *Proceso,* a neo-fascist regime persecuted homosexuals with particular vehemence.

RUSSIA

Even after the death of Stalin in 1953, the Soviet Union itself remained extremely hostile to homosexuals and homosexuality. In a country where state control was almost total, no homosexual groups, organizations, or publications were permitted, and gay bars and bathhouses were unknown. There were well-known gay male cruising spots in Moscow and other cities—certain parks and cafes and the hall of the Bolshoi Ballet—but they were closely watched by agents of the KGB. Books on gay subjects or by gay authors were not published; the first two volumes of Proust's *Remembrance of Things Past* were translated and published in the Soviet Union in the 1930s, but the fourth volume, *Sodom and Gomorrah,* never made it into print. Crowded living conditions made it extremely difficult, if not impossible, for gay people (and heterosexuals, too) to have sex outside of earshot of nosy neighbors. Because government bureaucrats controlled the allocation of apartments, it was virtually impossible for a gay or lesbian couple to receive permission to live together.

In the 1976 November issue of *Christopher Street* magazine, George Schuvaloff described the situation this way:

> *Basically, gay life takes place in certain parks in summer, in the dark entry halls to apartment buildings (never locked in Russia), in country houses, and most of all in certain apartments which attract gays like magnets—not to have sex but just to meet friends, to listen to music, to talk.*

Prosecutions of gay men under the sodomy laws continued. Article 121 of the Soviet Criminal Code, revised in 1960, punished consenting sexual relations between adult men with a maximum of five years in prison. Homosexual acts with "aggravating circumstances"—such as sex with a minor—were punishable by eight years in prison. These prohibitions did not extend to sex between women. It isn't known precisely how many men were sentenced under these laws: Estimates ranged from six hundred to twelve hundred a year in the 1960s and '70s. The most famous of those convicted was the Armenian filmmaker **Sergei Paradjanov** (1924–90), director of the highly acclaimed *Shadows of Forgotten Ancestors*. In April 1974, Paradjanov was sentenced to six years in prison for homosexual activity, although his case was complicated by what Schuvaloff calls his "passion for diamonds and antique furniture and an incorrigible habit of dabbling in the black market."

In the years of *glasnost* and *perestroika* in the late 1980s, repression eased. The first gay and lesbian organizations were established; the Moscow City Council granted permission for publication of the country's first gay newspaper. Yet prosecutions of gay men for consenting sexual activity continued. The Soviet Ministry of Justice reported that from 1989 until the breakup of the Soviet Union, an average of five hundred men were jailed each year for homosexual activity. In a May 1993 article in the American gay magazine *Out*, Russian émigré writer Masha Gessen described a visit that she and other journalists made to a block of gay prisoners at a prison outside St. Petersburg. The prison warden and psychiatrist praised the humane treatment of gay prisoners whom they claimed were kept on the "depraved" squad for their own protection. Gessen reported:

They led us to the barracks, where we stood getting used to the near darkness, the air even more stale, the bunk beds closer together than I had been told. The windows . . . let through just enough light to make out the faces of the men, framed by prison-issue haircuts and the dark blue cotton of their uniforms, shiny with wear. . . .

"Three and a half years because the guy I'd had a relationship with testified against me." "The other prisoners don't eat with us, but we are safe if we eat later. . . ." "They used to beat me up when I first got here, but on this squad nobody touches me." Before leaving, our group offered cigarettes and money and asked how we might help. The prisoners sounded apologetic: "You can't." As our bus struggled out of the mud outside, men mounted on one another's shoulders to extend their arms out the narrow windows for a farewell wave, hands barely visible over the concrete prison wall.

In the spring of 1993, under the government of **Boris Yelstin**, homosexuality was decriminalized in Russia. The newly independent Baltic republics of Latvia, Lithuania, and Estonia repealed their sodomy laws as well. At the time the Russian law was repealed, some 73 men remained incarcerated in Russia for consensual gay sex and 192 more were in prison under the sodomy law in combination with another offense. By the end of 1993, no mechanism for reviewing their cases had been put in place, and many continued to languish in prison. Meanwhile, the gay and lesbian movement remained in its infancy. When gay activists announced the formation of Russia's first nationwide gay rights group in August 1993, the group's chairwoman wore a brown paper bag over her head at a Moscow news conference. "I can't show my face because of society's attitude toward homosexuals," said the writing on the bag.

CHINA

Chinese history is full of references to male homosexuality, often in high places. The first ten emperors of the Han Dynasty (206 B.C.–220 A.D.) are said to have kept young men as favorites in addition to female concubines and wives. Most famous of the imperial favorites was **Dong Xian**, the lover of the emperor **Ai** (6 B.C.– 1 A.D.). By the age of twenty-two, he had attained the highest offices and titles possible. The story is told that once when the emperor and Dong Xian were taking a nap, the emperor awoke to find the long sleeve of his gown caught under his sleeping lover. Rather than wake him, the emperor cut the sleeve from the gown and freed himself. This story was repeated to demonstrate the emperor's love and thoughtfulness. After this incident, all of Ai's courtiers imitated the cut sleeve. Since then, the term "passions of the cut sleeve" has been a common Chinese literary term for homosexuality. (Upon his death, Ai proclaimed Dong Xian emperor, but Dong Xian was unable to retain power and was forced to commit suicide.)

Western travelers to China remarked—unfavorably—on Chinese acceptance of male homosexual relations. The sixteenth-century chronicler Galeote Pereira wrote, "The greatest fault we do find [among the Chinese] is sodomy, a vice very common in the meaner sort, and nothing strange among the best." When he visited Peking in 1583 and again in 1609, the Jesuit Matteo Ricci found male prostitution commonplace:

> [T]here are public streets full of boys got up like prostitutes. And there are people who buy these boys and teach them to play music, sing, and dance. And then, gallantly dressed and made up with rouge like women these miserable men are initiated into this terrible vice.

In the seventeenth century, Confucian scholars frequently referred to homosexual love in their writings, and novelists and playwrights celebrated it. Perhaps in response to what was considered the license of the previous dynasty, the Qing government in 1740 made consensual homosexual acts a punishable offense. Two centuries later, the novelist Christopher Isherwood described a bathhouse in 1930s Shanghai, where he was erotically soaped and massaged by young men who served him tea the entire time.

Once the Communists took power in 1948, though, homosexuality was all but erased from Chinese history and culture. It was explained away as an "evil product of capitalist society," as a "Western social disease," as the *Beijing Daily News* wrote in 1987. Officially, homosexuality did not exist in China. Although there was no law that explicitly punished homosexual relations, laws against "revolting behaviors" and "hooliganism" were used to arrest men partaking of homosexual sex. There were reports of periodic police sweeps, of shock treatments, and of disappearances of Chinese gay men. Social pressure to marry was intense. (A survey by a Shanghai sexologist of 254 homosexuals in six major Chinese cities found that 60 percent had been married.) Concern about mainland Chinese policies toward homosexuality was a factor in the 1990 decision of the Hong Kong legislative council to repeal the British crown colony's sodomy law in anticipation of the Communist Chinese takeover in 1997.

Whether the hostility of the Chinese authorities to homosexuality was completely a result of Communist ideology is questionable. Bret Hinsch, author of *Passions of the Cut Sleeve,* a book about the male homosexual tradition in Chinese history, suggests that the influence of Western missionaries and other antigay moralists may have been more important than Communism in this regard. He notes that attitudes toward homosexuality in non-Communist Taiwan and Hong Kong have been as negative as those on the mainland.

In any event, by 1992, rising numbers of AIDS cases in Chinese cities were forcing the government to deal with the issue of homosexuality in other than repressive ways. That summer, AIDS-prevention workers in Beijing began distributing safe-sex pamphlets to men in a downtown park known to be a gathering place for gay men. A *Washington Post* reporter described one park where young men sat in clusters on park benches near the men's toilet. The reporter, Lena H. Sun, wrote:

> Some wear tight jeans and spotless white sneakers. Some wear diamond studs in their ears or gold rings on their fingers. Sometimes there is a hint of eye-liner. . . .
> "I just want to find someone who can understand me," says one man, 31, ducking his head shyly. "It is hard to find someone I can talk to about this deepest, darkest secret."

Meanwhile, according to the *Shanghai Evening News,* police in Anhwei province in central China gave up trying to put a female couple on trial for being lesbians. The Ministry of State Security in Beijing told local officials to leave the women alone because no laws covered their alleged offenses.

But whether these developments indicated a shift in official hostility toward homosexuality was doubtful. When the film *Farewell My Concubine,* which chronicles the fifty-year friendship of two Beijing opera stars (including their homosexual relationship) was nominated for an Academy Award, the official *Beijing Evening*

News was sharply critical. "It is widely known that even in the West, homosexuality is social trash," the newspaper said. "Most people hate that kind of dirty behavior, even in capitalist society. In our country, homosexuality has been swept away since liberation in 1949."

CUBA

In 1963, so the story goes, **Ramiro Valdez,** Cuba's Interior Minister, was visiting China. He was particularly interested in meeting the mayor of Shanghai, a city with a long tradition of homosexuality. When Valdez asked the mayor about the subject, he is said to have replied, "We have no homosexuals here." Valdez was impressed. How had they "solved" their problem? The mayor explained that on a particular holiday, a number of the city's homosexuals had gathered in a park on a riverbank. Party officials descended on the scene and clubbed them to death. The bodies floated downstream for all to see. So ended homosexuality in Shanghai. According to the story, Valdez concluded that the Chinese method was too "brutal" for Cuba. But Cuba found other ways.

Fidel Castro's Cuba took Communist dictates about homosexuality with the utmost seriousness. In fact, probably more than any country except for Nazi Germany, it made its effort to root out homosexuality a national priority. If bodies didn't float down the river in Havana, the Castro regime nonetheless used tactics ranging from purges to public humiliations to a short-lived experiment with internment camps. All of this made life for gay men in Cuba a nightmare for many years.

When the ragtag bunch of Sierra Maestra guerillas ousted the dictatorship of **Fulgencio Batista** and seized control of Havana on New Year's Day 1959, they were determined to "clean up" the capital. For Havana was widely viewed as "Sin City"—a tourist paradise of gambling, sexual license, and prostitution (of both sexes). The tourist industry, much of it owned by the Mafia, had been the leading growth sector in the economy in the 1950s; large numbers of homosexuals were employed there. Cleaning up Havana meant primarily getting rid of prostitution and male homosexuality. Because of the gay connection to the *Yanqui*-owned tourist industry, it was easy to associate homosexuals with the enemies of the revolution, to paint them, Communist-style, as a manifestation of bourgeois decadence.

Male homosexual identity in Cuba, as in most Latin countries, took a different path from that in countries to the north. In anal sex between men, only the *pasivo* (receptive) partner was considered gay; the *activo* (insertive) partner was viewed as heterosexual. As a result, a large number of men who were attracted to other men and would have considered themselves gay in other cultures did not do so in Latin America. In Latin culture, homosexuality was equated with traditional notions of femininity; transvestism played an extremely important part in Latin gay life. At the same time, given the patriarchal nature of Latin culture, lesbians were even more invisible than in the U.S. and northern Europe. The result was a weak, vulnerable Cuban gay community, one that was easily stereotyped and easily persecuted.

Traditional Latin attitudes by themselves probably would not have explained the systematic crackdown on homosexuality that reached its height in Cuba in the mid-1960s. Two years after taking power, Castro declared himself a Marxist-Leninist; his government became increasingly dependent on the Cuban Communist Party, which followed the Soviet line on sexual matters. As a result, traditional cultural mores that held homosexuals in contempt were reinforced by an antigay political ideology. Fidel Castro himself expressed state policy in a 1965 interview with American journalist Lee Lockwood:

> *Nothing prevents a homosexual from professing revolutionary ideology, and, consequently, exhibiting a correct political position. In this case, he should not be considered politically negative. And yet, we would never come to believe that a homosexual could embody the conditions and requirements of conduct that would enable us to consider him a true Revolutionary, a true Communist militant. A deviation of that nature clashes with the concept we have of what a militant Communist should be.*

In line with Castro's position, no gays or lesbians were permitted to become members of the Cuban Communist Party, the key path to social and economic advancement in Cuban society.

Starting in 1965, a series of "moral purges" of homosexuals from the University of Havana and other institutions of higher learning took place. Often these were accompanied by public humiliations, in which gay students were brought before Communist youth assemblies and insults were hurled at them. That same year saw the establishment of the first UMAP camps (*Unidades Militares para el Aumento del Producción,* or Military Units for Aid to Production). Located in Camagüey province, in the east of Cuba, they were simply "a species of concentration camp," as Allen Young writes in his book *Gays Under the Cuban Revolution.* The camps were surrounded by barbed wire; their motto—"Work Will Make You Men"—echoed the inscription at the entrance to Auschwitz. Individuals deemed to be in need of "rehabilitation" were taken to the camps, put to work in the fields, and given daily indoctrination from Marxist-Leninist manuals. They were usually men of draft age: Jehovah's Witnesses, the unemployed, the politically suspect, and homosexual men.

Homosexuals were the "main target" of the UMAP camps, according to exiled Cuban poet **Heberto Padilla.** "They suffered the most," he said. (Few lesbians found their way into the camps, but they were nonetheless targets of "moral purges".)

Often the methods employed to determine who would be sent to the camps bordered on the absurd. Just having long hair or wearing tight pants could be enough. In the documentary film *Improper Conduct,* made by Cuban exiles and released in 1984, one man describes how he was brought to the authorities and told to walk around the interrogation room. By his walk, it was decided he should be sent to a camp. "We are going to make a man of you," he was told. An actor who dyed his hair blond to play a German character in a play was also sent to a camp; dyed hair, in the eyes of the authorities, implied homosexuality. The local Committees for the Defense of the Revolution—set up to keep an eye on counterrevolutionary activity after the abortive Bay of Pigs invasion—frequently denounced suspected homosexuals to the police.

There were protests against the UMAP camps. The Cuban Writers and Artists Union opposed them. French philosopher Jean-Paul Sartre, a supporter of the Cuban revolution, was quoted as saying, "Cuba does not have Jews, but has homosexuals." Yet the international political Left, which supported Cuba, was reluctant to criticize the regime and thus give aid and comfort to the counterrevolutionaries; right-wing opponents of Castro were unwilling to turn "moral purges" into a cause célèbre. Nonetheless, the camps were shut down after the sugar harvest of 1967.

The antigay purges and the ever-present threat of being sent to a UMAP camp failed to destroy homosexuality in Cuba. In his memoir, *Before Night Falls,* the Cuban gay novelist **Reinaldo Arenas** (1943–90) argues that the repression actually may have *increased* homosexual activity. Because of the danger that at any moment the police could arrest them, those not yet in an internment camp felt they had to take advantage of their freedom. And as the regime became increasingly unpopular, anything it opposed became perceived as desirable. Arenas writes:

> *I think that the sexual revolution in Cuba actually came about as a result of the existing sexual repression. Perhaps as a protest against the regime, homosexuality began to flourish with ever-increasing defiance. Moreover, since the dictatorship was considered evil, anything it proscribed was seen in a positive light by the nonconformists, who in the sixties were already almost the majority. I honestly believe that the concentration camps for homosexuals, and the police officers disguised as willing young men to entrap and arrest homosexuals, actually resulted in the promotion of homosexual activities.*

Although the camps had been shut, the first National Congress on Education and Culture, held in 1971, called for increased antigay measures. Among the conclusions of the conference was that homosexuals should not be permitted to work at places where they could come into contact with minors. It also called for a study of "how best to tackle the presence of homosexuals in the various institutions of our cultural sector." The government moved swiftly. It began to remove homosexuals from all teaching positions. Gay writers and artists were purged as well. In his memoir, Arenas describes some of the effects of the 1971 Congress:

> *Every gay writer, every gay artist, every gay dramatist, received a telegram telling that his behavior did not fall within the political and moral parameters necessary for his job, and that he was therefore either terminated or offered another job in the forced-labor camps. . . .*
> *Every artist who had a homosexual past or who had slipped politically ran the risk of losing his job. . . .*
> *One of the hottest scandals of the moment was Roberto Blanco's arrest and public trial. He had been a very important theater*

director in Cuba during the sixties, but had recently made the mistake of admiring the erect phallus of one of those splendid big boys of State Security; handcuffed, his hair close-shorn, Blanco was escorted to a public trial held in the very theater of which he had been the director.

In April 1980, a group of Cubans eager to leave the country commandeered a bus and crashed it into the grounds of the Peruvian embassy in Havana, killing a Cuban guard. The Cuban government announced that it was withdrawing protection from the embassy. Within hours, the embassy grounds swelled with people eager to leave Cuba. So began the Mariel boat-lift, in which the Cuban government permitted 117,000 of its citizens to leave for the United States. Large numbers of Cuban gays joined the "freedom flotilla" in the days that followed. The National Gay Task Force estimated some two thousand to ten thousand of the émigrés were homosexuals; a reporter for the *Washington Post* put the number as high as twenty thousand. (The number of lesbians among the gay refugees was relatively small, an indication that lesbians suffered less overt persecution than gay men and may have benefited from the enhanced status of women under the revolution.) The Cuban government tried to use the homosexuality of many of the refugees to discredit the boat-lift. A film, called *Escoria* (Scum)—after the term that the government applied to the refugees—was shown throughout Cuba; in the film, men taking refuge in the embassy were depicted in poses that made them appear as effeminate as possible.

As much as it was an acute political embarrassment, the Cuban government saw a positive aspect to the boat-lift: It provided an opportunity to encourage undesirables, particularly homosexuals, to leave the country. As Arenas notes, the best way to obtain an exit permit at the time was to provide documentary proof of being a homosexual. He himself went to the police station, where he was asked if he was a homosexual. He answered, "Yes." He was also asked if he was "active" or "passive." He replied that he was "passive" (a friend who said that he took the active role in homosexual sex had not been allowed to leave, since the Cuban government apparently did not look upon those who took the active role as "real" homosexuals). Then Arenas was made to parade in front of a group of psychologists to see whether he walked in an effeminate manner. After he passed this final "test," a police lieutenant yelled at another officer, "Send this one directly."

Although American immigration rules at the time barred the immigration of homosexuals to the United States, the Carter administration didn't try to stop gay refugees from entering the country. The Metropolitan Community Church played an important role in resettling them, placing Cubans in gay-sponsoring households and offering financial assistance. The Dade County Coalition for Human Rights, in Miami, and other national and local gay groups did the same.

When the film *Improper Conduct* was released in 1984, it brought Castro's persecution of homosexuals to a wider public for the first time. In response, the Cuban government sent a group of "official" homosexuals to Europe to state that gays were not persecuted in Cuba. Arenas claims they had to act "really queer before the public, and pretend to be more effeminate than they actually were to demonstrate that, without question, there was no persecution of homosexuals in Cuba."

In *Improper Conduct,* exiled Cuban and foreign intellectuals speculate on the reasons for the government's hostility toward homosexuals. The heterosexual novelist **Guillermo Cabrera Infante,** who defected in 1965, describes the revolutionary leadership as "obsessed" with the subject. "It's all tied up with the Spanish machismo so apparent in Castro. . . ." he argues. "But that's not all. Persecution of homosexuals—men and women—was persecution of dissidents. . . . Communists endorse conventional couples, marriage between men and women. Homosexuals threaten all that. That is why totalitarian states fear it." The American writer **Susan Sontag** saw the basis in power relationships. "If homosexuals are identifed with women, as weak elements, and the country's ideology is focused on strength—and strength is associated with virility—then male homosexuals are viewed as a subversive element," she noted. "It [homosexuality] is an element that in itself implies power is not the only goal." Heberto Padilla, the poet (also heterosexual) jailed under Castro, had his own interpretation: "Those in power always find some group who antagonize them. Homosexuals always question. . . . By nature they are active, never sad. . . ."

By the mid-1980s, Cuba faced a new challenge—AIDS. Although many of Cuba's cases were transmitted through heterosexual sex or drug use, the government responded in the same repressive manner it had when dealing with homosexuals twenty years before.

Cuba became one of the few governments in the world to respond to the epidemic with mandatory AIDS testing and was the only country to quarantine those who tested positive for HIV. By the year 1988, the country had set up a "sanitarium" for HIV carriers. At the time, 240 people—171 men and 69 women—were placed there, presumably for the rest of their lives. (They were permitted periodic visits home.)

One of the first Americans to visit the sanitarium was **Ronald Bayer,** a medical ethicist and associate professor at Columbia University's School of Public Health. In a November 1988 interview with the *Los Angeles Times,* Bayer described how he was taken on a tour of a group of featureless apartments that looked like typical Cuban suburban housing. "It was neither barracks-like nor dungeon-like, although I have to assume we were shown the best," he said. "It was impossible to determine whether the complex was surrounded by a wall or fence." Bayer was shown three two-bedroom apartments, each of which housed two married couples. The apartments were modestly furnished, with a common living room with a television set. (One featured a large picture of Cuban revolutionary **Che Guevara** on the wall.) Bayer found Cuban health officials well-informed about AIDS transmission; despite the use of quarantine, they didn't believe AIDS was spread by casual contact. "I pressed the health officials about the human burdens they were imposing," Bayer told the newspaper. "They replied with a little bit of pride in Cuban machismo, that Cuban men could not be expected to control their sexual behavior."

As of 1991, 75 percent of the Cuban population had been tested for AIDS, the highest percentage of any nation in the world. The country claimed far fewer cases of full-blown AIDS than its Caribbean neighbors. (As of January 1, 1992, according to the World Health Organization, Cuba had reported 95 cases of AIDS, as opposed to 3,086 in Haiti and 1,574 in the Dominican Republic.) Whether the small number of Cuban cases could be ascribed to its draconian policies is a matter of dispute. In part because of international criticism, the quarantine policies underwent some modifications as time went on. By 1993, those deemed "responsible and trustworthy" were permitted to leave the sanitarium and return home after six months. Finally, in January 1994, the policy of quarantine was discontinued.

As its AIDS policy eased, there were indications that official Cuban hostility toward homosexuality was diminishing as well. In

December 1993, **Tomás Gutiérrez Alea's** film *Fresa y Chocolate* ("Strawberry and Chocolate") opened a Latin American film festival in Havana, where it played to packed audiences and captured the major awards, including Best Picture. Set in the 1970s, the film tells the story of a gay man who overcomes the antigay feelings of a young Communist activist. (Some months later, however, the head of the film festival, **José Horta,** fled Cuba, fearing for his safety and suggesting that some of his current trouble might be connected to the showing of *Fresa y Chocolate*.) In July of that same year, Cuba voted in favor of granting consultative status at the United Nations Economic and Social Council to the International Lesbian and Gay Association (ILGA). Cuban representatives reportedly told ILGA that the country had "learned from its mistakes."

EAST GERMANY

Amid the unremitting hostility of virtually every Communist state toward homosexuality, there was one notable exception—East Germany. In most respects, East Germany—the German Democratic Republic, or the GDR, as it was known until it was absorbed into West Germany in 1990—was a harsh regime that allowed few personal freedoms. But its relative tolerance of homosexuality—particularly as monolithic state power began to wane in the 1980s—marked the only real attempt to test whether an orthodox Communist regime could co-exist with a recognized homosexual minority.

In the decade before Hitler came to power, the German Communist Party had been allied with Magnus Hirschfeld's attempts to repeal Paragraph 175, the law that criminalized sex between men. After World War II, this same Communist Party took power in East Germany. **Otto Grotewohl,** who served as the GDR's first prime minister from 1949 to 1969, had called for the repeal of Paragraph 175 in the Reichstag in 1931 under the Weimar Republic. Dr. **Rudolf Klimmer**, a Communist Party member who had been associated with Hirschfeld's Institute for Sexual Research in the pre-Nazi period, pressured the new government to repeal the law. But the force that put the German Communists in power—the Soviet Union— had a diametrically opposite view of homosexuality from its German protégés. The result, according to Dutch political scientist Hans Volk, was "a compromise." In 1948, the Supreme Court of East

Germany revoked the Nazi version of Paragraph 175, called Paragraph 175a, which had expanded upon the original law to make virtually every expression of affection between men a criminal offense. But it wouldn't revoke the basic provisions of Paragraph 175. (When the parliament of the state of Saxony in 1951 voted to eliminate Paragraph 175, the central government overruled it.) Meanwhile, **Hilde Benjamin,** the Minister of Justice from 1953 to 1967, wrote in professional publications that she considered Paragraph 175 to be a "monstrosity." **John Becker,** the Minister of Culture, is said to have lived openly with his gay lover, but would not make any public statements about the law or his own homosexuality.

In 1957, a year after **Nikita Khruschev** condemned Stalin's policies and inaugurated a period of relative liberalization in the Soviet Union (this did not extend to homosexuality), the East German government announced officially that it would no longer invoke Paragraph 175 in cases of consenting sexual activity. However, the law remained on the books. Finally, in 1968, East Germany revoked Paragraph 175 entirely, as part of a revision of the criminal code.

Despite the improved legal situation, East German gay life remained low-key and closeted throughout the 1970s. Many, particularly lesbians, married people of the opposite sex. Still, because of the GDR's proximity to the West—particularly the West German media—the growing openness regarding homosexuality spread East. The first homosexual groups were established in 1982, under the aegis of the Protestant Church, the only major independent force in the country outside of the Communist Party and state. Soon afterward, some gay social clubs, not affiliated with the Church, formed in Berlin and Leipzig. (In 1986, the Sonntags Club, which featured discussions, cultural programs, and recreational outings, became the first state-supported gay group.) In these groups, gay men and lesbians worked closely together. There were also a number of gay bars and cafes that opened in the Prenzlauer Berg section of East Berlin.

The party line ebbed and flowed. One year, gays and lesbians were permitted to place a wreath at the Buchenwald concentration camp to honor homosexuals murdered by the Nazis; the following year, permission was denied. Meanwhile, the ruling Communist Party monopolized all sources of information. No gay newspapers were permitted. Gays and lesbians were not allowed to place personal ads in newspapers, a restriction that particularly hurt lesbians, who had fewer social outlets than gay men. But by the mid-1980s, the rules were relaxed so that women could discreetly advertise "sensitive woman friend wanted," a code phrase understood by other lesbians.

One particularly revealing development came in August 1987, when, for all intents and purposes, the Supreme Court of East Germany lowered the legal age of consent for gay sexual relations (pegged at eighteen years old, as opposed to sixteen for heterosexuals). The decision came when the court overturned the conviction of a man who had had consensual sex with a minor. The court wrote:

> The starting point for a judgement about the sexual relations between persons of the same sex must be the principle that homosexuals just as much as hetereosexuals are members of the socialist society and are guaranteed the same rights of citizenship. . . .
>
> Homosexual relations between an adult and a person between the ages of 16 and 18 do not necessarily lead to an abnormal development and do not have any other harmful consequences than homosexual relations between two youths or heterosexual relations between an adult and a youth.

In 1988, a lesbian and gay political organization called Courage was established. Courage built channels of communication with the GDR youth movement—the Free German Youth; in 1989, it even had its own information booth and cafe at the youth movement's annual fair in East Berlin, which attracted hundreds of thousands of people. The first signs of gay culture emerged: the film *Coming Out*, which portrayed a young man's acceptance of his homosexuality; and **Jürgen Lemke's** book *Ganz Normal Anders (Normal but Different)*, a compilation of interviews with East German gay men. Both appeared in 1989; by coincidence, *Coming Out* had its East Berlin premiere the night the Wall that divided the two parts of the city was torn down.

During the year-long transition period between the fall of the Communist Party from power and the merger of the two Germanys, the homosexual movement began to flower in the East. Gay political groups could organize legally for the first time; Courage started chapters in a number of cities. A newspaper called *Die Andere Welt* appeared, the first gay and lesbian publication ever in East Germany.

The newly formed political parties, with the exception of the Christian Democratic Union (CDU), all endorsed gay rights. In fact, during the last session of the East German parliament, the restructured Communist Party actually proposed the legalization of gay and lesbian partnerships. The Christian Democrats who made up the majority in the new parliament opposed this, however. In the waning hours of the East German parliament, a compromise was reached: After unification, the legalization of gay partnerships would be introduced in the all-German parliament, the Bundestag, as a proposal from the former East German parliament. However, the Bundestag never acted on this unexpected legacy of East Germany.

East Germany, said Courage leader **Uvd Zobel,** "had good preconditions for the integration of gay people into society." Before it could get a chance to prove whether that was so, the country vanished, a historical anomaly in many respects, including that of gay rights.

ARGENTINA

In February 1975, a front-page article in the magazine published by the most influential adviser to Argentina's president, **Isabel Martínez de Perón,** called for the incarceration of homosexuals in "reeducation and work" camps. The headline was ACABAR CON LOS HOMOSEXUALES ("Finish Off the Homosexuals"). "We don't want more homosexuals," the article stated. The following year, Isabel Perón's government was overthrown in a right-wing military coup, ushering in a period called the *Proceso.* And although no concentration camps were established in Argentina, what followed were among the darkest years in the country's history for homosexuals. (Military governments in neighboring Chile and Uruguay also cracked down on gays but not with the same level of repression.)

If in Cuba, a combination of machismo, Communist ideology, and the personal obsessions of the country's leadership resulted in a campaign against homosexuals, in Argentina the ingredients were different. There, rigid social and sex roles and a cultural contempt for homosexuals were certainly in evidence. But, unlike in Cuba, the political ideology was right-wing and strongly influenced by a conservative Roman Catholic clergy. Populist-cum-fascist dictator **Juan Perón,** who ruled the country from 1943 to 1955 and was restored to power in 1973, had been strongly influenced by Mussolini's Italy. (Perón was succeeded by his third wife, Isabel, upon his death in 1974.) The country had a history of political repression, with brief interludes of civilian governments between military coups.

Argentina also had a long and colorful gay history. The tango originally evolved as a way for men to dance with one another. In the 1920s and '30s, there was a "whole range" of gay society in Buenos Aires, according to **Juan José Sebreli,** eminent sociologist and historian of gay Argentina. "There were tea-rooms and then in the upper classes, there were terrific parties," Sebreli notes. "There was a lot of transvestism. There was a famous judge who would have parties in his house where he dressed as a woman."

By the early 1940s, two scandals brought the gay subculture into the public eye. In 1942, it was revealed that cadets from the military college had been involved in wild parties with middle- and upper-class homosexual men. The result was a much-publicized scandal that made it appear that society—even the army—was utterly corrupt. The revelations were said to have been a contributing factor to the 1943 military coup that brought Perón to power. The following year, a national idol, the Spanish singer and dancer **Miguel de Molina,** was arrested in the middle of a performance. He was convicted of the corruption of minors and was expelled from the country.

In the 1950s, governments both military and civilian found it useful to harass the homosexual population. In 1955, for example, Juan Perón was feuding with the Catholic Church. If only to annoy the Church, Perón was determined to legalize prostitution. So the police launched a series of raids against homosexuals, which were reported with banner headlines in the newspapers. Perón claimed that young men were being compelled by necessity to have sexual relations with one another: With the brothels shut, there was no outlet for heterosexual activity. After fifteen days, the headlines (and the raids) ceased. "Policies regarding homosexuality were often incoherent," Sebreli notes, "because they had to do with other things." At the end of the decade, the civilian government of **Arturo Frondizi** reestablished friendly ties with the Church. This didn't make things any easier for Argentine homosexuals. During Frondizi's presidency, there was a spectacular raid in which bathhouses, gay cinemas, and the entire subway system of Buenos Aires were shut down simultaneously in a crackdown on male homosexual sex.

In the early 1970s, during a respite between military dictator-ships, the first gay group in Argentina, the Frente de Liberación Homosexual (FLH) was established. The FLH was influenced by the youth culture of the time and the radical ideas of gay liberation emanating from the United States and Western Europe. As in the United States, the fledgling Argentine gay movement saw itself as allied with the political Left, particularly the radical Peronist youth movement. But as the country moved toward repression and extre-mist violence under the rule of Isabel Perón, the FLH went under-ground. It formally dissolved when the military overthrew Perón in 1976.

The military government that took power in that year was the most vicious in modern Argentine history. In the "dirty war" against leftist guerillas and their sympathizers, thousands were killed or "disappeared." Stories of military atrocities are legion: suspected guerillas were dropped from the sky out of helicopters, small chil-dren of "disappeared" young couples were, essentially, kidnapped by families of high military officials. In part, because of the gay movement's links to the Left in the early 1970s, in part because of the military's close ties to right-wing and religious moralists, homo-sexuals were among the targets of military persecution.

During the period of military rule, gay bars were closed down, and no gay or lesbian organizations were permitted. Movies were heavily censored for any hint of homosexuality. Harassment of gay men on the streets and in gay cruising areas intensified, particularly at the time of the 1978 World Cup matches in Buenos Aires. Many gays fled the country, including author **Manuel Puig,** who went to Brazil. (Puig's book, *Kiss of the Spider Woman,* which tells the story of the relationship between a flamboyantly gay man and a het-erosexual political prisoner who share a jail cell, gives the flavor of the period.) Many gay men thought it best during this period to appear as heterosexual as possible. Some men married women. "You imitated traditionally masculine characteristics," one man said. "It was common for gay men to involve themselves in sports." With bars closed and no places permitted for gays to gather, many ex-perienced a strong sense of isolation.

Many gays in Argentina today contend that homosexuals were "disappeared" during the *Proceso* simply because they were gay. Nonetheless, unlike in Nazi Germany or in Cuba, there is no proof of a systematic state policy in this regard. According to **Alejandro**

Salazar, former president of the Comunidad Homosexual Argentina (CHA), the country's gay and lesbian organization, "People tended to be disappeared on the basis of political militancy, rather than homosexuality per se. The FLH [Gay Liberation Front] members who disappeared, disappeared as leftists. Still, after being arrested, the fact of being homosexual exacerbated the punishments these people were subjected to." Repression was so generalized, and police violence so random, that it is often impossible to say if someone was persecuted for being gay or for other reasons. "You might get arrested for cruising the Avenida Santa Fe," says sociologist Sebreli, "but you also might get arrested for standing on a street corner for too long waiting for a cab." As in Cuba, lesbians fared better than gay men in this period. In Argentina, Sebreli says, women were inconsequential in the eyes of the authorities.

By the early 1980s, the military government was losing support and repression lessened. Following the military defeat in the Falklands war against the British in 1983, the military government fell. Gays and lesbians shared in the generalized feeling of euphoria. Within two months of the restoration of democracy, the first gay disco opened in Buenos Aires. But for homosexuals that euphoria ended in March 1984 when the police raided a gay club, arresting a large number of people. In response, the CHA, the country's gay organization, was formed.

Even with the restoration of democracy in Argentina, strong antigay attitudes persisted. By the end of the 1980s, the police were again raiding gay bars in Buenos Aires. Although these weren't the spectacular raids the city had experienced in the past, the vice squad would arrive at certain bars and pluck five or ten or twenty or even forty people off the dance floor and hold them overnight for questioning. The constant threat of arrest created an atmosphere of fear. At the same time, the CHA was denied permission to register as a legal organization, which meant that it could not raise money or even have a post office box. In late 1991, the Argentine Supreme Court refused the right of homosexuals in the country to organize, stating that "the defense of homosexuality injures nature and the dignity of the human person." Finally, after strong pressure from the International Lesbian and Gay Association, President **Carlos Saúl Menem** personally intervened and granted legal status to the CHA. In the summer of 1994, the country's leading Roman Catholic prelate, Cardinal **Antonio Quarracino** told an interviewer that homosexuals were "an ignoble stain" on the face of society and suggested they should be put in a ghetto-like area "with their own laws, their own media . . . and even their own constitution." Later, the Cardinal claimed it was all a joke. Military rule appeared finally to be a thing of the past, but the situation of gays and lesbians remained precarious.

CHAPTER 29

ENGLAND: THE BATTLE OVER CLAUSE 28

WHILE THE POLITICAL AND SOCIAL SITUATION of gays and lesbians improved in the United States and most of the English-speaking world in the decade of the 1980s, that was not the case in England. There, the age of consent for male homosexual acts remained at twenty-one (as opposed to sixteen for heterosexuals)—the highest in Europe, except for Bulgaria. London's tabloid press spread hysteria about AIDS, and British newspapers generally tended to cover the epidemic with far less objectivity and compassion than their American counterparts. (As late as 1993, the influential *Times of London* was blaming AIDS on gay male promiscuity and casting doubt on the seriousness of the epidemic in the Third World.) In the middle of the decade, Margaret Thatcher's governing Conservative Party gained political mileage linking the left wing of the Labour Party with pro-gay policies. Then, in December 1987, Thatcherite parliamentarians proposed an amendment to a local government bill that would make it illegal for municipal councils to "intentionally promote homosexuality" or take any steps that might recognize homosexual relationships as "a pretended family relationship."

The amendment became known as Clause 28. For the first months of 1988 it emerged as a major issue nationwide, creating some of the most intense antigay feeling that Britain had experienced in years. The public mood was such that one alarmed writer, Bernard Levin, wrote in the *Times*, "This country seems to be in the grip of a galloping frenzy of hate, where homosexuals are concerned, that will soon, if not checked, lead to something like a pogrom."

The roots of Clause 28 can be found in the early 1980s when Labour Party politician **Ken Livingstone** became the leader of the Greater London Council (GLC), the city's local government. Livingstone was a colorful and somewhat eccentric figure who gained notoriety for his expressions of sympathy for the Irish Republican

Army and for statements like "I fear that within ten years there will be a coup and that all gays, trade union activists and left-wing politicians will be led off to the gas chambers." Still, in 1982, in a BBC "Man of the Year" poll, Livingstone rated second only to the Pope in popularity. Livingstone saw the GLC as the center of opposition to Thatcher's attempts to dismantle British socialism. He also wanted to create a new urban proletariat comprised of blacks, feminists, the Irish, the disabled, single-parent families, the homeless, and gays and lesbians. But many saw Livingstone as practicing a socialism that offered more style than substance. "What the GLC did under Livingstone was to make propaganda and give away money," writes British political commentator Peter Jenkins in his book *Mrs. Thatcher's Revolution*. One of the recipients of Livingstone's largesse was the gay community. By 1984, the GLC had allocated nearly £300,000 to gay and lesbian groups; another £750,000 in public money went to establish a London lesbian and gay center.

Needless to say, Livingstone's attempt to build "socialism in one city" while Thatcher was trying to destroy socialism across the country did not sit particularly well with Ten Downing Street. In their lavish spending and their support for marginalized constituencies, Livingstone's GLC and the Labour-controlled councils in other cities represented everything Thatcher abhorred. She was determined to abolish them altogether. Thatcher—and the tabloids—dubbed the councils the "loony Left," a term that stuck. Jenkins noted some examples of the "lunacy" of various London boroughs:

> *Haringey ruled that only Nicaraguan coffee should be purchased. . . . Hackney staged an "Open Day for Gays and Lesbians." Lambeth banned the use of the word "family" from council literature on the grounds that it was discriminatory. Ealing ordered a purge of all "racist" and "sexist" books from its libraries. Haringey introduced courses on homosexuality into its schools, including primary and nursery schools. At an ILEA [Inner London Education Authority] school in Kensington competitive games were discouraged and writing protest letters was made part of the time-table. . . .*

By early 1986, the Thatcherites had succeeded in abolishing the GLC. However, the equation of the "loony Left" with the "promotion" of homosexuality—specifically, the creation of "positive images" of gays and lesbians—continued. Just before the first post-GLC local elections, it was revealed that the Inner London Education Authority had recommended a picture book called *Jenny Lives with Eric and Martin* as an aid for teachers. Imported from Denmark, the book told the story of a five-year-old girl raised by her gay father and his lover; one scene was said to show the couple naked in bed with the child. The tabloids went berserk: VILE BOOK IN SCHOOL, headlined *The Sun,* while *Today* led with SCANDAL OF GAY PORN BOOKS READ IN SCHOOLS. In the end, *Jenny Lives with Eric and Martin* turned out to be a bit of a red (or lavender) herring. The book had apparently appeared in only one teacher resource library and had been checked out by a grand total of one teacher. No child in Britain, as far as was known, had ever seen it. But the public was alarmed and that had been the intention.

Thatcher's Conservative Party, like its Republican allies across the Atlantic, was becoming increasingly identified with opposition to homosexuality. In a November 1985 speech, Tory Party chairman **Norman Tebbit** fulminated against "the valueless values of the permissive society." (Peter Jenkins noted that the word *permissive* on Tebbit's lips sounded like a sexually transmitted disease.) Several months later, Tebbit declared, "Tolerance of sexual deviation has generated demands for deviance to be treated as the norm. . . . Love of the sinner has slipped into love of the sin." There were rumors that, in view of the spread of AIDS, the Conservative Party was going to propose recriminalization of homosexual acts. That, in fact, never occurred.

Meanwhile, the opposition Labour Party was moving in a very different direction. At its 1986 annual conference, it approved a motion calling for an end to discrimination against gays and lesbians. Two years before, Labour member of Parliament **Chris Smith** came out publicly as a gay man, the first time a sitting MP had ever revealed his homosexuality voluntarily.

In the 1987 general elections, the Tories played the "gay and lesbian card" against Labour. One Tory poster featured the cover of the book *Young, Gay, and Proud,* suggesting that this was Labour's idea of a "comprehensive education." A Tory TV spot attacked local governments engaged in wasteful spending—featuring dozens of little white teacups, each standing for a specific unnecessary expenditure. Predictably, the camera zeroed in on one teacup labeled "Gay Seminar."

In October 1987, in her closing speech to the Conservative Party Conference, Thatcher continued the offensive. "Children who need to be taught to respect traditional values are being taught that they have an unalienable right to be gay," she said. A month and a half later, Clause 28 was introduced in Parliament. Its provisions—banning local governments from "promoting" homosexuality—were theoretically intended to prevent the remaining Labour-controlled councils from supporting "positive images" of homosexuals and granting money to gay organizations and community centers. But the language of the proposed legislation was so broad as to be worrisome to many gays and lesbians. They feared that the vague term "promotion" could be used to shut down gay bars, bookstores, and theater groups—anything that required a municipal license.

Although the prime minister's office insisted that the idea for Clause 28 came from radical Tory backbenchers, *The Guardian* reported that Thatcher was the "driving force" behind the law. When the proposal came up for a vote in the House of Lords, the government sent out whips to "drag in the 'backwoodsmen'—the hereditary peers who rarely come to London, much less participate in parliamentary votes—from the far corners of the realm," as Michael Hodges noted in the American magazine *The Nation*.

At first, the Labour Party, reeling from yet another election defeat, was reluctant to oppose Clause 28, but within weeks, the leadership changed course. **Neil Kinnock,** the party leader, denounced it as a "pink triangle clause produced and supported by a bunch of bigots." Gays and lesbians demonstrated against the bill and, at one point, created such a disturbance in the House of Commons that debate had to be stopped for five minutes. **Ian McKellen,** the country's leading Shakesperean actor, came out as gay on a BBC radio show and emerged as the most prominent leader of the anti–Clause 28 campaign. When he accepted the award for Best Actor at the Olivier Awards (Britain's version of the Tony Awards), he used his speech to denounce the proposed legislation.

The debate in the House of Lords provided some of the most memorable moments of the Clause 28 battle. The first came when the Labour Peer, **Lord Rea,** admitted to being the product of a gay family:

I was brought up by two women, one of them was my mother, in an actual family relationship. There was no pretence there. . . . It was a good family and I maintain that there is nothing in-

*trinsically wrong with a homosexual couple bringing up a child.
I consider that I had as rich and happy a childhood as most
children who are reared by heterosexual couples. . . .*

The second memorable moment came just after Clause 28 was
passed by the Lords by a 202–122 vote. Suddenly, three women
sailed down on ropes from the heights of the public gallery to the
chamber floor amid shouts of "Lesbians are angry!" and "It's our
lives you're dealing with!" The women were quickly ushered out,
amid general horror. (When they were interrogated by the police,
the women refused to give their real identities, using the names of
famous lesbian historical figures instead; they were held for several
hours and released.) LESBIANS INVADE THE LORDS, went the *Daily
Express* headline, and the saga of the "leaping lesbians" (or the
"Tarzan lesbians," as the *Standard* referred to them) became legendary.

Finally, on March 9, 1988, the House of Commons voted 254–
201 to pass the legislation. A huge protest rally in London drew
thirty thousand. The day before the law was to come into force,
the same lesbians who had lowered themselves onto the floor
of the House of Lords found another target. They made their way
to the studio where the BBC's "Six O'Clock News" was being
televised and chained themselves to desks and cameras. "We have
rather been invaded," **Sue Lawley,** the show's co-anchor, announced
to the nation. The BBC cut awkwardly to a story about a nurses'
strike. The invaders were wrestled to the ground, gagged, and eventually removed.

Despite the hoopla, by the end it was unclear what effect Clause
28 would actually have. The law's vague language—which at first
had appeared so menacing—also made its provisions easy to cir-
cumvent. As **Stephen Jeffery-Poulter** notes in his book *Peers, Queers,
and Commons,* the Manchester City Council had been told that its
grant to the city's lesbian and gay center was legal, even under
Clause 28, because it was a "welfare" expenditure. Meanwhile, the
Department of Education sent a notice to all schools, advising teachers and school principals that their decisions regarding sex education and curriculum were not affected by the Clause. There were
a few isolated examples of censorship, but they were primarily cases
of self-censorship. Concerns about the closing down of gay bars
and bookstores proved unfounded. Indeed, some began to think
that the entire struggle, more than anything, had been a struggle

over symbolism. One of the Tory whips in Parliament was said to have told Ian McKellan that Clause 28 was merely "a piece of red meat which we have to throw to our wolves every now and then to keep them quiet."

But symbols can still be powerful. It was now enshrined in British law that homosexuality was a detriment to society that must not be "promoted" and that gay and lesbian family relationships were "pretended" ones, not to be recognized affirmatively by government policy. Chris Smith, the openly gay MP, summed it up during the debate in the House of Commons when he declared that those in favor of the legislation were essentially arguing that "there is only one form of relationship, one form of sexuality, and one form of lifestyle that is acceptable. That sexuality will be endorsed, approved, applauded and given enhanced legal status, and everything else will become second class."

The battle over Clause 28 was viewed by many as a step forward for the gay community. Homosexuality had been a subject of national discussion for three months; Parliament had spent twenty-five hours debating the subject, not all of it edifying, to be sure, but not always on the level of the tabloids, either. Meanwhile, the threat posed by Clause 28 had rallied the gay and lesbian community in a way that had never happened before. (The debate over law reform in the 1960s had been purely a parliamentary matter, with virtually no gay community participation.) As Stephen Jeffery-Poulter noted, "It could be argued that the gay and lesbian community in Britain had finally been faced with their own equivalent of the Stonewall riot." The newspaper *Capital Gay* saw it similarly:

We have seen the coming of age of the gay and lesbian movement. Well-known figures, previously quiet about their sexuality, have come out fighting, we have found support from across the political spectrum; ordinary homosexuals have written protest letters and taken to the streets in the biggest ever lesbian and gay demonstrations, the media coverage has been massive (and often sympathetic), and the visibility of our community has rarely, if ever, been greater.

Once again, attempts to repress homosexuality had wound up only giving the subject more visibility, "promoting" it more strongly than the "loony Left" councils ever had.

An interesting footnote came in 1991, when the Thatcher government conferred a knighthood upon actor Ian McKellen, the leading opponent of Clause 28. This made McKellen the first openly gay "sir." McKellen was strongly criticized by gay filmmaker **Derek Jarman,** who believed that he should never have accepted a knighthood from the government that was responsible for such a horrible piece of legislation. In response to Jarman's comments, a group of eighteen film and theater figures, including producer **Cameron Mackintosh** (*Miss Saigon* and *Les Misérables*), film director **John Schlesinger** (*Midnight Cowboy* and *Sunday Bloody Sunday*), and actors **Simon Callow** and **Anthony Sher,** defended McKellen in an open letter in which they themselves came out as gay. Thus, the capacity of Clause 28 to rally the gay community and bring gays and lesbians out of the closet continued even into the 1990s.

A modest gain was registered in February 1994 when Parliament voted to reduce the age of consent for male homosexual acts from twenty-one to eighteen. The amendment was passed, to the dismay of gay activists who had campaigned for the age of consent to be set at sixteen, in conformity with laws for heterosexuals and lesbians. But an amendment setting the lower age—supported by the Labour Party—was narrowly defeated. (Prime Minister **John Major** and most Conservative MPs supported the change to eighteen.) "Eighteen is not a compromise. It's discrimination," said **Peter Tatchell** of the gay rights group OutRage. Activists promised to take the inequality in the age of consent to the European Court of Human Rights. Meanwhile, the Ministry of Defence announced that it had no plans to change its policy that homosexuality was incompatible with service in the armed forces. Almost one hundred years after the trial of Oscar Wilde, it was clear that homosexuality was still a subject that made the British distinctly uncomfortable.

AND IN THE REST OF EUROPE . . .

If in many respects Britain seemed to be going backward on gay and lesbian rights in the 1980s, that wasn't true in much of the rest of Europe. France had had a discriminatory law—similar to that of Britain—that mandated an age of consent of twenty-one years old for sexual relations between two men and fifteen for everyone else. The law had originally been enacted by the Vichy government in 1942 and had remained in place after the War. (Homosexual activity between consenting adults had been legal in France since

1791.) In 1977, the French Socialist Party adopted a gay rights plank, so when François Mitterrand and the Socialists took power in the early 1980s, they quickly offered amnesty to 156 gay men who had been convicted under the age-of-consent law. In 1982, the age of consent was equalized for homosexuals and heterosexuals at fifteen years old. Soon after, the government licensed Fréquence Gaie, the first full-time gay radio station in the world, as part of the legalization of a number of pirate radio stations. In 1985, the National Assembly added sexual orientation to France's antiracism law.

But unquestionably the major development of the decade came in October 1989, when Denmark became the first country in the world to give legal recognition to same-sex partnerships. The Folketing, the Danish parliament, had enacted the law the previous May by a 71–47 vote. The decision came after a long campaign by the Danish gay and lesbian organization, the LBL, which had made the enactment of gay and lesbian partnerships a major priority. The Danish parliament had taken its first step in that direction in 1986 when it approved a law exempting cohabiting gay and lesbian couples from the high inheritance taxes in effect for individuals who wanted to leave money or property to someone other than a blood relative or legal spouse.

The 1989 partnership law was a compromise, however. While it gave registered gay and lesbian couples the same rights as heterosexual couples in terms of taxes, inheritance, insurance, and pension benefits, the partnership law also stated that gay couples could not be married in the Danish state church. In addition, registered same-sex partners were barred from adopting children, even the biological child of the other partner. (The law also insisted that one of the registered partners be a Danish citizen, ostensibly to prevent an influx of gays and lesbians from other countries from coming to Denmark to marry.) The adoption restrictions were strongly opposed by many Danish lesbians, and there was hope that they would eventually be repealed.

On the first day that the new law went into effect, six gay couples registered their partnerships and were married in the Bryllupsalon, or "wedding chamber," of Copenhagen's town hall. The first couple to be registered were two men, **Eigil** and **Axel Axgil**, who had lived together for thirty-nine years. (They had taken the same surname, a combination of their first names, in 1958.) Axel Axgil had been the original founder of the LBL, in 1948. The couple both wore suits, with carnations in their buttonholes, and the ceremony was followed by the traditional throwing of rice and confetti on the town hall front steps. A little more than a year later, 718 gay and lesbian couples had married. (There had also been seven divorces—under the law, gay couples could dissolve their partnerships by going through the same process as heterosexual couples to obtain a divorce.) "The only way to be able to move anything is to be open about it," said Eigil Axgil, sixty-seven on the day of his wedding. "You have to say that this is the way I am so society can be open to you. If everyone follows this lead in Denmark, if everyone goes out and says this is the way they are and go out of the closet, this event will also happen in the rest of the world."

That was beginning to be the case. In April 1993, the Norwegian parliament passed a similar partnership law—with the same restrictions on church marriages and adoption. On August 6 of that year, less than a week after the law went into effect, five gay couples registered their partnerships in Oslo, as a crowd of about a thousand watched. The following year Sweden's parliament followed suit, permitting couples of the same sex to register their partnerships and to wed in civil ceremonies. The new law—which featured the same caveats as the Danish and Norwegian laws—was to go into effect in January 1995. Meanwhile, in February 1994, the European parliament in Strasbourg passed a nonbinding resolution that gays and lesbians should be permitted to marry and adopt children. The resolution, drawn up by Green Party deputy **Claudia Roth,** was approved 159–96. (In Roth's Germany, however, the parliament refused to approve a constitutional amendment proposed by the opposition Social Democrats that would recognize long-term relationships between unmarried gay or heterosexual couples.)

The advances that were taking place in Scandinavia were particularly exasperating to British gay and lesbian activists. In April 1994, shortly after the British parliament refused to equalize the age of consent for homosexual and heterosexual activity, the gay civil rights group OutRage called on Denmark's **Queen Margrethe** to "liberate" their country. At a ceremony outside the Danish Embassy in London, members of OutRage tore up a British flag, played the Danish national anthem, and read an appeal to Queen Margrethe that read:

We, the Lesbian and Gay citizens of the territories of Great Britain, do hereby make supplication and humbly entreat Her

Majesty to mobilize her great forces, to progress westward, and liberate these benighted islands.

A Danish embassy official said that there was little chance that Queen Margrethe or her government would respond to the plea in any way. Buckingham Palace had no comment.

Simon Nkoli

IN NOVEMBER 1993, in the waning days of white minority rule, representatives of twenty South African parties—including **F. W. de Klerk's** ruling National Party and **Nelson Mandela's** African National Congress (the ANC)—approved a draft constitution for a post-apartheid South Africa. The new constitution featured a Bill of Rights outlawing discrimination on the basis of a number of personal characteristics, ranging from race and gender to age and physical disability. Included on this list was sexual orientation. It was a new South Africa, and homosexuals were part of it.

The symbol of the new visibility of gays and lesbians in South Africa was **Simon Nkoli** (b. 1957), a black man who was the founder and first president of the country's largest homosexual organization, Gays and Lesbians of the Witwatersrand (GLOW). During the apartheid period, Nkoli had been an activist with the United Democratic Front, the internal political arm of the ANC. Arrested in a rent boycott demonstration in his home township of Sebokeng in September 1986, he was one of twenty-two defendants in the Delmas Treason Trial, one of the most highly publicized political trials of the 1980s in South Africa. Eventually, Nkoli was acquitted, but not before he served four years in prison, including a year in solitary confinement with only the Bible to read.

Nkoli's father was a chef and his mother a chambermaid; like many black South Africans, his family was forced to lead a quasi-nomadic existence, because they lacked the necessary permit to stay in any one place. (One of his early memories was of locking his parents—illegal squatters—in a wardrobe to evade the police.) He studied to be a priest, then dropped out of the seminary. When he began to have relationships with men, Nkoli came face-to-face with the indignities of apartheid in his personal life. His lover—a white man—was injured in a motorcycle accident, and when Nkoli went to visit him in the hospital, he was denied entrance because he was black. He was admitted only by claiming that his lover was his employer. Later, he became involved with another white man and lived with him in an apartment building in Johannesburg. The only way he could live there legally was to register as the man's servant.

In the early 1980s, when Nkoli was first coming out, South Africa's gay community was closeted and almost totally white. Although the governing National Party was quite conservative on sexual matters (and although male homosexual acts were against the law), gay bars and gathering places existed in Johannesburg, Durban, and Cape Town. Johannesburg even had an identifiably gay neighborhood. For black gays and lesbians, however, there were few, if any, social outlets: They were trapped in the townships, denied entrance to white bars and clubs. Nkoli became involved with the all-white Gay Association of South Africa (GASA). In 1983 and 1984, he started a GASA adjunct for black men, publicizing it through an interview with a black Sunday newspaper. When more than seventy people showed up at the first meeting, Nkoli was stunned. "I believed I was the only black gay in South Africa," he said. The group met every second Saturday (it became known as Saturday Group) and started the first black gay bar in South Africa. Saturday Group dissolved shortly after Nkoli's imprisonment for antiapartheid activism; rumors circulated that the police had seized the organization's membership list when they arrested Nkoli.

During his years in prison, Nkoli became a hero to gays and lesbians around the world, but white members of GASA refused to assist him in any way. When Nkoli was released from prison in 1988, he was determined to establish a gay organization that was nonracial. He founded GLOW and began organizing black gays in townships around Johannesburg. In less than three years, GLOW boasted 350 members—60 percent of them black. In the fall of 1990, eight months after the government lifted its long-standing ban on marches and demonstrations, South Africa held its first gay and lesbian pride parade. Eight hundred people—black and white—marched through Johannesburg on a rainy Saturday morning, carrying signs like BLACK GAYS ARE BEAUTIFUL and GOD HET ALMAL

LIEF (Afrikaans for "God Loves Everyone"). "We had to show the ANC how strong we were," he said. "That first gay pride march was the first visible protest we had in this country."

During much of this period, the African National Congress was hesitant to take up the issue of gay rights. Like many other Third World liberation movements, the organization had been strongly influenced by orthodox Communist views on morality and the family. In the mid-1980s, **Ruth Mompati,** a member of the ANC executive committee in London, stated publicly that "in a normal society, there will be no gays because everyone will be normal." The remarks caused an uproar among gays and lesbians involved in the antiapartheid movement in Britain.

The controversy generated by Mompati's remarks led the ANC to rethink its official line on gay and lesbian rights. As a result, in 1990, the ANC included a clause banning discrimination on the basis of sexual orientation as part of a model Bill of Rights it hoped would become law. This made the ANC the first "liberation" organization in the world to support gay and lesbian rights. Many gay South Africans were convinced that the ban on antigay discrimination would never survive a constitutional agreement negotiated between the ANC and the National Party. Yet when the draft constitution was finally approved, the antidiscrimination protections remained.

Simon Nkoli was not the only person responsible for the ANC's support for gay rights. In fact, it was a group of mostly white, ANC-oriented intellectuals in Cape Town, members of an organization called OLGA (Organization of Lesbian and Gay Activists), that lobbied for the sexual orientation clause. But Nkoli's antiapartheid activism and his four years as a political prisoner gave him—and, by extension, the gay and lesbian community—the credibility necessary to win over the ANC. While countries like Britain and the United States were still far from enacting gay civil rights protections, in just a few short years South Africa had moved to the forefront.

CHAPTER 30

JAPAN

On November 25, 1970, Yukio Mishima, the most celebrated Japanese novelist of his generation, committed seppuku (hara-kiri) in the office of the commandant of the Japan Self-Defense Force. In his last act, Mishima shouted a traditional salute to the emperor and pierced his left side with a dagger, dragging it across his abdomen. His protégé, the cadet **Masakatsu Morita,** attempted to behead Mishima, striking at his neck with a long sword. When he failed, another cadet took the sword and did so. Morita then removed the dagger from Mishima's hand and drove it into his own abdomen. The cadet who had beheaded Mishima severed Morita's head as well. The ritual was over: It was the first public incident of hara-kiri in Japan since World War II.

Just an hour before, Mishima, Morita, and two other cadets of Mishima's private army, the Shield Society, had arrived at the Tokyo headquarters of the Eastern Army and taken the commandant prisoner at swordpoint. Mishima demanded that the entire 32nd Infantry Regiment assemble on the parade ground so he could address them. At a few minutes past noon, with Morita at his side, he stepped onto the balcony and exhorted the soldiers to rise up against Japan's postwar democratic government in the name of the emperor. Below, some eight hundred soldiers booed and jeered. Mishima, who had intended to speak for thirty minutes, gave up after seven. He and Morita returned to the commandant's office and took their own lives.

Yukio Mishima (1925–70) was born Kimitake Hiraoka, the eldest son of a government official, and descended on his mother's side from the samurai warrior class. At age twenty-four, with the publication of his autobiographical novel, *Confessions of a Mask,* he was hailed as a genius. In that book, published in 1949, Mishima's hero is quite explicit about his homosexual feelings, his attraction to sadomasochism, and his fascination with "Death and Night and Blood." These apparently had their roots in Mishima's own discovery, at age twelve, of a reproduction of a painting of the

Christian martyr St. Sebastian, in traditional pose, bound to a tree and pierced with arrows.

In 1950 and 1951, Mishima began to haunt Tokyo's gay bars, ostensibly to gather material for a new book about Japan's homosexual subculture, *Forbidden Colors,* which was published in 1951. (See "Excerpts from Mishima's *Confessions of a Mask* and *Forbidden Colors,*" page 522.) Inside the bars, he behaved as if he were a spectator. His biographer John Nathan noted, "He never let on that he was a participant in the world he was sketching on the note cards he always carried, and apparently his friends did not suspect him." Nathan says there is no evidence that Mishima was actively homosexual until his first journey to the West in 1952. Six years later, out of deference to his terminally ill mother—and because of rumors that he was homosexual—he married the daughter of one of Japan's most well-known traditional painters.

Mishima's creative output was prodigious. He wrote twenty-three novels, as well as numerous plays and essays; he sang on the stage and directed and acted in movies. He was considered to be a leading Japanese candidate for the Nobel Prize for literature, which was awarded instead to his fellow novelist (and former mentor) **Yasunari Kawabata** in 1968.

Mishima became obsessed with transforming himself into a modern version of a samurai. Starting in 1955, he began his famous regimen of body-building, which he continued faithfully until his death. He wrote in *Forbidden Colors,* "To samurai and homosexual the ugliest vice is femininity. Even though their reasons for it differ, the samurai and the homosexual do not see manliness as instinctive but rather as something gained only from moral effort." By the 1960s, Mishima had drifted into right-wing, nationalist political circles that advocated a revival of Japanese militarism and the veneration of the emperor, who had been discredited after Japan's defeat in World War II. In 1967, at forty-two years old, he enlisted secretly in the Army Self-Defense Force, undergoing a month and a half of basic training. His personal preoccupations and his political ideas merged when he formed his private army, the Shield Society, dedicated to the defense of the emperor.

At the Shield Society he met Morita, at the time a twenty-one-year-old university student. Morita had been orphaned at the age of two and raised by an older brother. The words most often used to describe him were "pure" and "simple." While at Waseda University, a hotbed of left-wing activity, Morita joined a tiny rightist

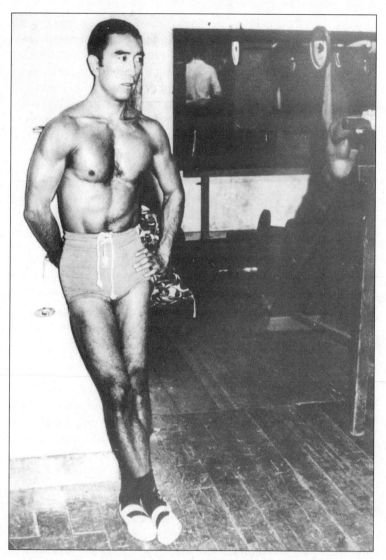

As part of his effort to transform himself into a modern-day samurai warrior, Yukio Mishima began a regimen of body-building in 1955. He continued it faithfully until his death in 1970. *(© UPI/Bettmann)*

student club. Passionately devoted to the emperor, he rose to become a leader of the Shield Society. During the last year of their lives, Mishima and Morita were frequently together; they are widely assumed to have been lovers. In Mishima's company, one friend described Morita as acting "like a confident fiancee," according to Nathan. For his part, Mishima played the role of proud protector. When he introduced Morita to friends, he told them, "I've pledged my life to the emperor and Morita has pledged his life to me."

Mishima became increasingly preoccupied with death, particularly the violent death of young men. "The samurai's profession is the business of death," he wrote. "No matter how peaceful the age in which he lives, death is the basis of all his action. The moment he fears and avoids death he is no longer a samurai." At some point, he and Morita decided to die together, in part to spark a nationalist rebellion, in part because of a shared fascination with death. One of Mishima's biographers, Henry Scott Stokes, quotes a friend of Mishima's who attributed the double suicide to a combination of homosexuality, emperor worship, and *Yomeigaku* (a complex system of Confucian Philosophy). "My speculation," writes Stokes, "is that he was having an affair with Masakatsu Morita and that the two committed a lovers' suicide."

In his attempt to recreate himself as a samurai, in his mentor-protégé relationship with Morita, in his preoccupation with violent death, Mishima can be seen as attempting to revive the proud traditions of a Japan that had resigned itself to U.S. political and military hegemony after its humiliating defeat in World War II. One aspect of these traditions was an acceptance of sex between men. For hundreds of years, from the feudal period through the end of the nineteenth century, male-male sexual relationships—known as *nanshoku* ("male colors")—flourished. Japanese literature is filled with stories of the suicides of homosexual lovers: samurai warriors and their pages, Buddhist monks and their servants, and even an epidemic of "double love" suicides by infatuated schoolgirls that gripped the country in the 1930s. One samurai treatise of the early Tokugawa, or Edo, Period (1603–1868) states, "To throw away one's life [for one's male lover] is the ultimate aim of *shudo*." (*Shudo*, or the "way of companions," is another term for *nanshoku*.)

Ejima Kiseki, a popular writer of the early eighteenth century, referred to *nanshoku* as "the pastime of the samurai." Samurai warriors pledged themselves to one another in "brotherhood bonds" in the manner of ancient Sparta, often with two lovers fighting side by side. As in ancient Greece, there was almost always an age difference between the male lovers, expressed in the terms "older brother" and "younger brother." (This terminology still lingers in Japanese gay usage today.) This military tradition of an "army of lovers" continued even in the late nineteenth century, when a European living in Tokyo wrote:

> In peace as in war, the Japanese soldier marches arm in arm with the friend with whom he is in an intimate relation. We can say, in fact, that in the homosexual liaison too, the old samurai spirit found exultant expression on the Manchu front (in the 1880–83 war between Japan and China). . . . Many officers have told me of scenes where a soldier in love with another had fought at the risk of his own life, rushing willingly to the deadly spot. This is not simply due to the warrior spirit and contempt for death characteristic of the Japanese soldier, but also to their passion for another soldier. . . .

The prevalence, even strong approval, of *nanshoku* within Japanese society was not restricted to the military class. The Buddhist clergy was apparently rife with same-sex relations: Saint Francis Xavier, the first Portuguese missionary to Japan, wrote in the sixteenth century that, among Buddhist monks, "the abominable vice against nature is so popular that they practice it without any feeling of shame." Historian Gary Leupp notes the names of twelve shoguns from 1147 to 1837 who were known for having sex with young men and boys. He also contends that among the urban classes of the Edo period a "cheerful bisexuality" was the norm, much of it centering around *nanshoku* teahouses and the Kabuki theater. Men made passes at boys quite openly, he writes, with the public baths being a site for such activity. Leupp notes that marriage did not preclude relationships with other men; in a society characterized by often loveless arranged marriages, same-sex relationships offered the possibility of romantic love. (There is little record of lesbian relationships within Japanese culture in this period, perhaps an indication of women's low social status.)

If as late as eighteenth- and early-nineteenth-century Japan, male-male relationships were an accepted part of the sexual landscape, that began to change with the accession to power of the Westernizing Meiji reign in 1868. *Nanshoku* was increasingly regarded as a cultural and social embarrassment, a feudal remnant in an era when Japan was keen to industrialize and catch up with the West. Negative Western views regarding same-sex relations became influential in a period coinciding with the appearance in Europe of biomedical conceptions of homosexuality. Japanese law began to reflect this change in perception as well: Anal intercourse between consenting adult males was briefly criminalized between the years 1874 and 1882. (This law, which mandated punishment of ninety days in prison, was apparently modeled on Chinese, not Western, law, however; its repeal was credited to the influence of the Napoleonic Code, which did not penalize homosexual relations between adults.)

Nonetheless, there appears to have been a revival of homosexuality among students in Tokyo toward the end of the nineteenth century. An 1898 article in the newspaper *Eastern World* stated "Male homosexuality . . . is so widespread among the students of Tokyo that adolescent boys cannot go out at night." The newspaper proposed the introduction of a law similar to Germany's Paragraph 175. This never occurred. Yet the cultural expression of male-male love continued to decline. In his work *The Aesthetics of Adolescent-Love,* the Japanese writer Tahuro Inagaki writes:

> *Without our noticing it, this cultural tradition has been lost to us. . . . When we were schoolboys, we often heard of an affair in which two students had quarreled on account of a beautiful young boy and had ended by drawing knives. It still happened occasionally that a boy would stab with his dagger someone who had attempted to take him by force. But since the new era of Taisho (1912–26), we no longer hear of this kind of thing. The* shudo, *which had clung on to life, has now reached its end.*

By the early-to-mid-twentieth century, a new word emerged in the Japanese language: *doseiai,* or "same-sex love." *Doseiai* applied to both men and women and it did not have the connotations of pederasty that *nanshoku* and *shudo* had. But *doseiai* was still *shumi*—a "hobby" or "pastime" or "personal interest," something that could be taken on and put off at will. It wasn't really serious and didn't constitute an identity. And while the Japanese didn't persecute (or prosecute) *doseiai,* they tended to view it as a Western import, something that had no cultural roots in Japan.

. . .

Viewed in the light of Japanese history, Mishima's *seppuku* represented a last gasp of feudal concepts of love between men. By the 1980s, the traditional notions had been replaced by a Western-style concept of gay and lesbian identity. In part, this was due to American and European cultural influence, but it was also the result of social and economic changes within Japanese society itself as the country moved into a more advanced stage of capitalism. Increasing affluence meant many young people no longer were compelled to live with their families. Although pressure to marry remained strong, it became acceptable to marry at a later age, which gave young gays and lesbians a "window of opportunity" to experiment with sexual feelings and attractions. Women began to enjoy a degree of economic independence and social freedom unknown in the past.

In the mid-to-late 1980s, the first gay organizations were established, as well as the country's first lesbian group. The emergence of gay magazines enabled gay men to feel less isolated, to communicate with one another, and hinted at the possibility of community. Because of the still unequal status of women in Japanese society, lesbians lagged behind gay men in developing a sense of themselves as a distinct social entity. But the emergence of a Japanese women's movement helped to foster the beginnings of lesbian identity. By the early 1990s there were all-women's dances in Tokyo, and a lesbian coffeehouse in Osaka.

Nonetheless, in many respects, the Japanese gay world remained the same closed universe that Mishima had described forty years before in *Forbidden Colors*. Most gays and lesbians remained in the closet. Family pressure to marry made it difficult for women, in particular, to take on a gay identity. Although Tokyo had some three hundred gay bars, they were largely hidden and unknown to most Japanese. Homosexuality remained a subject unsuitable for academic study. The government and media continued to deny that there was a significant number of gays and lesbians in the country. An article in the English-language *Japan Times* claimed that homosexuals made up only a half to one percent of the country's population. (The government gave out a figure of one hundred thousand, or one-tenth of one percent of Japan's population.) With most AIDS cases concentrated among hemophiliacs, the epidemic did not provide a basis for widespread gay organizing as in the West. And in a homogeneous society, with little tradition of recognition of minority groups, the idea of a separate homosexual "minority" remained an alien concept.

Japan remained a society of contradictions. Within a short period of time, feudal-based notions of same-sex relationships had given way to a more modern gay and lesbian identity. The idea that one could have a long-term relationship with someone of the same sex in place of heterosexual marriage was gaining currency among Japanese homosexuals. There was little social hostility: Pressure to marry—not homophobia—was the central issue for most young Japanese gays. But widespread denial that gays and lesbians even existed in Japan persisted. (As one Japanese man put it, regarding Tokyo's gay bars, "No Japanese go there, right? Only foreigners!") This social denial, combined with the absence of antigay laws or overt discrimination that could serve as rallying points, made gay organizing difficult.

Then, in August 1994, a remarkable development occurred: some 300 to 1,000 gays and lesbians marched down the streets of Shinjuku, Tokyo's "entertainment" district, to celebrate gay pride. It was the first public manifestation of a gay and lesbian presence in Japan, and a signal that change might be coming faster than anyone had anticipated. At the very least, one could no longer claim that homosexuals didn't exist in Japan.

Excerpts from Mishima's *Confessions of a Mask* and *Forbidden Colors*

Yukio Mishima's autobiographical novel, Confessions of a Mask, *published in 1949, gained him immediate acclaim. "I am dazzled by Mishima's mature talent," wrote his mentor, the novelist Yasunari Kawabata. "And at the same time I am disturbed by it. His novelty is not easy to understand. Some may think that Mishima is invulnerable, to judge from this work. Others will see that he has deep wounds." The novel recounts the experiences of a young man in postwar Japan who grapples with homosexual attractions. In the following excerpt, the narrator and his female friend, Sonoko, encounter a group of* yakuza—*gangsters—in a dance hall on a sweltering summer day. The passage illustrates Mishima's equation of masculinity, homosexual feelings, and violent death that so pervaded his imaginative life.*

THEN MY ATTENTION WAS DRAWN to the other boy. He was a youth of twenty-one or -two, with coarse but regular and swarthy features. He had taken off his shirt and stood there half naked, rewinding a belly-band about his middle. . . . His naked chest showed bulging muscles, fully developed and tensely knit. . . . His bare, sun-tanned shoulders gleamed as though covered in oil. And black tufts stuck out from the cracks of his armpits, catching the sunlight, curling and glittering with glints of gold.

At this sight, above all at the sign of the peony tattooed on his hard chest, I was beset by sexual desire. My fervent gaze was fixed upon that rough and savage, but incomparably beautiful, body. Its owner was laughing there under the sun. When he threw back his head I could see his thick, muscular neck. A strange shudder ran through my innermost heart. I could no longer take my eyes off him.

I had forgotten Sonoko's existence. I was thinking of but one thing: Of his going out onto the streets of high summer just as he was, half-naked, and getting into a fight with a rival gang. Of a sharp dagger cutting through that belly-band, piercing that torso. Of that soiled belly-band beautifully dyed with blood. Of his gory corpse being put on an improvised stretcher, made of a window shutter, and brought back here.

Forbidden Colors, Mishima's third novel, is a less personal work. It tells the story of a young man, Yuichi, who is used by an aging writer to exact revenge on women who have wronged him. The book also takes Yuichi on a journey through Tokyo's gay subculture of bars, parks, and parties. Forbidden Colors was first published in 1951, and, like most novels about homosexuality published in the West at the time, paints a bleak portrait of gay life. The following passage describes the kinds of people Yuichi meets at a gay bar called Rudon's.

As Yuichi's knowledge broadened, he came to be amazed at the unexpected scope of that world.

Muffled in a straw poncho, this world idled through the daylight hours. There was friendship, the love of comrades, philanthropy, the love of master and protégé; there were partners, assistants, managers, houseboys, leaders and followers, brothers, cousins, uncle and nephew, secretaries, amanuenses, drivers—and there were numbers of other capacities and stations of diverse kinds: executives, actors, singers, authors, artists, musicians, high and mighty college professors, white-collar workers, students. In the world of men they idled, in all kinds of ponchos made of straw. . . .

Bound by the spell of their common fate, they dreamed a dream of a simple truth. That dream was that the truth that man loves man would overthrow the old truth that man loves woman. Only the Jews were a match for them when it came to fortitude. In the abnormal degree to which they held fast to a single, humiliating point of view they were like the Jews. The emotion proper to this tribe gave birth to fanatical heroism during the war. After the war it embraced a pride at being in the van of decadence. It thrived on confusion. In that riven ground it grew clumps of tiny, dark violets.

THE GAY MOMENT

CHAPTER 31

THE CLINTON YEARS

AT THE FIRST-EVER GAY INAUGURAL BALL, held at the National Press Club in Washington, D.C., a crowd of seventeen hundred gays and lesbians—in tuxedos and evening dress—sang the "Star Spangled Banner." The Great Seal of the United States, redesigned for the occasion with a pink triangle emblazoned over the American Eagle, gazed down from above the stage. On the flanking video screens, a **Bill Clinton** campaign speech on AIDS and gay rights warmed up the crowd. Lesbian pop singer k.d. lang leaned over the balcony and told the audience, "The best thing I ever did in my life was to come out." The band struck up the Clinton campaign theme song, "Don't Stop Thinkin' About Tomorrow," as red, white, and blue balloons fell from the ceiling. The crowd toasted the new president. It was a moment of hope and expectation. The Clinton era had begun.

The hope and expectation had started several months earlier, in May, just before the California primary, when candidate Clinton gave a speech to six hundred gay and lesbian activists in Los Angeles. **David Mixner,** gay political organizer, longtime friend of Clinton, and cochair of his California campaign, stood next to him on the stage. "I have a vision and you're part of it," Clinton told an enthralled audience. Declaring that "we don't have a person to waste," he promised an end to the U.S. military's ban on homosexual servicemen and women; he also promised to appoint an AIDS czar and to initiate a Manhattan Project–like crash program to combat AIDS. He added:

> If I could, if I could wave my arm for those of you that are HIV positive and make it go away tomorrow, I would do it, so help me God I would. If I gave up my race for the White House and everything else, I would do that . . .

The moment was captured on videotape and was played over and over in gay living rooms across the country over the next few months. At the Democratic National Convention in New York City, there were 108 openly gay and lesbian delegates, alternates, and party officials. The party's platform called for an end to the ban on gays in the military and the passage of antidiscrimination legislation. **Bob Hattoy,** a gay man with AIDS, later to be a White House aide to Clinton, gave a moving, prime-time speech to the convention. In his acceptance address, Clinton mentioned gays as part of a list of groups that would find a place in the new administration. The gay and lesbian community had achieved a new legitimacy.

In contrast, before and during its convention in Houston, the Republican Party was making veiled and not-so-veiled appeals to antigay feeling. Representatives of gay and lesbian groups were barred from testifying at platform hearings. In his convention speech, Pat Buchanan, unsuccessful presidential candidate and long-time foe of gay rights, declared "religious war." Speaker after speaker extolled "family values," a term that, in GOP-speak, clearly excluded homosexuals. President **George Bush** asserted that homosexuality was not "normal." Vice President **Dan Quayle** questioned the suitability of gay and lesbian parents.

After the convention, the media reported that gay-bashing would be part of the GOP campaign strategy. "After Willie Horton Are Gays Next?" asked *Time* magazine, a reference to commercials about the furloughed black convict that the Bush campaign had used effectively to paint the Democrats as "soft on crime" in 1988. *The New York Times* quoted an unnamed senior Bush campaign official as saying, "When we talk about family values, part of it will be to point out that Clinton went out to California, had a fund-raiser by the biggest gay group there and bought into their agenda." Yet, the gay-bashing campaign never occurred. Postconvention polls showed that the antigay rhetoric of the Houston convention didn't play well with large segments of the American public. And, curiously, Bush failed to make an issue of Clinton's promise to end the ban on gays in the military—an issue that could have given the Republicans some political mileage, especially in the socially conservative South.

Even as the Republicans lowered the temperature of their antigay rhetoric, "no special rights" for homosexuals emerged as a major issue for the Religious Right. Christian fundamentalists and their allies attempted to overturn gay rights ordinances in Portland, Maine, and Tampa, Florida. They gathered enough signatures in the traditionally "live and let live" states of Oregon and Colorado to put referendum questions on the November ballot forbidding the enactment of gay antidiscrimination protections. (The Oregon initiative went the furthest, labeling homosexuality as "abnormal, wrong, unnatural, and perverse" and mandating that state-supported institutions—including schools and libraries—work actively to discourage such behavior.)

The combination of Clinton promises and the newest wave of backlash spurred the gay and lesbian community into action. As November neared, it appeared as if every apartment window in San Francisco's Castro district featured a Clinton-Gore placard. An estimated $3 million in gay money flowed into the Clinton campaign. "The gay community is the new Jewish community," **Rahm Emanuel,** Clinton campaign national finance director, told *The New York Times.* "It's highly politicized, with fundamental health and civil rights concerns. And it contributes money. All that makes for a potent political force, indeed."

As Election Day neared, the media, traditionally leery of gay issues, began to take notice. *The New York Times Magazine* featured a cover article, "Gay Politics Goes Mainstream," written by openly gay political reporter **Jeffrey Schmalz.** On the Thursday before Election Day, the "CBS Evening News" aired a long feature on the gay and lesbian vote, estimating that five million gays and lesbians would go to the polls. For the first time in a national race, exit pollsters queried voters as to their sexual orientation. When the votes were counted, it was clear that the gay vote had gone overwhelmingly for Clinton. Exit polls done for Cable News Network and the three major networks found Clinton winning 72 percent of the gay vote (with Bush and third-party candidate **Ross Perot** splitting the remainder); other polls put Clinton's total at closer to 90 percent. It wasn't clear how many American voters were gay or lesbian. The figure of one in seven was bandied about by Clinton campaign officials, but in fact the Voter Research and Survey Group (VRS), which did research for the major networks, found only 2.4 percent of voters willing to identify themselves as homosexual or bisexual. Since many people are reluctant to disclose their homosexuality to an exit pollster, VRS director **Murray Edelman** suggested that 4 or 5 percent was probably a more accurate number.

The day after Clinton's election, *The New York Times* headlined GAY AREAS ARE JUBILANT OVER CLINTON. Reporter Jeffrey Schmalz's lead went: "After a bitter year in which homosexual issues figured in a presidential election for the first time, men and women took

Bill Clinton, the great
gay hope, at the 1992
Democratic National
Convention. *(© Reuters/
Bettmann)*

to the street Tuesday night in gay enclaves like San Francisco and
West Hollywood, weeping, dancing, and hugging to celebrate the
victory of Gov. Bill Clinton." Gay spokespeople were exultant.
Urvashi Vaid, former executive director of the National Gay and
Lesbian Task Force, proclaimed, "This is a rite of passage for the
gay and lesbian movement. For the first time in our history, we're
going to be full and open partners in the Government." And David
Mixner told *The New York Times,* "I believe thousands of my
friends who wouldn't make it, who would die of AIDS, might make
it now because Bill Clinton is President."

Other results that November Election Day provided less cause
for celebration. While Oregon voters soundly defeated the antigay
initiative in that state, Colorado's less harsh ballot measure passed
by a narrow majority. Portland, Maine, rejected an effort to repeal
its gay and lesbian rights ordinance, but a similar ordinance was
overturned by voters in Tampa, Florida. The antigay forces were
undaunted, however, with the Oregon Citizens' Alliance promising

to move town by town and county by county in that state to enact laws barring gay rights protections. Despite Clinton's victory, gay and lesbian rights remained a controversial, polarizing issue. Just how controversial and how polarizing was to become evident as Inauguration Day neared.

The issue of the U.S. military's policy of banning homosexuals had never been a major issue for the gay movement, even though some 80,000 gay men and women had been discharged since the ban was initiated in 1943. The challenges to military policy by armed forces personnel like Leonard Matlovich, Vernon "Copy" Berg, Miriam Ben-Shalom, and others in the 1970s and '80s made headlines in the gay press, of course. Yet perhaps because the gay movement had its roots in the antiwar New Left, perhaps because it was weakest in small towns and in the South—the region of the country from which the military draws its greatest number of recruits—the issue was never a top priority. Instead, largely symbolic issues like sodomy law repeal and gay rights legislation took center stage. Later, AIDS became the major concern, eclipsing most other issues.

But unlike with gay rights legislation or sodomy law repeal or AIDS funding, the perception was widespread that the ban on discrimination against homosexuals in the military could be overturned with the stroke of a pen—in this case, a presidential pen, by means of an executive order. Polls showed a majority of the American public supported ending the ban. Even George Bush's Defense Secretary **Dick Cheney** had described the ban as "a bit of an old chestnut." Military witch-hunts against gays and lesbians seemed particularly retrograde in a society where there was a growing degree of tolerance of homosexuality. Australia and Canada had just overturned their restrictions on gays and lesbians in the military, with no apparent ill effect. The Dutch Navy was about to launch a promotional campaign to encourage gay and lesbian recruits, featuring a brochure that showed two lesbian sailors in an onshore embrace.

Most important, increasing numbers of gay and lesbian servicepeople were coming out and challenging military policy: **Joe Steffan,** the U.S. Naval Academy midshipman ousted for being gay in 1987 just a few weeks before graduation; **Tracy Thorne,** the dashing "Top Gun", who came out on ABC's "Nightline"; Navy Petty Officer **Keith Meinhold,** who revealed his homosexuality on "World

Perry Watkins (left) and Miriam Ben-Shalom (right) were both involved in lengthy court battles challenging the ban on gays in the U.S. military. Although at his draft physical Watkins had checked "yes" to a question about "homosexual tendencies," he successfully remained in the U.S. Army for sixteen years. After he was discharged, the Supreme Court reinstated him; however, his case did not contain the broad constitutional issues necessary to challenge the overall policy. Ben-Shalom, a drill sergeant in the army reserves, was honorably discharged in 1976 and successfully sued for reinstatement. Eventually, the high court upheld the army's right to dismiss her. Watkins and Ben-Shalom are pictured at a 1993 rally in Washington, D.C. (© *Lina Pallotta, Impact Visuals*)

News Tonight with Peter Jennings"; and Colonel **Margarethe Cammermeyer,** a twenty-eight-year veteran and chief nurse of the Washington State National Guard, who revealed she was a lesbian when she was being considered for the position of chief nurse for the entire National Guard of the United States. The armed forces were opposed to change, to be sure—but they were opposed to virtually *any* change. For Bill Clinton, lifting the ban through an executive order seemed the simplest way to pay his campaign debt to the gay community. It also was something he believed was right.

Candidate Clinton had first promised to lift the ban in October 1991, when asked about it by a student questioner at the John F.

Kennedy School of Government at Harvard University. Yet clearly he never expected that it would become the central issue—virtually the only issue—of the early days of his presidency. That is precisely what occurred. For the first ten days of the new administration, the issue that dominated the headlines was not the economy or health care: It was gays in the military. Before Clinton could issue his promised executive order, opposition mobilized: The Religious Right jammed the phone lines to the House and Senate; congressional mail overwhelmingly opposed overturning the ban (Senator **John Glenn's** (D-Ohio) office reported letters running 10 to 1 against); national gay groups seemed immobilized. The popular General **Colin Powell,** head of the Joint Chiefs of Staff, and Senator **Sam Nunn** (D-Georgia), the powerful chairman of the Senate Armed Services Committee whom Clinton had passed over for the post of Defense Secretary, led the charge against any change in policy.

Senators worried aloud about the effect of gays in the military on "unit cohesion," about openly homosexual and heterosexual GIs sharing close quarters and showers. (The entire debate was conducted as if all gay service personnel were male.) Senator **Bob Dole** (R-Kansas) announced that Republicans would offer an amendment to affirm the existing policy. Senate Majority Leader **George Mitchell** (D-Maine) reportedly told then–Defense Secretary **Les Aspin** that the White House could count on no more than thirty votes in the Senate.

The new president temporized, trying to find a way out of the quandary. But the opposition continued to gain strength. Faced with having an executive order overturned in Congress, Clinton announced a compromise. The ban would remain in place for six months, while the Pentagon drafted a plan for an executive order that would end the ban and establish "rigorous standards regarding sexual conduct to be applied to all military personnel." The formal discharge of homosexuals from the military would be halted, and new recruits would no longer be asked if they were homosexual. In the meantime, the military could continue discharge proceedings against avowed homosexuals; instead of being discharged, however, they would be put on unpaid "standby reserve." At Clinton's first presidential news conference—one entirely devoted to the military issue—he portrayed his action as "a dramatic step forward." He added, "This compromise is not everything I would have hoped for, or everything that I have stood for, but it is plainly a substantial step in the right direction."

Gays and lesbians—so jubilant in November when Clinton won—were stunned both by the intensity of the opposition and the new president's seeming lack of firmness. "Homosexuals Wake to See a Referendum: It's on Them" headlined *The New York Times*. Political analyst William Schneider told the *Times*, "I thought all along that the Willie Horton issue of the campaign would be gays and Clinton's support of gay rights. Well, instead of happening in the campaign, it has come true now." Meanwhile, intense feelings within the military were underscored when three Marine lance corporals stationed at Camp Lejeune, North Carolina, were accused of dragging a gay man out of a gay bar and beating him, allegedly shouting, "Clinton must pay." The man, **Crae Pridgen**, said he suffered a fractured skull. (The marines were later acquitted.)

Unable to compete with the firestorm of opposition, gay and lesbian groups attempted to regroup. With seed money from **David Geffen**, the Hollywood producer, and **Barry Diller**, the entertainment mogul, an organization called the Campaign for Military Service (CMS) was established to lobby for repeal of the ban. **Tom Stoddard**, former director of the Lambda Legal Defense and Education Fund, the national gay legal organization, was named to head the new group.

Yet with six months to go before the Pentagon made a final decision on the matter, the initiative clearly lay with Sam Nunn and opponents of lifting the ban. Nunn was preparing to put forth a compromise of his own, dubbed "Don't Ask, Don't Tell," permitting homosexuals to remain in the military if they kept their sexual orientation private. Nunn announced that he would schedule Senate hearings, not just in Washington, but also at military bases around the country, where there was intense opposition. That did not augur well for the gay side. President Clinton, seeking to move the spotlight on to other issues, said little. In late March, responding to a question at a news conference, the president surprised all sides by stating that he might consider a proposal to segregate troops by sexual orientation. Bob Hattoy, the White House aide who had made a prime-time speech on AIDS at the Democratic National Convention, likened this idea to "restricting gays and lesbians to jobs as florists and hairdressers" in civilian life. Although the White House quickly retreated, the fact that the president would even entertain such a notion was indication that he was less than committed to his earlier, stated position.

. . .

The hopes of November were slipping away, and it was only March. Yet amid the widespread public discussion about gays in the military, a kind of seismic shift had occurred regarding gay issues in general. Suddenly, the subject of homosexuality—always relegated to the margins of American discourse, always treated warily in the media, if at all—had arrived at the center of American life. It was now a legitimate public issue and a recognized part of American society and culture. The "Gay Moment" had arrived. As journalist **Andrew Kopkind** (who coined the term) wrote in an article in *The Nation*:

> *The gay moment is unavoidable. It fills the media, charges politics, saturates popular and elite culture. It is the stuff of everyday conversation and public discourse. Not for thirty years has a class of Americans endured the peculiar pain and exhilaration of having their civil rights and moral worth—their very humanness—debated at every level of public life. Lesbians and gay men today wake up to headlines alternately disputing their claim to equality under the law, supporting their right to family status, denying their desire, affirming their social identity. They fall asleep to TV talk shows where generals call them perverts, liberals plead for tolerance and politicians weigh their votes. "Gay invisibility," the social enforcement of the sexual closet, is hardly the problem anymore. Overexposure is becoming hazardous.*

The New York Times, which in the past had downplayed gay coverage (even refusing to use the word "gay"), now featured almost daily articles on various aspects of gay and lesbian life. *Times* reporter Jeffrey Schmalz provided extensive coverage of the gay movement and described his personal fight against AIDS in a Sunday "News of the Week in Review" piece. (See "Whatever Happened to AIDS," p. 545.) Gay *wunderkind* Andrew Sullivan became editor of *The New Republic*, arguably the most influential political magazine in the country. *Vanity Fair* ran an article on "The New Gay Power Elite," turning gay and lesbian activists into the stuff of celebrity profile. The newspapers were full of articles about discoveries of a possible biological basis for homosexuality—if it really *were* biological, all the more reason why it couldn't be ignored and why antigay discrimination couldn't be tolerated.

Within the arts in particular, works by openly gay authors treating gay subjects were gaining attention and winning prizes, the latter being something unheard of previously. **Paul Monette's** memoir, *Becoming a Man*, won a National Book Award. **Tony Kushner's** play *Angels in America* was the recipient of a Pulitzer prize. Gay-cum-Jewish plays such as Larry Kramer's *The Destiny of Me* and **William Finn**'s musical *Falsettos* became crossover hits on and off Broadway. These works all dealt with AIDS as well as gay issues, and this perhaps made them more palatable to mainstream audiences. As Kopkind noted, "The New York theater is now almost exclusively about gays, Jews, and blacks—with considerable overlap." Although Hollywood still remained wary of gay themes, an Irish import called *The Crying Game* proved one of the oddest gay love stories ever filmed—and one of the most successful. By year's end, the movie industry was stunned by the success of **Jonathan Demme's** *Philadelphia*, a film about a gay lawyer fired from his job because he has AIDS. Starring **Tom Hanks** and **Denzel Washington**, *Philadelphia* was the top-grossing movie in the country for several weeks. Hanks won an Oscar for Best Actor.

The "gay moment" culminated on April 25 with the long-planned Gay and Lesbian March on Washington. Unlike the two previous gay marches on the nation's capital in 1979 and 1987, this time there was extraordinary media attention: The public-affairs cable channel, C-Span, announced plans to broadcast the entire march and rally live. President Clinton declined to appear or speak by audio hookup, a sign of how much the White House feared his political standing had been eroded by his identification with gay rights. (He did send a letter of support, however, and met with gay leaders at the White House a few days before the event, in itself a first.) March organizers predicted a million people would attend.

And so, on April 25, they marched, hundreds of thousands of them, parading for six hours from the Ellipse, down Pennsylvania Avenue past the White House, and then on to the mall in front of the Capitol. If AIDS had dominated the 1987 march, this time, not surprisingly, it was the military: Among the marchers was **Dorothy Hadjys,** the mother of **Allen Schindler,** a gay sailor whose brutal murder by a shipmate the previous October had become a cause célèbre and symbol of hostility to gays within the military. Mrs.

Hadjys, who spoke at the rally afterward, marched surrounded by gay veterans in uniform.

One of the largest contingents came from Colorado, indication of the politicization of that state's gay community in the wake of the passage of the antigay referendum the previous fall (and the ensuing national boycott of the state). The Colorado marchers carried a massive banner that read "Under Siege" as well as a papier-mâché Statue of Liberty and scales of justice. AIDS was not entirely forgotten: ACT UP members lay down in front of the White House to focus attention on the issue, and the AIDS Quilt was displayed once again. A Lesbian Community Cancer Project group marched with placards featuring the names of lesbians who had died from breast cancer. Names held up included black lesbian writers, Audre Lorde and **Pat Parker,** and the comedian Pat Bond.

At the rally, California Representative **Nancy Pelosi** read a letter from President Clinton; there were scattered boos. David Mixner, Clinton friend and leader of the Lift-the-Ban campaign, told the throng, "Make no mistake, America. We won't compromise our freedom. We won't go back. We will win." Holly Near sang. Still, for all the anticipation, the rally largely lacked the big names of American politics or the entertainment world.

Although march organizers and the Park Police sparred over how many people were actually in attendance and some of the more X-rated aspects of the day received a full airing on C-Span, the march and rally received generally good notices from the media. Writing in *The New York Times,* Richard L. Berke noted in a page-one analysis that the march showed the general public "that gay America does have a face. And it was, in fact, a face that seemed rather well-behaved and conventional, and that was the image that Americans saw on the evening news." The *Washington Post* columnist E. J. Dionne, Jr., praised the march as a "serious and sober celebration of liberty" and was struck by "the infinite variety of political organizations, singing ensembles, mutual aid societies and support groups that came together not to shock but to talk about freedom."

These views were echoed in the middle of the country as well. Under the headline WE WON'T COMPROMISE OUR FREEDOM, the *Chicago Tribune* featured two front-page color photos: One showed two men embracing in front of the AIDS Quilt; another provided an air view of the Mall thronged with people. For its part, the conservative *Memphis Commercial Appeal* headlined its front-page

story GAYS MARCH ON WASHINGTON FOR CIVIL RIGHTS, ACCEP-
TANCE, and accompanied it with a large color photo of the ACT
UP die-in in front of the White House. The newspaper pulled a
quote from **Torie Osborn,** executive director of the National Gay
and Lesbian Task Force, and displayed it prominently on the front
page: "We are the new American refugees coming home from exile."

In fact, media coverage of the march was generally so favorable
that two weeks later, *Washington Post* media critic Howard Kurtz
was complaining that some of the more "flamboyant behavior and
vulgar language" had actually been "bleached out" of most news
accounts. This marked a complete turnabout from how most gay
marches had been covered in the past (coverage that usually consisted of pictures of men in drag) and emphasized the media's eagerness to portray the gay movement as a mainstream political force.

Despite the positive coverage, it wasn't clear how much the march
actually achieved. Richard Berke noted in his *New York Times*
article that although the massive civil rights marches and anti-Vietnam rallies are "defined as significant occasions in modern history,
there is little evidence that they created any immediate shifts in
public or political opinion." He suspected the same would be true
of this march. Openly gay U.S. Representative Barney Frank thought
that the major impact of demonstrations of this sort was on the
participants themselves. Frank was later to label the march a political failure because a relatively small number of participants went
to Capitol Hill in the days that followed to lobby their senators and
representatives to lift the ban. In fact, the march—planned long
before the military ban became an issue—was never sure whether
it wanted to be a giant gay and lesbian pride celebration or a show
of political strength to force the president and Congress to lift the
ban.

On the same day as the march, in Boston for a speech to the
Newspaper Association of America, President Clinton said, "A lot
of people think that I did a terrible political thing, and I know I
paid a terrible political price for saying that I thought the time had
come to end the categorical ban on gays and lesbians serving in
our military service . . ."

The hearings held by Sam Nunn's Senate Armed Services Committee, beginning in late March, turned out to be reasoned, un-
emotional affairs in which academics talked abstractly about "unit

cohesion," and Chairman Nunn always referred to homosexuals, in a courtly manner, as "gays and lesbians." But Nunn was in charge, while the White House adopted a posture of public silence as it ostensibly waited for the Pentagon to come up with its final report, due on July 15. And Nunn had some tricks up his sleeve. When Armed Services Committee members paid a visit to the submarine *Montpelier* in Norfolk, Virginia, in early May, Nunn and Senator **John Warner** (R-Virginia) were pictured on the TV evening news talking earnestly to a group of sailors on their bunks in what appeared to be extraordinarily cramped sleeping conditions. The photo was a turning point of sorts: It lent dramatic credence to arguments that close quarters on ships and submarines might make the presence of homosexuals a problematic factor.

The most memorable moment of the hearings came when Marine Colonel **Fred Peck,** just back from Somalia, testified. Peck presented the usual arguments for retaining the ban—discipline, good order, and unit cohesion. Then he dropped a bombshell: "My son **Scott** is a homosexual, and I don't think there's any place for him in the military." The reason was not that Scott couldn't be a good soldier: In his father's view, the twenty-four-year-old college senior was "a recruiter's dream." Instead, the senior Peck was concerned for his son's safety. "I've spent twenty-seven years of my life in the military, and I know what it would be like for him if he went in," Peck continued. "And it would be hell. I would be very fearful that his life would be in jeopardy from his own troops." He loved his son and respected him. "I think he is a fine person," he said. It was moving and riveting testimony but it was curious reasoning. To *Washington Post* columnist William Raspberry, Peck was engaging in the time-honored tradition of blaming the victim. Raspberry wrote, "But fearing that a homosexual Marine would 'be in jeopardy from his own troops'. . . What sort of outfit have you devoted your life to, Colonel? And shouldn't you be trying to fix it?"

But as the clock ticked toward July 15 it was becoming plain that there wasn't going to be much of an effort to fix anything, except the politics of the situation. The best that the gays were likely to get was a version of Sam Nunn's "Don't Ask, Don't Tell." One of the first to recognize this publicly was Representative Barney Frank. In mid-May, at a Washington news conference, the outspoken and openly gay Massachusetts congressman broke ranks with gay activists and proposed his own variation on "Don't Ask, Don't Tell." Frank's compromise was similar to Nunn's in that gays would be allowed to remain in the military as long as they didn't reveal their sexual orientation while on duty. Frank's plan was more flexible than Nunn's, however, in that his proposal would permit service personnel to be openly gay off-base, without fear of investigation or reprisal. "My sense was that many members of Congress had already made up their minds on this," Frank told *Advocate* reporter Chris Bull. "The choice seemed to be whether we would get zero or offer some kind of a compromise that was more permissive than Nunn's. I think my proposal reopens the battle for us."

Although Frank was universally criticized by gay activists, his endorsement of compromise provided Clinton with some important political cover. The president could now bow to the reality that overturning the ban was politically impossible. A week after Frank's comments, Clinton indicated at a town meeting that he was amenable to some form of "Don't Ask, Don't Tell": "Most Americans believe if you don't ask and you don't say and you're not forced to confront it, people should be able to serve. . . . We are trying to work this out so that our country . . . does not appear to be endorsing a gay lifestyle. But we accept people as people and give them a chance to serve if they play by the rules."

Now the question was simple. Which version of "Don't Ask, Don't Tell" would be approved: Sam Nunn's or Barney Frank's?

In the end, what the president and the Pentagon did approve was something closer to Nunn than to Frank, so much so that Frank repudiated the deal altogether. The final compromise stuck to the basics of "Don't Ask, Don't Tell": It stated that recruits would not be asked their sexual orientation but homosexual servicepeople could not reveal it either. While gay soldiers would have to remain in the closet—and stay celibate—the witch-hunts of the past would end. Strict guidelines would make it difficult for officers to pursue accusations of homosexuality without strong evidence of repeated homosexual conduct or public affirmation. Simply being present at a gay bar or reading homosexual publications or even marching in a gay rights parade would not "provide a basis for initiating an investigation or serve as the basis for an administrative discharge under this policy." But the bottom line was that gay or lesbian GIs who revealed their homosexuality—either to a friend in the next bunk or to a national TV audience—would be discharged. The closet remained in force.

On July 19, Clinton made his announcement of the new policy before a friendly audience of military officers at the National Defense University at Fort McNair in Washington, D.C. He was flanked by General Colin Powell and the top commanders of the armed forces; there wasn't a single gay or lesbian representative present. Oddly enough, the president's speech was perhaps his most eloquent on the subject since he was elected, the one that seemed to best argue the case for the inclusion of homosexuals in the U.S. military. David Mixner summed up the reaction of many gays and lesbians: "This was one of those moments in anyone's presidency where he either hears a call to greatness or surrenders. He made no principled fight. He didn't address the nation until today, and that was to concede defeat."

But Senator Nunn still wasn't satisfied. He was determined to codify the policy into law, instead of leaving it as an executive order, which could theoretically be made more flexible at some future date without congressional approval. He introduced an amendment to the defense authorization bill that incorporated the compromise agreed to by Clinton and the Joint Chiefs of Staff. The wily Nunn couldn't restrain himself from tinkering with the Clinton plan. His amendment added language that "persons who demonstrate a propensity or intent to engage in homosexual acts" were "an unacceptable risk" for inclusion in the military. It also stated that the Secretary of Defense could, if he wished, reinstate the practice of asking recruits to disclose their sexual orientation. And it omitted language in the Clinton policy intended to curb military antigay witch-hunts. The White House insisted that these changes would have little impact. They declined to fight Nunn on these points, and Nunn's amendment passed both houses. The president signed it.

In the eyes of some, the codification of "Don't Ask, Don't Tell" actually created a worse situation than what had prevailed before Clinton took office. In an op-ed piece that appeared in *The New York Times,* the Campaign for Military Service's Tom Stoddard called the final product "an utter capitulation to Mr. Nunn" that was "not consistent with Mr. Clinton's earlier stands." He contended that lesbians and gay men in the military were about to confront "the worst of all possibilities: an unprecedented declaration by Congress that they pose an 'unacceptable risk' to our national security. What's 'honorable' about that?"

Soon enough, the action moved to the judicial arena, where a number of cases of gay and lesbian military personnel came up for review. As the year came to a close, more and more judges were ruling in favor of gay servicepeople. The issue was far from settled. The fate of gays and lesbians in the military was probably going to be decided where many had long thought it would be decided—not in Congress but in the courts.

Voices from the Military Debate

Former Senator Barry M. Goldwater
(Republican presidential candidate, 1964)

After more than 50 years in the military and politics, I am still amazed to see how upset people can get over nothing. Lifting the ban on gays in the military isn't exactly nothing, but it's pretty damned close. . . .

When the facts lead to one conclusion, I say it's time to act, not to hide. The country and the military know that eventually the ban will be lifted. The only remaining questions are how much muck we will all be dragged through, and how many brave Americans like Tom Paniccia and Col. Margarethe Cammermeyer will have their lives and careers destroyed in a senseless attempt to stall the inevitable. . . .

I have served in the armed forces. I have flown more than 150 of the best fighter planes and bombers this country manufactured. I founded the Arizona National Guard. I chaired the Senate Armed Services Committee. And I think it's high time to pull the curtains on this charade of policy.

> —from an op-ed piece in the *Washington Post National Weekly,* June 21, 1993

Dorothy Hadjys *(mother of murdered gay sailor Allen Schindler)*

When I went to the funeral home the next day to view Allen's body, my minister tried to talk me out of going in and seeing him. . . . He's been a minister for 34 years, and he's seen a lot of dead people. He had never seen a body destroyed the way Allen was destroyed

just by someone using his hands or feet. His whole face was caved in. His whole face was destroyed. He didn't look anything like my son whatsoever. And I, I wanted to hug him and kiss him, and I wasn't even sure it was my son."
>—from a profile by Mark Schoofs in *The Advocate*,
>   July 13, 1993

BOB ESENWEIN (*twenty-six-year navy veteran*)
We despise gays and all these people usurping the country.
>—quoted in *The New York Times* at the Jacksonville,
>   North Carolina, forum on gays in the military,
>   March 25, 1993

JACKSONVILLE, NORTH CAROLINA, FORUM ON GAYS IN
    THE MILITARY
"Is being old a sin?" asked the citizen who did not identify himself.
    "No," the crowd yelled back.
    "Is being handicapped a sin?" one man then asked.
    "No!" the crowd screamed, louder this time.
    "Is being homosexual a sin?" he came back.
    "Yes!" roared the crowd, loudest of all.
>—"Forum on Military's Gay Ban Starts, and Stays,
>   Shrill," by Eric Schmitt, *The New York Times*,
>   March 25, 1993

ANDREW SULLIVAN (*editor of* The New Republic)
Lifting the ban is essentially a conservative measure. It is not a radical attempt to remake society but a pragmatic effort to react to a change that is already taking place: the presence of openly gay people in the military. The values that gays in the military are espousing, patriotism and public service, are traditional values. And the effect that ending the ban could have on the gay community is to embolden the forces of responsibility and integration and weaken the impulses of victimology and despair.
>—from a *New York Times* op-ed piece, February 9, 1993

TANYA DOMI *(retired lesbian army captain)*
These guys who operate multimillion-dollar aircraft and tanks are afraid somebody's going to hit on them. Maybe they'll understand how women feel all the time.
—quoted in *Newsweek,* June 21, 1993

URVASHI VAID *(lesbian and gay activist)*
The biggest myth about compromise is that it is mutual and consensual. In fact, compromise is the most coercive of strategies, and compromise is always a burden on the powerless.
—in *The Advocate,* June 29, 1993

JOSEPH ZUNIGA *(former Soldier of the Year for the 6th Army)*
This compromise ["Don't Ask, Don't Tell"] would work if we were dealing with automatons, but for human beings, not announcing one's sexual orientation isn't the simple request that proponents of this compromise believe. There is no on-off switch when dealing with human identity.
—from an op-ed piece in the *Washington Post,*
May 18, 1993

SENATOR SAM NUNN *(chairman of the Senate Armed Services Committee)*
He's [Clinton] focused on the discrimination aspect of it. I understand where he's coming from on that. I have my view. Mine is focused on the military side of it. . . . That's two different perspectives and you get two different answers.
—from a *Washington Post* profile, May 3, 1993

"Whatever Happened to AIDS?"

In the two years before his death from AIDS at the age of thirty-nine, New York Times *reporter Jeffrey Schmalz gave new prominence to gay and lesbian issues and AIDS in a newspaper that had traditionally been reticent in its coverage of both subjects. He profiled other people with HIV, such as* **Earvin "Magic" Johnson,** *Larry Kramer, Bob Hattoy,* **Elizabeth Glaser,** *and* **Mary Fisher,** *and covered gay politics during the watershed period beginning with the Clinton campaign through the battle over homosexuals in the military. He also wrote a personal article in December 1992 for the "Week in Review" section that broke the long-standing rule that daily journalists rarely, if ever, refer to themselves in their work. "Now I see the world through the prism of AIDS," he wrote. "I feel an obligation to write about it and an obligation to the newspaper to write what just about no other reporter in America can cover in quite the same way."*

Schmalz began his journalistic career as a night copy boy at the Times *while a student at Columbia University. He covered the early years of the Cuomo administration as the newspaper's Albany bureau chief and also served as Miami bureau chief, where he was so devoted to his job that he was famous for sleeping all night at his desk. He was the deputy national editor in December 1990 when he suffered a brain seizure at work that led to his AIDS diagnosis. At that point, he became open at the* Times *about his homosexuality and his illness and helped to transform the atmosphere both in the newsroom and on the news pages.*

His final (and unfinished) article, "Whatever Happened to AIDS?," appeared in the Times Sunday Magazine *on November 28, 1993, three weeks after his death. In what is part journalistic account and part personal statement, Schmalz expresses his growing despair that, despite two hundred thousand deaths in the United States and an estimated one million infections, AIDS is being forgotten.*

ONCE AIDS WAS A HOT TOPIC in America—promising treatments on the horizon, intense media interest, a political battlefield. Now, 12 years after it was first recognized as a new disease, AIDS has become normalized, part of the landscape. It is at once everywhere and nowhere, the leading cause of death among young men nationwide, but little threat to the core of American political power, the white heterosexual suburbanite. No cure or vaccine is in sight. And what small treatment advances had been won are now crumbling. The world is moving on, uncaring, frustrated and bored, leaving by the roadside those of us who are infected and who can't help but wonder: Whatever happened to AIDS? . . .

The AIDS movement was built on grass-roots efforts. Now those efforts are in disarray. Many Act Up leaders have died. The group's very existence was based on the belief that AIDS could be cured quickly if only enough money and effort were thrown at it—something that now seems increasingly in doubt. Besides, it is hard to maintain attacks against a Government that is seeking big increases in AIDS spending. . . .

Anyone questioning how AIDS ranks as an issue among gay groups need only look to the march on Washington on April 25. Six years earlier, in 1987, a similar gay march had one overriding theme: AIDS. If there was a dominant theme last April, it was homosexuals in the military. To be sure, AIDS was an element of the march, but *just* an element. Speaker after speaker ignored it. . . .

Increasingly, many homosexuals, especially those who test negative for HIV, do not want a disease to be what defines their community. . . .

What is to some a broadening of the gay agenda, however, is to others desertion. "It's one thing for politicians to abandon AIDS," Kevin Frost, a TAG [Treatment Action Group] member, said. "But for our own community to abandon the issue . . . Who brought this issue of gays in the military out in the open? A couple of flashy queers with checkbooks. Well, what about AIDS?" . . .

In my interviews for this article and others, I always ask people with AIDS if they expect to die of the disease. One reason for that is a genuine reporter's curiosity; the answer is part of the profile of who they are. But I am also searching for hope for myself. Increasingly, the answers come back the same, even from the most optimistic of Act Up zealots: Yes, we will die of AIDS. . . .

I had such hope when I interviewed Bill Clinton about AIDS and gay issues for this magazine in August 1992. He spoke so eloquently on AIDS. I really did see him as a white knight who might save me. How naive I was to think that one man could make that big a difference. At its core, the problem isn't a government; it's a virus.

Still, in interviews with researchers and Administration officials, it was clear that we are talking from different planets. I need help now, not five years from now. Yet the urgency just wasn't there. Compassion and concern, yes; even sympathy. But urgency, no. I felt alone, abandoned, cheated. . . .

I usually say that my epitaph is not a phrase but the body of my work. I am writing it with each article, including this one. But actually, there is a phrase that I want shouted at my funeral and written on the memorial cards, a phrase that captures the mix of cynicism and despair that I feel right now and that I will almost certainly take to my grave: *Whatever happened to AIDS?*

The Many Lives of Martina Navratilova

IN LATE AUGUST 1993 at Madison Square Garden in New York City, a fund-raising event called "A Gay and Lesbian Tribute to Martina" raised $250,000. The proceeds were to benefit Gay Games IV, a gathering of an expected more than 10,000 gay and lesbian athletes to be held in New York on the twenty-fifth anniversary of the Stonewall rebellion. **Martina Navratilova,** whose overpowering serve and stamina on the court had made her the nine-time winner of Wimbledon tennis singles titles and four-time U.S. Open champion, had thrust a relatively unknown gay athletic competition into the national spotlight.

Suddenly, at age thirty-seven, America's top female athlete emerged as the nation's most famous (and most marketable) gay and lesbian activist. As a *New York Times* headline put it, IN THE TWILIGHT OF HER PROFESSIONAL TENNIS CAREER, MARTINA NAVRATILOVA STEPS FORWARD WITH A NEW MISSION: SERVING AS A VOICE FOR LESBIANS AND GAY MEN. She joined an American Civil Liberties Union lawsuit to overturn the new Colorado law banning the enactment of gay and lesbian rights ordinances. She threatened to move out of Aspen, Colorado, where she lived, unless the law was

Martina Navratilova on the court. *(© Reuters/Bettmann)*

repealed. Her name adorned a fund-raising mailing for the National Gay and Lesbian Task Force. She was one of the speakers at the 1993 March on Washington. When a reporter asked her why she was doing all this, she replied, "I've got to practice what I preach and this feels right."

Being a gay activist was a new role for Navratilova. For many years, as the most visible figure in women's tennis, she walked a delicate line. She wanted to be open about her sexuality, but at the same time she didn't want the sport to be tarred with the brush of lesbianism (any more than it was already). "The media thinks if you're a female athlete, you're automatically gay," Navratilova noted. "And if you're a male athlete, then obviously you're straight. I happen to be gay but 90 percent of the women on tour are not." In 1993, she was the only major sports figure in the United States who was out of the closet, an indication of just how taboo homosexuality remained in the world of sports. (Four-time Olympic gold medal–winning diver **Greg Louganis** came out at the Gay Games that same year.)

Navratilova had never particularly hidden her sexuality. It wasn't very long after she defected from her native Czechoslovakia to the United States in 1975 at age eighteen that she recognized her attraction to women. "Looking back to when I was sixteen or seventeen, I can see I had some crushes on some women players and didn't really know it. I just liked being with them. By the time I was eighteen I knew I always had these feelings," she wrote in *Martina*, her autobiography, published in 1985, at the height of her career. The fact that she was earning a phenomenal amount of money for an eighteen-year-old and was on her own—her parents were unable to leave Czechoslovakia—made it easier for her to follow her own sexual inclinations. She did characterize herself as bisexual at one time, although there is no sign she was ever involved with a man.

But Navratilova was a public figure—she was extremely young; she had defected from a Communist country; she was a terrific tennis player (winning Wimbledon for six consecutive years, from 1982 to 1987, and the Grand Slam sweeps in 1984) at a time when women's tennis had an extremely high profile. Her love life became fodder for the gossip columns, particularly in the British tabloids. First came her relationship with author Rita Mae Brown, who met her in 1979 when Brown was researching a Czech character for a novel she was writing. Brown was the most stimulating person

Navratilova had ever met, according to Navratilova's account. Brown also made it clear from the start that she didn't care whether or not Navratilova was a great tennis player; in fact, she rather disparaged sports. Navratilova had never met anyone like *that* before. The couple bought a house together in Charlottesville, Virginia, and a Rolls-Royce Silver Cloud II with a quote from Virgil— "Amor Vincet Omnia"—plastered on the side. But when her career began to founder in the early eighties, Navratilova broke off the relationship. (Brown got her revenge, portraying Navratilova as a temperamental Argentine tennis player in her satirical novel about the women's tennis circuit, *Sudden Death*.) Later, Navratilova's seven-year relationship with **Judy Nelson** ended in an acrimonious palimony suit. To add insult to injury, eventually Brown and Nelson became lovers, resulting in a gossipy feature in the *Washington Post,* headlined, TOUGH MATCH FOR MARTINA: RITA MAE BROWN AND JUDY NELSON WERE HER LOVERS. NOW THEY'RE LOVERS.

Over the years, the press—on the sports page, at least—handled her rather gingerly, a testament to both her athletic abilities and personal qualities. Still, Navratilova had to endure a number of antigay slights. She recalled one woman cheering for her archrival **Chris Evert** at the 1983 U.S. Open finals at Forest Hills with, "Come on, Chris, I want a real woman to win." That same year, Navratilova won three of four events in tennis's Grand Slam, but *Sports Illustrated* gave its Sportswoman of the Year award to track star **Mary Decker.** Navratilova thought she deserved it. She noted how the article portrayed Decker as someone who "badly needed to be protected and loved and supported" and featured a picture of Decker in the arms of her new boyfriend. Once Navratilova's sexuality became known, she became anathema to advertisers who might have otherwise paid her vast sums for endorsements.

By 1994, the year she announced her retirement, any lingering hostility had vanished, however. Still ranked number three in women's tennis, Navratilova was a kind of elder stateswoman who had finally gained the adulation of the crowds. Spectators would cheer when her name was announced, and she was amused that she would receive a standing ovation even for a mediocre shot. "Now I'm the home team everywhere I go," she said. When she lost her bid for her tenth Wimbledon title to **Conchita Martinez,** virtually the entire tennis world was devastated.

Perhaps it was the slights she had endured over the years that propelled Navratilova into the gay political arena. Or maybe it was simply that at age thirty-seven, with those nine Wimbledon and four U.S. Open singles championships behind her, she didn't have anything to lose anymore. In any event, there she was at the Gay and Lesbian March on Washington, telling a crowd of hundreds of thousands of people, in one of the most heartfelt speeches of the day, "What our movement needs most, in my humble opinion, is for us to come out of the closet."

The fact that such a prominent sports figure was willing to be associated publicly with the gay and lesbian rights movement was an indication of the legitimacy the movement was achieving in the nineties. But despite the emphasis Navratilova put on coming out, it remained difficult for athletes who lacked her stature to follow in her footsteps—athletes who had more to lose and could easily be destroyed by hostile teammates and jeering crowds. Still, Navratilova's activism—and newfound adulation on the court—offered hope. As her mentor, **Billie Jean King,** put it, "One thing that I love about Martina is that she demands acceptance on equal terms for all of us. Not tolerance but acceptance. Because she is comfortable in her own skin, she helps all of us be more comfortable in ours."

The Year of the Lesbian

NINETEEN NINETY-THREE WAS THE YEAR of the lesbian. The print media discovered lesbians: They made the covers of *Newsweek* and *New York* magazines; openly lesbian singer k.d. lang posed in a barber's chair, getting her face shaved by model **Cindy Crawford,** on the cover of *Vanity Fair.* Television discovered lesbians: A lesbian character played by the bisexual actress **Sandra Bernhard** became a regular on the top-rated sitcom "Roseanne." The U.S. Senate took note of them as well (although women were curiously absent from the gays in the military debate), spending three days discussing the sexual orientation of **Roberta Achtenberg,** Bill Clinton's openly lesbian nominee to be the Assistant Secretary for Fair Housing at the Department of Housing and Urban Development. "Sometimes I think it's like the year of the woman squared," lesbian comic **Kate**

Clinton told *Newsweek*. "It's sort of like the year of the woman loving woman."

When asked by a *Washington Times* reporter if he would support the Achtenberg nomination, Senator Jesse Helms, scourge of gay rights, replied that he wouldn't do so "because she's a damn lesbian. I'm not going to put a lesbian in a position like that. If you want to call me a bigot, fine." The Achtenberg nomination was significant because it marked the first time a president had appointed an openly gay person to a position that required Senate confirmation.

Achtenberg herself was a natural choice to become the first openly gay person appointed to a high federal post. A forty-two-year-old San Francisco lawyer, she had been a law school dean and founded the Lesbian Rights Project, an organization that dealt with family and custody issues. She had run unsuccessfully for state assembly, and in 1990 was elected to the San Francisco Board of Supervisors. Her lover, **Mary Morgan,** was a San Francisco Municipal Court justice, the first openly lesbian judge appointed in the United States. And Achtenberg had been an early supporter of Bill Clinton's presidential bid. But San Francisco politics are different than politics in most other places in the United States. One issue that Achtenberg championed while on the board of supervisors was an effort to pressure the Boy Scouts of America to reverse their policy banning openly gay scoutmasters.

If Jesse Helms didn't mind being labeled a bigot, most other legislators did. So a number of Republican senators used the Boy Scout issue as a way to derail Achtenberg's nomination, without appearing to oppose her simply because she was a lesbian. Senator **Slade Gorton** (R-Washington) accused her of having "crossed the line from advocacy to misuse of government power" by introducing a resolution into the board of supervisors suggesting that San Francisco withdraw $6 million from the Bank of America because the bank had donated money to the Boy Scouts. Minority Leader Robert Dole characterized her as "a ringleader of an ideological crusade to remake the Boy Scouts in her image."

When Senator **Barbara Boxer** (D-California) contended that Achtenberg's critics were using the Boy Scout issue as "a smoke screen for disapproval of her private life," Jesse Helms was quick to respond. "She sure wasn't private when she was hugging and kissing in that homosexual parade in San Francisco," he said. The previous week, Helms had shown Republican colleagues a videotape that featured Achtenberg and her lover riding in a car in the San Francisco Lesbian and Gay Freedom Day parade.

In the midst of such arguments, Senator **Claiborne Pell** (D-Rhode Island) rose before the Senate on a Friday afternoon to announce that he had "a personal reason" for supporting Achtenberg. His daughter, **Julia,** was a lesbian, he declared; in fact, she was the head of Rhode Island's statewide Alliance for Gay and Lesbian Civil Rights. Pell told the senators that he didn't want to see his daughter "barred from a government job because of her orientation." It was believed to be the first time a senator had announced publicly that a member of his family was gay, certainly on the Senate floor. Pell's disclosure also provided a neat counterpoint to Marine Colonel Fred Peck's announcement before the Senate Armed Services Committee that his son Scott was gay and therefore should be kept out of the military. For her part, Julia Pell said she hadn't been told in advance of her father's speech. "I'm not surprised," she said. "He's very supportive of me."

On May 25, Achtenberg's nomination was confirmed by a 58–31 vote. First-term Senator **Patty Murray** (D-Washington) spoke for many when she said, "We're sitting here talking about the private life of an assistant secretary. This country is tired of people who view America as 'us' versus 'them.' " But it was more than just the private life of an assistant secretary that was at issue here. Achtenberg's confirmation had broken a barrier, one that would make it far easier for presidents to appoint openly gay people to high office in the years to come.

EPILOGUE

At the Lesbian and Gay March on Washington, April 25, 1993. *(© Rick Reinhard, Impact Visuals)*

EPILOGUE

Even if the military issue hadn't turned out the way many had hoped in those exhilarating days following Bill Clinton's election victory, the first years of the Clinton administration proved to be a remarkable period for the American gay movement. The serious treatment in the media that gays and lesbians were receiving—from *Vanity Fair* to ABC News "Nightline" to the *Memphis Commercial Appeal*—represented a watershed. And it was the media, as writer Mark Schoofs noted in an article in *Out* magazine, where the cultural battles of American society were increasingly being fought. Eight states now had gay civil rights protections, and Washington, D.C., repealed its sodomy law, without the expected congressional veto. (Almost half the states still had laws prohibiting homosexual sex, however.) Even in places where restrictions on gay rights had been approved by voters—Tampa, Florida, and the state of Colorado—judges had either limited their enforcement or voided them altogether. Meanwhile, Roberta Achtenberg, President Clinton's choice to be his Fair Housing Administrator, became the first openly gay person to be confirmed to a government post by the U.S. Senate (See "The Year of the Lesbian," page 551.) And, in one of the most significant developments of 1993, the Massachusetts State Legislature passed a bill outlawing discrimination against gay and lesbian students in the public schools. The legislation, the first of its kind in the country, passed after an extraordinary lobbying campaign by hundreds of high school students—gay and straight—and was strongly supported by socially liberal Republican governor **William Weld.** The new law would protect gay and lesbian students against harassment, enable them to form school clubs and support groups, and even take a date of the same sex to a prom.

In June 1994, the twenty-fifth anniversary of the Stonewall riots, "Gay Moment II" took place, at least in New York City, the national media capital. The combination of Gay Games IV, with its 11,000 participants, and a march to celebrate Stonewall (and to call attention to abuses of gay and lesbian human rights around the globe) resulted in another unprecedented degree of media coverage. "Is

Everybody Gay?" asked the front cover of *New York* magazine; *The New Yorker* featured a gay marriage on its cover and a listing of the cultural events surrounding Stonewall 25 in its "Goings On About Town" section; *The New York Times* ran full coverage of the Gay Games and interviewed Stonewall "veterans" on the front page. (The newspaper had all but ignored Stonewall back in 1969.) In an editorial, the *Times* urged the acceptance of all kinds of homosexuals, not just the more "respectable" elements. "[T]he measure of a just society is not how it treats people who dress in business clothes," wrote the newspaper. "A just society must offer the same protections to men in leather and chains as to those who wear Brooks Brothers suits." Meanwhile, Republican Mayor **Rudy Giuliani,** who had been elected the previous November with the support of the most fiercely antigay elements in the city, addressed the participants on opening night of the Gay Games as if they were just another tourist convention; Giuliani took part in the march past the United Nations. Outside of New York, Gay Moment II was less keenly felt, however. The *Washington Post* and *Boston Globe* relegated stories about the Stonewall 25 march to inside pages, in contrast to their lavish coverage of the March on Washington a year before. And *Time* and *Newsweek* scrapped cover stories on the gay movement to cover the O. J. Simpson saga instead.

Despite gains on a number of fronts, the overall situation of gays and lesbians remained difficult. As the battle over homosexuals in the military demonstrated, the national gay and lesbian rights organizations were ill-equipped to match their foes in organizational ability and financial resources. There were few, if any, national gay and lesbian leaders of commanding stature. Some had been tarnished by the military defeat, like David Mixner, who rose to prominence particularly because of his supposed access to Clinton. At the same time, partly because the Clinton administration was perceived as sympathetic, the steam had gone out of the militant side of the gay and lesbian movement, which had been so energized by Reagan and Bush policies. ACT UP and Queer Nation were in disarray, with chapters in many cities disbanding; the only direct-action group with any real dynamism was the Lesbian Avengers, a sign of increasing lesbian clout within the movement.

As backlash and polarization intensified, these weaknesses were cause for great concern. "In the 1990s homosexuality will become what the abortion issue was in the 1980s," said **Morris Chapman,** president of the Southern Baptist Convention. The outcome was far from clear. Although, in the 1994 midterm elections, anti-gay referendums were defeated in Oregon and Idaho, the Republican electoral sweep boded ill for gay issues ranging from AIDS funding to the passage of federal antidiscrimination legislation. (The Republican victory also brought the only out-of-the-closet gay Republican congressman, **Steve Gunderson** of Wisconsin, into prominence.) In post-election analyses, pundits contended that Clinton's stand in favor of gays in the military was a key factor in the defection of white heterosexual men to the GOP, particularly in the South.

Gays and lesbians were on the map, finally, but American society remained sharply divided on the subject.

Amid the political victories and defeats, the steps forward and back and forward again, it is easy to lose perspective, to become immersed in the events of the moment. In the United States, the early Clinton years appeared to be a watershed. Yet the development of homosexual identity and community of the previous 125 years and the strides of the political movement before and since Stonewall unquestionably led up to that moment when homosexuality arrived at the center of American political and cultural life. Historian John D'Emilio wrote, " 'Gay History': in 1970, this phrase was an oxymoron. Homosexuality had no history. It was a medical condition, a psychopathological state embodied in aberrant individuals. It had been and remained hidden, isolated, and marginal, a set of disconnected and fragmentary life stories." The life stories don't seem disconnected and fragmentary anymore. As one looks back on the last 125 years, one can see the larger forces that contributed to the creation of the modern sense of gay identity and community: the growth of capitalism and wage labor, the rise of secular societies, the emergence of sexual classifications and of the psychological worldview, changes in the role of women, the effects of two world wars, the arrival of the sexual revolution. More overtly political forces played a decisive role as well. With the rise of the political Left, with the growing self-awareness of racial and ethnic minorities and women, came the notion that average individuals—not just elites—could make history. It was these forces that, eventually, unleashed Stonewall and the post-Stonewall gay and lesbian movement. And one cannot discount the contributions of courageous individuals—the writers, the thinkers, the activists, from Walt Whitman to Radclyffe Hall, from Magnus Hirschfeld to Simon Nkoli.

If one takes the long view of these developments, the rise of gay identity, politics, and culture appears inevitable. The idea of a community based on little more than shared sexual orientation—something that would have been inconceivable just fifty years ago and still seems bizarre to many people today—continues to take root. Within a short period of time, a stigmatized identity and sexuality—condemned by most established religions, declared "sick" by psychiatry, ridiculed in the popular culture—has become "gay," taken on a positive, even celebratory, aspect, and emerged as the basis of community and culture. The more the opposition has attempted to crush it, the more stubborn is its development, the more resilient it appears. Even AIDS has failed to crush it, tens of thousands of deaths later.

The changes have been incremental—the "gay moments" of the American 1990s could not have taken place without the more modest gains and hard work of previous decades. These changes can be seen not just in political advances, but in other areas as well: in culture, in the media, in language, in social attitudes, in the small currencies of daily life. As *New York Times* columnist Anna Quindlen wrote in an April 6, 1994, column:

> *The time has come. You can feel it, in a hundred little ways year after year. It is so certain and inevitable, that the next century will be a time in which it is not simply safe, but commonplace, to be openly gay.*

Quindlen, who is not gay herself, was speaking from the comfortable pundit's perch of New York City in the middle of the Clinton administration. She probably wouldn't have written the same words if she lived in the American South or in Beijing or Havana. But in any historical survey of lesbians and gay men, it is hard not to be optimistic. Twenty-five years before, in the exhilaration of another "gay moment," Kate Millett asked the question "Are we trying to invent a new existence, whizzing through decades of social evolution in an afternoon? Or only joyriding?" An afternoon has stretched into years, but gay and lesbian identity and culture have become a permanent part of history and social development.

Notes

Introduction

xix. HISTORIANS OF HOMOSEXUALITY: Will Roscoe, "The Challenge of Gay and Lesbian Studies," *Journal of Homosexuality*, Vol. 15, Nos. 3/4, 1988.

xx. AMOROUS AND SPECIFIC: Blanche Wiesen Cook, *Eleanor Roosevelt*, p. 478.

xxiii. ONLY WHEN INDIVIDUALS BEGAN: John D'Emilio, *Making Trouble*, p. 8.

CHAPTER 1: THE AGE OF WHITMAN

3. Wilde's visit to Whitman: See Richard Ellman, *Oscar Wilde*, pp. 167–70.

4. CHOSE THE SPURIOUS SAFETY OF IGNORANCE: Peter Gay, *The Tender Passion*, p. 202.

4. A MAN WHO KISSED: E. Anthony Rotundo, *American Manhood*, p. 84.

5. PHYSICAL CONTACT WAS: Ibid., p. 85.

5. SAFER IN THE EARLIER DAYS: Gay, p. 202.

5. ABSOLUTELY CLEAN AND SWEET: Maurice Bucke, Introduction to *Calamus*, p. 11.

6. HE HAD THE FREE AND EASY MANNERS: Justin Kaplan, *Walt Whitman*, p. 15.

6. HIMSELF, HIS NATION, AND HIS CENTURY: Ibid., p. 21.

6. THE MOST EXTRAORDINARY PIECE: Ibid., pp. 202–3.

6. I NEVER KNEW A CASE: Bucke, p. 25.

6. MY DARLING BOY: Charley Shively, ed., *Calamus Lovers*, p. 77.

6. LEW IS SO GOOD: Ibid., p. 73.

7. DEAR COMRADE, YOU MUST NOT: Ibid., pp. 73–74.

7. MIGHT JUST AS WELL HAVE DEALT: Kaplan, p. 286.

7. WALT, YOU WILL BE A SECOND FATHER: Ibid., p. 287.

8. DAN'L SPENCER . . . SOMEWHAT FEMININE: Jonathan Ned Katz, *Gay American History*, p. 500.

8. OCTOBER 9, 1863 JERRY TAYLOR: Shively, p. 58.

8. THE POET'S PRACTICE: Katz, p. 499.

8. WE FELT TO OTHER AT ONCE: Bucke, p. 23.

9. WE WERE AWFUL CLOSE: Ibid., p. 25.

9. DEPRESS THE ADHESIVE NATURE: Kaplan, p. 316.

9. REMEMBER WHERE I AM MOST WEAK: Ibid.

9. I NEVER DREAMED: Ibid.

10. "MY (ADOPTED) SON" AND "MY NEPHEW": Shively, p. 139.

10. RESOLV'D TO SING NO SONGS: Walt Whitman, *Leaves of Grass and Selected Prose*, p. 93.

10. MANY WILL SAY: Ibid., p. 505 n.

11. YOU HAVE MADE MEN TO BE: Katz, p. 359.

11. FOR THE FIRST TIME I ACT: Ibid., p. 501–502.
11. I MIGHT HAVE BEEN A MERE ENGLISH: Ibid., p. 355.
11. I HAVE PORED: Ibid., p. 342.
12. AB'T THE QUESTIONS ON CALAMUS: Ibid., p. 349.
12. WHY HE [WHITMAN] KNEW THAT THE MOMENT: Ibid., p. 364.
12. THERE IS NO DOUBT IN MY MIND: Ibid., p. 365.
12. KISS OF WALT WHITMAN IS STILL ON MY LIPS: Ellman, p. 171.

CHAPTER 2: PIONEERS OF SEXOLOGY

13. NOTHING THAT WENT INTO: Michel Foucault, *History of Sexuality,* Vol. I, p. 43.
15. ONE EVENING I WAS SEATED: Peter Gay, *The Tender Passion,* pp. 230–31.
15. IN ALMOST ALL CASES [OF HOMOSEXUALS]: David F. Greenberg, *The Construction of Homosexuality,* p. 414.
16. TANTALIZING AND TROUBLING MATERIALS: Gay, p. 231.
18. SEX LIES AT THE ROOT OF LIFE: Ibid., p. 232.
19. THE FEMALE EMERGES: Phyllis Grosskurth, *Havelock Ellis,* p. 188.
19. THE BRUSQUE, ENERGETIC: Havelock Ellis, *Studies in the Psychology of Sex,* Vol. I, Part IV, p. 250.
20. THESE UNQUESTIONABLE INFLUENCES: Ibid., Part IV (*Sexual Inversion*), p. 262.
21. WORK DOWN AMONG THE MASS-PEOPLE: P. N. Furbank, *E. M. Forster: A Life,* Vol. 1, p. 256.
21. IT WAS NOT TILL (AT THE AGE OF TWENTY FIVE): Jeffrey Weeks, *Coming Out,* p. 69.
21. BY EMOTION AND TEMPERAMENT: Edward Carpenter, "The Intermediate Sex" in *Love's Coming of Age,* pp. 120–21.
21. A RATHER GENTLE, EMOTIONAL DISPOSITION: Ibid., p. 130.
21. FORWARD FORCE IN HUMAN EVOLUTION: Edward Carpenter, *Intermediate Types Among Primitive Folk,* p. 59.
21. INVENTORS, TEACHERS, MUSICIANS: Ibid., p. 58.
21. HE BELIEVES AND PRACTICES THE PHYSICAL VERY FRANKLY: Noel Annan, *Our Age,* p. 107.
22. I HAVE RECEIVED NO END OF LETTERS: Weeks, p. 79.
22. WHEN IS THAT LITTLE LADY: Grosskurth, p. 157.
22. CARPENTER WAS ALMOST ALONE: Weeks, p. 76.
24. FOR FREUD, HETEROSEXUAL, GENITAL LOVEMAKING: Gay, p. 251.
24. SPECIALLY HIGH INTELLECTUAL DEVELOPMENT: Ronald Bayer, Homosexuality and American Psychiatry, p. 22.
24. HOMOSEXUALITY IS ASSUREDLY NO ADVANTAGE: Sigmund Freud, *Letters,* pp. 423–24.

Two Case Studies from Havelock Ellis's *Sexual Inversion*

25. HISTORY XXXVI from Ellis, *Studies in the Psychology of Sex,* Vol. I, Part IV, pp. 224–26.
27. CASE HISTORY XII: Ellis, p. 120.

CHAPTER 3: WE'WHA GOES TO WASHINGTON: THE BERDACHE

29. I KNOW NOT THROUGH WHAT SUPERSTITION: Katz, *Gay American History*, p. 287.
29. We'wha's visit to Washington: See Will Roscoe, "The Zuni Man-Woman," *OUT/LOOK*, Summer 1988, pp. 58–59.
29. THE MOST INTELLIGENT OF THE ZUNI TRIBE: Roscoe, p. 57.
31. FOLKS WHO HAVE FORMED POETIC IDEAS: Ibid., p. 58.
31. THERE IS A SIDE TO THE LIVES OF THESE MEN: Walter L. Williams, *The Spirit and the Flesh*, p. 185.
32. A SUBGROUP OF HOMOSEXUALS: Ibid., p. 125.
32. ALLIED HIMSELF TO A MAN: Katz, p. 314.
33. DURING THE TIME I WAS THUS: Ibid., p. 285.
33. BASIC CHARACTER: Williams, p. 25.
34. THESE OLD TIME SCALP DANCES: Maurice Kenny, "Tinselled Bucks," in Will Roscoe, ed., *Living the Spirit*, p. 23.
35. WE'WHA'S DEATH WAS REGARDED: Williams, p. 63
35. THEY WEAR THE HAIR CUT: Ibid., p. 233.
36. THE STORY OF THE WOMAN CHIEF OF THE CROW INDIANS: Katz, pp. 309–11.
36. LONG BEFORE SHE HAD VENTURED: Ibid., p. 309.
36. OLD MEN BEGAN TO BELIEVE: Ibid., p. 310.
37. STRANGE COUNTRY THIS: Ibid.
37. ARE ALL SODOMITES: Williams, p. 137.
37. FOUGHT MOST COURAGEOUSLY: Ibid.
37. A FINE ACTION OF AN HONORABLE AND CATHOLIC SPANIARD: Ibid., p. 137.
37. IN THE ACT OF COMMITTING THE NEFARIOUS SIN: Katz, p. 292.
38. AT THE PRESENT TIME THIS HORRIBLE CUSTOM: Williams, p. 139.
38. CONDEMNED OUR TRADITIONS: Ibid., p. 183.
38. THE INDIAN AGENT WROTE TO VICTORIA: Ibid., p. 180.
39. THEY BEGAN TO LOOK DOWN ON THE *WINKTE*: Ibid., p. 182.
39. IT MAY BE THAT THE BACHELORS IN THEIR THIRTIES: Ibid., p. 183.

On the Frontier

40. MRS. NASH, THE COMPANY LAUNDRESS: Katz, pp. 509–10.
40. THEY [COWBOYS] DRINK, SWEAR, AND FIGHT: Clifford P. Westermeir, "Cowboy Sexuality: A Historical No-No?," *Red River Valley Historical Review*, Spring 1975, p. 94.
41. WE JUST DON'T KNOW: Author conversation with Robert French.
41. COWBOYS ATTENDING DANCES: Westermeir, p. 104.
41. COCKED JAUNTILY OVER HIS RIGHT EYE: Edgar Beecher Bronson, *Reminiscences of a Ranchman*, pp. 269–70.
42. FEMININE LOOKS AND BEARING: Westermeir, p. 104.
42. THIS IS NOT TO SUGGEST: Williams, p. 169.
42. I HATE THE STEADY SUN: Katz, p. 511.

CHAPTER 4: OSCAR WILDE

44. THE TALK IN DORMITORIES AND STUDIES: John Chandos, *Boys Together*, pp. 307–8.
46. THE YOUNGEST SON OF THE MARQUESS OF QUEENSBERRY: Ellman, p. 324.
47. TO MY ASTONISHMENT: Frank Harris, *Oscar Wilde*, p. 90.
48. THE AFFECTION AND LOVE OF THE ARTIST: Ellman, p. 449.
48. NEVER WAS PARIS SO CROWDED: Harris, pp. 146–47.
49. THE "LOVE THAT DARE NOT SPEAK ITS NAME": Ellman, p. 463.
49. THREE PERMANENT PUNISHMENTS: Ibid., p. 484.
50. MY DEAREST BOY, THIS IS TO ASSURE YOU: Ibid., p. 461.
50. THE BASIS OF CHARACTER IS WILL POWER: Wilde, *De Profundis*, p. 10.
50. A YOUNG AMERICAN FROM HOT SPRINGS: See Thomas Beer, *The Mauve Decade*, pp. 130–33.
50. WILDE IS NOW SUFFERING FOR BEING A URANIAN: Ellman, p. 502.
51. I'M AN UNSPEAKABLE OF THE OSCAR WILDE SORT: E. M. Forster, *Maurice*, p. 145.
51. MAY HAVE BROUGHT CONVICTION OF THEIR PERVERSION TO MANY INVERTS: Ellis, p. 63.

An Excerpt from Wilde's *De Profundis*

51. Oscar Wilde, *De Profundis*, pp. 62–63.

Wilde and Bosie in Algiers

52. André Gide, *If It Die*, pp. 278–83.

CHAPTER 5: ROMANTIC FRIENDSHIPS BETWEEN WOMEN

55. THE FALL: Nancy Sahli, "Smashing: Women's Relationships Before the Fall," *Chrysalis* 8 (Summer 1979), p. 17.
56. HOW MUCH I WANT TO SEE YOU and NOW WHEN ARE YOU COMING TO NEW YORK: Ibid., p. 18.
57. I AM SO GLAD THAT I HAVE GOT YOU FOR MY DARLING: Ibid.
57. WOMEN WHO LOVE WOMEN: Ibid.
57. A COHORT OF MIDDLE- AND UPPER-MIDDLE-CLASS AMERICAN WOMEN: Carroll Smith-Rosenberg, "Discourses of Sexuality and Subjectivity: The New Woman, 1870–1936," in Martin Duberman et al., eds., *Hidden from History*, p. 265.
58. IN ENGLAND, TOO: For a discussion of women's friendship networks in England, see Rosemary Auchmuty, "By Their Friends We Shall Know Them," in Lesbian History Group, *Not a Passing Phase*, pp. 80–98.
59. IT IS PRETTY CERTAIN THAT SUCH COMRADE-ALLIANCES: Lillian Faderman, *Surpassing the Love of Men*, p. 189.
59. THE LOVES OF WOMEN FOR EACH OTHER GROW MORE NUMEROUS EACH DAY: Jonathan Ned Katz, *Gay/Lesbian Almanac*, pp. 217–18.
59. MORE THAN ANY PHENOMENON, EDUCATION: Lillian Faderman, *Odd Girls and Twilight Lovers*, p. 13.

60. WHILE ONLY 10 PERCENT OF AMERICAN WOMEN REMAINED UNMARRIED: Ibid., p. 14.

60. WHEN A VASSAR GIRL TAKES A SHINE TO ANOTHER: Sahli, p. 21.

60. ONE THING WHICH DAMAGED THE HEALTH OF THE GIRLS: Katz, *Gay/Lesbian Almanac*, p. 178.

61. WANDA FRAIKEN NEFF'S 1928 NOVEL: See Faderman, *Odd Girls and Twilight Lovers*, p. 25.

61. WHAT A SHAME THAT FEMININE FRIENDSHIP SHOULD BE UNNATURAL: Sharon O'Brien, *Willa Cather: The Emerging Voice*, p. 132.

62. I LIKE A GIRL TO HAVE MANY GIRL-FRIENDS: Ibid., p. 133.

62. UNWISE COLLEGE FRIENDSHIPS: Faderman, *Odd Girls and Twilight Lovers*, p. 53.

62. ALL-FEMALE ENVIRONMENTS: Ellis, pp. 219 and 262.

62. JEWETT'S BIOGRAPHER SUGGESTED OMITTING: Faderman, *Surpassing the Love of Men*, p. 197.

62. THE POET EMILY DICKINSON'S NIECE CENSORED: Ibid., pp. 174–77.

63. AS LONG AS WOMEN LOVED EACH OTHER AS THEY DID: Sahli, p. 27.

Willa Cather

64. IN 1916, WHEN . . . : The information in this sidebar comes from Sharon O'Brien, *Willa Cather: The Emerging Voice*.

64. SHE WAS THE FIRST GIRL THAT I EVER SAW IN SUSPENDERS: Ibid., p. 121.

64. WHILE THE STUDENTS WERE SITTING IN THE CLASSROOM: Ibid.

66. GRAND ROMANCE, HER MUSE, HER IDEAL READER: Ibid., p. 353.

66. CATHER'S ALICE B. TOKLAS: Author conversation with Sharon O'Brien.

The Reporter and the First Lady

67. DURING THE 1932 PRESIDENTIAL CAMPAIGN . . . : Most of the information in this sidebar comes from Blanche Wiesen Cook, *Eleanor Roosevelt*.

69. THEIRS WAS A POWERFUL ATTRACTION: Ibid., p. 479.

69. I'VE BEEN TRYING TODAY TO BRING BACK YOUR FACE: Ibid.

70. HICK, DARLING: Ibid., p. 488–89.

70. THOUGH SHE [HICK] HAD COME TO ACCEPT: Doris Kearns Goodwin, *No Ordinary Time*, p. 225.

71. THE FACT IS THAT E.R. AND HICK: Cook, p. 479.

71. SIGMUND FREUD NOTWITHSTANDING: Ibid.

A "Passing Woman": The Strange Case of Murray Hall

71. AN IMPRESSIVE NUMBER OF SUCH STORIES: Katz, *Gay American History*, pp. 211–12.

71. APPROXIMATELY FOUR HUNDRED WOMEN MASQUERADED AS MEN: Faderman, *Odd Girls and Twilight Lovers*, pp. 42–43.

72. THERE MUST HAVE BEEN THOUSANDS OF WOMEN: Ibid., p. 43.

72. EARLY FORM OF FEMALE REVOLT: Katz, p. 210.

72. THIS WORLD IS MADE BY MEN: Ibid., p. 256.

72. TAMMANY HALL POLITICIAN AND BAIL BONDSMAN MURRAY HALL: Most of the information about Hall here comes from Katz, pp. 232–38.

73. MURRAY HALL FOOLED MANY SHREWD MEN: *New York Times,* Jan. 19, 1901.

73. HALL'S ORIGINS WERE UNCLEAR: For Havelock Ellis's comments on Hall, see *Studies in the Psychology of Sex,* Vol. I, Part IV, pp. 246–47.

CHAPTER 6: SAPPHO COMES TO PARIS

75. THEN I REPLIED TO THEM, THE DELIGHTFUL WOMEN: Sappho, translation by Elizabeth Kaye.

76. WOMEN OF THE *DEMI-MONDE* MIXED WITH AGED DUCHESSES: Shari Benstock, *Women of the Left Bank,* p. 40.

76. THE UNJUST STIGMA WHICH CONDEMNED THE NATIVES OF SODOM: Quoted in Michèle Sarde, *Colette: Free and Fettered,* p. 227.

76. ALL THE NOTEWORTHY WOMEN ARE DOING IT: Benstock, p. 47.

77. The Colette Scandal: See Sarde, pp. 197–202.

77. AN ASSORTMENT OF SHIRTS AND WOOLEN WAISTCOATS: Allan Massie, *Colette,* p. 58.

77. I AM THE MARQUISE OF BELBEUF: Sarde, p. 221.

78. SOME OF THESE LADIES FONDLY KEPT: Colette, *The Pure and the Impure,* p. 69.

78. WORE A MONOCLE, A WHITE CARNATION IN THE BUTTONHOLE: Ibid., p. 72.

8–79. VEILED IN BLACK OR PURPLE, ALMOST INVISIBLE: Ibid., p. 81. For Colette's portrait of Renée Vivien, see *The Pure and the Impure,* pp. 79–98.

79. POWDERED AND ROUGED, HOLLOW-EYED: Ibid., p. 89.

79. MUST HAVE BEEN IN REALITY HORRID: Karla Jay, *The Amazon and the Page,* p. 73.

79. THE WILD GIRL FROM CINCINNATI: Sarde, p. 225.

80. THE ONLY CITY WHERE YOU CAN LIVE: George Wickes, *The Amazon of Letters,* p. 44.

80. A CREATURE BORN OUT OF HER EPOCH: Radclyffe Hall, *The Well of Loneliness,* p. 281.

80. GLASS COACH AND HORSES: Benstock, p. 88.

80. HER WILD, OVERGROWN GARDEN: Ibid., pp. 302–03.

81. NO LONGER RESEMBLED THE WOOD NYMPHS: Ibid., p. 304.

81. BARNEY'S SALONS AND TEMPLE OF FRIENDSHIP: See Diana Souhami, *Gertrude and Alice,* pp. 159–60.

81. PARIS ONES AND THOSE ONLY PASSING THROUGH TOWN: Ibid., p. 160.

An Excerpt from Colette's *The Pure and the Impure*

82. COLETTE'S LESBOS IS A MORE COMFORTING WOMB: Sarde, p. 228.

82. THERE WAS ALSO A CELLAR IN MONTMARTRE . . . : Colette, *The Pure and the Impure,* pp. 77–78.

An Excerpt from Proust's *Sodom and Gomorrah*

84. PROUST CONSCIOUSLY TREATED HOMOSEXUAL URGES AS A CURSE: Gay, p. 200.

85. I NOW UNDERSTOOD . . . : Proust, *Sodom and Gomorrah,* pp. 19–44.

An Excerpt from Baudelaire's "Lesbos"

86–87. Charles Baudelaire, *Poems*, pp. 175–76.

André Gide

88. WILDE, I BELIEVE: André Gide, *Journals*, Vol. 1, p. 12.

88. A MARVELLOUS YOUTH: Gide, *If It Die*, p. 285.

88. *DEAR*, WOULD YOU LIKE: Ibid., p. 286.

88. A RESOUNDING LAUGH: Ibid.

88. EVERY TIME SINCE THEN: Ibid., p. 288.

89. MANY PEOPLE FOUND THAT GIDE RESEMBLED: Edmund White, *Genet*, p. 97.

89. SLIPPERY AS A TROUT, E. M. Forster, "Gide's Death," in *Two Cheers for Democracy*, p. 232.

89. IT WAS MY DUTY TO DENY: Gide, *If It Die*, p. 239.

89. THERE WAS NOTHING NOW I COULD ATTACH: Ibid., p. 310.

90. I READ EVERY ONE BEFORE DESTROYING THEM: George D. Painter, *André Gide*, p. 85.

91. YOU UNDERSTAND THAT IN HOMOSEXUALITY: Gide, *Corydon*, p. 18.

91. A FAINTLY RIDICULOUS DEFENCE: White, p. 97.

91. HE OUGHT TO HAVE LEANED: James Baldwin, "The Male Prison," in *The Price of the Ticket*, p. 102.

91. FREE MIND [AND] FREE MINDS ARE AS RARE: Forster, "Gide's Death," p. 233.

CHAPTER 7: ENGLAND DURING THE GREAT WAR

92. CLEANSING PURGE: Samuel Hynes, *A War Imagined*, pp. 15–16.

92. IT IS JUST AS IMPORTANT TO CIVILIZATION THAT LITERARY ENGLAND: Ibid., p. 223.

92. NO ONE TURNING FROM THE POETRY: Paul Fussell, *The Great War and Modern Memory*, pp. 279–80.

93. FAUNLIKE GOOD LOOKS, INNOCENCE, VULNERABILITY, AND "CHARM": Ibid., p. 272.

93. WE DID NOT CALL IT LOVE: Martin Taylor, *Lads: Love Poetry in the Trenches*, p. 33.

93. A RECOGNISABLE OR SELF-CONFESSED ADULT HOMOSEXUAL: J. R. Ackerley, *My Father and Myself*, p. 117.

94. MY PERSONAL RUNNERS: Ibid., p. 115.

94. WELL-KNOWN PREDILECTION OF BRITISH UPPER-CLASS HOMOSEXUALS: Peter Parker, *Ackerley*, p. 93.

94. I WONDER WHETHER HE WOULD HAVE CARED SO MUCH: P. N. Furbank, *E. M. Forster: A Life*, Vol. 2, p. 55.

94. TOMMY DEAD; AND BOBBIE HANMER AT SALONIKA: Siegfried Sassoon, *Diaries*, 1915–18, p. 53.

95. THEN I SAW HIM, DIGGING AWAY AT ROAD-MENDING: Sassoon, p. 262.

95. SUCH A REALIZATION OFTEN PRECIPITATED A PERSONAL CRISIS: Taylor, pp. 32–33.

95. GREATEST STAND-BY: Richard Perceval Graves, *Robert Graves, The Assault Heroic*, p. 127.

95. THIS NEWS WAS NEARLY THE END OF ME: Ibid., p. 177.

96. GIBSON IS A GHOST: Sassoon, *Diaries: 1920–22*, pp. 73–74. Also quoted in Taylor, pp. 56–57.

96. THE PAPERS ARE FULL OF THIS FOUL "BILLING CASE": Sassoon, *Diaries: 1915–18*, pp. 259–60.

96. The Billing affair and Black Book trial: Samuel Hynes, *A War Imagined*, pp. 226–31, and H. Montgomery Hyde, *Lord Alfred Douglas*, pp. 221–28.

98. IT WAS AT NO POINT A TRIAL OF THE ACCUSED: Hynes, *A War Imagined*, pp. 227–28.

98. A GOOD SECOND-RATE LITERRATEUR: Rupert Croft-Cooke, *Bosie*, p. 287.

99. OSCAR WILDE WROTE FILTHY WORKS, AS YOU KNOW: Hynes, p. 228.

99. THERE CAN BE NO DOUBT THAT MR. PEMBERTON BILLING HAD A VERY GREAT: Ibid., p. 231.

99. FOR A FEW DAYS LONDON FORGOT ALL ABOUT THE WAR: Maureen Borland, *Wilde's Devoted Friend*, p. 282.

100. THE ROMANTIC MOOD OF THE PLACE: Martin Green, *Children of the Sun*, p. 203.

100. THE HEARTIES WENT IN FOR BEER: Ibid., p. 232.

100. THE HOMOSEXUALS OF THE TWENTIES CAME OUT OF THE CLOSET: Noel Annan, *Our Age*, p. 113.

101. SO LONG AS ONE ACTED CONSISTENTLY: Robert Graves and Alan Hodge, *The Long Weekend*, pp. 101–2.

The Sexual Labyrinth of T. E. Lawrence

103. OUR YOUTHS BEGAN INDIFFERENTLY TO SLAKE: T. E. Lawrence, *Seven Pillars of Wisdom*, p. 30.

103. I REMEMBERED THE CORPORAL KICKING: Ibid., p. 445.

104. LAWRENCE COULD NEVER HAVE BEEN AT DERA: Lawrence James, *The Golden Warrior*, pp. 214–21.

104. THE TURKS, AS YOU PROBABLY KNOW: P. N. Furbank, *E. M. Forster: A Life*, Vol. 2, p. 150.

An Excerpt from E. M. Forster's *Maurice*

105. IN MAURICE, I TRIED TO CREATE: E. M. Forster, *Maurice*, p. 236.

105. AS THE SPRING WORE AWAY: Ibid., pp. 142–46.

J. R. Ackerley and the Quest for the Ideal Friend

107. "HOMO" OR "HETERO": J. R. Ackerley, *My Father and Myself*, p. 117.

107. ON THE SEXUAL MAP: Ibid., p. 118.

107. SOMETHING OF A PUBLICIST: Ibid.

108. REMAINED LOYAL TO THEM: Peter Parker, *Ackerley*, p. 108.

108. SADDEST DAY OF HIS LIFE: Parker, p. 380.

108. LIKE MANY WIDOWERS: Ibid.

108. HE SHOULD NOT BE EFFEMINATE: Ackerley, pp. 125–26.

Noel Coward

109. WEARING A CHINESE DRESSING GOWN: Graves and Hodge, p. 144.
109. THE DRAMATIST OF DISILLUSION: Ibid., p. 147.
109. HE WAS A VERY DIGNIFIED MAN: Cole Lesley, *Remembered Laughter*, p. 93.
111. I LOVE YOU. YOU LOVE ME: Quoted in Michael Bronski, *Culture Clash*, p. 112.
111. HIDING BEHIND HIS DANDY PROSE: Ibid.
111. COWARD'S CAREER FLOUNDERED: Ibid., p. 70.

CHAPTER 8: GERMANY'S GOLDEN AGE

114. COULD EASILY HAVE BEEN TAKEN FOR A BUSINESSMAN OR A BANKER: Charlotte Wolff, *Magnus Hirschfeld*, p. 57.
115. AT THE BEGINNING OF THIS VERY WEEK, A WELL-KNOWN HOMOSEXUAL STUDENT: John Lauritsen and David Thorstad, *The Early Homosexual Rights Movement (1864–1935)*, p. 23.
115. CENSUS, MODERN STYLE: James D. Steakley, *The Homosexual Emancipation Movement in Germany*, p. 34.
116. FALSE PREMISE THAT LOVE OF A MALE: Benedikt Friedländer, "Memoir for the Friends and Contributors of the Scientific Humanitarian Committee in the Name of the Secession of the Scientific Humanitarian Committee," *Journal of Homosexuality*, Vol. 22, Nos. 1/2, 1991, p. 79.
116. THUS WE SHALL NOT SPEAK OF "URNINGS": Ibid., p. 81.
116. MOST CASES OF SAME-SEX LOVE: Ibid.
116. THE LARGE AND INFLUENTIAL ORGANIZATIONS OF THE MOVEMENT: Anna Rueling, "What Interest Does the Women's Movement Have in the Homosexual Question" in Lillian Faderman and Brigitte Eriksson, eds., *Lesbians in Germany, 1890s–1920s*, p. 88.
117. INTELLECTUAL MURDER: William Manchester, *The Arms of Krupp*, p. 239. For the Krupp scandal, see Manchester, pp. 214–40.
117. THE EULENBURG AFFAIR: See Steakley, "Iconography of a Scandal," in *Hidden from History*, pp. 233–57; also Steakley, *The Homosexual Emancipation Movement in Germany;* Robert K. Massie, *Dreadnought;* Virginia Cowles, *The Kaiser;* and Wolff, *Magnus Hirschfeld*.
118. A PALE, GREY-HAIRED, SOMEWHAT WEARY-LOOKING: Quoted in Virginia Cowles, *The Kaiser*, p. 79.
118. MY BOSOM FRIEND: Steakley, "Iconography of a Scandal" in *Hidden from History*, p. 236.
118. AMBASSADOR OF THE GERMAN GOVERNMENT: Robert K. Massie, *Dreadnought: Britain, Germany, and the Coming of the Great War*, p. 668.
119. UNHEALTHY, LATE ROMANTIC AND CLAIRVOYANT: Ibid., p. 673.
119. "THE HARPEST" AND "SWEETIE": Steakley, "Iconography of a Scandal," p. 239.
120. PHILI, MY PHILI: Ibid., p. 241.
120. HAD HIS "FEMININE SIDE": Ibid., p. 242.
120. PATH OVER CORPSES: Ibid., p. 243.
121. IT HAS BEEN A VERY DIFFICULT YEAR: Massie, p. 679.

121. ABSOLUTELY INNOCENT: Ibid.
121. AT THE MOMENT WHEN THE FRESHEST: Steakley, "Iconography of a Scandal," p. 252.
122. AMAZING TACTICAL BLUNDER: Steakley, *The Homosexual Emancipation Movement in Germany*, p. 38.
122. WEALTHY CONTRIBUTORS: Ibid.
122. *LE VICE ALLEMAND*: Steakley, "Iconography of a Scandal," p. 247.
122. INTERNATIONAL JEWRY: Ibid., p. 235.
122. WOULD NOT REMOVE INEQUALITY: Steakley, *The Homosexual Emancipation Movement in Germany*, p. 42.
124. ALONG THE ENTIRE *KUNFURSTENDAMM*: Quoted in Garry Wotherspoon, *City of the Plain*, p. 61.
124. A MAD WHIRL: Quoted in Barry D. Adam, *The Rise of a Gay and Lesbian Movement*, p. 24.
124. HIRSCHFELD WAS CONDUCTING HIS PSYCHOANALYTIC SCHOOL: Robert McAlmon and Kay Boyle, *Being Geniuses Together*, p. 107.
125. BERLIN MEANT BOYS: Christopher Isherwood, *Christopher and His Kind*, p. 2.
125. BOYS STRIPPED OFF THEIR SWEATERS: Ibid., p. 30.
125. GOVERNED BY THE CODE: Ibid., pp. 26–27.
125. DENS OF "PSEUDO-VICE": Ibid., p. 29.
126. HOTHOUSE FOR THE FORCED GROWTH OF SEXUAL NOTIONS AND INCITEMENT: Adolf Hitler, *Mein Kampf*, p. 145.
126. IT IS NOT WITHOUT CHARM: Steakley, p. 88.
126. EXCEPT FOR A FEW MINOR CLIQUES: Steakley, p. 82.
127. WE CONGRATULATE YOU, MR. HIRSCHFELD: Richard Plant, *The Pink Triangle*, p. 49.

Strindberg Goes to a Gay Ball in Berlin, Circa 1890

128. BEFORE GOING TO THE CAFÉ NATIONAL: August Strindberg, *The Cloister*, pp. 12–13.

Christopher Isherwood in Berlin

129. THE BUILDING WHICH WAS NOW OCCUPIED: Christopher Isherwood, *Christopher and His Kind*, pp. 15–17.

Two Films: *Different from the Others* and *Mädchen in Uniform*

131. Isherwood's description of *Different from the Others*: In *Christopher and His Kind*, pp. 34–35.
132. Conrad Veidt at gay ball: See Ibid., p. 34.
133. THE MOST FAMOUS PLEA FOR LESBIAN LIBERATION: George Mosse, *Nationalism and Sexuality*, p. 188.
133. BEST FILM OF THE YEAR IN GERMANY: Siegfried Kracauer, *From Caligari to Hitler*, p. 227. For an extensive discussion of *Mädchen*'s attitudes toward authoritarianism, see Kracauer, pp. 228–29.

133. THIS DELETION, A POLITICAL ACT: Vito Russo, *The Celluloid Closet*, p. 58. For more on *Mädchen* in America, see Russo, pp. 57–58.

134. MADLY IN LOVE WITH HER: Peter Kurth, *American Cassandra*, p. 178. For more on Christa Winsloe's relationship with Dorothy Thompson, see Kurth, pp. 177–82 and 188–95.

CHAPTER 9: GREENWICH VILLAGE

137. YOU COULD RENT A FURNISHED HALL-BEDROOM: Malcolm Cowley, *Exile's Return*, p. 48.

138. THEY EVEN DRESSED DIFFERENTLY: Steven Watson, *Strange Bedfellows*, pp. 126–27.

138. IT IS BOUNDED ON THE NORTH BY THE FEMINIST MOVEMENT: Huchins Hapgood quoted in Watson, *Strange Bedfellows*, p. 122. For more on the Village in this period, see Watson, pp. 122–66.

138. PRIVATE WAR BETWEEN GREENWICH VILLAGE AND THE *SATURDAY EVENING POST*: Cowley, p. 53.

138. A FATAL TENDENCY TO ASSUME THAT ALL MOTHERS: Leslie Fishbein, *Rebels in Bohemia*, pp. 95–96.

138. IT WAS A MORE DELICIOUS LIFE I FELT: Katz, *Gay American History*, p. 521.

139. IT WAS BOHEMIAN CHIC: Lillian Faderman, *Odd Girls and Twilight Lovers*, p. 82.

139. I WONDER IF IT HAS EVER OCCURRED TO YOU: Ibid., p. 82.

139. ENCHANTED GARDEN OF CHILDHOOD: Anne Cheney, *Millay in Greenwich Village*, p. 64. For more on Floyd Dell's attempt to "rescue" Edna St. Vincent Millay from lesbianism and the general ambivalence of the Village regarding homosexuality: See Faderman, pp. 85–88.

140. I CAME TO BELIEVE THAT A GENERAL OFFENSIVE WAS ABOUT TO BE MADE AGAINST MODERN ART: Cowley, p. 190.

140. YOU WOULD SET ABOUT HANGING POLICEMEN: Ibid., p. 52.

140. SURER OF MYSELF, MORE DETERMINED TO PLEAD FOR EVERY VICTIM: Katz, p. 377.

141. Webster Hall dances: See description in George Chauncey, *Gay New York*, pp. 235–36.

141. For description of "fairy" subculture, see Ibid., pp. 33–127.

141. THE LOWEST AND MOST DISGUSTING PLACE: Luc Sante, *Low Life*, p. 192.

141. COME ALL YE REVELERS: Chauncey, "The Way We Were," *Village Voice*, July 1, 1986.

143. HANGOUT OF DAINTY ELVES AND STERN WOMEN: Chauncey, *Gay New York*, p. 240.

143. THE QUEEN OF THE THIRD SEX: Ibid.

143. The Everard Baths: See Chauncey, pp. 216–18.

143. Clara Bow film, *Call Her Savage*: See Vito Russo, *The Celluloid Closet*, pp. 42–43, and Chauncey, *Gay New York*, pp. 234–35.

144. Legal troubles of *The Captive*: See Katz, *Gay American History*, pp. 82–90. For Mae West's *The Drag*, see Chauncey, pp. 312–13.

144. INFORMAL "UNDERSTANDING": Chauncey, p. 356.

145. RESTAURANTS, SPEAKEASIES, AND EVEN BATHHOUSES: Ibid.

145. Pansy Clubs: Ibid., pp. 314–321.

145. CLOSED LITERALLY HUNDREDS OF BARS: Ibid., p. 339. For a detailed description of State Liquor Authority crackdowns, see Chauncey, pp. 335–53.

Degenerates of Greenwich Village

146. A NEW YORKER WHO RETURNED: "Degenerates of Greenwich Village," *Current Psychology and Psychoanalysis*, December 1936. Reprinted in Martin Duberman, *About Time*, pp. 160–62.

CHAPTER 10: RENAISSANCE IN HARLEM

148. THERE'S TWO THINGS GOT ME PUZZLED: Bessie Smith, "Foolish Man Blues," *The Empress*, Columbia CG 30818.

148. I WAS IN LOVE WITH HARLEM: Arnold Rampersad, *The Life of Langston Hughes*, Vol. 1, p. 51.

149. WHITES SNICKERED AND LEERED: Faderman, *Odd Girls and Twilight Lovers*, p. 68.

149. ROUGH TRADE: Eric Garber, "A Spectacle in Color," in *Hidden from History*, pp. 323–24.

150. NOTHING BUT FAGGOTS AND BULLDAGGERS: Chris Albertson, *Bessie*, p. 74.

150. ALTHOUGH UNALLOYED HOMOSEXUALITY MAY STILL HAVE CONNOTED: Faderman, p. 75.

150. "Prove It to Me Blues": See Ibid., pp. 74–75.

151. Bessie Smith flees Detroit: Albertson, pp. 123–25.

151. THAT'S HOW I LOST THE ONLY FUR COAT I EVER HAD: Ibid., p. 125.

151. BECAUSE SO MUCH OF POPULAR CULTURE IS CONCERNED: Bronski, p. 75.

151. FOR TWO OR THREE AMAZING YEARS, MISS BENTLEY SAT: Langston Hughes, *The Big Sea*, pp. 225–26.

151. FOR MANY YEARS I LIVED IN A PERSONAL HELL: Gladys Bentley, "I Am a Woman Again," *Ebony*, August 1952, p. 92.

152. WE YOUNGER NEGRO ARTISTS: Quoted in Rampersad, Vol. 1, p. 131.

153. WE JUST TOOK IT FOR GRANTED, AS A FACT: Rampersad, Vol. 2, p. 335.

153. HE WAS DEFINITELY CURIOUS: Ibid., p. 149.

153. WHO SEEMED TO THRIVE WITHOUT HAVING SEX: Rampersad, Vol. 1, p. 133.

154. A GORGEOUS DARK AMAZON: Hughes, p. 245.

154. CROWDED AS THE NEW YORK SUBWAY: Ibid., p. 244.

154. BECAUSE A'LELIA ADORED THE COMPANY OF LESBIANS AND GAY MEN: Garber, p. 322.

154. THE BEGINNING OF PATRONAGE BY TOP-DRAWER SOCIETY FOLK: Bentley, in *Ebony*, p. 93.

154. STARK NAKED, SAVE FOR A DECORATIVE *CACHE SEX* AND SILVER SANDALS: Bruce Kellner, *Carl Van Vechten and the Irreverent Decades*, p. 201.

155. HE LOVED THEM BOTH: Garber, p. 330.

155. WALLY [THURMAN] AND I THOUGHT THAT THE MAGAZINE: Charles Michael Smith, "Bruce Nugent: Bohemian of the Harlem Renaissance," in Joseph Beam, ed., *In the Life*, p. 214.

155. I HAVE JUST TOSSED: Ibid.

155. I'VE ALWAYS BEEN FLAMBOYANT: Ibid., p. 209.

155. I JUST DON'T SEE WHY EVERYONE HAS TO BE LABELED: Samuel R. Delany and Joseph Beam, "The Possibility of Possibilities," in *In the Life*, p. 204.

156. THERE IS A GREAT DIFFERENCE BETWEEN LUST AND LOVE: Smith, pp. 216–17.

156. ADAM CLAYTON POWELL, SR., HARLEM'S MOST POWERFUL: George Chauncey, *Gay New York*, pp. 254–55.

156. STRUTTING ABOUT: Rampersad, Vol. 1, p. 171.

156. AWFULLY BAD COLORED SHOWS: Ibid., p. 172.

A Drag Ball in Harlem

157. THE "GAY ELEMENT": George Chauncey, *Gay New York*, p. 257.

157. SINGER ETHEL WATERS: Ibid., p. 258. For more on the balls, see Chauncey, pp. 257–63.

157. STRANGEST AND GAUDIEST: Langston Hughes, *The Big Sea*, pp. 273–74.

CHAPTER 11: PARIS IN THE TWENTIES

159. PARIS WAS THE ONE PLACE WHERE YOU COULD LIVE AND EXPRESS YOURSELF: George Wickes, *The Amazon of Letters*, p. 44.

159. THE POPULACE HAD GROWN SO HARDENED TO ARTISTS: George Orwell, "Inside the Whale," in *An Age Like This*, p. 493.

161. I CONSIDERED MYSELF WITHOUT SHAME: Faderman, *Odd Girls and Twilight Lovers*, p. 58.

161. THE LESBIANS OF THIS PERIOD INTO TWO GROUPS: Benstock, p. 174.

161. NOT LONG AFTER I HAD OPENED MY BOOKSHOP: Diana Souhami, *Gertrude and Alice*, p. 148.

162. EDITOR, AMANUENSIS, SECRETARY: Ibid., p. 94.

162. MOST OF THE TIME, THOUGH, GERTRUDE AND ALICE: Ibid., p. 127.

163. AN INDIVIDUAL PROBLEM: Ibid., p. 80.

163. THE ACT THAT MALE HOMOSEXUALS COMMIT: Ibid., p. 152.

163. I MARVEL AT MY BABY: Ibid., p. 111.

164. I CAME TO EUROPE TO GET CULTURE: Andrew Field, *Djuna*, p. 37.

164. INCREDIBLY LONG SILENCES IN THE CAFÉS: Ibid., p. 118.

164. THEY WALKED DOWN 1922 AND THE BOULEVARD DU MONTPARNASSE: Ibid., p. 37.

164. I'M NOT A LESBIAN, I JUST LOVED THELMA and I AM NOT OFFENDED IN THE LEAST: Benstock, p. 245.

164. THREE GATEWAYS: Field, p. 121.

164. PARLIAMENT OF THE EXPATRIATION: Ibid., p. 120.

164. HOMEY AND PICTURESQUE, IT WAS DECORATED: Souhami, p. 147.

165. MY LOVES WERE ADRIENNE MONNIER AND JAMES JOYCE: Noel Riley Fitch, *Sylvia Beach and the Lost Generation*, p. 11.

166. Shutting down of *Inversions*: See Adam, p. 31.

167. I THINK OF ALL OF US WITH AMAZEMENT: Benstock, p. 235.

Marguerite Yourcenar

167. THE LAST ECHO OF A HEROIC CHORUS: Edmund White, "The Celebration of Passion," *The New York Times Book Review*, October 17, 1993, p. 1.

167. SHE WAS THE VERY EPITOME OF A WOMAN WHO LOVES WOMEN: Josyane Savigneau, *Marguerite Yourcenar*, p. 102.

168. I HAVE BEEN PARTICULARLY GRATEFUL: Ibid., pp. 276–77.

169. NATURALLY, I WAS MUCH TOO YOUNG: Marguerite Yourcenar, *Alexis*, pp. 22–23.

CHAPTER 12: BLOOMSBURY

170. WITH THAT ONE WORD ALL BARRIERS OF RETICENCE: Quentin Bell, *Virginia Woolf*, Vol. I, p. 124.

170. IT NEVER STRUCK ME THAT THE ABSTRACTNESS: Leon Edel, *Bloomsbury: A House of Lions*, p. 124.

170. I KNEW THERE WERE BUGGERS: Ibid., p. 149.

171. A MIXTURE OF HOMOSEXUALS WITH YOUNG VIRGINS: Ibid., p. 148.

172. SUFFERING FROM HEMORRHOIDS, HE BROUGHT: Ibid., pp. 202–3.

172. HE IS THE FULL MOON OF HEAVEN: Michael Holroyd, *Lytton Strachey: The Unknown Years, 1880–1910*, p. 266.

172. THE FRANKNESS OF STRACHEY AND KEYNES'S CORRESPONDENCE: Ibid., p. 212.

173. ONE OF THE FINEST HARMONIES: Edel, p. 147.

173. Strachey and Carrington reading Macaulay instead of copulating: Ibid., p. 223.

173. IF I HAD TO CHOOSE BETWEEN BETRAYING MY COUNTRY: E. M. Forster, "What I Believe," in *Two Cheers for Democracy*, p. 68.

173. Forster's visit to Edward Carpenter: In P. N. Furbank, *E. M. Forster: A Life*, Vol. I, p. 257.

174. INSPIRATION FOR THE NOVEL LAY IN THE SUICIDE OF A HOMOSEXUAL FRIEND: See Nicola Beauman, *E. M. Forster*, pp. 226–31.

174. WISH I WAS WRITING THE LATTER HALF OF *MAURICE*: Furbank, Vol. 2, p. 40.

174. THAT MORGAN AND BOB WERE DEFINITELY LOVERS: Beauman, p. 350.

175. HAPPINESS: Furbank, Vol. 2, p. 169.

175. BUT GIDE HASN'T GOT A MOTHER!: Peter Parker, *Ackerley*, p. 338.

175. REGARDED SEX, NOT SO MUCH WITH HORROR: Bell, Vol. 2, p. 6.

175. DISLIKES THE POSSESSIVENESS: Victoria Glendinning, *Vita*, p. 201.

175. CERTAINLY A VERY BEAUTIFUL WOMAN, IN A LAZY, MAJESTIC, RATHER MELANCHOLY WAY: Bell, Vol. 2, pp. 115–16.

176. I LOVE VIRGINIA, AS WHO WOULDN'T?: Glendinning, p. 165.

176. THERE MAY HAVE BEEN—ON BALANCE: Bell, Vol. 2, p. 119.

176. AND VITA COMES TO LUNCH: Ibid., p. 119.

176. LONGEST AND MOST CHARMING LOVE-LETTER: Glendinning, p. 202.

177. BUT *ORLANDO*! IMAGINE THOSE TWO: Nigel Nicolson, *Portrait of a Marriage*, p. 231.

178. THERE HAD BEEN NO QUARREL, NO OUTWARD SIGN OF COLDNESS: Bell, Vol. 2, p. 183.

Vita and Harold

179. HIS GENERALLY LIGHT-HEARTED HOMOSEXUAL FRIENDSHIPS: Glendinning, p. 48.
179. YOU WERE OLDER AND BETTER INFORMED: Ibid., p. 47.
180. VITA'S ELOPEMENT WITH VIOLET TREFUSIS: Nicolson, p. 207.

An Excerpt from Virginia Woolf's *Orlando*

180. DIFFERENT THOUGH THE SEXES ARE, THEY INTERMIX: Virginia Woolf, *Orlando*, p. 123.
180. PHANTASMAGORIA OF IMAGES AND INCIDENTS: Glendinning, p. 203.
181. [E]ACH WAS SO SURPRISED: Woolf, p. 168.
181. BUT TO GIVE AN EXACT AND PARTICULAR ACCOUNT: Woolf, pp. 144–45.

CHAPTER 13: *THE WELL OF LONELINESS*

183. [L]ESS THAN FOUR YEARS AFTER THE PUBLICATION: Michael Baker, *Our Three Selves*, p. 197.
185. YOU ARE GOING TO TELL THE WHOLE WORLD THAT THERE IS SUCH AN OFFENCE: Jeffrey Weeks, *Coming Out*, pp. 106–7.
185. I WROTE THE BOOK FROM A DEEP SENSE OF DUTY: Ibid., p. 107.
185. GOD . . . WE BELIEVE: Radclyffe Hall, *The Well of Loneliness*, p. 506.
186. NOTABLE PSYCHOLOGICAL AND SOCIOLOGICAL SIGNIFICANCE: Ibid., Commentary.
186. I HAVE SEEN THE PLAGUE STALKING: Baker, p. 223.
187. [HALL'S] MERITORIOUS DULL BOOK: Virginia Woolf, *The Diary of Virginia Woolf*, Vol. 3, p. 193.
187. SCREAMED LIKE A HERRING GULL, MAD WITH EGOTISM & VANITY: Ibid.
187. THE SUBJECT-MATTER OF THE BOOK EXISTS AS A FACT: P. N. Furbank, *E. M. Forster: A Life*, Vol. 2, p. 154.
188. RADCLYFFE HALL SAT AT THE SOLICITOR'S TABLE: Baker, p. 239. The description of the trial comes from Baker.
188. WE WERE ALL PACKED IN: Virginia Woolf, pp. 206–7.
188. A SCHOOLGIRL CRUSH: Baker, p. 240.
188. A FACT OF GOD'S OWN CREATION: Ibid., p. 242.
189. THEN THE MAGISTRATE, INCREASINGLY DELIBERATE & COURTEOUS: Woolf, p. 207.
189. SIR CHARTRES BIRON DELIVERED HIS JUDGMENT: Baker, p. 243.
189. THESE HORRIBLE PRACTICES: Ibid.
189. I PROTEST!: Ibid.
189. I CLAIM EMPHATICALLY THAT THE TRUE INVERT IS BORN: Ibid., p. 238.
190. A DISGUSTING BOOK: Baker, p. 245.
190. ALL THE CHARACTER OF A BURSTING DAM: Rosemary Auchmuty, "You're a Dyke, Angela! Elsie J. Oxenham and the Rise and Fall of the Schoolgirl Story," in Lesbian History Group, *Not a Passing Phase*, p. 135.
190. WHEN I READ *THE WELL OF LONELINESS*: Quoted in Weeks, p. 100.
191. BRITISH SCHOOLGIRL ROMANCE NOVELS: Auchmuty, pp. 133–35.

191. "LESBIAN-BAITING" OF SPINSTER SCHOOLTEACHERS: Alison Oram, " 'Embittered, Sexless or Homosexual': Attacks on Spinster Teachers, 1918–39," in *Not a Passing Phase*, pp. 99–118.

An Excerpt from Radclyffe Hall's *The Well of Loneliness*

191. AS LONG AS SHE LIVED STEPHEN NEVER FORGOT: Radclyffe Hall, *The Well of Loneliness*, pp. 447–51.

Quentin Crisp's 1920s

193. IN THOSE FAR-OFF DAYS: Quentin Crisp, *The Naked Civil Servant*, pp. 18–23.

CHAPTER 14: CZARS AND COMMISSARS: HOMOSEXUALITY IN RUSSIA

199. Gogol's death: See Simon Karlinsky, *The Sexual Labyrinth of Nikolai Gogol*, pp. 272–80.

199. ENOUGH! STOP IT!: Ibid., p. 273.

199. STRANGEST PROSE-POET RUSSIA EVER PRODUCED: Vladimir Nabokov, *Nikolai Gogol*, p. 1.

199. CLEANSING FROM WHAT?: Karlinsky, pp. 273–74.

201. RITUAL MURDER: Ibid., p. 279.

201. Tchaikovsky's death: See "Doubts About Tchaikovsky," in *The New York Times*, August 9, 1981, and "The Great Suicide Debate," in the *Washington Post*, March 28, 1982. See also Karlinsky, "Russia's Gay Literature and Culture," in *Hidden from History*, p. 352.

202. WHERE'S THE HARM?: Leo Tolstoy, *Resurrection*, pp. 269–71.

202. TO RECONCEPTUALIZE HOMOSEXUALITY IN SECULAR TERMS: Laura Engelstein, *The Keys to Happiness*, p. 58.

202. DEEPLY REPUGNANT: Ibid., p. 67.

202. FROM THE MORAL POINT OF VIEW: Ibid.

203. THE CULTURAL RELATIVITY OF MORAL STANDARDS: Ibid., p. 69.

203. SHE KISSED MY EYES AND LIPS: Ibid., p. 392.

203. AN ETHEREAL PLANE: Ibid.

203. IT IS CLEAR THAT NOT EVEN THE MOST CULTURALLY RADICAL CREAM: Ibid., p. 394.

204. REALLY, IT CAN ONLY HAPPEN IN GERMANY: Richard Plant, *The Pink Triangle*, p. 38.

204. THEY ARE OLD-FASHIONED SLAVES: Karlinsky, in *Hidden from History*, p. 355.

205. IN THE ADVANCED CAPITALIST COUNTRIES, THE STRUGGLE: John Lauritsen and David Thorstad, *The Early Homosexual Rights Movement*, pp. 64–65.

205. SCIENCE HAS NOW ESTABLISHED: Karlinsky, p. 358.

205. IN THE LITERARY AND INTELLECTUAL SPHERES: Karlinsky, p. 358.

206. HAD IT NOT BEEN FOR LEONARDO, MARX, LENIN, FREUD, AND THE MOVIES: Marie Seton, *Sergei M. Eisenstein*, p. 119.

206. MY OBSERVATIONS LED ME TO THE CONCLUSION THAT HOMOSEXUALITY IS IN ALL WAYS: Ibid., p. 134.

206. ONE REVOLTS AT EVEN MENTIONING THE HORRORS: Lauritsen and Thorstad, p. 69.

207. EITHER THE DREGS OF SOCIETY, OR REMNANTS OF THE EXPLOITING CLASSES: Ben DeJong, "An Intolerable Kind of Moral Degeneration: Homosexuality in the Soviet Union," in ILGA Pink Book, 1985, p. 77.

207. SOME 3,000 MOSCOW HOMOSEXUALS WERE INCARCERATED: Robert Conquest, The Great Terror: A Reassessment, p. 317.

207. SO SICK OF VIRTUE: Quoted in Lauritsen and Thorstad, p. 70.

Diaghilev, Nijinsky, and the Ballets Russes

208. I NEVER SAW ANYTHING SO BEAUTIFUL: Martin Green, Children of the Sun, p. 52.

208. NOW I KNEW WHERE I STOOD: Ibid., p. 55.

208. IF THE THEATRE WERE TO BURN DOWN: Arnold Haskell, Diaghileff: His Artistic and Private Life, p. 151.

209. CYRIL CONNOLLY HAS SPOKEN OF THE GREAT HOMOSEXUAL TRAIL-BLAZERS: Green, p. 52.

209. I AM FIRSTLY A GREAT CHARLATAN: Ibid.

209. THE CREATOR MUST LOVE ONLY BEAUTY: Ibid., p. 53.

210. Zinadia Gippius's pursuit of Filosofov: See Simon Karlinsky, "Sergei Diaghilev: Public and Private," in Christopher Street, March 1980, pp. 51–52.

210. EXEMPLIFIED THE FINEST FEATURES OF THE ANCIENT GREEK LOVE: Karlinsky, p. 53.

212. A COMBINATION OF HOMOPHOBIA AND A POPULAR TASTE FOR MELODRAMA: Ibid.

212. DID NOT END IN LOSS: Ibid., p. 54.

212. IT IS ABSURD, IN FACT: Haskell, pp. 41–42.

213. IT IS BECAUSE OF DIAGHILEV THAT I AM WHATEVER I AM: Green, p. 290.

Love Between Women in the Gulag—An Excerpt from Vasily Grossman's *Forever Flowing*

213. THERE WERE SPECIAL HARD-LABOR CAMPS FOR WOMEN: Vasily Grossman, Forever Flowing, pp. 116–17.

CHAPTER 15: THE NAZI PERSECUTION OF HOMOSEXUALS

215. Destruction of Hirschfeld's institute: See Steakley, The Homosexual Emancipation Movement in Germany, pp. 104–5, and Isherwood, Christopher and His Kind, p. 129.

215. INTERNATIONAL CENTER OF THE WHITE-SLAVE TRADE: Steakley, p. 104.

215. THAT JEWISH PESTILENCE: George L. Mosse, Nationalism & Sexuality, p. 158.

216. THE NAZI PARTY "TEEMED": Adolf Brand, "Political Criminals: A Word About the Röhm Case," Journal of Homosexuality, Vol. 22, Nos. 1/2, 1991, p. 236.

216. NATIONALIST AND NAZI TYPOLOGIES: Mosse, pp. 140–49.

216. BOTH JEWS AND HOMOSEXUALS WERE REGARDED: Ibid., p. 138.

216. The Roehm affair: Richard Plant, *The Pink Triangle*, pp. 54–69.

216. SWASHBUCKLING MERCENARY: Plant, p. 62.

217. NOBODY CAN CALL ME A PURITAN: Ibid., pp. 59–60.

218. [THE SA] IS NOT AN INSTITUTE FOR THE MORAL EDUCATION OF GENTEEL YOUNG LADIES: Ibid., p. 61.

218. ROEHM HAD PROVIDED AS EASY A TARGET FOR HIS ENEMIES: Ibid., p. 68.

219. OUR *VOLK* IS BEING DESTROYED BY THIS EPIDEMIC: Peter Padfield, *Himmler*, p. 185.

219. WE MUST BE CLEAR ABOUT IT: Ibid., p. 187.

219. THESE PEOPLE WILL OBVIOUSLY BE PUBLICLY DEGRADED: Ibid.

219. DEDICATED TO THE WORSHIP OF MASCULINITY: Mosse, p. 176.

220. LOOK, IF I HAVE THE CHOICE BETWEEN A LOVELY BUT INCOMPETENT GIRL: Padfield, p. 186.

220. Early Nazi moves against homosexuals: See Plant, pp. 106–17.

221. THE SACRISTY HAS BECOME A BORDELLO: Plant, p. 135.

221. HERE OBEDIENT TO THEIR LAWS WE LIE: Noel Annan, *Our Age*, p. 123.

221. MOST LESBIANS MANAGED TO SURVIVE UNSCATHED: Plant, p. 116.

221. Fate of Non-German gays under Occupation: See Plant pp. 117–23.

222. BELIEVE IT OR NOT, THOSE WORTHIES HAVE DECIDED: Francis Steegmuller, *Cocteau*, p. 441.

222. DANGEROUSLY NAIVE POLITICALLY: Edmund White, *Genet*, p. 191.

223. DEATH RATES WERE HIGH: Rüdiger Lautmann, "Categorization in Concentration Camps as a Collective Fate: A Comparison of Homosexuals, Jehovah's Witnesses, and Political Prisoners," in *Journal of Homosexuality*, Vol. 19 (1), 1990, p. 81.

223. FIVE TO FIFTEEN THOUSAND GAYS PERISHED: Plant, p. 154.

223. THE LOWEST, MOST EXPENDABLE: Ibid., p. 172.

223. AMONG THE HOMOSEXUALS WERE EXCEPTIONAL PEOPLE: Ibid., p. 167.

223. WHEN MY NAME WAS CALLED: Heinz Heger, *The Men with the Pink Triangle*, p. 33.

224. THEY WERE FORBIDDEN TO SPEAK WITH PRISONERS FROM OTHER BLOCKS: Ibid., p. 35.

224. THE WINDOWS HAD A CENTIMETER OF ICE ON THEM: Ibid., pp. 34–35.

224. CLAY PITS OF THE BRICK WORKS AT SACHSENHAUSEN: Ibid., pp. 38–39.

225. ALREADY SO NUMBED AND INDIFFERENT: Ibid., p. 39.

225. WE LEARNED THAT WE WERE TO BE SEGREGATED: Plant, pp. 173–74.

225–226. SHOULD ONE OF THESE [PINK TRIANGLES] LOSE HIS "FRIEND": Quoted in Adam, p. 54.

226. A SLAVE-BOY MARKET IN ANCIENT ROME: Heger, p. 48.

226. MY WILL TO SURVIVE: Ibid., p. 75.

226. RÜDIGER LAUTMANN . . . STRONGLY DISPUTES: Lautmann, p. 86.

227. MANOEUVRES ESPECIALLY CLEVERLY IN THE CAMP GHETTO: Lautmann, p. 86.

227. A BROTHEL . . . IN PART TO "CURE" HOMOSEXUAL INMATES: Heger, p. 96.

227. MEDICAL EXPERIMENTS: Plant, pp. 176–78.

228. CAMP DID NOT TECHNICALLY CONSTITUTE A PRISON: Ibid., p. 181.

228. A BIT OF A FUSS: Heger, pp. 114–15.

228. ALTHOUGH THEY WERE NO LONGER COMPELLED TO WEAR: Plant, p. 181.

An Excerpt from Heinz Heger's
The Men with the Pink Triangle

229. AT THE END OF FEBRUARY 1941: Heinz Heger, *The Men with the Pink Triangle*, pp. 64–66.

CHAPTER 16: THE UNITED STATES IN WORLD WAR II

231. A SUBSTANTIALLY NEW "EROTIC SITUATION": John D'Emilio, *Sexual Politics, Sexual Communities*, p. 24.

232. THE CONCEPT OF THE HOMOSEXUAL AS A PERSONALITY TYPE: Allan Berube, *Coming Out Under Fire*, p. 2.

232. SEXUAL PSYCHOPATHS: Ibid., p. 14.

232. FEMININE BODILY CHARACTERISTICS: Ibid, p. 19.

233. I WAS AFRAID I WOULD NEVER GET INTO THE ARMY: Merle Miller, *On Being Different*, pp. 19–20.

233. ASKING AND ANSWERING THE HOMOSEXUAL QUESTION: Berube, p. 22.

234. THE THREE OF US STOOD THERE LOOKING AT THESE GUYS: Ibid., p. 185.

234. IT WOULD BE IMPOSSIBLE TO CALCULATE THE CONTRIBUTION OF THE ASTOR BAR: Ibid., p. 115.

234. A PROCESS OF MULTIPLICATION AND SPECIALIZATION: Ibid., p. 126.

234. THE BRILLIANT CROWD, THE SWISHY CROWD: Ibid.

235. MY SAILOR'S NAME WAS EARL: Donald Vining, *A Gay Diary, 1933–1946*, pp. 334–35.

235. THE WAR IS A TRAGEDY TO MY MIND AND SOUL: Ibid., p. 220.

235. IT WAS NOT UNTIL AFTER PEARL HARBOR: Donald Webster Cory, *The Homosexual in America*, p. 107.

235. ALMOST QUINTESSENTIAL LESBIAN INSTITUTION: D'Emilio, p. 27.

235. 80 PERCENT OF THE WOMEN: Randy Shilts, *Conduct Unbecoming*, p. 140.

235. OLD GYM TEACHERS IN DRAG: Berube, p. 32.

236. EVERYONE WAS GOING WITH SOMEONE OR HAD A CRUSH ON SOMEBODY: Ibid., p. 42.

236. THERE WAS A WHOLE WING OF THAT HUGE PRISON: Ibid., p. 145.

237. DO YOU [AND YOUR LOVER] KISS LONG CLINGING KISSES?: Ibid., p. 206.

237. IT'S OBVIOUS TO ME, SOLDIER: Marvin Liebman, *Coming Out Conservative*, p. 42.

237. I WAS ABSOLUTELY CERTAIN THAT I WOULD BE KILLED: Ibid., p. 44.

238. I WOULD LIKE YOU MEN TO SEE HOW A NEW YORK JEW FAGGOT DRILLS: Ibid., p. 45.

238. I OBEYED HIS ORDERS: Ibid., pp. 45–46.

239. GAY AND LESBIAN GIS SWELLED THE POPULATION OF PORT CITIES: D'Emilio, p. 31.

Homosexuals in Uniform

239. ALTHOUGH ARMY REGULATIONS: *Newsweek*, June 9, 1947, p. 54.

An Excerpt from Gore Vidal's *The City and the Pillar*

241. "COLDLY CYNICAL," "BORING": Jonathan Ned Katz, *Gay/Lesbian Almanac*, p. 630.

242. "SHOCK" and "DISBELIEF": Gore Vidal, *The City and the Pillar*, (1965 edition), p. 247.

242. "THERE SHOULD BE NO NEED TO HIDE ...": Gore Vidal, *The City and the Pillar* (1948 edition), pp. 140–41.

CHAPTER 17: THE RISE AND FALL OF THE "GAY IS SICK" SHRINKS

247. HIDDEN BUT INCAPACITATING FEARS: Quoted in Cornelia B. Wilbur, "Clinical Aspects of Female Homosexuality," in Judd Marmor, ed., *Sexual Inversion*, p. 268. For more on Rado's views, see his essay "A Critical Examination of the Concept of Bisexuality," in Marmor.

247. EVERY HOMOSEXUAL IS A LATENT HETEROSEXUAL: Ronald Bayer, *Homosexuality and American Psychiatry*, p. 30.

247. DETACHED, HOSTILE FATHER: Irving Bieber, "Clinical Aspects of Male Homosexuality," in Marmor, ed., p. 250.

247. INTENSELY RIVALROUS AND MURDEROUS: Ibid., p. 251.

248. PASSIVE, UNASSERTIVE, GENTLE, AND DETACHED FATHER: Wilbur in Marmor, ed., p. 276.

248. LOOKING FOR ILLNESS: Martin Duberman, *Cures*, p. 66.

248. A HETEROSEXUAL SHIFT IS A POSSIBILITY: Quoted in Bayer, p. 33.

248. HETEROSEXUAL OBJECT CHOICE IS DETERMINED: Ibid., p. 34.

249. THEY HOPE TO ACHIEVE A "SHOT" OF MASCULINITY: Ibid., p. 36.

249. COOPERATION, SOLACE, STIMULATION: Ibid.

249. GREAT AMBIVALENCE, BY GREAT LONGING FOR LOVE: Wilbur in Marmor, ed., pp. 280–81.

250. FOUR MEN COLLECTED THE INFORMATION: *Time*, August 24, 1953, p. 51.

250. Kinsey's findings (men): Alfred Kinsey et al., *Sexual Behavior in the Human Male*, pp. 650–51.

251. Kinsey's findings (women): Kinsey et al., *Sexual Behavior in the Human Female*, pp. 472–74.

251. IS THERE A MRS. KINSEY?: David Halberstam, *The Fifties*, p. 278.

251. IT IS IMPOSSIBLE TO ESTIMATE THE DAMAGE THIS BOOK WILL DO: Ibid., p. 280.

251. A PREVAILING DEGRADATION: Ibid., p. 280.

252. RARE AND THEREFORE ABNORMAL OR UNNATURAL: Kinsey et al., *Sexual Behavior in the Human Male*, pp. 659–60.

253. AM TRYING TO GET [HOMOSEXUAL] CASES IN ALL CLASSES: Wardell B. Pomeroy, *Dr. Kinsey and the Institute for Sex Research*, pp. 72–73.

253. [W]E ASKED ABOUT A DOZEN QUESTIONS: Ibid., pp. 133–34.

254. BY REVEALING THE WIDE DIVERGENCE: D'Emilio, p. 37.

254. WE HAVE LET YOU SEE US AS WE ARE: Eric Marcus, *Making History*, p. 18.

255. YOU MUST DO IT, EEE-VAH-LEEEEN!: Ibid., p. 19.

255. AT THAT TIME, THE 1950S, EVERY CLINICAL PSYCHOLOGIST: Ibid., p. 24.

256. TEARS WERE STREAMING: Ibid., p. 25.

256. American Psychiatric Association removal of homosexuality from nomenclature of disorders: Bayer, pp. 101–54.

257. SEVERE DAMAGE TO THE IMAGE OF AMERICAN PSYCHIATRY: Charles W. Socarides et al., "Homosexuality," in Letters to the Editor, *Psychiatric News,* December 3, 1993.

CHAPTER 18: THE AGE OF McCARTHY

258. I HAVE HERE IN MY HAND: Quoted in David Halberstam, *The Fifties,* p. 50.

258. ALMOST BY INADVERTENCE: Richard H. Rovere, *Senator Joe McCarthy,* p. 4.

258–59. NINETY-ONE PERSONS IN THE SHADY CATEGORY: "Never Condoned Disloyalty, says Acheson on His Stand," *New York Times,* March 1, 1950.

259. PERHAPS AS DANGEROUS AS THE ACTUAL COMMUNISTS: "Perverts Called Government Peril," *New York Times,* April 19, 1950.

259. THE PRIMARY ISSUE IS . . . THE CHARGE THAT THE FOREIGN POLICY OF THE U.S.: Quoted in Nicholas von Hoffman, *Citizen Cohn,* p. 127.

259. HITLER HAD COMPILED A LIST: Ibid., p. 130.

260. THE GOOD PEOPLE SHOOK THEIR HEADS IN DISBELIEF: Jack Lait and Lee Mortimer, *Washington Confidential,* p. 90–91.

260. FOREIGN CHANCELLERIES LONG AGO LEARNED: Ibid., p. 96.

260. DR. KINSEY WASN'T APPALLED: Ibid., p. 98.

260. THE MERRY MORTICIAN and IT IS MY UNANIMOUS OPINION: David M. Oshinsky, *A Conspiracy So Immense,* pp. 130–31.

261. YOU CAN HARDLY SEPARATE HOMOSEXUALS FROM SUBVERSIVES: Max Lerner, "The Senator and the Purge," *New York Post,* July 17, 1950.

261. A CORROSIVE INFLUENCE UPON HIS FELLOW EMPLOYEES: U.S. Senate, 81st Congress, 2nd Session, Committee on Expenditures in Executive Departments, *Employment of Homosexuals and Other Sex Perverts in Government,* pp. 3–5.

261. Dismissals of homosexuals: D'Emilio, p. 44.

262. The FBI and Post Office surveillance: See Ibid., pp. 46–47.

262. The experience of B.D.H.: Ibid., p. 47.

263. The Mounties: John Sawatsky, *Men in the Shadows,* pp. 112–29.

264. Drew Pearson's files: Drew Pearson, *Diaries: 1949–1959,* pp. 188–92.

264. JOE MCCARTHY IS A BACHELOR OF 43 YEARS: Quoted in Oshinsky, p. 310.

264. THE YOUNG REPUBLICANS HELD: Quoted in von Hoffman, p. 186.

265. A GOOD-LOOKING YOUNG MAN: Rovere, p. 193.

265. A STUDY IN CONTRASTS: Oshinsky, p. 256.

266. YOU SEE, WE DON'T WORK FOR THE STATE DEPARTMENT: Rovere, p. 202.

266. Nature of Cohn and Schine's relationship: von Hoffman, pp. 188–89.

266. ANYONE WHO KNOWS ME: Ibid., p. 132.

266. EMBARRASSED, THICK-TONGUED DENIAL: Ibid.

267. The Reber affair: Ibid., p. 148.

267. Death of Senator Hunt: Ibid., pp. 231–32.

267. THE MODUS OPERANDI WAS THE SAME: Ibid., p. 232.

268. IT WAS COHN'S LOYALTY TO SCHINE AND MCCARTHY'S TO COHN: Rovere, pp. 206–07. For Cohn and Schine in Europe, see Rovere, pp. 199–205.

268. REAL HEART: von Hoffman, p. 230.
269. FIRST, I WILL ASK YOU IF YOU HAVE ANY SPECIAL INTEREST IN MR. SCHINE?: Ibid., p. 240.
270. I FIND MYSELF SO PUZZLED: Robert Goldston, *The American Nightmare*, pp. 159–60.
270. MALICIOUS, WICKED, INDECENT: von Hoffman, p. 202.
271. Police sweeps and bar raids: See D'Emilio, p. 334.
271. Johns's committee: "Florida Reviews an Era of Fear," *The New York Times*, July 4, 1993, p. 14.
272. CRUSH THE MONSTER: John Gerassi, *The Boys of Boise*, p. 3. For extensive documentation of the Boise witch-hunt, see Gerassi's book; also *Time*, December 12, 1955. Jonathan Ned Katz's *Gay American History* features an interview with a Boise witch-hunt victim, pp. 109–19.
272. WORD IS OUT THEY'RE NOT WELCOME IN SIOUX CITY ANYMORE: *One*, February 1956.
272. WILL HOMOSEXUAL ACTS NOW CEASE TO OCCUR AMONG IOWA'S 2,700,000?: Ibid.
273. ACLU position on gay rights: See D'Emilio, p. 156.

Lieutenant Blick of the Vice Squad

274. . . . LIEUTENANT BLICK IS A TOUGH COP: Max Lerner, "Lieutenant Blick of the Vice Squad," *New York Post*, July 18, 1950.

Garden of Pansies—The Hand-on-Hip Set Wins the Battle of Washington

276. WE ARE NOT REFORMERS: Jack Lait and Lee Mortimer, *Washington Confidential*, pp. ix–x.
276. IF YOU'RE WONDERING WHERE YOUR WANDERING SEMI-BOY IS: Ibid., pp. 90–95.

The Fruit Machine

This sidebar draws extensively from John Sawatsky, *Men in the Shadows*, pp. 133–38.
278. SHADES OF GEORGE ORWELL AND WOODY ALLEN: Sawatsky, p. 134.
279. LOOKED LIKE SOMETHING OUT OF SCIENCE FICTION: Ibid., pp. 135–36.

CHAPTER 19: THE STRUGGLE FOR BRITISH LAW REFORM, 1950–1967

280. THE MOST ENLIGHTENED METHOD OF DEALING: Peter Parker, *Ackerley*, p. 229.
281. WEEDING OUT BOTH SEXUAL AND POLITICAL PERVERTS: Andrew Hodges, *Alan Turing: The Enigma*, p. 501.
281. For alleged American role in British crackdown: Stephen Jeffery-Poulter, *Peers, Queers, and Commons*, p. 25.
281. ABSOLUTELY NO CONCEPTION OF THE DANGER IN YOUR MIDST: Nancy Mitford,

The Blessing, p. 110–111, Penguin edition, quoted in Garry Wotherspoon, *City of the Plain*, pp. 114–15.

282. EXHIBITIONISTS AND PROSELYTIZERS: Weeks, *Coming Out*, p. 159.

282. STRENGTHEN THEIR [HOMOSEXUALS'] RESOLVE: Annan, *Our Age*, p. 126.

282. THE TWO GREATEST THREATS FACING AUSTRALIA: Wotherspoon, p. 113.

283. THE CASE FOR REFORM OF THE LAW: Jeffery-Poulter, p. 18.

284. VICE OFFICIAL: NO WHITEWASH: Ibid., p. 32.

285. IT ALSO BEGAN TO BE RECOGNIZED HOW MUCH HOMOSEXUALS: Annan, p. 124.

286. ARRAN HOMO: Jeffery-Poulter, pp. 84–85.

286. THE ONLY GREAT MOMENT OF MY SMALL LIFE: Ibid., p. 71.

286. I REGARD THE ACT OF HOMOSEXUALITY IN ANY FORM: Quoted in *A Queer Reader*, Patrick Higgins, ed, pp. 192–93.

287. SOME SORT OF INSIDIOUS SICKNESS: Jeffery-Poulter, p. 83.

287. HOMOSEXUALS MUST CONTINUE TO REMEMBER: Ibid., p. 89.

287. Law reform in Northern Ireland: See Jeffery-Poulter, pp. 147–54.

289. AN OPEN FLAUNTING OF THE NEW AND LEGAL FREEDOM OF OUTLET: Ibid., p. 95.

289. SEXUAL INTERCOURSE BEGAN: Phillip Larkin, "Annus Mirabilis," in *Collected Poems*, p. 167.

Victim

290. WITH CREDENTIALS ENOUGH TO GET INTO HEAVEN: Vito Russo, *The Celluloid Closet*, p. 130.

291. IT IS EXTRAORDINARY, IN THIS OVER-PERMISSIVE AGE: Dirk Bogarde, *Snakes and Ladders*, p. 201.

291. WHOLE PROJECT WAS TREATED, AT THE BEGINNING: Ibid., p. 202.

291. CANDID AND CLINICAL DISCUSSION: Russo, p. 128.

Alan Turing, Secret Hero

Most of the information here comes from Andrew Hodges, *Alan Turing: The Enigma*.

292. HE WAS A CROSS-COUNTRY RUNNER OF INTERNATIONAL STATURE: Annan, p. 237.

292. POWERFUL BRAIN: Hodges, 474.

293. FILLED WITH KNOWLEDGE OF THE BRITISH CRYPTOGRAPHIC AND CRYPTANA-LYTIC: Ibid., p. 502.

Piccadilly Polari

293. IN THE 1960S, LONDON GAYS: Peter Burton, *Parallel Lives*, p. 38 passim.

Canada Reforms Its Laws

The material in this sidebar comes from Gary Kinsman, *The Regulation of Desire: Sexuality in Canada*.

295. THE PROBLEM IN CANADA WAS NOT PERSECUTION: Gary Kinsman, *The Regulation of Desire*, p. 148.

296. WHETHER THE CRIMINAL LAW . . . SHOULD BE CHANGED: Ibid., p. 163.

296. SUPREME COURT RULING MAKES HOMOSEXUAL LIABLE FOR LIFE: Ibid.

296. THE STATE HAS NO PLACE IN THE BEDROOMS: Ibid.

CHAPTER 20: THE OTHER SIDE OF THE 1950S

297. REMARKABLE COLLECTION OF ANGELS: Barry Miles, *Allen Ginsberg*, p. 195.

297. I SAW THE BEST MINDS OF MY GENERATION: Allen Ginsberg, *Collected Poems, 1947–1980*, p. 126.

297. CHANTING LIKE A JEWISH CANTOR: Miles, p. 196.

297. DETONATION IN A MUSEUM: John Tytell, *Naked Angels*, p. 104.

297. ABSOLUTELY COMPELLING INCANTATORY QUALITY: David Halberstam, *The Fifties*, p. 306.

298. CRISS-CROSSED THE CONTINENT: Barbara Ehrenreich, *The Hearts of Men*, p. 53.

298. TO HEIGHTEN EXPERIENCE AND GET OUT OF ONE'S USUAL SELF: Paul Goodman, *Growing Up Absurd*, p. 180.

299. SPINDLY JEWISH KID: Miles, p. 44.

299. FELLOW TRAVELLER OF HOMOSEXUALS: Catharine R. Stimpson, "The Beat Generation and the Trials of Homosexual Liberation," in *Salamagundi*, Nos. 58–59, Fall 1982–Winter 1983, p. 385.

299. SEX WAS THE ONE AND ONLY HOLY: Quoted in Tytell, p. 161.

299. CONSTRUED AN UNFETTERED, UNCENSORED SEXUALITY AS A GOOD IN ITSELF: Stimpson, p. 374.

299. THEY RE-IMAGINED AND REVISED MALE HOMOSEXUALITY: Ibid.

300. I'M HAPPY, KEROUAC, YOUR MADMAN ALLEN'S: Ginsberg, *Collected Poems*, p. 123.

300. WE MADE A VOW TO EACH OTHER: Miles, p. 180.

300. DARK RUSSIAN MOODS: Ibid., p. 182.

300. MORE THAN ONE MÉNAGE À TROIS OF UNUSUAL COMPLEXITY: Ibid., p. 181.

301. HOMOSEXUALITY WEAVED ITS WAY: D'Emilio, p. 179.

301. THROUGH THE BEATS' EXAMPLE, GAYS COULD PERCEIVE THEMSELVES: Ibid., p. 181.

301. SMUGGLERS, COUNTERFEITERS, SLEIGHT-OF-HAND BANKERS: Michelle Green, *The Dream at the End of the World*, pp. 9–10.

302. VIRTUALLY EVERY TANGERINE IS ENSCONCED THERE: Quoted in Andrew Sinclair, *Francis Bacon*, pp. 137–38.

302. ALTHOUGH HOMOSEXUALITY WAS STILL A CRIMINAL OFFENSE: Green, p. 11.

303. NEITHER QUEER NOR AVAILABLE: Ibid., p. 131.

303. NOT TOO MANY GOOD VIBRATIONS: Ibid., p. 176.

303. DIPLOMATS, SCANDAL-HUNGRY JOURNALISTS, NYMPHOMANIACAL HEIRESSES: Ibid., p. 49.

303. ARRIVE IN THE MAR CHICA, ALL-NIGHT BAR: Ibid., p. 129.

304. THE BEST AMERICAN PLAY OF OUR TIME: Brad Gooch, *City Poet*, p. 246.

304. SMALL, PIQUANT, DARTING BETWEEN: Millicent Dillon, *A Little Original Sin*, p. 179.

304. I ALWAYS THOUGHT OF PAUL AND JANE: Green, p. 145.

305. I HAVE NEVER UNDERSTOOD WHY, BUT I AM TERRIFIED: Ibid., p. 51.

305. AND DON'T IMAGINE I'M BEING PARANOID: Dillon, p. 286.

305. THAT CHERIFA POISONED JANE: Ibid., pp. 286–87.

306. TANGIER IS FINISHED. THE ARAB DOGS ARE UPON US: Green, p. 206.

306. TO STICK A NEEDLE EVERY HOUR: Ibid., p. 129.

307. FROM THE FIRST DAY, MOROCCO SEEMED MORE DREAMLIKE THAN REAL: Ibid., p. 338.

Joe Orton in Tangier

307–309. Excerpt from The Orton Diaries, pp. 175–77.

Tennessee Williams and Fifties Theater

310. THE DISTASTEFUL TRAPPINGS: Gerald Clarke, Capote, p. 155.

310. SMALL PEOPLE WITH SMALL PROBLEMS: Michael Bronski, Culture Clash, p. 115.

310. BY HIS OWN ADMISSION, HOWEVER: Georges-Michel Sarotte, Like a Brother, Like a Lover, p. 118.

310. PORTRAYING MARRIAGE NEGATIVELY: Bronski, p. 125.

311. CREATED SOME OF THE BEST WOMEN CHARACTERS: Gore Vidal, "Tennessee Williams: Someone to Laugh at the Squares With," in United States: Essays, 1952–1992, p. 443.

311. TENNESSEE, YOU ARE BLANCHE: Don Lee Keith interview, "New Tennessee Williams Rises from 'Stoned Age,' " in Conversations with Tennessee Williams, Albert J. Devlin, ed., p. 159.

311. [H]IS SYMPATHIES WERE ALWAYS: Vidal, p. 443.

311. HE SHOWED THE MALE NOT ONLY AS SEXUALLY ATTRACTIVE IN THE FLESH: Ibid., p. 448.

311. SO CLOSE TO LIFE!: Dotson Rader interview, "The Art of Theatre V: Tennessee Williams," in Conversations with Tennessee Williams, p. 340.

312. THE ONLY ONE OF TENNESSEE'S CLOSE COMPANIONS: Maria St. Just, Five O'Clock Angel, p. 14.

312. I SLEEP WITH MR. WILLIAMS: Clarke, p. 196.

312. I'VE COVERED THE WATERFRONT: David Frost interview, "Will God Talk Back to a Playwright?" in Conversations with Tennessee Williams, p. 146.

312. I'VE NEVER HIDDEN MY HOMOSEXUALITY: Don Lee Keith, "New Tennessee Williams Arises from 'Stoned Age' " in Conversations, p. 159.

312. A MOST GLAMOROUS CRACKUP: Vidal, p. 439.

312. AFTER FRANK [MERLO]'S DEATH, TENNESSEE FELT: St. Just, p. 187.

313. I ONCE FOUND HIM REVISING A SHORT STORY: Vidal, p. 446.

313. WHEN YOUR CANDLE BURNS LOW: St. Just, p. 186.

James Baldwin and Giovanni's Room

313. AN INCANDESCENT NEGRO BOY: James Baldwin, "The New Lost Generation" in The Price of the Ticket, p. 305.

313. FOR WHAT IT'S WORTH: James Baldwin, "Introduction: The Price of the Ticket," in Ibid., p. xii.
314. IT TOOK ME NEARLY NO TIME TO DESPISE THE WORLD: Baldwin, "The New Lost Generation," in Ibid., p. 305.
314. A MAN IS NOT A MAN: Ibid., p. 312.
315. FINDING OLDER "PROTECTORS": For a description of Baldwin's early experiences as a gay man in New York, see his essay "Here Be Dragons" in The Price of the Ticket, pp. 677–90.
316. THE REALLY HORRIBLE THING: Baldwin, "The Male Prison," in Ibid., p. 104.
316. THE PEOPLE I HAD BEEN RAISED AMONG: Baldwin, "The New Lost Generation," in Ibid., p. 309.
316. I LOVED A FEW PEOPLE AND THEY LOVED ME: Richard Goldstein interview, "Go the Way Your Blood Beats," in James Baldwin: The Legacy, p. 183.
316. BEST ADVICE I EVER GOT: Ibid., p. 185.
316. IT'S ABOUT WHAT HAPPENS TO YOU IF YOU'RE AFRAID TO LOVE: Ibid., p. 176.
317. Excerpt from Giovanni's Room: pp. 82–84 and 94.

CHAPTER 21: THE OTHER SIDE OF THE FIFTIES, PART II: LESBIAN BUTCH/FEMME CULTURE

319. THE MANAGER WAS SAID TO WANDER: Lillian Faderman, Odd Girls and Twilight Lovers, p. 164.
319. I WASN'T CUTE OR PASSIVE ENOUGH: Audre Lorde, Zami: A New Spelling of My Name, p. 224.
320. TWO BATHROOMS—ONE MARKED "BUTCH" AND ONE MARKED "FEMME": Faderman, p. 169.
321. GROWING INFLUENCE OF THE PERRY COMO LOOK: Elizabeth Lapovsky Kennedy and Madeline D. Davis, Boots of Leather, Slippers of Gold, p. 159.
321. "SWEATER GIRL" LOOK: Ibid., p. 162.
321. YEAH, THERE WAS A LOT OF PRESSURE TO LOOK BUTCH: Nancy Adair and Casey Adair, Word Is Out, pp. 57–59.
322. HALL'S NOVEL THE WELL OF LONELINESS: Faderman, p. 173.
322. A POLICEWOMAN WOULD AUTOMATICALLY STAND OUT: Ibid., pp. 164–65.
322. SOMEDAY I EXPECT THE "DISCRETE" LESBIAN WILL NOT TURN HER HEAD: Lorraine Hansberry, The Ladder, No. 1, May 1957, p. 28.
322. FOR SOME OF US, ROLE-PLAYING REFLECTED ALL THE DEPRECATING ATTITUDES: Lorde, p. 221.
323. [BUTCH/FEMME RELATIONSHIPS] WERE FILLED WITH A DEEPLY LESBIAN LANGUAGE: Joan Nestle, A Restricted Country, p. 100.
323. "ARE YOU SEXUAL" and "ARE YOU SAFE?": Ibid., p. 102.
324. EROTIC AUTONOMY: Ibid., p. 102.
324. YOU WERE THERE, YOU WERE GAY, YOU WERE QUEER: Kennedy and Davis, p. 183.
324. A WEEKEND WASN'T A WEEKEND IF THERE WASN'T A FIGHT: Ibid., p. 91.
324. GLASSES WERE FLYING: Ibid., p. 94.
324. CUSTOMARY FOR BUTCHES TO ACCOMPANY THEIR FEMMES TO THE BATHROOM: Ibid., p. 309.
324. THE BIG THING WAS THEY USED TO LEAVE NOTES: Ibid., pp. 310–11.

325. THE "STONE BUTCH," OR THE "UNTOUCHABLE": Ibid., pp. 204–14.
325. I FEEL THAT IF WE'RE IN BED: Ibid., p. 208.
325. YOU HAD TO BE MORE FRIENDLY: Ibid., p. 123.
325. LESBIANS WERE PROBABLY THE ONLY BLACK AND WHITE WOMEN: Lorde, p. 179.

Black Poet in a White Butch/Femme World

327. Excerpt from *Zami: A New Spelling of My Name,* pp. 176–177, 224, and 226.

Lorraine Hansberry

328. NEVER BEFORE IN THE ENTIRE HISTORY: James Baldwin, "Sweet Lorraine," in *The Price of the Ticket,* p. 444.
329. WAS NOT A PERIPHERAL OR CASUAL PART: Steven R. Carter, *Hansberry's Drama,* p. 6.
330. OFTEN, JUST WHEN I WAS CERTAIN: Baldwin, pp. 443–44.
331. I'M GLAD AS HECK THAT YOU EXIST: Quoted in Katz, *Gay American History,* p. 425.
331. I THINK IT IS ABOUT TIME: Ibid., 425.
331. TANTAMOUNT TO THE CRIMINAL: Carter, pp. 6–7.
331. IF SOMEBODY INSULTS YOU: Lorraine Hansberry, *The Sign in Sidney Brustein's Window,* pp. 269–70.

CHAPTER 22: THE HOMOPHILES

333. BACHELORS FOR WALLACE: D'Emilio, *Sexual Politics, Sexual Communities,* p. 60.
333. HENRY GERBER and THE SOCIETY FOR HUMAN RIGHTS: See Katz, *Gay American History,* pp. 385–93.
334. AN ETHICAL HOMOSEXUAL CULTURE: Ibid., p. 412.
334. NAME MATTACHINE DERIVED FROM: Ibid., pp. 412–13.
334. MASKED PEOPLE, UNKNOWN AND ANONYMOUS: Ibid., p. 413.
334. SECRET, CELL-LIKE: D'Emilio, p. 64.
335. THERE WERE ABOUT 180 PEOPLE PRESENT: Eric Marcus, *Making History,* p. 48.
335. THAT WAS VERY DISTURBING: Ibid., p. 49.
336. STRANGE NEW PRESSURE GROUP: Quoted in D'Emilio, p. 76 and Katz, p. 416.
336. MANY MEMBERS OF THE MEETINGS . . . FEEL THAT MR. COATES ASKED LEGITIMATE QUESTIONS: D'Emilio, p. 76.
336. *EVERYONE* HAD SOMETHING TO HIDE: Ibid., p. 77.
336. A VERY STRONG STATEMENT CONCERNING OUR STAND ON SUBVERSIVE ELEMENTS: Ibid., p. 79.
337. ANY ORGANIZED PRESSURE: Ibid., p. 83.
337. SPECIAL PLEAS FOR A MINORITY GROUP: Ibid., pp. 83–84.
337. THE PEOPLE WHO REMAINED: Nancy Adair and Casey Adair, *Word Is Out,* p. 242.

337. THE [EARLY MATTACHINE] CLAIM: D'Emilio, p. 91.

338. WE THOUGHT THAT "DAUGHTERS OF BILITIS": Del Martin and Phyllis Lyon, *Lesbian Woman*, pp. 238–40.

338. INTEGRATION OF THE HOMOSEXUAL INTO SOCIETY: Katz, p. 426.

338. DOB EXISTED AS A SELF-HELP EFFORT FOR WOMEN: D'Emilio, p. 104.

339. MY INTRODUCTION TO THE DAUGHTERS: Marcus, p. 131.

339. AT EVERY ONE OF THESE CONVENTIONS: Quoted D'Emilio, p. 105 and Katz, p. 431.

340. SCOLDING-TEACHER ATTITUDE: Marcus, p. 118.

340. THE LITTLE LESBIAN WAS BEGINNING TO CLIMB THE LADDER: Ibid., p. 119.

340. PRETTY MUCH AS A TRANSVESTITE: D'Emilio, p. 106.

340. AT FIRST WE WERE GRATEFUL JUST TO HAVE PEOPLE—ANYBODY—PAY ATTENTION TO US: Katz, pp. 426–27.

341. 1959 Denver Mattachine convention: See D'Emilio, pp. 119–21.

342. CARE, DISCRETION, AND RESTRAINT: Vito Russo, *The Celluloid Closet*, p. 121.

342. PATHOLOGICAL, PREDATORY, AND DANGEROUS: Ibid., p. 122.

343. MY DISMISSAL AMOUNTED TO A DECLARATION OF WAR AGAINST ME BY MY GOVERNMENT: Marcus, p. 94.

343. THE ENTIRE MOVEMENT IS GOING TO STAND OR FALL: D'Emilio, p. 163.

343. A CLEAR AND COMPELLING VISION: Marcus, p. 120.

343. GOT THE ARRESTED MEN TO SIGN AFFIDAVITS: D'Emilio, p. 157.

344. THE MAN WHO CONTRIBUTED THE MOST: Ibid.

344. MOVE AWAY FROM THE COMFORTINGLY DETACHED RESPECTABILITY: Ibid., p. 170.

345. PURGES FROM THE ARMED FORCES: John D'Emilio, "Gay Politics, Gay Community," in *Making Trouble*, p. 77.

345. THE CITY HAD SOME THIRTY GAY BARS: Ibid. For a discussion of the demographic changes in San Francisco during this period, see Ibid., pp. 76–77.

346. THE NATIONAL HEADQUARTERS OF THE ORGANIZED HOMOSEXUALS: D'Emilio, *Sexual Politics, Sexual Communities*, p. 121.

346. THE GREATEST GAY BAR: Ibid., pp. 186–87.

347. THE FIRST GAY NEWS SERVICE: Randy Shilts, *The Mayor of Castro Street*, p. 52.

347. A BLUE FUNGUS HAS HIT THE PARKS: Ibid.

347. IT SOUNDS SILLY, BUT IF YOU LIVED AT THAT TIME: Adair, *Word Is Out*, p. 73.

348. THEY COULD NOT HAVE BEEN ANY BETTER PREPARED: Marcus, p. 153.

348. FOR ALL INTENTS AND PURPOSES, THE POLICE WERE JUST RUNNING ROUGHSHOD: Ibid., p. 157.

348. DELIBERATE HARASSMENT: D'Emilio, p. 194.

349. THERE WEREN'T, BUT WHEN THEY CARRY IT ON THE WIRE SERVICES: Marcus, pp. 191–92.

350. HOW DO I KNOW YOU'RE HOMOSEXUALS?: Martin Duberman, *Stonewall*, p. 115.

352. THE LESBIAN, AFTER ALL, IS FIRST OF ALL A *WOMAN:* D'Emilio, p. 228.

"The Raid"—An Excerpt from *One* Magazine

353. IT WAS A TYPICAL FRIDAY NIGHT: Chas. K. Robinson, "The Raid," *One*, July 1960, pp. 26–27.

The Secret Life of J. Edgar Hoover

355. I THINK WE SHOULD TAKE THIS CROWD ON: Randy Shilts, *Conduct Unbecoming*, p. 109.

355. I DIDN'T REALLY UNDERSTAND ANYTHING ABOUT HOMOSEXUALITY: Quoted in Anthony Summers, *Official and Confidential: The Secret Life of J. Edgar Hoover*, p. 85.

355. SOME OF MY BEST FRIENDS ARE HOMOSEXUAL: Quoted in Ibid., 84.

355. FLUFFY BLACK DRESS: Ibid., p. 254.

356. IT'S BEEN A LONG SLIDE FROM NATIONAL HERO TO DEVIL IN A BLACK DRESS: Henry Allen, *Washington Post National Weekly Edition*, March 29–April 4, 1993, p. 10.

356. IT IS CURIOUS THAT, AT A TIME WHEN THE LEFT IS MARSHALING: Ibid., p. 11.

357. THE ELEGANT ONES WHO HAVE DECIDED TO EXPRESS THEIR SOCIAL HOSTILITY: *One*, November 1955.

357. IT WAS RATHER HILARIOUS: Marcus, p. 101.

The Word *Gay*

358. HOW, WHEN, AND WHERE THIS WORD: Donald Webster Cory, *The Homosexual in America*, p. 107 ff.

Bayard Rustin, "Outside Agitator"

360. A GLORIOUS PASSAGE . . . ARRIVING CRIMINALS WERE BEING CELEBRATED: Taylor Branch, *Parting the Waters: America in the King Years 1954–63*, p. 177.

361. A VAGABOND MINSTREL: Ibid., p. 168.

362. GRAB ONE LITTLE BROTHER: Ibid., p. 861.

362. WAS NOT SOMEONE WHO EVER CONCEALED HIS IDENTITY: Quoted in Lisa Sragovicz, "Bayard Rustin's Legacy," *Washington Blade*, August 20, 1993, p. 17.

CHAPTER 23: STONEWALL AND THE BIRTH OF GAY AND LESBIAN LIBERATION

365. MANY SAW IT AS AN OASIS: Duberman, *Stonewall*, p. 182.

366. SUDDENLY, THE PADDYWAGON ARRIVED: Lucian Truscott IV, "Gay Power Comes to Sheridan Square," *Village Voice*, July 3, 1969, p. 1.

366. WE ARE THE STONEWALL GIRLS: Duberman, p. 201.

367. YOU KNOW THE GUYS THERE WERE SO BEAUTIFUL: Quoted in Donn Teal, *The Gay Militants*, p. 22.

367. BOSTON TEA PARTY: Dennis Altman, *Homosexual Oppression and Liberation*, p. 117.

367. THE HAIRPIN DROP HEARD AROUND THE WORLD: Toby Marotta, *The Politics of Homosexuality*, p. 77.

367. PITY: JUST WHEN MIDDLE AMERICA FINALLY DISCOVERED THE HOMOSEXUAL: Tom Burke, "The New Homosexuality," *Esquire*, December 1969, p. 178.

367–68. A DEPENDABLE, FORTYISH CARTIER SALESCLERK: Ibid., p. 316.

368. A TENSE BOY WITH LEONINE HAIR: Ibid.

369. NO LONGER IS THE CLAIM MADE THAT GAY PEOPLE CAN FIT INTO AMERICAN SOCIETY: Altman, pp. 118–19.

369. THE KEY PHRASE IS COME OUT: Jill Johnston, " 'Of This Pure But Irregular Passion,' " *Village Voice*, July 2, 1970, p. 29.

370. THOSE WHO SAY THEY LIKE THE WORD HOMOSEXUAL BETTER THAN GAY: Charles P. Thorp, "I.D., Leadership and Violence," in Karla Jay and Allen Young, eds., *Out of the Closets*, p. 353.

370. SO BUSY PLAYING HUNTER OR GAME: Marcus Overseth, quoted in Teal, p. 56.

371. TO BE A FREE TERRITORY: Carl Wittman, "A Gay Manifesto," reprinted in Jay and Young, eds., p. 339.

371. THE BLACK, THE FEMINIST, THE SPANISH-AMERICAN, THE INDIAN, THE HIPPIE: Teal, p. 54.

372. A CROSS BETWEEN A QUAKER MEETING AND AN INFORMAL RAP SESSION: Altman, p. 125.

372. CHARACTERS WERE DEFINED: Arthur Bell, *Dancing the Gay Lib Blues*, p. 14.

372. "A CRAZY" INTERRUPTED: Ibid., p. 17.

373. WHITE MAN'S WEAKNESS: Teal, p. 94.

373. HOMOSEXUALITY IS A SICKNESS: Quoted in Marotta, p. 135.

374. LAVENDER MENACE: Sidney Abbott and Barbara Love, *Sappho Was a Right-On Woman*, p. 110.

374. LESBIAN IS THE ONE WORD THAT CAN CAUSE THE EXECUTIVE COMMITTEE A COLLECTIVE HEART ATTACK: Abbott and Love, p. 112.

374. BEJEWELLED AND WELL-DRESSED WOMEN: Rita Mae Brown, "Take a Lesbian to Lunch," in Jay and Young, eds., p. 189.

375. A DIFFERENT WAY OF LIVING: Ibid., p. 192.

375. WE ARE NO LONGER WILLING TO BE TOKEN LESBIANS: Ibid., p. 194.

375. BE IT RESOLVED THAT WOMEN'S LIBERATION IS A LESBIAN PLOT: Abbott and Love, p. 115.

376. WHAT IS A LESBIAN? A LESBIAN IS THE RAGE OF ALL WOMEN: Radicalesbians Statement, "The Woman-Identified Woman," in Jay and Young, eds., p. 177.

376. LESBIANS MUST BECOME FEMINISTS: Charlotte Bunch, "Lesbians in Revolt," in Nancy Myron and Charlotte Bunch, eds., *Lesbianism and the Women's Movement*, p. 31.

377. ARE YOU A LESBIAN? SAY IT. ARE YOU?: Kate Millett, *Flying*, p. 15.

377. FEMINISM IS THE THEORY AND LESBIANISM IS THE PRACTICE: Marotta, p. 258.

377. IS BOUND TO DISCREDIT HER AS A SPOKESMAN FOR HER CAUSE: *Time*, December 14, 1970, p. 50.

378. BE IT RESOLVED THAT N.O.W. RECOGNIZES THE DOUBLE OPPRESSION OF LESBIANS: Abbott and Love, p. 134.

378. COMPLETE TURNABOUT: Ibid., p. 131.

378. THE LEADERSHIP WOULD, IN OTHER CIRCUMSTANCES: Altman, p. 122.

379. IF ONE LOOKS LIKE A DUCK, WALKS LIKE A DUCK, QUACKS LIKE A DUCK: Marotta, pp. 204–5.

379. THE REAL SIGNIFICANCE OF ZAPPING A POLITICAL FIGURE: Altman, p. 131.

379. I THINK THERE ARE MORE IMPORTANT THINGS TO TALK ABOUT: Marotta, p. 158.

381. WHAT IF WE EMPLOY A MR. SCHULTZ ON MONDAY?: Ibid., p. 219.

381. HETEROSEXUAL BASTARDS!: Ibid.

381. JUSTICE! JUSTICE! JUSTICE!: Ibid., p. 221.

381. WHEN GAA UNDERTOOK INTRO 475, IT WAS NOT ADVOCATED AS THE GOAL: Ibid., pp. 225–26.

382. THE OLD HOMOPHILE AND THE REFORMIST GAY AND LESBIAN LIBERATIONIST: Ibid., p. 322.

383. THEY STRETCHED IN A LINE, FROM GIMBELS TO TIMES SQUARE, THOUSANDS AND THOUSANDS: Jonathan Black, "A Happy Birthday for Gay Liberation," *Village Voice*, July 2, 1970, p. 1.

384. SENSATION-SATED HOLLYWOOD HAD NEVER SEEN ANYTHING LIKE IT: "1200 Parade in Hollywood; Crowds Line Boulevard," *The Advocate*, July 22, 1970, p. 2.

384. A GROUP WENT TO THE PLAYBOY CLUB: David Steinecker, "Several Hundred Gays March in Chicago Pride Celebration," *The Advocate*, July 22, 1970, p. 2.

384. ARE WE TRYING TO INVENT A NEW EXISTENCE?: Millett, *Flying*, p. 90.

"A Gay Manifesto"

385. IN THE PAST YEAR THERE HAS BEEN AN AWAKENING: Carl Wittman, "A Gay Manifesto," reprinted in *Out of the Closets*, pp. 330–40.

Lesbianism and the Women's Movement

388. LESBIANISM, POLITICALLY ORGANIZED: Rita Mae Brown, "The Shape of Things to Come," in Myron and Bunch, eds., *Lesbianism and the Women's Movement*, pp. 70–73.

Gay Liberation Comes to London

389. COULD NEVER HAPPEN IN LONDON: Jeffrey Weeks, *Coming Out*, p. 189.

390. BADGES WITH SLOGANS LIKE "GAY POWER" AND "GAY IS GOOD": Ibid., p. 191.

390. THE COTTAGE IS THE COFFIN: Ibid., pp. 192–93.

391. THE ESSENCE OF GLF WAS TO CHANGE CONSCIOUSNESS: Ibid., p. 205.

391. SUCH DIFFERING ASPECTS OF OUR SOCIETY: Stephen Jeffery-Poulter, *Peers, Queers, and Commons*, p. 107.

391. ANY FORM OF OSTENTATIOUS BEHAVIOR: Ibid., p. 90.

Gay Liberation Comes to Paris

392. ONLY PERSONS OF "GOOD MORALITY": David Macey, *The Lives of Michel Foucault*, p. 30.

392. SOCIAL SCOURGE: Ibid., p. 91.

392. HOMOSEXUAL "APOLOGETICS": White, *Genet*, p. 382.

393. I ARRIVED AT A SMALL ROOM: Michael Moon, Introduction to Guy Hocquenghem, *Homosexual Desire*, p. 12.

393. ABORTION AND CONTRACEPTION ON DEMAND: Ibid.

393. *LE SEXISME, LE PHALLOCRATISME, ET L'HÉTÉROFLIQUISME:* Barry D. Adam, *The Rise of a Gay and Lesbian Movement*, p. 87.

393. A LARGE, IF VERY ALIENATING, COMMERCIAL GAY WORLD: Dennis Altman, "Three Views of France," in *Coming Out in the Seventies*, p. 90.

393. THE GAY MILITANTS OF THE LATIN WORLD: Ibid., p. 93.

394. EXPLOSION OF ENERGY: Ibid., p. 101.

394. A LITTLE BIT OF GAY PRIDE WEEK AMID THE FRENCH LEFT: Ibid., p. 99.

394. A NEW LIFE STYLE FOR MARGINAL HOMOSEXUALS: Ibid., p. 102.

394. A SOCIETY WHERE THE POSSIBILITIES OF MAJOR POLITICAL CHANGE: Ibid., p. 100.

CHAPTER 24: THE 1970S: THE TIMES OF HARVEY MILK AND ANITA BRYANT

396. WELL-ORGANIZED LIGHTNING STRIKE: Randy Shilts, *The Mayor of Castro Street*, p. 63.

396. WE DO NOT COME TO YOU PLEADING: Ibid., p. 64.

397. WE'RE LIKE THE CATHOLIC CHURCH: Ibid., p. 74.

398. VEST-POCKET CITY HALL: Ibid., p. 87.

399. THAT GUY HAS CHARISMA: Ibid., pp. 97–98.

400. MIGHT BE REFUGEES FROM OPPRESSION: Frances FitzGerald, *Cities on a Hill*, pp. 59–60.

400. AND THE YOUNG GAY PEOPLE IN THE ALTOONA, PENNSYLVANIAS: Mike Weiss, *Double Play*, p. 106.

401. YOU MUST REALIZE THAT THERE ARE THOUSANDS UPON THOUSANDS OF FRUSTRATED, ANGRY PEOPLE: Ibid., p. 52.

402. VIOLATE MY RIGHTS AND THE RIGHTS OF ALL DECENT: Anita Bryant, *The Anita Bryant Story*, p. 25.

402. THE CAMPAIGN IS OVER GAY RIGHTS: Ibid., p. 49.

402. MILITANT HOMOSEXUALS: Ibid., p. 15.

403. NEVER VIEWED THE HOMOSEXUAL LIFESTYLE AS SOMETHING: Martin Duberman, "The Anita Bryant Brigade," in *About Time*, p. 344.

403. WELL-ORGANIZED, HIGHLY FINANCED: Bryant, p. 21.

403. TONIGHT THE LAWS OF GOD AND THE CULTURAL VALUES OF MAN: Ibid., p. 125.

403. MY SON'S BLOOD IS ON HER [BRYANT'S] HANDS: Shilts, p. 164.

404. LIKE THE UNION ARMY AT THE SECOND MANASSAS: Anita Bryant and Bob Green, *At Any Cost*, p. 26.

404. MOST OF THEM ARE IN THE CLOSET: Shilts, p. 229.

404. IF YOU LET ONE HOMOSEXUAL TEACHER STAY: Ibid., p. 239.

404. WHATEVER ELSE IT IS, HOMOSEXUALITY IS NOT A CONTAGIOUS DISEASE: Ibid., p. 243.

405. LIKE TWO WORLD WAR II BUDDIES: Ibid., p. 248.

405. DAN WHITE IS JUST STUPID: Ibid., p. 185.

405. JUST DIDN'T HOLD UP UNDER FIRE: Weiss, p. 124.

406. IF YOU HAD TO GUESS: Ibid., p. 288.

407. DAN WHITE WOULD TRULY BE JUDGED BY A JURY OF HIS PEERS: Shilts, p. 309.

407. GOOD PEOPLE, FINE PEOPLE: Weiss, p. 293. The account of Dan White's trial relies on Weiss, pp. 284–404. See also Shilts, pp. 308–23.

407. WITHOUT A BELIEVABLE MOTIVE: Weiss, p. 392.

407. I WANTED TO TALK TO HIM: Shilts, p. 313.

408. AS I LOOK AT THE LAW: Ibid., p. 326.

408. THE CASTRO MOURNED HARVEY MILK: FitzGerald, p. 81.

409. PLEASE REMEMBER, HOMOSEXUALS DO NOT REPRODUCE!: Adam, *The Rise of a Gay and Lesbian Movement*, p. 113.

410. CAN'T LET MILITANT GAYS: Ibid.

410. Similarities between gays and lesbians and evangelical Christians: Shilts, p. 216.

Leonard Matlovich: A Soldier's Story

411. I HAVE A LETTER I'D LIKE FOR YOU TO READ: Mike Hippler, *Matlovich: The Good Soldier*, p. 48.

411. AFTER SOME YEARS OF UNCERTAINTY: Ibid., p. 47.

412. I'VE ALWAYS BEEN VERY CONSERVATIVE: Ibid., p. 16.

412. EVERY DAY, HE REMINDED HIS CLASSES OF THE PLEA: Randy Shilts, *Conduct Unbecoming*, p. 186.

413. WHY DON'T THEY KICK *ME* OUT?: Ibid., p. 228.

414. ARGUABLY THE MOST INFLUENTIAL GAY ACTIVIST OF HIS GENERATION: Ibid., p. 623.

In the Statehouse: Noble and Spear

415. For a portrait of Spear, see Neil Miller, *In Search of Gay America*, pp. 269–71.

The Man Who Saved the President

417. ONE OF THE HEROES OF THE DAY: Shilts, *The Mayor of Castro Street*, p. 122.

417. HARVEY MILK WHO LEAKED: Ibid.

418. I WANT YOU TO KNOW THAT MY MOTHER TOLD ME TODAY: Ibid., pp. 122–23.

The Rise of the Gay Press

420. LIBERATION BY ACCUMULATION: Bronski, *Culture Clash*, p. 149.

420. I'M TRYING TO REACH THE GAYS WE DON'T ORDINARILY SEE: Edmund White, *States of Desire*, p. 39.

CHAPTER 25: SEX AND MUSIC IN THE SEVENTIES

422. I HAVE CRUISED RICH, POOR, MIDDLE CLASS: Paul Goodman, "The Politics of Being Queer," in *Nature Heals: The Psychological Essays of Paul Goodman*, p. 219.

422. THE COFFEE SHOP/DANCE HALLS, RURAL RETREATS: Carl Wittman, "A Gay Manifesto," reprinted in Jay and Young, eds., p. 339.

422. PROFOUNDLY DEMOCRATIZING, THROWING TOGETHER EVERY CLASS AND GROUP: Goodman, p. 221.

423. THE *LINGUA FRANCA*, THE ESPERANTO OF THE MALE HOMOSEXUAL COMMUNITY: Andrew Holleran, "Notes on Promiscuity," in *Ground Zero*, p. 115.

423. DATES LEADING TO ORGASM: Larry Kramer, *Faggots*, p. 14.

423. SEX IS CASUAL, ROMANCE SHORT-LIVED: Edmund White, *States of Desire*, p. 286.

424. SIX TYPES OF TWINING'S TEA: Dennis Altman, "Fear and Loathing and Hepatitis," in *Coming Out in the Seventies*, p. 84.

424. THE BRIGHT LIGHTS AND GLITTER: Altman, "Gay Oppression in the Baths," in Ibid., p. 43.

424. PARTICULAR FRISSON: Ibid., p. 42.

424. A GAY MAN WITH $15: Ibid., p. 45.

424. STREET CRUISING GAVE WAY: White, pp. 266–67.

425. HIRED MUSCLEMEN GARBED AS CENTURIONS: Ibid., p. 270.

425. WE WERE FORCED TO SLITHER ACROSS: Ibid.

425–26. THE MAIN UPSTAIRS ROOM, CALLED THE "PLAYGROUND": Joel I. Brodsky, "The Mineshaft: A Retrospective Ethnography," *Journal of Homosexuality*, Vol. 24, Nos. 3/4 1993, p. 244. See also White, pp. 282–85.

426. YOU TOUCH, WITH YOUR BLIND HAND: White, p. 284.

426. WATCHING SOMETHING UNSPEAKABLE: Ibid., p. 283.

426. GROWING HEDONISM DOES NOT: Altman, p. 84.

426. IF I WERE PERSUADED THAT THESE REPRESENTED A WORKING OUT: Ibid., pp. 84–85.

427. I OPPOSE THE GAY OBSESSION WITH SEX: White, p. 37.

427. COULD NOT STOP DANCING: Andrew Holleran, *Dancer from the Dance*, p. 111.

427. OVERLAPPED SOUL AND PHILLY: Anthony Thomas, "The House That Kids Built: The Gay Black Imprint on American Dance Music," *OUT/LOOK*, Summer 1989, p. 26.

429. IF I CAN GET THE BLACKS, THE HISPANICS, AND THE GAYS: Neil Miller, "Lavender Capitalism," *Boston Phoenix*, July 8, 1980, Sec. 2, p. 4.

429. FOR THAT IS THE CURIOUS QUALITY OF THE DISCOTHEQUE: Holleran, p. 132.

CHAPTER 26: LESBIAN NATION AND WOMEN'S MUSIC

431. POLISHING THEIR CHAINS: Rita Mae Brown, "The Shape of Things to Come," in Myron and Bunch, eds., *Lesbianism and the Women's Movement*, p. 71.

431. WHEN I CAME OUT [IN THE SEVENTIES]: Miller, *In Search of Gay America*, p. 166.

432. LESBIAN CONTINUUM: Adrienne Rich, "Compulsory Heterosexuality and Lesbian Existence," in *Blood, Bread, and Poetry,* p. 51.

433. THEIR OWN QUASI-LEGAL SYSTEM: Faderman, *Odd Girls and Twilight Lovers,* p. 226.

433. "DOGMAS" OF LESBIAN-FEMINISM: Ibid., pp. 230–33.

434. WERE SUPPOSED TO LOOK BUTCH AND TO HAVE SEX WITH OTHER WOMEN WHO LOOKED BUTCH: Faderman, "The Return of Butch and Femme," in *American Sexual Politics,* John C. Fout and Maura Shaw Tantillo, eds., p. 336.

434. AT GATHERINGS OF THE SEVENTIES, IF A WOMAN WALKED IN WEARING MAKEUP: Miller, p. 175.

434. A FIXTURE ON THE [BLACK] GHETTO SCENE: Faderman, "The Return of Butch and Femme," p. 338.

434. WHO WERE THESE PEOPLE TO COME OUT OF THEIR MIDDLE CLASS: Ibid., p. 340.

435. WE WERE GOING TO CHANGE THE WORLD: Author interview with Holly Near.

435. THERE WAS AN INHERENT UNDERSTANDING ON THE PART OF LESBIANS: Ibid.

436. IN A BIG CITY, THE FIRST CONCERT WOULD DRAW: Author interview with Judy Dlugacz.

436. WHAT WE WERE SAYING WAS THAT THERE HAD NEVER BEEN A PLACE FOR WOMEN TO SEE EACH OTHER: Ibid.

437. PEOPLE COULD SAY, "MARGIE ADAM, I KNOW HER STORY": Author interview with Lissa LeGrand.

437. YOU'D FIND MORE DYKES AT A TINA TURNER CONCERT: Author interview with Holly Near.

CHAPTER 27: THE 1980S: THE AGE OF AIDS

439. IMMUNOLOGIST DR. MICHAEL GOTTLIEB WAS MYSTIFIED: "The AIDS Epidemic: The Search for a Cure," *Newsweek,* April 18, 1983, p. 74.

441. TODAY I MUST TELL YOU THAT 120 GAY MEN IN THE UNITED STATES: Larry Kramer, *Reports from the Holocaust,* pp. 8–9.

442. READ ANYTHING BY KRAMER CLOSELY: Ibid., p. 16.

443. WE HAVE NEVER ENCOUNTERED SO MUCH LOVE: Ibid., p. 30.

443. LIVED WITH FURIES INSIDE HIM: Bruce Nussbaum, *Good Intentions,* p. 92.

444. IF THIS ARTICLE DOESN'T SCARE THE SHIT OUT OF YOU: Kramer, p. 33.

444. INARGUABLY ONE OF THE MOST INFLUENTIAL: Randy Shilts, *And the Band Played On,* p. 245.

445. WE BELIEVE THAT IT IS TIME TO SPEAK THE SIMPLE TRUTH: Ibid., p. 259.

445. YOU HAVE GIVEN THE MORAL MAJORITY AND THE RIGHT WING THE GASOLINE: Frances FitzGerald, *Cities on a Hill,* p. 108.

445. THE GAY LIBERATION MOVEMENT IN SAN FRANCISCO ALMOST DIED: Shilts, p. 445.

446. RUSSIAN ROULETTE: Ibid., p. 489.

447. THE COMMUNITY HAS NOW ACCEPTED AIDS: FitzGerald, p. 116.

447. THE GAY BARS WERE STILL THERE: Ibid., pp. 120–21.

447. SHRUNK TO A SINGLE FACT: Holleran, "Ground Zero," in *Ground Zero,* p. 19.

447. DARK AND QUIET AND CALM: Ibid., p. 21.

447. NO CLUMPS, NO ORGIES: Ibid., p. 27.

448. THE FUTURE WAS ALWAYS BRIGHT: Miller, *In Search of Gay America*, pp. 138–40.

450. I CAN PICTURE WISER PEOPLE IN THE NEXT CENTURY: White, *States of Desire*, p. 282.

451. THE SEXUAL REVOLUTION HAS BEGUN TO DEVOUR ITS CHILDREN: Shilts, p. 311.

451. AIDS: HOMOSEXUAL DISEASES THREATEN AMERICAN FAMILIES: Charles Krauthammer, "The Politics of a Plague," *The New Republic*, August 1, 1983, p. 19.

451. THERE HAS EVEN BEEN SPECULATION THAT AIDS VICTIMS COULD DELIBERATELY CONTAMINATE: Ibid., p. 20.

452. PROPOSED *REDUCING* AIDS FUNDING: Shilts, p. 525.

456. AT THE RATE WE ARE GOING: Kramer, p. 128.

457. TODAY'S FRONT PAGE OF *THE NEW YORK TIMES*: Ibid., pp. 134–35.

458. THE COMBINATION OF NEARING DEATH AND POLITICAL ACTIVISM: Andrew Sullivan, "Gay Life, Gay Death," *The New Republic*, December 19, 1990, p. 24.

458. ACT UP at the FDA: See Nussbaum, pp. 205–206.

460. MANICHEAN VISION: Sullivan, p. 24.

460. HE IS NO MAN OF GOD—HE IS THE DEVIL: Michelangelo Signorile, *Queer in America*, p. 57.

460. WHAT DO YOU THINK CAUSED YOUR HETEROSEXUALITY?: Phyllis Burke, *Family Values*, p. 83.

461. I FELT THAT THE HISTORICAL RECORD HAD TO BE CORRECTED: Signorile, p. 73.

461. SINGULAR CASE: Ibid., p. 128.

461. BROWNSHIRTS and LAVENDER FASCISTS: Ibid., p. 153.

461. ACT UP FOR NEGATIVES: Sullivan, p. 20.

462. WE'RE HERE. WE'RE QUEER: Burke, p. 76.

An Excerpt from *And the Band Played On*

463. THE LOUDEST OVATIONS: Randy Shilts, *And the Band Played On*, p. 570.

The Vatican Cracks Down

464. OPEN ITS EYES TO REALITY: Joseph Berger, "Religions Confront the Issue of Homosexuality," *The New York Times*, March 2, 1987, p. A-13.

465. A RESPONSIBILITY TO DEVELOP A THEOLOGY OF SEXUALITY: Miller, *In Search of Gay America*, p. 229.

465. THEREFORE SPECIAL CONCERN AND PASTORAL ATTENTION: Loren Jenkins, "Vatican Adamant on Gays," *Washington Post*, October 31, 1986, p. A-1.

466. HOMOSEXUALITY MAY SERIOUSLY THREATEN THE LIVES AND WELL-BEING: Robert Suro, "Vatican Reproaches Homosexuals with a Pointed Allusion to AIDS," *The New York Times*, October 31, 1986, p. A-17.

466. WHICH ARE AMBIGUOUS ABOUT IT OR NEGLECT IT ENTIRELY: "Bishop Bars Homosexuals," *Washington Post*, February 13, 1987, p. A-19.

466. I WOULD SEE NO OTHER WAY TO INTERPRET THE DECREE: "O'Connor Supports

Ban on a Homosexual Group," *The New York Times*, February 16, 1987, p. A-31.

466. WE'VE DONE WHAT THE ARCHDIOCESE HAS FAILED MISERABLY TO DO: Joseph Berger, "Roman Catholic Mass for Homosexuals Banned," *The New York Times*, March 6, 1987, p. B-3.

The Great Lesbian Sex Debates

467. I DO WANT A XANADU: Rita Mae Brown, "Queen for a Day: A Stranger in Paradise," in *The Real Paper*, October 8, 1975.

468. FREQUENCY OF SEXUAL RELATIONS AMONG 788 LESBIAN COUPLES: Philip Blumstein and Pepper Schwartz, *American Couples*, p. 196.

469. THE NOBLE SOUL WHO WILL ALWAYS PUT HER PRINCIPLES: Miller, *In Search of Gay America*, p. 167.

469. THERE IS THE SENSE OF CONFIDENCE: Ibid.

469. VALIDATED THE SYSTEM OF PATRIARCHY: Faderman, *Odd Girls and Twilight Lovers*, p. 250.

469. WHICH HAVE MISTAKENLY BEEN CORRELATED WITH LESBIAN/GAY RIGHTS: Ibid., p. 252.

470. THE ENCOURAGEMENT OF THE SEXUAL RADICALS: Ibid., p. 270.

Michel Foucault

470. I WASN'T ALWAYS SMART: James Miller, *The Passion of Michel Foucault*, p. 56.

70–71. IN THE EYES OF HIS ADMIRERS: Ibid., p. 13.

471. NO PHILOSOPHER HAS EVER MATCHED: Alexander Nehamas, "Subject and Object," *The New Republic*, February 15, 1993, p. 27.

471. IT MADE POSSIBLE THE FORMATION OF A "REVERSE" DISCOURSE: Michel Foucault, *The History of Sexuality*, p. 101.

472. IT'S NOT ENOUGH AS A PART OF A GENERAL WAY OF LIFE: Interview with Gilles Barbedette, "The Social Triumph of the Sexual Will," *Christopher Street*, No. 64, May 1982, p. 36.

472. I HAVE LIVED FOR EIGHTEEN YEARS: Miller, p. 186.

473. THAT DAY, I SAID TO HIM: David Macey, *The Lives of Michel Foucault*, pp. 479–80.

The Contradictions of the Gay Conservative: Terry Dolan

474. LARRY KRAMER CLAIMS TO HAVE THROWN A DRINK IN HIS FACE: Shilts, *And the Band Played On*, p. 407.

474. SOME OF THE RHETORIC THAT SOME OF MY FRIENDS ON THE RIGHT: Elizabeth Kastor, "The Cautious Closet of the Gay Conservative," *Washington Post*, May 11, 1987, p. B-2.

474. OUR NATION'S MORAL FIBER: Ibid.

475. TERRY WAS BEGINNING: Ibid.

The Gay Fiction Boom of the 1980s

477. A LITERATURE OF GUILT AND APOLOGY: Richard Hall, "Gay Fiction Comes Home," *The New York Times Book Review*, June 19, 1988, p. 1.
478. FINDING A FAMILY: Hall, p. 25.

CHAPTER 28: COMMUNISM AND FASCISM

RUSSIA

484. BASICALLY, GAY LIFE TAKES PLACE IN CERTAIN PARKS IN SUMMER: George Schuvaloff, "Gay Life in Russia," in *Christopher Street*, September 1976, p. 16.
484. PASSION FOR DIAMONDS AND ANTIQUE FURNITURE: Ibid., p. 17.
485. THEY LED US TO THE BARRACKS: Masha Gessen, "Red Army of Lovers," *Out*, April/May 1993, p. 59.
485. I CAN'T SHOW MY FACE: "Gays in Russia Organize," *Boston Globe*, August 17, 1993, p. 10.

CHINA

486. THE GREATEST FAULT WE DO FIND: Quoted in Bret Hinsch, *Passions of the Cut Sleeve*, p. 2.
486. [T]HERE ARE PUBLIC STREETS FULL OF BOYS: David F. Greenberg, *The Construction of Homosexuality*, p. 162.
486. EROTICALLY SOAPED AND MASSAGED BY YOUNG MEN: Isherwood, *Christopher and His Kind*, p. 308.
486. EVIL PRODUCT OF CAPITALIST SOCIETY: Stephan Likosky, ed., *Coming Out*, p. 39.
487. SURVEY BY A SHANGHAI SEXOLOGIST: Lena H. Sun, "China's Secrets Are Coming Out," *Washington Post National Weekly*, January 11–17, 1993, p. 17.
487. INFLUENCE OF WESTERN MISSIONARIES AND OTHER ANTIGAY MORALISTS: Hinsch, p. 167.
487. SOME WEAR TIGHT JEANS: Sun, *Washington Post National Weekly*, p. 17.
488. IT IS WIDELY KNOWN THAT EVEN IN THE WEST: "Chinese Paper Denounces Gay Film," *Washington Blade*, February 18, 1984, p. 13.

CUBA

488. WE HAVE NO HOMOSEXUALS HERE: Guillermo Gabrera Infante, interviewed in the documentary film *Improper Conduct*, Nestor Almendros and Orlando Jimenez Leal, directors, 1984.
489. NOTHING PREVENTS A HOMOSEXUAL FROM PROFESSING REVOLUTIONARY IDEOLOGY: Lee Lockwood, *Castro's Cuba, Cuba's Fidel*, p. 107.
490. A SPECIES OF CONCENTRATION CAMP: Allen Young, *Gays Under the Cuban Revolution*, p. 21.
490. THEY SUFFERED THE MOST: Heberto Padilla, interviewed in *Improper Conduct*.
490. CUBA DOES NOT HAVE JEWS: Henk van den Boogard and Kathelijne van Kammen, "We Cannot Jump Over Our Own Shadow" in *ILGA Pink Book 1985*, p. 31.

491. I THINK THAT THE SEXUAL REVOLUTION IN CUBA ACTUALLY CAME ABOUT: Reinaldo Arenas, *Before Night Falls*, p. 107.

491. EVERY GAY WRITER, EVERY GAY ARTIST: Ibid., p. 138.

492. HE HIMSELF WENT TO THE POLICE STATION, WHERE HE WAS ASKED IF HE WAS HOMOSEXUAL: Ibid., p. 280.

493. REALLY QUEER: Ibid., p. 300.

494. IT WAS NEITHER BARRACKS-LIKE: Victor F. Zonana, "Cuba's AIDS Quarantine Center Called 'Frightening,' " *Los Angeles Times*, November 4, 1988, Sec. 1, p. 1.

EAST GERMANY

495. A COMPROMISE: Hans Vonk, "Homosexuality in the GDR," *ILGA Pink Book: 1985*, p. 44.

496. A MONSTROSITY: Ibid., p. 45.

497. THE STARTING POINT FOR A JUDGEMENT: John Parsons, "East Germany Faces Its Past," *OUT/LOOK*, Summer 1989, p. 51.

498. GOOD PRECONDITIONS FOR THE INTEGRATION OF GAY PEOPLE: Neil Miller, *Out in the World*, p. 334.

ARGENTINA

498. ACABAR CON LOS HOMOSEXUALES: Juan José Sebreli, "Historia Secreta de los Homosexuales Porteños," *Perfil*, No. 27, November 1983, p. 12.

499. THERE WERE TEA-ROOMS: Author conversation with Juan José Sebreli.

499. POLICIES REGARDING HOMOSEXUALITY WERE OFTEN INCOHERENT: Miller, pp. 195–96.

500. YOU IMITATED TRADITIONALLY MASCULINE CHARACTERISTICS: Ibid., p. 197.

501. PEOPLE TENDED TO BE DISAPPEARED: Ibid.

501. YOU MIGHT GET ARRESTED FOR CRUISING THE AVENIDA SANTA FE: Ibid., p. 198.

CHAPTER 29: ENGLAND: THE BATTLE OVER CLAUSE 28

503. THIS COUNTRY SEEMS TO BE IN THE GRIP OF A GALLOPING FRENZY OF HATE: Jeffery-Poulter, *Peers, Queers, and Commons*, p. 223.

504. MAKE PROPAGANDA AND GIVE AWAY MONEY: Peter Jenkins, *Mrs. Thatcher's Revolution*, p. 243.

504. SOCIALISM IN ONE CITY: Ibid., p. 246.

504. HARINGEY RULED: Ibid., p. 245.

505. *JENNY LIVES WITH ERIC AND MARTIN*: See Jeffery-Poulter, pp. 207–208, and 221–222.

505. THE WORD *PERMISSIVE*: Jenkins, pp. 326–27.

505. TOLERANCE OF SEXUAL DEVIATION: Jeffery-Poulter, p. 202.

505. LABOUR'S IDEA OF A "COMPREHENSIVE EDUCATION": Michael H. Hodges, "No Gays, Please, We're British," *The Nation*, February 6, 1989, p. 158.

506. CHILDREN WHO NEED TO BE TAUGHT TO RESPECT: Jeffery-Poulter, p. 218.

506. THATCHER WAS THE "DRIVING FORCE": Hodges, p. 156.

506. DRAG IN THE "BACKWOODSMEN": Ibid.

506. PINK TRIANGLE CLAUSE: Jeffery-Poulter, p. 226.

506. I WAS BROUGHT UP BY TWO WOMEN: Ibid., p. 229.

507. TARZAN LESBIANS: Ibid., p. 230.

507. WE HAVE RATHER BEEN INVADED: Hodges, p. 160.

507. "WELFARE" EXPENDITURE: Jeffery-Poulter, p. 233.

508. A PIECE OF RED MEAT: Ibid., p. 234.

508. THERE IS ONLY ONE FORM OF RELATIONSHIP: Ibid., p. 218.

508. IT COULD BE ARGUED THAT THE GAY AND LESBIAN COMMUNITY: Ibid., p. 234.

508. WE HAVE SEEN THE COMING OF AGE OF THE GAY AND LESBIAN MOVEMENT: Ibid., p. 234.

509. THE FIRST OPENLY GAY "SIR": Lawrence O'Toole, "Sympathy for the Devil," *The New York Times Magazine*, April 5, 1992, p. 24.

509. EIGHTEEN IS NOT A COMPROMISE: "British Cut Age of Gay Consent," *Boston Globe*, February 22, 1994, p. 9.

AND IN THE REST OF EUROPE . . .

511. THE ONLY WAY TO BE ABLE TO MOVE ANYTHING: "Denmark Permits Gay 'Partnerships,'" *The New York Times*, October 2, 1989, p. I-8.

511. WE, THE LESBIAN AND GAY CITIZENS: "British Gays Ask Denmark to 'liberate'," *Washington Blade*, April 29, 1994, p. 12.

Simon Nkoli

512. ONE OF HIS EARLY MEMORIES: Simon Nkoli, "Wardrobes," in Mark Gevisser and Edwin Cameron, eds., *Defiant Desire*, p. 249.

513. I BELIEVED I WAS THE ONLY BLACK GAY: Author's conversation with Simon Nkoli.

514. WE HAD TO SHOW THE ANC HOW STRONG WE WERE: Author's interview.

514. IN A NORMAL SOCIETY, THERE WILL BE NO GAYS: Miller, *Out in the World*, p. 61.

CHAPTER 30: JAPAN

515. DEATH AND NIGHT AND BLOOD: Henry Scott-Stokes, *The Life and Death of Yukio Mishima*, p. 308. For a description of Mishima's suicide, see Stokes, pp. 27–54.

516. HE NEVER LET ON: John Nathan, *Mishima: A Biography*, p. 106.

516. TO SAMURAI AND HOMOSEXUAL: Yukio Mishima, *Forbidden Colors*, p. 380.

518. LIKE A CONFIDENT FIANCEE: Nathan, p. 258.

518. I'VE PLEDGED MY LIFE: Ibid.

518. THE SAMURAI'S PROFESSION: Ibid., p. 223.

518. MY SPECULATION: Stokes, p. 303.

518. TO THROW AWAY ONE'S LIFE: Gary Leupp, *Male Colors*, forthcoming.

518. THE PASTIME OF THE SAMURAI: Ibid.

519. IN PEACE AS IN WAR: Tsuneo Watanabe and Jun'ichi Iwata, *The Love of the Samurai*, p. 122.

519. THE ABOMINABLE VICE: Ibid., p. 20.

519. CHEERFUL BISEXUALITY: Leupp.

520. MALE HOMOSEXUALITY . . . IS SO WIDESPREAD: Watanabe and Iwata, p. 122.

520. WITHOUT OUR NOTICING IT, THIS CULTURAL TRADITION: Ibid., p. 124.

522. NO JAPANESE GO THERE, RIGHT?: Miller, *Out in the World*, p. 152.

Excerpts from Mishima's *Confessions of a Mask* and *Forbidden Colors*

522. I AM DAZZLED BY MISHIMA'S MATURE TALENT: Scott-Stokes, p. 121.

523. THEN MY ATTENTION WAS DRAWN: Mishima, *Confessions of a Mask*, pp. 251–52.

524. AS YUICHI'S KNOWLEDGE BROADENED: Mishima, *Forbidden Colors*, pp. 95–96.

CHAPTER 31: THE CLINTON YEARS

527. IF I COULD, IF I COULD WAVE MY ARM: Andrew Kopkind, "The Gay Moment," *The Nation*, May 3, 1993, p. 596.

528. AFTER WILLIE HORTON, ARE GAYS NEXT?: Priscilla Painton, *Time*, August 3, 1992, p. 42.

528. WHEN WE TALK ABOUT FAMILY VALUES: Ibid.

529. THE GAY COMMUNITY IS THE NEW JEWISH COMMUNITY: Jeffrey Schmalz, "Gay Politics Goes Mainstream," *The New York Times Magazine*, October 11, 1992, p. 21.

529. AFTER A BITTER YEAR: Schmalz, "Gay Areas Are Jubilant Over Clinton," *The New York Times*, November 5, 1992, p. B-8.

530. THIS IS A RITE OF PASSAGE: Ibid.

530. I BELIEVE THOUSANDS OF MY FRIENDS: Ibid.

533. A DRAMATIC STEP FORWARD: Gwen Ifill, "Clinton Accepts Delay in Lifting Military Gay Ban," *The New York Times*, January 30, 1993, p. A-1.

534. I THOUGHT ALL ALONG THAT THE WILLIE HORTON ISSUE: Schmalz, "Homosexuals Awake to See a Referendum: It's on Them," *The New York Times*, January 31, 1993, Sec. 4, p. 1.

534. RESTRICTING GAYS AND LESBIANS TO JOBS AS FLORISTS: Eric Schmitt, "Clinton Tries to Erase Impression He Would Set Gay Troops Apart," *The New York Times*, March 26, 1993, p. A-1.

535. THE GAY MOMENT IS UNAVOIDABLE: Kopkind, *The Nation*, May 3, 1993, cover.

536. THE NEW YORK THEATER IS NOW ALMOST EXCLUSIVELY ABOUT GAYS, JEWS, AND BLACKS: Ibid., p. 594.

536. HUNDREDS OF THOUSANDS: Schmalz, "Gay Americans Throng Capital in Appeal for Rights," *The New York Times*, April 26, 1993, p. A-1; Renee Sanchez and Linda Wheeler, "Gays Demand Rights in 6-Hour March," *Washington Post*, April 26, 1993, p. A-1.

537. THAT GAY AMERICA DOES HAVE A FACE: Richard L. Berke, "Crossroad for Gay Rights," *The New York Times*, April 26, 1993, p. A-1.

537. SERIOUS AND SOBER CELEBRATION: E. J. Dionne, Jr., "Isn't Bigotry a Sin?," *Washington Post*, April 27, 1993, p. A-17.

537. WE WON'T COMPROMISE OUR FREEDOM: *Chicago Tribune*, April 26, 1993, p. 1.

538. GAYS MARCH ON WASHINGTON: *Memphis Commercial Appeal*, April 26, 1993, p. 1.

538. WE ARE THE NEW AMERICAN REFUGEES: Ibid.

538. FLAMBOYANT BEHAVIOR AND VULGAR LANGUAGE: Howard Kurtz, "Don't Read All About It!," *Washington Post*, May 9, 1993, p. C-1.

538. DEFINED AS SIGNIFICANT OCCASIONS: Berke, *The New York Times*, April 27, 1993, p. A-1.

538. A LOT OF PEOPLE THINK THAT I DID A TERRIBLE POLITICAL THING: Berke, p. B-8.

539. MY SON SCOTT IS A HOMOSEXUAL: William Raspberry, "What Fred Peck Said," *Washington Post*, May 17, 1993, p. A-21.

539. BUT FEARING THAT A HOMOSEXUAL MARINE: Ibid.

540. MY SENSE WAS THAT MANY MEMBERS OF CONGRESS: Chris Bull, "No Frankness," *The Advocate*, June 29, 1993, p. 27.

540. MOST AMERICANS BELIEVE IF YOU DON'T ASK: Richard L. Berke, "President Backs a Gay Compromise," *The New York Times*, May 28, 1993, p. A-1.

541. THIS WAS ONE OF THOSE MOMENTS: Thomas L. Friedman, "Chiefs Back Clinton on Gay-Troop Plan," *The New York Times*, July 20, 1993, p. A-16.

541. AN UTTER CAPITULATION: Tom Stoddard, "Nunn 2, Clinton 0," *The New York Times*, September 20, 1993, p. A-19.

Voices from the Military Debate

542. FORMER SENATOR BARRY M. GOLDWATER: Barry M. Goldwater, "The Gay Ban: Just Plain Un-American," *Washington Post National Weekly*, July 21–27, p. 28.

542. DOROTHY HADJYS: Mark Schoofs, "Life After Death," *The Advocate*, July 13, 1993, p. 35.

543. BOB ESENWEIN: Eric Schmitt, "Forum on Military's Gay Ban Starts, and Stays, Shrill," *The New York Times*, March 25, 1993, p. A-16.

543. JACKSONVILLE, NORTH CAROLINA, FORUM: Ibid.

543. ANDREW SULLIVAN: Andrew Sullivan, "Gay Values, Truly Conservative," *The New York Times*, February 9, 1993, p. A-21.

544. TONYA DOMI: Melinda Beck, "A (Quiet) Uprising in the Ranks," *Newsweek*, June 21, 1993, p. 60.

544. URVASHI VAID: Urvashi Vaid, "Compromising Positions," *The Advocate*, June 29, 1993, p. 96.

544. JOSEPH ZUNIGA: Joseph Zuniga, " 'Don't Ask, Don't Tell,' Won't Do," *Washington Post*, May 18, 1993, p. A-21.

544. SAM NUNN: David Von Drehle and Helen Dewar, "The Contrary Democrat: What is Sam Nunn Thinking?," *Washington Post*, May 3, 1993, p. A-1.

"Whatever Happened to AIDS?"

545. NOW I SEE THE WORLD: Jeffrey Schmalz, "Covering AIDS and Living It: A Reporter's Testimony," *The New York Times*, December 20, 1992, Sec. 4, p. 5.

546. ONCE AIDS WAS A HOT TOPIC: Schmalz, "Whatever Happened to AIDS?" *The New York Times Magazine*, November 28, 1993, pp. 58–60, 81, 85, 86.

The Many Lives of Martina Navratilova

547. IN THE TWILIGHT: Kimberly J. McLarin, "Center-Court Star at Center Stage," *The New York Times*, August 1, 1993, Sec. 4, p. 4.

549. I'VE GOT TO PRACTICE WHAT I PREACH: Ibid.

549. THE MEDIA THINKS IF YOU'RE A FEMALE ATHLETE: Ibid.

549. LOOKING BACK TO WHEN I WAS SIXTEEN OR SEVENTEEN: Martina Navratilova (with George Vecsey), *Martina*, p. 137.

550. TOUGH MATCH FOR MARTINA: *Washington Post*, May 17, 1993, p. B-1.

550. COME ON, CHRIS: Navratilova, p. 55.

550. BADLY NEEDED TO BE PROTECTED AND . . . SUPPORTED: Navratilova, p. 56.

550. NOW I'M THE HOME TEAM EVERYWHERE I GO: Interview with Alison Carlson, "It's Only a Game," WBUR-FM (Boston), January 8, 1994.

551. WHAT OUR MOVEMENT NEEDS MOST: "Gays Demand Rights in 6-Hour March," *Washington Post*, April 26, 1993, p. A-10.

551. ONE THING THAT I LOVE ABOUT MARTINA: *New York Times*, August 1, 1993.

The Year of the Lesbian

551. SOMETIMES I THINK IT'S LIKE THE YEAR OF THE WOMAN SQUARED: *Newsweek*, June 21, 1993, p. 54.

552. BECAUSE SHE'S A DAMN LESBIAN: "Helms on Nominee: 'She's a Damn Lesbian,' " *Washington Post*, May 7, 1993, p. A-19.

552. CROSSED THE LINE: Helen Dewar, "Senate Votes to Confirm Achtenberg," *Washington Post*, May 25, 1993, p. A-7.

552. A RINGLEADER OF AN IDEOLOGICAL CRUSADE: Ibid.

552. SMOKE SCREEN FOR DISAPPROVAL: Ibid.

552. SHE SURE WASN'T PRIVATE WHEN SHE WAS HUGGING AND KISSING: Ibid.

553. "A PERSONAL REASON" FOR SUPPORTING ACHTENBERG: John Aloysius Farrell, "Senators Hear Pell Talk of Gay Daughter," *Boston Globe*, May 22, 1993, p. 3.

553. WE'RE SITTING HERE TALKING: Dewar, *Washington Post*, p. A-7.

EPILOGUE

558. [T]HE MEASURE OF A JUST SOCIETY: "After Stonewall: Pride and Prejudice," *New York Times*, June 26, 1994, p. A-16

558. IN THE 1990S HOMOSEXUALITY WILL BECOME WHAT THE ABORTION ISSUE WAS: Quoted in "Gays Under Fire," *Newsweek*, September 14, 1992, p. 37.

559. "GAY HISTORY": IN 1970, THIS PHRASE WAS AN OXYMORON: John D'Emilio, "Gay History," in *Making Trouble*, p. 96.

560. THE TIME HAS COME: Anna Quindlen, "Happy and Gay," *The New York Times*, April 6, 1994, p. A-21.

560. ARE WE TRYING TO INVENT A NEW EXISTENCE: Kate Millett, *Flying*, p. 90.

BIBLIOGRAPHICAL SUMMARY

IN THIS SHORT SUMMARY, I will highlight the major sources that I used in compiling this work. My purpose is to describe the works that were of particular value to me and to assist the reader who wishes to read more widely on various aspects of gay and lesbian history. I should caution that this summary does not mention every source I used in the book—for that, the reader will have to go to the bibliography and endnotes. (For publication information on various source material, readers should refer to the bibliography as well.)

There are several important works of gay and lesbian history that span much of the period covered in this book and to which I am particularly indebted. Jonathan Ned Katz's *Gay American History* is a treasure trove of documents about American gays and lesbians from the colonial period to the present. Lillian Faderman's *Odd Girls and Twilight Lovers* (1991) provides a narrative account of U.S. lesbian history from the romantic friendships of the late nineteenth century through the sex wars of the 1980s. The British gay historian Jeffrey Weeks's *Coming Out* is an account of British gay and lesbian history from the early sexual pioneers to the gay liberation movement of the 1970s, albeit from a liberationist, antireformist perspective. *Hidden from History*, edited by Martin Duberman, George Chauncey, and Martha Vicinus, offers a variety of essays on gay and lesbian history from antiquity through World War II and the postwar era. George Chauncey's *Gay New York* looks at homosexuality in that city from the turn of the century to 1940. Michael Bronski's *Culture Clash* charts the development of a male sensibility from Whitman to Judy Garland and Boy George. The late Vito Russo's *The Celluloid Closet* (1981) is the definitive work on the portrayal of gays and lesbians in the movies.

INTRODUCTION: Readers interested in the subject of same-sex love in the period before 1870 are urged to read, among others: John Boswell's *Christianity, Social Tolerance, and Homosexuality,* for ancient Rome and the Middle Ages, as well as his *Same-Sex Unions in Premodern Europe;* Bret Hinsch's *Passions of the Cut Sleeve,* for ancient China; Michel Foucault's *The Use of Pleasure,* for ancient Greece, and *The Care of the Self,* for ancient Rome; Robert Bray's *Homosexuality in Renaissance England;* Jonathan Ned Katz's *Gay American History,* for eighteenth- and nineteenth-century America; Lillian Faderman's *Surpassing the Love of Men,* for relationships between women from the Renaissance to the present day; and the essays in Duberman, Chauncey, and Vicinus's *Hidden from History*. David M. Halperin's *One Hundred Years of Homosexuality* contains a lucid discussion of the constructivist-essentialist debate on gay history, primarily from the constructivist point of view; Boswell's essay, "Revolutions, Universals, and Sexual Categories," in *Hidden From History*, takes up the same subject from an essentialist perspective.

CHAPTER 1—THE AGE OF WHITMAN: Justin Kaplan's *Walt Whitman* remains the most exhaustive biography of the poet; while hardly written from a gay perspective, it treats Whitman's sexuality and relationships in a balanced manner. Charlie Shively's *Calamus Lovers* includes a set of Whitman's letters to his young men friends. Katz's *Gay American History* includes a number of extracts from Whitman's letters and notebooks as well as his correspondence from gay admirers. For a larger picture of how the era viewed same-sex love and gay identity, I highly recommend Peter Gay's *The Tender Passion* and E. Anthony Rotundo's *American Manhood*.

CHAPTER 2—PIONEERS OF SEXOLOGY: For the work of the German sexologists, particularly Ulrichs, see James Steakley's *The Homosexual Emancipation Movement in Germany*. Weeks's *Coming Out* provides an accessible account of the British sexual pioneers Havelock Ellis, John Aldington Symonds, and Edward Carpenter. Ellis's *Sexual Inversion* remains a fascinating and readable book, even the case studies. Peter Gay's *The Tender Passion* offers a (perhaps overly sympathetic) summing up of Freud's ideas on homosexuality and also of those of Symonds, Ellis, and Kraft-Ebbing. George Chauncey's essay, "From Sexual Inversion to Homosexuality," examines how the early sexologists conceptualized lesbianism. For a look at the implications of the new psychological worldview, see Katz's "treatment" section in *Gay American History*. And Michel Foucault's *The History of Sexuality* is indispensable for an overall view of how the early sexologists created sexual categories.

CHAPTER 3—WE'WHA GOES TO WASHINGTON: THE BERDACHE: Walter Williams's *The Spirit and the Flesh* remains, in my estimation, the most comprehensive overall treatment of the American Indian berdache, as well as that of other Native cultures. Once again, Katz's *Gay American History* includes a number of documents from which subsequent historians of the berdache have drawn. Will Roscoe's *Living the Spirit* contains source documents, as well as perspectives of gay American Indians today. Roscoe's article "The Zuni Man-Woman" was the basis of my account of We'wha's visit to Washington. Ramón Gutíerrez's "Must We Deracinate Indians to Find Gay Roots?" challenges conventional thinking about the berdache.

CHAPTER 4—OSCAR WILDE: Richard Ellman's *Oscar Wilde* is the best source about Wilde's life. The account of Wilde's life by his friend Frank

Harris is full of colorful anecdotes but is not necessarily always reliable. For the impact of Wilde's trial and notoriety on America, see Thomas Beer's *The Mauve Decade*. André Gide's encounters with Wilde are recounted in Gide's autobiography, *If It Die*.

CHAPTER 5—ROMANTIC FRIENDSHIPS BETWEEN WOMEN: For this section, Faderman's *Surpassing the Love of Men* and *Odd Girls and Twilight Lovers* proved particularly valuable. *Odd Girls* offers a perceptive examination of the transition from romantic friendship to a more Freudian, psychologized view of relationships between women. Nancy Sahli's essay, "Smashing," was another valuable source, as was the work of Carroll Smith-Rosenberg. Sharon O'Brien's book *Willa Cather: The Emerging Voice* and Blanche Wiesen Cook's *Eleanor Roosevelt* both treat their subjects' lesbian relationships openly and without apology. In my brief examination of "passing women," I am indebted to Faderman and to Katz.

CHAPTER 6—SAPPHO COMES TO PARIS: Shari Benstock's *Women of the Left Bank* offers a revealing look at Belle Époque attitudes toward lesbianism. Among the many biographies of Colette, I found Michèle Sarde's to be the most useful. Colette's writing offers a vivid picture of Paris-Lesbos, and her portrait of lesbian poet Renée Vivien in *The Pure and the Impure* is a classic in itself. On male homosexuality of the period there are fewer source materials, of which Proust's novels must rank as the best.

CHAPTER 7—ENGLAND DURING THE GREAT WAR: For a look at the homosexuality of the war poets, I recommend the introduction to Martin Taylor's anthology, *Lads: Love Poetry of the Trenches*. Paul Fussell's social and literary history of World War I, *The Great War and Modern Memory*, offers a lush treatment of the homoerotic nature of the period's writings and relationships. The poet Siegfried Sassoon's diaries provide a more personal view. For information on the Billing case, I relied on Samuel Hynes's *A War Imagined* and Montgomery Hyde's biography of Lord Alfred Douglas. For the postwar mood and the revival of dandyism, see Martin Green's *Children of the Sun*.

CHAPTER 8—GERMANY'S GOLDEN AGE: James Steakley's *The Homosexual Emancipation Movement in Germany* was particularly helpful to me. Charlotte Wolff's biography of Magnus Hirschfeld provides useful information on Hirschfeld's life and work but one awaits a more complete work on the subject. A special issue of the *Journal of Homosexuality* includes essays by Benedikt Friedländer, Adolf Brand, and others, although it is biased toward the "masculinist" side of the movement. For documents on lesbians in the pre-war period, see Faderman and Eriksson's *Lesbians in Germany.* For the Eulenburg affair, I used Steakley's essay, "Iconography of a Scandal" in *Hidden from History,* as well as Robert K. Massie's *Dreadnought* and Virginia Cowles's *The Kaiser.* Christopher Isherwood's *Christopher and His Kind* remains the best source in English on the Weimar gay scene and gay movement. For more on the gay and lesbian films, see Russo.

CHAPTER 9—GREENWICH VILLAGE: In this chapter, I drew on George Chauncey's exhaustive and groundbreaking *Gay New York* (1994). Faderman's *Odd Girls* explores the contradictions of the Village's view of lesbianism, particularly the case of Edna St. Vincent Millay. Katz includes documents relating to the anarchists Emma Goldman and Alexander Berkman and their views on homosexuality. Katz also offers extensive documentation of the censorship that faced gay-themed plays in New York in the 1920s. For more on the Village in this period (although not from a gay point of view), see Malcolm Cowley's *Exile's Return,* Leslie Fishbein's *Rebels in Bohemia,* and Steven Watson's *Strange Bedfellows.*

CHAPTER 10—RENAISSANCE IN HARLEM: For an overview of the ambiguous sexuality of the period, I once again recommend Faderman's *Odd Girls.* I also relied on Langston Hughes's own writings and Arnold Rampersad's two-volume biography of the poet. Chris Albertson's *Bessie* presents a lively account of Bessie Smith and the bisexual world of female blues singers. Another helpful overview is Eric Garber's "Harlem, A Spectacle in Color," in *Hidden from History.* Charles Michael Smith's interview with Bruce Nugent in *In the Life* offers a look at an important and openly gay Renaissance figure.

CHAPTER 11—PARIS IN THE TWENTIES: Shari Benstock's *Women of the Left Bank* is a major source on the expatriate women of the period and paints a "group portrait" of Paris in the twenties. I am also endebted to Diana Souhami's biography of Gertrude Stein and Alice B. Toklas, *Gertrude and Alice,* and Andrew Field's *Djuna* (his life of Djuna Barnes). George Wickes's biography of Natalie Barney, *The Amazon of Letters,* provides a readable account of Barney's life.

CHAPTER 12—BLOOMSBURY: Leon Edel's *Bloomsbury: A House of Lions* provides a group portrait. I relied on the standard biographies of Bloomsbury figures: Quentin Bell's *Virginia Woolf,* Victoria Glendinning's *Vita,* Michael Holroyd's *Lytton Strachey,* Robert Sidelsky's biography of John Maynard Keynes, and P. N. Furbank and Nicola Beauman's lives of E. M. Forster. *Portrait of a Marriage,* Nigel Nicolson's book about his parents, Vita Sackville-West and Harold Nicolson, is essential reading.

Nonetheless, a book that looks at Bloomsbury from a gay or lesbian point of view has yet to be written.

CHAPTER 13—THE WELL OF LONELINESS: Michael Baker's *Our Three Selves* is the major source on the life of Radclyffe Hall and on the *Well of Loneliness* trial. Virginia Woolf's diary entries on the trial provide a maddening point of view on the proceedings. For the effects of the trial on social and cultural attitudes, see the essays by Rosemary Auchmuty and Alison Oram in the Lesbian History Project's *Not A Passing Phase.*

CHAPTER 14—CZARS AND COMMISSARS: HOMOSEXUALITY IN RUSSIA: For prerevolutionary Russia, I found Laura Engelstein's *The Keys to Happiness* particularly helpful. Although Simon Karlinsky's revisionist essay "Russia's Gay Literature and Culture," in *Hidden from History,* may somewhat romanticize gay life under the czars, it provides a good overview. Karlinsky's *The Sexual Labyrinth of Nikolai Gogol* was my source on the novelist's appalling demise. For postrevolutionary Russia, I drew again on Karlinsky's essay and also on Lauritsen and Thorstad's *The Early Homosexual Rights Movement.*

CHAPTER 15—THE NAZI PERSECUTION OF HOMOSEXUALS: I relied on Richard Plant's *The Pink Triangle,* the best and most balanced account available of the Nazi persecution of homosexuals. For Nazi attitudes toward homosexuality, I recommend George Mosse's *Nationalism and Sexuality* and Peter Padfield's *Himmler.* One of the few personal accounts of the gay experience in Nazi concentration camps is Heinz Heger's *The Men with the Pink Triangles.* For an examination of the gay situation in Nazi-occupied Europe, also see Plant's *The Pink Triangle*; this subject area is in need of more extensive documentation, however.

CHAPTER 16—THE UNITED STATES IN WORLD WAR II: I am indebted to Allen Berube's *Coming Out Under Fire,* the definitive account of the American gay and lesbian experience in World War II. For the war's role in forming the gay community and as a turning-point in gay identity in the U.S., see John D'Emilio's *Sexual Politics, Sexual Communities.*

CHAPTER 17—THE RISE AND FALL OF THE "GAY IS SICK" SHRINKS: Ronald Bayer's *Homosexuality and American Psychiatry* offers a comprehensive account of changing psychiatric views and of the political maneuvering that led to the American Psychiatric Association's decision to remove homosexuality from its official list of mental illnesses. For essays representing a variety of psychiatric viewpoints of the time, see Judd Marmor's *Sexual Inversion.* David Halberstam's *The Fifties* provides a lively portrait of Kinsey. For a look at Kinsey's attitudes toward homosexuality and how the great sex researcher conducted his interviews, I recommend Dr. Wordell Pomeroy's *Dr. Kinsey and the Institute for Sex Research*. Eric Marcus's *Making History* provides an informative interview with Dr. Evelyn Hooker.

CHAPTER 18—THE AGE OF MCCARTHY: Nicholas von Hoffman's *Citizen Cohn* offers a damning (and gossipy) view of Roy Cohn. I also used the standard biographical works on McCarthy: Richard Rovere's *Senator Joe McCarthy* and Thomas Reeves's *The Life and Times of Joe McCarthy*. For the effect of the McCarthy period on gays and lesbians, I recommend D'Emilio's *Sexual Politics, Sexual Communities*, the most thorough account. Also helpful were back issues of *ONE* magazine.

CHAPTER 19—THE STRUGGLE FOR BRITISH LAW REFORM: Stephen Jeffery-Poulter's *Peers, Queers, and Commons* offers a detailed account of the struggle for British law reform. I also found Noel Annan's *Our Age* helpful. Andrew Hodges's biography *Allen Turing* gives a good sense of Britain during the McCarthy era. For Australia in this period, see Garry Wotherspoon's book on Sydney, *City of the Plain;* for Canada's law reform struggle, see Gary Kinsman's *The Regulation of Sexuality*.

CHAPTER 20—THE OTHER SIDE OF THE 1950S: For a literary and biographical examination of the Beats, I recommend John Tytell's *Naked Angels*. Barry Miles's *Allen Ginsberg* offers a good look at the Ginsberg-Orlovsky relationship. The works of the Beats themselves—Kerouac's *On the Road,* Ginsberg's *Howl,* and Burroughs's *Naked Lunch,* among others—are, of course, essential. For a portrait of the Tangier expatriate subculture, Michelle Green's entertaining *The Dream at the End of the World* is the most thorough work so far. Millicent Dillon's biography of Jane Bowles, *A Little Original Sin,* offers another view.

CHAPTER 21—THE OTHER SIDE OF THE FIFTIES, PART II: Lapovsky and Kennedy's examination of the butch/femme subculture in Buffalo, New York, provides a truly fascinating anthropological look at that world. Faderman's *Odd Girls* and her essay "The Return of Butch and Femme" are also illuminating. For the point of view of a black lesbian and also of a woman who felt alienated from the prevailing butch-femme culture, see Audre Lorde's autobiography, *Zami: A New Spelling of My Name*. For a deeply felt but somewhat romanticized view of butch/femme mores and culture, Joan Nestle's *A Restricted Country* is essential. One still awaits a full-scale biography of Lorraine Hansberry that deals forthrightly with her lesbianism.

CHAPTER 22—THE HOMOPHILES: John D'Emilio's superb *Sexual Politics, Sexual Communities* is the definitive book on the gay movement of the 1950s and '60s. Eric Marcus's *Making History* offers a number of interesting interviews with fifties and sixties gay and lesbian political figures, using an oral history approach. Katz contains a number of documents in this regard, as well as interviews with lesbian activists Barbara Gittings and Kay Tobin. Phyllis Lyon and Del Martin's *Lesbian Woman* provides an early view of the Daughters of Bilitis by that organization's founders.

CHAPTER 23—STONEWALL AND THE BIRTH OF GAY AND LESBIAN LIBERATION: There are a number of books on this heavily documented period. Martin Duberman's *Stonewall* (1993) provides a close look at the events surrounding the Stonewall riots and the lives of some of the people who participated in them. Donn Teal's *The Gay Militants* presents a detailed account of the first year of gay liberation; Sydney Abbot and Barbara Love's *Sappho Was a Right-On Woman* tells the lesbian side. Dennis Altman's *Homosexual* offers a thoughtful summary of the ideas behind the gay (male) liberation movement; the essays in *Lesbianism and the Women's Movement* do the same for lesbians. Toby Marotta's *The Politics of Homosexuality* takes the story further into the seventies. For the spirit of the early movement, I recommend Arthur Bell's *Dancing the Gay Lib Blues* and Kate Millett's autobiographical *Flying*. The essays in Karla Jay and Allen Young's *Out of the Closet* offer a wide variety of perspectives. For the arrival of gay liberation in London, see Jeffrey Weeks's *Coming Out*. Barry D. Adam's *The Rise of a Lesbian and Gay Movement* puts the gay and lesbian liberation movement in an international perspective.

CHAPTER 24—THE 1970S: THE TIMES OF HARVEY MILK AND ANITA BRYANT: Randy Shilts's *The Mayor of Castro Street* offers an invaluable depiction of the rise of Harvey Milk and gay politics in San Francisco. For an up-close look at Milk, Moscone, and Dan White and the assassinations, I recommend Mike Weiss's *Double Play*. Shilts, in *Conduct Unbecoming,* offers a sympathetic look at military rights pioneer Leonard Matlovich; so does Matlovich's biography, *The Good Soldier,* written by Mike Hippler, with participation (and extensive quotes) from Matlovich. For Oliver Sipple, the man who saved President Ford's life, see Shilts's *The Mayor of Castro Street.*

CHAPTER 25—SEX AND MUSIC IN THE SEVENTIES: Edmund White's *States of Desire* offers a fascinating examination of gay male culture in the decade before AIDS. Dennis Altman's essays in *Coming Out in the Seventies* take a critical look at the effects of sexual liberation. But Andrew Holleran's novel, *Dancer from the Dance,* probably evokes the era better than any other work.

CHAPTER 26—LESBIAN NATION AND WOMEN'S MUSIC: Faderman's *Odd Girls* gives a good perspective on the period, while frequently taking a critical stance. For the theoretics behind "Lesbian Nation," see Jill Johnston's book of the same name, Rita Mae Brown and Charlotte Bunch's essays, and Adrienne Rich's "Compulsory Heterosexuality and Lesbian Existence." The material on women's music and its role in creating lesbian culture comes largely from interviews I conducted previously with singer Holly Near and Judy Dlugacz, head of Olivia Records.

CHAPTER 27—THE AGE OF AIDS: As with the years immediately following Stonewall, the Age of AIDS is probably the most documented period in contemporary U.S. gay history. Despite its biases, Randy Shilts's *And the Band Played On* remains the most valuable source on the early days of the epidemic. In view of the role that Larry Kramer played as the catalyst for so much of the decade's AIDS organizing, his collection of essays and speeches, *Reports from the Holocaust,* represents an important record. Frances FitzGerald's *Cities on a Hill* offers a superb journalistic portrait of San Francisco during the early AIDS years; Andrew Holleran's essays in *Ground Zero* provide an inside look at gay New York City. Bruce Nussbaum's *Best Intentions* examines AIDS organizing and the politics of AIDS research. Michaelangelo Signorile's *Queer in America* portrays the radicalism of ACT UP and Queer Nation from the point of view of the leading proponent of "outing." Phyllis Burke's *Family Values* gives a West Coast perspective on Queer Nation. (Burke also provides an engaging account of lesbian parenthood.)

CHAPTER 28—COMMUNISM AND FASCISM: For a look at Communism in the Soviet Union and China and its effect on homosexuals, I drew on newspaper and magazine articles from sources ranging from *Christopher Street* to the *Washington Post*. Bret Hinsch's *Passions of the Cut Sleeve* explores same-sex love in ancient China, although it does not attempt to treat the modern period. For Cuba, Allen Young's *Gays Under the Cuban Revolution* is a good introduction. Cuban novelist Reinaldo Arenas's memoir, *Before Night Falls,* is a vital source, despite its violently anti-Castro tone. Extremely antagonistic to Castro but also important is the 1984 documentary film *Improper Conduct*. For Argentina, I made use of an essay on Argentine gay history by the eminent sociologist Juan José Sebreli, as well as my own reportage in *Out in the World.*

CHAPTER 29—ENGLAND: THE BATTLE OVER CLAUSE 28: Once again, Stephen Jeffery-Poulter's *Peers, Queers, and Commons* documents the period most thoroughly. Peter Jenkins's book *Mrs. Thatcher's Revolution* gives a good picture of the general political background to Clause 28. For the South Africa section, I referred to Mark Gevisser and Edwin Cameron's anthology *Defiant Desire,* as well as my own interviews with Simon Nkoli.

CHAPTER 30—JAPAN: I made use of biographies of Yukio Mishima by Henry Scott-Stokes and John Nathan. Mishima's novel *Forbidden Colors* presents a portrait of gay life in 1950s Japan. For a look at Japanese attitudes toward same-sex love among males in the premodern period, see Gary Leupp's forthcoming *Male Colors*. For the more modern period, see my *Out in the World*.

CHAPTER 31—THE CLINTON YEARS: For my discussion of the battle over gays in the military, I used newspaper coverage, particularly *The New York Times* and the *Washington Post*, as well as magazines ranging from *Newsweek* to *The New Republic* to *The Advocate*. Andrew Kopkind's article "The Gay Moment," published in *The Nation*, provides a good account of the social and cultural changes that marked the first year of the Clinton presidency. For an analysis of gay political failures of the military battle, I recommend Chris Bull's article "And the Ban Played On," in *The Advocate*, and Mark Schoofs's piece, "No Quick Fix," in *Out*.

BIBLIOGRAPHY

BOOKS

Abbot, Sidney, and Barbara Love. *Sappho Was a Right-On Woman*. New York: Stein and Day, 1972.

Ackerley, J. R. *My Father and Myself*. New York: Coward-McCann, 1969.

Adair, Nancy, and Casey Adair. *Word Is Out*. San Francisco: New Glide Publications, 1978.

Adam, Barry D. *The Rise of a Gay and Lesbian Movement*. Boston: Twayne Publishers, 1987.

Annan, Noel. *Our Age: Portrait of a Generation*. London: Weidenfeld and Nicolson, 1990.

Albertson, Chris. *Bessie*. New York: Stein and Day, 1972.

Altman, Dennis. *Homosexual Oppression and Liberation*. New York: Avon Books, 1973.

———. *Coming Out in the Seventies*. Sydney and Eugene, Ore.: Wild and Woolley, 1979.

Arenas, Reinaldo. *Before Night Falls*. New York: Viking, 1993.

Auchmuty, Rosemary. "You're a Dyke, Angela! Elsie J. Oxenham and the Rise and Fall of the Schoolgirl Story" in Lesbian History Group, *Not a Passing Phase*, q.v.

Baker, Michael. *Our Three Selves*. New York: William Morrow, 1985.

Baldwin, James. *Giovanni's Room*. New York: Dial Press, 1956.

———. *The Price of the Ticket*. New York: St. Martin's Press, 1985.

Baudelaire, Charles. *Poems* (Richard Howard, tr.). New York: Everyman's Library, 1993.

Bayer, Ronald. *Homosexuality and American Psychiatry*. New York: Basic Books, 1981.

Beam, Joseph, ed. *In the Life: A Black Gay Anthology*. Boston: Alyson Publications, Inc., 1986.

Beauman, Nicola. *E. M. Forster*. New York: Alfred A. Knopf, 1994.

Beer, Thomas. *The Mauve Decade*. New York: Alfred A. Knopf, 1926.

Bell, Arthur. *Dancing the Gay Lib Blues*. New York: Simon and Schuster, 1971.

Bell, Quentin. *Virginia Woolf*. New York: Harcourt, Brace. 1972.

Benstock, Shari. *Women of the Left Bank*. Austin: University of Texas Press, 1986.

Berube, Allan. *Coming Out Under Fire.* New York: The Free Press, 1990.

Bieber, Irving. "Clinical Aspects of Male Homosexuality," in Marmor, Judd, ed., *Sexual Inversion,* q.v.

Blumstein, Philip, and Pepper Schwartz. *American Couples.* New York: William Morrow, 1983.

Bogarde, Dirk. *Snakes and Ladders.* New York: Holt, Rinehart, 1978.

Borland, Maureen. *Wilde's Devoted Friend: A Life of Robert Ross.* Oxford: Lennard Publishing Company, 1990.

Boswell, John. *Christianity, Social Tolerance, and Homosexuality.* Chicago: University of Chicago Press, 1980.

———. "Revolutions, Universals and Sexual Categories," in Duberman, Vicinus, and Chauncey, eds., *Hidden from History,* q.v.

Boyd, Brian. *Vladimir Nabokov.* Princeton: Princeton University Press, 1990.

Branch, Taylor, *Parting the Waters: America in the King Years 1954–63.* New York: Simon and Schuster, 1988.

Bronski, Michael. *Culture Clash: The Making of Gay Sensibility.* Boston: South End Press, 1984.

Bronson, Edgar Beecher. *Reminiscences of a Ranchman.* New York: McClure Company. 1908.

Brown, Rita Mae. "Take a Lesbian to Lunch," in Jay and Young, eds., *Out of the Closets,* q.v.

———. "The Shape of Things to Come," in Myron and Bunch, eds., *Lesbianism and the Women's Movement,* q.v.

Bryant, Anita. *The Anita Bryant Story.* Old Tappan, N.J.: Fleming H. Revell Company, 1977.

Bryant, Anita, and Bob Green. *At Any Cost.* Old Tappan, N.J.: Fleming H. Revell Company, 1978.

Bucke, Maurice, ed. *Calamus.* London: G. P. Putnam's Sons, London, 1898.

Bunch, Charlotte. "Lesbians in Revolt," in Myron and Bunch, eds., *Lesbianism and the Women's Movement,* q.v.

Burke, Phyllis. *Family Values.* New York: Random House, 1993.

Burton, Peter. *Parallel Lives.* London: Gay Men's Press, 1985.

Campbell, James. *Talking at the Gates.* New York: Viking, 1991.

Carpenter, Edward. *Love's Coming of Age.* New York: Boni and Liveright, 1911.

Carpenter, Edward. *Intermediate Types Among Primitive Folk.* New York: Arno Press, 1975.

Carter, Stephen R. *Hansberry's Drama.* Urbana and Chicago: University of Illinois Press, 1991.

Chandos, John. *Boys Together.* New Haven, Conn.: Yale University Press, 1984.

Chauncey, George. *Gay New York: Gender, Urban Culture, and the Making of the Gay Male World, 1890–1940.* New York: Basic Books, 1994.

Cheney, Anne. *Millay in Greenwich Village*. Tuscaloosa, Alabama: University of Alabama Press, 1975.

Clarke, Gerald. *Capote*. New York: Simon and Schuster, 1988.

Colette. *The Pure and the Impure*. New York: Farrar, Straus, and Giroux, 1966.

Conquest, Robert. *The Great Terror: A Reassessment*. New York and Oxford: Oxford University Press, 1990.

Cook, Blanche Wiesen. *Eleanor Roosevelt, Volume 1, 1884–1933*. New York: Viking, 1992.

Cory, Donald Webster. *The Homosexual in America*. New York: Greenberg [Ayer Publishers], 1951.

Costello, John. *Virtue Under Fire*. Boston: Little Brown, 1987.

Cowles, Virginia. *The Kaiser*. New York: Harper and Row, 1963.

Cowley, Malcolm. *Exile's Return*. New York: Viking, 1951.

Crisp, Quentin. *The Naked Civil Servant*. New York: Holt, Rinehart, and Winston, 1977.

Croft-Cooke, Rupert. *Bosie*. London: W. H. Allen, 1963.

Crompton, Louis. *Byron and Greek Love*. Berkeley and Los Angeles: University of California Press, 1985.

Davis, Allen F. *American Heroine: The Life and Legend of Jane Addams*. Oxford and New York: Oxford University Press, 1973.

D'Emilio, John. *Sexual Politics, Sexual Communities*. Chicago and London: University of Chicago Press, 1983.

———. *Making Trouble*. New York and London: Routledge, 1992.

de Grazia, Edward. *Girls Lean Back Everywhere*. New York: Random House, 1992.

De Jong, Ben. " 'An Intolerable Kind of Moral Degeneration': Homosexuality in the Soviet Union," in *ILGA Pink Book, 1985,* q.v.

Delany, Samuel R., and Joseph Beam. "Samuel R. Delany: The Possibility of Possibilities," in Beam, ed., *In the Life,* q.v.

Devlin, Albert J., ed. *Conversations with Tennessee Williams*. Jackson, Miss. and London: University Press of Mississippi, 1986.

Dillon, Millicent. *A Little Original Sin: The Life and Work of Jane Bowles*. New York: Holt, Rinehart, and Winston, 1981.

Driberg, Tom. *Ruling Passions*. New York: Stein and Day, 1978.

Duberman, Martin. *About Time*. New York: Meridian, 1991.

———. *Cures*. New York: Dutton, 1991.

———. *Stonewall*. New York: Dutton, 1993.

Duberman, Martin Bauml, Martha Vicinus and George Chauncey, Jr., eds. *Hidden from History*. New York: New American Library, 1989.

Edel, Leon. *Bloomsbury: A House of Lions*. Philadelphia and New York: J. P. Lippincott, 1979.

Ehrenreich, Barbara. *The Hearts of Men*. New York: Anchor Press, 1983.

Ellis, Havelock. *Studies in the Psychology of Sex*. New York: Random House, 1936.

Ellman, Richard. *Oscar Wilde*. New York: Alfred A. Knopf, 1988.

Engelstein, Laura. *The Keys to Happiness: Sex and the Search for Modernity in Fin-de-Siecle Russia*. Ithaca, N.Y., and London: Cornell University Press, 1992.

Faderman, Lillian. *Surpassing the Love of Men*. New York: William Morrow and Company, 1981.

———. *Odd Girls and Twilight Lovers*. New York: Columbia University Press, 1991.

———. "The Return of Butch and Femme," in Fout and Tantillo, eds., *American Sexual Politics*, q.v.

Faderman, Lillian, and Brigitte Eriksson, eds. *Lesbians in Germany: 1890s–1920s*. Tallahassee: Naiad Press.

Feinberg, David B. *Eighty-Sixed*. New York: Viking, 1989.

Field, Andrew. *Djuna: The Life and Times of Djuna Barnes*. New York: G. P. Putnam's Sons, 1983.

Fishbein, Leslie. *Rebels in Bohemia*. Chapel Hill: University of North Carolina Press, 1982.

Fitch, Noel Riley. *Sylvia Beach and the Lost Generation*. New York: W. W. Norton, 1993.

FitzGerald, Frances. *Cities on a Hill*. New York: Simon and Schuster, 1986.

———. *Maurice*. Toronto: Macmillan of Canada, 1971.

———. *Selected Letters, Volume 2*. Mary Lago and P. N. Furbank, eds. Cambridge, Massachusetts: Harvard University Press, 1985.

Forster, E. M. *Two Cheers for Democracy*. New York: Harcourt Brace, 1938.

Foucault, Michel. *The History of Sexuality*, Volume 1. New York: Pantheon Books, 1978.

———. *The Use of Pleasure: The History of Sexuality*, Volume 2. New York: Pantheon Books, 1985.

Fout, John C., and Maura Shaw Tantillo, eds. *American Sexual Politics*. Chicago and London: University of Chicago Press, 1993.

Freud, Sigmund. *The Letters of Sigmund Freud*. New York: Basic Books, 1960.

Furbank, P. N. *E. M. Forster: A Life*. New York and London: Harcourt Brace Jovanovich, 1978.

Fussell, Paul. *The Great War and Modern Memory*. Oxford: Oxford University Press, 1975.

Garber, Eric. "A Spectacle in Color: The Lesbian and Gay Subculture of Jazz Age Harlem" in Duberman, Vicinus, and Chauncey, eds., *"Hidden from History,"* q.v.

Garber, Marjorie. *Vested Interests*. New York: Routledge, 1992.

Gay, Peter. *The Tender Passion: The Bourgeois Experience,* Volume 2. New York and Oxford: Oxford University Press, 1986.

Gerassi, John. *The Boys of Boise.* New York: The Macmillan Company, 1966.

Gevisser, Mark, and Edwin Cameron, eds., *Defiant Desire: Gay and Lesbian Lives in South Africa.* Johannesburg: Ravan Press, 1994.

Gide, André. *Journals,* Volume 1. New York: Vintage, 1956.

———. *If It Die.* New York: Vintage, 1963.

———. *Corydon.* New York: Farrar, Straus, and Giroux, 1981.

Ginsberg, Allen. *Collected Poems, 1947–1980.* New York: Harper and Row, 1984.

Girard, Jacques. *Le Mouvement Homosexual en France.* Paris: Editions Syros, 1981.

Glendinning, Victoria. *Vita.* New York: Alfred A. Knopf, 1983.

Goldstein, Richard. " 'Go the Way Your Blood Beats': An Interview with James Baldwin," in Troupe, ed., *James Baldwin: The Legacy,* q.v.

Goldston, Robert. *The American Nightmare: Senator Joseph R. McCarthy and the Politics of Hate.* Indianapolis and New York: Bobbs-Merrill, 1973.

Gooch, Brad. *City Poet: The Life and Times of Frank O'Hara.* New York: Alfred A. Knopf, 1993.

Goodman, Paul. *Growing Up Absurd.* New York: Random House, 1956.

———. *Nature Heals: The Psychological Essays of Paul Goodman.* New York: Free Life Editions, 1977.

Goodwin, Doris Kearns. *No Ordinary Time.* New York: Simon and Schuster, 1994.

Graves, Richard Perceval. *Robert Graves: The Assault Heroic.* New York: Viking Press, 1987.

Graves, Robert, and Alan Hodge. *The Long Week-End: A Social History of Great Britain, 1918–39.* New York: W. W. Norton, 1963.

Green, Martin. *Children of the Sun.* London: Constable, 1977.

Green, Michelle. *The Dream at the End of the World.* New York: HarperCollins, 1991.

Greenberg, David F. *The Construction of Homosexuality.* Chicago and London: University of Chicago Press, 1988.

Grosskurth, Phyllis. *Havelock Ellis.* New York: Alfred A. Knopf, 1980.

Grossman, Vasily. *Forever Flowing.* New York: Harper & Row, 1972.

Halberstam, David. *The Fifties.* New York: Villard Books, 1993.

Hall, Radclyffe. *The Well of Loneliness.* Garden City, N.Y.: Sun Dial Press, 1928.

Halperin, David M. *One Hundred Years of Homosexuality.* New York: Routledge, 1990.

Hansberry, Lorraine. *A Raisin in the Sun* and *The Sign in Sidney Brustein's Window.* New York: Plume, 1987.

Harris, Frank. *Oscar Wilde*. Lansing: Michigan State University Press, 1959.

Haskell, Arnold. *Diaghileff: His Artistic and Private Life*. New York: Simon and Schuster, 1935.

Heger, Heinz. *The Men with the Pink Triangle*. Boston: Alyson Publications, 1980.

Higgins, Patrick, ed. *A Queer Reader*. London: Fourth Estate, 1993.

Hinsch, Bret. *Passions of the Cut Sleeve: The Male Homosexual Tradition in China*. Berkeley and Los Angeles: University of California Press, 1990.

Hippler, Mike. *Matlovich: The Good Soldier*. Boston: Alyson Publications, 1989.

Hitler, Adolf. *Mein Kampf* (James Murphy, tr.). London: Hurst and Blackett, 1939.

Hocquenghem, Guy. *Homosexual Desire*. Durham, N.C., and London: Duke University Press, 1993.

Hodges, Andrew. *Alan Turing: The Enigma*. New York: Simon and Schuster, 1983.

Holleran, Andrew. *Dancer from the Dance*. New York: William Morrow, 1978.

———. *Ground Zero*. New York: William Morrow, 1988.

Holroyd, Michael. *Lytton Strachey: The Unknown Years, 1880–1910*. London: Penguin, 1971.

Hughes, Langston. *The Big Sea*. New York: Hill and Wang, 1963.

Hyde, H. Montgomery. *Lord Alfred Douglas*. New York: Dodd, Mead, and Company, 1985.

Hynes, Samuel. *A War Imagined*. New York: Atheneum, 1991.

ILGA Pink Book, 1985: A Global View of Lesbian and Gay Oppression. Amsterdam: International Association of Lesbians and Gay Men, 1985.

Isherwood, Christopher. *Christopher and His Kind*. New York: Farrar, Straus, and Giroux, 1976.

James, Lawrence. *The Golden Warrior: The Life and Legend of Lawrence of Arabia*. New York: Paragon House, 1993.

Jay, Karla. *The Amazon and the Page*. Bloomington: Indiana University Press, 1988.

Jay, Karla, and Allen Young. *Out of the Closets*. New York: Pyramid Books, 1972.

Jeffery-Poulter, Stephen. *Peers, Queers, and Commons*. New York and London: Routledge, 1991.

Jenkins, Peter. *Mrs. Thatcher's Revolution*. Cambridge, Mass.: Harvard University Press, 1988.

Jenkins, Roy. *A Life at the Center*. New York: Random House, 1991.

Kaplan, Justin. *Walt Whitman.* New York: Simon and Schuster, 1980.

Karlinsky, Simon. *The Sexual Labyrinth of Nikolai Gogol.* Cambridge, Mass., and London: Harvard University Press, 1976.

———. "Russia's Gay Literature and Culture," in Duberman, Vicinus, and Chauncey, eds., *Hidden From History,* q.v.

Katz, Jonathan Ned. *Gay American History.* New York: Thomas Y. Crowell Company, 1976.

———. *Gay/Lesbian Almanac.* New York: Harper and Row, 1983.

Keith, Don Lee. "New Tennessee Williams Rises from 'Stoned Age.' " In Devlin, Albert J., ed., *Conversations with Tennessee Williams,* q.v.

Kellner, Bruce. *Carl Van Vechten and the Irreverent Decades.* Norman: University of Oklahoma Press, 1968.

Kennedy, Elizabeth Lapovsky, and Madeline D. Davis. *Boots of Leather, Slippers of Gold.* New York and London: Routledge, 1993.

Kerouac, Jack. *On the Road.* New York: New American Library, 1957.

Kinsey, Alfred C. et al. *Sexual Behavior in the Human Male.* Philadelphia: Saunders, 1948.

———. *Sexual Behavior in the Human Female.* Philadelphia: Saunders, 1953.

Kinsman, Gary. *The Regulation of Desire: Sexuality in Canada.* Montreal: Black Rose Books, 1987.

Kenan, Randall. *James Baldwin.* New York: Chelsea House, 1994.

Kracauer, Siegfried. *From Caligari to Hitler.* Princeton, N.J.: Princeton University Press, 1947.

Kramer, Larry. *Faggots.* New York: Random House, 1978.

———. *Reports from the Holocaust.* New York: St. Martin's Press, 1987.

Kurth, Peter. *American Cassandra: The Life of Dorothy Thompson.* Boston: Little Brown, 1990.

Lait, Jack, and Lee Mortimer. *Washington Confidential.* New York: Crown Publishers, 1951.

Larkin, Philip. *Collected Poems.* New York: Farrar, Straus, and Giroux, 1989.

Lauritsen, John, and David Thorstad. *The Early Homosexual Rights Movement (1864–1935).* New York: Times Change Press, 1974.

Lawrence, T. E. *Seven Pillars of Wisdom.* Garden City, N. Y.: Doubleday, Doran, and Company, 1936.

Lerner, Max. *The Unfinished Country.* New York: Simon and Schuster, 1959.

Lesbian History Group. *Not a Passing Phase.* London: The Women's Press, 1989.

Lesley, Cole. *Remembered Laughter: The Life of Noel Coward.* New York: Alfred A. Knopf, 1976.

Leupp, Gary. *Male Colors: The Construction of Homosexuality in Toka-*

gawa Japan. Berkeley: University of California Press (forthcoming, 1995).

Liebman, Martin. *Coming Out Conservative*. San Francisco: Chronicle Books, 1992.

Likosky, Stephan. *Coming Out*. New York: Pantheon Books, 1992.

Lockwood, Lee. *Castro's Cuba, Cuba's Fidel*. New York: Vintage Books, 1969.

Lorde, Audre. *Zami: A New Spelling of My Name*. Trumansburg, N. Y.: Crossing Press, 1983.

McAlmon, Robert, and Kay Boyle. *Being Geniuses Together*. New York: Doubleday, 1968.

Macey, David. *The Lives of Michel Foucault*. New York: Pantheon Books, 1993.

Manchester, William. *The Arms of Krupp*. Boston: Little, Brown, 1968.

Mann, Klaus. *André Gide*. New York: Creative Age Press, 1943.

Marcus, Eric. *Making History*. New York: HarperCollins, 1992.

Marmor, Judd, ed. *Sexual Inversion*. New York: Basic Books, 1965.

Marotta, Toby. *The Politics of Homosexuality*. Boston: Houghton Mifflin Company, 1981.

Marr, David. *Patrick White: A Life*. New York: Alfred A. Knopf, 1992.

Martin, Del, and Phyllis Lyon. *Lesbian Woman*. New York: Bantam, 1972.

Massie, Allan. *Colette*. London: Penguin, 1986.

Massie, Robert K. *Dreadnought: Britain, Germany, and the Coming of The Great War*. New York: Random House, 1991.

Masur, Gerhard. *Imperial Berlin*. New York: Basic Books, 1970.

Miles, Barry. *Ginsberg: A Biography*. New York: Simon and Schuster, 1989.

Miller, James. *The Passion of Michel Foucault*. New York: Simon and Schuster, 1993.

Miller, Merle. *On Being Different*. New York: Random House, 1971.

Miller, Neil. *In Search of Gay America*. New York: Atlantic Monthly Press, 1989.

———. *Out in the World: Gay and Lesbian Life from Buenos Aires to Bangkok*. New York: Random House, 1992.

Millett, Kate. *Flying*. New York: Alfred A. Knopf, 1974.

Mishima, Yukio. *Confessions of a Mask*. New York: New Directions, 1958.

———. *Forbidden Colors*. New York: Alfred A. Knopf, 1968.

Mosse, George. *Nationalism and Sexuality*. New York: H. Fertig, 1987.

Myron, Nancy, and Charlotte Bunch, eds. *Lesbianism and the Women's Movement*. Baltimore: Diana Press, 1975.

Nabokov, Vladimir. *Nikolai Gogol*. New York: New Directions: 1944.

Nathan, John. *Mishima: A Biography*. Boston: Little Brown, 1974.

Navratilova, Martina (with George Vecsey). *Martina*. New York: Alfred A. Knopf, 1985.

Nestle, Joan. *A Restricted Country*. Ithaca, N.Y.: Firebrand Books, 1987.

Nicolson, Nigel. *Portrait of a Marriage*. New York: Atheneum, 1973.

Nkoli, Simon. "Wardrobes: Coming Out as a Black Gay Activist in South Africa," in Gevisser, Mark, and Edwin Cameron, eds., *Defiant Desire*, q.v.

Norton, Rictor. *Mother Clap's Molly House*. London: Gay Men's Press, 1992.

Nussbaum, Bruce. *Good Intentions*. New York: Atlantic Monthly Press, 1990.

O'Brien, Sharon. *Willa Cather: The Emerging Voice*. New York and Oxford: Oxford University Press, 1987.

Oram, Alison, "Embittered, Sexless or Homosexual: Attacks on Spinster Teachers, 1918–39" in Lesbian History Group, *Not a Passing Phase*, q.v.

Orton, Joe. *The Orton Diaries*. John Lahr, ed. New York: Harper & Row, 1986.

Orwell, George. *An Age Like This: The Collected Essays, Journalism and Letters of George Orwell*. New York: Harcourt, Brace, Jovanovich, 1968.

Oshinsky, David M. *A Conspiracy So Immense*. New York: The Free Press, 1983.

Padfield, Peter. *Himmler*. New York: Henry Holt and Company, 1990.

Painter, George D. *André Gide*. New York: Atheneum, 1968.

Parker, Peter. *Ackerley*. New York: Farrar, Straus, and Giroux, 1989.

Pearson, Drew. *Diaries. 1949–1959*. New York: Holt, Rinehart, 1974.

Plant, Richard. *The Pink Triangle*. New York: Henry Holt and Company, 1986.

Pomeroy, Wardell B. *Dr. Kinsey and the Institute for Sex Research*. New York: Harper & Row, 1972.

Powers, Richard. *Secrecy and Power: The Life of J. Edgar Hoover*. New York and London: The Free Press, 1987.

Proust, Marcel. *Sodom and Gomorrah*. New York: The Modern Library (Random House Inc.), 1993.

Rader, Dotson. "The Art of Theatre V," in Devlin, Albert J., ed., *Conversations with Tennessee Williams*, q.v.

Rampersad, Arnold. *The Life of Langston Hughes*, Volumes 1 and 2. New York and Oxford: Oxford University Press, 1985 and 1986.

Reeves, Thomas C. *The Life and Times of Joe McCarthy*. New York: Stein and Day, 1982.

Rich, Adrienne. *Blood, Bread, and Poetry*. New York: Norton, 1986.

Roscoe, Will, ed. *Living the Spirit: A Gay American Indian Anthology*. New York: St. Martin's Press, 1988.

Rosenbaum, S. P. *The Bloomsbury Group*. Toronto: University of Toronto Press, 1975.

Rotundo, E. Anthony. *American Manhood*. New York: Basic Books, 1993.

Rovere, Richard H. *Senator Joe McCarthy*. New York: Harcourt, Brace, 1959.

Russo, Vito. *The Celluloid Closet*. New York: Harper & Row, 1981.

St. Just, Maria. *Five O'Clock Angel: Letters from Tennessee Williams to Maria St. Just: 1948–82*. New York: Alfred A. Knopf, 1990.

Sante, Luc. *Low Life*. New York: Farrar, Straus, and Giroux, 1991.

Sarde, Michèle. *Colette: Free and Fettered*. New York: William Morrow, 1980.

Sarotte Georges-Michel. *Like a Brother, Like a Lover*. Garden City, N.Y.: Anchor/Doubleday, 1978.

Sassoon, Siegfried. *Diaries, 1915–1918*. London: Farber and Faber, 1983.

———. *Diaries, 1920–1922*. London: Faber and Faber, 1983.

Savigneau, Josyane. *Marguerite Yourcenar: Inventing a Life*. Chicago and London: University of Chicago Press, 1993.

Sawatsky, John. *Men in the Shadows*. Toronto: Doubleday, Canada, 1980.

Scott-Stokes, Henry. *The Life and Death of Yukio Mishima*. New York: Farrar, Straus, and Giroux, 1974.

Seton, Marie. *Sergei M. Eisenstein*. London: Dennis Dobson, 1978.

Shilts, Randy. *The Mayor of Castro Street*. New York: St. Martin's Press, 1982.

———. *And the Band Played On*. New York: St. Martin's Press, 1987.

———. *Conduct Unbecoming*. New York: St. Martin's Press, 1993.

Shively, Charley, ed. *Calamus Lovers: Walt Whitman's Working Class Camerados*. San Francisco: Gay Sunshine Press, 1987.

Sidelsky, Robert. *John Maynard Keynes: Hopes Betrayed, 1883–1920*. New York: Viking, 1986.

Signorile, Michelangelo. *Queer in America*. New York: Random House, 1993.

Sinclair, Andrew. *Francis Bacon: His Life and Violent Times*. New York: Crown Publishers, 1993.

Smith, Charles Michael. "Bruce Nugent: Bohemian of the Harlem Renaissance," in Beam, ed., *In the Life*, q.v.

Smith-Rosenberg, Carroll. "Discourses of Sexuality and Subjectivity: The New Woman, 1870–1936," in Duberman, Vicinus, and Chauncey, eds., *Hidden from History*, q.v.

Souhami, Diana. *Gertrude and Alice*. London: Pandora Press, 1991.

Steakley, James D. *The Homosexual Emancipation Movement in Germany*. New York: Arno Press, 1975.

———. "Iconography of a Scandal," in Duberman, Vicinus, and Chauncey, eds., *Hidden from History*, q.v.

Steegmuller, Francis. *Cocteau.* Boston: Atlantic Monthly Press, 1970.

Strindberg, August. *The Cloister.* New York: Hill and Wang, 1969.

Summers, Anthony. *Official and Confidential: The Secret Life of J. Edgar Hoover.* London: Victor Gollancz, 1993.

Taylor, Martin. *Lads: Love Poetry of the Trenches.* London: Constable, 1989.

Teal, Donn. *The Gay Militants.* New York: Stein and Day, 1971.

Thompson, Mark, ed. *Gay Spirit.* New York: St. Martin's Press, 1987.

Thorp, Charles P. "I.D., Leadership and Violence," in Jay and Young, eds., *Out of the Closets,* q.v.

Tobin, Kay, and Randy Wicker. *The Gay Crusaders.* New York: Paperback Library, 1972.

Tolstoy, Leo. *Resurrection.* New York: New American Library, 1961.

Troupe, Quincy, ed. *James Baldwin: The Legacy.* New York: Touchstone, 1989.

Tytell, John *Naked Angels: The Lives and Literature of the Beat Generation.* New York: McGraw Hill, 1976.

Van den Boogaard, Henk, and Kathelijne van Kammen. "We Cannot Jump Over Our Own Shadow," in *ILGA Pink Book, 1985,* q.v.

van Naerssen, A. X., ed. *Gay Life in Dutch Society.* New York: Harrington Park Press, 1987.

Vidal, Gore. *The City and the Pillar.* New York: E. P. Dutton, 1948 and 1965.

———. *United States: Essays, 1952–1992.* New York: Random House, 1993.

Vining, Donald. *A Gay Diary: 1933–1946.* New York: The Pepys Press, 1979.

von Hoffman, Nicholas. *Citizen Cohn.* New York: Doubleday, 1988.

Vonk, Hans. "Homosexuality in the GDR," in *ILGA Pink Book, 1985,* q.v.

Watanabe, Tsuneo, and Jun'ichi Iwata. *The Love of the Samurai: A Thousand Years of Japanese Homosexuality.* London: GMP Publications Ltd., 1989.

Watson, Steven. *Strange Bedfellows: The First American Avant-Garde.* New York: Abbeville Press, 1991.

Weatherby, W. J. *James Baldwin: Artist on Fire.* New York: Donald I. Fine, 1989.

Weeks, Jeffrey. *Coming Out.* London: Quartet Books, 1977.

Weiss, Mike. *Double Play: The San Francisco City Hall Killings.* Reading, Mass.: Addison-Wesley, 1984.

White, Edmund. *States of Desire.* New York: E. P. Dutton, 1983.

———. *Genet.* New York: Alfred A. Knopf, 1993.

Whitman, Walt. *Leaves of Grass and Selected Prose*. New York: Random House, 1950.

Wickes, George. *The Amazon of Letters*. New York: G. P. Putnam's Sons, 1976.

Wilde, Oscar. *De Profundis*. New York: Philosophical Library, 1960.

Wilbur, Cornelia B. "Clinical Aspects of Female Homosexuality," in Marmor, Judd, ed., *Sexual Inversion*, q.v.

Williams, Walter L. *The Spirit and the Flesh*. Boston: Beacon Press, 1986.

Winterson, Jeanette. *Oranges Are Not the Only Fruit*. New York: Atlantic Monthly Press, 1987.

The Wolfenden Report. *Report of the Committee on Homosexual Offenses and Prostitution*. New York: Stein and Day, 1963.

Wolff, Charlotte. *Magnus Hirschfeld*. London: Quartet Books, 1986.

Woolf, Virginia. *Orlando*. New York: New American Library, 1960.

———. *The Diary of Virginia Woolf, 1925–1930*. New York: Harcourt, Brace, 1980.

Wotherspoon, Garry. *Being Different*. Sydney: Hale and Iremonger, 1986.

———. *City of the Plain*. Sydney: Hale and Iremonger, 1991.

Yourcenar, Marguerite. *Alexis*. New York: Farrar, Straus, Giroux, 1984.

Young, Allen. *Gays Under the Cuban Revolution*. San Francisco: Grey Fox Press, 1981.

ARTICLES

Allen, Henry. "J. Edgar Hoover's Fall from Fashion," *Washington Post Weekly Edition*, March 29–April 4, 1993.

Barbedette, Gilles. "The Social Triumph of the Sexual Will," *Christopher Street*, No. 64, May 1982.

Beck, Melinda. "A (Quiet) Uprising in the Ranks," *Newsweek*, June 21, 1993.

Bentley, Gladys. "I Am a Woman Again," *Ebony*, August 1952.

Berger, Joseph. "Religions Confront the Issue of Homosexuality," *The New York Times*, March 2, 1987.

———. "Roman Catholic Mass for Homosexuals Banned," *The New York Times*, March 6, 1987.

Berke, Richard L. "Crossroad for Gay Rights," *The New York Times*, April 26, 1993.

———. "President Backs a Gay Compromise," *The New York Times*, May 28, 1993.

Black, Jonathan. "A Happy Birthday for Gay Liberation," *Village Voice*, July 2, 1970.

Brand, Adolf. "Political Criminals: A Word About the Röhm Case," *Journal of Homosexuality*, Vol. 22, Nos. 1/2, 1991.

Brodsky, Joel I. "The Mineshaft: A Retrospective Ethnography," *Journal of Homosexuality*, Vol. 24, Nos. 3/4, 1993.

Brown, Rita Mae. "Queen for a Day: A Stranger in Paradise," *The Real Paper* (Boston), October 8, 1975.

Brule, Tyler. "In the Navy," *Out*, May 1994.

Bull, Chris. "And the Ban Played On," *The Advocate*, March 9, 1993.

———. "No Frankness," *The Advocate*, June 29, 1993.

Burke, Tom. "The New Homosexual," *Esquire*, December 1969.

Campbell, Linda. "Clinton Gay Policy Gets Legal Alert," *Chicago Tribune*, November 17, 1993.

Chauncey, George, Jr. "From Sexual Inversion to Homosexuality: Medicine and the Changing Conceptualization of Female Deviance," *Salamagundi*, Nos. 58–59, Fall 1982–Winter 1983.

———. "The Way We Were," *Village Voice*, July 1, 1986.

Dionne, E. J. Jr. "Isn't Bigotry a Sin?" *Washington Post*, April 27, 1993.

Dewar, Helen. "Senate Votes to Confirm Achtenberg," *Washington Post*, May 25, 1993.

Farrell, John Aloysius, "Senators Hear Pell Talk of Gay Daughter," *Boston Globe*, May 22, 1993.

Feray, Jean-Claude, and Manfred Herzer. "Homosexual Studies and Politics in the 19th Century: Karl Maria Kertbeny," *Journal of Homosexuality*, Vol. 19 (1), 1990.

Friedländer, Benedikt. "Memoir for the Friends and Contributors of the Scientific Humanitarian Committee in the Name of the Secession of the Scientific Humanitarian Committee," *Journal of Homosexuality*, Vol. 22, Nos. 1/2, 1991.

Friedman, Thomas L. "Chiefs Back Clinton on Gay-Troop Plan," *The New York Times*, July 20, 1993.

Gessen, Masha. "Red Army of Lovers," *Out*, April/May 1993.

Goldwater, Barry M. "The Gay Ban: Just Plain Un-American," *Washington Post National Weekly*, July 21–27, 1993.

Gutierrez, Ramon A. "Must We Deracinate Indians to Find Gay Roots?" *OUT/LOOK*, Winter 1989.

Hall, Richard. "Gay Fiction Comes Home," *The New York Times Book Review*, June 19, 1988.

Hodges, Michael H. "No Gays, Please, We're British," *The Nation*, February 6, 1989.

Ifill, Gwen. "Clinton Accepts Delay in Lifting Military Gay Ban," *The New York Times*, January 30, 1993.

Jenkins, Loren. "Vatican Adamant on Gays," *Washington Post*, October 31, 1986.

Johnston, Jill. "Of This Pure But Irregular Passion," *Village Voice*, July 2, 1970.

Karlinsky, Simon, "Sergei Diaghilev: Public and Private," *Christopher Street*, March 1980.

Kastor, Elizabeth. "The Cautious Closet of the Gay Conservative," *Washington Post*, May 11, 1987.

Kopkind, Andrew. "The Gay Moment," *The Nation*, May 3, 1993.

Krauthammer, Charles. "The Politics of a Plague," *The New Republic*, August 1, 1983.

Kurtz, Howard. "Don't Read All About It!" *Washington Post*, May 9, 1993.

Lautmann, Rüdiger. "Categorization in Concentration Camps as a Collective Fate: A Comparison of Homosexuals, Jehovah's Witnesses, and Political Prisoners," *Journal of Homosexuality*, Vol. 19, No. 1, 1990.

Lerner, Max. "The Senator and the Purge," *New York Post*, July 17, 1950.

McLarin, Kimberly J. "Center-Court Star at Center Stage," *The New York Times*, August 1, 1993.

Miller, Neil. "A Make-or-Break Year for Gay Civil Rights," *In These Times*, April 13, 1977.

———. "Lavender Capitalism," *Boston Phoenix*, July 8, 1980.

———. "Gay Culture Since AIDS," *Boston Phoenix*, June 18, 1985.

Nehamas, Alexander. "Subject and Abject: The Examined Life of Michel Foucault," *The New Republic*, February 15, 1993.

O'Toole, Lawrence. "Sympathy for the Devil," *The New York Times Magazine*, April 5, 1992.

Parsons, John. "East Germany Faces Its Past," *Out/look*, Summer 1989.

Painton, Priscilla. "After Willie Horton, Are Gays Next?" *Time*, August 3, 1992.

Quindlen, Anna. "Happy and Gay," *The New York Times*, April 6, 1994.

Raspberry, William. "What Fred Peck Said," *Washington Post*, May 17, 1993.

Robinson, Charles K. "The Raid," *One,* July 1960.

Roscoe, Will. "The Challenge of Gay and Lesbian Studies," *Journal of Homosexuality,* Volume 15, Nos. 3/4, 1988.

———. "The Zuni-Man Woman," *OUT/LOOK,* Summer 1988.

Sahli, Nancy. "Smashing: Women's Relationships Before the Fall," *Chrysalis* 8, Summer 1979.

Sanchez, Renee, and Linda Wheeler. "Gays Demand Rights in 6-Hour March," *Washington Post,* April 26, 1993.

Schoofs, Mark. "Life After Death," *The Advocate,* July 13, 1993.

———. "No Quick Fix," *Out,* December/January 1994.

Schmalz, Jeffrey. "Gay Politics Goes Mainstream," *The New York Times Magazine,* October 11, 1992.

———. "Gay Areas Are Jubilant Over Clinton," *The New York Times,* November 5, 1992.

———. "Covering AIDS and Living It: A Reporter's Testimony," *The New York Times,* December 20, 1992.

———. "Homosexuals Awake to See a Referendum: It's On Them," *The New York Times,* January 31, 1992.

———. "Gay Americans Throng Capital in Appeal for Rights," *The New York Times,* April 26, 1993.

———. "Whatever Happened to AIDS?" *The New York Times Magazine,* November 28, 1993.

Schmitt, Eric. "Forum on Military's Gay Ban Starts, and Stays, Shrill," *The New York Times,* March 25, 1993.

———. "Clinton Tries to Erase Impression He Would Set Gay Troops Apart," *The New York Times,* March 26, 1993.

Schuvaloff, George. "Gay Life in Russia," *Christopher Street,* September 1976.

Sebreli, Juan José. "Historia Secreta de los Homosexuales Porteños," *Perfil* (Buenos Aires), No. 27, November 1983.

Socarides, Charles W. et al. "Homosexuality," *Psychiatric News,* December 3, 1993.

Sragovicz, Lisa. "Bayard Rustin's Legacy," *Washington Blade,* August 20, 1993.

Stimpson, Catharine R. "The Beat Generation and the Trials of Homosexual Liberation," *Salamagundi,* Nos. 58–59, Fall–Winter, 1983.

Stoddard, Tom. "Nunn 2, Clinton 0," *The New York Times,* September 20, 1993.

Sullivan, Andrew. "Gay Life, Gay Death," *The New Republic,* December 19, 1990.

———. "Gay Values, Truly Conservative," *The New York Times,* February 9, 1993.

Sun, Lena H. "China's Secrets Are Coming Out," *Washington Post National Weekly,* January 11–17, 1993.

Suro, Robert. "Vatican Reproaches Homosexuals with a Pointed Allusion to AIDS," *The New York Times,* October 31, 1986.

Thomas, Anthony. "The House That Kids Built: The Gay Black Imprint on American Dance Music," *OUT/LOOK,* Summer 1989.

Truscott, Lucian IV. "Gay Power Comes to Sheridan Square," *Village Voice,* July 3, 1969.

Vaid, Urvashi. "Compromising Positions," *The Advocate,* June 29, 1993.

Von Drehle, David, and Helen Dewar. "The Contrary Democrat: What Is Sam Nunn Thinking?" *Washington Post,* May 3, 1993.

Westermeir, Clifford P. "Cowboy Sexuality: A Historical No-No?" *Red River Valley Historical Review,* Spring 1975.

White, Edmund. "The Celebration of Passion," *The New York Times Book Review,* October 17, 1993.

Zonana, Victor F. "Cuba's AIDS Quarantine Center Called 'Frightening'," *Los Angeles Times,* November 4, 1988.

Zuniga, Joseph. " 'Don't Ask, Don't Tell' Won't Do," *Washington Post,* May 18, 1993.

NEWSPAPERS, MAGAZINES, AND JOURNALS CONSULTED

The Advocate. The Body Politic. Boston Globe. Boston Phoenix. Chicago Tribune. Christopher Street. Chrysalis. Ebony. Esquire. Gay Community News. In These Times. Journal of Homosexuality. The Ladder. Los Angeles Times. Mattachine Review. Memphis Commercial Appeal. The Nation. Newsweek. The New Republic. New York Native. New York Post. The New York Times. One. Out. OUT/LOOK. Perfil. Psychiatric News. The Real Paper. Red River Historical Review. Salamagundi. Time. Village Voice. Washington Blade. Washington Post.

Index

Page numbers in italics refer to illustrations.

Abbot, Sidney, 378

Abernathy, Ralph, 360

Abzug, Bella, 380

Acheson, Dean, 259

Achtenberg, Roberta, 453, 551, 552–553, 557

Ackerley, J.R., 93–94, 108, 175, 280, 289
  excerpt from *My Father and Myself*, 108–109

Acquired Immune Deficiency Syndrome, *see* AIDS

ACT UP, 382, 457–460, 537, 546, 558

Acton, Harold, 100

Adam, Margie, 437

Adams, Joan Vollner, 301

Adam's Breed, 183, 191

Addams, Eve, 143

Addams, Jane, 58

"adhesiveness," 4, 9

Advise and Consent, 342

The Advocate, 419, 420, 427, 429, 461, 475, 540, 543, 544

Aesthetic Movement, 3

African National Congress (ANC), 512, 514

After Delores, 477

AIDS (Acquired Immune Deficiency Syndrome)
  in Britain, 503
  changes in gay lifestyles, 447–450
  in China, 487
  in Cuba, 493–494
  early cases of, 439–440
  early reaction in gay community, 441
  excerpt from "Whatever Happened to AIDS?," 546–547
  first named, 439–440
  and gay bathhouses, 444–446
  in Japan, 521
  as lesbian issue, 452–453, 462
  novels on, 478–479
  numbers of cases, 440
  as political issue, 441, 450, 452–453, 462
  and sodomy laws, 455
  as struggle over sex, 441–442
  transmission of, 440, 446–447

AIDS Coalition to Unleash Power, *see* ACT UP

AIDS quilt, 455

Alamo Club, 271

Albee, Edward, 310

Albertson, Chris, 151

Alea, Tomás Gutiérrez, 495

Alexandrovich, Grand Duke Sergei, 204

Alexis, 167, 168–169

Alioto, Joseph, 396

Allégret, Marc, 90

Allen, Maud, 97, 98, 99, 185

Allen, Robert, 341

Alliance for Gay and Lesbian Civil Rights, 553

Altman, Dennis
  as chronicler, 369
  view of French gay liberation, 393–394
  view of Stonewall, 367
  views on gay rights organizations, 372, 378, 379
  views on liberated gay lifestyle, 424, 426–427

Amato, Richard, 381

Amburgy, Victor, 464

American Civil Liberties Union, 262, 273, 348, 350

American Conservative Union, 476

American Law Institute, 342

American Psychiatric Association, 249, 256, 257

American West, 40–43

And the Band Played On, 463
  excerpt from, 463–464
Anderson, Cora, 72
Anderson, Margaret, 138, 159, 165
Anderson, Mary, *see* Hall, Murray
Anderson, Richard, 475
Angels in America, 536
Annan, Noel, 100, 285, 292
Anthony, Susan B., 56
Arab society, and homosexuality, 302
Arcadie (French homophile organization), 392, 393
Arenas, Reinaldo, 491–492
Argentina, 498–502
Army-McCarthy hearings, 263, 268–271
Arran, Lord, 286, 287, 289, 391
Ashmore, Ruth, 61
Ashton, Frederick, 285
Askew, Reuben, 403
Aspin, Les, 533
Astor Bar (New York City), 234
Atkin, Gabriel, 96
Atkinson, Ti-Grace, 377
Auchmuty, Rosemary, 190
Auden, W.H., 285
Auletta, Ken, 266
Australia
  gay liberation groups in, 389
  homosexuality among bushrangers, 41
  influence of British colonial law, 282
  legal reforms in, 288
  policy on gays in military, 531
  Religious Right in, 410
Axgil, Axel, 510–511
Axgil, Eigil, 510–511
AZT (drug), 457

"backroom" bars, 424, 425–426
Bacon, Francis, 285, 303
Bad Attitude, 469
Baker, Jack, 373
Baker, Josephine, 150
Baker, Michael, 183, 188
Balanchine, George, 213
Baldwin, James, 91, 309, 313–317, 315, 328, 330, 342

excerpt from *Giovanni's Room,* 317–318
Ballets Russes, 208, 210
Bannon, Ann, 320
Barger, Florence, 174
Barnard College, 468
Barnes, Djuna, 80, 139, 161, 163–164, 165, 166–167, 478
Barney, Natalie, 79–81, 159, 161, 164, 166, 167, 168, 183, 185
Barry Sisters, 252
bathhouses
  closing of, 444–446
  and lesbians, 467
  movement view of, 370–371
  popularity of, 143, 424
Batista, Fulgencio, 488
Batten, Mabel, 183
Battle of the Rosebud, 34, 38
Baudelaire, Charles, 44, 75, 79, 87
  excerpt from "Lesbos," 87
Baudry, André, 392
Bauman, Robert, 474, 476
Bay Area Reporter, 419, 444, 445
Bayer, Ronald, 494
Bayh, Birch, 474
Baylis, Lilian, 59
Beach, Sylvia, 81, 159, 161, 164–165, 167
Beat Generation, 297–301
Beauman, Nicola, 174
Bebel, August, 112
Becker, John, 496
Becoming a Man, 536
Bee Gees, 429
Before Night Falls, 491
Belbeuf, Marquise de, 77, 78, 82
Bell, Arthur, 372
Bell, Clive, 171
Bell, Quentin, 170, 175, 176, 178
Bell, Vanessa Stephen, 170, 171
Belle Époque, 76, 159–167
Benjamin, Hilde, 496
Bennett, Arnold, 99
Ben-Shalom, Miriam, 413, 532
Benson, Elmer, 416
Benstock, Shari, 76, 80, 161
Bentley, Gladys, 149, 151–152, 154
Benton, William, 264

berdaches
  defined, 31
  equivalents in other cultures, 31
  female, 35–37
  latter day views of, 37–40
  marriages of, 31, 32, 33
  modern view of, 39–40
  prevalence of, 31
  role in tribal society, 32–35
  sexuality of, 31, 32
  We'wha as, 29–31
Berg, Vernon "Copy" III, 413
Berke, Richard L., 537, 538
Berkman, Alexander, 204
Bernhard, Sandra, 551
Bertolucci, Bernardo, 304
Berube, Allan, 232, 234, 236
Beyria, Gustave-Léon, 166
Bieber, Irving, 247, 248, 249, 256
The Big Sea, excerpt from, 157–158
Bilitis, Daughters of, see Daughters of
  Bilitis
Birkett, K.C. Norman, 188
Biron, Sir Chartres, 188, 189
bisexuality
  and Arab world, 302
  and Eisenstein, 206
  Freudian belief in, 23–24, 247
  in Jazz Age Harlem, 150
Black Book, 96, 97, 98–99, 259
Black Cat (gay bar), 346–347
Black Panthers, 373
Black Rabbit (gay club), 143
Blackfeet Indians, 36
Blackwell, Alice Stone, 60–61
The Blessing, 281
  excerpt from, 281–282
Blick, Roy E., 259, 273–275
Blinder, Dr. Marty, 407
Bloomsbury group, 170–178
"blue" discharge, 237, 238
Blumstein, Philip, 468
The Body Politic (newspaper), 389,
  421
Bogarde, Dirk, 285, 290, 291
Bogart, Neil, 429
bohemian enclaves, defined, 137. See
  also Bloomsbury; Greenwich Vil-
  lage; Harlem; Paris

Bolsheviks, 204
Bond, Pat, 235–236, 239, 321, 537
Boots of Leather, Slippers of Gold,
  320, 325
Boston marriages, 58, 72
The Bostonians, 58, 62
Bourdet, Edouard, 144
Bow, Clara, 143
Bowers v. Hardwick, 455, 457
Bowie, David, 289
Bowles, Jane, 304, 305, 306, 307
Bowles, Paul, 165, 304–305, 306, 307
Boxer, Barbara, 552
The Boys in the Band, 342, 367
A Boy's Own Story, 477
Brackett, Louise, 56
Bradley, Jack T., 270
Bram, Christopher, 478
Branch, Taylor, 360, 361
Brand, Adolf, 117, 119, 120, 216, 221
Brando, Marlon, 311
Brazil, female warriors in, 35
Bridges, Styles, 267
Briggs, John, 404
Briggs Initiative, 404, 409, 452
Bright, Susie, 431, 469
Britain
  age of consent in, 287, 503, 509
  and AIDS, 503
  Bloomsbury group, 170–178
  and Clause 28, 503–509
  gay liberation movement in London,
    389–391
  gay press in, 289, 391, 421
  legal reforms in Empire, 288–289
  passage of legal reforms, 284–287,
    391, 509
  press coverage of gay issues, 186,
    284, 503, 505, 506, 507
  Religious Right in, 410
  romantic friendships among women,
    58–59
  during World War I, 92–100
Britt, Harry, 408, 414, 446
Britten, Benjamin, 285
Brodsky, Joel I., 425
Bronski, Michael, 111, 151, 310, 385,
  420
Bronson, Edgar Beecher, 41

Brooks, Romaine, 81, 161
Broom (magazine), 140
Broshears, Rev. Ray, 417
Brown, David, 201
Brown, Howard, 382
Brown, Jerry, 404
Brown, Lewy, 6, 7
Brown, Rita Mae
  as author, 351, 433, 467–468, 476,
    477
  and Congress to Unite Women, 375–
    376
  excerpt from Furies essay, "The
    Shape of Things to Come," 388–
    389
  and Navratilova, 549–550
  as radical lesbian, 431–432
  views on sex, 467–468, 470
  and women's movement, 374–375,
    387
Brown, W.B., 272
Brownmiller, Susan, 377
Bruce, Richard, 155
Bryant, Anita, 355, 401–403, 409,
  410, 452
Bryher (Winifred Ellerman), 159, 165
Buchanan, Pat, 404, 450–451, 474,
  528
Buchenwald, 227
Bucke, Maurice, 5
Buckingham, Robert, 174
Bull, Chris, 540
Bullard, Laura Curtis, 57
Bülow, Bernhard Prince von, 119,
  120
Bunch, Charlotte, 376, 431
Burden, Carter, 381
Burgess, Guy, 100, 281
Burke, Phyllis, 460
Burke, Tom, 367
Burns, John Horne, 234, 241
Burns, Richard, 420
Burroughs, William, 298, 299, 301,
  302, 303, 306, 342
Burroughs Wellcome, 457
Burton, Peter, excerpt from *Parallel
  Lives*, 294–295
Burton, Philip, 445
Bush, George, 462, 528

butch/femme culture
  after Stonewall, 326, 433–434
  characteristics of, 319–322
  class distinctions in, 322–326
  origins of, 322
Byron, Lord, 104

Cabeza de Vaca, Alvar Núñez, 33
Caen, Herb, 417
Calamus poems, 3, 6, 10, 11, 12
California. *See also* San Francisco
  Briggs Initiative, 404, 409, 452
  legal reforms in, 395
Call, Hal, 336
Call Her Savage, 143–144
Callow, Simon, 509
Cameron, Peter, 478
Cammermeyer, Margarethe, 532, 541
CAMP Inc., 389
Campaign for Military Service, 541
Campbell, Jack, 403
Canada
  bars homosexuals from entering, 263
  gay liberation groups in, 389
  gay press in, 421
  homophile movement in, 351
  legal reforms in, 288, 295–296
  policy on gays in military, 531
  Religious Right in, 410
Cape, Jonathan, 186, 187, 189
Capital Gay, 508
Capote, Truman, 302, 303, 305, 309
The Captive, 144
Carpenter, Edward
  as homosexual, 21–22
  influence of, 22, 173
  view of Walt Whitman, 11, 12, 21
  view of women's romantic friend-
    ships, 59
  views on homosexuality, 20–22
Carrington, Dora, 173
Carson, Sir Edward, 48
Carter, Jimmy, 401, 404
Cassady, Neal, 299, 300
Castro, Fidel, 488, 489
Castro neighborhood, San Francisco,
  397, 399–400
Cathcart, Kevin, 420

Cather, Willa, 58, 61, 64–67, 65
Catholic Church, 465–467
Catholic University, 465
Cavafy, Constantine, 168
Cavett, Dick, 379
Caviano, Ray, 429
Cellini, Benvenuto, 16
Centers for Disease Control, 439, 442
Chaliapin, Feodor, 210
Channell, Carl "Spitz," 475–476
Chapman, Morris, 559
Chapman, Tracy, 437
Chatwin, Bruce, 104
Chauncey, George, 141, 142, 143, 144–145, 157
Cheney, Dick, 531
Cherifa, 305, 306
Chesley, Robert, 442
Chester, Alfred, 307
Cheyenne Indians, 33, 34
China, 485–488
Christian, Meg, 435, 436, 437
Christian Coalition, 451
Christian Voice, 409–410
Christopher, George, 346
Christopher and His Kind, 129
  excerpt from, 129–131
Christopher Street, 419, 429, 472, 477
Church, Frank, 474
Church of St. Francis Xavier, 466, 467
Cities of the Plain, see Sodom and Gomorrah
Cities on a Hill, 446
Citizens Committee to Outlaw Entrapment, 335
The City and the Pillar, 241–242, 309, 477
  excerpt from, 242–243
City of Night, 478
Civil Rights Act of 1964, 362
Civil War
  Walt Whitman during, 6, 231, 235
  women passing as men in, 71
Clam House (Harlem club), 151
Clark, Badger, 42
Clark, Karen, 415
Clause 28
  background of, 503–504
  debate over, 506–507

impact of, 507–509
  introduced in Parliament, 506
  passage of, 507
  as symbol, 508
Cleaver, Eldridge, 373
Cleaver, Scott, 464
Cleveland, Grover, 29
Clift, Montgomery, 311
Clingan, Eldon, 381
Clinton, Bill
  campaign promise to lift ban on gays in military, 532–533
  campaign speech on AIDS, 527
  compromises on issue of gays in military, 533–534, 538, 540
  disappointment in, 534, 541
  and "Don't Ask, Don't Tell," 540–541
  and Gay and Lesbian March on Washington, 536, 537
  Jeffrey Schmalz view of, 546–547
  wins gay vote, 529
Clinton, Kate, 551–552
The Cloister, 127
  excerpt from, 128–129
Coates, Paul, 336
Cochran, C.B., 109
Cocteau, Jean, 166, 209, 222, 392
Code Napoléon, 48, 76
Cohn, Roy M.
  and AIDS quilt, 455
  and Army-McCarthy hearings, 268–271
  and G. David Schine, 263, 265–266, 268, 269
  homosexuality of, 265, 266–267
  and J. Edgar Hoover, 355
  and McCarthy, 263, 267–268
Colette, 77–78, 83, 166
  excerpt from *The Pure and the Impure,* 82, 84
Collins, Capt. Dennis, 411
Colorado
  antigay initiative in, 411, 528, 530, 557
  gay contingent in March on Washington, 537
  Navratilova response to antigay law, 547

Columbia University, 298–299, 351, 377, 494
Come Together, 390
Coming Out (book), 391
Coming Out (film), 497
Coming Out Conservative, 237–238
Coming Out Under Fire, 232
Committee of the Special, 115–116
Communism
  and formation of Mattachine Society, 333, 336
  and McCarthy, 258, 259
  in past of Bayard Rustin, 360
  in pre-Nazi Germany, 126
  in Soviet Union, 204–208
concentration camps, homosexuals in, 222–227
Concerned Americans for Individual Rights, 414, 475
Conduct Unbecoming, 235, 355
Confessions of a Mask, 515, 522–523
  excerpt from, 523
Congress of Racial Equality, 361
Congress to Unite Women, 375–376
Connolly, Cyril, 209
Conquest, Robert, 207
Constanza, Margaret (Midge), 401
Contact Press, 165
Continental Baths, 424
Cook, Blanche Wiesen, 57, 67, 69, 70, 71
Cook, Nancy, 70
Cortés, Hernán, 37
Cory, Donald Webster, 235, 358
  excerpt from *The Homosexual in America*, 358–359
Corydon, 90–91
Cotton Club, 148, 355
Coughlin, Timothy J., 467
Council on Religion and the Homosexual, 348
Coup de Grace, 168
Covici Friede (publisher), 190
Coward, Noel, 100, 109–111, *110*
  comparison to Oscar Wilde, 109, 111
cowboys, homosexuality among, 40–43
Cowley, Malcolm, 137, 138, 140

Coyle, Brian, 415, 451
Crane, Philip, 475
Cranston, Alan, 474
Crawford, Cindy, 551
Crazy Horse, 33
Crisp, Quentin, 193
  excerpt from *The Naked Civil Servant*, 193–196
Crow Indians, 33, 34, 36, 38
Crowley, Matt, 342
The Crying Game, 356, 536
C-Span, 536, 537
Cuba
  and AIDS, 493–494
  homosexuality in, 488–495
  internment camps in, 490, 491
  and Mariel boat-lift, 492
Cullen, Countee, 152, 153, 154
Culver, John, 474
Curran, Fr. Charles E., 465
Custer, George Armstrong, 40

da Vinci, Leonardo, 16
Dachau, 223
Daly, Jo, 399
Dancer from the Dance, 427, 429–430, 476, 478
dancing, 372–373, 427–430
Dark, Alvin, 402
Darling, Justice, 97–99
Dasbach, Kaplan, 117
Daughters of Bilitis, 76, 322, 331, 338–340, 344
  and first anniversary of Stonewall, 383
  militant challenge to, 342
  and NOW, 375
  and women's movement, 352, 375, 376, 377
Daughter's Press, 433
Davidson, Jaye, 356
Davis, Madeline D., 320, 322, 324, 325, 326
de Gaulle, Charles, 392
de Klerk, F.W., 512
De Marco, Michael, 381
De Profundis, 50, 51
  excerpt from, 51–52

Dean, James, 311
Dearden, Basil, 290
Debussy, Claude, 76
Decker, Mary, 550
Defert, Daniel, 472–473
degeneracy theory, 15–16
Delaney, C.J., 282
Delaney, Samuel, 155
Delaney, Shelagh, 285
Dell, Floyd, 139, 140
Delmas Treason Trial, 512
D'Emilio, John, 231, 235, 254, 261,
    262, 301, 334, 335, 337, 339, 341,
    345, 352, 559
Demme, Jonathan, 536
Democratic National Convention
    (1992), 527–528
Democratic Vistas, 10
Demuth, Charles, 138, 143
Denig, Edwin T., 36–37
Denmark, recognizes same-sex partner-
    ships, 510
Denneny, Michael, 477
DePuyster, Jake, 41
Desart, Lord, 185
The Destiny of Me, 536
Diaghilev, Sergei, 204, 208–213
Diagnostic and Statistical Manual,
    249, 257
Dickerman, Marion, 702
Dickinson, Anna E., 55–57
Dickinson, Emily, 62
Dickinson, Goldsworthy Lowes, 21
Diels, Rudolf, 219–220
Different from the Others (film), 124,
    131–133
Dignity (Catholic organization), 465,
    466–467
Diller, Barry, 534
Diller, Phyllis, 379
Dinkins, David, 453
Dionne, E.J. Jr., 537
disco music, 427–430
Dlugacz, Judy, 436
Dolan, John Terrence "Terry," 474–
    476
Dole, Robert, 533, 552
domestic partners, 453
Domi, Tanya, 544

Donaldson, Herb, 348, 349
Dong Xian, 485–486
"Don't Ask, Don't Tell" policy
    Barney Frank compromise, 539–540
    codification of, 541
    introduction of, 534
Doolittle, Hilda, 159
Dorn, Bill, 465
doseiai, 520
Douglas, James, 186
Douglas, Lord Alfred "Bosie," 45, 46
    in later life, 92, 98
    and Natalie Barney, 80
    relationship with Oscar Wilde, 46,
    47, 53–54, 88
Dowdy, Rep. John, 344
Doyle, Peter, 5, 6, 8–10
The Drag, 144
Dreier, Mary Elisabeth, 56
DSM (Diagnostic and Statistical Man-
    ual), 249, 257
Du Bois, W.E.B., 152, 153
Du Bois, Yolande, 153
Duberman, Martin, 146, 248, 365,
    366, 382
Dukakis, Michael, 455
Duncan, Isadora, 137
Duncan, Robert, 301
Dutch Scientific Humanitarian Com-
    mittee, 123, 222
Dymally, Mervyn, 395

Eagleton, Thomas, 474
East Germany, gay life in, 495–498
Eastern World, 520
Ebony, 151–152
Edel, Leon, 171, 172, 173
Edelman, Murray, 529
Ehrenreich, Barbara, 298
Eighty-Sixed, 479
Eisenhower, Dwight David, 261–262
Eisenstein, Sergei M., 205–206, 207
El Adl, Mohammed, 174
Eliot, T.S., 163, 165
Ellerman, Winifred (Bryher), 159, 165
Ellis, Havelock, 16, 17, 18
    case studies from Sexual Inversion,
    25–28

Ellis, Havelock (*cont.*)
  influence on Radclyffe Hall, 185–186, 188
  marriage of, 18–19
  and *Sexual Inversion*, 18, 25–28, 185
  view of degeneracy theory, 16
  view of inversion, 19–20
  view of lesbians, 19–20, 62
  view of Murray Hall, 73
  view of Oscar Wilde, 51
  views on homosexuality, 16–20, 22–23
Ellmann, Richard, 46
Emanuel, Rahm, 529
Emerson, Ralph Waldo, 6
The Empty Closet, 419
Engels, Friedrich, 204
Engelstein, Laura, 202–203
Enigma machine, 292
entrapment, 350
Ephron, Nora, 379
Episcopal Church, 464–465, 467
Erasmus, 16
Erhard, Werner, 420
Esenwein, Bob, 543
Esquire, 367
Eulenberg, Prince Phillip zu, 117–118, 119, 120–121
European Parliament, 511
Evankovich, George, 399
Evans, Arthur, 378
Everard (bathhouse), 143
Evert, Chris, 550
Extraordinary Women, 283

Faderman, Lillian, 57, 58, 59–60, 61, 62, 71–72, 139, 140, 149, 322, 432, 433, 434, 469, 470
Fag Rag, 419
Faggots, 423, 442
Faggots' Ball, 157
Falsettos, 536
Falwell, Jerry, 409
family issues, 453
Farewell My Concubine, 487
Fauci, Anthony, 459
FBI. *See also* Hoover, J. Edgar
  and gay witch-hunts, 262

and Mattachine Society, 341, 357–358
Feinberg, David, B., 479
Feinstein, Dianne, 349, 406, 408, 453
Fellowship of Metropolitan Community Churches, 351, 435
Fellowship of Reconciliation, 360, 361
female impersonators, as GIs, 234
female warriors, 35–37
feminism, *see* women's movement
fiction, gay, 241, 476–479
  The City and the Pillar, 241–242, 309, 477
  Dancer from the Dance, 427, 429–430, 476, 478
  To a Friend Who Did Not Save My Life, 473
  pulp, lesbian, 320
Field, Andrew, 164
Field, William, 282
Fields, Annie, 58, 62
Filippov, Tertius, 199–200
Filosofov, Dima, 209, 210, 212
Finn, William, 536
Firbank, Ronald, 80
Fire!, 155
firsts
  anniversary of Stonewall, 383–384
  Denmark recognizes same-sex partnerships, 510
  gay publications in Britain, 289
  gay publications in U.S., 236
  gay rights ordinance upheld in popular vote, 405
  gay rights organizations in U.S., 123, 333
  homosexuality as U.S. public issue, 263
  lesbian appearance in film, 133
  N.Y. gay community media coverage, 349
  openly gay legislator, 395
  uses of term *homosexual*, 13, 18
Fishbein, Leslie, 138
Fisher, Mary, 545
FitzGerald, Frances, 400, 408, 446, 447, 450
Flanders, Ralph, 268
Flanner, Janet, 159, 166

Fleiss, Wilhelm, 247
Flossenbürg (concentration camp), 226–227
Flying (book), 377
Forbes, Malcolm, 461
Forbidden Colors, 516, 521, 523
  excerpt from, 524
Ford, Gerald, 404, 417
Forever Flowing, 213
  excerpt from, 213–214
Forster, E.M., 105, 173–175, 178, 283, 285
  excerpt from Maurice, 105–107
  influence of Carpenter, 22
  and Maurice, 22, 51, 105, 171, 173, 174, 175, 391
  and T.E. Lawrence, 104
  view of Gide, 89, 91
  and The Well of Loneliness, 186, 187, 188, 285
Foster, Jim, 396, 397
Foucault, Michel, 13–14, 421, 470–473
Fouratt, James, 369
Fox, Elijah Douglas, 7
Fraigneau, André, 167, 168
France. See also Paris
  and age of consent, 509, 510
  Code Napoléon, 48, 76
  gay liberation groups in, 392–394
  gay press in, 421
  legal reforms in, 510
  Mirguet Amendment, 392
  trend in attitude toward homosexuality, 199
  Vichy government, 222, 392, 509
Frank, Barney, 416, 455, 538, 539–540
French, Robert, 41
Frente de Liberación Homosexual (Argentina), 500
Freud, Sigmund
  and bisexuality issue, 247
  opposes legal penalties, 24
  views on homosexuality, 23–25
Frick, Grace, 167
Frick, Wilhelm, 215
Friedan, Betty, 374, 376
Friedländer, Benedikt, 116

Friedman-Kien, Dr. Alvin, 439, 442, 443
friendship, see romantic friendships
Fritsch, Baron Werner von, 221
Frondizi, Arturo, 499
Front Homosexuel d'Action Révolutionnaire, 392–393
The Front Runner, 476
Frost, David, 312
Frost, Kevin, 546
Fry, Roger, 171
the Furies, 387
Fussell, Paul, 92–93

Gabrielson, Guy George, 259
Gai Pied, 421, 472
Gallagher, W.C., 74
The Gallery, 241
Gallo, Dr. Robert, 440, 446
Garber, Eric, 154
Garelik, Sanford, 350
Garland, Judy, 367
Garrett, Mary, 58
Garvey, Marcus, 152
Gauthier-Villars, Henri, 77–78
Gautier, Henri, 75
Gay, Peter
  view of Freud, 24
  view of Havelock Ellis, 16
  view of Krafft-Ebing, 15
  view of nineteenth century romantic friendships, 5
  view of Proust, 84
  view of Whitman, 4
gay (term)
  becomes term of choice, 370
  use of, 358–359
Gay Activists Alliance, 372, 378–382, 383
Gay and Come Out!, 419
Gay Association of South Africa, 513
gay bars
  "backroom," 424, 425–426
  excerpt from bar raid article, 353–354
  harrassment of, 346, 347, 350–351, 365
  Mafia-run, 370, 372

gay bars (cont.)
  in New York, 350–351, 370
  in San Francisco, 346–347
  Stonewall Inn, 145, 365–367, 372
  during World War II, 234
"gay cancer," 439
Gay Community News, 362, 418, 419,
  420, 434
gay dances, 372–373, 427–430
Gay Days, 390
Gay Games, 449, 547, 549, 557, 558
Gay Inaugural Ball, 527
gay liberation, 382–384. See also gay
  rights
  beginning of era, 352
  as change in consciousness, 369, 372
  divisions within movement, 349–
    350, 373, 376, 378, 382, 383, 422
  first media coverage of New York
    gay community, 349
  as part of world revolutionary strug-
    gle, 371, 373
  in South Africa, 512–514
  as stepchild social movement, 368–
    369
Gay Liberation Front
  in Argentina, 501
  as consciousness-raising, 369, 372
  fading of, 382
  and first anniversary of Stonewall, 383
  formation of, 368, 369
  vs. Gay Activists Alliance, 378
  in London, 389–391
  similarity of ACT UP to, 458
Gay Life, 419
"A Gay Manifesto," 369, 371, 384–
  385
  excerpt from, 385–387
gay marches
  first anniversary of Stonewall, 383–
    384
  in London, 390
  in Washington, D.C., 455, 536–538,
    549, 551, 553
Gay Men's Health Crisis, 442–443
"gay moments," 535–538, 557–558,
  559
Gay News (British newspaper), 391,
  421

Gay Pravda, 421
gay press, 351, 418–421
  in Britain, 89, 391, 421
  first publications, 236, 289
gay rights. See also gay liberation
  in Argentina, 501
  backlash against, 402–404, 409–411
  first organizations, 123, 333
  impact of AIDS on, 452–453
  military ban as issue, 531
  opposition emerges, 402–404
  picketing of White House, 344
  recognition of domestic partnerships,
    453–454
  and Religious Right, 409–411
  in Russia, 485
gay sports, 449
Gay Sunshine, 419
Gay Sweatshop, 391
Gay Women's Liberation, 376
Gaynor, Gloria, 428
Gay-Related Immune Deficiency
  (GRID), 440
Gays and Lesbians of the Witwaters-
  rand (GLOW), 512
The Gazette, 357
Geffen, David, 534
Genet, Jean, 342, 478
Gentet, Simone, 134
Georgetown University, 466
Gerassi, John, 272
Gerber, Henry, 333
Gerke, August, 200
German Democratic Republic (East
  Germany), gay life in, 495–498
Germany. See also East Germany
  Berlin as "gayest" city, 114, 123–
    127
  Communist party in, 126
  early gay rights movement in, 14,
    112
  gay life and culture after World War
    I, 123–127
  homosexuals become scapegoats, 122
  impact of Eulenburg affair, 121–123
  lesbians in, 116–117, 122–123
  rise of Nazism, 125–126, 127
  trial over romantic friendships, 117–
    121

Gesell, Jedge Gerhard, 413
Gessen, Masha, 484
Gide, André, 167, 175, 207, 209, 222, 315
  affair with Elisabeth van Rysselberghe, 90
  and *Corydon*, 90–91
  excerpt from *If It Die*, 53–54
  homosexuality of, 87–91
  and *If It Die*, 89, 90
  and *The Immoralist*, 90
  at Institute for Sexual Science, 131
  marriage of, 89–90
  and Oscar Wilde, 52–53, 87–88
Gielgud, John, 282
Giese, Karl, 130
Gilbert, Sue, 62
Gilbert and Sullivan, 3
Gingrich, Rev. John, 474
Ginsberg, Allen, 297, *298*, 298–300, 304, 306, 346, 366
Giovanni's Room, 309, 314, 316–317, 477
  excerpt from, 317–318
Gippius, Zinadia, 210
Gittings, Barbara, 340, 343, 344, 382
Giuliani, Rudy, 558
Glaser, Elizabeth, 545
glasnost, 484
Glendinning, Victoria, 179, 180
Glenn, John, 533
Gloeden, Baron Wilhelm von, 210
Goebbels, Joseph, 221
Gogol, Nikolai, 199–200, 201
Gold, Ron, 256
Goldberg, Arthur, 379–380
Goldman, Emma, 137, 140, 141, 204
Goldstein, Richard, 316
Goldwater, Barry, 397, 541
Goodman, Paul, 298, 422, 423, 424
Goodstein, David B., 420, 427
Goodwin, Doris Kearns, 70
Gorky, Maxim, 204, 206
Gorton, Slade, 552
Got, Ambroise, 124
Gottlieb, Dr. Michael, 439, 442
Graham, Billy, 251
Grand United Order of Odd Fellows, 157

Grant, Duncan, 171, 172, 173
Graves, Robert, 44, 46, 95–96, 101, 109
Green, Martin, 100, 209
Green, Michelle, 301, 302, 303
Greenspun, Hank, 264
Greenwich Village
  as bohemian enclave, 137–145
  end of isolation era, 142–143
  as gay community, 137–145
  social life, 141–142
  Stonewall Inn, 145, 365–367, 372
  viewed by *Current Psychology and Psychoanalysis*, 146–147
  during World War I, 141
Greenwich Village Quill, 143
Greeves, George, 309
Grein, J.T., 97, 99
Greitzer, Carol, 380–381
Grinnell, George, 34
Grosskurth, Phyllis, 16, 19
Grossman, Vasily, 213
  excerpt from *Forever Flowing*, 213–214
Grosvenor, Rosamund, 177
Grotewohl, Otto, 495
Grove Press, 342
Gründgens, Gustav, 221
Guibert, Hervé, 473
Gunderson, Steve, 559
Guzman, Nuno de, 37
Gwinn, Mary, 58

Hadjys, Dorothy, 536–537, 541–542
Hall, Radclyffe, 80, 101, 159, 161, 171, *184*, 322, 559
  excerpt from *The Well of Loneliness*, 191–193
  and obscenity trial, 187–190
  and *The Well of Loneliness*, 183, 185–191
Hall, Richard, 478
Halliwell, Kenneth, 303, 306, 307
Hamilton Lodge Ball, 157
Han Dynasty, 485
Hanks, Tom, 536
Hansberry, Carl, 330
Hansberry, Harry, 151

Hansberry, Lorraine, 322, 328–332
Happersberger, Lucien, 314
Harden, Maximilian, 119–120, 121
Harding, Carl, 341
Hari, Mata, 80
Harlem
    blackness vs. sexuality as focus,
        154–156
    as bohemian enclave, 148–156
    as center of black American culture,
        148
    intellectual ferment in, 152–156
    in Jazz Age, 148–156
    salons in, 154–156
    sexual fluidity in, 149–152
Harris, Frank, 46–47, 48
Hart, Lois, 369
Hartley, Marsden, 138
Haskell, Arnold, 212
Hatch, Orrin, 474
Hattoy, Bob, 528, 534, 545
Hauptmann, Gerhart, 112
Havana, 488–489
Hay, Harry, 333, 334, 336, 337
Hayden, Tom, 384
Heap, Jane, 138, 165
Heckler, Margaret, 446
Heger, Heinz, 223, 229
    excerpts from The Men with the
        Pink Triangle, 223, 229–230
Helms, Jesse, 456, 552–553
Hemingway, Ernest, 163, 165
Henry, Stuart, 42
Herbart, Pierre, 207
Hess, Rudolf, 224, 225–226
Heyman, Richard, 451
Hickey, Archbishop James A., 466
Hickok, James Butler "Wild Bill," 42
Hickok, Lorena "Hick," 67–71, 68
Hidden Pictures, 478
High Gear, 419
Hill, Octavia, 58–59
Hiller, Kurt, 126, 220
Hillsborough, Robert, 403
Himmler, Heinrich, 216, 218–219,
    221, 227
Hinsch, Bret, 487
Hippler, Mike, 412

Hiraoka, Kimitake, see Mishima,
    Yukio
Hirschfeld, Magnus
    attempt to count homosexuals, 114–
        115
    beliefs about homosexuality, 113–
        115, 559
    and Institute for Sexual Science, 112,
        125, 129–131, 206, 215, 495
    and Moltke vs. Harden, 119, 121–
        122
    and politics, 125, 126, 127, 215
    World League for Sexual Reform,
        112, 205
Hitchens, Donna, 453
Hitler, Adolf. See also Nazis
    and homosexuality, 126, 219–220,
        259
    view of Roehm, 217–218
HIV (Human Immunodeficiency
    Virus), 440, 446. See also AIDS
    (Acquired Immune Deficiency Syn-
    drome)
Hocquenghem, Guy, 392–393
Hodge, Alan, 101, 109
Hodges, Andrew, 293
Hodges, Julian, 349
Hodges, Michael, 506
Holiday, Billie, 428
Holleran, Andrew, 423, 427, 429–
    430, 447, 448, 476
Hollinghurst, Alan, 479
Holman, Libby, 304, 305
Holroyd, Michael, 172
Holstein, Friedrich von, 118–119
homophile movement, 333–352
The Homosexual in America, 358
    excerpt from, 358–359
Homosexual Law Reform Society,
    285–286
homosexuality. See also gay liberation
    as "arrested development," 23–25
    becomes mainstream issue, 535–538,
        557–560
    black, 155, 325, 434
    crackdown on "perverts" in 1950s,
        258–259, 260–261, 271–273
    and degeneracy theory, 15–16

efforts to transform men, 23
female, 18. See also lesbians
gays as consumers, 429
gays as security risks, 261–262
gays as voters, 529
impact of World War II on subculture, 231–239
and Jewishness in Nazi Germany, 126, 127, 216
and Kinsey reports, 249–254
in Latin countries, 489
and McCarthy, 259
as medical condition to be cured, 23–24
men shift toward domesticity, 449–450
middle-class, 422, 452
Native American view, 39–40
Nazi war against, 215–228
in Nazi-occupied countries, 221–222
in Old West, 40–43
origin of term, 13
as pathology, 247–249
and post-war mental health profession, 247–256
public health/disease model for, 451
and religion, 464–467
scientific study of, 13–25
in Soviet Union, 204–208, 421, 483–484
under Stalin, 206–208
states, legal status, 557
toleration by sexual pioneers, 22–23
and totalitarian regimes, 204–206, 483–484
Ulrichs' theory about, 14–15, 22–23
view of Greenwich Village in Current Psychology and Psychoanalysis, 146–147
in World War I, 92–100
Hong Kong, legal reforms in, 289
Hooker, Evelyn, 254–256
Hoover, J. Edgar, 355–358, 362
Hoppe, Marianne, 221
Horta, José, 495
House Un-American Activities Committee, 336, 337
Howard, Brian, 100

Hudson, Rock, 451, 452, 455, 463
Hughes, Langston, 148, 149, 151, 152, 154, 156
    excerpt from The Big Sea, 157–158
    sexuality of, 153
Human Events, 451
Human Immunodeficiency Virus, see HIV
Human Rights Campaign Fund, 453
Hunt, Lester, 267
Hunter, Alberta, 150
Hunthausen, Archbishop Raymond, 465
Hurston, Zora Neale, 152
Hutton, Barbara, 302
Huxley, Julian, 286
Hynes, Samuel, 92, 97

Idaho Statesman, 272
If It Die, 89, 90
    excerpt from, 53–54
Image, Selwyn, 92
The Importance of Being Earnest, 44, 47, 48
Improper Conduct (Cuban film), 490, 493
Infante, Guillermo Cabrera, 493
Inagaki, Tahuro, 520
Inge, William, 310
Institute for Sexual Science, 112, 125, 129–131, 206, 215, 495
"intermediate sex"
    defined, 13
    effect of characterization, 23
    as theorized by Carpenter, 21
    as theorized by Ulrichs, 14–15
inversion, see sexual inversion
Inversions (French magazine), 166
The Irreversible Decline of Eddie Sockett, 479
Isherwood, Christopher, 124–125, 303
    excerpt from Christopher and His Kind, 129–131
    at Hirschfeld's Institute, 129–131, 132
    in Shanghai, 486
Italy, homosexuality under Nazis, 222

Jackman, Harold, 153
Jackson, Jesse
Jacobi, Nicolai Borisovich, 200
Jagger, Mick, 289
James, Henry, 58, 62
James, Lawrence, 104
Jameson, Storm, 188
Japan
    AIDS in, 521
    lesbians in, 519
    and Mishima, 515–518
    modern gay identity, 521–522
    traditional acceptance of male homo-
        sexuality, 518–520
Jarman, Derek, 509
Jeffery-Poulter, Stephen, 283, 287, 507,
    508
Jenkins, Peter, 504, 505
Jenkins, Roy, 286
Jennings, Dale, 335
Jenny Lives with Eric and Martin, 505
Jeremy (British publication), 289
Jewett, Sarah Orne, 58, 62
Joachim, Joseph, 129
John Paul II, Pope, 465
Johns, Charley, 271
Johnson, Earvin "Magic," 545
Johnston, Jill, 369, 370, 432
Johnstone, G.H., 95
Jones, Cleve, 455
Jones, James Earl, 379
Jones, Leroi, 373
Joya, 37
Joyce, James, 138, 164, 165
Joynson-Hicks, Sir William, 186, 187
Juarez, Teresa, 377
Juliana, James N., 270
Julius (gay bar), 350–351

Kameny, Frank, 342–344, 357, 382,
    395
Kaplan, Justin, 5, 6, 7, 9
Kaposi's sarcoma, 439
Karlinsky, Simon, 199, 201, 203–204,
    205, 210, 212
Katz, Jonathan Ned, 8, 37, 71, 72,
    340, 352
Kawabata, Yasunari, 516, 522

Keith, Rudolf "Skip," 413
Kellor, Frances, 56
Kennedy, Elizabeth Lapovsky, 320,
    322, 324, 325, 326
Kennedy, Flo, 377
Kennedy, John F., 341
Kennedy, Robert F., 265, 330
Kepner, Jim, 335
Kerouac, Jack, 297, 298, 299, 300,
    302, 303, 304, 306
Kerr, Jean, 264
Kertbeny, Karl Maria, first to use term
    homosexuality, 13
Kerwinieo, Ralph, 72
Keynes, John Maynard, 171, 172–173
Khruschev, Nikita, 496
King, Billie Jean, 551
King, Martin Luther Jr., 356, 360,
    361, 362, 412
Kinnock, Neil, 506
Kinsey, Alfred C., 249–254, 337
Kinsey reports, 138, 249–254
Kiseki, Ejima, 518
Kiss of the Spider Woman, 500
Klimmer, Dr. Rudolf, 495
Klippert, Everett, 295–296
Klopfer, Bruno, 255
Koch, Ed, 443, 444
Konstantinovsky, Fr. Matthew, 199–
    200, 201
Kopay, Dave, 395
Kopkind, Andrew, 535, 536
Kotchover, Eva, 143
Kowalski, Sharon, 454
Krafft-Ebing, Richard von
    influence on Radclyffe Hall, 185
    use of hypnosis, 23
    views on homosexuality, 15–16
Kramer, Larry, 423, 474, 536, 545
    and founding of ACT UP, 456–457
    and Gay Men's Health Crisis, 442–
        444
    writes "1,112 and Counting," 444
    writes "A Personal Appeal," 441–
        442
Kraus, Bill, 444–445, 446
Krupp, Alfred, 117
Krylenko, Nikolai, 207
Kurtz, Howard, 538

Kushner, Tony, 536
Kuzmin, Mikhail, 203, 204, 205
Kwakiutl Indians, 38–39

LaBelle, Patti, 437
Labouchère Amendment, 47, 185, 280
The Ladder, 322, 329, 330–331, 339,
   340, 344, 352, 419
Ladies Almanack, 163–164
Lady Chatterley's Lover, 285
Lafayette Baths, 143
Lait, Jack, 259–260, 276
   excerpts from *Washington Confiden-
   tial*, 260, 276–278
Lakota Sioux Indians, 33, 34, 39
Lambda Legal Defense and Education
   Fund, 420, 534
L'Amitié, 166
The Lamp and the Bell, 139
lang, k.d., 437, 527, 551
Lape, Esther, 70
Larkin, Philip, 289
Lauper, Cyndi, 437
Lautmann, Rüdiger, 226–227
Lavender Menace, 374, 375–376, 383
Lawley, Sue, 507
Lawrence, D.H., 285, 442
Lawrence, T.E., 101–104, *102*
Lawrence of Arabia, *see* Lawrence,
   T.E.
Le Bivre Blanc, 166
Le Navire d'Argent, 165
Leadbelly, 361
Leary, Timothy, 369
Leaves of Grass, 3, 6, 10, 11, 12
Leavitt, David, 478
Lees, Edith, 18–19, 22
   in *Sexual Inversion*, 25–27
LeGrand, Lissa, 437
Leitsch, Dick, 349, 350, 367–368, 369
Lemke, Jürgen, 497
Leno, Jay, 356
Lépine, M., 76
Lerner, Max, 261, 263, 273–274
   excerpt from *New York Post* article,
   274–275
Lesbian Avengers, 558
Lesbian Nation, 432

Lesbian Rights Project, 552
Lesbian Woman, 338
lesbians. *See also* Lees, Edith
   and ACT UP, 458
   and AIDS issue, 452–453, 470
   in Argentina, 501
   baby boom among, 450, 453
   become mainstream, 551–553
   in Belle Époque Paris, 160–167
   black vs. white, 325, 434
   butch/femme culture, 319–326, 433–
   434
   changing interests of, 437–438
   class differences among, 323–325,
   433–434
   in Cuba, 492
   in Czarist Russia, 201
   and feminist activism, 375–376, 387,
   431–435
   in fin de siècle France, 76–77, 78
   first appearance in film, 133
   the Furies, 387–389
   and Gay Liberation Front, 374, 390
   and gay press, 419
   in Germany, 116–117, 122–123
   in Greenwich Village, 139–140
   impact of *The Well of Loneliness*,
   190–191
   in Japan, 519
   music of, 431, 435–437
   under Nazi regime, 221
   and NOW, 374, 375, 376, 377, 378
   and pornography, 469–470
   relationships with gay men, 375,
   434–435, 438, 450
   in Russian labor camps, 213–214
   and sex, 467–470
   in U.S. military, 233, 235–236, 413
   views of, 19–20, 62, 139–140, 190–
   191, 248, 249
   and women's movement, 352, 374–
   378
Lesbos, 75, 79
"Lesbos" (poem), 87
   excerpt from, 87
Lestrade, Gaston, 166
Leupp, Gary, 519
Levin, Bernard, 503
Lewis, Edith, 58, 66–67

Liberace, 455
Libération, 473
Liberation News Service, 369
Liddy, G. Gordon, 356
Liebman, Marvin, 237–238, 239
The Life and Times of Harvey Milk (film), 408
Lincoln, Abraham
 bedmate of Joshua Speed, 4
 Whitman elegy for, 6
Lindsay, John, 350, 379
The Little Review, 138, 165
Littlejohn, Larry, 445, 446
Livingstone, Ken, 503–504
Locke, Alain Leroy, 152, 156
The Long Weekend, 100–101, 109
Lopokova, Lydia, 173
Lorde, Audre, 319–320, 322, 325, 326, 537
 excerpt from *Zami: A New Spelling of My Name*, 327–328
Los Angeles Advocate, 351, 383. *See also The Advocate*
Louganis, Greg, 549
Louys, Pierre, 75, 338
Love, Barbara, 378
"love of comrades," 4, 8, 10
"the love that dare not speak its name," 49, 51, 107
Lucifer with a Book, 241
Luhan, Mabel Dodge, 138
Lunn, Arthur, 107
Lvov, Prince Pavel, 210
Lyon, Phyllis, 338, 352, 399, 406

Mabley, Jackie "Moms," 150
Mackenzie, Compton, 283
Mackintosh, Cameron, 509
Maclean, Donald, 100, 281
Mädchen in Uniform (film), 133–134
Magalhães de Gandavo, Pedro de, 35
Major, John, 509
Mandela, Nelson, 512
Manilow, Barry, 424
Mann, Heinrich, 112
Mann, Klaus, 221
Mann, Thomas, 112, 167

Marais, Jean, 222
March on Washington (1963), 361–362
March on Washington (1987), 455
March on Washington (1993), 536–538, 553
 Navratilova at, 549, 551
 press coverage of, 536, 537–538
Marcus, Eric, 254, 339, 348
Marcus, Frank, 284
Margrethe, Queen, 511–512
Mariel boat-lift, 492
Marks, Jeanette, 58, 62
Marotta, Toby, 382
Marquess of Queensberry, 47, 48, 49
Mars-Jones, Adam, 479
Martin, Barney, 73
Martin, Del, 338, 339, 352, 399, 406
Martinez, Conchita, 550
Marx, Eleanor, 16
Marx, Karl, 16, 204
Massachusetts, enacts gay rights laws, 455, 557
The Masses, 137–138, 141
Massine, Léonide, 209, 210, 212
Matlovich, Leonard, 395, 411–414, 475
Matson, Bill, 341
Mattachine Review, 337, 419
Mattachine Society
 activities of, 334–338, 341
 and aftermath of Stonewall, 367–368
 and FBI, 341, 357–358
 and first anniversary of Stonewall, 383
 formation of, 333, 334
 militant challenge to, 342
 New York branch, 349–351
 Washington D.C. branch, 343
Maupin, Armistead, 478
Maurice, 22, 51, 105, 171, 173, 174, 175, 186, 391
 excerpt from, 105–107
Maxwell-Fyfe, Sir David, 282
The Mayor of Castro Street (book), 347
McAlmon, Robert, 124, 165

McCarthy, Joseph, 258, 333
  and Army-McCarthy hearings, 268–271
  and homosexual issue, 100, 259, 260
  and Roy Cohn, 263, 267–268
  sexuality of, 263–264
McCarthy, Mary, 342
McCarty, Jack, 463, 464
McCauley, Stephen, 478
McClellan, John, 269
McClung, Isabelle, 64, 66
McEnery, Peter, 290
McGovern, George, 396, 474
McKay, Claude, 156
McKellen, Ian, 506, 508, 509
McKusick, Leon, 446
McMahon, William, 264
McNeill, Fr. John J., 465
media, see gay press; press coverage
Meinhold, Keith, 531
Melville, James B., 188
Memoir Club, 171, 173
Memoirs of Hadrian, 168
Memphis Commercial Appeal, 537–538, 557
Men in the Shadows, 278
Men on Men, 477
The Men with the Pink Triangle, 223, 229
  excerpts from, 223, 229–230
Mendenhall, George, 347
Menem, Carlos Saúl, 501
Merezhkovski, 210
Merill, George, 173
Merlo, Frank, 311–312
Merman, Ethel, 355
Merrill, George, 21
Methodist Church, 465
Metzenbaum, Howard, 356
Michelangelo, 16
Midler, Bette, 424
Migden, Carole, 453
Miles, Barry, 297, 300
Milk, Harvey
  aftermath of his death, 408
  assassination of, 406
  elected to San Francisco board of supervisors, 398, 401

  "Hope Speech" of, 400
  moves to San Francisco, 397
  and Oliver Sipple, 417
  as political organizer, 397–399, 400, 452
  relationship with Dan White, 405–406
  runs for board of supervisors, 395, 397
Millay, Edna St. Vincent, 94, 138–139, 166
Miller, James, 471, 473
Miller, Merle, 232–233
Millett, Kate, 320, 377, 384, 433, 560
Mineshaft (bar), 425–426
Mirguet Amendment, 392
Mishima, Yukio, 168, 517
  death of, 515
  excerpt from Confessions of a Mask, 523
  excerpt from Forbidden Colors, 524
  and Morita, 516, 518
  writings of, 515–516, 522–523
Mitchell, George, 533
Mitford, Nancy, excerpt from The Blessing, 281–282
Mitterrand, François, 394, 510
Mixner, David, 527, 530, 537, 541, 558
modernism, in Belle Époque Paris, 161–167
Mohave Indians, 35
Molina, Miguel de, 499
Moltke, Kuno Count von, 119–120, 121
Mompati, Ruth, 514
Monette, Paul, 536
Monnier, Adrienne, 165
Monroe, Vaughn, 265
Montagu, Lord, 282
Montgomery, Viscount, 286
Montpelier (submarine), 539
Moore, Sara Jane, 417
Moral Majority, 409, 451
Morgan, Mary, 552
Morgan, Ted, 297
Morita, Masakatsu, 515, 516, 518
Morrison, Jack, 349

Mortimer, Lee, 259–260, 276
    excerpts from *Washington Confidential*, 260, 276–278
Moscone, George, 395, 399, 406
Mosse, George L., 133, 216, 219
Motion Picture Production Code, 291, 342
Mrabet, Mohammed, 305
Murray, Arnold, 292
Murray, Patty, 553
music
    disco, 427–430
    women's, 431, 435–437
Mussolini, Benito, 222
Muste, A.J., 360
My Father and Myself, 108
    excerpt from, 108–109
Myrtle Beach Bitch, 236

NAACP, 152
Nabokov, Sergei, 204
Nabokov, V.D., 202–203
Nabokov, Vladimir, 199, 202, 477
Naiad Press, 433, 477
The Naked Civil Servant, excerpt from, 193–196
Names Project Quilt, 455
nanshoku, 518–519, 520
Nash, Mrs., 40
Nathan, John, 516
The Nation, 535
National Conservative Political Action Committee (NCPAC), 474
National Gay and Lesbian Task Force, 420, 434, 453, 530, 538, 549
National Gay Liberation Front Student Conference, 370
National Gay Task Force, 382, 434, 492
National Institute of Allergy and Infectious Diseases, 459
National Organization for Women (NOW)
    and lesbianism, 374, 375, 376, 377, 378, 469
    in San Francisco, 377
National Public Radio, 475
Native Americans. *See also* berdaches

women passing as men, 72
Navajo Indians, 33, 34, 38
Navratilova, Martina
    as gay activist, 547, 549, 550–551
    and Rita Mae Brown, 549–550
Nazis. *See also* Hitler, Adolf
    destroy Hirschfeld's Institute for Sexual Science, 215
    homosexuals within party, 216
    rise of Nazism in Germany, 125–126, 127
    war against homosexuals, 215–228
Neagle, Walter, 362
Near, Holly, 431, 435, 436, 437, 537
Neff, Wanda Fraiken, 61
Nehamas, Alexander, 471
Nelson, Judy, 550
Nemiroff, Robert, 329–330
Nestle, Joan, 323, 324, 326, 434, 469
the Netherlands
    gay rights group established in, 123
    Nazi crackdown on gays, 222
    policy on gays in military, 531
The New Republic, 458, 535
New Woman, 57–58, 59
New York City. *See also* Greenwich Village; Harlem
    enacts gay rights bill, 454
    homophile movement in, 349–351
    press coverage of gay issues in, 349, 419
    response to AIDS crisis, 443, 444
New York Native, 419, 441, 442, 444
The New York Times, 73, 74, 259, 349, 383, 529–530, 534, 535, 537, 538, 547, 558, 560
The New York Times Book Review, 241, 251, 478
The New York Times Sunday Magazine, excerpt from "Whatever Happened to AIDS?," 546–547
New York University, 374
The New Yorker, 166, 383, 558
New Zealand
    legal reforms in, 289
    Religious Right in, 410
Newsweek magazine, 239–241, 551
Newton, Huey, 373
Nicholas II, Czar, 204

Nichols, Jack, 343
Nicolson, Harold, 175, 176, 179–180, 181
Nicolson, Nigel, 175, 176, 179
Nigger Heaven, 154
Nightwood, 163, 164
Nijinsky, Romola, 210–211, 212
Nijinsky, Vaslav, 204, 209, 210–212, 211
Nile, Fred, 410
Nixon, E.D., 360
Nkoli, Simon, 512–513, 514, 559
Nkrumah, Kwame, 361
Noble, Elaine, 395, 415–416, 433
The Normal Heart, 444
Norman, Tom, 407
North, Oliver, 475
Northern Ireland (Ulster), 287–288
Norway, enacts partnership law, 511
Nott-Bower, Sir John, 281
novels, *see* fiction, gay
Nugent, Bruce, 149, 153, 155–156
Numantius, Numa, 14
Núñez de Balboa, Vasco, 37
Nunn, Sam, 533, 534, 538–539, 541, 544
Nussbaum, Bruce, 443

O'Beirne, John A., 357
O'Brien, Don, 272
O'Brien, Larry F., 262
O'Brien, Sharon, 64, 66
Obscene Publications Act of 1857, 187
O'Connor, John Cardinal, 460, 467
Odd Fellows, 157
Odd Girls and Twilight Lovers, 433
O'Donnell, John, 259
O'Hara, Frank, 304
O'Horgan, Tom, 397
O'Leary, Jean, 434
Olivia Records, 435–436
Omega Workshops, 171
On Our Backs, 469
One magazine, 272–273, 329, 330, 335, 338, 419
  excerpt from bar raid article, 353–354
"1,112 and Counting," 444

O'Neill, Eugene, 137
Oram, Alison, 191
Oranges Are Not the Only Fruit, 478, 479
Oregon, antigay initiative in, 411, 528, 529, 530
Oregon Citizens' Alliance (OCA), 530–531
Organization of Lesbian and Gay Activists (OLGA), 514
Orlando, 176–178, 180–181
  excerpt from, 181–182
Orlova, Alexandra, 200, 201
Orlovsky, Peter, 300, 304
Orton, Joe, 284, 303, 306, 307
  excerpt from Tangier diary, 307–309
Orwell, George, 159
Osborn, Torie, 538
Oshinsky, David M., 265–266
Osh-Tisch, 34, 38
Ostrander, Horace, 8
Other Voices, Other Rooms, 309–310
Out magazine, 484, 557
outing, 461
OUTLOOK (magazine), 427
OutRage, 509, 511
OutWeek, 461
Owen, Wilfred, 92
Owles, Jim, 378, 380

Pabich, Dick, 405
Pabst, G.W., 133
Padilla, Herberto, 490, 493
Painter, George, 76
Paniccia, Tom, 541
Pansy Club, 145
Paradjanov, Sergei, 484
Paragraph 175
  after World War I, 125–126
  after World War II, 228
  aftermath of Eulenburg affair, 121, 122
  background of, 112
  efforts to abolish, 112, 125–126
  extended under Nazis, 220
  Krafft-Ebing supports repeal of, 16
  and lesbians, 116–117, 122–123

Parallel Lives, 294
excerpt from, 294–295
Paresis Hall, 141
Paris
as bohemian enclave, 159–167
breakup of expatriate scene, 166–167
during Nazi occupation, 167, 222
Parker, Pat, 537
Parker, Peter, 94, 108
Passions of the Cut Sleeve, 487
Pasteur Institute, 440
Paul and Joe's (speakeasy), 143
Pearson, Drew, 263–264
Peck, Fred, 539, 553
Peck, Scott, 539
Peers, Queers, and Commons, 507
Pell, Claiborne, 553
Pell, Julia, 553
Pelosi, Nancy, 537
Pemberton Billing, Noel, 96–99
Penn Post Baths, 143
Pereira, Galeote, 486
perestroika, 484
Perón, Isabel Martínez, 498
Perón, Juan, 498–499
Perot, Ross, 529
Perry, Rev. Troy, 351
Petrelis, Michael, 461
Peurifoy, John, 258–259
Philadelphia (film), 536
Philadelphia Gay News, 419
The Picture of Dorian Gray, 44, 46, 48
pink triangle, 215
fate of wearers in concentration camps, 222–227
The Pink Triangle, 216–217, 218
Pitt-Rivers, Michael, 282
Plant, Richard, 216–217, 218, 221, 223, 228
Plato, 14–15
Playboy Club, 384
Pneumocystis carinii pneumonia (PCP), 439
Poland, homosexuality under Nazis, 222
polari, defined, 293–295
political lesbians, 377
Pomeroy, Wardell B., 253

Popham, Paul, 443
Portrait of a Marriage, 175, 177, 179–180
Pougy, Liane de, 80
Pound, Ezra, 166
Pound, Louise, 61, 64–65
Powell, Adam Clayton Jr., 361
Powell, Adam Clayton Sr., 156
Powell, Colin, 533, 541
Powell, Lewis, 455
Preminger, Otto, 342
press coverage. *See also* gay press
in Britain, 186, 284, 503, 505, 506, 507
of gay issues, 349, 419, 536, 537–538
inclusion of gays and lesbians, 551, 558
Pridgen, Crae, 534
Proceso, 498, 500
Produce Exchange Baths, 143
Prohibition, 143, 145, 149
promiscuity, 423–427
Proust, Marcel, 76, 84, 208, 209, 478
excerpt from *Sodom and Gomorrah,* 85–86
Puig, Manuel, 500
The Pure and the Impure, 82
excerpt from, 82, 84

Quarracino, Antonio Cardinal, 501–502
Quayle, Dan, 528
Queensberry, Marquess of, 47, 48, 49
Queer Nation, 382, 460–462, 558
"queer," use of term, 370, 461
quilt, *see* Names Project Quilt
Quindlen, Anna, 560

Radicalesbians, 376
Rado, Sandor, 247
Rainey, Ma, 150–151
Randolph, A. Philip, 360, 361
Randolph, Barbara, 413
Raspberry, William, 539
Ratzinger, Joseph Cardinal, 460
Rea, Lord, 506–507

Read, Elizabeth, 70
Read, Herbert, 93
Reagan, Ronald
    and AIDS, 441, 452, 462
    elected president, 409, 450
    as governor of California, 404
The Real Paper, 467
Reber, Samuel, 267
Rechy, John, 342, 478
The Red Shoes, 212
Reddy, Tom, 234
Redl affair, 99
Reed, John, 138
Rees-Davis, Dai, 309
Reeves, Thomas C., 264
religion
    and homosexuality issue, 464–467
    liberal church leaders, 348
    as response to AIDS crisis, 449
Religious Right, 409–411, 450–451,
    474, 475, 528, 533, 559
Republican National Convention
    (1992), 528
A Restricted Country, 323
Resurrection, 201–202
Revolution, 57
Reynard, William, 341
Ricci, Matteo, 486
Rich, Adrienne, 432
Rieger, Marilyn, 336
Rilke, Rainer Maria, 112
Rivera, Ray "Sylvia," 378–379, 381
Robeson, Paul, 152, 330
Robinson, Charles K., excerpt from
    bar raid article in One, 353–354
Robinson, Marty, 378, 380, 381
Rockefeller, Nelson, 380
Rockefeller Foundation, 252
Rockland Palace (Harlem casino), 154
Roditi, Edouard, 305
Rodwell, Craig, 349, 350, 351, 365
Roehm, Ernst, 216–218
Rofes, Eric, 421
Roman Catholic Church, 465–467
romantic friendships
    in 1970s, 432
    boundaries of, 4–5, 10
    German trial over, 117–121
    Hoover and Tolson, 356

between men, 4–5, 44, 46
and "smashing," 60–61
between women, 5, 55–63
Roosevelt, Eleanor, 57, 67–71, 68
Roren, Ned, 303
Roscoe, Will, 32
"Roseanne," 551
Rosenberg, Julius and Ethel, 265
Rosensteil, Susan, 355
Ross, Diana, 428
Ross, Robbie, 46, 99
Roth, Claudia, 511
Rotundo, E. Anthony, 4–5
Rouilard, Richard, 461
Rovere, Richard H., 258, 265
Rowland, Chuck, 336
Royal Canadian Mounted Police, 263
Rubyfruit Jungle, 433, 476, 477
Rueling, Anna, 116
Russell, Bertrand, 286
Russell, Ken, 442
Russia. See also Soviet Union
    after revolution, 204–205
    Czarist, 199, 201
    legal reforms in, 485
Russo, Vito, 290, 342
Rustin, Bayard, 360–362

Sachsenhausen (concentration camp),
    223–226
Sackville-West, Vita, 172, 175–176,
    177, 178, 179–180
safe sex, 448–449
Sagan, Leontine, 133
Sahaykwisa (Mohave hwame), 35
Sahli, Nancy, 55, 56, 63
"Saint's disease," 440
Salazar, Alejandro, 501
Salomé (Wilde play), 97, 98, 99
salons
    in Belle Époque Paris, 164–165
    in Harlem, 154–156
San Francisco
    and Beat Generation, 297–301
    Castro neighborhood, 397, 399–400
    election of George Moscone, 395
    and gay bathhouses, 444–446
    as gay capital of U.S., 349, 396

San Francisco (*cont.*)
Gay Liberation Front in, 373
gay rights movement in, 345–349
San Francisco Chronicle, 417, 418,
444, 463
Sanders, Doug, 295
Sanger, Margaret, 137
Sappho, 16, 75–76, 79, 358
Sappho (magazine), 391
Sarde, Michle, 82
Saroyan, William, 346
Sarria, José, 346–347
Sarton, May, 477
Sartre, Jean-Paul, 393, 471, 490
Sassoon, Siegfried, 92, 94–95, 96, 231
Savigneau, Josyane, 167
Savoy Ballroom (Harlem), 154
Sawatsky, John, 278
Sawyer, Tom, 6, 7
Saypol, Irving, 265
Scandinavia, partnership laws in, 510–
511
Schindler, Allen, 536, 542
Schine, G. David, 263, 265–266, 268,
269
Schlesinger, John, 509
Schmalz, Jeffrey, 529–530, 535, 545
excerpt from "Whatever Happened
to AIDS?," 546–547
Schmidt, Doug, 407
Schmitt, Eric, 543
Schnabel, Raimund, 223
Schneider, Romy, 134
Schneider, William, 534
Schoofs, Mark, 543, 557
Schorer, Jacob, 123
Schreiner, Olive, 16
Schulman, Sarah, 477, 478
Schuvaloff, George, 484
Schwartz, Pepper, 468
Scientific Humanitarian Committee,
112, 116, 117, 220
Scondras, David, 415, 451
Scotland Yard, 281
Seattle, upholds gay rights ordinance
in popular vote, 405
Sebreli, Juan José, 499, 501
Senate Armed Services Committee,
538–539

Sencer, David, 444
Seton, Marie, 206
Seven Pillars of Wisdom, 103
sexology, 13–25, 62
Sexual Inversion, 18, 185
case studies from, 25–28
sexual inversion
defined, 13, 14
and Havelock Ellis, 18, 19–20, 25–
28, 185
and *The Well of Loneliness*, 185, 188
and women, 19–20, 62, 185–186
Shakespeare and Company (bookstore), 161, 164–165, 167
Shanti Project, 421, 464
"The Shape of Things to Come"
(essay), 387
excerpt from, 388–389
Sharison, Saul, 381
Sher, Anthony, 509
Shield Society, 515, 516
Shillito, Violet, 138
Shilts, Randy, *398*, 405, 407, 414,
420, 461, 463
and *And the Band Played On*, 444,
463–464
and *Conduct Unbecoming*, 235, 355,
412, 463
excerpt from *And the Band Played
On*, 463–464
and *Mayor of Castro Street*, 347,
397, 410, 417
Shively, Charley, 419
shudo, 518, 520
The Sign in Sidney Brustein's Window,
329, 331
Signorile, Michelangelo, 460, 461
Silver, Carol Ruth, 407
Silverman, Mervyn, 445, 446
Simpson, Lillian, 151
Sims, Sylvia, 290, 291
Sinclair, Upton, 207
Sipple, Oliver W. "Bill," 417–418
Sitwell, Osbert, 208
Slide (gay bar), 141
"smashing," 60–61
Smith, Bessie, 150–151
Smith, Chris, 505, 508
Smith, Evander, 348

Smith, Mary Rozet, 58
Smith-Rosenberg, Carroll, 57, 62
Snider, Fred, 336
Socarides, Charles W., 248–249, 256, 257
Society for Human Rights, 333
Society for Individual Rights, 347, 349, 373, 396
Sodom and Gomorrah, 84
  excerpt from, 85–86
sodomy
  and AIDS, 455
  historical view of, 4, 13–14
  relationship to homosexuality, 13
Sokolsky, George, 265
Songs of Bilitis, 75–76
Sontag, Susan, 493
Souhami, Diana, 162
South Africa, 512–514
Soviet Union. *See also* Russia
  after revolution, 204–205
  gay press in, 421
  and *glasnost*, 484
  hostility toward homosexuality, 483–484
  and *perestroika*, 484
  under Stalin, 206–208
Spartacus (British publication), 289
speakeasies, 143
Spear, Allen, 395, 415–416
Speed, Joshua, 4
Spencer, Daniel, 8
Spencer, Harold, 98
Spicer, Jack, 301
Sports Illustrated, 550
St. Cloud University, 465
St. Just, Maria, 312
St. Martin's Press, 477
Stafford, Harry, 5, 10
Stalin, Joseph, 206–208
Stambolian, George, 477
Starr, Ellen, 58
States of Desire: Travels in Gay America, 423, 424–425, 450
Steakley, James, 121–122
Steffan, Joe, 531
Stein, Gertrude, 159, 161–163, 165, 166, 167, 478
Steinbeck, John, 346

Steinem, Gloria, 377
Stenbok-Fermor, Duke, 200
Stephen, Adrian, 170
Stephen, Virginia, *see* Woolf, Virginia
Stevens, Robert, 270
Stevenson, Matilda Coxe, 29, 31, 32, 34
Stewart, James, 356
Stimpson, Catharine R., 299
Stöcker, Helene, 122
Stoddard, Charles Warren, 11
Stoddart, J.W., 3
Stokes, Henry Scott, 518
Stokes, Rick, 400
Stonewall Editions, 477
Stonewall Inn, 145, 372
  25th anniversary of riots, 557
  first anniversary of riots, 383–384
  police raid, 365–367
Strachey, Lytton, 46, 170, 171, 172–173, 178
Strindberg, August, 127
  excerpt from *The Cloister*, 128–129
Stuart, Eileen Villiers, 98
Stuart, Luisa, 355
Studds, Gerry, 455
Student Homophile League, 374
Students for a Democratic Society, 369
Sullivan, Andrew, 458, 460, 535, 543
Summer, Donna, 428
Summers, Anthony, 355
Sun, Lena H., 487
Supreme Court, and *Bowers* v. *Hardwick*, 455, 457
Sweden, enacts partnership law, 511
The Swimming Pool Library, 479
Sylvester (black gay singer), 428
Symonds, John Addington, 44, 76
  correspondence with Walt Whitman, 11–12
  first use of term *homosexual* in English, 18
  and Havelock Ellis, 18

Tammany Hall, 72–73
Tangier
  attraction of, 301–302

Tangier (*cont.*)
  excerpt from Joe Orton's diary, 307–309
  as gay and lesbian haven, 302–307
tango, origin of, 499
Tarn, Pauline, *see* Vivien, Renée
Tatchell, Peter, 509
Taubman, Howard, 310
Tavern Guild, 347
Tay-Bush Inn, 346
Taylor, Elizabeth, 451–452, 461
Taylor, Jerry, 8
Taylor, Martin, 95
Taylor, Valerie, 320
Tchaikovsky, Modest, 201
Tchaikovsky, Peter Illych, 200–201
Tebbit, Norman, 505
Tennant, Stephen, 96
Tennyson, Alfred Lord, 46
Thatcher, Margaret, 284, 503, 504, 506
"the Fruit Machine," 278–279
Thiele, Hertha, 133, 134
Thin Ice, 283
"third sex"
  defined, 13
  effect of characterization, 23
  in Germany, 115
  as theorized by Carpenter, 21
  as theorized by Hirschfeld, 113, 114
  as theorized by Ulrichs, 14–15
Thirty-three Abominations, 203
Thomas, Anthony, 427
Thomas, M. Carey, 58
Thompson, Dorothy, 134
Thompson, Karen, 454
Thomson, Meldrim, 401
Thorne, Tracy, 531
Thorp, Charles P., 370
Thurman, Wallace, 153, 155, 156
Thurmond, Strom, 362
Tillery, Linda, 436
Time magazine, 413
Times Square, 144, 145, 146
Timm (British publication), 289
To a Friend Who Did Not Save My Life, 473
Tobin, Kay, 340
Toklas, Alice B., 159, 161–163, 167

Tolson, Clyde, 355, 356, 357
Tolstoy, Count Alexander, 199
Tolstoy, Leo, 201–202
Topham, Anne, 118
Tory Party, 505
Travolta, John, 429
Trefusis, Violet, 175, 179, 180, 181
Troubridge, Una, 159, 183, 185
Trudeau, Pierre, 296
Trull, Teresa, 436
Truman, Harry S, 259
Truscott, Lucian IV, 365, 366
Turing, Alan, 291–293
Turner, Tina, 437
"Twinkie defense," 407
The Twyborn Affair, 479

UCLA Medical Center, 439
Ulrichs, Karl Heinrich
  Engels' view of, 204
  influence on Hirschfeld, 113
  theory of "third" or "intermediate" sex, 14–15
  and toleration of homosexuals, 22–23
Ulysses, 165
Unitarian Universalists, 464
United Church of Christ, 465
United Methodist Church, 465
Uranians, use of term, 15, 21, 358
U.S. Civil Service Commission, 343, 395
U.S. Food and Drug Administration, 440, 456, 457, 458–459
U.S. military
  ambivalence toward gay GIs, 233–234
  discharge systems for homosexuals, 237–239
  homosexual ban as political issue, 531
  homosexual challenges to, 412–413
  and Leonard Matlovich, 411–414
  lesbians in, 233, 235–236, 413
  pre–World War II policy toward homosexuals, 231
  World War II policy toward homosexuals, 231–232, 233
U.S. Post Office, 262, 335

Vaernet, Carl, 227
Vaid, Urvashi, 420, 530, 544
Valdez, Ramiro, 488
Van Dusen, Henry Pitney, 251
van Rysselberghe, Elisabeth, 90
Van Vechten, Carl, 138, 153, 154, 156
Vanity Fair, 535, 551, 557
Vatican, 465–467
Veidt, Conrad, 124, 131, 132
Verlaine, 75, 79
Vichy government, 222, 392, 509
Victim (film), 285, 290–291
Vida, Ginny, 434
Vidal, Gore, 241, 242, 303, 309, 311,
    312–313
    excerpt from The City and the Pillar,
    242–243
Village People, 428, 429
Village Voice, 316, 349, 362, 365–
    366, 369–370, 381–382, 383, 419
Vining, Donald, 234–235
Visconti, Luchino, 311
Vivien, Renée, 78–79, 166
Voeller, Bruce, 382
Voitov, Alexander, 201
Volk, Hans, 495
von Classen-Neudegg, L.D., 224
von Hoffman, Nicholas, 265–266, 267
Voris, Ralph, 253
Voter Research and Survey Group, 529
Voting Rights Act of 1965, 362

Walker, A'Lelia, 154
Walker, James "Gentleman Jimmy,"
    144
Walker, Ruby, 150, 151
Wallace, Henry, 333
Walpole, Hugh, 188
Warner, Jack, 312
Warner, John, 539
Warren, Patricia Nell, 476
Washington, Denzel, 536
Washington Blade, 419
Washington Confidential, 259–260
    excerpts from, 260, 276–278
Washington Post, 537, 538, 550, 558
Waters, Ethel, 150, 157
Watkins, Mary, 436

Watkins, Perry, 532
Watson, Debbie, 413
The Weary Blues, 154
Webster Hall, 141–142
Weeks, Jeffrey, 22, 23, 389, 390, 391
Weimar Republic, gay life and culture
    in, 123–127
Weir, John, 479
Weiss, Mike, 406, 407
Welch, Joseph, 270
Weld, William, 557
The Well of Loneliness, 80, 81, 101,
    159, 171, 183–191, 285, 322,
    477
    excerpt from, 191–193
West, Mae, 144
West, Old, 40–43
West, Rebecca, 109, 285
Westphal, Karl, 13
We'wha
    death of, 34–35
    photograph, 30
    in Washington, D.C., 29, 31
"Whatever Happened to AIDS?," 545
    excerpt from, 546–547
Wherry, Kenneth, 260–261
White, Dan
    confession of, 407–408
    elected to board of supervisors, 401
    kills Moscone and Milk, 406
    murder trial of, 406–408
    relationship with Harvey Milk, 405–
    406
    riots follow manslaughter conviction,
    408
    suicide of, 409
    and "Twinkie defense," 407
White, Edmund, 167, 222, 392, 426,
    427, 470, 477
    and States of Desire: Travels in Gay
    America, 423, 424–425, 450
    view of Gide, 89, 91
White, Josh, 361
White, Kevin, 416
White, Marie, 72
White, Patrick, 479
Whitehead, Bill, 477
Whitehouse, Mary, 410
Whitemore, Hugh, 293

Whitman, Walt, 3, 4, 5–6, 559
  and "adhesiveness," 4, 9
  and *Calamus* poems, 3, 6, 10, 11, 12
  during Civil War, 6, 231, 235
  and *Leaves of Grass*, 3, 6, 10, 11, 12
  and "love of comrades," 4, 8, 10
  relationship with Peter Doyle, 8–10
  relationships with men, 6–10
  sexual contradictions in, 12
  viewed as homoerotic writer, 10–11
  visits from Oscar Wilde, 3, 12
Who's Afraid of Virginia Woolf?, 310
Wicker, Randy, 349
Wieck, Dorothea, 133, 134
Wilbur, Cornelia, 248, 249
Wilde, Oscar, 44, *45*
  and André Gide, 52–53, 87–88
  and *De Profundis*, 50, 51
  effect of trials, 50–51, 98, 99, 100,
    190
  excerpt from *De Profundis*, 51–52
  films about, 285
  and Noel Coward, 109, 111
  in prison, 49–50
  recklessness of, 46–47
  relationship with Lord Alfred Doug-
    las, 46, 47, 53–54, 88
  and "the love that dare not speak its
    name," 49, 51
  trials of, 44, 48, 49, 50
  visits Walt Whitman, 3, 12
Wildeblood, Peter, 281, 282–283
Wilhelm II, Kaiser, 117–118, 121
Willard, Frances, 59
Willer, Shirley, 339
Williams, Pete, 461
Williams, Tennessee, 303, 304, 310–
    313
Williams, Walter L., 31, 32, 33, 38,
    39, 42
Williams, William Carlos, 166
Williamson, Cris, 431, 435, 436
Wilson, David, 8
Wilson, Jerry, 168
Wilson, Woodie, 236–237
Winchell, Walter, 265
Wings, 203
Winsloe, Christa, 133, 134
Winterson, Jeanette, 478, 479

Wittman, Carl, 369, 371, 384–385
  excerpt from "A Gay Manifesto,"
    385–387
Wolden, Russell, 346
Wolfenden, Sir John, 283
Wolfenden Committee, 283–284
Wolff, Charlotte, 113, 114, 190
Wolitzer, Meg, 478
A Woman of No Importance, 44, 48
women. *See also* lesbians
  passing as men, 71–74
  romantic friendships of, 5, 55–63
Women Against Pornography, 469
Women in Love, 442
Women's Army Corps, 233, 235–236,
    413
women's movement
  and lesbian-feminist activism, 375–
    376, 387, 431–435
  lesbians in, 352, 374–378
Wood, Thelma, 139, 164
Wooley, Mary, 58
Woolf, Leonard, 171, 175, 187
Woolf, Virginia, 170, 171, 173, 175,
    176, 178, 180, 181, 188, 189
  excerpt from *Orlando*, 181–182
  view of *The Well of Loneliness*, 187
Word Is Out (film), 321, 347
World League for Sexual Reform, 112,
    205
The World of Art, 209–210, 212
World War I
  Britain during, 92–100
  Greenwich Village during, 141
  homosexuality in, 92–100
  and J.R. Ackerley, 107
World War II, U.S. policy toward
    homosexuals, 231–241
Worth, Eugene, 313–314

Xanadu (bathhouse), 467
Xavier, Saint Francis, 519

Yacoubi, Ahmed, 304–305, 306
Yeltsin, Boris, 485
Yorke, Harriet, 59
Young, Allen, 369, 490

Young, Frank, 457
Young, Gay, and Proud, 505
Young, Joseph, 73
Yourcenar, Marguerite, 167–169

Zami: A New Spelling of My Name,
  320, 322, 326

excerpt from, 327–328
"zapping," 379
Zinov'eva-Annibal, Lidiia, 203
Zobel, Uvd, 498
Zuni Indians, 34–35. *See* We'wha
Zuniga, Joseph, 544
Zuylan, Baroness de, 79
Zweig, Stefan, 124

Grateful acknowledgement is made to the following for permission to reprint previously published material:

The ADVOCATE: Excerpts from "Life After Death" by Mark Schoofs (*The ADVOCATE,* July 13, 1993). Reprinted by permission of *The ADVOCATE,* the national gay and lesbian newsmagazine.

Alyson Publications, Inc.: Excerpt from *The Men with the Pink Triangle* by Heinz Heger, copyright © 1980 by Merlin-Verlag, Germany. U.S. edition published by Alyson Publications, Inc. Reprinted by permission of Alyson Publications, Inc.

Ayer Company Publishers: Excerpt from *The Homosexual in America* by Donald Webster Cory (Ayer Company Publishers, 1975, originally published in 1951 by Greenburg Publishers). Reprinted by permission of Ayer Company Publishers.

BasicBooks and *A. W. Freud et al./Mark Paterson & Associates:* Excerpt from 1935 "Letter to an American Mother" from *Letters of Sigmund Freud,* edited by Ernst L. Freud, copyright © 1960 by Sigmund Freud Copyrights Ltd., copyright renewed. Rights in the United Kingdom administered by A. W. Freud et al./Mark Paterson & Associates, London. Reprinted by permission of BasicBooks, a division of HarperCollins Publishers, Inc., and A. W. Freud et al./Mark Paterson & Associates.

Brandt & Brandt Literary Agents, Inc. and *A. M. Heath & Company Limited:* Excerpt from *The Well of Loneliness* by Radclyffe Hall, copyright © 1928 by Radclyffe Hall, copyright renewed 1956 by Una Lady Troubridge. Rights outside the United States administered by A. M. Heath & Company Limited, London. Reprinted by permission of Brandt & Brandt Literary Agents, Inc., and A. M. Heath & Company Limited on behalf of the Estate of the late Radclyffe Hall.

The Crossing Press: Excerpt from *Zami: A New Spelling of My Name* by Audre Lorde, copyright © 1982 by Audre Lorde. Reprinted by permission of The Crossing Press, Freedom, Calif.

Doubleday: Excerpts from *Giovanni's Room* by James Baldwin, copyright © 1956 by James Baldwin. Reprinted by permission of Doubleday, a division of Bantam Doubleday Dell Publishing Group, Inc.

Dutton Signet and *Connie Clausen Associates:* Excerpts from *The Naked Civil Servant* by Quentin Crisp, copyright © 1968 by Quentin Crisp. Reprinted by permission of Dutton Signet, a division of Penguin Books USA Inc., and Connie Clausen Associates.

Esquire Magazine: Excerpt from "The New Homosexuality" by Tom Burke (*Esquire,* December 1969). Reprinted by permission of *Esquire Magazine,* a member of The Hearst Corporation.

Farrar, Straus & Giroux, Inc.: Excerpt from *Christopher and His Kind* by Christopher Isherwood, copyright © 1976 by Christopher Isherwood. Reprinted by permission of Farrar, Straus & Giroux, Inc.

Farrar, Straus & Giroux, Inc. and *Martin Secker & Warburg Ltd.:* Excerpts from

THE CULTURE OF DESIRE
PARADOX AND PERVERSITY IN GAY LIVES
by Frank Browning

Nowhere has America's gay culture been observed with greater intelligence, liveliness, and sensitivity than in this provocative and deeply personal book. Taking in Cuban couples in Miami and farmers in Kentucky, AIDS activists, sexual theorists, and dedicated hedonists, *The Culture of Desire* is an intriguing insider's guide to gay America and a sharp look at the conflicts that arise when who we are is defined by whom we love.

"Absolutely cutting edge—a portrait of modern sexual politics [that] should be required reading."
　　　　　　　　　　　　　　　　　　　　　　　　—Armistead Maupin

Gay Studies/Sociology/0-679-75030-4

FAMILY VALUES
A LESBIAN MOTHER'S FIGHT FOR HER SON
by Phyllis Burke

When Phyllis Burke's lesbian partner bore a child by donor insemination, it seemed natural for Phyllis to adopt him: baby Jesse, after all, was calling her Mama. But Burke soon discovered that, even in liberated San Francisco, there were forces that would deny lesbians the legal right to be mothers.

"An important book...about motherhood, identity, honesty and love for a child. It is about homosexuals and it is pro-family. A strong challenge to prevailing 'mainstream' sensibilities."
　　　　　　　　　　　　　　　　　　　　　　　　—*Chicago Sun-Times*

Gay Studies/Sociology/0-679-75249-8

THE QUEEN'S THROAT
OPERA, HOMOSEXUALITY, AND THE MYSTERY OF DESIRE
by Wayne Koestenbaum

The Queen's Throat is at once a passionate love letter to opera and a work that triumphantly overturns our received notions of culture and sexuality. It is an innovative, profound, and wildly playful book that reveals the ways in which opera has served as a source of gay identity and gay personal style.

"[A] high-spirited and very personal book...laced with moral reflections and warmed with comedy.... A work of formidable and curious learning...a dazzling performance."
　　　　　　　　　　　　　　　　　　　　　　　　—*The New York Times Book Review*

Gay Literature/Music/0-679-74985-3

OUT IN THE WORLD
by Neil Miller

In this eye-opening and vastly entertaining book, Neil Miller travels from the black townships of South Africa to the sex clubs of Bangkok to deliver a front-line report on the lives of gays and lesbians around the world.

"Sharp, informative, and always engaging, this is first-rate work." —*The Advocate*

Vintage Departures
Gay Studies/Travel/0-679-74551-3

CLOSE TO THE KNIVES
A MEMOIR OF DISINTEGRATION
by David Wojnarowicz

David Wojnarowicz's powerful and iconoclastic memoir takes us from a violent childhood in suburbia to eventual homelessness on the streets of New York City, to recognition as one of the most provocative artists of his generation. Street life, drugs, art and nature, family, AIDS, politics, friendship and acceptance: he challenges us to examine our lives—politically, socially, emotionally, and aesthetically.

"Wojnarowicz has caught the age-old voice of the road, the voice of the traveler, the outcast, the thief, the whore, the same voice that was heard in Villon's Paris, in the Rome of Petronius. Pick up his book and listen."

—William S. Burroughs

Nonfiction/Literature/0-679-73227-6

role models
rumor
independence
outing